CONTENTS

SECTION 1: PROBLEM SOLVING 1
    1.1 PROGRAM DEVELOPMENT CYCLE 3
    1.2 PROGRAMMING TOOLS 5

SECTION 2: FUNDAMENTALS OF PROGRAMMING IN VISUAL BASIC 15
    2.1 VISUAL BASIC OBJECTS 17
    2.2 VISUAL BASIC EVENTS 27
    2.3 NUMBERS 34
    2.4 STRINGS 42
    2.5 INPUT AND OUTPUT 49
    2.6 BUILT-IN FUNCTIONS 58
    SUMMARY 67
    PROGRAMMING PROJECTS 68

SECTION 3: GENERAL PROCEDURES 71
    3.1 SUB PROCEDURES, PART I 73
    3.2 SUB PROCEDURES, PART II 80
    3.3 FUNCTION PROCEDURES 87
    3.4 MODULAR DESIGN 93
    SUMMARY 97
    PROGRAMMING PROJECTS 97

SECTION 4: DECISIONS 101
    4.1 RELATIONAL AND LOGICAL OPERATORS 103
    4.2 IF BLOCKS 106
    4.4 SELECT CASE BLOCKS 112
    4.4 A CASE STUDY: WEEKLY PAYROLL 119
    SUMMARY 126
    PROGRAMMING PROJECTS 126

SECTION 5: REPETITION 129
    5.1 DO LOOPS 131
    5.2 PROCESSING LISTS OF DATA WITH DO LOOPS 135
    5.3 FOR...NEXT LOOPS 141
    5.4 A CASE STUDY: ANALYZE A LOAN 146
    SUMMARY 153
    PROGRAMMING PROJECTS 153

SECTION 6: ARRAYS 159
    6.1 CREATING AND ACCESSING ARRAYS 161
    6.2 USING ARRAYS 171
    6.3 CONTROL ARRAYS 179
    6.4 SORTING AND SEARCHING 184
    6.5 TWO-DIMENSIONAL ARRAYS 196
    6.6 A CASE STUDY: CALCULATING WITH A SPREADSHEET 200

SUMMARY 209
PROGRAMMING PROJECTS 209

SECTION 7: SEQUENTIAL FILES 215
7.1 SEQUENTIAL FILES 217
7.2 USING SEQUENTIAL FILES 223
7.3 A CASE STUDY: RECORDING CHECKS AND DEPOSITS 228
SUMMARY 237
PROGRAMMING PROJECTS 237

SECTION 8: RANDOM-ACCESS FILES 243
8.1 USER DEFINED DATA TYPES 245
8.2 RANDOM-ACCESS FILES 251
SUMMARY 255
PROGRAMMING PROJECTS 255

SECTION 9: THE GRAPHICAL DISPLAY OF DATA 257
9.1 INTRODUCTION TO GRAPHICS 259
9.2 LINE CHARTS 267
9.3 BAR CHARTS 273
9.4 PIE CHARTS 277
SUMMARY 282
PROGRAMMING PROJECTS 282

SECTION 10: ADDITIONAL CONTROLS AND OBJECTS 285
10.1 LIST BOXES AND COMBO BOXES 287
10.2 NINE ELEMENTARY CONTROLS 294
10.3 FIVE ADDITIONAL OBJECTS 303
SUMMARY 316
PROGRAMMING PROJECTS 317

SECTION 11: DATABASE MANAGEMENT 321
11.1 AN INTRODUCTION TO DATABASES 323
11.2 RELATIONAL DATABASES AND SQL 330
11.3 THREE ADDITIONAL DATA-BOUND CONTROLS; CREATING AND DESIGNING DATABASES 338
SUMMARY 350
PROGRAMMING PROJECTS 350

SECTION 12: OBJECT-ORIENTED PROGRAMMING 353
12.1 CLASSES AND OBJECTS 355
12.2 COLLECTIONS AND EVENTS 365
12.3 CLASS RELATIONSHIPS 373
SUMMARY 380
PROGRAMMING PROJECTS 381

SECTION 13: COMMUNICATING WITH OTHER APPLICATIONS 383
13.1 OLE 385
13.2 ACCESSING THE INTERNET WITH VISUAL BASIC 392

Computer Programming Concepts and Visual Basic

David I. Schneider

UNIVERSITY OF PHOENIX
COLLEGE OF INFORMATION SYSTEMS AND TECHNOLOGY

Pearson
Custom
Publishing

Cover Art: Copyright © Stock Illustration Source, Inc./Kelly Brother.

Excerpts taken from:

An Introduction to Programming Using Visual Basic 6.0, Fourth Edition,
by David I. Schneider
Copyright © 1999, 1998, 1997, 1995 by Prentice-Hall, Inc.
A Pearson Education Company
Upper Saddle River, New Jersey 07458

Copyright © 2000 by Pearson Custom Publishing.

This special edition published in cooperation with
Pearson Custom Publishing

Printed in the United States of America

10 9 8 7 6 5 4 3 2

Please visit our web site at www.pearsoncustom.com

ISBN 0–536–60446–0

BA 990807

PEARSON CUSTOM PUBLISHING
75 Arlington Street, Boston, MA 02116
A Pearson Education Company

13.3 WEB PAGE PROGRAMMING WITH VBSCRIPT 397

SUMMARY 403

APPENDICES

A. ANSI VALUES 407

B. HOW TO 409

C. VISUAL BASIC STATEMENTS, FUNCTIONS, METHODS, PROPERTIES, EVENTS,
DATA TYPES, AND OPERATORS 423

D. VISUAL BASIC DEBUGGING TOOLS 457

INDEX 465

CONGRATULATIONS…

You have just purchased access to a valuable website that will open many doors for you! The University of Phoenix has chosen to enhance and expand your course's material with a dynamic website that contains an abundance of rich and valuable online resources specifically designed to help you achieve success!

This website provides you with material selected and added to powerful online tools that have been seamlessly integrated with this textbook, resulting in a dynamic, course-enhancing learning system. These exciting tools include:

> Online Study Guide
> Online glossary
> Links to selected, high-quality websites
> And more!

You can begin to access these tremendous resources immediately!

www.pearsoncustom.com/uop: The opening screen of the University of Phoenix website includes book covers of all the Pearson Custom Publishing books in the BSBIS and BSIT programs. Click on the book cover representing your course. This will launch the online study guide for the course in which you are currently enrolled **and** the glossary of key terms for all the University of Phoenix BSBIS and BSIT courses.

CD-ROM: The accompanying CD-ROM includes key terms underlined within the online book that are linked to the World Wide Web. Use the enclosed CD-ROM to launch websites selected to reinforce your learning experience.

TAKE THE FIRST STEP ON THE ROAD TO SUCCESS TODAY!

Pearson
Custom
Publishing

PROBLEM SOLVING

1.1 PROGRAM DEVELOPMENT CYCLE

Hardware refers to the machinery in a computer system (such as the monitor, keyboard, and CPU) and software refers to a collection of instructions, called a **program** (or **project**), that directs the hardware. Programs are written to solve problems or perform tasks on a computer. Programmers translate the solutions or tasks into a language the computer can understand. As we write programs, we must keep in mind that the computer will only do what we instruct it to do. Because of this, we must be very careful and thorough with our instructions.

■ PERFORMING A TASK ON THE COMPUTER

The first step in writing instructions to carry out a task is to determine what the **output** should be—that is, exactly what the task should produce. The second step is to identify the data, or **input**, necessary to obtain the output. The last step is to determine how to **process** the input to obtain the desired output, that is, to determine what formulas or ways of doing things can be used to obtain the output.

This problem-solving approach is the same as that used to solve word problems in an algebra class. For example, consider the following algebra problem:

How fast is a car traveling if it goes 50 miles in 2 hours?

The first step is to determine the type of answer requested. The answer should be a number giving the rate of speed in miles per hour (the output). The information needed to obtain the answer is the distance and time the car has traveled (the input). The formula

rate distance / time

is used to process the distance traveled and the time elapsed in order to determine the rate of speed. That is,

$$rate = 50 miles / 2$$
$$= 25\ miles / hour$$

A pictorial representation of this problem-solving process is

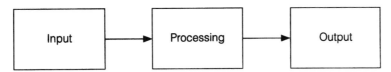

We determine what we want as output, get the needed input, and process the input to produce the desired output.

In the following chapters we discuss how to write programs to carry out the preceding operations. But first we look at the general process of writing programs.

■ PROGRAM PLANNING

A recipe provides a good example of a plan. The ingredients and the amounts are determined by what is to be baked. That is, the *output* determines the *input* and the *processing*. The recipe, or plan, reduces the number of mistakes you might make if you tried to bake with no plan at all. Although it's difficult to imagine an architect building a bridge or a factory without a detailed plan, many programmers (particularly students in their first programming course) frequently try to write programs without first making a careful plan. The more complicated the problem, the more complex the plan must be. You will spend much less time working on a program if you devise a carefully thought out step-by-step plan and test it before actually writing the program.

Many programmers plan their programs using a sequence of steps, referred to as the **program development cycle**. The following step-by-step process will enable you to use your time efficiently and help you design error-free programs that produce the desired output.

1. *Analyze:* Define the problem.

   Be sure you understand what the program should do, that is, what the output should be. Have a clear idea of what data (or input) are given and the relationship between the input and the desired output.

2. *Design:* Plan the solution to the problem.

   Find a logical sequence of precise steps that solve the problem. Such a sequence of steps is called an **algorithm**. Every detail, including obvious steps, should appear in the algorithm. In the next section, we discuss three popular methods used to develop the logic plan: flowcharts, pseudocode, and top-down charts. These tools help the programmer break a problem into a sequence of small tasks the computer can perform to solve the problem.

   Planning also involves using representative data to test the logic of the algorithm by hand to ensure that it is correct.

3. *Choose the interface:* Select the objects (text boxes, command buttons, etc.).

   Determine how the input will be obtained and how the output will be displayed. Then create objects to receive the input and display the output. Also, create appropriate command buttons to allow the user to control the program.

4. *Code:* Translate the algorithm into a programming language.

   Coding is the technical word for writing the program. During this stage, the program is written in Visual Basic and entered into the computer. The programmer uses the algorithm devised in Step 2 along with a knowledge of Visual Basic.

5. *Test and debug:* Locate and remove any errors in the program.

   Testing is the process of finding errors in a program, and **debugging** is the process of correcting errors that are found. (An error in a program is called a **bug**.) As the program is typed, Visual Basic points out certain types of program errors. Other types of errors will be detected by Visual Basic when the program is executed; however, many errors due to typing mistakes, flaws in the algorithm, or incorrect usages of the Visual Basic language rules only can be uncovered and corrected by careful detective work. An example of such an error would be using addition when multiplication was the proper operation.

6. ***Complete the documentation:*** Organize all the material that describes the program.

Documentation is intended to allow another person, or the programmer at a later date, to understand the program. Internal documentation consists of statements in the program that are not executed, but point out the purposes of various parts of the program. Documentation might also consist of a detailed description of what the program does and how to use the program (for instance, what type of input is expected). For commercial programs, documentation includes an instruction manual. Other types of documentation are the flowchart, pseudocode, and top-down chart that were used to construct the program. Although documentation is listed as the last step in the program development cycle, it should take place as the program is being coded.

1.2 PROGRAMMING TOOLS

This section discusses some specific algorithms and develops three tools used to convert algorithms into computer programs: flowcharts, pseudocode, and hierarchy charts.

You use algorithms every day to make decisions and perform tasks. For instance, whenever you mail a letter, you must decide how much postage to put on the envelope. One rule of thumb is to use one stamp for every five sheets of paper or fraction thereof. Suppose a friend asks you to determine the number of stamps to place on an envelope. The following algorithm will accomplish the task.

1. Request the number of sheets of paper; call it Sheets.   *(input)*
2. Divide Sheets by 5.   *(processing)*
3. Round the quotient up to the next highest whole number;
   call it Stamps.   *(processing)*
4. Reply with the number Stamps.   *(output)*

The preceding algorithm takes the number of sheets (Sheets) as input, processes the data, and produces the number of stamps needed (Stamps) as output. We can test the algorithm for a letter with 16 sheets of paper.

1. Request the number of sheets of paper; Sheets = 16.
2. Dividing 5 into 16 gives 3.2.
3. Rounding 3.2 up to 4 gives Stamps = 4.
4. Reply with the answer, 4 stamps.

This problem-solving example can be pictured by

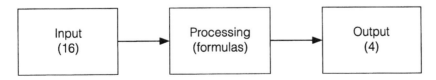

Of the program design tools available, the three most popular are the following:

Flowcharts: Graphically depict the logical steps to carry out a task and show how the steps relate to each other.

Pseudocode: Uses English-like phrases with some Visual Basic terms to outline the task.

Hierarchy charts: Show how the different parts of a program relate to each other.

■ FLOWCHARTS

A flowchart consists of special geometric symbols connected by arrows. Within each symbol is a phrase presenting the activity at that step. The shape of the symbol indicates the type of operation that is to occur. For instance, the parallelogram denotes input or output. The arrows connecting the symbols, called **flowlines**, show the progression in which the steps take place. Flowcharts should "flow" from the top of the page to the bottom. Although the symbols used in flowcharts are standardized, no standards exist for the amount of detail required within each symbol.

A table of the flowchart symbols adopted by the American National Standards Institute (ANSI) follows. Figure 1-1 shows the flowchart for the postage stamp problem.

The main advantage of using a flowchart to plan a task is that it provides a pictorial representation of the task, which makes the logic easier to follow. We can clearly see every step and how each step is connected to the next. The major disadvantage with flowcharts is that when a program is very large, the flowcharts may continue for many pages, making them difficult to follow and modify.

Symbol,	Name,	Meaning
→	*Flowline*	Used to connect symbols and indicate the flow of logic.
⬭	*Terminal*	Used to represent the beginning (Start) or the end (End) of a task.
▱	*Input/Output*	Used for input and output operations, such as reading and printing. The data to be read or printed are described inside.
▭	*Processing*	Used for arithmetic and data-manipulation operations. The instructions are listed inside the symbol.
◇	*Decision*	Used for any logic or comparison operations. Unlike the input/output and processing symbols, which have one entry and one exit flowline, the decision symbol has one entry and two exit paths. The path chosen depends on whether the answer to a question is "yes" or "no."
○	*Connector*	Used to join different flowlines.
⬠	*Offpage Connector*	Used to indicate that the flowchart continuesto a second page.
▯	*Predefined Process*	Used to represent a group of statements that perform one processing task.
⌐	*Annotation*	Used to provide additional information about another flowchart symbol.

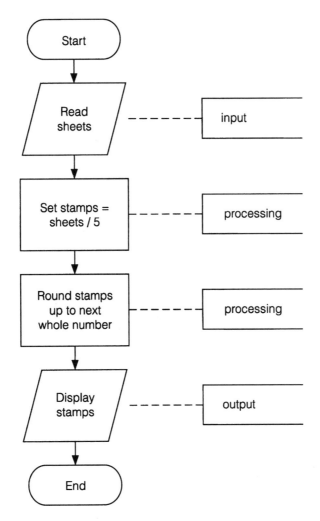

FIGURE 1-1 *Flowchart for the Postage Stamp Problem*

◼ PSEUDOCODE

Pseudocode is an abbreviated version of actual computer code (hence, *pseudocode*). The geometric symbols used in flowcharts are replaced by English-like statements that outline the process. As a result, pseudocode looks more like computer code than does a flowchart. Pseudocode allows the programmer to focus on the steps required to solve a problem rather than on how to use the computer language. The programmer can describe the algorithm in Visual Basic-like form without being restricted by the rules of Visual Basic. When the pseudocode is completed, it can be easily translated into the Visual Basic language.

The following is pseudocode for the postage stamp problem:

> ***Program:*** Determine the proper number of stamps for a letter
>
> | | |
> |---|---|
> | Read Sheets | *(input)* |
> | Set the number of stamps to Sheets / 5 | *(processing)* |
> | Round the number of stamps up to the next whole number | *(processing)* |
> | Display the number of stamps | *(output)* |

Pseudocode has several advantages. It is compact and probably will not extend for many pages as flowcharts commonly do. Also, the plan looks like the code to be written and so is preferred by many programmers.

■ HIERARCHY CHART

The last programming tool we'll discuss is the **hierarchy chart**, which shows the overall program structure. Hierarchy charts are also called structure charts, HIPO (Hierarchy plus Input-Process-Output) charts, top-down charts, or VTOC (Visual Table of Contents) charts. All these names refer to planning diagrams that are similar to a company's organization chart.

Hierarchy charts depict the organization of a program but omit the specific processing logic. They describe what each part, or **module**, of the program does and they show how the modules relate to each other. The details on how the modules work, however, are omitted. The chart is read from top to bottom and from left to right. Each module may be subdivided into a succession of submodules that branch out under it. Typically, after the activities in the succession of submodules are carried out, the module to the right of the original module is considered. A quick glance at the hierarchy chart reveals each task performed in the program and where it is performed. Figure 1-2 shows a hierarchy chart for the postage stamp problem.

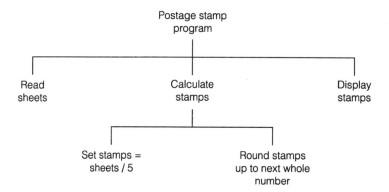

FIGURE 1-2 *Hierarchy Chart for the Postage Stamp Problem*

The main benefit of hierarchy charts is in the initial planning of a program. We break down the major parts of a program so we can see what must be done in general. From this point, we can then refine each module into more detailed plans using flowcharts or pseudocode. This process is called the **divide-and-conquer** method.

The postage stamp problem was solved by a series of instructions to read data, perform calculations, and display results. Each step was in a sequence; that is, we moved from one line to the next without skipping over any lines. This kind of structure is called a **sequence structure**. Many problems, however, require a decision to determine whether a series of instructions should be executed. If the answer to a question is "Yes," then one group of instructions is executed. If the answer is "No," then another is executed. This structure is called a **decision structure**. Figure 1-3 contains the pseudocode and flowchart for a decision structure.

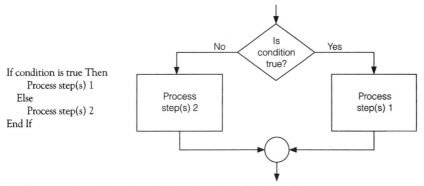

If condition is true Then
    Process step(s) 1
Else
    Process step(s) 2
End If

FIGURE 1-3   *Pseudocode and Flowchart for a Decision Structure*

The sequence and decision structures are both used to solve the following problem.

■ DIRECTION OF NUMBERED NYC STREETS ALGORITHM

Problem: Given a street number of a one-way street in New York, decide the direction of the street, either eastbound or westbound.

Discussion: There is a simple rule to tell the direction of a one-way street in New York: Even numbered streets run eastbound.

Input: Street number

Processing: Decide if the street number is divisible by 2.

Output: "Eastbound" or "Westbound"

Figures 1-4 through 1-6 show the flowchart, pseudocode, and hierarchy chart for the New York numbered streets problem.

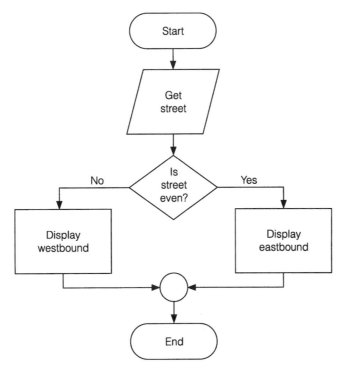

FIGURE 1-4   *Flowchart for the New York Numbered Streets Problem*

Program: Determine the direction of a numbered NYC street.

Get Street
If Street is even Then
        Display Eastbound
    Else
        Display Westbound
End If

FIGURE 1-5   *Pseudocode for the New York Numbered Streets Problem*

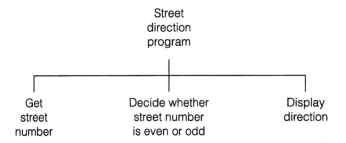

FIGURE 1-6   *Hierarchy Chart for the New York Numbered Streets Problem*

The solution to the next problem requires the repetition of a series of instructions. A programming structure that executes instructions many times is called a **loop structure**.

We need a test (or decision) to tell when the loop should end. Without an exit condition, the loop would repeat endlessly (an infinite loop). One way to control the number of times a loop repeats (often referred to as the number of passes or iterations) is to check a condition before each pass through the loop and continue executing the loop as long as the condition is true. See Figure 1-7.

Do While condition is true
    Process step(s)
Loop

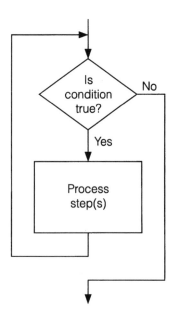

FIGURE 1-7   *Pseudocode and Flowchart for a Loop*

■ CLASS AVERAGE ALGORITHM

Problem: Calculate and report the grade-point average for a class.

Discussion: The average grade equals the sum of all grades divided by the number of students. We need a loop to read and then add (accumulate) the grades for each student in the class. Inside the loop, we also need to total (count) the number of students in the class. See Figures 1-8 to 1-10.

Input: Student grades

Processing: Find the sum of the grades; count the number of students; calculate average grade = sum of grades / number of students.

Output: Average grade

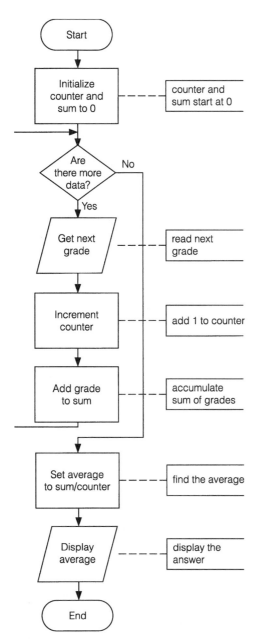

FIGURE 1-8   *Flowchart for the Class Average Problem*

Program: Determine the average grade of a class
Initialize Counter and Sum to 0
Do While there are more data
   Get the next Grade
   Add the Grade to the Sum
   Increment the Counter Loop
Compute Average = Sum / Counter
Display Average

FIGURE 1-9   *Pseudocode for the Class Average Problem*

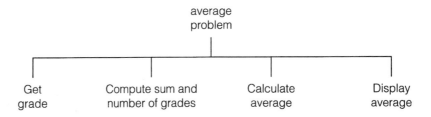

FIGURE 1-10   *Hierarchy Chart for the Class-Average Problem*

COMMENTS

1. Tracing a flowchart is like playing a board game. We begin at the Start symbol and proceed from symbol to symbol until we reach the End symbol. At any time, we will be at just one symbol. In a board game, the path taken depends on the result of spinning a spinner or rolling a pair of dice. The path taken through a flowchart depends on the input.

2. The algorithm should be tested at the flowchart stage before being coded into a program. Different data should be used as input, and the output checked. This process is known as **desk checking**. The test data should include nonstandard data as well as typical data.

3. Flowcharts, pseudocode, and hierarchy charts are universal problem-solving tools. They can be used to construct programs in any computer language, not just Visual Basic.

4. Flowcharts are used throughout this text to provide a visualization of the flow of certain programming tasks and Visual Basic control structures. Major examples of pseudocode and hierarchy charts appear in the case studies.

5. There are four primary logical programming constructs: sequence, decision, loop, and unconditional branch. Unconditional branch, which appears in some languages as Goto statements, involves jumping from one place in a program to another. Structured programming uses the first three constructs but forbids the fourth. One advantage of pseudocode over flowcharts is that pseudocode has no provision for unconditional branching and thus forces the programmer to write structured programs.

6. Flowcharts are time-consuming to write and difficult to update. For this reason, professional programmers are more likely to favor pseudocode and hierarchy charts. Because flowcharts so clearly illustrate the logical flow of programming techniques, however, they are a valuable tool in the education of programmers.

7. There are many styles of pseudocode. Some programmers use an outline form, whereas others use a form that looks almost like a programming language. The pseudocode appearing in the case studies of this text focuses on the primary tasks to be performed by the program and leaves many of the routine details to be completed during the coding process. Several Visual Basic keywords, such as, Print, If, Do, and While, are used extensively in the pseudocode appearing in this text.

8. Many people draw rectangles around each item in a hierarchy chart. In this text, rectangles are omitted to encourage the use of hierarchy charts by making them easier to draw.

2

FUNDAMENTALS OF PROGRAMMING IN VISUAL BASIC

2.1 VISUAL BASIC OBJECTS

Visual Basic programs display a Windows style screen (called a **form**) with boxes into which users type (and edit) information and buttons that they click to initiate actions. The boxes and buttons are referred to as **controls**. Forms and controls are called **objects**. In this section, we examine forms and four of the most useful Visual Basic controls.

Note: If Visual Basic has not been installed on your computer, you can install it by following the steps outlined on the first page of Appendix B.

Invoking Visual Basic 6.0: To invoke Visual Basic, click the Start button, point to Programs, point to Microsoft Visual Basic 6.0, and click on Microsoft Visual Basic 6.0 in the final list.

With all versions of Visual Basic 6.0, the center of the screen will contain the New Project window of Figure 2-1. The main part of the window is a tabbed dialog box with three tabs—New, Existing, and Recent. (If the New tab is not in the foreground, click on it to bring it to the front.) The number of project icons showing are either three (with the Working Model and Learning Editions) or thirteen (with the Professional and Enterprise Editions).

FIGURE 2-1   *New Project Window from the Working Model Edition of VB 6.0*

Double-click the Standard EXE icon to bring up the initial Visual Basic screen in Figure 2-2. The appearance of this screen varies slightly with the different versions of Visual Basic.

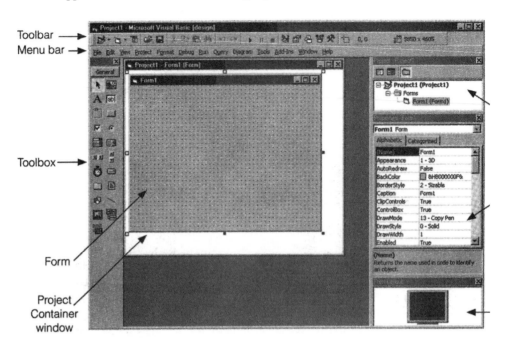

FIGURE 2-2   *The Initial Visual Basic Screen*

The **Menu bar** of the Visual Basic screen displays the commands you use to work with Visual Basic. Some of the menus, like File, Edit, View, and Window, are common to most Windows applications. Others, such as Project, Format, and Debug, provide commands specific to programming in Visual Basic.

The **Toolbar** is a collection of icons that carry out standard operations when clicked. For example, the fifth icon, which looks like a diskette, can be used to save the current program to a disk. To reveal the function of a Toolbar icon, position the mouse pointer over the icon for a few seconds.

The large stippled **Form window**, or **form** for short, becomes a Windows window when a program is executed. Most information displayed by the program appears on the form. The information usually is displayed in controls that have been placed on the form. The **Form Layout window** allows you to position the location of the form at run time relative to the entire screen using a small graphical representation of the screen.

The **Project Explorer window** is seldom needed for our purposes until Section 12. The **Properties window** is used to change how objects look and react.

The icons in the **Toolbox** represent controls that can be placed on the form. The four controls discussed in this section are text boxes, labels, command buttons, and picture boxes.

Text boxes: You use a text box primarily to get information, referred to as **input**, from the user.

Labels: You place a label to the left of a text box to tell the user what type of information to enter into the text box. You also use labels to display output.

Command buttons: The user clicks a command button to initiate an action.

Picture boxes: You use a picture box to display text or graphics output.

A TEXT BOX WALKTHROUGH

1. Double-click on the text box icon. (The text box icon consists of the letters ab and a vertical bar cursor inside a rectangle and is the fourth icon in the Toolbox.) A rectangle with eight small squares, called **sizing handles**, appears at the center of the form. See Figure 2-3.

 Sizing handles

FIGURE 2-3   *A Text Box with Sizing Handles*

2. Click anywhere on the form outside the rectangle to remove the handles.

3. Click on the rectangle to restore the handles. An object showing its handles is (said to be) **selected**. A selected object can have its size altered, location changed, and other properties modified.

4. Move the mouse arrow to the handle in the center of the right side of the text box. The cursor should change to a double arrow (◀▬▶). Hold down the left mouse button, and move the mouse to the right. The text box is stretched to the right. Similarly, grabbing the text box by one of the other handles and moving the mouse stretches the text box in another direction. For instance, you use the handle in the upper-left corner to stretch the text box up and to the left. Handles also can be used to make the text box smaller.

5. Move the mouse arrow to any point of the text box other than a handle, hold down the left mouse button, and move the mouse. You can now drag the text box to a new location. Using Steps 4 and 5, you can place a text box of any size anywhere on the form.

   Note: The text box should now be selected; that is, its sizing handles should be showing. If not, click anywhere inside the text box to select it.

6. Press the delete key, Del, to remove the text box from the form. Step 7 gives an alternative way to place a text box of any size at any location on the form.

7. Click on the text box icon in the Toolbox. Then move the mouse pointer to any place on the form. (When over the form, the mouse pointer becomes a pair of crossed thin lines.) Hold down the left mouse button, and move the mouse on a diagonal to generate a rectangle. Release the mouse button to obtain a selected text box. You can now alter the size and location as before.

   Note: The text box should now be selected; that is, its sizing handles should be showing. If not, click anywhere inside the text box to select it.

8. Press F4 to activate the Properties window. (You can also activate the properties window by clicking on it or clicking on the Properties window icon in the Toolbar.) See Figure 2-4. The first line of the Properties window (called the **Object box**) reads "Text1 TextBox". Text1 is the current name of the text box. The two tabs permit you to view the list of properties either alphabetically or grouped into categories. Text boxes have 43 properties that can be grouped into 7 categories. Use the up- and down-arrow keys (or the up- and down-scroll arrows) to glance through the list. The left column gives the property and the right column gives the current setting of the property. We discuss four properties in this walkthrough.

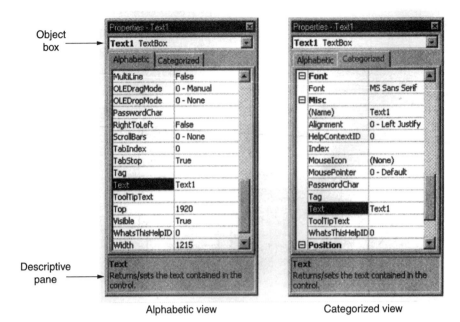

Alphabetic view   Categorized view

FIGURE 2-4   *Text Box Properties Window*

9. Move to the Text property with the up- and down-arrow keys. (Alternatively, scroll until the property is visible and click on the property.) The Text property is now highlighted. The Text property determines the words in the text box. Currently, the words are set to "Text1" in the **Settings box** on the right.

10. Type your first name. As you type, your name replaces "Text1" in both the Settings box and the text box. See Figure 2-5. (Alternatively, you could have clicked on the Settings box and edited its contents.)

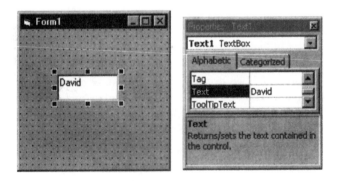

FIGURE 2-5   *Setting the Text Property to David*

11. Click at the beginning of your name in the Settings box and add your title, such as Mr., Ms., or The Honorable. (If you mistyped your name, you can easily correct it now.)

12. Press Shift+Ctrl+F to move to the first property that begins with the letter F. Now use the down-arrow key or the mouse to highlight the property ForeColor. The foreground color is the color of the text.

13. Click on the down arrow in the right part of the Settings box, and then click on the Palette tab to display a selection of colors. See Figure 2-6. Click on one of the solid colors, such as blue or red. Notice the change in the color of your name.

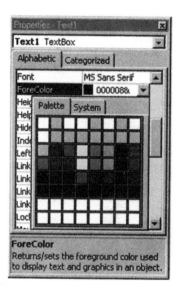

FIGURE 2-6   *Setting the ForeColor Property*

14. Highlight the Font property with a single click of the mouse. The current font is named MS Sans Serif.

15. Click on the ellipsis (...) box in the right part of the settings box to display a dialog box. See Figure 2-7. The three lists give the current name (MS Sans Serif), current style (Regular), and current size (8) of the font. You can change any of these attributes by clicking. Click on Bold in the style list, and click on 12 in the size list. Now click on the OK button to see your name displayed in a larger bold font.

16. Click on the text box and resize it to be about 3 inches wide and 1 inch high.

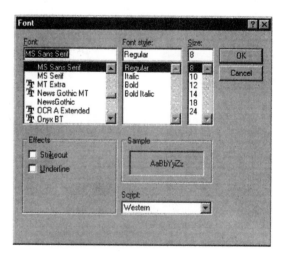

FIGURE 2-7   *The Font Dialog Box*

Visual Basic programs consist of three parts—interface, values of properties, and code. Our interface consists of a form with a single object, a text box. We have set a few properties for the text box—the text (namely, your name), the foreground color, the font style, and the font size. In Section 2.2, we see how to place code into a program. Visual Basic endows certain capabilities to programs that are independent of any code. We will now run the existing codeless program and experience these capabilities.

17. Press F5 to run the program. (Alternatively, a program can be run from the menu by pressing Alt/R/S or by clicking on the Start icon 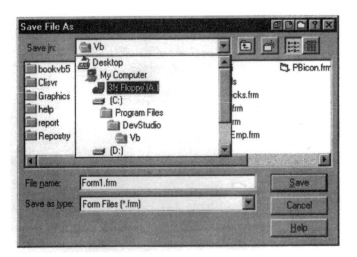, the twelfth icon on the Toolbar.) Notice that the dots have disappeared from the form.

18. The cursor is at the beginning of your name. Press the End key to move the cursor to the end of your name. Now type in your last name, and then keep typing. Eventually, the words will scroll to the left.

19. Press Home to return to the beginning of the text. You have a full-fledged word processor at your disposal. You can place the cursor anywhere you like to add or delete text. You can drag the cursor across text to create a block, place a copy of the block in the clipboard with Ctrl+C, and then duplicate it anywhere with Ctrl+V.

20. To terminate the program, press Alt+F4. Alternatively, you can end a program by clicking on the End icon , the fourteenth icon on the Toolbar, or clicking on the form's close button .

21. Select the text box, activate the Properties window, select the MultiLine property, click on the down-arrow button, and finally click on True. The MultiLine property has been changed from False to True.

22. Run the program, and type in the text box. Notice that now words wrap around when the end of a line is reached. Also, text will scroll up when it reaches the bottom of the text box.

23. End the program.

24. Press Alt/F/V, or click on the Save Project icon to save the work done so far. A Save File As dialog box appears. See Figure 2-8. Visual Basic creates two disk files to store a program. The first, with the extension .frm, is entered into the Save File As dialog box and the second, with the extension .vbp, into a Save Project As dialog box. Visual Basic refers to programs as **projects**.

FIGURE 2-8   *The Save File As Dialog Box*

25. Type a file name, such as *testprog* into the "File name" box. The extension .frm automatically will be appended to the name. Do not press the Enter key yet. (Pressing the Enter key has the same effect as clicking Save.) The selection in the "Save in" box tells where your program will be saved. Alter it as desired. (**Suggestion:** If you are using a computer in a campus computer lab, you probably should use a diskette to save your work. If so, place the diskette in a drive, say, the A drive, and select 3 1/2 Floppy (A:) in the "Save in" box.)

26. Click the Save button when you are ready to go on. (Alternatively, press Tab several times until the Save button is highlighted and then press Enter.) The Save Project As dialog box appears.

27. Type a file name into the File name box. You can use the same name, such as *testprog*, as before. Then proceed as in Steps 25 and 26. (The extension .vbp will be added.)

28. Press Alt/F/N to begin a new program. (As before, select Standard EXE.)

29. Place three text boxes on the form. (Move each text box out of the center of the form before creating the next.) Notice that they have the names Text1, Text2, and Text3.

30. Run the program. Notice that the cursor is in Text1. We say that Text1 has the **focus**. (This means that Text1 is the currently selected object and any keyboard actions will be sent directly to this object.) Any text typed will display in that text box.

31. Press Tab once. Now, Text2 has the focus. When you type, the characters appear in Text2.

32. Press Tab several times and then press Shift+Tab a few times. With Tab, the focus cycles through the objects on the form in the order the objects were created. With Shift+Tab, the focus cycles in the reverse order.

33. End the program.

34. Press Alt/F/O, or click on the Open Project icon to reload your first program. When a dialog box asks if you want to save your changes, click the No button or press N. An Open Project dialog box appears on the screen. Click on the Recent tab to see a list of the programs most recently opened or saved. Your first program and its location should appear at the top of the list. (*Note:* You can also find any program by clicking on the Existing tab and using the dialog box to search for the program.)

35. Click on the name of your first program and then click on the Open button. Alternatively, double-click on the name. (You also have the option of typing the name into the File Name box and then clicking the Open button.)

A COMMAND BUTTON WALKTHROUGH

1. Press Alt/F/N and double-click on Standard EXE to start a new program. There is no need to save anything.

2. Double-click on the command button icon to place a command button in the center of the form. (The rectangular-shaped command button icon is the sixth icon in the Toolbox.)

3. Activate the Properties window, highlight the Caption property, and type "Please Push Me". See Figure 2-9. Notice that the letters appear on the command button as they are typed. The button is too small.

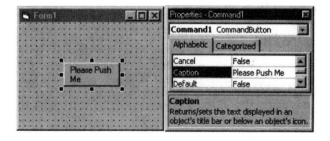

FIGURE 2-9 *Setting the Caption Property*

4. Click on the command button to select it, and then enlarge it to accommodate the phrase "Please Push Me" on one line.

5. Run the program, and click on the command button. The command button appears to move in and then out. In Section 2.2, we write code that is activated when a command button is pushed.

6. End the program, and select the command button.

7. From the Properties window, edit the Caption setting by inserting an ampersand (&) before the first letter, P. Notice that the ampersand does not show on the button. However, the letter following the ampersand is now underlined. See Figure 2-10. Pressing Alt+P while the program is running executes the same code as clicking the command button. Here, P is referred to as the **access key** for the command button. (The access key is always specified by the character following the ampersand.)

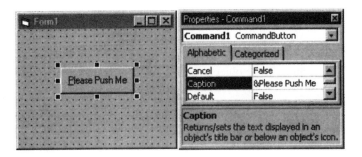

FIGURE 2-10   *Designating P as an Access Key*

 A LABEL WALKTHROUGH

1. Press Alt/F/N and double-click on Standard EXE to start a new program. There is no need to save anything.

2. Double-click on the label icon to place a label in the center of the form. (The label icon, a large letter A, is the third icon in the Toolbox.)

3. Activate the Properties window, highlight the Caption property, and type "Enter Your Phone Number". Such a label would be placed next to a text box into which the user will enter a phone number.

4. Click on the label to select it, and then widen it until all words are on the same line.

5. Make the label narrower until the words occupy two lines.

6. Activate the Properties window, and double-click on the Alignment property. Double-click two more times and observe the label's appearance. The combination of sizing and alignment permits you to design a label easily.

7. Run the program. Nothing happens, even if you click on the label. Labels just sit there. The user cannot change what a label displays unless you write code to allow the change.

8. End the program.

 A PICTURE BOX WALKTHROUGH

1. Press Alt/F/N and double-click on Standard EXE to start a new program. There is no need to save anything.

2. Double-click on the picture box icon to place a picture box in the center of the form. (The picture box icon is the second icon in the Toolbox. It contains a picture of the sun shining over a desert.)

3. Enlarge the picture box.

4. Run the program. Nothing happens and nothing will, no matter what you do. Although picture boxes look like text boxes, you can't type in them. However, you can display text in them with statements discussed later in this section, you can draw lines and circles in them with statements discussed in Section 9, and you can insert pictures into them.

5. End the program and click the picture box to select it.

6. Activate the Properties window, and double-click on the Picture property. A Load Picture dialog box appears. See Figure 2-11.

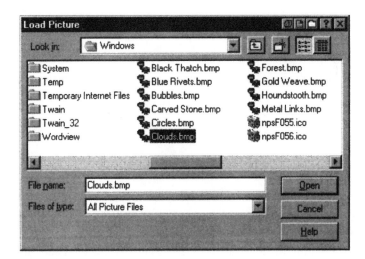

FIGURE 2-11   *The Load Picture Dialog Box*

7. Select the Windows folder and then double-click on one of the picture files. Good candidates are Clouds.bmp, shown in Figure 2-12, and Setup.bmp. (Also, the CD accompanying this textbook contains several picture files in the folder Pictures.)

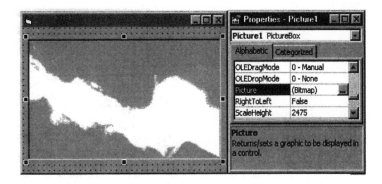

FIGURE 2-12   *A Picture Box Filled with the Clouds.bmp Picture*

8. Click on the picture box and press Del to remove the picture box.

COMMENTS

1. When selecting from a list, double-clicking has the same effect as clicking once and pressing Enter.

2. On a form, the Tab key cycles through the objects that can get the focus, and in a dialog box, it cycles through the items.

3. The form itself is also an object and has properties. For instance, you can change the text in the title bar with the Caption property. You can move the form by dragging the title bar of its Project Container window.

4. The name of an object is used in code to refer to the object. By default, objects are given names like Text1 and Text2. You can use the Properties window to change the Name property of an object to a more suggestive name. (The Name property is always the first property in the list of properties. An object's Name must start with a letter and can be a maximum of 40 characters. It can include numbers and underline (_) characters, but can't include punctuation or spaces.) Also, Microsoft recommends that each name begin with a three-letter prefix that identifies the type of the control. See the table below. Beginning with Section 2.2, we will use suggestive names and these prefixes whenever possible.

Object	Prefix	Example
command button	cmd	cmdComputeTotal
form	frm	frmPayroll
label	lbl	blInstructions
picture box	pic	picClouds
text box	txt	txtAddress

5. The Name and Caption properties of a command button are both initially set to something like Command1. However, changing one of these properties does not affect the setting of the other property. Similarly for the Name and Caption properties of forms and labels, and for the Name and Text properties of text boxes.

6. The color settings appear as strings of digits and letters preceded by &H and trailed with &. Don't concern yourself with the notation.

7. Here are some fine points on the use of the Properties window.

   (a) Press Shift+Ctrl+*letterkey* to highlight the first property that begins with that letter. Successive pressings highlight successive properties that begin with that letter.

   (b) To change the selected object from the Properties window, click on the down-arrow icon at the right of the Object box of the Properties window. Then select the new object from the drop-down list.

8. Some useful properties that have not been discussed are the following:

   (a) BorderStyle: Setting the BorderStyle to "0 – None" removes the border from an object.

   (b) Visible: Setting the Visible property to False hides an object when the program is run. The object can be made to reappear with code.

   (c) BackColor: Specifies the background color for a text box, label, picture box, or form. Also specifies the background color for a command button having the Style property set to "1 – Graphical." (Such a command button can display a picture.)

   (d) BackStyle: The BackStyle property of a label is opaque by default. The rectangular region associated with the label is filled with the label's background color and caption. Setting the background style of a label to transparent causes whatever is behind the label to remain visible; the background color of the label essentially becomes "see through."

(e) Font: Can be set to any of Windows' fonts, such as Courier and Times New Roman. Two unusual fonts are Symbol and Wingdings. For instance, with the Wingdings font, pressing the keys for %, &, ', and J yield a bell, a book, a candle, and a smiling face, respectively. To view the character sets for the different Windows' fonts, click on the Start button, and successively select Programs, Accessories, and Character Map. Then click on Character Map or press the Enter key. After selecting a font, hold down the left mouse button on any character to enlarge it and obtain the keystroke that produces that character.

9. When you click on a property in the Properties window, a description of the property appears just below the window. Additional information about many of the properties can be found in Appendix C. With the Learning, Professional, and Enterprise Editions of VB6.0 you can obtain very detailed (and somewhat advanced) information about a property by clicking on the property and pressing F1 for Help.

10. Most properties can be set or altered with code as the program is running instead of being preset from the Properties window. For instance, a command button can be made to disappear with a line such as Command1.Visible = False. See Section 2.2 for details.

11. The BorderStyle and MultiLine properties of a text box can be set only from the Properties window. You cannot alter them during run time.

12. Of the objects discussed in this section, only command buttons have true access keys.

13. If you inadvertently double-click an object in a form, a window containing two lines of text will appear. (The first line begins Private Sub.) This is a code window and is discussed in the next section. To remove this window, click on its Close button.

14. To enlarge (or decrease) the Project Container window, position the mouse cursor anywhere on the right or bottom edge and drag the mouse. To enlarge (or decrease) the form, select the form and drag one of its sizing handles. Alternatively, you can enlarge either the Project Container window or the form by clicking on its Maximize button.

15. We will always be selecting the Standard EXE icon from the New Project window.

2.2 VISUAL BASIC EVENTS

When a Visual Basic program is run, a form and its controls appear on the screen. Normally, nothing happens until the user takes an action, such as clicking a control or pressing the Tab key. Such an action is called an **event**.

The three steps to creating a Visual Basic program are as follows:

1. Create the interface; that is, generate, position, and size the objects.

2. Set properties; that is, set relevant properties for the objects.

3. Write the code that executes when the events occur.

This section is devoted to Step 3.

Code consists of statements that carry out tasks. Visual Basic has a repertoire of over 200 statements and we will use many of them in this text. In this section, we limit ourselves to statements that change properties of objects while a program is running.

Properties of an object are changed in code with statements of the form

```
objectName.property = setting
```

where *objectName* is the name of the form or a control, *property* is one of the properties of the object, and *setting* is a valid setting for that object. Such statements are called **assignment statements**. They assign values to properties. Here are three other assignment statements.

The statement

```
txtBox.Font.Size = 12
```

sets the size of the characters in the text box named txtBox to 12.

The statement

```
txtBox.Font.Bold = True
```

converts the characters in the text box to boldface.

The statement

```
txtBox.Text = ""
```

clears the contents of the text box; that is, it invokes the blank setting.

Most events are associated with objects. The event *clicking cmdButton* is different from the event *clicking picBox*. These two events are specified cmdButton_Click and picBox_Click. The statements to be executed when an event occurs are written in a block of code called an **event procedure**. The structure of an event procedure is

```
Private Sub objectName_event()
   statements
End Sub
```

The word Sub in the first line signals the beginning of the event procedure, and the first line identifies the object and the event occurring to that object. The last line signals the termination of the event procedure. The statements to be executed appear between these two lines. (***Note:*** The word Private indicates that the event procedure cannot be invoked by an event from another form. This will not concern us until much later in the text. The word *Sub* is an abbreviation of *Subprogram*.) For instance, the event procedure

```
Private Sub cmdButton_Click()
   txtBox.Text = ""
End Sub
```

clears the contents of the text box when the command button is clicked.

■ AN EVENT PROCEDURE WALKTHROUGH

The form in Figure 2-13, which contains a text box and a command button, will be used to demonstrate what event procedures are and how they are created. Three event procedures will be used to alter the appearance of a phrase that is typed into the text box. The event procedures are txtPhrase_LostFocus, txtPhrase_GotFocus, and cmdBold_Click.

Object	Property	Setting
frmWalkthrough	Caption	Demonstration
txtPhrase	Text	(blank)
cmdBold	Caption	Make Phrase Bold

FIGURE 2-13   *The Interface for the Event Procedure Walkthrough*

1. Create the interface in Figure 2-13. The Name properties of the form, text box, and command button should be set as shown in the Object column. The Caption property of the form should be set to Demonstration, the Text property of the text box should be made blank, and the Caption property of the command button should be set to Make Phrase Bold.

2. Double-click on the text box. A window, called the **Code window**, appears. See Figure 2-14. Just below the title bar are two drop-down list boxes. The left box is called the **Object box** and the right box is called the **Procedure box**. (When you position the mouse pointer over one of these list boxes, its type appears.)

Object
box
Procedure
box

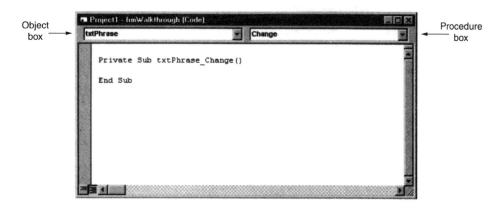

FIGURE 2-14   *A Code Window*

3. Click on the down-arrow button to the right of the Procedure box. The drop-down menu that appears contains a list of all possible event procedures associated with text boxes. See Figure 2-15.

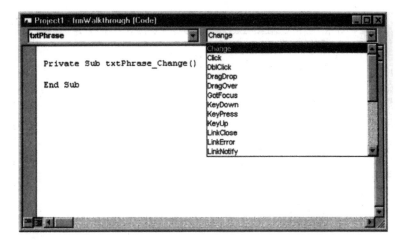

FIGURE 2-15   *Drop-Down Menu of Event Procedures*

4. Scroll down the list of event procedures and click on LostFocus. (LostFocus is the 14th event procedure.) The lines

```
Private Sub txtPhrase_LostFocus()

End Sub
```

appear in the code window with a blinking cursor poised at the beginning of the blank line.

5. Type the line

```
txtPhrase.Font.Size = 12
```

between the existing two lines. (We usually indent lines inside procedures.) (After you type each period, the editor displays a list containing possible choices of items to follow the period. See Figure 2-16. This feature is called "List Properties/Methods." In Figure 2-16, instead of typing the word "Size," you can double-click on "Size" in the displayed list or highlight the word "Size" and press Tab.) The screen appears as in Figure 2-17. We have now created an event procedure that is activated whenever the text box loses the focus.

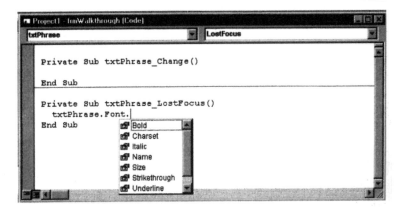

FIGURE 2-16   *A LostFocus Event Procedure*

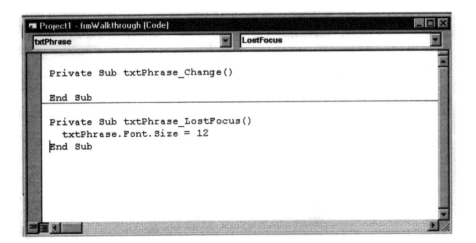

FIGURE 2-17   *A LostFocus Event Procedure*

6. Let's create another event procedure for the text box. Click on the down-arrow button to the right of the Procedure box, scroll up the list of event procedures, and click on GotFocus. Then type the lines

```
txtPhrase.Font.Size = 8txtPhrase.Font.Bold = False
```

between the existing two lines. See Figure 2-18.

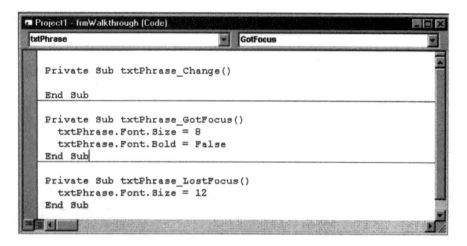

FIGURE 2-18 *A GotFocus Event Procedure*

7. The txtPhrase_Change event procedure in Figure 2-18 was not used and can be deleted. To delete the procedure, highlight it by dragging the mouse across the two lines of code, and then press the Del key.

8. Let's now create an event procedure for the command button. Click on the down-arrow button to the right of the Object box. The drop-down menu contains a list of the objects, along with a mysterious object called (General). See Figure 2-19. [We'll discuss (General) in the next section.]

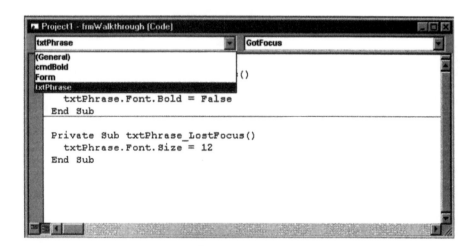

FIGURE 2-19 *List of Objects*

9. Click on cmdBold. The event procedure cmdBold_Click is displayed. Type in the line

```
txtPhrase.Font.Bold = True
```

The screen appears as in Figure 2-20, and the program is complete.

```
Project1 - frmWalkthrough (Code)
cmdBold                                    Click

    Private Sub cmdBold_Click()
        txtPhrase.Font.Bold = True
    End Sub

    Private Sub txtPhrase_GotFocus()
        txtPhrase.Font.Size = 8
        txtPhrase.Font.Bold = False
    End Sub

    Private Sub txtPhrase_LostFocus()
        txtPhrase.Font.Size = 12
    End Sub
```

FIGURE 2-20   *The Three Event Procedures*

10. Now run the program by pressing F5.

11. Type something into the text box. In Figure 2-21, the words "Hello Friend" have been typed. (A text box has the focus whenever it is ready to accept typing; that is, whenever it contains a blinking cursor.)

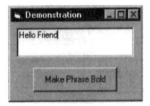

FIGURE 2-21   *Text Box Containing Input*

12. Press the Tab key. The contents of the text box will be enlarged as in Figure 2-22. When Tab was pressed, the text box lost the focus; that is, the event Lost-Focus happened to txtPhrase. Thus, the event procedure txtPhrase_ LostFocus was called, and the code inside the procedure was executed.

FIGURE 2-22   *Text Box After It Has Lost the Focus*

13. Click on the command button. This calls the event procedure cmd Bold_Click, which converts the text to boldface. See Figure 2-23.

FIGURE 2-23   *Text Box After the Command Button Has Been Clicked*

14. Click on the text box or press the Tab key to move the cursor (and, therefore, the focus) to the text box. This calls the event procedure txtPhrase_GotFocus, which restores the text to its original state.

15. You can repeat Steps 11 through 14 as many times as you like. When you are finished, end the program by pressing Alt+F4, clicking the End icon on the Toolbar, or clicking the Close button (X) on the form.

COMMENTS

1. To hide the code window, press the right mouse button and click on Hide. You can also hide it by clicking on the icon at the left side of the title bar and clicking on Close. To view a hidden code window, press Alt/View/Code. To hide a form, close its container. To view a hidden form, press Alt/View/Object.

2. The form is the default object in Visual Basic code. That is, code such as

```
Form1.property = setting
```

can be written as

```
property = setting
```

Also, event procedures associated with Form1 appear as

```
Form_event()
```

rather than

```
Form1_event()
```

3. Another useful command is SetFocus. The statement

```
object.SetFocus
```

moves the focus to the object.

4. We have ended our programs by clicking the End icon or pressing Alt+F4. A more elegant technique is to create a command button, call it cmdQuit, with caption Quit and the event procedure:

```
Private Sub cmdQuit_Click()
  End
End Sub
```

5. Certain words, such as Sub, End, and False, have special meanings in Visual Basic and are referred to as **keywords** or **reserved words**. The Visual Basic editor automatically capitalizes the first letter of a keyword and displays the word in blue.

6. Visual Basic can detect certain types of errors. For instance, consider the line

```
txtPhrase.Font.Bold = False
```

from the walkthrough. Suppose you neglected to type the word False to the right of the equal sign before leaving the line. Visual Basic would tell you something was missing by displaying the left message box at the top of page 66. (Also, the line would turn red.) On the other hand, suppose in the CmdBold_Click procedure you misspell the keyword "Bold" as "bolt." You might notice something is wrong when the letter "b" is not capitalized. If not, you will certainly know about the problem when the program is run because Visual Basic will display the right message box at the top of page 66 when you click on the command button. After you click on Debug, the line containing the offending word will be highlighted.

 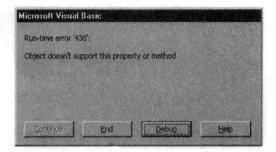

7. At design time, colors are selected from a palette. At run time, the eight most common colors can be assigned with the color constants vbBlack, vbRed, vbGreen, vbYellow, vbBlue, vbMagenta, vbCyan, and vbWhite. For instance, the statement

    ```
    picBox.BackColor = vbYellow
    ```

    gives picBox a yellow background.

8. For statements of the form *object.property = setting*, with properties Caption, Text, or Font.Name, the setting must be surrounded by quotes. (For instance, lblTwo.Caption = "Name", txtBox.Text = "Fore", and picBox.Font.Name = "Courier".) When the words True or False appear to the right of the equal sign, they should *not* be surrounded by quotation marks.

9. Code windows have many features of word processors. For instance, the operations cut, copy, paste, find, undo, and redo can be carried out with the sixth through eleventh icons of the Toolbar. These operations, and several others, also can be initiated from the Edit menu.

10. Names of existing event procedures associated with an object are *not* automatically changed when you rename the object. You must change them yourself and also must change any references to the object. Therefore, you should finalize the names of your objects before you put any code into their event procedures.

11. If you find the automatic List Properties/Methods feature distracting, you can turn it off by pressing Tools/Options, selecting the Editor page, and clicking on Auto List Members. If you do so, you can still display a list manually at the appropriate time by pressing Ctrl+J.

12. Earlier versions of Visual Basic used the property FontSize instead of Font.Size. Although Font.Size is preferred, FontSize is allowed for compatibility. Similarly, properties such as FontBold, FontItalic, and FontName have been included for compatibility with earlier versions of Visual Basic.

13. Assignment statements can be written preceded with the keyword Let. For instance, `txtBox.Text = "Hello"` also can be written `Let txtBox.Text = "Hello"`. Therefore, assignment statements are also known as Let statements.

2.3 NUMBERS

Much of the data processed by computers consists of numbers. In "computerese," numbers are often called **numeric constants**. This section discusses the operations that are performed with numbers and the ways numbers are displayed.

■ ARITHMETIC OPERATIONS

The five arithmetic operations in Visual Basic are addition, subtraction, multiplication, division, and exponentiation. (Because exponentiation is not as familiar as the others, it is reviewed in detail in Comment 10.) Addition, subtraction, and division are denoted in Visual Basic by the standard symbols +, −, and /, respectively. However, the notations for multiplication and exponentiation differ from the customary mathematical notations.

Mathematical Notation	Visual Basic Notation
$a \cdot b$ or $a \times b$	$a * b$
a^r	$a \wedge r$

(The asterisk [*] is the upper character of the 8 key. The caret [^] is the upper character of the 6 key.) *Note:* In this book, the proportional font used for text differs from the monospaced font used for programs. In the program font, the asterisk appears as a five-pointed star (*).

One way to show a number on the screen is to display it in a picture box. If n is a number, then the instruction

```
picBox.Print n
```

displays the number n in the picture box. If the picBox.Print instruction is followed by a combination of numbers and arithmetic operations, it carries out the operations and displays the result. Print is a reserved word and the Print operation is called a **method**. Another important method is Cls. The statement

    picBox.Cls

erases all text and graphics from the picture box picBox.

EXAMPLE 1

The following program applies each of the five arithmetic operations to the numbers 3 and 2. Notice that 3/2 is displayed in decimal form. Visual Basic never displays numbers as common fractions. *Note 1:* The star in the fifth and eighth lines is the computer font version of the asterisk. *Note 2:* The word "Run" in the phrasing [Run ...] indicates that F5 should be pressed to execute the program. *Note 3:* All programs appearing in examples and case studies are provided on the CD accompanying this book. See the discussion on the next to last page of the book for details.

Below is the form design and a table showing the names of the objects on the form and the settings, if any, for properties of these objects. This form design is also used in the discussion and examples in the remainder of this section.

Object	Property	Setting
frm3_3_1	Caption,	3-3-1
picResults		
cmdCompute	Caption	Compute

```
Private Sub cmdCompute_Click()
  picResults.Cls
  picResults.Print 3 + 2
  picResults.Print 3 - 2
  picResults.Print 3 * 2
  picResults.Print 3 / 2
  picResults.Print 3 ^ 2
  picResults.Print 2 * (3 + 4)
End Sub
```

[Run and then click the command button.]

■ SCIENTIFIC NOTATION

Let us review powers of 10 and scientific notation. Our method of decimal notation is based on a systematic use of exponents.

$$10^1 = 10 \qquad\qquad 10^{-1} = 1/10 = .1$$
$$10^2 = 100 \qquad\qquad 10^{-2} = .01$$
$$10^3 = 1000 \qquad\qquad 10^{-3} = .001$$

$$\cdot$$
$$\cdot$$
$$\cdot$$

$$10^n = \underbrace{1000...0}_{n \text{ zeros}} \qquad\qquad 10^{-n} = \underbrace{.001...01}_{n \text{ digits}}$$

Scientific notation provides a convenient way of writing numbers by using powers of 10 to stand for zeros. Numbers are written in the form $b \cdot 10^r$, where b is a number from 1 up to (but not including) 10, and r is an integer. For example, it is much more convenient to write the diameter of the sun (1,400,000,000 meters) in scientific notation: $1.4 \cdot 10^9$ meters. Similarly, rather than write .0000003 meters for the diameter of a bacterium, it is simpler to write $3 \cdot 10{-}7$ meters.

Any acceptable number can be entered into the computer in either standard or scientific notation. The form in which Visual Basic displays a number depends on many factors, with size being an important consideration. In Visual Basic, $b \cdot 10^r$ is usually written as bEr. (The letter E is an abbreviation for *exponent*.) The following forms of the numbers just mentioned are equivalent.

1.4 * 10^9	1.4E+09 1	4E+9	1.4E9	1400000000
3 * 10^-7	3E-07	3E-7	.0000003	

The computer displays r as a two-digit number, preceded by a plus sign if r is positive and a minus sign if r is negative.

EXAMPLE 2

The following program illustrates scientific notation. The computer's choice of whether to display a number in scientific or standard form depends on the magnitude of the number.

```
Private Sub cmdCompute_Click()
  picResults.Cls
  picResults.Print 1.2 * 10 ^ 34
  picResults.Print 1.2 * 10 ^ 8
  picResults.Print 1.2 * 10 ^ 3
  picResults.Print 10 ^ -20
  picResults.Print 10 ^ -2
End Sub
```

[Run and then click the command button.]

■ VARIABLES

In applied mathematics problems, quantities are referred to by names. For instance, consider the following high school algebra problem. "If a car travels at 50 miles per hour, how far will it travel in 14 hours? Also, how many hours are required to travel 410 miles?" The solution to this problem uses the well-known formula

$$\text{distance} = \text{speed} \times \text{time elapsed}$$

Here's how this problem would be solved with a computer program.

```
Private Sub cmdCompute_Click()
   picResults.Cls speed = 50
   timeElapsed = 14
   distance = speed * timeElapsed
   picResults.Print distance
   distance = 410
   timeElapsed = distance / speed
   picResults.Print timeElapsed
End Sub
```

[Run, and then click the command button. The following is displayed in the picture box.]

```
700
8.2
```

The third line of the event procedure sets the speed to 50, and the fourth line sets the time elapsed to 14. The fifth line multiplies the value for the speed by the value for the time elapsed and sets the distance to this product. The next line displays the answer to the first question. The three lines before the End Sub statement answer the second question in a similar manner.

The names *speed*, *timeElapsed*, and *distance*, which hold numbers, are referred to as **variables**. Consider the variable *timeElapsed*. In the fourth line, its value was set to 14. In the eighth line, its value was changed as the result of a computation. On the other hand, the variable *speed* had the same value, 50, throughout the program.

In general, a variable is a name that is used to refer to an item of data. The value assigned to the variable may change during the execution of the program. In Visual Basic, variable names can be up to 255 characters long, must begin with a letter, and can consist only of letters, digits, and underscores. (The shortest variable names consist of a single letter.) Visual Basic does not distinguish between uppercase and lowercase letters used in variable names. Some examples of variable names are *total*, *numberOfCars*, *taxRate_1999*, and *n*. As a convention, we write variable names in lowercase letters except for the first letters of additional words (as in *numberOfCars*).

If *var* is a variable and *num* is a constant, then the statement

```
var = num
```

assigns the number *num* to the variable *var*. (Such a statement is called an **assignment statement**.) Actually, the computer sets aside a location in memory with the name *var* and places the number *num* in it. The statement

```
picBox.Print var
```

looks into this memory location for the value of the variable and displays the value in the picture box.

A combination of constants, variables, and arithmetic operations that can be evaluated to yield a number is called a **numeric expression**. Expressions are evaluated by replacing each variable by its value and carrying out the arithmetic. Some examples of expressions are 2 * distance + 7, n + 1, and (a + b) / 3.

EXAMPLE 3

The following program displays the value of an expression.

```
Private Sub cmdCompute_Click()
  picResults.Cls
  a = 5
  b = 4
  picResults.Print a * (2 + b)
End Sub
```

[Run, and then click the command button. The following is displayed in the picture box.]

30

If *var* is a variable, then the statement

```
var = expression
```

first evaluates the expression on the right and *then* assigns its value to the variable. For instance, the event procedure in Example 3 can be written as

```
Private Sub cmdCompute_Click()
  picResults.Cls
  a = 5
  b = 4
  c = a * (2 + b)
  picResults.Print c
End Sub
```

The expression a * (2 + b) is evaluated to 30 and then this value is assigned to the variable *c*.

Because the expression on the right side of an assignment statement is evaluated *before* an assignment is made, a statement such as

```
n = n + 1
```

is meaningful. It first evaluates the expression on the right (that is, it adds 1 to the original value of the variable *n*), and then assigns this sum to the variable *n*. The effect is to increase the value of the variable *n* by 1. In terms of memory locations, the statement retrieves the value of *n* from *n*'s memory location, uses it to compute *n* + 1, and then places the sum back into *n*'s memory location.

■ PRINT METHOD

Consider the following event procedure.

```
Private Sub cmdDisplay_Click()
  picResults.Cls
  picResults.Print 3
  picResults.Print -3
End Sub
```

[Run and then click the command button.]

Notice that the negative number –3 begins directly at the left margin, whereas the positive number 3 begins one space to the right. The Print method always displays nonnegative numbers with a leading space. The Print method also displays a trailing space after every number. Although the trailing spaces are not apparent here, we will soon see evidence of their presence.

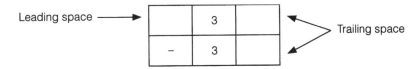

The Print methods used so far display only one number per line. After displaying a number, the cursor moves to the leftmost position and down a line for the next display. Borrowing from typewriter terminology, we say that the computer performs a carriage return and a line feed after each number is displayed. The carriage return and line feed, however, can be suppressed by placing a semicolon at the end of the number.

EXAMPLE 4

The following program illustrates the use of semicolons in Print methods. The output reveals the presence of the space trailing each number. For instance, the space trailing –3 combines with the leading space of 99 to produce two spaces between the numbers.

```
Private Sub cmdDisplay_Click()
   picResults.Cls
   picResults.Print 3;
   picResults.Print -3;
   picResults.Print 99;
   picResults.Print 100
End Sub
```

[Run, and then click the command button.]

Semicolons can be used to display several numbers with one Print method. If *m*, *n*, and *r* are numbers, a line of the form

```
picBox.Print m; n; r
```

displays the three numbers, one after another, separated only by their leading and trailing spaces. For instance, the Print methods in preceding Example 4 can be replaced by the single line

```
picResults.Print 3; -3; 99; 100
```

COMMENTS

1. Numbers must not contain commas, dollar signs, or percent signs. Also, mixed numbers, such as 8 1/2, are not allowed.

2. Some people think of the equal sign (=) in an assignment statement as an arrow pointing to the left. This stresses the fact that the value on the right is assigned to the variable on the left.

3. Parentheses should be used when necessary to clarify the meaning of an expression. When there are no parentheses, the arithmetic operations are performed in the following order: (1) exponentiations; (2) multiplications and divisions; (3) additions and subtractions. In the event of ties, the leftmost operation is carried out first. Table 2-1 summarizes these rules.

TABLE 2-1
Level of Precedence for Arithmetic Operations

( )	Inner to outer, left to right
^	Left to right in expression
*/	Left to right in expression
+ −	Left to right in expression

4. Restricted keywords cannot be used as names of variables. For instance, the statements print = 99 and end = 99 are not valid. Some other common restricted keywords are Call, If, Let, Select, and Sub. If a keyword is used as a variable name, you will soon be warned that something is wrong. As soon as the cursor is moved from the line, an error message will appear, and the line will turn red. The use of some other keywords (such as Error, Height, Name, Rate, Time, Val, Width, and Year) as variable names does not trigger an immediate warning, but generates an error message when the program is run. Although there is a way to get Visual Basic to accept this last group of keywords as variable names, we will never use keywords as variable names. Most of the items in Appendix C, other than properties, are reserved words. You can tell immediately when you inadvertently use a reserved word as a variable in an assignment statement because Visual Basic automatically capitalizes the first letter of keywords. For instance, if you type "rate = 50" and press the Enter key, the line will change to "Rate = 50".

5. Grammatical errors, such as misspellings or incorrect punctuations, are called **syntax errors**. Certain types of syntax errors are spotted by the smart editor when they are entered, whereas others are not detected until the program is executed. When Visual Basic spots an error, it displays a dialog box. Some incorrect statements and their errors are given below.

Statement	**Reason for Error**
picBox.Primt 3	Misspelling of keyword
picBox.Print 2 +	No number follows the plus sign
9W = 5	9W is not a valid variable name

6. Errors detected while a program is running are called **run-time errors**. Although some run-time errors are due to improper syntax, others result from the inability of the computer to carry out the intended task. For instance, if the value of *numVar* is 0, then the statement

```
numVarInv = 1/numVar
```

interrupts the program with the run-time error "Division by zero." If the file DATA.TXT is not in the root folder of the C drive, then a statement that refers to the file by the filespec "C:\DATA.TXT" produces the run-time error "File not found."

The dialog box generated by a run-time error states the type of error and has a row of four command buttons captioned Continue, End, Debug, and Help. If you click on the Debug command button, Visual Basic will highlight in yellow the line of code that caused the error. (***Note:*** After a run-time error occurs, the program is said to be in break mode. See the first page of Appendix D for a discussion of the three program modes.)

7. A third type of error is the so-called **logical error**. Such an error occurs when a program does not perform the way it was intended. For instance, the line

```
ave = firstNum + secondNum / 2
```

is syntactically correct. However, the missing parentheses in the first line are responsible for an incorrect value being generated. Appendix D discusses debugging tools that can be used to detect and correct logical errors.

8. The omission of the asterisk to denote multiplication is a common error. For instance, the expression a(b + c) is not valid. It should read a * (b + c).

9. The largest number that most of the numeric variables considered in this text can represent is 3.402823E+38. Attempting to generate larger values produces the message "Overflow." The numbers generated by the programs in this text usually have a maximum of seven digits.

10. *A Review of Exponents.* The expression 2^3 means $2 \cdot 2 \cdot 2$, the product of three 2's. The number 3 is called the **exponent**, and the number 2 is called the **base**. In general, if r is a positive integer and a is a number, then a is defined as follows:

$$a^r = \underbrace{a \cdot a. \ldots a}_{r \text{ factors}}$$

The process of calculating a^r is called *raising a to the rth power*. Some other types of exponents are the following:

$a^{1/2} = \sqrt{a}$ $9^{1/2} = 3$

$a^{1/n} = \sqrt[n]{a}$ n positive integer $16^{1/4} = 2$

$a^{m/n} = (\sqrt[n]{a})^m$ m, n positive integers $8^{2/3} = (\sqrt[3]{8})^2 = 4$

$a^{-r} = 1/a^r$ $a \neq 0$ $10^{-2} = .01$

11. More than one statement can be placed on a single line of a program provided the statements are separated by colons. For instance, the code inside the event procedure in Example 3 can be written as

```
picResults.Cls: a = 5: b = 4: picResults.Print a * (2 + b)
```

In general, though, programs are much easier to follow if just one statement appears on each line. In this text, we almost always use single-statement lines.

12. When you first open a program that has been saved on disk, the Code window may not appear. If so, run and then terminate the program to see the Code window. To see the Form window, click on Object in the View menu or press Shift+F7. To return to the Code window, click on Code in the View window or press F7.

2.4 STRINGS

Two primary types of data can be processed by Visual Basic: numbers and strings. Sentences, phrases, words, letters of the alphabet, names, telephone numbers, addresses, and social security numbers are all examples of strings. Formally, a **string constant** is a sequence of characters that is treated as a single item. Strings can be assigned names with assignment statements, can be displayed with Print methods, and can be combined by an operation called concatenation (denoted by &).

■ VARIABLES AND STRINGS

A **string variable** is a name used to refer to a string. The allowable names of string variables are identical to those of numeric variables. The value of a string variable is assigned or altered with assignment statements and displayed with Print methods just like the value of a numeric variable.

EXAMPLE 1

The following code shows how assignment statements and Print are used with strings. The string variable *today* is assigned a value by the fourth line and this value is displayed by the fifth line. The quotation marks surrounding each string constant are not part of the constant and are not displayed by the Print method. (The form design for Examples 1 through 5 consists of a command button and picture box.)

```
Private Sub cmdButton_Click()
   picBox.Cls
   picBox.Print "hello"
   today = "9/17/99"
   picBox.Print today
End Sub
```

[Run, and then click the command button. The following is displayed in the picture box.]

```
hello
9/17/99
```

If *x, y, ..., z* are characters and *strVar1* is a string variable, then the statement

```
strVar1 = "xy...z"
```

assigns the string constant *xy...z* to the variable, and the statement

```
picBox.Print "xy...z"
```

or

```
picBox.Print strVar1
```

displays the string *xy...z* in a picture box. If *strVar2* is another string variable, then the statement

```
strVar2 = strVar1
```

assigns the value of the variable *strVar1* to the variable *strVar2*. (The value of *strVar1* will remain the same.) String constants used in assignment or picBox.Print statements must be surrounded by quotation marks, but string variables are never surrounded by quotation marks.

As with numbers, semicolons can be used with strings in picBox.Print statements to suppress carriage returns and line feeds. However, picBox.Print statements do not display leading or trailing spaces along with strings.

EXAMPLE 2

The following program illustrates the use of the assignment statement and Print method with text.

```
Private Sub cmdShow_Click()
  picOutput.Cls
  phrase = "win or lose that counts."
  picOutput.Print "It's not whether you "; phrase
  picOutput.Print "It's whether I "; phrase
End Sub
```

[Run, and then click the command button. The following is displayed in the picture box.]

```
It's not whether you win or lose that counts.
It's whether I win or lose that counts.
```

EXAMPLE 3

The following program has strings and numbers occurring together in a picBalance.Print statement.

```
Private Sub cmdCompute_Click()
  picBalance.Cls
  interestRate = 0.0655
  principal = 100
  phrase = "The balance after a year is"
  picBalance.Print phrase; (1 + interestRate) * principal
End Sub
```

[Run, and then click the command button. The following is displayed in the picture box.]

```
The balance after a year is 106.55
```

■ CONCATENATION

Two strings can be combined to form a new string consisting of the strings joined together. The joining operation is called **concatenation** and is represented by an ampersand (&). For instance, "good" & "bye" is "goodbye". A combination of strings and ampersands that can be evaluated to form a string is called a **string expression**. The assignment statement and Print method evaluate expressions before assigning them to variables or displaying them.

EXAMPLE 4

The following program illustrates concatenation.

```
Private Sub cmdDisplay_Click()
  picQuote.Cls
  quote1 = "The ballgame isn't over, "
  quote2 = "until it's over."
  quote = quote1 & quote2
  picQuote.Print quote & " Yogi Berra"
End Sub
```

[Run, and then click the command button. The following is displayed in the picture box.]

```
The ballgame isn't over, until it's over. Yogi Berra
```

■ DECLARING VARIABLE TYPES

So far, we have not distinguished between variables that hold strings and variables that hold numbers. There are several advantages to specifying the type of values, string or numeric, that can be assigned to a variable. A statement of the form

```
Dim variableName As String
```

specifies that only strings can be assigned to the named variable. A statement of the form

```
Dim variableName As Single
```

specifies that only numbers can be assigned to the named variable. The term Single derives from *single-precision real number*. After you type the space after the word "As," the editor displays a list of all the possible next words. In this text we use only a few of the items from this list.

A Dim statement is said to **declare** a variable. From now on we will declare all variables. However, all the programs will run correctly even if the Dim statements are omitted. Declaring variables at the beginning of each event procedure is regarded as good programming practice because it makes programs easier to read and helps prevent certain types of errors.

EXAMPLE 5

The following rewrite of Example 3 declares all variables.

```
Private Sub cmdCompute_Click()
    Dim interestRate As Single
    Dim principal As Single
    Dim phrase As String
    picBalance.Cls
    interestRate = 0.0655
    principal = 100
    phrase = "The balance after a year is"
    picBalance.Print phrase; (1 + interestRate) * principal
End Sub
```

Several Dim statements can be combined into one. For instance, the first three Dim statements of Example 5 can be replaced by

```
Dim interestRate As Single, principal As Single, phrase As String
```

Visual Basic actually has several different types of numeric variables. So far, we have used only single-precision numeric variables. Single-precision numeric variables can hold numbers of magnitude from as small as 1.4×10^{-45} to as large as 3.4×10^{38}. Another type of numeric variable, called **Integer**, can hold only whole numbers from –32768 to 32767. Integer-type variables are declared with a statement of the form

```
Dim intVar As Integer
```

The Integer data type uses less memory than the Single data type and statements using the Integer type execute faster. (This is only useful in programs with many calculations, such as the programs in later sections that use For...Next loops.) Of course, Integer variables are limited because they cannot hold decimals or large numbers. We will use Integer variables extensively with For...Next loops in Section 6 and occasionally when the data clearly consist of small whole numbers.

Other types of numeric variables are Long, Double, and Currency. We do not use them in this text. If you want to learn about them, consult Appendix C. Whenever we refer to a numeric variable without mentioning a type, we mean Single or Integer.

■ USING TEXT BOXES FOR INPUT AND OUTPUT

The contents of a text box is always a string. Therefore, statements such as

```
strVar = txtBox.Text
```

and

```
txtBox.Text = strVar
```

can be used to assign the contents of the text box to the string variable *strVar* and vice versa.

Numbers are stored in text boxes as strings. Therefore, they should be converted to numbers before being assigned to numeric variables. If *str* is a string representation of a number, then

```
Val(str)
```

is that number. Conversely, if *num* is a number, then

```
Str(num)
```

is a string representation of the number. Therefore, statements such as

```
numVar = Val(txtBox.Text)
```

and

```
txtBox.Text = Str(numVar)
```

can be used to assign the contents of the text box to the numeric variable *numVar* and vice versa. *Note:* When a non-negative number is converted to a string with Str, its first character (but not its last character) is a blank space.

EXAMPLE 6

The following program converts miles to furlongs and vice versa. *Note:* A furlong is 1/8th of a mile.

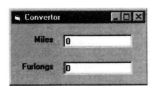

Object	Property	Setting
frm3_4_6	Caption,	Convertor
lblMile	Caption	Miles
txtMile	Text	0
lblFurlong	Caption	Furlongs
txtFurlong	Text	0

The two text boxes have been named txtMile and txtFurlong. With the Event procedures shown, typing a number into a text box and pressing Tab results in the converted number being displayed in the other text box.

```
Private Sub txtMile_LostFocus()
   txtFurlong.Text = Str(8 * Val(txtMile.Text))
End Sub

Private Sub txtFurlong_LostFocus()
   txtMile.Text = Str(Val(txtFurlong.Text) / 8)
End Sub
```

■ ANSI CHARACTER SET

Each of the 47 different keys in the center typewriter portion of the keyboard can produce two characters, for a total of 94 characters. Adding 1 for the space character produced by the space bar makes 95 characters. These characters have numbers ranging from 32 to 126 associated with them. These values, called the ANSI (or ASCII) values of the characters, are given in Appendix A. Table 2-2 shows a few of the values.

TABLE 2-2
A Few ANSI Values

32 (space)	48 0	66 B	122 z
33 !	49 1	90 Z	123 {
34 "	57 9	97 a	125 }
35 #	65 A	98 b	126 ~

Most of the best-known fonts, such as Ariel, Courier, Helvetica, and Times New Roman, are essentially governed by the ANSI standard, which assigns characters to the numbers from 32 to 255. Table 2-3 shows a few of the higher ANSI values.

TABLE 2-3
A Few Higher ANSI Values

162 ¢	177 ±	181 μ	190 $3/4$
169 ©	178 ^{2}	188 $1/4$	247 ÷
176 °	179 ^{3}	189 $1/2$	248 Ø

If *n* is a number between 32 and 255, then

    Chr(*n*)

is the string consisting of the character with ANSI value *n*. If *str* is any string, then

    Asc(*str*)

is the ANSI value of the first character of *str*. For instance, the statement

    txtBox.Text = Chr(65)

displays the letter A in the text box and the statement

    picBox.Print Asc("Apple")

displays the number 65 in the picture box.

Concatenation can be used with Chr to obtain strings using the higher ANSI characters. For instance, with one of the fonts that conforms to the ANSI standard, the statement

    txtBox.Text = "32" & Chr(176) & " Fahrenheit"

displays 32° Fahrenheit in the text box.

■ THE KEYPRESS EVENT PROCEDURE

When a text box has the focus and the user presses a key, the KeyPress event procedure identifies the key pressed. When a key is pressed, the event procedure assigns the ANSI value of the key to an Integer variable called *KeyAscii*. The general form of the procedure is

    Private Sub *ControlName*_KeyPress(KeyAscii As Integer)
       statements
    End Sub

The statements usually involve the variable *KeyAscii*. Also, a character does not appear in the text box until End Sub is reached. At that time, the character with ANSI value *KeyAscii* is displayed.

EXAMPLE 7

The following program allows the user to determine the ANSI values of the standard (typewriter) keys of the keyboard. The statement txtCharacter. Text = "" removes any previously typed character from the text box.

Object	Property	Setting
frm3_4_7	Caption,	ANSI Values
lblPress	Caption	Press any key
txtCharacter	Text	(blank)
picOutput		

```
Private Sub txtCharacter_KeyPress(KeyAscii As Integer)
   txtCharacter.Text = ""
   picOutput.Cls
   picOutput.Print Chr(KeyAscii);
   " has ANSI value"; KeyAscii
End Sub
```

[Run, and then press a key. For instance, if A is pressed, the following is displayed in the picture box.]

```
A has ANSI value 65
```

The KeyPress event procedure can alter the character typed into the text box. For instance, if the statement

```
KeyAscii = 65
```

is placed in a KeyPress event procedure, the letter A is displayed when any standard key is pressed. In Section 4, we use a decision structure to prevent the user from typing unwanted keys. For instance, if we want the user to enter a number into a text box, we can intercept and discard any key presses that are not digits. The statement

```
KeyAscii = 0
```

placed in a KeyPress event procedure discards the key pressed. Finally, a program can be made more friendly by letting the Enter key (ANSI value 13) move the focus in the same way that the Tab key moves the focus. This requires having a KeyPress event procedure for each object that is to respond to the Enter key and then setting the focus to the next object when the value of *KeyAscii* is 13.

COMMENTS

1. The string "" contains no characters and is called the **null string** or the **empty string**. It is different than the string containing a single space (" "). String variables that have not been assigned values initially have "" as their default values. (Numeric variables have default value 0.)

2. The statement picBox.Print, with no string or number, simply skips a line in the picture box.

3. Assigning a string value to a numeric variable can result in the error message "Type mismatch."

4. In Visual Basic 6.0, the maximum allowable number of characters in a string is approximately 2 billion.

5. The quotation-mark character (") can be placed into a string constant by using Chr(34). For example, after the statement

```
txtBox.Text = "George " & Chr(34) & "Babe" & Chr(34) & " Ruth"
```

is executed, the text box contains

```
George "Babe" Ruth
```

6. Most major programming languages require that all variables be declared before they can be used. Although declaring variables with Dim statements is optional in Visual Basic, you can tell Visual Basic to make declaration mandatory. The steps are as follows:

   (a) From any code window, click on the down-arrow to the right of the Object box and click on (General).

   (b) Type

   ```
   Option Explicit
   ```

   and press Enter.

   Then, if you use a variable without first declaring it in a Dim statement, the message "Variable not defined" will appear as soon as you attempt to run the program. One big advantage of using Option Explicit is that mistypings of variable names will be detected. Otherwise, malfunctions due to typing errors are often difficult to detect.

7. You can have Visual Basic automatically place Option Explicit in every program you write. The steps are as follows:

   (a) Press Alt/T/O and click on the Editor tab to invoke the editor options.

   (b) If the square to the left of "Require Variable Declaration" does not contain a check mark, click on the square and press the OK button.

8. Variables that are not (explicitly) declared with Dim statements are said to be **implicitly declared**. Such variables, which have a data type called Variant, can hold strings, numbers, and several other kinds of information.

9. You can display the type of a variable with the following steps—position the cursor over the word, press the right mouse button, and click on Quick Info.

10. Val can be applied to strings containing nonnumeric characters. If the beginning of the string *str* represents a number, then Val(*str*) is that number; otherwise, it is 0. For instance, Val("123Blastoff") is 123, and Val("ab3") is 0.

11. The KeyPress event also applies to command buttons and picture boxes.

12. Concatenation of strings also can be represented by a plus sign (+). However, restricting the plus sign to operations on numbers eliminates ambiguity and provides self-documenting code.

13. If Val is omitted from the statement

    ```
    numVar = Val(txtBox.Text)
    ```

    or Str is omitted from the statement

    ```
    txtBox.Text = Str(numVar)
    ```

    Visual Basic does not complain, but simply makes the conversion for you. However, errors can arise from omitting Val and Str. For instance, if the contents of txtBox1.Text is 34 and the contents of txtBox2.Text is 56, then the statement

    ```
    numVar = txtBox1.Text + txtBox2.Text
    ```

    assigns the number 3456 rather than 90 to *numVar*. (This is because Visual Basic does not perform the conversion until just before the assignment.) If txtBox1 is empty, then the statement

    ```
    3 * txtBox1.Text
    ```

    will stop the program and produce the error message "Type mismatch." We follow the standards of good programming practice by always using Val and Str to convert values between text boxes and numeric variables. Similar considerations apply to conversions involving label captions.

14. Variable names should describe the role of the variable. Also, some programmers use a prefix, such as sng or str, to identify the type of a variable. For example, they would use names like sngInterestRate and strFirstName.

2.5 INPUT AND OUTPUT

So far we have relied on assignment statements to assign values to variables. Data also can be stored in files and accessed through Input # statements, or data can be supplied by the user in a text box or input box. The Print method, with a little help from commas and the Tab function, can spread out and align the display of data in a picture box or on a printer. Message boxes grab the user's attention and display temporary messages. Comment statements allow the programmer to document all aspects of a program, including a description of the input used and the output to be produced.

■ READING DATA FROM FILES

In Section 1, we saw how to create data files with Windows' Notepad. (As a rule of thumb, and simply as a matter of style, we enclose each string in quotation marks.) A file can have either one item per line or many items (separated by commas) can be listed on the same line. Usually, related items are grouped together on a line. For instance, if a file consisted of payroll information, each line would contain the name of a person, that person's hourly wage, and the number of hours that person worked during the week, as shown in Figure 2-24.

```
"Mike Jones", 7.35, 35
"John Smith", 6.75, 33
```

FIGURE 2-24 *Contents of STAFF.TXT*

The items of data will be assigned to variables one at a time in the order they appear in the file. That is, "Mike Jones" will be the first value assigned to a variable. After all the items from the first line have been assigned to variables, subsequent requests for values will be read from the next line.

Data stored in a file can be read in order (that is, sequentially) and assigned to variables with the following steps.

1. Choose a number from 1 to 255 to be the **reference number** for the file.

2. Execute the statement

```
Open "filespec" For Input As #n
```

where *n* is the reference number. This procedure is referred to as **Opening a file for input**. It establishes a communications link between the computer and the disk drive for reading data *from* the disk. Data then can be input from the specified file and assigned to variables in the program.

3. Read items of data in order, one at a time, from the file with Input # statements. The statement

```
Input #n, var
```

causes the program to look in the file for the next available item of data and assign it to the variable *var*. In the file, individual items are separated by commas or line breaks. The variable in the Input # statement should be the same type (that is, string versus numeric) as the data to be assigned to it from the file.

4. After the desired items have been read from the file, close the file with the statement

```
Close #n
```

EXAMPLE 1

Write a program that uses a file for input and produces the same output as the following code. (The form design for all examples in this section consists of a command button and a picture box.)

```
Private Sub cmdDisplay_Click()
   Dim houseNumber As Single, street As String
   picAddress.Cls
   houseNumber = 1600
   street = "Pennsylvania Ave."
   picAddress.Print "The White House is located at"; houseNumber; street
End Sub
```

[Run and then click the command button. The following is displayed in the picture box.]

```
The White House is located at 1600 Pennsylvania Ave.
```

SOLUTION:

Use Windows' Notepad to create the file DATA.TXT containing the following two lines:

1600
"Pennsylvania Ave."

In the following code, the fifth line looks for the first item of data, 1600, and assigns it to the numeric variable *houseNumber*. (Visual Basic records that this piece of data has been used.) The sixth line looks for the next available item of data, "Pennsylvania Ave.", and assigns it to the string variable *street*. ***Note:*** You will have to alter the Open statement in the fourth line to tell it where the file DATA.TXT is located. For instance, if the file is in the root directory (that is, folder) of a diskette in drive A, then the line should read Open "A:\DATA.TXT" For Input As #1. If the file is located in the subdirectory (that is, folder) VB6 of the C drive, then the statement should be changed to Open "C:\VB6\DATA.TXT" For Input As #1. See Comment 1 for another option.

```
Private Sub cmdReadFile_Click()
   Dim houseNumber As Single, street As String
   picAddress.Cls
   Open "DATA.TXT" For Input As #1
   Input #1, houseNumber
   Input #1, street
   picAddress.Print "The White House is located at"; houseNumber; street
   Close #1
End Sub
```

A single Input # statement can assign values to several different variables. For instance, the two Input # statements in the solution of Example 1 can be replaced by the single statement

```
Input #1, houseNumber, street
```

In general, a statement of the form

```
Input #n, var1, var2, ..., varj
```

has the same effect as the sequence of statements

```
Input #n, var1
Input #n, var2
   .
   .
   .
Input #n, varj
```

EXAMPLE 2

The following program uses the file STAFF.TXT in Figure 2-24 to compute weekly pay. Notice that the variables in the Input # statement are the same types (String, Single, Single) as the constants in each line of the file.

```
Private Sub cmdCompute_Click()
   Dim nom As String, wage As Single, hrs As Single
   picPay.Cls
   Open "STAFF.TXT" For Input As #1
   Input #1, nom, wage, hrs
   picPay.Print nom; hrs * wage
   Input #1, nom, wage, hrs
   picPay.Print nom; hrs * wage
   Close #1
End Sub
```

[Run, and then click the command button. The following will be displayed in the picture box.]

```
Mike Jones 257.25
John Smith 222.75
```

In certain situations, we must read the data in a file more than once. This is accomplished by closing the file and reopening it. After a file is closed and then reopened, subsequent Input # statements begin reading from the first entry of the file.

EXAMPLE 3

The following program takes the average annual amounts of money spent by single-person households for several categories and converts these amounts to percentages. The data are read once to compute the total amount of money spent and then read again to calculate the percentage for each category. ***Note:*** These figures were compiled for the year 1995 by the Bureau of Labor Statistics.

COSTS.TXT consists of the following four lines:

"Transportation", 3887
"Housing", 7643
"Food", 3017
"Other", 7804

```
Private Sub cmdCompute_Click()
   Dim total As Single, category As String, amount As Single
   Open "COSTS.TXT" For Input As #1
   picPercent.Cls
   total = 0
   Input #1, category, amount
   total = total + amount
   Input #1, category, amount
   total = total + amount
   Input #1, category, amount
   total = total + amount
   Input #1, category, amount
   total = total + amount
   Close #1
   Open "COSTS.TXT" For Input As #1
   Input #1, category, amount
   picPercent.Print category; amount / total
   Input #1, category, amount
   picPercent.Print category; amount / total
   Input #1, category, amount
```

```
    picPercent.Print category; amount / total
    Input #1, category, amount
    picPercent.Print category; amount / total
    Close #1
End Sub
```

[Run and then click the command button. The following is displayed in the picture box.]

```
Transportation 0.1739072
Housing 0.3419534
Food 0.1349828
Other 0.3491566
```

■ INPUT FROM AN INPUT BOX

Normally, a text box is used to obtain input described by a label. Sometimes, we want just one piece of input and would rather not have a text box and label stay on the screen forever. The problem can be solved with an **input box**. When a statement of the form

```
stringVar = InputBox(prompt, title)
```

is executed, an input box similar to the one shown in Figure 2-25 pops up on the screen. After the user types a response into the text box at the bottom of the screen and presses Enter (or clicks OK), the response is assigned to the string variable. The *title* argument is optional and gives the caption to appear in the Title bar. The *prompt* argument is a string that tells the user what information to type into the text box.

FIGURE 2-25 *Sample Input Box*

When you type the parenthesis following the word InputBox, the editor displays a line containing the general form of the InputBox statement. See Figure 2-26. This feature, which was added in Visual Basic 5.0, is called **Quick Info**. Optional parameters are surrounded by brackets. All the parameters in the general form of the InputBox statement are optional except for *prompt*.

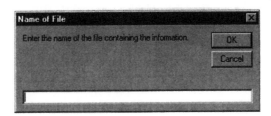

FIGURE 2-26 *Quick Info Feature*

EXAMPLE 4

In the following solution to Example 1, the file name is provided by the user in an input box.

```
Private Sub cmdDisplay_Click()
  Dim fileName As String, prompt As String, title As String
  Dim houseNumber As Single, street As String
  picAddress.Cls
  prompt = "Enter the name of the file containing the information."
  title = "Name of File"
  fileName = InputBox(prompt, title)
  Open fileName For Input As #1
  Input #1, houseNumber
  Input #1, street
  picAddress.Print "The White House is located at"; houseNumber; street
  Close #1
End Sub
```

[Run, and then click the command button. The input box of Figure 2-25 appears on the screen. Type DATA.TXT (possibly preceded with a path) into the input box and click on OK. The input box disappears and the following appears in the picture box.]

```
The White House is located at 1600 Pennsylvania Ave.
```

The response typed into an input box is treated as a single string value, no matter what is typed. (Quotation marks are not needed and, if included, are considered as part of the string.) Numeric data typed into an input box should be converted to a number with Val before it is assigned to a numeric variable or used in a calculation.

■ FORMATTING OUTPUT WITH PRINT ZONES

Each line in a picture box can be thought of as being subdivided into zones, as shown in Figure 2-27. Each zone contains 14 positions, where the width of a position is the average width of the characters in the font.

FIGURE 2-27   *Print Zones*

We have seen that when the Print method is followed by several items separated by semicolons, the items are displayed one after another. When commas are used instead of semicolons, the items are displayed in consecutive zones. For instance, if the Font property of picBox is set to Courier, when the motto of the state of Alaska is displayed with the statements

```
picBox.Print "North", "to", "the", "future."
picBox.Print "12345678901234567890123456789012345678901234567890"
```

the resulting picture box is

```
North         to          the          future.
12345678901234567890123456789012345678901234567890
```

where each word is in a separate print zone. This same output can be achieved with the code

```
Dim a As String, b As String, c As String, d As String
  a = "North"
  b = "to"
  c = "the"
  d = "future."
  picBox.Print a, b, c, d
picBox.Print "1234567890123456789012345678901234567890123456789"
```

EXAMPLE 5

The following program uses Print zones to organize expenses for public and private schools into columns of a table. The data represent the average expenses for 1995–96. (The Font setting for picTable is the default font MS Sans Serif.)

```
Private Sub cmdDisplay_Click()
  picTable.Cls
  picTable.Print " ", "Pb 2-yr", "Pr 2-yr", "Pb 4-yr", "Pr 4-yr"
  picTable.Print
  picTable.Print "Tuit & Fees", 1387, 6350, 2860, 12432
  picTable.Print "Bks & Suppl", 577, 567, 591, 601
  picTable.Print "Board", 1752, 1796, 1721, 1845
  picTable.Print "Trans", 894, 902, 929, 863
  picTable.Print "Other Exp", 1142, 1220, 1348, 1169
  picTable.Print " ", "-------", "-------", "-------", "-------"
  picTable.Print "Total", 5752, 10835, 7449, 16910
End Sub
```

[Run and then click the command button. The following is displayed in the picture box.]

	Pb 2-yr	Pr 2-yr	Pb 4-yr	Pr 4-yr
Tuit & Fees	1387	6350	2860	12432
Bks & Suppl	577	567	591	601
Board	1752	1796	1721	1845
Trans	894	902	929	863
Other Exp	1142	1220	1348	1169
	------	------	------	------
Total	5752	10835	7449	16910

■ **TAB FUNCTION**

If an item appearing in a Print statement is preceded by

Tab(n);

where n is a positive integer, that item will be displayed (if possible) beginning at the nth position of the line. (Exceptions are discussed in Comment 10.)

EXAMPLE 6

The following program uses the Tab function to organize data into columns of a table. The data represent the number of bachelor's degrees conferred (in units of 1000). (*Source:* National Center of Educational Statistics.)

```
Private Sub cmdDisplay_Click()
picTable.Cls
picTable.Print Tab(10); "1970-71"; Tab(20); "1980-81"; Tab(30); "1990-91"
picTable.Print
picTable.Print "Male"; Tab(10); 476; Tab(20); 470; Tab(30); 490
```

```
     picTable.Print "Female"; Tab(10); 364; Tab(20); 465; Tab(30); 560
     picTable.Print "Total"; Tab(10); 840; Tab(20); 935; Tab(30); 1050
End Sub
```

[Run and then click the command button. The resulting picture box is shown.]

	1970-71	1980-81	1990-91
Male	476	470	490
Female	364	465	560
Total	840	935	1050

■ USING A MESSAGE BOX FOR OUTPUT

Sometimes you want to grab the user's attention with a brief message such as "Correct" or "Nice try, but no cigar." You want this message only to appear on the screen until the user has read it. This mission is easily accomplished with a **message box** such as the one shown in Figure 2-28. When a statement of the form

```
     MsgBox prompt, , title
```

is executed, where *prompt* and *title* are strings, a message box with *prompt* displayed and the title bar caption *title* appears, and stays on the screen until the user presses Enter or clicks OK. For instance, the statement MsgBox "Nice try, but no cigar.", , "Consolation" produces Figure 2-28. If you use double quotation marks ("") for *title*, the title bar will be blank.

FIGURE 2-28 *Sample Message Box*

■ LINE CONTINUATION CHARACTER

Up to 1023 characters can be typed in a line of code. If you use a line with more characters than can fit in the window, Visual Basic scrolls the window toward the right as needed. However, most programmers prefer having lines that are no longer than the width of the code window. This can be achieved with the underscore character (_) preceded by a space. Make sure the underscore doesn't appear inside quotation marks though. For instance, the line

```
     msg = "640K ought to be enough for anybody. (Bill Gates, 1981)"
```

can be written as

```
     msg = "640K ought to be enough for " & _
     "anybody. (Bill Gates, 1981)"
```

■ OUTPUT TO THE PRINTER

You print text on a sheet of paper in the printer in much the same way you display text in a picture box. Visual Basic treats the printer as an object named Printer. If *expr* is a string or numeric expression, then the statement

```
     Printer.Print expr
```

sends *expr* to the printer in exactly the same way picBox.Print sends output to a picture box. You can use semicolons, commas for print zones, and Tab.

Font properties can be set with statements like

```
Printer.Font.Name = "Script"
Printer.Font.Bold = True
Printer.Font.Size = 12
```

Another useful printer command is

```
Printer.NewPage
```

which starts a new page.

Windows' print manager usually waits until an entire page has been completed before starting to print. To avoid losing information, execute the statement

```
Printer.EndDoc
```

when you are finished printing.

The statement

```
PrintForm
```

prints the content of the form.

■ INTERNAL DOCUMENTATION

Now that we have the capability to write more complicated programs, we must concern ourselves with program documentation. **Program documentation** is the inclusion of comments that specify the intent of the program, the purpose of the variables, the nature of the data in the files, and the tasks performed by individual portions of the program. To create a comment line, just begin the line with an apostrophe. Such a line is completely ignored when the program is executed. (The keyword Rem can be used instead of an apostrophe. Rem is an abbreviation of Remark.) Program documentation appears whenever the program is displayed or printed. Also, a line of code can be documented by adding an apostrophe, followed by the desired information, to the end of the line. Comments (also known as Rem statements) appear green on the screen.

EXAMPLE 7

Document the program in Example 2.

SOLUTION

In the following program, the first comment describes the entire program, the next three comments give the meanings of the variables, and the final comment describes the items in each line of the file.

```
Private Sub cmdCompute_Click()
    'Compute weekly pay
    Dim nom As String    'Employee name
    Dim wage As Single   'Hourly pay
    Dim hrs As Single    'Number of hours worked during week
    picPay.Cls
    Open "STAFF.TXT" For Input As #1
    'Get person's name, hourly pay, and hours worked
    Input #1, nom, wage, hrs
    picPay.Print nom; hrs * wage Input #1, nom, wage,
    hrs picPay.Print nom; hrs * wage
    Close #1
End Sub
```

Some of the benefits of documentation are as follows:

1. Other people can easily comprehend the program.

2. The program can be understood when read later.

3. Long programs are easier to read because the purposes of individual pieces can be determined at a glance.

COMMENTS

1. Visual Basic provides a convenient device for accessing a file that resides in the same folder as the (saved) program. After a program has been saved in a folder, the value of App.Path is the string containing the name of the folder. Therefore, if a program contains a line such as

```
Open App.Path & "\DATA.TXT" For Input As #1
```

Visual Basic will look for the file DATA.TXT in the folder containing the program.

   The programs from this book, as well as the data files they use, all are contained in the folder Programs on the CD accompanying this book. On the CD, App.Path is used in every Open statement. Therefore, even after you copy the contents of the Programs folder onto a hard drive or diskette, the programs will continue to execute properly without your having to alter any paths.

2. The text box and input box provide a whole new dimension to the capabilities of a program. The user, rather than the programmer, can provide the data to be processed.

3. A string used in a file does not have to be enclosed by quotation marks. The only exceptions are strings containing commas or leading and trailing spaces.

4. If an Input # statement looks for a string and finds a number, it will treat the number as a string. Suppose the first two entries in the file DATA.TXT are the numbers 2 and 3.

```
Private Sub cmdButton_Click()
   Dim a As String, b As String
   picBox.Cls
   Open "DATA.TXT" For Input As #1
   Input #1, a, b
   picBox.Print a + b
   Close #1
End Sub
```

[Run and then click the command button. The following is displayed in the picture box.]

```
23
```

5. If an Input # statement looks for a number and finds a string, the Input # statement will assign the value 0 to the numeric variable. For instance, suppose the first two entries in the file DATA.TXT are "ten" and 10. Then after the statement

```
Input #1, num1, num2
```

is executed, where um1 and *num2* are numeric variables, the values of these variables will be 0 and 10.

6. If all the data in a file have been read by Input # statements and another item is requested by an Input # statement, a box will appear displaying the message "Input past end of file."

7. Numeric data in a text box, input box, or file must be a constant. It *cannot* be a variable or an expression. For instance, num, 1 / 2, and 2 + 3 are not acceptable.

8. To skip a Print zone, just include two consecutive commas.

9. Print zones are usually employed to align information into columns. Since most fonts have proportionally-spaced characters, wide characters occupy more than one fixed-width column and narrow characters occupy less. The best and most predictable results are obtained when a fixed-pitch font (such as Courier) is used with print zones.

10. The Tab function cannot be used to move the cursor to the left. If the position specified in a Tab function is to the left of the current cursor position, the cursor will move to that position on the next line. For instance, the line

```
picBox.Print "hello"; Tab(3); "good-bye"
```

results in the output

```
hello
  good-bye
```

11. The statement Close, without any reference number, closes all open files.

12. Windows allows you to alternate between Visual Basic and Notepad without exiting either application. To invoke Notepad with Windows, click on the Start button; successively select Programs, Accessories, and Notepad; and then click on Notepad or press the Enter key. Now that both Visual Basic and Notepad have been invoked, you can go from one application to the other by holding down the Alt key and repeatedly pressing the Tab key until the name of the other application appears. When the Alt key is released, the named application becomes active.

2.6 BUILT-IN FUNCTIONS

Visual Basic has a number of built-in functions that greatly extend its capability. These functions perform such varied tasks as taking the square root of a number, counting the number of characters in a string, and capitalizing letters. Functions associate with one or more values, called the *input*, a single value, called the *output*. The function is said to **return** the output value. The three functions considered in what follows have numeric input and output.

■ NUMERIC FUNCTIONS: SQR, INT, ROUND

The function Sqr calculates the square root of a number. The function Int finds the greatest integer less than or equal to a number. Therefore, Int discards the decimal part of positive numbers. The value of Round (n, r) is the number n rounded to r decimal places. The parameter r can be omitted. If so, n is rounded to a whole number. Some examples follow:

```
Sqr(9) is 3.          Int(2.7) is 2.      Round(2.7) is 3.
   Sqr(0) is 0.       Int(3) is 3.        Round(2.317, 2) is 2.32.
Sqr(2) is 1.414214.   Int(-2.7) is -3.    Round(2.317, 1) is 2.3.
```

The terms inside the parentheses can be either numbers (as shown), numeric variables, or numeric expressions. Expressions are first evaluated to produce the input.

EXAMPLE 1

The following program evaluates each of the functions for a specific input given by the value of the variable *n*.

```
Private Sub cmdEvaluate_Click()
   Dim n As Single, root As Single
   'Evaluate functions at a variable
   picResults.Cls
   n = 6.76
   root = Sqr(n)
   picResults.Print root; Int(n); Round(n,1)
End Sub
```

[Run and then click the command button. The following is displayed in the picture box.]

```
2.6 6 6.8
```

EXAMPLE 2

The following program evaluates each of the preceding functions at an expression.

```
Private Sub cmdEvaluate_Click()
   Dim a As Single, b As Single
   'Evaluate functions at expressions
   picResults.Cls
   a = 2
   b = 3
   picResults.Print Sqr(5 * b + 1); Int(a ^ b); Round(a / b, 3)
End Sub
```

[Run and then click the command button. The following is displayed in the picture box.]

```
4 8 0.667
```

EXAMPLE 3

The following program shows an application of the Sqr function.

```
Private Sub cmdComputeHyp_Click()
   Dim leg1 As Single, leg2 As Single, hyp As Single
   'Find the length of the hypotenuse of a right triangle
   picHyp.Cls
   leg1 = Val(txtFirst.Text)
   leg2 = Val(txtSecond.Text)
   hyp = Sqr(leg1 ^ 2 + leg2 ^ 2)
   picHyp.Print "The length of the hypotenuse is"; hyp
End Sub
```

[Run, type 3 and 4 into the text boxes, and then click the command button.]

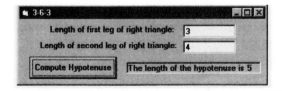

EXAMPLE 4

The following program shows how Int is used to carry out long division. When the integer *m* is divided into the integer *n* with long division, the result is a quotient and a remainder. See Figure 2-29.

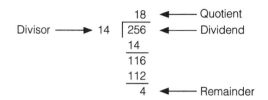

FIGURE 2-29 *Long Division*

```
Private Sub cmdDivide_Click()
  Dim divisor As Single, dividend As Single
  Dim quotient As Single, remainder As Single
  'Long division
  picResult.Cls
  divisor = Val(txtDivisor.Text)
  dividend = Val(txtDividend.Text)
  quotient = Int(dividend / divisor)
  remainder = dividend - quotient * divisor
  picResult.Print "The quotient is"; quotient
  picResult.Print "The remainder is"; remainder
End Sub
```

[Run, type 14 and 256 into the text boxes, and then click the command button.]

■ STRING FUNCTIONS: LEFT, MID, RIGHT, UCASE, TRIM

The functions Left, Mid, and Right are used to extract characters from the left end, middle, and right end of a string. Suppose *str* is a string and *m* and *n* are positive integers. Then Left(*str*, *n*) is the string consisting of the first *n* characters of *str* and Right(*str*, *n*) is the string consisting of the last *n* characters of *str*. Mid(*str*, *m*, *n*) is the string consisting of *n* characters of *str*, beginning with the *m*th character. UCase(*str*) is the string *str* with all of its lowercase letters capitalized. Trim(*str*) is the string *str* with all leading and trailing spaces removed. Some examples are as follows:

```
Left("fanatic", 3) is "fan".          Right("fanatic", 3) is "tic".
Left("12/15/99", 2) is "12".          Right("12/15/99", 2) is "99".
Mid("fanatic", 5, 1) is "t".          Mid("12/15/99", 4, 2) is "15".
UCase("Disk") is "DISK".              UCase("12three") is "12THREE".
Trim(" 1 2 ") is "1 2".               Trim("-12 ") is "-12".
```

The strings produced by Left, Mid, and Right are referred to as **substrings** of the strings from which they were formed. For instance, "fan" and "t" are substrings of "fanatic". The substring "fan" is said to begin at position 1 of "fanatic" and the substring "t" is said to begin at position 5.

Like the numeric functions discussed before, Left, Mid, Right, UCase, and Trim also can be evaluated for variables and expressions.

EXAMPLE 5

The following program evaluates the functions above for variables and expressions. Note that spaces are counted as characters.

```
Private Sub cmdEvaluate_Click()
  Dim str1 As String, str2 As String
  'Evaluate functions at variables and expressions.
  picResults.Cls
  str1 = "Quick as "
  str2 = "a wink"
  picResults.Print Left(str1, 7)
  picResults.Print Mid(str1 & str2, 7, 6)
  picResults.Print UCase(str1 & str2)
  picResults.Print "The average "; Right(str2, 4); " lasts .1 second."
  picResults.Print Trim(str1); str2
End Sub
```

[Run and then click the command button. The following is displayed in the picture box.]

```
Quick a
  as a w
  QUICK AS A WINK
  The average wink lasts .1 second.
Quick asa wink
```

■ STRING-RELATED NUMERIC FUNCTIONS: LEN, INSTR

The functions Len and InStr operate on strings but produce numbers. The function Len gives the number of characters in a string. The function InStr searches for the first occurrence of one string in another and gives the position at which the string is found. Suppose *str1* and *str2* are strings. The value of Len(*str1*) is the number of characters in *str1*. The value of InStr(*str1*, *str2*) is 0 if *str2* is not a substring of *str1*. Otherwise, its value is the first position of *str2* in *str1*. Some examples of Len and InStr follow:

```
Len("Shenandoah") is 10.        InStr("Shenandoah", "nand") is 4.
Len("Just a moment") is 13.     InStr("Just a moment", " ") is 5.
Len(" ") is 1.                  InStr("Croissant", "ist") is 0.
```

EXAMPLE 6

The following program evaluates functions at variables and expressions. The ninth line locates the position of the space separating the two names. The first name will end one position to the left of this position and the last name will consist of all but the first *n* characters of the full name.

```
Private Sub cmdAnalyze_Click()
  Dim nom As String   'Name
  Dim n As Integer    'Location of space
  Dim first As String 'First name
  Dim last As String  'Last name
  'Evaluate functions at variables and expressions.
  picResults.Cls
  nom = txtFullName.Text
  n = InStr(nom, " ")
  first = Left(nom, n - 1)
```

```
   last = Right(nom, Len(nom) - n)
   picResults.Print "Your first name is "; first
   picResults.Print "Your last name has"; Len(last); "letters."
End Sub
```

[Run, type John Doe into the text box, and then click the command button.]

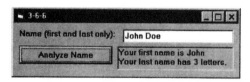

■ FORMAT FUNCTIONS

The Format functions are used to display numbers and dates in familiar forms and to right-justify numbers. Here are some examples of how numbers are converted to strings with Format functions.

Function	String Value
FormatNumber(12345.628, 1)	12,345.6
FormatCurrency(12345.628, 2)	$12,345.63
FormatPercent(.185, 2)	18.50%

The value of FormatNumber(n, r) is the string containing the number n rounded to r decimal places and displayed with commas every three digits to the left of the decimal point. The value of FormatCurrency(n, r) is the string consisting of a dollar sign followed by the value of FormatNumber(n, r). FormatCurrency uses the accountant's convention of using surrounding parentheses to denote negative amounts. The value of FormatPercent(n, r) is the string consisting of the number n displayed as a percent and rounded to r decimal places.

With all three functions, r can be omitted. If so, the number is rounded to 2 decimal places. Strings corresponding to numbers less than 1 in magnitude have a zero to the left of the decimal point. Also, n can be a either a number, a numeric expression, or even a string corresponding to a number.

Function	String Value
FormatNumber(1 + Sqr(2), 3)	2.414
FormatCurrency(-1000)	($1,000.00)
FormatPercent(".005")	0.50%

If *dateString* represents a date in a form such as "7-4-1999", "7-4-99", or "7/4/99", then the value of FormatDateTime(*dateString*, vbLongDate) is a string giving the date as Sunday, July 04, 1999.

Function	String Value
FormatDateTime("9-15-99", vbLongDate)	Wednesday, September 15, 1999
FormatDateTime("10-23-00", vbLongDate)	Monday, October 23, 2000

The value of Format(*expr*, "@@ ... @"), where "@@ ... @" is a string of n "at" symbols, is the string consisting of the value of *expr* right-justified in a field of n spaces. This function is used with fixed-width fonts, such as Courier or Terminal, to display columns of numbers so that the decimal points and commas are lined up or to display right-justified lists of words. The following examples use a string of 10 "at" symbols.

Function	String Value
Format(1234567890, "@@@@@@@@@@")	1234567890
Format(FormatNumber(1234.5), "@@@@@@@@@@")	1,234.50
Format(FormatNumber(12345.67), "@@@@@@@@@@")	12,345.67
Format(FormatCurrency(13580.17), "@@@@@@@@@@")	$13,580.17

EXAMPLE 7

The following program produces essentially the first two columns of the table in Example 5 of Section 2.5. However, Format is used to right-justify the expense categories and to align the numbers.

Object	Property	Setting
frmExpenses	Caption	Public 2-year College Expenses
cmdDisplay	Caption	Display Expenses
picTable	Font.Name	Courier

```
Private Sub cmdDisplay_Click()
  Dim fmt1 As String, fmt2 As String
  Dim col1 As String, col2 As String
  'Average expenses of commuter students (1995-96)
  picTable.Cls
  picTable.Print Tab(19); "Pb 2-yr"
  picTable.Print
  fmt1 = "@@@@@@@@@@@@@@@@@" '17 @ symbols
  fmt2 = "@@@@@" '6 @ symbols
  col1 = Format("Tuition & Fees", fmt1)
  col2 = FormatNumber(1387, 0)
  col2 = Format(col2, fmt2)
  picTable.Print col1; Tab(19); col2
  col1 = Format("Books & Supplies", fmt1)
  col2 = FormatNumber(577, 0)
  col2 = Format(col2, fmt2)
  picTable.Print col1; Tab(19); col2
  col1 = Format("Board", fmt1)
  col2 = FormatNumber(1752, 0)
  col2 = Format(col2, fmt2)
  picTable.Print col1; Tab(19); col2
  col1 = Format("Transportation", fmt1)
  col2 = FormatNumber(894, 0)
  col2 = Format(col2, fmt2)
  picTable.Print col1; Tab(19); col2
  col1 = Format("Other Expenses", fmt1)
  col2 = FormatNumber(1142, 0)
  col2 = Format(col2, fmt2)
  picTable.Print col1; Tab(19); col2
  picTable.Print Tab(19); "——"
  col1 = Format("Total", fmt1)
  col2 = FormatNumber(5752, 0)
  col2 = Format(col2, fmt2)
  picTable.Print col1; Tab(19);
  col2
End Sub
```

[Run, and then click the command button.]

```
                    Pb 2-Yr
    Tuition & Fees  1,387
  Books & Supplies  577
             Board  1,752
    Transportation  894
    Other Expenses  1,142
                    -----
             Total  5,752
```

■ GENERATING RANDOM NUMBERS: RND

Consider a specific collection of numbers. We say that a process selects a number at **random** from this collection if any number in the collection is just as likely to be selected as any other and the number cannot be predicted in advance. Some examples follow:

Collection	Process
1, 2, 3, 4, 5, 6	toss a die
0 or 1,	toss a coin: 0 = tails, 1 = heads
−1, 0, 1, . . . , 36	spin a roulette wheel (interpret −1 as 00)
1, 2, . . . , n	write numbers on slips of paper, pull one from hat
numbers from 0 to 1	flip the spinner in Figure 2-30

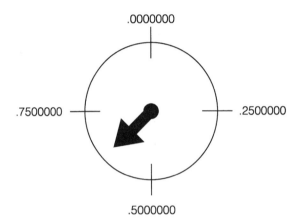

FIGURE 2-30   *Spinner to Randomly Select a Number Between 0 and 1*

The function Rnd, which acts like the spinner in Figure 2-30, returns a random number. The statement

```
picBox.Print Rnd
```

randomly displays a number from 0 up to (but not including) 1. The statement

```
numVar = Rnd
```

randomly assigns a number between 0 and 1 to the variable *numVar*. A different number will be assigned each time Rnd is called in the program, and any number greater than or equal to 0 and less than 1 is just as likely to be generated as any other. Therefore, although Rnd looks like a numeric variable, it does not act at all like a variable.

With appropriate scaling, the Rnd function can generate random numbers from other collections. The statement

```
picBox.Print Int(6 * Rnd) + 1;
```

displays a number from the set 1, 2, 3, 4, 5, 6. Because Rnd always has a value from 0 to 1, excluding 1, 6 * Rnd has a value from 0 to 6 (excluding 6), and Int(6 * Rnd) has one of the values 0, 1, 2, 3, 4, 5. Adding 1 shifts the resulting number into the desired range.

Suppose the preceding statement is repeated many times. The integers generated should exhibit no apparent pattern. They should look very much like a sequence of integers obtained from successively rolling a die. For instance, each of the six integers should appear about one-sixth of the time and be reasonably spread out in the sequence. The longer the sequence, the more likely this is to occur.

Rnd normally generates the same sequence of numbers each time a program is run. However, Visual Basic has another function, Randomize, that changes the sequence of numbers generated by Rnd. This statement will be used in all programs in this text.

EXAMPLE 8

The DC Lottery number is obtained by selecting a Ping-Pong ball from each of three separate bowls. Each ball is numbered with an integer from 0 through 9. Write a computer program to produce a lottery number. (Such a program is said to simulate the selection of Ping-Pong balls.)

SOLUTION:

The value of Int(10 * Rnd) will be an integer from 0 through 9, and each of these integers has the same likelihood of occurring. Repeating the process three times produces the requested digits.

```
Private Sub cmdDisplayANumber_Click()
   'Display a lottery number
   picNumber.Cls
   Randomize
   picNumber.Print Int(10 * Rnd);
   picNumber.Print Int(10 * Rnd);
   picNumber.Print Int(10 * Rnd)
End Sub
```

[Run and then click the command button. One possible output to be displayed in the picture box is as follows.]

8 3 9

Note: Run the program in Example 8 several times and notice that the output changes each time. Then delete the Randomize statement and run the program several times.

COMMENTS

1. Requesting the square root of a negative number terminates the execution of the program and gives the error message "Invalid procedure call or argument."

2. If n is greater than the length of str, then the value of Left(str, n) will be the entire string str. A similar result holds for Mid and Right.

3. Visual Basic has a function called LCase that is analogous to UCase. LCase converts all uppercase letters in a string to lowercase letters.

4. Because the values of the functions Left, Mid, Right, UCase, and the Format functions are strings, they are referred to as **string-valued functions**.

5. Mid is an important function. It will be used several times in this book to examine each letter of a string.

6. Trim is useful when reading data from a text box. Sometimes users type spaces at the end of input. Unless the spaces are removed, they can cause havoc elsewhere in the program. Also, Trim is useful in trimming the leading spaces from numbers that have been converted to strings with Str.

7. The InStr function has a useful extension. The value of InStr(n, $str1$, $str2$) is the position of the first occurrence of $str2$ in $str1$ in position n or greater. For instance, InStr(5, "Mississippi", "ss") is 6.

8. In Example 4, we found that 4 is the remainder when 256 is divided by 14. Mathematicians say "4 = 256 modulo 14." Visual Basic has an operation, Mod, that performs this calculation directly. If m and n are positive integers, then n Mod m is the remainder when n is divided by m. Visual Basic also has an operation called **integer division**, denoted by \, which gives the quotient portion of a long division problem. For instance, 14/4 is 3.5 whereas 14\4 is the integer 3.

9. Recall that the function Mid has the form Mid(str, m, n) and returns the substring of str starting with position m and having length n. Visual Basic does its best to please for unexpected values of m and n. If m is greater than the length

of the string or *n* is 0, then the empty string is returned. If *m* + *n* is greater than the length of the string, then Mid(*str*, *m*, *n*) is the right part of the string beginning with the mth character. The same is true for Mid(*str*, *m*). For instance, the values of Mid("abcdef", 3, 9) and Mid("abcdef", 3) are both "cdef".

10. With FormatCurrency(*n*, *r*), fractional values are preceded by a leading zero, and negative values are surrounded by parentheses instead of beginning with a minus sign. The function has additional optional parameters. FormatCurrency(*exp*, , vbFalse) suppresses leading zeros for fractional values. FormatCurrency(*exp*, , , vbFalse) uses minus signs for negative numbers. For instance, the value of FormatCurrency(–3/4, 3, vbFalse, vbFalse) is –$.750.

11. With FormatNumber(*n*, *r*), fractional values are preceded by a leading zero. The function has additional optional parameters. FormatNumber(*exp*, , vbFalse) suppresses leading zeros for fractional values. For instance, the value of FormatNumber(3/4, 3) is 0.750 and the value of FormatNumber(3/4, 3, vbFalse) is .750. FormatNumber(*exp*, , , , vbFalse) suppresses commas.

12. When *n* is a number that is halfway between two whole numbers (such as 1.5, 2.5, 3.5, and 4.5), then *n* is rounded by Round(*n*) to the nearest even number. That is, half the time *n* is rounded up and half the time is rounded down. For instance, Round(2.5) is 2 and Round(3.5) is 4. Similar results hold for any number whose decimal part ends in 5. For instance, Round(3.65, 1) is 3.6 and Round(3.75, 1) is 3.8. On the other hand, FormatNumber, FormatCurrency, and FormatPercent always round 5's up. For instance, FormatNumber(2.5) is "3.00".

13. The value of `FormatDateTime(Now, vbLongDate)` is today's date. For any positive number *n*, `FormatDateTime(Now + n, vbLongDate)` is the date *n* days from today and `FormatDateTime(Now - n, vbLongDate)` is the date *n* days ago.

14. The functions FormatNumber, FormatCurrency, FormatPercent, and FormatDateTime were added to Visual Basic in VB6.0. The same results can be obtained with the Format function alone. However, these new functions execute faster than Format and are easier to use. In addition, they can be placed in VBScript programs that are used to make Web pages interactive.

15. Each time the function Rnd appears in a program, it will be reassigned a value. For instance, the task attempted (but not accomplished) by the first set of lines that follows is achieved by the second set of lines. Because each of the Rnd's in the first set of lines will assume a different value, it is highly unlikely that the square of the first one will equal the product of the last two.

```
'Generate the square of a randomly chosen number
Randomize
picBox.Print "The square of"; Rnd; "is"; Rnd * Rnd'

Generate the square of a randomly chosen number
Randomize
numVar = Rnd
picBox.Print "The square of"; numVar; "is"; numVar * numVar
```

16. Additional information about the keywords, functions, methods, and properties discussed in this section appear in Appendix C. With the Learning, Professional, and Enterprise Editions of Visual Basic you can obtain a detailed (and somewhat advanced) discussion about an item appearing in code by clicking on the item and pressing F1. Other ways of obtaining help with these editions are presented in Appendix B.

SUMMARY

1. The Visual Basic screen consists of a collection of objects for which various properties can be set. Some examples of *objects* are text boxes, labels, command buttons, picture boxes, and the form itself. Objects placed on the form are called *controls*. Some useful properties are Text (set the text displayed by a text box), Caption (set the title of a form, the contents of a label, or the words on a command button), Font.Size (set the size of the characters displayed), Alignment (set the placement of the contents of a label), MultiLine (text box to display text on several lines), Picture (display drawing in picture box), ForeColor (set foreground color), BackColor (set background color), Visible (show or hide object), BorderStyle (alter and possibly remove border), Font.Bold (display boldface text), and Font.Italic (display italic text).

2. An event procedure is called when a specific event occurs to a specified object. Some event procedures are *object*_Click (*object* is clicked), *object*_LostFocus (*object* loses the focus), *object*_GotFocus (*object* receives the focus), and *object*_KeyPress (a key is pressed while *object* has the focus).

3. Visual Basic methods such as Print and Cls are applied to objects and are coded as *object*.Print and *object*.Cls.

4. Two types of *constants* that can be stored and processed by computers are *numbers* and *strings*.

5. The arithmetic *operations* are +, −, *, /, and ^. The only string operation is &, concatenation. An *expression* is a combination of constants, variables, functions, and operations that can be evaluated.

6. A *variable* is a name used to refer to data. Variable names can be up to 255 characters long, must begin with a letter, and may contain letters, digits, and underscores. Dim statements explicitly declare variables and specify the types of the variables. In this book, variables have types Single, Integer, and String.

7. Values are assigned to variables by assignment and Input # statements. The values appearing in assignment statements can be constants, variables, or expressions. Input # statements look to data files for constants. String constants used in assignment statements must be surrounded by quotation marks, whereas quotation marks are optional for string constants input with Input #. InputBox can be used to request that the user type in data.

8. The Print method displays information in a picture box or on the printer. *Semicolons*, *commas*, and *Tab* control the placement of the items on a particular line. A temporary message can be displayed on the screen using the MsgBox statement.

9. You control the printer with the Printer object and write to it with statements of the form Printer.Print *expression*. You set properties with statements of the form Printer.*property* = *setting*. Printer.NewPage starts a new page and PrintForm does a screen dump. A series of commands to the Printer object must end with EndDoc, which actually produces the final printed page.

10. Comment statements are used to explain formulas, state the purposes of variables, and articulate the purposes of various parts of a program.

11. The Format functions provide detailed control of how numbers, dates, and strings are displayed. Numbers can be made to line up uniformly and be displayed with dollar signs, commas, and a specified number of decimal places. Dates can be converted to a long form. Strings can be right-justified.

12. *Functions* can be thought of as accepting numbers or strings as input and returning numbers or strings as output.

Function	Input	Output
Asc	string	number
Chr	number	string
InStr	string, string	number
Int	number	number
LCase	string	string
Left	string, number	string
Len	string	number
Mid	string, number, number	string
Right	string,, number	string
Rnd		number
Round	number, number	number
Sqr	number	number
Str	number	string
Trim	string	string
UCase	string	string
Val	string	number

PROGRAMMING PROJECTS

1. Write a program that allows the user to specify two numbers and then adds, subtracts, or multiplies them when the user clicks on the appropriate command button. The output should give the type of arithmetic performed and the result.

2. Suppose automobile repair customers are billed at the rate of $35 per hour for labor. Also, costs for parts and supplies are subject to a 5 percent sales tax. Write a program to print out a simplified bill. The customer's name, the number of hours of labor, and the cost of parts and supplies should be entered into the program via text boxes. When a command button is clicked, the customer's name (indented) and the three costs should be displayed in a picture box, as shown in the sample run in Figure 2-31.

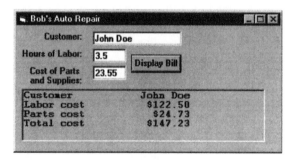

FIGURE 2-31 *Sample Run for Programming Project 2*

3. Write a program to generate the following personalized form letter. The person's name and address should be read from text boxes.

```
Mr. John Jones
123 Main Street
Juneau, Alaska 99803

Dear Mr. Jones,
```

```
    The Jones family has been selected as the
first family on Main Street to have the opportunity
to purchase an Apex solar-powered flashlight. Due to limited
supply, only 1000 of these amazing inventions will be available
in the entire state of Alaska. Don't delay. Order today.
                    Sincerely,
                    Cuthbert J. Twillie
```

4. At the end of each month, a credit card company constructs the table in Figure 2-32 to summarize the status of the accounts. Write a program to produce this table. The first four pieces of information for each account should be read from a data file. The program should compute the finance charges (1.5 percent of the unpaid past due amount) and the current amount due. Format the last column to be aligned right.

Account Number	Past Due Amount	Payments	Purchases	Finance Charges	Current Amt Due
123-AB	123.45	10.00	934.00	1.70	$1,049.15
456-CD	134.56	134.56	300.00	0.00	$300.00

FIGURE 2-32   *Status of Credit Card Accounts*

5. Table 2-11 gives the distribution of the U.S. population (in thousands) by age group and sex. Write a program to produce the table shown in Figure 2-33. For each age group, the column labeled %Males gives the percentage of the people in that age group that are male, similarly for the column labeled %Females. The last column gives the percentage of the total population in each age group. *Note:* Store the information in Table 2-11 in a data file. For instance, the first line in the file should be "Under 20", 39168, 37202. Read and add up the data once to obtain the total population, and then read the data again to produce the table.)

TABLE 2-11
U.S. Resident Population in Thousands (1996)

Age Group	Males	Females
Under 20	39,168	37,202
20–64	76,761	78,291
Over 64	13,881	19,980

```
              U.S. Population (in thousands)

Age group   Males    Females    %Males    %Females    %Total

Under 20    39,168   37,202     51.29%    48.71%      28.79%

20-64       76,761   78,291     49.51%    50.49%      58.45%

Over 64     13,881   19,980     40.99%    59.01%      12.76%
```

FIGURE 2-33   *Output of Programming Project 5*

6. Write a program to convert a U.S. Customary System length in miles, yards, feet, and inches to a Metric System length in kilometers, meters, and centimeters. A sample run is shown in Figure 2-34. After the number of miles, yards, feet, and inches are read from the text boxes, the length should be converted entirely to inches and then divided by 39.37 to obtain the value in meters. The Int function should be used to break the total number of meters into a whole

number of kilometers and meters. The number of centimeters should be displayed to one decimal place. Some of the needed formulas are as follows:

total inches = 63360 * miles + 36 * yards + 12 * feet + inches

total meters = total inches / 39.37

kilometers = Int(meters / 1000)

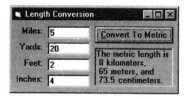

FIGURE 2-34   *Sample Run for Programming Project 6*

GENERAL PROCEDURES

3.1 SUB PROCEDURES, PART I

Structured program design requires that problems be broken into small problems to be solved one at a time. Visual Basic has two devices, **Sub procedures** and **Function procedures**, that are used to break problems into manageable chunks. To distinguish them from event procedures, Sub and Function procedures are referred to as **general procedures**. General procedures also eliminate repetitive code, can be reused in other programs, and allow a team of programmers to work on a single program.

In this section we show how Sub procedures are defined and used. The programs in this section are designed to demonstrate the use of Sub procedures rather than to accomplish sophisticated programming tasks. Later chapters of the book use them for more substantial programming efforts.

A **Sub procedure** is a part of a program that performs one or more related tasks, has its own name, is written as a separate part of the program. The simplest type of Sub procedure has the form

```
Private Sub ProcedureName()
   statement(s)
End Sub
```

A Sub procedure is invoked with a statement of the form

```
Call ProcedureName
```

The rules for naming general procedures are identical to the rules for naming variables. The name chosen for a Sub procedure should describe the task it performs. Sub procedures can be either typed directly into the code window, or into a template created with the following steps:

1. Press Alt/T/P to select Add Procedure from the Tools menu.

2. Type in the name of the procedure. (Omit parentheses.)

3. Select Sub from the Type box.

4. Select Private from the Scope box. *Note:* Actually either Public or Private is OK. A Public procedure is available to all forms, whereas a Private procedure is only available to the form in which it is defined.

5. Press the Enter key or click on OK.

Consider the following program that calculates the sum of two numbers. This program will be revised to incorporate Sub procedures.

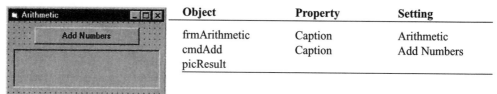

Object	Property	Setting
frmArithmetic	Caption	Arithmetic
cmdAdd	Caption	Add Numbers
picResult		

```
Private Sub cmdAdd_Click()
   Dim num1 As Single, num2 As Single
   'Display the sum of two numbers
   picResult.Cls
   picResult.Print "This program displays a sentence "
   picResult.Print "identifying two numbers and their sum."
   picResult.Print num1 = 2 num2 = 3
   picResult.Print "The sum of"; num1; "and"; num2; "is"; num1 + num2
End Sub
```

[Run, and then click the command button. The following is displayed in the picture box.]

```
This program displays a sentence
identifying two numbers and their sum.

The sum of 2 and 3 is 5
```

The tasks performed by this program can be summarized as follows:
Explain purpose of program.

Display numbers and their sum.

Sub procedures allow us to write and read the program in such a way that we first focus on the tasks and later on how to accomplish each task.

EXAMPLE 1

The following program uses a Sub procedure to accomplish the first task of the preceding program. When the statement Call ExplainPurpose is reached, execution jumps to the Sub ExplainPurpose statement. The lines between Sub ExplainPurpose and End Sub are executed, and then execution continues with the line following the Call statement.

```
Private Sub cmdAdd_Click()
   Dim num1 As Single, num2 As Single
   'Display the sum of two numbers
   picResult.Cls
   Call ExplainPurpose
   picResult.Print
   num1 = 2
   num2 = 3
   picResult.Print "The sum of"; num1; "and"; num2; "is"; num1 + num2
End Sub

Private Sub ExplainPurpose()
   'Explain the task performed by the program
   picResult.Print "This program displays a sentence"
   picResult.Print "identifying two numbers and their sum."
End Sub
```

The second task performed by the addition program also can be handled by a Sub procedure. The values of the two numbers, however, must be transmitted to the Sub procedure. This transmission is called **passing**.

EXAMPLE 2

The following revision of the program in Example 1 uses a Sub procedure to accomplish the second task. The statement Call Add(2, 3) causes execution to jump to the Private Sub Add(num1 As Single, num2 As Single) statement, which assigns the number 2 to *num1* and the number 3 to *num2*.

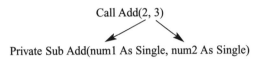

After the lines between Private Sub Add (num1 As Single, num2 As Single) and End Sub are executed, execution continues with the line following Call Add(2, 3), namely, the End Sub statement in the event procedure. *Note 1:* When you create the Sub procedure Add, you must type in "(num1 As Single, num2 As Single)" after leaving the Add Procedure dialog box.

```
Private Sub cmdAdd_Click()
   'Display the sum of two numbers
   picResult.Cls
   Call ExplainPurpose
   picResult.Print
   Call Add(2, 3)
End Sub

Private Sub Add(num1 As Single, num2 As Single)
   'Display numbers and their sum
   picResult.Print "The sum of"; num1; "and"; num2; "is"; num1 + num2
End Sub

Private Sub ExplainPurpose()
   'Explain the task performed by the program
   picResult.Print "This program displays a sentence"
   picResult.Print "identifying two numbers and their sum."
End Sub
```

Sub procedures make a program easy to read, modify, and debug. The event procedure gives a description of what the program does and the Sub procedures fill in the details. Another benefit of Sub procedures is that they can be called several times during the execution of the program. This feature is especially useful when there are many statements in the Sub procedure.

EXAMPLE 3

The following extension of the program in Example 2 displays several sums.

```
Private Sub cmdAdd_Click()
   'Display the sums of several pairs of numbers
   picResult.Cls
   Call ExplainPurpose
   picResult.Print
   Call Add(2, 3)
   Call Add(4, 6)
   Call Add(7, 8)
End Sub
```

```
Private Sub Add(num1 As Single, num2 As Single)
   'Display numbers and their sum picResult.Print "The sum of"; num1; "and";
   num2; "is"; num1 + num2
End Sub

Private Sub ExplainPurpose()
   'Explain the task performed by the program
   picResult.Print "This program displays sentences"
   picResult.Print "identifying pairs of numbers and their sums."
End Sub
```

[Run and then click the command button. The following is displayed in the picture box.]

```
This program displays sentences
identifying pairs of numbers and their sums.

The sum of 2 and 3 is 5
The sum of 4 and 6 is 10
The sum of 7 and 8 is 15
```

The variables *num1* and *num2* appearing in the Sub procedure Add are called **parameters**. They are merely temporary place holders for the numbers passed to the Sub procedure; their names are not important. The only essentials are their type, quantity, and order. In this Add Sub procedure, the parameters must be numeric variables and there must be two of them. For instance, the Sub procedure could have been written

```
Private Sub Add(this As Single, that As Single)
   'Display numbers and their sum
   picResult.Print "The sum of"; this; "and"; that; "is"; this + that
End Sub
```

A string also can be passed to a Sub procedure. In this case, the receiving parameter in the Sub procedure must be followed by the declaration As String.

EXAMPLE 4

The following program passes a string and two numbers to a Sub procedure. When the Sub procedure is first called, the string parameter *state* is assigned the string constant "Hawaii", and the numeric parameters *pop* and *area* are assigned the numeric constants 1184000 and 6471, respectively. The Sub procedure then uses these parameters to carry out the task of calculating the population density of Hawaii. The second Call statement assigns different values to the parameters.

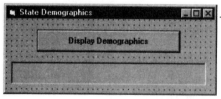

Object	Property	Setting
frmStates	Caption	State Demographics
cmdDisplay	Caption	Display Demographics
picDensity		

```
Private Sub cmdDisplay_Click()
   'Calculate the population densities of states
   picDensity.Cls
   Call CalculateDensity("Hawaii", 1184000, 6471)
   Call CalculateDensity("Alaska", 607000, 591000)
End Sub

Private Sub CalculateDensity(state As String, pop As Single, area As Single)
   Dim rawDensity As Single, density As Single
```

```
    'The density (number of people per square mile)
    'will be displayed rounded to a whole number
    rawDensity = pop / area
    density = Round(rawDensity) 'round to whole number
    picDensity.Print "The density of "; state; " is"; density;
    picDensity.Print "people per square mile."
End Sub
```

[Run, and then click the command button. The following is displayed in the picture box.]

```
    The density of Hawaii is 183 people per square mile.
    The density of Alaska is 1 people per square mile.
```

The parameters in the density program can have any names, as with the parameters in the addition program of Example 3. The only restriction is that the first parameter be a string variable and that the last two parameters be numeric variables. For instance, the Sub procedure could have been written

```
Private Sub CalculateDensity(x As String, y As Single, z As Single)
    Dim rawDensity As Single, density As Single
    'The density (number of people per square mile)
    'will be rounded to a whole number
    rawDensity = y / z
    density = Round(rawDensity)
    picDensity.Print "The density of "; x; " is"; density;
    picDensity.Print "people per square mile."
End Sub
```

When nondescriptive names are used for parameters, the Sub procedure should contain comments giving the meanings of the variables. Possible comments for the preceding program are

```
    'x name of the state'
    y population of the state'
    z area of the state
```

■ VARIABLES AND EXPRESSIONS AS ARGUMENTS

The items appearing in the parentheses of a Call statement are called **arguments**. These should not be confused with parameters, which appear in the heading of a Sub procedure. In Example 3, the arguments of the Call Add statements were constants. These arguments also could have been variables or expressions. For instance, the event procedure could have been written as follows. See Figure 3-1.

```
Private Sub cmdAdd_Click()
    Dim x As Single, y As Single, z As Single
    'Display the sum of two numbers
    picResult.Cls
    Call ExplainPurpose
    picResult.Print
    x = 2
    y = 3
    Call Add(x, y)
    Call Add(x + 2, 2 * y) z = 7
    Call Add(z, z + 1)
End Sub
```

```
        Arguments                              Arguments
        ┌──┴──┐                              ┌────┴────┐
Call Add( x,    y)                   Call Add(x + 2,   2 * y)
          │      \                            │          │
          ▼       \                           ▼          ▼
Private Sub Add (num1 As Single, num2 As Single)  Private Sub Add (num1 As Single, num2 As Single)
                └──────────┬──────────┘                     └──────────┬──────────┘
                      Parameters                                   Parameters
```

FIGURE 3-1   *Passing Arguments to Parameters*

This feature allows values obtained as input from the user to be passed to a Sub procedure.

EXAMPLE 5

The following variation of the addition program requests the two numbers as input from the user. Notice that the names of the arguments, *x* and *y*, are different from the names of the parameters. The names of the arguments and parameters may be the same or different; what matters is that the order, number, and types of the arguments and parameters match.

Object	Property	Setting
frmAdd	Caption	Add Two Numbers
lblFirstNum	Caption	First Number
txtFirstNum	Text	(blank)
lblSecondNum	Caption	Second Number
txtSecondNum	Text	(blank)
cmdCompute	Caption	Compute Sum
picResult		

```
Private Sub cmdCompute_Click()
   Dim x As Single,, y As Single
   'This program requests two numbers and
   'displays the two numbers and their sum.
   x = Val(txtFirstNum.Text)
   y = Val(txtSecondNum.Text)
   Call Add(x,, y)
End Sub

Private Sub Add(num1 As Single,, num2 As Single)
   'Display numbers and their sum
   picResult.Cls
   picResult.Print "The sum of"; num1; "and"; num2; "is"; num1 + num2
End Sub
```

[Run, type 23 and 67 into the text boxes, and then click the command button.]

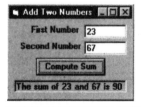

EXAMPLE 6

The following variation of Example 4 obtains its input from the file DEMOGRAP.TXT. The second Call statement uses different variable names for the arguments to show that using the same argument names is not necessary. See Figure 3-2.

DEMOGRAP.TXT contains the following two lines:

"Hawaii", 1184000, 6471
"Alaska", 607000, 591000

```
Private Sub cmdDisplay_Click()
   Dim state As String, pop As Single, area As Single
   Dim s As String, p As Single, a As Single
   'Calculate the population densities of states
   picDensity.Cls Open "DEMOGRAP.TXT" For Input As #1
   Input #1, state, pop, area
   Call CalculateDensity(state, pop, area)
   Input #1, s, p, a
   Call CalculateDensity(s, p, a)
   Close #1
End Sub

Private Sub CalculateDensity(state As String, pop As Single, area As Single)
   Dim rawDensity As Single, density As Single
   'The density (number of people per square mile)
   'will be rounded to a whole number
   rawDensity = pop / area density = Round(rawDensity)
   picDensity.Print "The density of "; state; " is "; density;
   picDensity.Print "people per square mile."
End Sub
```

[Run, and then click the command button. The following is displayed in the picture box.]

```
The density of Hawaii is 183 people per square mile.
The density of Alaska is 1 people per square mile.
```

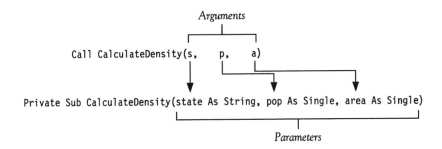

FIGURE 3-2   *Passing Arguments to Parameters in Example 6*

Arguments and parameters also can be used to pass values from Sub procedures back to event procedures or other Sub procedures. This important property is explored in detail in the next section.

COMMENTS

1. In this text, Sub procedure names begin with uppercase letters in order to distinguish them from variable names. Like variable names, however, they can be written with any combination of upper- and lowercase letters. To improve readability, the Visual Basic editor will automatically ensure that the capitalization of a Sub procedure name is consistent throughout a program. For instance, if you type Private Sub PROCEDURENAME and also type Call ProcedureName, the second name will be changed to match the first. *Note:* Parameters appearing in a Sub statement are not part of the Sub procedure name.

2. To obtain a list of the general procedures in a program, select (General) from the Code window's Object box and then click on the down-arrow at the right side of the Procedure box.

3. Sub procedures allow programmers to focus on the main flow of the program and defer the details of implementation. Modern programs use them liberally. An event procedure acts as a supervisor, delegating tasks to the Sub procedures. This method of program construction is known as **modular** or **top-down** design.

4. As a rule, a Sub procedure should perform only one task, or several closely related tasks, and should be kept relatively small.

5. After a Sub procedure has been defined, Visual Basic automatically reminds you of the Sub procedure's parameters when you type in Call statements. As soon as you type in the left parenthesis of a Call statement, a banner appears giving the names and types of the parameters. The help feature is called **Parameter Info**. See Figure 3-3.

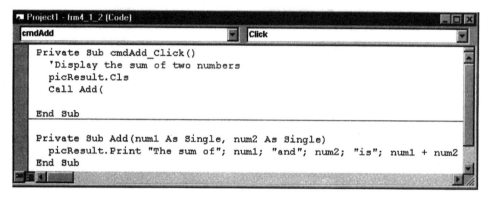

FIGURE 3-3 *The Parameter Info Help Feature*

6. In this text, the first line inside a Sub procedure is often a comment statement describing the task performed by the Sub procedure. If necessary, several comment statements are devoted to this purpose. Conventional programming practice also recommends that all variables used by the Sub procedure be listed in comment statements with their meanings. In this text, we give several examples of this practice but only adhere to it when the variables are especially numerous or lack descriptive names.

7. Although both constants and expressions can be used as arguments in Call statements, only variables can be used as parameters in Sub statements.

8. A Sub procedure can call another Sub procedure. If so, after the End Sub of the called Sub procedure is reached, execution continues with the line in the calling Sub procedure that follows the Call statement.

9. When you write a Sub procedure without parameters, Visual Basic automatically adds a pair of empty parentheses at the end of the Sub procedure name. However, Call statements should not use the empty parentheses.

10. The first lines of event procedures and Sub procedures end with a pair of parentheses. With the event procedures we have discussed, the parentheses are usually empty, whereas with Sub procedures, the parentheses often contain parameters.

3.2 SUB PROCEDURES, PART II

The previous section introduced the concept of a Sub procedure but left some questions unanswered. Why can't the value of a variable be passed from an event procedure to a Sub procedure by just using the variable in the Sub procedure? How do Sub procedures pass values back to an event procedure? The answers to these questions provide a deeper understanding of the workings of Sub procedures and reveal their full capabilities.

■ PASSING VALUES BACK FROM SUB PROCEDURES

Suppose a variable, call it *arg*, appears as an argument in a Call statement, and its corresponding parameter in the Sub statement is *par*. After the Sub procedure is executed, *arg* will have whatever value *par* had in the Sub procedure. Hence, not only is the value of *arg* passed to *par*, but the value of *par* is passed back to *arg*.

EXAMPLE 1

The following program illustrates the transfer of the value of a parameter to its calling argument.

```
Private Sub cmdDisplay_Click()
   Dim amt As Single
   'Illustrate effect of value of parameter on value of argument
   picResults.Cls
   amt = 2
   picResults.Print amt;
   Call Triple(amt)
   picResults.Print amt
End Sub

Private Sub
   Triple(num As Single)
   'Triple a number picResults.Print num;
   num = 3 * num
   picResults.Print num;
End Sub
```

[Run and then click the command button. The following is displayed in the picture box.]

2   2   6   6

Although this feature may be surprising at first glance, it provides a vehicle for passing values from a Sub procedure back to the place from which the Sub procedure was called. Different names may be used for an argument and its corresponding parameter, but only one memory location is involved. Initially, the cmdDisplay_Click( ) event procedure allocates a memory location to hold the value of *amt* (Figure 3-4(a)). When the Sub procedure is called, the parameter *num* becomes the Sub procedure's name for this memory location (Figure 3-4(b)). When the value of *num* is tripled, the value in the memory location becomes 6 (Figure 3-4(c)). After the completion of the procedure, the parameter name *num* is forgotten; however, its value lives on in *amt* (Figure 3-4(d)). The variable *amt* is said to be **passed by reference**.

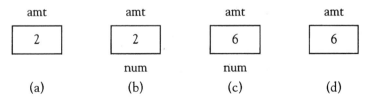

FIGURE 3-4   *Passing a Variable by Reference to a Sub Procedure*

Passing by reference has a wide variety of uses. In the next example, it is used as a vehicle to transport a value from a Sub procedure back to an event procedure.

EXAMPLE 2

The following variation of the addition program from the previous section uses a Sub procedure to acquire the input. The variables x and y are not assigned values prior to the execution of the first Call statement. Therefore, before the Call statement is executed, they have the value 0. After the Call statement is executed, however, they have the values 2 and 3. These values then are passed by the second Call statement to the Sub procedure Add.

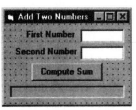

Object	Property	Setting
frmAdd	Caption	Add Two Numbers
lblFirstNum	Caption	First Number
txtFirstNum	Text	(blank)
lblSecondNum	Caption	Second Number
txtSecondNum	Text	(blank)
cmdCompute	Caption	Compute Sum
picResult		

```
Private Sub cmdCompute_Click()
    Dim x As Single, y As Single
    'Display the sum of the two numbers
    Call GetNumbers(x, y)
    Call Add(x, y)
End Sub

Private Sub Add(num1 As Single, num2 As Single)
    Dim sum As Single
    'Display numbers and their sum
    picResult.Cls
    sum = num1 + num2
    picResult.Print "The sum of"; num1; "and"; num2; "is"; sum
End Sub

Private Sub GetNumbers(num1 As Single, num2 As Single)
    'Record the two numbers in the text boxes
    num1 = Val(txtFirstNum.Text)
    num2 = Val(txtSecondNum.Text)
End Sub
```

[Run, type 2 and 3 into the text boxes, and then click the command button.]

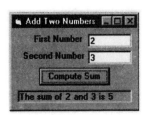

In most situations, a variable with no preassigned value is used as an argument of a Call statement for the sole purpose of carrying back a value from the Sub procedure.

EXAMPLE 3

The following variation of Example 2 allows the cmdCompute_Click event procedure to be written in the input-process-output style.

```
Private Sub cmdCompute_Click()
    Dim x As Single, y As Single, s As Single
    'Display the sum of two numbers
    Call GetNumbers(x, y)
```

```
   Call CalculateSum(x, y, s)
   Call DisplayResult(x, y, s)
End Sub

Private Sub CalculateSum(num1 As Single, num2 As Single, sum As Single)
   'Add the values of num1 and num2
   'and assign the value to sum
   sum = num1 + num2
End Sub

Private Sub DisplayResult(num1 As Single, num2 As Single, sum As Single)
   'Display a sentence giving the two numbers and their sum
   picResult.Cls
   picResult.Print "The sum of"; num1; "and"; num2; "is"; sum
End Sub

Private Sub GetNumbers(num1 As Single, num2 As Single)
   'Record the two numbers in the text boxes
   num1 = Val(txtFirstNum.Text)
   num2 = Val(txtSecondNum.Text)
End Sub
```

■ PASSING BY VALUE

Sometimes you want to pass a variable to a Sub procedure, but you want to ensure that the variable will retain its original value after the Sub procedure terminates—regardless of what was done to the corresponding parameter inside the Sub procedure. Such a variable is said to be **passed by value**. There are two ways to pass a variable by value.

1. In the Call statement, enclose the variable in an extra pair of parentheses.

2. In the Private Sub statement, precede the corresponding parameter with the word ByVal.

For instance, in Example 1, if you change the Call statement to

```
   Call Triple((amt))
```

then the output will be

```
2   2   6   2
```

The same output results if you change the Private Sub statement to

```
   Private Sub Triple(ByVal num As Single)
```

   When a variable is passed by value, two memory locations are involved. At the time the Sub procedure is called, a temporary second memory location for the parameter is set aside for the Sub procedure's use and the value of the argument is copied into that location. After the completion of the Sub procedure, the temporary memory location is released and the value in it is lost.

■ LOCAL VARIABLES

When the same variable name appears in two different Sub procedures or in a Sub procedure and an event procedure, Visual Basic gives the variables separate identities and treats them as two different variables. A value assigned to a variable in one part of the program will not affect the value of the like-named variable in the other part of the program, unless, of course, the values are passed by a Call statement. Also, each time a Sub procedure is called, all declared variables that are not parameters assume their default values. (Numeric variables have default value 0, and string variables default to the empty string.) The variables in a Sub procedure are said to be local to the Sub procedure in which they reside.

EXAMPLE 4

The following program illustrates the fact that each time a Sub procedure is called, its variables are set to their default values; that is, numerical variables are set to 0 and string variables are set to the empty string.

```
Private Sub cmdDisplay_Click()
    'Demonstrate that variables in a Sub procedure do
    'not retain their values in subsequent calls
    picResults.Cls
    Call Three
    Call Three
End Sub

Private Sub Three()
    Dim num As Single
    'Display the value of num and assign it the value 3
    picResults.Print num;
    num = 3
End Sub
```

[Run, and then click the command button. The following is displayed in the picture box.]

0 0

EXAMPLE 5

The following program illustrates the fact that variables are local to the part of the program in which they reside. The variable x in the event procedure and the variable x in the Sub procedure are treated as different variables. Visual Basic handles them as if their names were separate, such as *xcmdDisplay_Click* and *xTrivial*. Also, each time the Sub procedure is called, the value of variable x inside the Sub procedure is reset to 0.

```
Private Sub cmdDisplay_Click()
    Dim x As Single
    'Demonstrate the local nature of variables
    picResults.Cls
    x = 2
    picResults.Print x;
    Call Trivial
    picResults.Print x;
    Call Trivial
    picResults.Print x;
End Sub

Private Sub Trivial()
    Dim x As Single
    'Do something trivial
    picResults.Print x;
    x = 3
    picResults.Print x;
End Sub
```

[Run and then click the command button. The following is displayed in the picture box.]

2 0 3 2 0 3 2

■ FORM-LEVEL VARIABLES

Visual Basic provides a way to make a variable visible to *every* procedure in a form's code without being passed. Such a variable is called a **form-level variable**. Form-level variables appear at the top of the code window and are separated from the rest of the code by a horizontal separator line. Inside the code window, you can move to them either by pressing Ctrl+Home or clicking on General in the Object list box. Form-level variables are said to reside in the (Declarations) section of (General) and are declared with the following steps.

1. Invoke a code window if one is not already active.

2. Click on the down-arrow to the right of the Object list box.

3. Click on (General).

4. Click on (Declarations) in the Procedure list box.

5. Type in a declaration statement, such as Dim strVar As String, and press the Enter key.

When a form-level variable is assigned a value by a procedure, it retains that value when the procedure is exited. In this text, we rarely use form-level variables until Section 6.

EXAMPLE 6

The following program contains the form-level variables *num1* and *num2*. Their Dim statement does not appear inside a procedure.

```
Dim num1 As Single, num2 As Single 'In (Declarations) section of (General)

Private Sub cmdDisplay_Click()
   'Display the sum of two numbers
   num1 = 2
   num2 = 3
   picResults.Cls
   Call AddAndIncrement
   picResults.Print
   picResults.Print "num1 = "; num1
   picResults.Print "num2 = "; num2
End Sub


Private Sub AddAndIncrement()
   'Display numbers and their sum
   picResults.Print "The sum of"; num1; "and"; num2; "is"; num1 + num2
   num1 = num1 + 1
   num2 = num2 + 1
End Sub
```

[Run, and click the command button. The following is displayed in the picture box.]

```
The sum of 2 and 3 is 5

num1 = 3
num2 = 4
```

In the preceding example, we had to click a command button to assign values to the form-level variables. In some situations, we want to assign a value immediately to a form-level variable, without requiring the user to perform some specific action. Visual Basic has a special event procedure called Form_Load that is automatically activated as soon as the program is run, even before the form is created. The Form_Load template is invoked by double-clicking on the form itself.

EXAMPLE 7

The following program demonstrates the use of Form_Load.

```
Dim pi As Single 'In (Declarations) section of (General)

Private Sub Form_Load()
   'Assign a value to pi
   pi = 3.14159
End Sub

Private Sub cmdCompute_Click()
   'Display the area of a circle of radius 5
   picArea.Cls
   picArea.Print "The area of a circle of radius 5 is"; pi * 5 * 5
End Sub
```

[Run, and then click the command button. The following is displayed in the picture box.]

```
The area of a circle of radius 5 is 78.53975
```

COMMENTS

1. In addition to the reasons presented earlier, some other reasons for using Sub procedures follow:

   (a) Programs with Sub procedures are easier to debug. Each Sub procedure can be checked individually before being placed into the program.

   (b) The task performed by a Sub procedure might be needed in another program. The Sub procedure can be reused with no changes. Programmers refer to the collection of their most universal Sub procedures as a **library** of Sub procedures. (The fact that variables appearing in Sub procedures are local to the Sub procedures is quite helpful when reusing Sub procedures in other programs. There is no need to worry if a variable name in the Sub procedure is used for a different purpose in another part of the program.)

   (c) Often, programs are written by a team of programmers. After a problem has been broken into distinct and manageable tasks, each programmer is assigned a single Sub procedure to write.

   (d) Sub procedures make large programs easier to understand. Some programming standards insist that each Sub procedure be at most two pages long.

   (e) Sub procedures permit the following program design, which provides a built-in outline of an event procedure. A reader can focus on the main flow first, and then go into the specifics of accomplishing the secondary tasks.

   ```
   Private Sub Object_Event()
      'An event procedure written entirely as Sub procudures
      Call FirstSubprocedure 'Perform first task
      Call SecondSubprocedure 'Perform second task
      Call ThirdSubprocedure 'Perform third task
   End Sub
   ```

2. Sub procedures can call other Sub procedures. In such cases, the calling Sub procedure plays the role of the event procedure with respect to the called Sub procedure. Complex problems are thereby broken into simpler tasks, which are then broken into still more elementary tasks. This approach to problem solving is called **top-down design**.

3. In Appendix D, the section "Stepping Through a Program Containing a Procedure: Section 3" uses the Visual Basic debugger to trace the flow through a program and observe the interplay between arguments and parameters.

4. You can use the Print method in a Form_Load event procedure. If so, you must set the AutoRedraw property of the picture box to True. Otherwise the contents of the picture box will be erased when the event procedure terminates.

3.3 FUNCTION PROCEDURES

Visual Basic has many built-in functions. In one respect, functions are like miniature programs. They use input, they process the input, and they have output. Some functions we encountered earlier are listed in Table 3.1.

TABLE 3.1
Some Visual Basic Built-In Functions

Function	Example	Input	Output
Int	Int(2.6) is 2	number	number
Chr	Chr(65) is "A"	number	string
Len	Len("perhaps") is 7	string	number
Mid	Mid("perhaps",4,2) is "ha"	string, number, number	string
InStr	InStr("to be"," ") is 3	string,string	number

Although the input can involve several values, the output always consists of a single value. The items inside the parentheses can be constants (as in Table 3.1), variables, or expressions.

In addition to using built-in functions, we can define functions of our own. These new functions, called **Function procedures** or **user-defined functions**, are defined in much the same way as Sub procedures and are used in the same way as built-in functions. Like built-in functions, Function procedures have a single output that can be string or numeric. Function procedures can be used in expressions in exactly the same way as built-in functions. Programs refer to them as if they were constants, variables, or expressions. Function procedures are defined by function blocks of the form

```
Private Function FunctionName(var1 As Type1, var2 As Type2, ...) As dataType
    statement(s)
    FunctionName = expression
End Function
```

The variables in the top line are called **parameters**, and variables inside the function block that are not parameters have local scope. Function names should be suggestive of the role performed and must conform to the rules for naming variables. The type *dataType*, which specifies the type of the output, will be one of String, Integer, Single, and so on. In the preceding general code, the next-to-last line assigns the output, which must be of type *dataType*, to the function name. Two examples of Function procedures are as follows:

```
Private Function FtoC(t As Single) As Single
    'Convert Fahrenheit temperature to Celsius
    FtoC = (5 / 9) * (t - 32)
End Function
```

```
Private Function FirstName(nom As String) As String
    Dim firstSpace As Integer
    'Extract the first name from the full name nom
    firstSpace = InStr(nom, " ")
```

```
    FirstName = Left(nom, firstSpace - 1)
End Function
```

The value of each of the preceding functions is assigned by a statement of the form *FunctionName = expression*. The variables *t* and *nom* appearing in the preceding functions are parameters. They can be replaced with any variable of the same type without affecting the function definition. For instance, the function FtoC could have been defined as

```
Private Function FtoC(temp As Single) As Single
  'Convert Fahrenheit temperature to Celsius
  FtoC = (5 / 9) * (temp - 32)
End Function
```

Like Sub procedures, Function procedures can be created from a code window with Alt/T/P. The only difference is that the circle next to the word Function should be selected. After the name is typed and the OK button is clicked, the lines Private Function *FunctionName*( ) and End Function will be placed automatically (separated by a blank line) in the code window.

EXAMPLE 1

The following program uses the function FtoC.

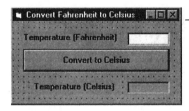

Object	Property	Setting
frm4_3_1	Caption	Convert Fahrenheit to Celsius
lblTempF	Caption	Temperature (Fahrenheit)
txtTempF	Text	(blank)
cmdConvert	Caption	Convert to Celsius
lblTempC	Caption	Temperature (Celsius)
picTempC		

```
Private Sub cmdConvert_Click()
  picTempC.Cls
  picTempC.Print FtoC(Val(txtTempF.Text))
End Sub

Private Function FtoC(t As Single) As Single
  'Convert Fahrenheit temperature to Celsius
  FtoC = (5 / 9) * (t - 32)
End Function
```

[Run, type 212 into the text box, and then click the command button.]

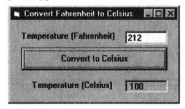

EXAMPLE 2

The following program uses the function FirstName.

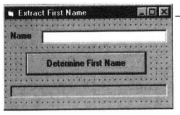

Object	Property	Setting
frm4_3_2	Caption	Extract First Name
lblName	Caption	Name
txtFullName	Text	(blank)
cmdDetermine	Caption	Determine First Name
picFirstName		

```
Private Sub cmdDetermine_Click()
   Dim nom As String
   'Determine a person's first name
   nom = txtFullName.Text
   picFirstName.Cls
   picFirstName.Print "The first name is "; FirstName(nom)
End Sub

Private Function FirstName(nom As String) As String
   Dim firstSpace As Integer
   'Extract the first name from a full name
   firstSpace = InStr(nom, " ")
   FirstName = Left(nom, firstSpace - 1)
End Function
```

[Run, type Thomas Woodrow Wilson into the text box, and then click the command button.]

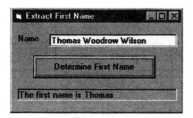

The input to a user-defined function can consist of one or more values. Two examples of functions with several parameters follow. One-letter variable names have been used so the mathematical formulas will look familiar and be readable. Because the names are not descriptive, the meanings of these variables are carefully stated in comment statements.

```
Private Function Hypotenuse(a As Single, b As Single) As Single
   'Calculate the hypotenuse of a right triangle
   'having sides of lengths a and b
   Hypotenuse = Sqr(a ^ 2 + b ^ 2)
End Function

Private Function FV(p As Single,r As Single,c As Single,n As Single)
   As Single Dim i As Single, m As Single
   'Find the future value of a bank savings account
   'p principal, the amount deposited
   'r annual rate of interest
   'c number of times interest is compounded per year
   'n number of years
   'i interest rate per period
   'm total number of times interest is compounded
   i = r / c
   m = c * n
   FV = p * ((1 + i) ^ m)
End Function
```

EXAMPLE 3

The following program uses the Hypotenuse function.

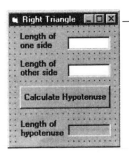

Object	Property	Setting
frm4_3_3	Caption	Right Triangle
lblSideOne	Caption	Length of one side
txtSideOne	Text	(blank)
lblSideTwo	Caption	Length of other side
txtSideTwo	Text	(blank)
cmdCalculate	Caption	Calculate Hypotenuse
lblHyp	Caption	Length of hypotenuse
picHyp		

```
Private Sub cmdCalculate_Click()
  Dim a As Single, b As Single
  'Calculate length of the hypotenuse of a right triangle
  a = Val(txtSideOne.Text)
  b = Val(txtSideTwo.Text)
  picHyp.Cls
  picHyp.Print Hypotenuse(a, b)
End Sub

Private Function Hypotenuse(a As Single, b As Single) As Single
  'Calculate the hypotenuse of a right triangle
  'having sides of lengths a and b
  Hypotenuse = Sqr(a ^ 2 + b ^ 2)
End Function
```

[Run, type 3 and 4 into the text boxes, and then click the command button.]

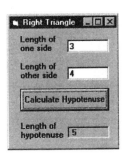

EXAMPLE 4

The following program uses the future value function. With the responses shown, the program computes the balance in a savings account when $100 is deposited for 5 years at 4% interest compounded quarterly. Interest is earned 4 times per year at the rate of 1% per interest period. There will be 4 * 5 or interest periods.

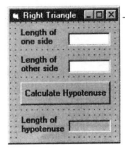

Object	Property	Setting
frm4_3_4	Caption	Bank Deposit
lblAmount	Caption	Amount of bank deposit
txtAmount	Text	(blank)
lblRate	Caption	Annual rate of interest
txtRate	Text	(blank)
lblNumComp	Caption	Number of times interest is compounded per year
txtNumComp	Text	(blank)
lblNumYrs	Caption	Number of years
txtNumYrs	Text	(blank)
cmdCompute	Caption	Compute Balance
lblBalance	Caption	Balance
picBalance		

```
Private Sub cmdCompute_Click()
  Dim p As Single, r As Single, c As Single, n As Single
  'Find the future value of a bank deposit
  Call InputData(p, r, c, n)
  Call DisplayBalance(p, r, c, n)
End Sub

Private Sub DisplayBalance(p As Single,r As Single,c As Single,n As Single)
  Dim balance As Single
  'Display the balance in the picture box
  picBalance.Cls
  balance = FV(p, r, c, n)
  picBalance.Print FormatCurrency(balance)
End Sub

Private Function FV(p As Single,r As Single,c As Single,n As Single) As Single
  Dim i As Single, m As Single
  'Find the future value of a bank savings account
  'p principal, the amount deposited
  'r annual rate of interest
  'c number of times interest is compounded per year
  'n number of years
  'i interest rate per period
  'm total number of times interest is compounded
  i = r / c
  m = c * n
  FV = p * ((1 + i) ^ m)
End Function

Private Sub InputData(p As Single, r As Single, c As Single, n As Single)
  'Get the four values from the text boxes
  p = Val(txtAmount.Text)
  r = Val(txtRate.Text)
  c = Val(txtNumComp.Text)
  n = Val(txtNumYrs.Text)
End Sub
```

[Run, type 100, .04, 4, and 5 into the text boxes, then click the command button.]

EXAMPLE 5

Some computer languages have a useful built-in function called Ceil that is similar to the function Int, except that it rounds noninteger numbers up to the next integer. For instance, Ceil(3.2) is 4 and Ceil(–1.6) is –1. The following program creates Ceil in Visual Basic as a user-defined function.

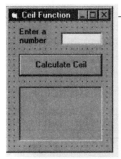

Object	Property	Setting
frm4_3_5	Caption	Ceil Function
lblNumber	Caption	Enter a number
txtNumber	Text	(blank)
cmdCalculate	Caption	Calculate Ceil
picResults		

```
Private Function Ceil(x As Single) As Single
  'Round nonintegers up
  Ceil = -Int(-x)
End Function

Private Sub cmdCalculate_Click()
  'Demonstrate the Ceil function
  picResults.Print "Ceil("; txtNumber.Text; ") ="; Ceil(Val(txtNumber.Text))
  txtNumber.Text = ""
  txtNumber.SetFocus
End Sub
```

[Run, type 4.3 into the text box, click the command button, type 4 into the text box, and then click the command button again.]

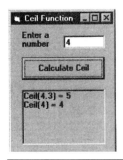

There are many reasons for employing user-defined functions.

1. User-defined functions are consistent with the modular approach to program design. Once we realize a particular function is needed, we can give it a name but save the task of figuring out the computational details until later.

2. Sometimes a single formula must be used several times in a program. Specifying the formula as a function saves repeated typing of the same formula, improves readability, and simplifies debugging.

3. Functions written for one program can be used in other programs. Programmers maintain a collection, or library, of functions that might be needed.

COMMENTS

1. By default, variables passed to a Function procedure are passed by reference; that is, their values are subject to being changed by the Function procedure. Variables also can be passed by value to Function procedures and thereby have their values persist. As with Sub procedures, a variable is passed by value if the variable is enclosed in an extra pair of parentheses when the function is invoked, or if the corresponding parameter in the Private Function statement is

preceded with the word ByVal. Built-in functions have all their arguments passed by value. Some programmers feel that "by value" should have been the default for Function procedures, rather than "by reference."

2. Function procedures can perform the same tasks as Sub procedures. For instance, they can request input and display text; however, they are primarily used to calculate a single value. Normally, Sub procedures are used to carry out other tasks.

3. Function procedures differ from Sub procedures in the way they are accessed. Sub procedures are invoked with Call statements, whereas functions are invoked by placing them where you would otherwise expect to find a constant, variable, or expression. Unlike a Function procedure, a Sub procedure can't be used in an expression.

4. Function procedures can invoke other Function procedures or Sub procedures.

5. Function procedures, like Sub procedures need not have any parameters. Unlike Sub procedures, when a parameterless function is used, the function name may be followed by an empty set of parentheses. The following program uses a "parameterless" function.

```
Private Sub cmdButton_Click()
   'Request and display a saying
   picBox.Cls
   picBox.Print Saying() '() is optional
End Sub

Private Function Saying() As String
   'Retrieve a saying from the user
   Saying = InputBox("What is your favorite saying?")
End Function
```

[Run, click the command button, and then type *Less is more.* into the message box.]

The saying *Less is more.* is displayed in the picture box.

6. An alternative method of creating a Function procedure is to move the cursor to a blank line outside of any procedure, type Private Function *FunctionName*, and press the Enter key.

3.4 MODULAR DESIGN

■ TOP-DOWN DESIGN

Large problems usually require large programs. One method programmers use to make a large problem more understandable is to divide it into smaller, less complex subproblems. Repeatedly using a "divide-and-conquer" approach to break up a large problem into smaller subproblems is called **stepwise refinement**. Stepwise refinement is part of a larger methodology of writing programs known as **top-down design**. The term top-down refers to the fact that the more general tasks occur near the top of the design and tasks representing their refinement occur below. Top-down design and structured programming emerged as techniques to enhance programming productivity. Their use leads to programs that are easier to read and maintain. They also produce programs containing fewer initial errors, with these errors being easier to find and correct. When such programs are later modified, there is a much smaller likelihood of introducing new errors.

The goal of top-down design is to break a problem into individual tasks, or modules, that can easily be transcribed into pseudocode, flowcharts, or a program. First, a problem is restated as several simpler problems depicted as modules. Any modules that remain too complex are broken down further. The process of refining modules continues until the smallest modules can be coded directly. Each stage of refinement adds a more complete specification of what tasks must be performed. The main idea in top-down design is to go from the general to the specific. This process of dividing and organizing a problem into tasks can be pictured using a hierarchy chart. When using top-down design, certain criteria should be met:

1. The design should be easily readable and emphasize small module size.

2. Modules proceed from general to specific as you read down the chart.

3. The modules, as much as possible, should be single-minded. That is, they should only perform a single well-defined task.

4. Modules should be as independent of each other as possible, and any relationships among modules should be specified.

This process is illustrated with the following example.

EXAMPLE 1

Write a hierarchy chart for a program that gives certain information about a car loan. The amount of the loan, the duration (in years), and the interest rate should be input. The output should consist of the monthly payment and the amount of interest paid during the first month.

SOLUTION:

In the broadest sense, the program calls for obtaining the input, making calculations, and displaying the output. Figure 3-5 shows these tasks as the first row of a hierarchy chart.

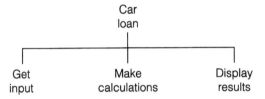

FIGURE 3-5   *Beginning of a Hierarchy Chart for the Car Loan Program*

Each of these tasks can be refined into more specific subtasks. (See Figure 3-6 for the final hierarchy chart.) Most of the subtasks in the second row are straightforward and so do not require further refinement. For instance, the first month's interest is computed by multiplying the amount of the loan by one-twelfth of the annual rate of interest. The most complicated subtask, the computation of the monthly payment, has been broken down further. This task is carried out by applying a standard formula found in finance books; however, the formula requires the number of payments.

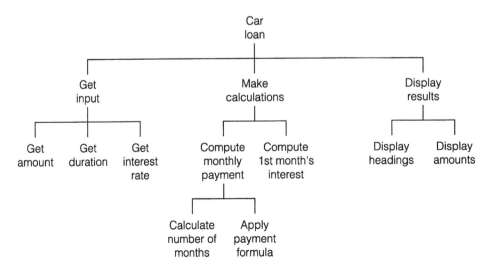

FIGURE 3-6   *Hierarchy Chart for the Car Loan Program*

It is clear from the hierarchy chart that the top modules manipulate the modules beneath them. While the higher-level modules control the flow of the program, the lower-level modules do the actual work. By designing the top modules first, specific processing decisions can be delayed.

■ STRUCTURED PROGRAMMING

A program is said to be **structured** if it meets modern standards of program design. Although there is no formal definition of the term **structured program**, computer scientists are in uniform agreement that such programs should have modular design and use only the three types of logical structures discussed in Section 1: sequences, decisions, and loops.

Sequences: Statements are executed one after another.

Decisions: One of two blocks of program code is executed based on a test for some condition.

Loops (iteration): One or more statements are executed repeatedly as long as a specified condition is true.

Sections 4 and 5 are devoted to decisions and loops, respectively.

One major shortcoming of the earliest programming languages was their reliance on the GoTo statement. This statement was used to branch (that is, jump) from one line of a program to another. It was common for a program to be composed of a convoluted tangle of branchings that produced confusing code referred to as *spaghetti code*. At the heart of structured programming is the assertion of E. W. Dijkstra that GoTo statements should be eliminated entirely because they lead to complex and confusing programs. Two Italians, C. Bohm and G. Jacopini, were able to prove that GoTo statements are not needed and that any program can be written using only the three types of logic structures discussed before.

Structured programming requires that all programs be written using sequences, decisions, and loops. Nesting of such statements is allowed. All other logical constructs, such as GoTos, are not allowed. The logic of a structured program can be pictured using a flowchart that flows smoothly from top to bottom without unstructured branching (GoTos). The portion of a flowchart shown in Figure 3-7(a) contains the equivalent of a GoTo statement and, therefore, is not structured. A correctly structured version of the flowchart in which the logic flows from the top to the bottom appears in Figure 3-7(b).

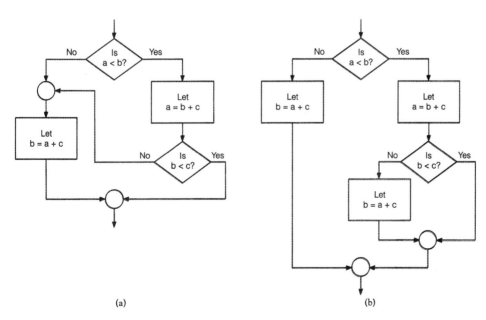

(a)   (b)

FIGURE 3-7   *Flowcharts Illustrating the Removal of a GoTo Statement*

◼ ADVANTAGES OF STRUCTURED PROGRAMMING

The goal of structured programming is to create correct programs that are easy to write, understand, and change. Let us now take a closer look at the way modular design, along with a limited number of logical structures, contributes to attaining these goals.

1. *Easy to write.*

   Modular design increases the programmer's productivity by allowing him or her to look at the big picture first and focus on the details later. During the actual coding, the programmer works with a manageable chunk of the program and does not have to think about an entire complex program.

   Several programmers can work on a single large program, each taking responsibility for a specific module.

   Studies have shown structured programs require significantly less time to write than standard programs.

   Often, procedures written for one program can be reused in other programs requiring the same task. Not only is time saved in writing a program, but reliability is enhanced, because reused procedures will already be tested and debugged. A procedure that can be used in many programs is said to be **reusable**.

2. *Easy to debug.*

   Because each procedure is specialized to perform just one task, a procedure can be checked individually to determine its reliability. A dummy program, called a **driver**, is set up to test the procedure. The driver contains the minimum definitions needed to call the procedure to be tested. For instance, if the procedure to be tested is a function, the driver program assigns diverse values to the arguments and then examines the corresponding function value. The arguments should contain both typical and special-case values.

   The program can be tested and debugged as it is being designed with a technique known as **stub programming**. In this technique, the key event procedures and perhaps some of the smaller procedures are coded first. Dummy procedures, or stubs, are written for the remaining procedures. Initially, a stub procedure might consist of a Print method to indicate that the procedure has been called, and thereby confirm that the procedure was called at the right time. Later, a stub might simply display values passed to it in order to confirm not only that the procedure was called, but also that it received the correct values from the calling procedure. A stub also can assign new values to one or more of its parameters to simulate either input or computation. This provides greater control of the conditions being tested. The stub procedure is always simpler than the actual procedure it represents. Although the stub program is only a skeleton of the final program, the program's structure can still be debugged and tested. (The stub program consists of some coded procedures and the stub procedures.)

   Old-fashioned unstructured programs consist of a sequence of instructions that are not grouped for specific tasks. The logic of such a program is cluttered with details and therefore difficult to follow. Needed tasks are easily left out and crucial details easily neglected. Tricky parts of the program cannot be isolated and examined. Bugs are difficult to locate because they might be present in any part of the program.

3. *Easy to understand.*

   The interconnections of the procedures reveal the modular design of the program.

The meaningful procedure names, along with relevant comments, identify the tasks performed by the modules.

The meaningful variable names help the programmer to recall the purpose of each variable.

4. *Easy to change.*

Because a structured program is self-documenting, it can easily be deciphered by another programmer.

Modifying a structured program often amounts to inserting or altering a few procedures rather than revising an entire complex program. The programmer does not even have to look at most of the program. This is in sharp contrast to the situation with unstructured programs that require an understanding of the entire logic of the program before any changes can be made with confidence.

SUMMARY

1. A *general procedure* is a portion of a program that is accessed by event procedures or other general procedures. The two types of general procedures are *Sub procedures* and *Function procedures*.

2. Sub procedures are defined in blocks beginning with Sub statements and ending with End Sub statements. They are accessed by Call statements.

3. Function procedures are defined in blocks beginning with Function statements and ending with End Function statements. A function is activated by a reference in an expression and returns a value.

4. In any procedure, the arguments appearing in the calling statement must match the parameters of the Sub or Function statement in number, type, and order. They need not match in name.

5. A variable declared in the (Declarations) section of (General) is *form-level*. Such a variable is available to every procedure in the form's code and retains its value from one procedure invocation to the next. Form-level variables are often initialized in the Form_Load event procedure.

6. A variable appearing inside a procedure is *local* to the procedure if it is declared in a Dim statement within the procedure or if it is not a form-level variable and does not appear in the parameter list. The values of these variables are reinitialized each time the procedure is called. A variable with the same name appearing in another part of the program is treated as a different variable.

7. Structured programming uses modular design to refine large problems into smaller subproblems. Programs are coded using the three logical structures of sequences, decisions, and loops.

PROGRAMMING PROJECTS

1. The numbers of calories per gram of carbohydrate, fat, and protein are 4, 9, and 4, respectively. Write a program that requests the nutritional content of a 1-ounce serving of food and displays the number of calories in the serving. The input and output should be handled by Sub procedures and the calories computed by a function. A sample run for a typical breakfast cereal is shown in Figure 3-8.

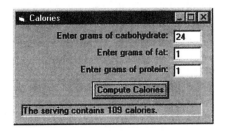

FIGURE 3-8   *Sample Run for Programming Project 1*

2. About seven million notebook computers were sold during 1997. Table 3.2 gives the market share for the four largest vendors. Write a program that displays the number of computers sold by each of the Big Four. The input and output should be handled by Sub procedures and the number of computers calculated by a Function procedure.

TABLE 3.2
1997 Market Shares of the Top Notebook Vendors

Company	Market Share
Toshiba	20%
IBM	11%
Compaq	9%
Dell	6%

Source: PC Magazine, January 20, 1998.

3. Table 3.3 gives the advertising expenditures (in millions of dollars) for the four most advertised soft drink brands during the first nine months of 1995 and 1996. Write a program that displays the percentage change in advertising for each brand. Sub procedures should be used for input and output and the percentage change should be computed with a Function procedure. *Note:* The percentage change is 100 * ([1996 expenditure] − [1995 expenditure]) / [1995 expenditure].

TABLE 3.3
Most Advertised Soft Drinks

Brand	1995 Expenditure	1996 Expenditure
Coca-Cola classic	60.7	121.6
Pepsi-Cola	94.8	83.0
Diet Coke	43.7	70.0
Dr. Pepper	46.3	51.8

Source: Beverage World, March 1997.

4. A fast-food vendor sells pizza slices ($1.25), fries ($1.00), and soft drinks ($.75). Write a program to compute a customer's bill. The program should request the quantity of each item ordered in a Sub procedure, calculate the total cost with a Function procedure, and use a Sub procedure to display an itemized bill. A sample output is shown in Figure 3-9.

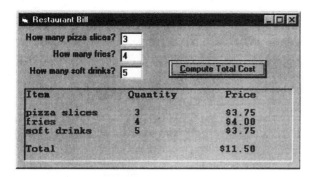

FIGURE 3-9   *Sample Run for Programming Project 4*

5. Write a program to generate a Business Travel Expense attachment for an income tax return. The program should request as input the name of the organization visited, the date and location of the visit, and the expenses for meals and entertainment, airplane fare, lodging, and taxi fares. (Only 50% of the expenses for meals and entertainment are deductible.) A possible form layout and run are shown in Figures 3.10 and 3.11, respectively. Sub procedures should be used for the input and output.

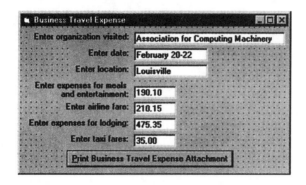

FIGURE 3-10   *Form with Sample Data for Programming Project 5*

```
Business Travel Expense
Trip to attend meeting of
Association for Computing Machinery
February 25-28 in Atlanta

Meals and entertainment $190.10
Airplane fare           $210.15
Lodging                 $475.35
Taxi fares              $35.00


Total other than Meals and Entertainment: $720.50
50% of Meals and Entertainment: $95.05
```

FIGURE 3-11   *Output on Printer for Sample Run of Programming Project 5*

4

DECISIONS

4.1 RELATIONAL AND LOGICAL OPERATORS

A **condition** is an expression involving relational operators (such as < and =) that is either true or false. Conditions also may incorporate logical operators (such as And, Or, and Not).

The relational operator *less than* (<) can be applied to both numbers and strings. The number a is said to be less than the number b if a lies to the left of b on the number line. For instance, $2 < 5$, $-5 < -2$, and $0 < 3.5$.

The string a is said to be less than the string b if a precedes b alphabetically when using the ANSI (or ASCII) table to alphabetize their values. For instance, "cat" < "dog", "cart" < "cat", and "cat" < "catalog". Digits precede uppercase letters, which precede lowercase letters. Two strings are compared working from left to right, character by character, to determine which one should precede the other. Therefore, "9W" < "bat", "Dog" < "cat", and "Sales-99" < "Sales-retail".

Table 4.1 shows the different mathematical relational operators, their representations in Visual Basic, and their meanings.

TABLE 4.1
Relational Operators

Mathematical Notation	Visual Basic Notation	Numeric Meaning	String Meaning
=	=	equal to	identical to
≠	<>	unequal to	different from
<	<	less than	precedes alphabetically
>	>	greater than	follows alphabetically
≤	<=	less than or equal to	precedes alphabetically or is identical to
≥	>=	greater than or equal to	follows alphabetically or is identical to

EXAMPLE 1

Determine whether each of the following conditions is true or false.

(a) $1 <= 1$

(b) $1 < 1$

(c) "car" "cat"

(d) "Dog" < "dog"

SOLUTION:

(a) True. The notation <= means "less than *or* equal to." That is, the condition is true provided either of the two circumstances holds. The second one (equal to) holds.

(b) False. The notation < means "strictly less than" and no number can be strictly less than itself.

(c) True. The characters of the strings are compared one at a time working from left to right. Because the first two match, the third character decides the order.

(d) True. Because uppercase letters precede lowercase letters in the ANSI table, the first character of "Dog" precedes the first character of "dog."

Conditions also can involve variables, numeric operators, and functions. To determine whether a condition is true or false, first compute the numeric or string values and then decide if the resulting assertion is true or false.

EXAMPLE 2

Suppose the numeric variables *a* and *b* have values 4 and 3, and the string variables *c* and *d* have values "hello" and "bye". Are the following conditions true or false?

(a) $(a + b) < 2 * a$

(b) $(Len(c) - b) = (a / 2)$

(c) $c < ($"good" $\& d)$

SOLUTION:

(a) The value of $a + b$ is 7 and the value of $2 * a$ is 8. Because $7 < 8$, the condition is true.

(b) True, because the value of $Len(c) - b$ is 2, the same as $(a / 2)$.

(c) The condition "hello" < "goodbye" is false, because "h" follows "g" in the ANSI table.

■ **LOGICAL OPERATORS**

Programming situations often require more complex conditions than those considered so far. For instance, suppose we would like to state that the value of a numeric variable, *n*, is strictly between 2 and 5. The proper Visual Basic condition is

$$(2 < n) \text{ And } (n < 5)$$

The condition $(2 < n)$ And $(n < 5)$ is a combination of the two conditions $2 < n$ and $n < 5$ with the logical operator And.

The three main logical operators are And, Or, and Not. If *cond1* and *cond2* are conditions, then the condition

```
cond1 And cond2
```

is true if both *cond1* and *cond2* are true. Otherwise, it is false. The condition

```
cond1 Or cond2
```

is true if either *cond1* or *cond2* (or both) is true. Otherwise, it is false. The condition

```
Not cond1
```

is true if *cond1* is false, and is false if *cond1* is true.

EXAMPLE 3

Suppose the numeric variable *n* has value 4 and the string variable *answ* has value "Y". Determine whether each of the following conditions is true or false.

(a) $(2 < n)$ And $(n < 6)$

(b) $(2 < n)$ Or $(n = 6)$

(c) Not $(n < 6)$

(d) (answ = "Y") Or (answ = "y")

(e) (answ = "Y") And (answ = "y")

(f) Not (answ = "y")

(g) $((2 < n)$ And $(n = 5 + 1))$ Or (answ = "No")

(h) $((n = 2)$ And $(n = 7))$ Or (answ = "Y")

(i) $(n = 2)$ And $((n = 7)$ Or (answ = "Y"))

SOLUTION:

(a) True, because the conditions $(2 < 4)$ and $(4 < 6)$ are both true.

(b) True, because the condition $(2 < 4)$ is true. The fact that the condition $(4 = 6)$ is false does not affect the conclusion. The only requirement is that at least one of the two conditions be true.

(c) False, because $(4 < 6)$ is true.

(d) True, because the first condition becomes ("Y" = "Y") when the value of *answ* is substituted for *answ*.

(e) False, because the second condition is false. Actually, this compound condition is false for every value of *answ*.

(f) True, because ("Y" = "y") is false.

(g) False. In this logical expression, the compound condition $((2 < n)$ And $(n = 5 + 1))$ and the simple condition (answ = "No") are joined by the logical operator Or. Because both of these conditions are false, the total condition is false.

(h) True, because the second Or clause is true.

(i) False. Comparing (h) and (i) shows the necessity of using parentheses to specify the intended grouping.

The use of parentheses with logical operators improves readability; however, they can be omitted sometimes. Visual Basic has an operator hierarchy for deciding how to evaluate logical expressions without parentheses. First, all arithmetic operations are carried out, and then all expressions involving >, <, and = are evaluated to true or false. The logical operators are next applied, in the order Not, then And, and finally Or. For instance, the logical expression in part (g) of Example 3 could have been written $2 < n$ And $n = 5 + 1$ Or answ = "No". In the event of a tie, the leftmost operator is applied first.

EXAMPLE 4

Place parentheses in the following condition to show how it would be evaluated by Visual Basic.

$a < b + c$ Or $d < e$ And Not $f = g$

SOLUTION:
$((a < (b + c))$ Or $((d < e)$ And (Not $(f = g))))$

The step-by-step analysis of the order of operations is

$a < (b + c)$, Or$d < e$, AndNot $f = g$	arithmetic operation
$(a < (b + c))$, Or$(d < e)$, AndNot $(f = g)$	relational expressions
$(a < (b + c))$, Or$(d < e)$, And, (Not $(f = g))$	Not
$(a < (b + c))$, Or, $((d < e)$, And, (Not $(f = g)))$	And
$((a < (b + c))$, Or, $((d < e)$, And, (Not $(f = g))))$	Or

1. A condition involving numeric variables is different from an algebraic truth. The assertion $(a + b) < 2 * a$, considered in Example 2, is not a valid algebraic truth because it isn't true for all values of a and b. When encountered in a Visual Basic program, however, it will be considered true if it is correct for the current values of the variables.

2. Conditions evaluate to either true or false. These two values often are called the possible **truth values** of the condition.

3. A condition such as $2 < n < 5$ should never be used, because Visual Basic will not evaluate it as intended. The correct condition is $(2 < n)$ And $(n < 5)$.

4. A common error is to replace the condition Not $(2 < 3)$ by condition $(3 > 2)$. The correct replacement is $(3 >= 2)$.

4.2 IF BLOCKS

An **If block** allows a program to decide on a course of action based on whether a certain condition is true or false. A block of the form

```
If condition Then
    action1
  Else
    action2
End If
```

causes the program to take *action1* if *condition* is true and *action2* if *condition* is false. Each action consists of one or more Visual Basic statements. After an action is taken, execution continues with the line after the If block. Figure 4.1 contains the pseudocode and flowchart for an If block.

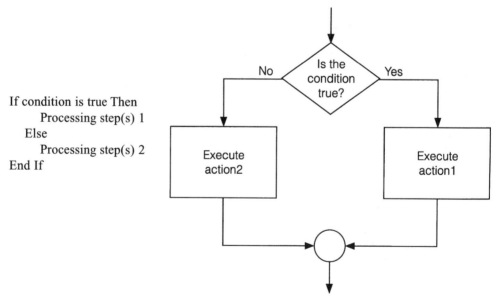

```
If condition is true Then
    Processing step(s) 1
  Else
    Processing step(s) 2
End If
```

FIGURE 4-1   *Pseudocode and Flowchart for an If Block*

EXAMPLE 1

Write a program to find the larger of two numbers input by the user.

SOLUTION:

In the following program, the condition is Val(txtFirstNum.Text) > Val(txtSecond Num.Text), and each action consists of a single assignment statement. With the input 3 and 7, the condition is false, and so the second action is taken.

Object	Property	Setting
frmMaximum	Caption	Maximum
lblFirstNum	Caption	First Number
Alignment	Right Justify	
txtFirstNum	Text	(blank)
lblSecondNum	Caption	Second Number
Alignment	Right Justify	
txtSecondNum	Text	(blank)
cmdFindLarger	Caption	Find Larger Number
picResult		

```
Private Sub cmdFindLarger_Click()
   Dim largerNum As Single
   picResult.Cls
   If Val(txtFirstNum.Text) > Val(txtSecondNum.Text) Then
        largerNum = Val(txtFirstNum.Text)
     Else
        largerNum = Val(txtSecondNum.Text)
   End If
   picResult.Print "The larger number is"; largerNum
End Sub
```

[Run, type 3 and 7 into the text boxes, and press the command button.]

EXAMPLE 2

Write a program that requests the costs and revenue for a company and displays the message "Break even" if the costs and revenue are equal or otherwise displays the profit or loss.

SOLUTION:

In the following program, the action following Else is another If block.

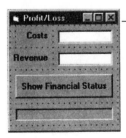

Object	Property	Setting
frm5_2_2	Caption	Profit/Loss
lblCosts	Caption	Costs
	Alignment	Right justify
txtCosts	Text	(blank)
lblRev	Caption	Revenue
	Alignment	Right justify
txtRev	Text	(blank)
cmdShow	Caption	Show Financial Status
picResult		

```
Private Sub cmdShow_Click()
   Dim costs As Single, revenue As Single, profit As Single, loss As Single
```

```
    costs = Val(txtCosts.Text) revenue = Val(txtRev.Text)
        picResult.Cls If costs = revenue Then picResult.Print "Break even"
      Else
  If costs < revenue Then
            profit = revenue - costs
            picResult.Print "Profit is "; FormatCurrency(profit)
        Else
  loss = costs - revenue
            picResult.Print "Loss is "; FormatCurrency(loss)
  End If
  End If
End Sub
```

[Run, type 9500 and 8000 into the text boxes, and press the command button.]

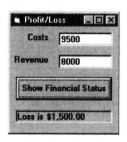

EXAMPLE 3

The If block in the following program has a logical operator in its condition

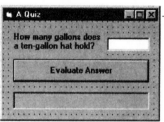

Object	Property	Setting
frmQuiz	Caption	A Quiz
lblQuestion	Caption	How many gallons does a ten-gallon hat hold?
txtAnswer	Text	(blank)
cmdEvaluate	Caption	Evaluate Answer
picSolution		

```
Private Sub cmdEvaluate_Click()
  Dim answer As Single 'Evaluate answer picSolution.Cls
  answer = Val(txtAnswer.Text)
  If (answer >= .5) And (answer <= 1) Then
      picSolution.Print "Good, ";
    Else
      picSolution.Print "No, ";
  End If
  picSolution.Print "it holds about 3/4 of a gallon."
End Sub
```

[Run, type 10 into the text box, and press the command button.]

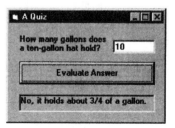

The Else part of an If block can be omitted. This important type of If block appears in the next example.

EXAMPLE 4

The following program offers assistance to the user before presenting a quotation.

Object	Property	Setting
frm5_2_4	Caption	Quotation
lblQuestion	Caption	Do you know what the game of skittles is (Y/N)?
txtAnswer	Text	(blank)
cmdDisplay	Caption	Display Quotation
picQuote		

```
Private Sub cmdDisplay_Click()
  Dim message As String
  message = "Skittles is an old form of bowling in which a wooden" & _ " disk is used
            to knock down nine pins arranged in a square."
  If UCase(txtAnswer.Text) = "N" Then
    MsgBox message, , ""
  End If
  picQuote.Cls picQuote.Print "Life ain't all beer and skittles. - Du Maurier
  (1894)"
End Sub
```

[Run, type N into the text box, and press the command button.]

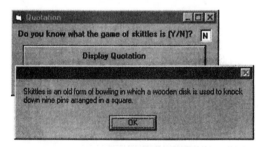

[Press OK.]

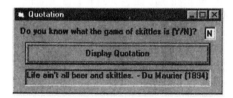

Note: Rerun the program, type Y into the text box, press the command button, and observe that the description of the game is bypassed.

An extension of the If block allows for more than two possible alternatives with the inclusion of ElseIf clauses. A typical block of this type is

```
If condition1 Then
    action1
  ElseIf condition2 Then
    action2
  ElseIf condition3 Then
    action3
  Else action4
End If
```

This block searches for the first true condition, carries out its action, and then skips to the statement following End If. If none of the conditions is true, then Else's action is carried out. Execution then continues with the statement following the block. In general, an If block can contain any number of ElseIf clauses. As before, the Else clause is optional.

EXAMPLE 5

Redo Example 1 so that if the two numbers are equal, the program so reports.

SOLUTION:

```
Private Sub cmdFindLarger_Click()
  picResult.Cls
  If Val(txtFirstNum.Text) > Val(txtSecondNum.Text) Then
      picResult.Print "The larger number is "; txtFirstNum.Text
    ElseIf Val(txtSecondNum.Text) > Val(txtFirstNum.Text) Then
      picResult.Print "The larger number is "; txtSecondNum.Text
    Else
      picResult.Print "The two numbers are equal."
  End If
End Sub
```

[Run, type 7 into both text boxes, and press the command button.]

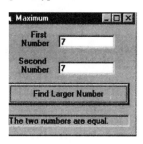

If blocks allow us to define functions whose values are not determined by a simple formula. The function in Example 6 uses an If block.

EXAMPLE 6

The Social Security or FICA tax has two components—the Social Security benefits tax, which in 1999 is 6.2 percent on the first $72,600 of earnings for the year, and the Medicare tax, which is 1.45 percent of earnings. Write a program to calculate an employee's FICA tax for the current pay period.

SOLUTION:

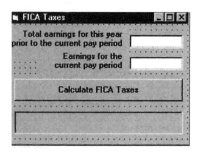

Object	Property	Setting
frmFICA	Caption	FICA Taxes
lblToDate	Caption	Total earnings for this year prior to the current pay period
	Alignment	Right Justify
txtToDate	Text	(blank)
lblCurrent	Caption	Earnings for the current pay period
	Alignment	Right Justify
txtCurrent	Text	(blank)
cmdCalculate	Caption	Calculate FICA Taxes
picTax		

```
Private Sub cmdCalculate_Click()
  Dim FicaTaxes As Single
  FicaTaxes = FICA(Val(txtToDate.Text), Val(txtCurrent.Text))
```

```
    picTax.Cls
    picTax.Print "Your FICA taxes for the current"
    picTax.Print "pay period are "; FormatCurrency(FicaTaxes)
End Sub

Private Function FICA(ytdEarnings As Single, curEarnings As Single) As Single
    Dim socialSecurityBenTax As Single, medicare As Single
    'Calculate Social Security benefits tax and Medicare tax
    'for a single pay period in 1999
    socialSecurityBenTax = 0
    If (ytdEarnings + curEarnings) <= 72600 Then
        socialSecurityBenTax = .062 * curEarnings
      ElseIf ytdEarnings < 72600 Then
        socialSecurityBenTax = .062 * (72600 - ytdEarnings)
    End If
    medicare = .0145 * curEarnings
    FICA = socialSecurityBenTax + medicare
End Function
```

[Run, type 12345.67 and 543.21 into the text boxes, and press the command button.]

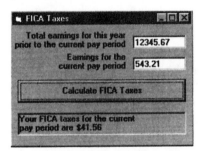

COMMENTS

1. The actions of an If block and the words Else and ElseIf do not have to be indented. For instance, the If block of Example 1 can be written

```
If Val(txtFirstNum.Text) > Val(txtSecondNum.Text) Then
largerNum = Val(txtFirstNum.Text)
Else
largerNum = Val(txtSecondNum.Text)
End If
```

However, because indenting improves the readability of the block, it is regarded as good programming style. As soon as you see the word If, your eyes can easily scan down the program to find the matching End If and the enclosed Else and ElseIf clauses. You then immediately have a good idea of the size and complexity of the block.

2. Constructs in which an If block is contained inside another If block are referred to as **nested** If blocks.

3. Care should be taken to make If blocks easy to understand. For instance, in Figure 4.2, the block on the left is difficult to follow and should be replaced by the clearer block on the right.

```
          If cond1 Then                 If cond1 And cond2 Then
            If cond2 Then                 action
              action                    End If
            End If
          End If
```

FIGURE 4-2   *A Confusing If Block and an Improvement*

4. Some programs call for selecting among many possibilities. Although such tasks can be accomplished with complicated nested If blocks, the Select Case block (discussed in the next section) is often a better alternative.

5. In Appendix D, the section "Stepping Through Programs Containing Decision Structures: Section 4" uses the Visual Basic debugging tools to trace the flow through an If block.

6. Visual Basic also has a single-line If statement of the form

```
If condition Then action1 Else action2
```

which is a holdover from earlier, unstructured versions of BASIC; it is seldom used in this text.

4.3 SELECT CASE BLOCKS

A Select Case block is an efficient decision-making structure that simplifies choosing among several actions. It avoids complex nested If constructs. If blocks make decisions based on the truth value of a condition; Select Case choices are determined by the value of an expression called a **selector**. Each of the possible actions is preceded by a clause of the form

```
Case valueList
```

where *valueList* itemizes the values of the selector for which the action should be taken.

EXAMPLE 1

The following program converts the finishing position in a horse race into a descriptive phrase. After the variable *position* is assigned a value from txtPosition, Visual Basic searches for the first Case statement whose value list contains that value and executes the succeeding statement. If the value of *position* is greater than 5, then the statement following Case Else is executed.

Object	Property	Setting
frmRace	Caption	Horse Race
lblPosition	Caption	Finishing position (1, 2, 3, . . .)
txtPosition	Text	(blank)
cmdDescribe	Caption	Describe Position
picOutcome		

```
Private Sub cmdDescribe_Click()
  Dim position As Integer 'selector
  position = Val(txtPosition.Text)
  picOutcome.Cls Select Case position
    Case 1
      picOutcome.Print "Win"
    Case 2
      picOutcome.Print "Place"
    Case 3
      picOutcome.Print "Show"
```

```
      Case 4, 5
         picOutcome.Print "You almost placed"
         picOutcome.Print "in the money." Case Else
         picOutcome.Print "Out of the money."
   End Select
End Sub
```

[Run, type 2 into the text box, and press the command button.]

EXAMPLE 2

In the following variation of Example 1, the value lists specify ranges of values. The first value list provides another way to specify the numbers 1, 2, and 3. The second value list covers all numbers from 4 on.

```
Private Sub cmdDescribe_Click()
   Dim position As Integer
   'Describe finishing positions in a horse race
   position = Val(txtPosition.Text)
   picOutcome.Cls
   Select Case position
      Case 1 To 3
         picOutcome.Print "In the money."
         picOutcome.Print "Congratulations"
      Case Is > 3
         picOutcome.Print "Not in the money."
   End Select
End Sub
```

[Run, type 2 into the text box, and press the command button.]

The general form of the Select Case block is

```
Select Case selector
   Case valueList1
      action1
   Case valueList2
      action2
      .
      .
   Case Else
      action of last resort
End Select
```

where Case Else (and its action) is optional, and each value list contains one or more of the following types of items separated by commas:

1. A constant

2. A variable

3. An expression

4. An inequality sign preceded by Is and followed by a constant, variable, or expression

5. A range expressed in the form *a* To *b*, where *a* and *b* are constants, variables, or expressions

Different items appearing in the same list must be separated by commas. Each action consists of one or more statements. After the selector is evaluated, Visual Basic looks for the first value-list item containing the value of the selector and carries out its associated action. Figure 4-3 contains the flowchart for a Select Case block. The pseudocode for a Select Case block is the same as for the equivalent If block.

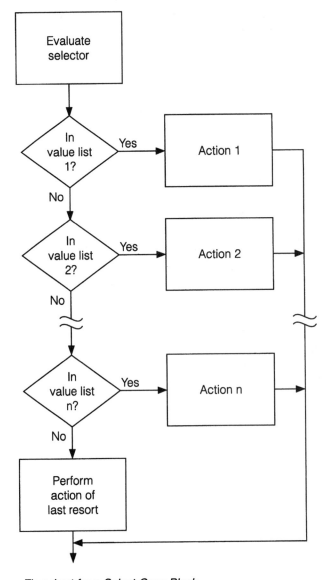

FIGURE 4-3   *Flowchart for a Select Case Block*

EXAMPLE 3

The following program uses several different types of value lists. With the response shown, the first action was selected because the value of y − x is 1.

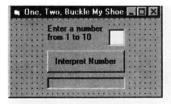

Object	Property	Setting
frm5_3_3	Caption	One, Two, Buckle My Shoe
lblEnterNum	Caption	Enter a number from 1 to 10
txtNumber	Text	(blank)
cmdInterpret	Caption	Interpret Number
picPhrase		

```
Private Sub cmdInterpret_Click()
  Dim x As Integer, y As Integer, num As Integer
  'One, Two, Buckle My Shoe
  picPhrase.Cls
  x = 2
  y = 3
  num = Val(txtNumber.Text)
  Select Case num
    Case y - x, x
      picPhrase.Print "Buckle my shoe."
    Case Is <= 4
      picPhrase.Print "Shut the door."
    Case x + y To x * y
      picPhrase.Print "Pick up sticks."
    Case 7, 8
      picPhrase.Print "Lay them straight."
    Case Else
      picPhrase.Print "Start all over again."
  End Select
End Sub
```

[Run, type 4 into the text box, and press the command button.]

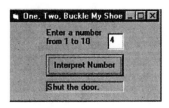

In each of the three preceding examples the selector was a numeric variable; however, the selector also can be a string variable or an expression.

EXAMPLE 4

The following program has the string variable *firstName* as a selector.

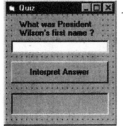

Object	Property	Setting
frmQuiz	Caption	Quiz
lblQuestion	Caption	"What was President Wilson's first name ?"
txtName	Text	(blank)
cmdInterpret	Caption	Interpret Answer
picAnswer		

```
Private Sub cmdInterpret_Click()
   Dim firstName As String
   'Quiz
   picAnswer.Cls
   firstName = txtName.Text
   Select Case firstName
      Case "Thomas"
         picAnswer.Print "Correct."
      Case "Woodrow"
         picAnswer.Print "Sorry, his full name was"
         picAnswer.Print "Thomas Woodrow Wilson."
      Case "President"
         picAnswer.Print "Are you for real?"
      Case Else
         picAnswer.Print "Nice try, but no cigar."
   End Select
End Sub
```

[Run, type Woodrow into the text box, and press the command button.]

EXAMPLE 5

The following program has the selector Left(anyString, 1), a string expression. In the sample run, only the first action was carried out, even though the value of the selector was in both of the first two value lists. The computer stops looking as soon as it finds the value of the selector.

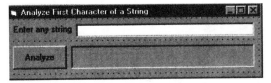

Object	Property	Setting
frm5_3_5	Caption	Analyze First [~]Character of a String
lblEnter	Caption	Enter any string
txtString	Text	(blank)
cmdAnalyze	Caption	Analyze
picResult		

```
Private Sub cmdAnalyze_Click()
   Dim anyString As String
   'Analyze the first character of a string
   picResult.Cls
   anyString = UCase(txtString.Text)
   Select Case Left(anyString, 1)
      Case "S", "Z"
         picResult.Print "The string begins with a sibilant."
      Case "A" To "Z"
         picResult.Print "The string begins with a nonsibilant."
      Case "0" To "9"
         picResult.Print "The string begins with a digit."
      Case Is < "0"
         picResult.Print "The string begins with a character of ANSI"
         picResult.Print "value less than 48 (e.g. +, &, #, or %)."
```

```
      Case Else
         picResult.Print "The string begins with one of the following:"
         picResult.Print " : ; < = > ? @ [ \ ] ^ _ ` "
   End Select
End Sub
```

[Run, type Sunday into the text box, and press the command button.]

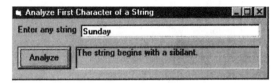

EXAMPLE 6

The color of the beacon light atop Boston's John Hancock Building forecasts the weather according to the following rhyme. Write a program that requests a color (blue or red) and a mode (steady or flashing) as input and displays the weather forecast. The program should contain a Select Case block with a string variable as selector.

Steady blue, clear view.
Flashing blue, clouds due.
Steady red, rain ahead.
Flashing red, snow instead.

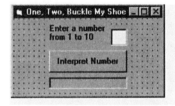

frmWeather	Caption	Weather Beacon
lblColor	Caption	Color of the light
txtColor	Text	(blank)
lblMode	Caption	Mode (S or F)
txtMode	Text	(blank)
cmdInterpret	Caption	Interpret Beacon
picForecast		

```
Private Sub cmdInterpret_Click()
   Dim color As String, mode As String
   'Interpret a weather beacon
   picForecast.Cls
   color = txtColor.Text
   mode = txtMode.Text
   Select Case UCase(mode) & UCase(color)
      Case "SBLUE"
         picForecast.Print "CLEAR VIEW"
      Case "FBLUE"
         picForecast.Print "CLOUDS DUE"
      Case "SRED"
         picForecast.Print "RAIN AHEAD"
      Case "FRED"
         picForecast.Print "SNOW AHEAD"
   End Select
End Sub
```

[Run, type red and S into the text boxes, and press the command button.]

EXAMPLE 7

Select Case is useful in defining functions that are not determined by a formula. The following program assumes the current year is not a leap year.

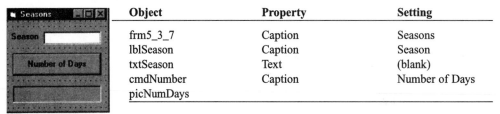

Object	Property	Setting
frm5_3_7	Caption	Seasons
lblSeason	Caption	Season
txtSeason	Text	(blank)
cmdNumber	Caption	Number of Days
picNumDays		

```
Private Sub cmdNumber_Click()
   Dim season As String
   'Determine the number of days in a season
   picNumDays.Cls
   season = txtSeason.Text
   picNumDays.Print season; " has"; NumDays(season); "days."
End Sub

Private Function NumDays(season As String) As Integer
   'Look up the number of days in a given season
   Select Case UCase(season)
     Case "WINTER"
        NumDays = 87
     Case "SPRING"
        NumDays = 92
     Case "SUMMER", "AUTUMN", "FALL"
        NumDays = 93
   End Select
End Function
```

[Run, type Summer into the text box, and press the command button.]

COMMENTS

1. Some programming languages do not allow a value to appear in two different value lists; Visual Basic does. If the value of the selector appears in two different value lists, the action associated with the first value list will be carried out.

2. In Visual Basic, if the value of the selector does not appear in any of the value lists and there is no Case Else clause, execution of the program will continue with the statement following the Select Case block.

3. The Case statements and their actions do not have to be indented; however, because indenting improves the readability of the block, it is regarded as good programming style. As soon as you see the words Select Case, your eyes can easily scan down the block to find the matching End Select statement. You immediately know the number of different cases under consideration.

4. The items in the value list must evaluate to a constant of the same type, string or numeric, as the selector. For instance, if the selector evaluates to a string value, as in

```
Dim firstName A String
firstName = txtBox.Text
Select Case first Name
```

then the clause

```
Case Len(firstNme)
```

would be meaningless.

5. If the word Is, which should precede an inequality sign in a value list, is accidentally omitted, the smart editor will automatically insert it when checking the line.

6. A Case clause of the form Case b To c selects values from *b* to *c* inclusive. However, the extreme values can be excluded by placing the action inside an If block beginning with If (*selector* <> b) And (*selector* <> c) Then.

7. The value of *b* must be less than or equal to the value of *c* in a Case clause of the form Case b To c.

8. Every Select Case block can be replaced by an If block. Select Case is preferable to an If block when the possible choices have more or less the same importance.

9. In Appendix D, the section "Stepping Through Programs Containing Selection Structures: Section 4" uses the Visual Basic debugging tools to trace the flow through a Select Case block.

4.4 A CASE STUDY: WEEKLY PAYROLL

This case study processes a weekly payroll using the 1998 Employer's Tax Guide. Table 4.2 shows typical data used by a company's payroll office. These data are processed to produce the information in Table 4.3 that is supplied to each employee along with his or her paycheck. The program should request the data from Table 4.2 for an individual as input and produce output similar to that in Table 4.3.

The items in Table 4.3 should be calculated as follows:

Current Earnings: Hourly wage times hours worked (with time-and-a-half after 40 hours)

Year-to-Date Earnings: Previous year-to-date earnings plus current earnings

FICA Tax: Sum of 6.2 percent of first $68,400 of earnings (Social Security benefits tax) and 1.45 percent of total wages (Medicare tax)

Federal Income Tax Withheld: Subtract $51.92 from the current earnings for each withholding exemption and use Table 4.4 or Table 4.5, depending on marital status

Check Amount: [Current earnings] – [FICA taxes] – [Income tax withheld]

TABLE 4.2
Employee Data

Name	Hourly Wage	Hours Worked	Withholding Exemptions	Marital Status	Previous Year-to-Date Earnings
Al Clark	$45.50	38	4	Married	$68,925.50
Ann Miller	$44.00	35	3	Married	$68,200.00
John Smith	$17.95	50	1	Single	$30,604.75
Sue Taylor	$25.50	43	2	Single	$36,295.50

TABLE 4.3
Payroll Information

Name	Current Earnings	Yr. to Date Earnings	FICA Taxes	Income Tax Wh.	Check Amount
Al Clark	$1,729.00	$70,654.50	$25.07	$290.50	$1,413.43

TABLE 4.4
1998 Federal Income Tax Withheld for a Single Person Paid Weekly

Adjusted Weekly Income	Income Tax Withheld
$0 to $51	$0
Over $51 to $517	15% of amount over $51
Over $517 to $1,105	$69.90 + 28% of excess over $517
Over $1,105 to $2,493	$234.54 + 31% of excess over $1,105
Over $2,493 to $5,385	$664.82 + 36% of excess over $2,493
Over $5,385	$1,705.94 + 39.6% of excess over $5,385

TABLE 4.5
1998 Federal Income Tax Withheld for a Married Person Paid Weekly

Adjusted Weekly Income	Income Tax Withheld
$0 to $124	$0
Over $124 to $899	15% of excess over $124
Over $899 to $1,855	$116.25 + 28% of excess over $899
Over $1,855 to $3,084	$383.93 + 31% of excess over $1,855
Over $3,084 to $5,439	$764.92 + 36% of excess over $3,084
Over $5,439	$1,612.72 + 39.6% of excess over $5,439

■ DESIGNING THE WEEKLY PAYROLL PROGRAM

After the data for an employee have been gathered from the text boxes, the program must compute the five items appearing in Table 4.3 and then display the payroll information. The five computations form the basic tasks of the program.

1. Compute current earnings.
2. Compute year-to-date earnings.
3. Compute FICA tax.
4. Compute federal income tax withheld.
5. Compute paycheck amount (that is, take-home pay).

   Tasks 1, 2, 3, and 5 are fairly simple. Each involves applying a formula to given data. (For instance, if hours worked is at most 40, then Current Earnings = Hourly Wage times Hours Worked.) Thus, we won't break down these tasks any further. Task 4 is more complicated, so we continue to divide it into smaller subtasks.

4. *Compute Federal Income Tax Withheld.* First, the employee's pay is adjusted for exemptions, and then the amount of income tax to be withheld is computed. The computation of the income tax withheld differs for married and single individuals. Task 4 is, therefore, divided into the following subtasks:

   4.1 Compute pay adjusted by exemptions.
   4.2 Compute income tax withheld for single employee.
   4.3 Compute income tax withheld for married employee.

The hierarchy chart in Figure 4-4 shows the stepwise refinement of the problem.

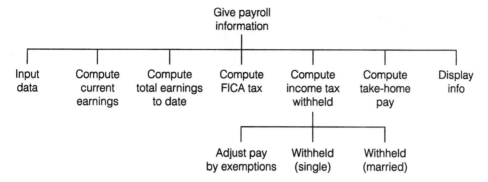

FIGURE 4-4   *Hierarchy Chart for the Weekly Payroll Program*

■ PSEUDOCODE FOR THE DISPLAY PAYROLL EVENT

INPUTemployee data (Sub procedure InputData)
COMPUTE CURRENT GROSS PAY (Function Gross_Pay)
COMPUTE TOTAL EARNINGS TO DATE (Function Total_Pay)
COMPUTE FICA TAX (Function FICA_Tax)
COMPUTE FEDERAL TAX (Function Fed_Tax)
   Adjust pay for exemptions
   If employee is single Then
      COMPUTE INCOME TAX WITHHELD from adjusted pay using tax brackets for
      single taxpayers (Function TaxSingle)
   Else
      COMPUTE INCOME TAX WITHHELD from adjusted pay using taxbrackets for
      married taxpayers (Function TaxMarried)
   End If
COMPUTE CHECK (Function Net_Check)
Display payroll information (Sub procedure ShowPayroll)

■ WRITING THE WEEKLY PAYROLL PROGRAM

The cmdDisplay event procedure calls a sequence of seven procedures. Table 4.6 shows the tasks and the procedures that perform the tasks.

TABLE 4.6
Tasks and Their Procedures

Task	Procedure
0. Input employee data.	InputData
1. Compute current earnings.	Gross_Pay
2. Compute year-to-date earnings.	Total_Pay
3. Compute FICA tax.	FICA_Tax
4. Compute federal income tax withheld.	Fed_Tax
4.1 Compute adjusted pay.	Fed_Tax
4.2 Compute amount withheld for single employee.	TaxSingle
4.3 Compute amount withheld for married employee.	TaxMarried
5. Compute paycheck amounts.	Net_Check
6. Display payroll information.	ShowPayroll

■ THE USER INTERFACE

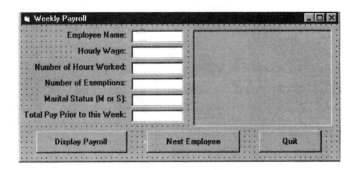

FIGURE 4-5   *Template for Entering Payroll Data*

TABLE 4.7
Objects and Initial Properties for the Weekly Payroll Program

Object	Property	Setting
frmPayroll	Caption	Weekly Payroll
lblName	Alignment	1 – Right Justify
	Caption	Employee Name
txtName	Text	(blank)
lblWage	Alignment	1 – Right Justify
	Caption	Hourly Wage
txtWage	Text	(blank)
lblHours	Alignment	1 – Right Justify
	Caption	Number of Hours Worked
txtHours	Text	(blank)
lblExempts	Alignment	1 – Right Justify
	Caption	Number of Exemptions
txtExempts	Text	(blank)
lblMarital	Alignment	1 – Right Justify
	Caption	Marital Status (M or S)
txtMarital	Text	(blank)
lblPriorPay	Alignment	1– Right Justify
	Caption	Total Pay Prior to this Week
txtPriorPay	Text	(blank)
cmdDisplay	Caption	Display Payroll
cmdNext	Caption	Next Employee
cmdQuit	Caption	Quit
picResults		

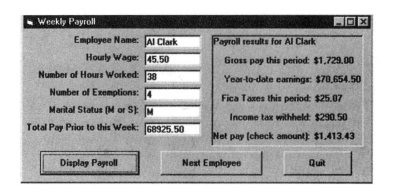

FIGURE 4-6   *Sample Run of Weekly Payroll*

```
'Program to compute employees' weekly payroll

Private Sub cmdDisplay_Click()
    Dim empName As String          'Name of employee
    Dim hrWage As Single           'Hourly wage
    Dim hrsWorked As Single        'Hours worked this week
    Dim exemptions As Integer      'Number of exemptions for employee
    Dim mStatus As String          'Marital status: S for Single; M for Married
    Dim prevPay As Single          'Total pay for year excluding this week
    Dim pay As Single              'This week's pay before taxes
    Dim totalPay As Single         'Total pay for year including this week
    Dim ficaTax As Single          'FICA taxes for this week
    Dim fedTax As Single           'Federal income tax withheld this week
    Dim check As Single            'Paycheck this week (take-home pay)
    'Obtain data, compute payroll, display results
    Call InputData(empName, hrWage, hrsWorked, exemptions,
                        mStatus, prevPay)                            'Task 0
    pay = Gross_Pay(hrWage, hrsWorked)                               'Task 1
    totalPay = Total_Pay(prevPay, pay)                               'Task 2
    ficaTax = FICA_Tax(pay, prevPay, totalPay)                       'Task 3
    fedTax = Fed_Tax(pay, exemptions, mStatus)                       'Task 4
    check = Net_Check(pay, ficaTax, fedTax)                          'Task 5
    Call ShowPayroll(empName, pay, totalPay, ficaTax, fedTax, check) 'Task 6
End Sub


Private Sub cmdNext_Click()
    'Clear all text boxes for next employee's data
    txtName.Text = " "
    txtWage.Text = " "
    txtHours.Text = " "
    txtExempts.Text = " "
    txtMarital.Text = " "
    txtPriorPay.Text = " "
    picResults.Cls
End Sub


Private Sub cmdQuit_Click()
    End
End Sub


Private Function Fed_Tax(pay As Single, exemptions As Integer, mStatus As String)
    Dim adjPay As Single
    'Task 4.1: Compute federal income tax
    adjPay = pay - (51.92 * exemptions)
    If adjPay < 0 Then
        adjPay = 0
    End If
    If mStatus = "S" Then
        Fed_Tax = TaxSingle(adjPay)        'Task 4.2
      Else
        Fed_Tax = TaxMarried(adjPay)       'Task 4.3
    End If
    Fed_Tax = Round(Fed_Tax, 2)            'Round to nearest cent
End Function


Private Function FICA_Tax(pay As Single, prevPay As Single, totalPay As Single)
```

```
       Dim socialSecurity As Single          'Social Security tax for this week
       Dim medicare As Single                'Medicare tax for this week
       'Task 3: Compute social security and medicare tax
       If totalPay <= 68400 Then
           socialSecurity = 0.062 * pay
         ElseIf prevPay < 68400 Then
           socialSecurity = 0.062 * (68400 - prevPay)
       End If
       medicare = 0.0145 * pay
       FICA_Tax = socialSecurity + medicare
       FICA_Tax = Round(FICA_Tax, 2) 'Round to nearest cent
   End Function

   Private Function Gross_Pay(hrWage As Single, hrsWorked As Single)
      'Task 1: Compute weekly pay before taxes
      If hrsWorked <= 40 Then
          Gross_Pay = hrsWorked * hrWage
        Else
          Gross_Pay = 40 * hrWage + (hrsWorked - 40) * 1.5 * hrWage
      End If
   End Function

   Private Sub InputData(empName As String, hrWage As Single, _ hrsWorked As
                         Single, exemptions As Integer, _ mStatus As String,
                         prevPay As Single)
      'Get payroll data for employee empName = txtName.Text
      hrWage = Val(txtWage.Text)
      hrsWorked = Val(txtHours.Text)
      exemptions = Val(txtExempts.Text)
      mStatus = Left(UCase(txtMarital.Text), 1) 'M or S
      prevPay = Val(txtPriorPay.Text)
   End Sub

   Private Function Net_Check(pay As Single, ficaTax As Single, fedTax As Single)
      'Task 5: Compute amount of money given to employee
      Net_Check = pay - ficaTax - fedTax
   End Function

   Private Sub ShowPayroll(empName As String, pay As Single, _ totalPay As
                Single, ficaTax As Single, fedTax As Single, check As Single)
      'Display results of payroll computations
      picResults.Cls
      picResults.Print "Payroll results for "; empName
      picResults.Print
      picResults.Print " Gross pay this period: "; FormatCurrency(pay)
      picResults.Print
      picResults.Print " Year-to-date earnings: "; FormatCurrency(totalPay)
      picResults.Print
      picResults.Print " Fica Taxes this period: "; FormatCurrency(ficaTax)
      picResults.Print
      picResults.Print " Income tax withheld: "; FormatCurrency(fedTax)
      picResults.Print
      picResults.Print "Net pay (check amount): "; FormatCurrency(check)
   End Sub
```

```
Private Function TaxMarried(adjPay As Single) As Single
   'Task 6.3: Compute federal tax for married person based on adjusted pay
   Select Case adjPay
      Case 0 To 124
         TaxMarried = 0
      Case 124 To 899
         TaxMarried = 0.15 * (adjPay - 124)
      Case 899 To 1855
         TaxMarried = 116.25 + 0.28 * (adjPay - 899)
      Case 1855 To 3084
         TaxMarried = 383.93 + 0.31 * (adjPay - 1855)
      Case 3084 To 5439
         TaxMarried = 764.92 + 0.36 * (adjPay - 3084)
      Case Is > 5439
         TaxMarried = 1612.72 + 0.396 * (adjPay - 5439)
   End Select
End Function


Private Function TaxSingle(adjPay As Single) As Single
   'Task 6.2: Compute federal tax for single person based on adjusted pay
   Select Case adjPay
      Case 0 To 51
         TaxSingle = 0
      Case 51 To 517
         TaxSingle = 0.15 * (adjPay - 51)
      Case 517 To 1105
         TaxSingle = 69.6 + 0.28 * (adjPay - 517)
      Case 1105 To 2493
         TaxSingle = 234.54 + 0.31 * (adjPay - 1105)
      Case 2493 To 5385
         TaxSingle = 664.82 + 0.36 * (adjPay - 2493)
      Case Is > 5385
         TaxSingle = 1705.94 + 0.396 * (adjPay - 5385)
   End Select
End Function

Private Function Total_Pay(prevPay As Single, pay As Single)
   'Compute total pay before taxes
   Total_Pay = prevPay + pay
End Function
```

COMMENTS

1. In the function FICA_Tax, care has been taken to avoid computing Social Security benefits tax on income in excess of $68,400 per year. The logic of the program makes sure an employee whose income crosses the $68,400 threshold during a given week is taxed only on the difference between $68,400 and his previous year-to-date income.

2. The two functions TaxMarried and TaxSingle use Select Case to incorporate the tax brackets given in Tables 4.4 and 4.5 for the amount of federal income tax withheld. The upper limit of each Case clause is the same as the lower limit of the next Case clause. This ensures fractional values for adjPay, such as 51.50 in

the TaxSingle function, will be properly treated as part of the higher salary range.

SUMMARY

1. The *relational operators* are <, >, =, <>, <=, and >=.
2. The principal *logical operators* are And, Or, and Not.
3. A *condition* is an expression involving constants, variables, functions, and operators (arithmetic, relational, and/or logical) that can be evaluated as either True or False.
4. An If block decides what action to take depending on the truth values of one or more conditions. To allow several courses of action, the If and Else parts of an If statement can contain other If statements.
5. A Select Case block selects one of several actions depending on the value of an expression, called the *selector*. The entries in the *value* lists should have the same type (string or numeric) as the selector.

PROGRAMMING PROJECTS

1. Table 4.8 gives the price schedule for Eddie's Equipment Rental. Full-day rentals cost one-and-a-half times half-day rentals. Write a program that displays Table 4.8 in a picture box when an appropriate command button is clicked and displays a bill in another picture box based on the item number and time period chosen by a customer. The bill should include a $30.00 deposit.

TABLE 4.8
Price Schedule for Eddie's Equipment Rental

Piece of Equipment	Half-Day	Full Day
1. Rug cleaner	$16.00	$24.00
2. Lawn mower	$12.00	$18.00
3. Paint sprayer	$20.00	$30.00

A possible form layout and sample run is shown in Figure 4-7.

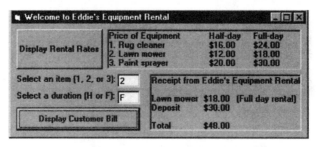

FIGURE 4-7   *Form Layout and Sample Run for Programming Project 1*

2. The American Heart Association suggests that at most 30 percent of the calories in our diet come from fat. Although food labels give the number of calories and amount of fat per serving, they often do not give the percentage of calories from fat. This percentage can be calculated by multiplying the number of grams of fat in one serving by 9, dividing that number by the total number of calories per serving, and multiplying the result by 100. Write a program that requests the name, number of calories per serving, and the grams of fat per serving as input,

and tells us whether the food meets the American Heart Association recommendation. A sample run is as follows:

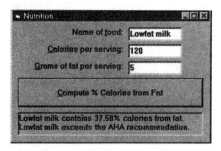

3. Table 4.9 gives the 1998 federal income tax rate schedule for single taxpayers. Write a program that requests the taxable income and calculates the federal income tax. Use a Sub procedure for the input and a Function procedure to calculate the tax.

TABLE 4.9
1998 Federal Income Tax Rates for Single Taxpayers

Taxable Income Over	But Not Over	Your Tax Is	Of Amount Over
$0	$25,350	15%	$0
$25,350	$61,400	$3,802.50 + 28%	$25,350
$61,400	$128,100	$13,896.50 + 31%	$61,400
$128,100	$278,450	$34,573.50 + 36%	$128,100
$278,450		$86,699.50 + 39.6%	$278,450

4. Write a program to determine the real roots of the quadratic equation $ax + bx + c = 0$ (where $a \neq 0$) after requesting the values of a, b, and c. Use a sub procedure to ensure that a is nonzero. *Note:* The equation has 2, 1, or 0 solutions depending on whether the value of $b\,^2 - 4 * a * c$ is positive, zero, or negative. In the first two cases, the solutions are given by the quadratic formula $(-b \pm Sqr(b^2 - 4 * a * c)) / (2 * a)$. (Test the program with the following sets of coefficients.)

$a = 1$	$b = -11$	$c = 28$	Solutions are 4 and 7.
$a = 1$	$b = -6$	$c = 9$	Solution is 3.
$a = 1$	$b = 4$	$c = 1$	No solution.

5. Table 4.10 contains seven proverbs and their truth values. Write a program that presents these proverbs one at a time and asks the user to evaluate them as true or false. The program should then tell the user how many questions were answered correctly and display one of the following evaluations: Perfect (all correct), Excellent (5 or 6 correct), You might consider taking Psychology 101 (less than 5 correct).

TABLE 4.10
Seven Proverbs

Proverb	Truth Value
The squeaky wheel gets the grease.	True
Cry and you cry alone.	True
Opposites attract.	False
Spare the rod and spoil the child.	False
Actions speak louder than words.	True
Familiarity breeds contempt.	False
Marry in haste, repent at leisure.	True

Source: "You Know What They Say . . .," by Alfie Kohn, *Psychology Today,* April 1988.

6. Write a program to analyze a mortgage. The user should enter the amount of the loan, the annual rate of interest, and the duration of the loan in months. When the user clicks on the command button, the information that was entered should be checked to make sure it is reasonable. If bad data have been supplied, the user should be so advised. Otherwise, the monthly payment and the total amount of interest paid should be displayed. The formula for the monthly payment is

```
payment = p * r / (1 - (1 + r) ^ (-n))
```

where p is the amount of the loan, r is the monthly interest rate (annual rate divided by 12) given as a number between 0 (for 0 percent) and 1 (for 100 percent), and n is the duration of the loan. The formula for the total interest paid is

```
total interest = n * payment - p
```

(Test the program for a mortgage of $140,000 at 8% annual rate of interest, and duration 360 months. Such a mortgage will have a monthy payment of $1,027.27.)

7. Write a program using the form in Figure 4-8. Each time the command button is pressed, Rnd is used to simulate a coin toss and the values are updated. The figure shows the status after 27 coin tosses. *Note:* You can produce tosses quickly by just holding down the Enter key. Although the percentage of heads initially will fluctuate considerably, it should stay close to 50% after many (say, 1000) tosses.

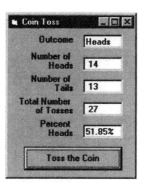

FIGURE 4-8   *Form for Programming*

REPETITION

5.1 DO LOOPS

A loop, one of the most important structures in Visual Basic, is used to repeat a sequence of statements a number of times. At each repetition, or pass, the statements act upon variables whose values are changing. The **Do loop** repeats a sequence of statements either as long as or until a certain condition is true. A Do statement precedes the sequence of statements, and a Loop statement follows the sequence of statements. The condition, along with either the word While or Until, follows the word Do or the word Loop. When Visual Basic executes a Do loop of the form

```
Do While condition
    statement(s)
Loop
```

it first checks the truth value of *condition*. If *condition* is false, then the statements inside the loop are not executed, and the program continues with the line after the Loop statement. If *condition* is true, then the statements inside the loop are executed. When the statement Loop is encountered, the entire process is repeated, beginning with the testing of *condition* in the Do While statement. In other words, the statements inside the loop are repeatedly executed only as long as (that is, while) the condition is true. Figure 5-1 contains the pseudocode and flowchart for this loop.

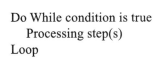

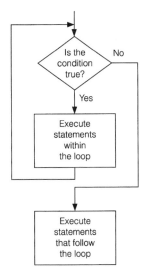

FIGURE 5-1   *Pseudocode and Flowchart for a Do While Loop*

EXAMPLE 1

Write a program that displays the numbers from 1 through 10.

SOLUTION:
The condition in the Do loop is "num <= 10"

```
Private Sub cmdDisplay_Click()
  Dim num As Integer
  'Display the numbers from 1 to 10
  num = 1
  Do While num <= 10
    picNumbers.Print num;
    num = num + 1
  Loop
End Sub
```

[Run, and click the command button. The following is displayed in the picture box.]

```
1 2 3 4 5 6 7 8 9 10
```

Do loops are commonly used to ensure that a proper response is received from the Input-Box function.

EXAMPLE 2

The following program requires the user to give a password before a secret file can be accessed.

Object	Property	Setting
frm6_1_2	Caption	Read File
lblFiles	Caption	The available files are: HUMOR.TXT, INSULTS.TXT, and SECRET.TXT.
lblName	Caption	Name of file to open
txtName	Text	(blank)
cmdDisplay	Caption	Display First Item of File
picItem		

```
Private Sub cmdDisplay_Click()
  Dim passWord As String, info As String
  If UCase(txtName.Text) = "SECRET.TXT"Then
    passWord = ""
    Do While passWord <> "SHAZAM"
      passWord = InputBox("What is the password?")
      passWord = UCase(passWord)
    Loop
  End If
  Open txtName.Text For Input As #1
  Input #1, info
  picItem.Cls
  picItem.Print info
  Close #1
End Sub
```

[Run, type SECRET.TXT into the text box, and click the command button.]

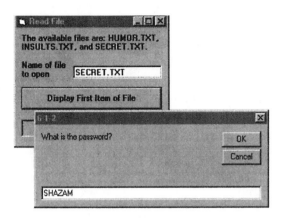

Note: If a file other than SECRET.TXT is requested, the statements inside the loop are not executed.

In Examples 1 and 2 the condition was checked at the top of the loop—that is, before the statements were executed. Alternatively, the condition can be checked at the bottom of the loop when the statement Loop is reached. When Visual Basic encounters a Do loop of the form

```
Do
    statement(s)
Loop Until condition
```

it executes the statements inside the loop and then checks the truth value of *condition*. If *condition* is true, then the program continues with the line after the Loop statement. If *condition* is false, then the entire process is repeated beginning with the Do statement. In other words, the statements inside the loop are executed at least once and then are repeatedly executed *until* the condition is true. Figure 5-2 shows the pseudocode and flowchart for this type of Do loop.

Do
    statement(s)
Loop Until condition is true

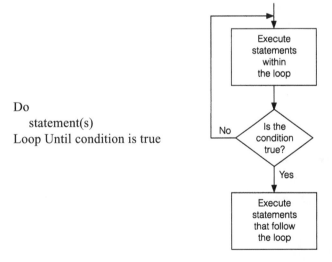

FIGURE 5-2   *Pseudocode and Flowchart for a Do Loop with Condition Tested at the Bottom*

EXAMPLE 3

The following program is equivalent to Example 2, except that the condition is tested at the bottom of the loop.

```
Private Sub cmdDisplay_Click()
    Dim passWord As String, info As String
```

```
    If UCase(txtName.Text) = "SECRET.TXT"Then
      Do
        passWord = InputBox("What is the password?")
        passWord = UCase(passWord)
      Loop Until passWord = "SHAZAM"
    End If
    Open txtName.Text For Input As #1
    Input #1, info
    picItem.Cls
    picItem.Print info
    Close #1
End Sub
```

Do loops allow us to calculate useful quantities for which we might not know a simple formula.

EXAMPLE 4

Suppose you deposit $100 into a savings account and let it accumulate at 7 percent interest compounded annually. The following program determines when you will be a millionaire.

Object	Property	Setting
frmInterest	Caption	7% Interest
lblAmount	Caption	Amount Deposited
txtAmount	Text	(blank)
cmdYears	Caption	Years to become a millionaire
picWhen		

```
Private Sub cmdYears_Click()
   Dim balance As Single, numYears As Integer
   'Compute years required to become a millionaire
   picWhen.Cls
   balance = Val(txtAmount.Text)
   numYears = 0
   Do While balance < 1000000
      balance = balance + .07 * balance
      numYears = numYears + 1
   Loop
   picWhen.Print "In"; numYears; "years you will have a million dollars."
End Sub
```

[Run, type 100 into the text box, and press the command button.]

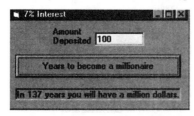

COMMENTS

1. Be careful to avoid infinite loops—that is, loops that are never exited. The following loop is infinite, because the condition "num < > 0"will always be true. *Note:* The loop can be terminated by pressing Ctrl+Break.

```
Private Sub cmdButton_Click()
   Dim num As Single
   'An infinite loop
   num = 7
   Do While num <> 0
     num = num - 2
   Loop
End Sub
```

Notice that this slip-up can be avoided by changing the condition to "num >= 0"

2. The statements between Do and Loop do not have to be indented. However, because indenting improves the readability of the program, it is regarded as good programming style. As soon as you see the word Do, your eyes can easily scan down the program to find the matching Loop statement. You know immediately the size of the loop.

3. Visual Basic allows the use of the words While and Until either at the top or bottom of a Do loop. In this text, the usage of these words is restricted for the following reasons.

   (a) Because any While statement can be easily converted to an Until statement and vice versa, the restriction produces no loss of capabilities and the programmer has one less matter to think about.

   (b) Restricting the use simplifies reading the program. The word While proclaims testing at the top, and the word Until proclaims testing at the bottom.

   (c) Certain other major structured languages, such as Pascal, only allow While at the top and Until at the bottom of a loop. Therefore, following this convention will make life easier for people already familiar with Pascal or planning to learn it.

   (d) Standard pseudocode uses the word While to denote testing a loop at the top and the word Until to denote testing at the bottom.

4. Good programming practice requires that all variables appearing in a Do loop be assigned values before the loop is entered rather than relying on default values. For instance, the code at the left in what follows should be replaced with the code at the right.

```
'Add 1 through 10                    'Add 1 through 10
Do While num < 10                    num = 0
   num = num + 1                     sum = 0
   sum = sum + num                   Do While num < 10
Loop                                    num = num + 1
                                        sum = sum + num
                                     Loop
```

5.2 PROCESSING LISTS OF DATA WITH DO LOOPS

One of the main applications of programming is the processing of lists of data from a file. Do loops are used to display all or selected items from lists, search lists for specific items, and perform calculations on the numerical entries of a list. This section introduces several devices that facilitate working with lists. **Counters** calculate the number of elements in lists, **accumulators** sum numerical values in lists, **flags** record whether certain events have occurred, and the **EOF function** indicates the end of a file. **Nested loops** add yet another dimension to repetition.

■ EOF FUNCTION

Data to be processed are often retrieved from a file by a Do loop. Visual Basic has a useful function, EOF, that tells us if we have reached the end of the file from which we are reading. Suppose a file has been opened with reference number n. At any time, the condition

```
EOF(n)
```

will be true if the end of the file has been reached, and false otherwise.

One of the first programs I wrote when I got my computer stored a list of names and phone numbers and printed a phone directory. I first had the program display the directory on the screen and later changed the picNumbers.Print statements to Printer.Print statements to produce a printed copy. I stored the names in a file so I could easily add, change, or delete entries.

EXAMPLE 1

The following program displays the contents of a telephone directory. The names and phone numbers are contained in the file PHONE.TXT. The loop will repeat as long as the end of the file is not reached.

PHONE.TXT contains the following four lines:

"Bert", "123-4567"
"Ernie", "987-6543"
"Grover", "246-8321"
"Oscar", "135-7900"

Object	Property	Setting
frmPhone	Caption	Directory
cmdDisplay	Caption	Display Phone Numbers
picNumbers		

```
Private Sub cmdDisplay_Click()
    Dim nom As String, phoneNum As String
    picNumbers.Cls
    Open "PHONE.TXT"For Input As #1
    Do While Not EOF(1)
        Input #1, nom, phoneNum
        picNumbers.Print nom, phoneNum
    Loop
    Close #1
End Sub
```

[Run, and press the command button.]

The program in Example 1 illustrates the proper way to process a list of data contained in a file. The Do loop should be tested at the top with an end-of-file condition. (If the file is empty, no attempt is made to input data from the file.) The first set of data should be input *after* the Do statement, and then the data should be processed. Figure 5-3 contains the pseudocode and flowchart for this technique.

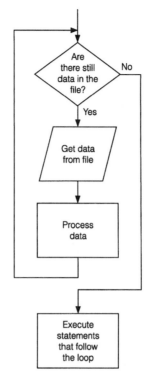

Do While there are still data in the file
    Get an item of data
    Process the item
Loop

FIGURE 5-3   *Pseudocode and Flowchart for Processing Data from a File*

Sequential files can be quite large. Rather than list the entire contents, we typically search the file for a specific piece of information.

EXAMPLE 2

Modify the program in Example 1 to search the telephone directory for a name specified by the user. If the name does not appear in the directory, so notify the user.

SOLUTION:

We want to keep searching as long as there is no match *and* we have not reached the end of the list. Therefore, the condition for the Do While statement is a compound logical expression with the operator And. After the last pass through the loop, we will know whether the name was found and be able to display the requested information.

Object	Property	Setting
frmPhone	Caption	Phone Number
lblName	Caption	Name to look up
txtName	Text	(blank)
cmdDisplay	Caption	Display Phone Number
picNumber		

```
Private Sub cmdDisplay_Click()
  Dim nom As String, phoneNum As String
  Open "PHONE.TXT"For Input As #1
  Do While (nom txtName.Text) And (Not EOF(1))
    Input #1, nom, phoneNum
  Loop
  Close #1
  picNumber.Cls
  If nom = txtName.Text Then
      picNumber.Print nom, phoneNum
```

```
        Else
            picNumber.Print "Name not found."
        End If
End Sub
```

[Run, type Grover into the text box, and press the command button.]

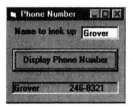

■ COUNTERS AND ACCUMULATORS

A **counter** is a numeric variable that keeps track of the number of items that have been processed. An **accumulator** is a numeric variable that totals numbers.

EXAMPLE 3

The following program counts and finds the value of coins listed in a file.

COINS.TXT contains the following entries: 1, 1, 5, 10, 10, 25

Object	Property	Setting
frmCoins	Caption	Coins
cmdAnalyze	Caption	Analyze Change
picValue		

```
Private Sub cmdAnalyze_Click()
    Dim numCoins As Integer, sum As Single, value As Single
    Open "COINS.TXT" For Input As #1
    numCoins = 0
    sum = 0
    Do While Not EOF(1)
        Input #1, value
        numCoins = numCoins + 1
        sum = sum + value
    Loop
    picValue.Cls
    picValue.Print "The value of the"; numCoins; "coins is"; sum; "cents."
    Close #1
End Sub
```

[Run, and press the command button.]

The value of the counter, *num*Coins, was initially 0 and changed on each execution of the loop to 1, 2, 3, 4, 5, and finally 6. The accumulator, *sum,* initially had the value 0 and increased with each execution of the loop to 1, 2, 7, 17, 27, and finally 52.

■ FLAGS

A flag is a variable that keeps track of whether a certain situation has occurred. The data type most suited to flags is the **Boolean data type.** Variables of type Boolean can assume just two values—True and False. Flags are used within loops to provide information that will be utilized after the loop terminates. Flags also provide an alternative method of terminating a loop.

EXAMPLE 4

The following program counts the number of words in the file WORDS.TXT and then reports whether the words are in alphabetical order. In each execution of the loop, a word is compared to the next word in the list. The flag variable, called *orderFlag,* is initially assigned the value True and is set to False if a pair of adjacent words is out of order. The technique used in this program will be used in Section 6 when we study sorting. ***Note:*** The statement in line 7, word1 = "", is a device to get things started. Each word must first be read into the variable *word2.*
WORDS.TXT contains the following winning words from the U.S. National Spelling Bee:
"cambist", "croissant", "deification"
"hydrophyte", "incisor", "maculature"
"macerate", "narcolepsy", "shallon"

Object	Property	Setting
frmWords	Caption	Word Analysis
cmdAnalyze	Caption	Analyze Words
picReport		

```
Private Sub cmdAnalyze_Click()
   Dim orderFlag As Boolean, wordCounter As Integer
   Dim word1 As String, word2 As String
   'Count words. Are they in alphabetical order?
   orderFlag = True
   wordCounter = 0
   word1 = ""
   Open "WORDS.TXT"For Input As #1
   Do While Not EOF(1)
     Input #1, word2
     wordCounter = wordCounter + 1
     If word1 > word2 Then    'Two words are out of order
          orderFlag = False
     End If
     word1 = word2
   Loop
   Close #1
   picReport.Print "The number of words is"; wordCounter
   If orderFlag = True Then
       picReport.Print "The words are in alphabetical order."
     Else
       picReport.Print "The words are not in alphabetical order."
   End If
End Sub
```

[Run, and press the command button.]

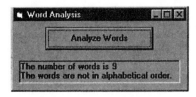

■ NESTED LOOPS

The statements inside of a Do loop can consist of another Do loop. Such a configuration is referred to as **nested loops** and is useful in repeating a single data-processing routine several times.

EXAMPLE 5

Modify the program in Example 2 to allow the user to look through several lists of names. Suppose we have several different phone directories, the names of which are listed in the file LISTS.TXT. (For instance, the file LISTS.TXT might contain the entries CLIENTS.TXT, FRIENDS.TXT, and KINFOLK.TXT.) A sought-after name might be in any one of the files.

SOLUTION:

The statements in the inner Do loop will be used to look up names as before. At least one pass through the outer Do loop is guaranteed and passes will continue as long as the name is not found and phone lists remain to be examined.

```
Private Sub cmdDisplay_Click()
    Dim foundFlag As Boolean, fileName As String
    Dim nom As String, phoneNum As String
    Open "LISTS.TXT" For Input As #1
    foundFlag = False
    nom = ""
    Do While (foundFlag = False) And (Not EOF(1))
        Input #1, fileName
        Open fileName For Input As #2
        Do While (nom <> txtName.Text) And (Not EOF(2))
            Input #2, nom, phoneNum
        Loop
        Close #2
        picNumber.Cls
        If nom = txtName.Text Then
            picNumber.Print nom, phoneNum
            foundFlag = True
        End If
    Loop
    Close #1
    If foundFlag = False Then
        picNumber.Print "Name not found."
    End If
End Sub
```

COMMENT

1. In Appendix D, the section "Stepping Through a Program Containing a Do Loop: Section 5" uses the Visual Basic debugging tools to trace the flow through a Do loop.

2. When flagVar is a variable of Boolean type, the statements

   ```
   True Then and If flagVar = False Then
   ```

   can be replaced by

   ```
   If flagVar Then    and    If Not flagVar Then
   ```

Similarly, the statements

```
Do While flagVar = True    and    Do While flagVar = False
```

can be replaced by

```
Do While flagVar    and    Do While Not flagVar
```

5.3 FOR...NEXT LOOPS

When we know exactly how many times a loop should be executed, a special type of loop, called a For...Next loop, can be used. For...Next loops are easy to read and write, and have features that make them ideal for certain common tasks. The following code uses a For...Next loop to display a table.

```
Private Sub cmdDisplayTable_Click()
  Dim i As Integer
  'Display a table of the first 5 numbers and their squares
  picTable.Cls
  For i = 1 To 5
    picTable.Print i; i ^ 2
  Next i
End Sub
```

[Run and click on cmdDisplayTable. The following is displayed in the picture box.]

```
1  1
2  4
3  9
4  16
5  25
```

The equivalent program written with a Do loop is as follows.

```
    Private Sub cmdDisplayTable_Click()
Dim i As Integer
  'Display a table of the first 5 numbers and their squares
  picTable.Cls
  i = 1
  Do While i <= 5
    picTable.Print i; i ^ 2
    i = i + 1
  Loop
End Sub
```

In general, a portion of a program of the form

```
initial value ───────┐   ┌─────┐
                     ┌┴───┴─┐   │
control variable ────┘ For i = m To n ◄────── terminating value
                       statement(s) ◄──────── body
                       Next i
```

constitutes a For...Next loop. The pair of statements For and Next cause the statements between them to be repeated a specified number of times. The For statement designates a numeric variable, called the **control variable,** that is initialized and then automatically changes after each execution of the loop. Also, the For statement gives the range of values this variable will assume. The Next statement increments the control variable. If $m \leq n$, then i is assigned the values m, $m + 1,..., n$ in order, and the body is executed once for each of these values. If $m > n$, then execution continues with the statement after the For...Next loop.

When program execution reaches a For...Next loop, such as the one shown previously, the For statement assigns to the control variable i the initial value m and checks to see whether it is greater than the terminating value n. If so, then execution jumps to the line following the Next statement. If $i <= n$, the statements inside the loop are executed. Then, the Next statement increases the value of i by 1 and checks this new value to see if it exceeds n. If not, the entire process is repeated until the value of i exceeds n. When this happens, the program moves to the line following the loop. Figure 5-4 contains the pseudocode and flowchart of a For...Next loop.

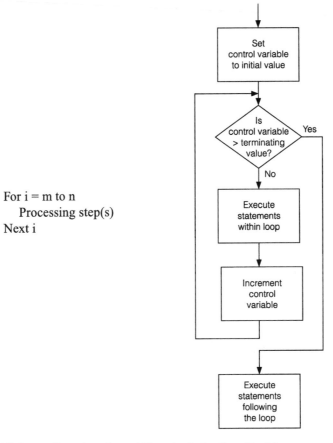

```
For i = m to n
    Processing step(s)
Next i
```

FIGURE 5-4   *Pseudocode and Flowchart of a For...Next Loop*

The control variable can be *any* numeric variable. The most common single-letter names are *i, j,* and *k*; however, if appropriate, the name should suggest the purpose of the control variable.

EXAMPLE 1

Suppose the population of a city is 300,000 in the year 1998 and is growing at the rate of 3 percent per year. The following program displays a table showing the population each year until 2002.

Object	Property	Setting
frm6_3_1	Caption	POPULATION GROWTH
cmdDisplay	Caption	Display Population
picTable		

```
Private Sub cmdDisplay_Click()
   Dim pop As Single, yr As Integer
   'Display population from 1998 to 2002
   picTable.Cls
   pop = 300000
   For yr = 1998 To 2002
     picTable.Print yr, FormatNumber(pop, 0)
     pop = pop + .03 * pop
   Next yr
End Sub
```

[Run, and click the command button.]

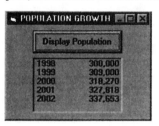

The initial and terminating values can be constants, variables, or expressions. For instance, the For statement in the preceding program can be replaced by

```
firstYr = 1998
lastYr = 2002
For yr = firstYr To lastYr
```

In Example 1, the control variable was increased by 1 after each pass through the loop. A variation of the For statement allows any number to be used as the increment. The statement

```
For i= m To n Step s
```

instructs the Next statement to add s to the control variable instead of 1. The numbers m, n, and s do not have to be whole numbers. The number *s* is called the **step value** of the loop.

EXAMPLE 2

The following program displays the values of the index of a For...Next loop for terminating and step values input by the user.

Object	Property	Setting
frm6_3_2	Caption	For index = 0 To n Step s
lblN	Caption	n:
txtEnd	Text	(blank)
lblS	Caption	s:
txtStep	Text	(blank)
cmdDisplay	Caption	Display Values of index
picValues		

```
Private Sub cmdDisplay_Click()
   Dim n As Single, s As Single, index As Single
   'Display values of index ranging from 0 to n Step s
   picValues.Cls
   n = Val(txtEnd.Text)
   s = Val(txtStep.Text)
   For index = 0 To n Step s
```

```
      picValues.Print index;
   Next index
End Sub
```

[Run, type 3.2 and .5 into the text boxes, and click the command button.]

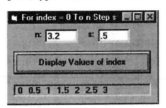

In the examples considered so far, the control variable was successively increased until it reached the terminating value. However, if a negative step value is used and the initial value is greater than the terminating value, then the control value is decreased until reaching the terminating value. In other words, the loop counts backward or downward.

EXAMPLE 3

The following program accepts a word as input and displays it backward.

Object	Property	Setting
frm6_3_3	Caption	Write Backwards
lblWord	Caption	Enter Word
txtWord	Text	(blank)
cmdReverse	Caption	Reverse Letters
picTranspose		

```
Private Sub cmdReverse_Click()
   picTranspose.Cls
   picTranspose.Print Reverse(txtWord.Text)
End Sub

Private Function Reverse(info As String) As String
   Dim m As Integer, j As Integer, temp As String
   m = Len(info)
   temp = ""
   For j = m To 1 Step -1
      temp = temp + Mid(info, j, 1)
   Next j
   Reverse = temp
End Function
```

[Run, type SUEZ into the text box, and click the command button.]

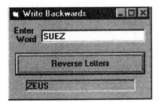

Note: The initial and terminating values of a For...Next loop can be expressions. For instance, the third and fifth lines of the function in Example 3 can be consolidated to

```
   For j = Len(info) To 1 Step -1
```

The body of a For...Next loop can contain any sequence of Visual Basic statements. In particular, it can contain another For...Next loop. However, the second loop must be completely contained inside the first loop and must have a different control variable. Such a configuration is called **nested loops.** Figure 5-5 shows several examples of valid nested loops.

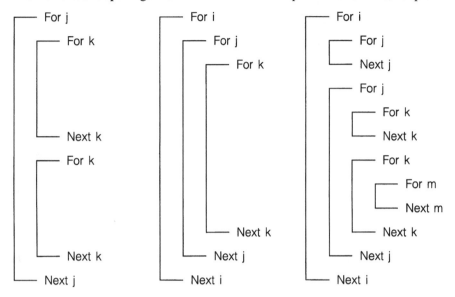

FIGURE 5-5   *Nested Loops*

EXAMPLE 4

Write a program to display a multiplication table for the integers from 1 to 4.

SOLUTION:

In the following program, j denotes the left factors of the products, and k denotes the right factors. Each factor takes on a value from 1 to 4. The values are assigned to j in the outer loop and to k in the inner loop. Initially, j is assigned the value 1, and then the inner loop is traversed four times to produce the first row of products. At the end of these four passes, the value of j will still be 1, and the value of k will have been incremented to 5. The picTable.Print statement just before Next j guarantees that no more products will be displayed in that row. The first execution of the outer loop is then complete. Following this, the statement Next j increments the value of j to *2*. The statement beginning **For** k is then executed. It resets the value of k to 1. The second row of products is displayed during the next four executions of the inner loop and so on.

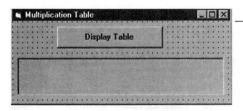

Object	Property	Setting
frmMultiply	Caption	Multiplication Table
cmdDisplay	Caption	Display Table
picTable		

```
Private Sub cmdDisplay_Click()
   Dim j As Integer, k As Integer
   picTable.Cls
   For j = 1 To 4
     For k = 1 To 4
        picTable.Print j; "x"; k; "="; j * k,
     Next k
     picTable.Print
   Next j
End Sub
```

[Run and press the command button.]

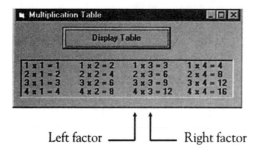

Left factor ——⌐ ⌐—— Right factor

COMMENTS

1. The body of a For...Next loop need not be indented. However, because indenting improves the readability of the program, it is good programming style. As soon as you see the word For, your eyes can easily scan down the program to find the matching Next statement. You then know two facts immediately: the number of statements in the body of the loop and the number of passes that will be made through the loop.

2. For and Next statements must be paired. If one is missing, the program will generate the error message "For without Next" or "Next without For."

3. Consider a loop beginning with For $i = m$ To n Step s. The loop will be executed exactly once if m equals n no matter what value s has. The loop will not be executed at all if m is greater than n and s is positive, or if m is less than n and s is negative.

4. The value of the control variable should not be altered within the body of the loop; doing so might cause the loop to repeat indefinitely or have an unpredictable number of repetitions.

5. Noninteger step values can lead to roundoff errors with the result that the loop is not executed the intended number of times. For instance, a loop beginning with For i = 1 To 2 Step .1 will be executed only 10 times instead of the intended 11 times. It should be replaced with For i = 1 To 2.01 Step .1.

5.4 A CASE STUDY: ANALYZE A LOAN

This case study develops a program to analyze a loan. Assume the loan is repaid in equal monthly payments and interest is compounded monthly. The program should request the amount (principal) of the loan, the annual rate of interest, and the number of years over which the loan is to be repaid. The four options to be provided by command buttons are as follows.

1. Calculate the monthly payment. The formula for the monthly payment is

$$\text{payment} = p * r / (1 - (1 + r) \wedge (-n))$$

where p is the principal of the loan, r is the monthly interest rate (annual rate divided by 12) given as a number between 0 (for 0 percent) and 1 (for 100 percent), and n is the number of months over which the loan is to be repaid. Because a payment computed in this manner can be expected to include fractions of a cent, the value should be rounded up to the next nearest cent. This corrected payment can be achieved using the formula

$$\text{correct payment} = \text{Round(payment} + .005, 2)$$

2. Display an amortization schedule, that is, a table showing the balance on the loan at the end of each month for any year over the duration of the loan. Also show how much of each monthly payment goes toward interest and how much is used to repay the principal. Finally, display the total interest paid over the duration of the loan. The balances for successive months are calculated with the formula

$$\text{balance} = (1 + r) * b - m$$

where r is the monthly interest rate (annual rate / 12, a fraction between 0 and 1), b is the balance for the preceding month (amount of loan left to be paid), and m is the monthly payment.

3. Show the effect of changes in the interest rate. Display a table giving the monthly payment for each interest rate from 1 percent below to 1 percent above the specified annual rate in steps of one-eighth of a percent.

4. Quit

■ DESIGNING THE ANALYZE-A-LOAN PROGRAM

For each of the tasks described in preceding options 1 to 4, the program must first look at the text boxes to obtain the particulars of the loan to be analyzed. Thus, the first division of the problem is into the following tasks:

1. Input the principal, interest, and duration.
2. Calculate the monthly payment.
3. Calculate the amortization schedule.
4. Display the effects of interest rate changes.
5. Quit.

Task 1 is a basic input operation and Task 2 involves applying the formula given in Step 1; therefore, these tasks need not be broken down any further. The demanding work of the program is done in Tasks 3 and 4, which can be divided into smaller subtasks.

3. *Calculate amortization schedule.* This task involves simulating the loan month by month. First, the monthly payment must be computed. Then, for each month, the new balance must be computed together with a decomposition of the monthly payment into the amount paid for interest and the amount going toward repaying the principal. That is, Task 3 is divided into the following subtasks:

   3.1 Calculate monthly payment.
   3.2 Calculate new balance.
   3.3 Calculate amount of monthly payment for interest.
   3.4 Calculate amount of monthly payment for principal.

4. *Display the effects of interest-rate changes.* A table is needed to show the effects of changes in the interest rate on the size of the monthly payment. First, the interest rate is reduced by one percentage point and the new monthly payment is computed. Then the interest rate is increased by regular increments until it reaches one percentage point above the original rate, with new monthly payment amounts computed for each intermediate interest rate. The subtasks for this task are then:

   4.1 Reduce the interest rate by 1 percent.
   4.2 Calculate the monthly payment.
   4.3 Increase the interest rate by 1/8 percent.

The hierarchy chart in Figure 5-6 shows the stepwise refinement of the problem.

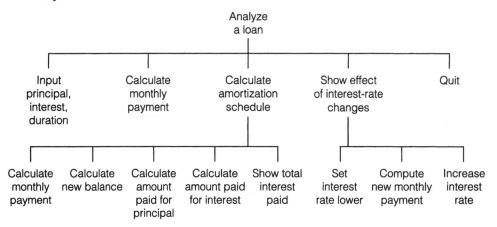

FIGURE 5-6 *Hierarchy Chart for the Analyze a Loan Program*

■ THE USER INTERFACE

Figure 5-7 shows a possible form design. Figures 5-8 and 5-9 show possible runs of the program for each task available through the command buttons. The width and height of the picture box were adjusted by trial and error to handle the extensive output generated.

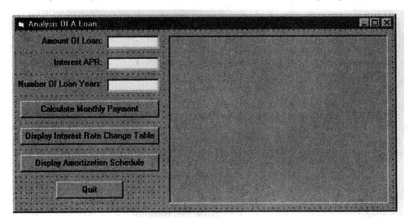

FIGURE 5-7 *Template for Loan Analysis*

TABLE 5.1
Objects and Initial Properties for the Loan Analysis Program

Object	Property	Setting
frmLoan	Caption	Analysis of a Loan
lblAmt	Alignment	1 – Right Justify
	Caption	Amount of Loan:
txtAmt	Text	(blank)
lblApr	Alignment	1 – Right Justify
	Caption	Interest APR:
txtApr	Text	(blank)
lblYrs	Alignment	1 – Right Justify
	Caption	Number of Loan Years
txtYrs	Text	(blank)
cmdPayment	Caption	Calculate Monthly Payment
cmdRateTable	Caption	Display Interest Rate Change Table
cmdAmort	Caption	Display Amortization Schedule
cmdQuit	Caption	Quit

picDisp

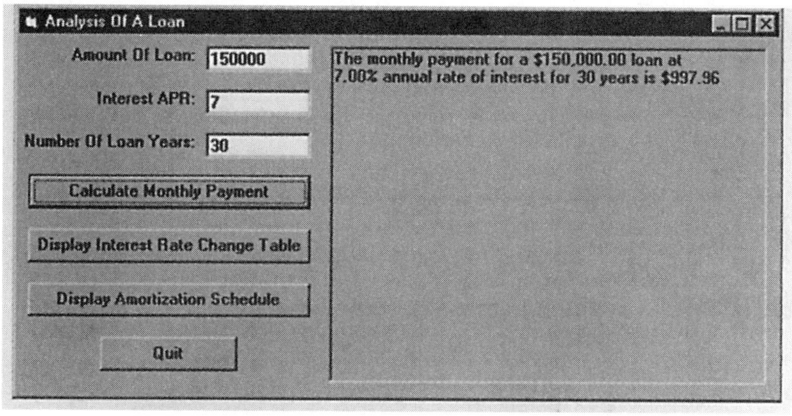

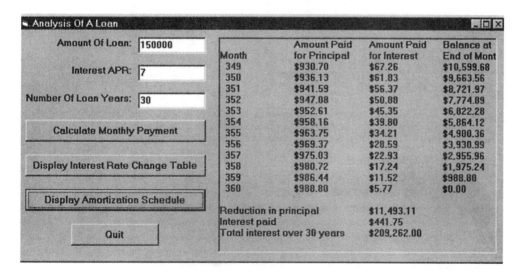

FIGURE 5-8 *Monthly Payment on a 30-Year Loan*

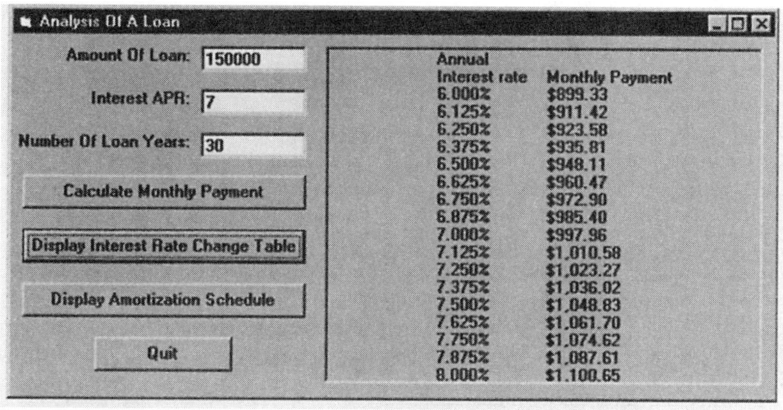

FIGURE 5-9 *Interest Rate Change Table for a 30-Year Loan*

FIGURE 5-10 *Amortization of Year 30 of a Loan*

■ WRITING THE ANALYZE-A-LOAN PROGRAM

Table 5.2 shows each task discussed before and the procedure that carries out the task.

■ **PSEUDOCODE FOR THE ANALYZE-A-LOAN PROGRAM**

Calculate Monthly Payment command button:
    INPUT LOAN DATA (Sub procedure InputData)
    COMPUTE MONTHLY PAYMENT (Function Payment)
    DISPLAY MONTHLY PAYMENT (Sub procedure ShowPayment)

Display Interest Rate Change Table command button:
    INPUT LOAN DATA (Sub procedure InputData)
    DISPLAY INTEREST RATE CHANGE TABLE
       (Sub procedure ShowInterestChanges)
    Decrease annual rate by .01
    Do
       Display monthly interest rate
       COMPUTE MONTHLY PAYMENT (Function Payment)
       Increase annual rate by .00125
    Loop Until annual rate > original annual rate + .01

Display Amortization Schedule command button:
    INPUT LOAN DATA (Sub procedure InputData)
    DISPLAY AMORTIZATION SCHEDULE (Sub procedure ShowAmortSched)
    Compute monthly interest rate
    COMPUTE MONTHLY PAYMENT (Function Payment)
    Display amortization table
    Display total interest paid

TABLE 5.2
Tasks and Their Procedures

Task	Procedure
1. Input principal, interest, duration.	InputData
2. Calculate monthly payment.	ShowPayment
3. Calculate amortization schedule.	ShowAmortSched
3.1 Calculate monthly payment.	Payment
3.2 Calculate new balance.	Balance
3.3 Calculate amount paid for loan.	ShowAmortSched
3.4 Calculate amount paid for interest.	ShowAmortSched
4. Show effect of interest rate changes.	ShowInterestChanges
4.1 Reduce interest rate.	ShowInterestChanges
4.2 Compute new monthly payment.	Payment
4.3 Increase interest rate.	ShowInterestChanges

```
'Analyze a loan

Private Function Balance(mPayment As Single, prin As Single, mRate As Single) As Single
    Dim newBal As Single 'Compute balance at end of month
    newBal = (1 + mRate) * prin
    If newBal <= mPayment Then
        mPayment = newBal
        Balance = 0
      Else
        Balance = newBal - mPayment
    End If
End Function

Private Sub cmdAmort_Click()
    Dim principal As Single       'Amount of loan
    Dim yearlyRate As Single      'Annual rate of interest
    Dim numMonths As Integer      'Number of months to repay loan
```

```
      Call InputData(principal, yearlyRate, numMonths)
      Call ShowAmortSched(principal, yearlyRate, numMonths)
End Sub

Private Sub cmdPayment_Click()
   Dim principal As Single       'Amount of loan
   Dim yearlyRate As Single      'Annual rate of interest
   Dim numMonths As Integer      'Number of months to repay loan
   Call InputData(principal, yearlyRate, numMonths)
   Call ShowPayment(principal, yearlyRate, numMonths)
End Sub

Private Sub cmdQuit_Click()
   End
End Sub

Private Sub cmdRateTable_Click()
   Dim principal As Single       'Amount of loan
   Dim yearlyRate As Single      'Annual rate of interest
   Dim numMonths As Integer      'Number of months to repay loan
   Call InputData(principal, yearlyRate, numMonths)
   Call ShowInterestChanges(principal, yearlyRate, numMonths)
End Sub

Private Sub InputData(prin As Single, yearlyRate As Single, numMs As Integer)
   Dim percentageRate As Single, numYears As Integer
   'Input the loan amount, yearly rate of interest, and duration
   prin = Val(txtAmt.Text)
   percentageRate = Val(txtApr.Text)
   numYears = Val(txtYrs.Text)
   yearlyRate = percentageRate / 100
   numMs = numYears * 12
End Sub

Private Function Payment(prin As Single, mRate As Single, numMs As Integer) As Single
   Dim payEst As Single
   If numMs = 0 Then
       payEst = prin
     ElseIf mRate = 0 Then
       payEst = prin / numMs
     Else
       payEst = prin * mRate / (1 - (1 + mRate) ^ (-numMs))
   End If
   If payEst <> Round(payEst, 2) Then
       Payment = Round(payEst + .005, 2) 'round up to nearest cent
   End If
End Function

Private Sub ShowAmortSched(prin As Single, yearlyRate As Single, numMs As Integer)
   Dim msg As String, startMonth As Integer, mRate As Single
   Dim monthlyPayment As Single, totalInterest As Single
   Dim yearInterest As Single, oldBalance As Single
   Dim monthNum As Integer, newBalance As Single
   Dim principalPaid As Single, interestPaid As Single
   Dim reducPrin As Single, loanYears As Integer
   'Display amortization schedule
```

```
         msg = "Please enter year (1-"& Str(numMs / 12)
         msg = msg & ") for which amorization is to be shown:"
         startMonth = 12 * Val(InputBox(msg)) - 11 picDisp.Cls
         picDisp.Print "", "Amount Paid ",
         picDisp.Print "Amount Paid", "Balance at"
         picDisp.Print "Month", "for Principal",
         picDisp.Print "for Interest", "End of Month"
         mRate = yearlyRate / 12 'monthly rate
         monthlyPayment = Payment(prin, mRate, numMs)
         totalInterest = 0
         yearInterest = 0
         oldBalance = prin
         For monthNum = 1 To numMs
            newBalance = Balance(monthlyPayment, oldBalance, mRate)
            principalPaid = oldBalance - newBalance
            interestPaid = monthlyPayment - principalPaid
            totalInterest = totalInterest + interestPaid
            If (monthNum >= startMonth) And (monthNum <= startMonth + 11) Then
               picDisp.Print Tab(2); FormatNumber(monthNum, 0),
               picDisp.Print FormatCurrency(principalPaid),
               picDisp.Print FormatCurrency(interestPaid),
               picDisp.Print FormatCurrency(newBalance)
               yearInterest = yearInterest + interestPaid
            End If
            oldBalance = newBalance
         Next monthNum
         reducPrin = 12 * monthlyPayment - yearInterest
         loanYears = numMs / 12
         picDisp.Print
         picDisp.Print "Reduction in principal",
         picDisp.Print FormatCurrency(reducPrin)
         picDisp.Print "Interest paid", ,
         picDisp.Print FormatCurrency(yearInterest)
         picDisp.Print "Total interest over"; loanYears; "years",
         picDisp.Print FormatCurrency(totalInterest)
End Sub

Private Sub ShowInterestChanges(prin As Single, yearlyRate As Single, numMs As Integer)
   Dim newRate As Single, mRate As Single, py As Single
   Dim pymnt As String
   'Display affect of interest changes
   picDisp.Cls
   picDisp.Print , "Annual"
   picDisp.Print , "Interest rate", "Monthly Payment"
   newRate = yearlyRate - .01
   Do
      mRate = newRate / 12 'monthly rate
      py = Payment(prin, mRate, numMs)
      pymnt = FormatCurrency(py)
      picDisp.Print , FormatPercent(newRate, 3) , pymnt
      newRate = newRate + .00125
   Loop Until newRate > yearlyRate + .01
End Sub

Private Sub ShowPayment(prin As Single, yearlyRate As Single, numMs As Integer)
   Dim mRate As Single, prn As String, apr As String
```

```
Dim yrs As String, pay As Single, pymnt As String
'Display monthly payment amount
mRate = yearlyRate / 12 'monthly rate
prn = FormatCurrency(prin)
apr = FormatNumber(yearlyRate * 100)
yrs = FormatNumber(numMs / 12, 0)
pay = Payment(prin, mRate, numMs)
pymnt = FormatCurrency(pay)
picDisp.Cls
picDisp.Print "The monthly payment for a "& prn & "loan at "
picDisp.Print apr & "% annual rate of interest for ";
picDisp.Print yrs & "years is "& pymnt
End Sub
```

COMMENTS

1. Tasks 3.1 and 3.2 are performed by functions. Using functions to compute these quantities simplifies the computations in ShowAmortSched.

2. Because the payment was rounded up to the nearest cent, it is highly likely that the payment needed in the final month to pay off the loan will be less than the normal payment. For this reason, ShowAmortSched checks if the balance of the loan (including interest due) is less than the regular payment, and if so, makes appropriate adjustments.

3. The standard formula for computing the monthly payment cannot be used if either the interest rate is zero percent or the loan duration is zero months. Although both of these situations do not represent reasonable loan parameters, provisions are made in the function Payment so that the program can handle these esoteric situations.

SUMMARY

1. A Do loop repeatedly executes a block of statements either as long as or until a certain condition is true. The condition can be checked either at the top of the loop or at the bottom.

2. The EOF function tells us if we have read to the end of a file.

3. As various items of data are processed by a loop, a *counter* can be used to keep track of the number of items, and an *accumulator* can be used to sum numerical values.

4. A *flag* is a Boolean variable, used to indicate whether or not a certain event has occurred.

5. A For...Next loop repeats a block of statements a fixed number of times. The *control variable* assumes an initial value and increments by one after each pass through the loop until it reaches the terminating value. Alternative increment values can be specified with the Step keyword.

PROGRAMMING PROJECTS

1. Write a program to display a company's payroll report in a picture box. The program should read each employee's name, hourly rate, and hours worked from a

file and produce a report in the form of the sample run shown in Figure 5-11. Employees should be paid time-and-a-half for hours in excess of 40.

```
Payroll Report for Week ending 4/15/99

Employee      Hourly Rate     Hours Worked     Gross Pay
Al Adams      $6.50                     38     $247.00
Bob Brown     $5.70                     50     $313.50
Carol Coe     $7.00                     40     $280.00
FinalTotal    $840.50
```

FIGURE 5-11   *Sample Output from Programming Project 1*

2. Table 5.3 shows the standard prices for items in a department store. Suppose prices will be reduced for the annual George Washington's Birthday Sale. The new price will be computed by reducing the old price by 10 percent, rounding up to the nearest dollar, and subtracting 1 cent. If the new price is greater than the old price, the old price is used as the sale price. Write a program to display in a picture box the output shown in Figure 5-12.

TABLE 5.3
Washington's Birthday Sale

Item	Original Price
GumShoes	39.00
SnugFoot Sandals	21.00
T-Shirt	7.75
Maine Handbag	33.00
Maple Syrup	6.75
Flaked Vest	24.00
Nightshirt	26.00

Item	Sale Price
GumShoes	35.99
SnugFoot Sandals	18.99
T-Shirt	6.99
Maine Handbag	29.99
Maple Syrup	6.75
Flaked Vest	21.99
Nightshirt	23.99

FIGURE 5-12   *Output of Project 2*

3. The Rule of 72 is used to make a quick estimate of the time required for prices to double due to inflation. If the inflation rate is r percent, then the Rule of 72 estimates that prices will double in 72/r years. For instance, at an inflation rate of 6 percent, prices double in about 72/6 or 12 years. Write a program to test the accuracy of this rule. The program should display a table showing, for each value of r from 1 to 20, the rounded value of 72/r and the actual number of years required for prices to double at an *r* percent inflation rate. (Assume prices increase at the end of each year.) Figure 5-13 shows the first few rows of the output.

Interest Rate (%)	Rule of 72	Actual
1	72	70
2	36	36
3	24	24

FIGURE 5-13   *Rule of 72*

4. Table 5.4 shows the number of bachelor degrees conferred in 1980 and 1994 in certain fields of study. Tables 5.5 and 5.6 show the percentage change and a his-

togram of 1994 levels, respectively. Write a program that allows the user to display any one of these tables as an option and quit as a fourth option.

TABLE 5.4
Bachelor Degrees Conferred in Certain Fields

Field of Study	1980	1994
Business and management	185,361	246,654
Computer and info. science	11,154	24,200
Education	118,169	167,600
Engineering	68,893	62,220
Social sciences	103,519	133,680

Source: U.S. National Center of Educational Statistics

TABLE 5.5
Percentage Change in Bachelor Degrees Conferred

Field of Study	% Change (1980–1994)
Business and management	33.1
Computer and info. science	117.0
Education	41.8
Engineering	–9.7
Social sciences	29.1

TABLE 5.6
Bachelor Degrees Conferred in 1994 in Certain Fields

Business and management	************************* 246,654
Computer and info. science	*** 24,200
Education	**************** 167,600
Engineering	****** 62,220
Social sciences	************* 133,680

5. *Least-Squares Approximation.* Table 5.7 shows the 1988 price of a gallon of fuel and the consumption of motor fuel for several countries. Figure 5-14 displays the data as points in the xy plane. For instance, the point with coordinates (1, 1400) corresponds to the USA. Figure 5-14 also shows the straight line that best fits these data in the least squares sense. (The sum of the squares of the distances of the 11 points from this line is as small as possible.) In general, if (x_i, y_1), (x_2, y_2), . . , (x_n, y_n) are n points in the xy coordinate system, then the least squares approximation to these points is the line $y = mx + b$, where

$$m = \frac{n * (\text{sum of } x_i * y_i) - (\text{sum of } x_i) * *=(\text{sum of } y_i)}{n * (\text{sum of } x_i * x_i) - (\text{sum of } x_i)^2}$$

and

$$b = ((\text{sum of } y_i) - m * (\text{sum of } x_i))/n$$

Write a program that calculates and displays the equation of the least squares line, and then allows the user to enter a fuel price and uses the equation of the line to predict the corresponding consumption of motor fuel. (Place the numeric data from the table in a data file.) A sample run is shown in Figure 5-15.

TABLE 5.7
A Comparison of 1988 Fuel Prices and Per Capita Motor Fuel Use

Country	Price per gallon in U.S. Dollars	Tons of Oil per 1000 Person	Country	Price per gallon in U.S. Dollars	Tons of Oil per 1000 Person
USA	$1.00	1400	France	$3.10	580
W. Ger.	$2.20	620	Norway	$3.15	600
England	$2.60	550	Japan	$3.60	410
Austria	$2.75	580	Denmark	$3.70	570
Sweden	$2.80	700	Italy	$3.85	430
Holland	$3.00	490			

Source: World Resources Institute

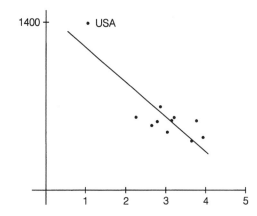

FIGURE 5-14   *Least-Squares Fit to Data from Table 5.7*

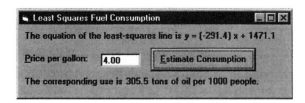

FIGURE 5-15   *Sample Run of Programming Project 5*

6. Write a program to provide information on the height of a ball thrown straight up into the air. The program should request the initial height, *h* feet, and the initial velocity, *v* feet per second, as input. The four options to be provided by command buttons are as follows:

(a) Determine the maximum height of the ball. *Note:* The ball will reach its maximum height after *v*/32 seconds.

(b) Determine approximately when the ball will hit the ground. *Hint:* Calculate the height after every .1 second and observe when the height is no longer a positive number.

(c) Display a table showing the height of the ball every quarter second for 5 seconds or until it hits the ground.

(d) Quit.

The formula for the height of the ball after t seconds, $h + v * t - 16 * t * t$, should be specified in a user-defined function. (Test the program with $v = 148$ and $h = 0$. This velocity is approximately the top speed clocked for a ball thrown by a professional baseball pitcher.)

7. Depreciation to a Salvage Value of 0. For tax purposes an item may be depreciated over a period of several years, n. With the straight-line method of depreciation, each year the item depreciates by $1/n$th of its original value. With the double-declining-balance method of depreciation, each year the item depreciates by $2/n$ths of its value at the beginning of that year. (In the last year it is depreciated by its value at the beginning of the year.) Write a program that

(a) Requests a description of the item, the year of purchase, the cost of the item, the number of years to be depreciated (estimated life), and the method of depreciation. The method of depreciation should be chosen by clicking one of two command buttons.

(b) Displays a depreciation schedule for the item similar to the schedule shown in Figure 5-16.

```
Description: Computer
Year of purchase: 1999
Cost: $2000.00
Estimated life: 5
Method of depreciation: double-declining-balance

          Value at      Amount Deprec   Total Depreciation
Year      Beg of Yr     During Year     to End of Year
1999      2,000.00      800.00          800.00
2000      1,200.00      480.00          1,280.00
2001      720.00        288.00          1,568.00
2002      432.00        172.80          1,740.80
2003      259.20        259.20          2,000.00
```

FIGURE 5-16   *Depreciation Schedule*

8. *The Twelve Days of Christmas.* Each year, Provident National Bank of Philadelphia publishes a Christmas price list. See Table 5.8. Write a program that requests an integer from 1 through 12 and then lists the gifts for that day along with that day's cost. On the nth day, the n gifts are 1 partridge in a pear tree, 2 turtle doves, ... n of the nth item. The program also should give the total cost of all twelve days. As an example, Figure 5-17 shows the output in the picture box when the user enters 3.

TABLE 5.8
Christmas Price Index

Item	Cost	Item	Cost
partridge in a pear tree	27.50	swan-a-swimming	1000.00
turtle dove	25.00	maid-a-milking	4.25
French hen	5.00	lady dancing	289.50
calling bird	70.00	lord-a-leaping	292.50
gold ring	60.00	piper piping	95.75
geese-a-laying	25.00	drummer drumming	95.00

```
The gifts for day 3 are
1 partridge in a pear tree
2 turtle doves
3 French hens
Cost: $92.50

Total cost for the twelve days: $71,613.50
```

FIGURE 5-17   *Sample Output for Programming Project 8*

ARRAYS

6.1 CREATING AND ACCESSING ARRAYS

A **variable** (or simple variable) is a name to which Visual Basic can assign a single value. An **array variable** is a collection of simple variables of the same type to which Visual Basic can efficiently assign a list of values.

Consider the following situation. Suppose you want to evaluate the exam grades for 30 students. Not only do you want to compute the average score, but you also want to display the names of the students whose scores are above average. You might place the 30 pairs of student names and scores in a data file and run the program outlined.

```
Private Sub cmdButton_Click()
    Dim student1 As String, score1 As Single
    Dim student2 As String, score2 As Single
    Dim student3 As String, score3 As Single
    .
    .
    .
    Dim student30 As String, score30 As Single
    'Analyze exam grades
    Open "SCORES.TXT" For Input As #1
    Input #1, student1, score1
    Input #1, student2, score2
    Input #1, student3, score3
    .
    .
    .
    Input #1, student30, score30
    'Compute the average grade
    .
    .
    .
    'Display names of above average students
    .
    .
    .
End Sub
```

This program is going to be uncomfortably long. What's most frustrating is that the 30 Dim statements and 30 Input # statements are very similar and look as if they should be condensed

161

into a short loop. A shorthand notation for the many related variables would be welcome. It would be nice if we could just write

```
For i = 1 To 30
   Input #1, studenti, scorei
Next i
```

Of course, this will not work. Visual Basic will treat *studenti* and *scorei* as two variables and keep reassigning new values to them. At the end of the loop they will have the values of the thirtieth student.

Visual Basic provides a data structure called an **array** that lets us do what we tried to accomplish in the loop. The variable names will be similar to those in the Input # statement. They will be

```
student(1), student(2), student(3), ..., student(30)
```

and

```
score(1), score(2), score(3), ..., score(30).
```

We refer to these collections of variables as the array variables *student( )* and *score( )*. The numbers inside the parentheses of the individual variables are called **subscripts**, and each individual variable is called a **subscripted variable** or **element**. For instance, *student(3)* is the third subscripted variable of the array *student( )*, and *score( )* is the 20th subscripted variable of the array *score( )*. The elements of an array are assigned successive memory locations. Figure 6-1 shows the memory locations for the array *score( )*.

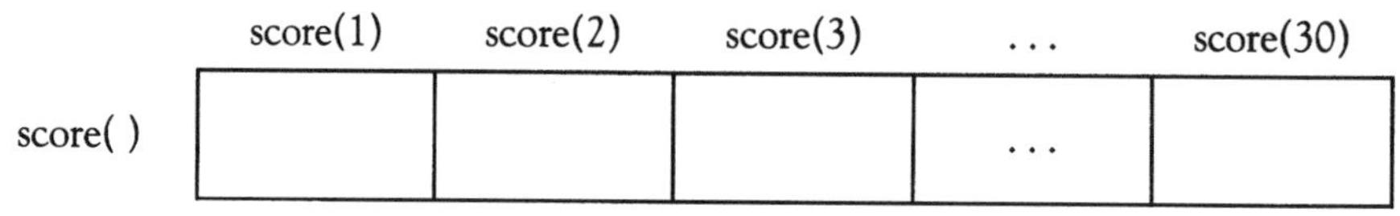

FIGURE 6-1   *The Array Score( )*

Array variables have the same kinds of names as simple variables. If *arrayName* is the name of an array variable and *n* is a whole number, then the statement

```
Dim arrayName(1 To n) As varType
```

placed in the (Declarations) section of (General) reserves space in memory to hold the values of the subscripted variables *arrayName*(1), *arrayName*(2), *arrayName*(3), . . . , *arrayName*(n). (Recall from Section 3.1 that the (Declarations) section of (General) is accessed from any code window by selecting these values in the Object and Procedure boxes.) The spread of the subscripts specified by the Dim statement is called the **range** of the array, and the Dim statement is said to **dimension** the array. The subscripted variables will all have the same data type; namely, the type specified by varType. For instance, they could be all String variables or all Integer variables. In particular, the statements

```
Dim student(1 To 30) As String
Dim score(1 To 30) As Integer
```

dimension the arrays needed for the preceding program.

As with any variable created in the (Declarations) section of (General), these array variables are form-level as discussed in Section 3. Recall that form-level variables can be accessed from any procedure in the program and continue to exist and retain their values as long as the program is running.

Values can be assigned to subscripted variables with assignment statements and displayed with Print methods. The statement

```
Dim score(1 To 30) As Integer
```

sets aside a portion of memory for the numeric array *score*( ) and places the default value 0 in each element.

	score(1)	score(2)	score(3)	. . .	score(30)
score( )	0	0	0	. . .	0

The statements

```
score(1) = 87
score(3) = 92
```

assign values to the first and third elements.

	score(1)	score(2)	score(3)	. . .	score(30)
score( )	87	0	92	. . .	0

The statements

```
For i = 1 To 4
  picBox.Print score(i);
Next i
```

then produce the output   87   0   92   in picBox.

EXAMPLE 1

The following program creates a string array consisting of the names of the first five World Series winners. Figure 6-2 shows the array created by the program.

```
'Create array for five strings
Dim teamName(1 To 5) As String 'in (Declarations) section of (General)

Private Sub cmdWhoWon_Click()
  Dim n As Integer
  'Fill array with World Series Winners
  teamName(1) = "Red Sox"
  teamName(2) = "Giants"
  teamName(3) = "White Sox"
  teamName(4) = "Cubs"
  teamName(5) = "Cubs" '
  Access array of five strings
  n = Val(txtNumber.Text)
  picWinner.Cls
  picWinner.Print "The "; teamName(n); " won World Series number"; n
End Sub
```

[Run, type 2 into the text box, and click the command button.]

	teamName(1)	teamName(2)	teamName(3)	teamName(4)	teamName(5)
teamName( )	Red Sox	Giants	White Sox	Cubs	Cubs

FIGURE 6-2   *The Array TeamName( ) of Example 1*

In Example 1, the array *teamName* was assigned values within the cmdWhoWon_Click event procedure. Every time the command button is clicked, the values are reassigned to the array. This manner of assigning values to an array can be very inefficient, especially in programs with large arrays where the task of the program (in Example 1, looking up a fact) may be repeated numerous times for different user input. When, as in Example 1, the data to be placed in an array are known at the time the program first begins to run, a more efficient location for the statements that fill the array is in Visual Basic's Form_Load event procedure. The Form_Load event procedure is executed by Visual Basic as soon as the program is run, and this execution is guaranteed to occur before the execution of any other event or general procedure in the program. Example 2 uses the Form_Load procedure to improve on Example 1.

EXAMPLE 2

Modify Example 1 to request the name of a baseball team as input and search the array to determine whether or not the team name appears in the array. Load the array values only once.

```
'Create array for five strings
Dim teamName(1 To 5) As String 'in (Declarations) section of (General)

Private Sub cmdDidTheyWin_Click()
   Dim team As String, foundFlag As Boolean, n As Integer
   'Search for an entry in a list of strings
   team = txtName.Text
   foundFlag = False
   n = 0
   Do
     n = n + 1
     If UCase(teamName(n)) = UCase(team) Then
       foundFlag = True
     End If
   Loop Until (foundFlag = True) Or (n = 5)
   'Above line can be replaced with Loop Until (foundFlag) or (n = 5)
   picWinner.Cls
   If foundFlag = False Then 'Can be replaced by If Not foundFlag Then
     picWinner.Print "The "; team; " did not win any";
     picWinner.Print " of the first five World Series."
   Else
     picWinner.Print "The "; teamName(n); " won World Series number"; n
   End If
End Sub

Private Sub Form_Load()
   'Fill array with World Series winners
   teamName(1) = "Red Sox"
   teamName(2) = "Giants"
   teamName(3) = "White Sox"
   teamName(4) = "Cubs"
   teamName(5) = "Cubs"
```

```
End Sub
```

[Run, type White Sox into the text box, and click the command button.]

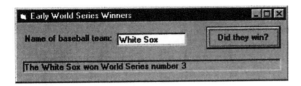

We could have written the program in Example 2 with a For...Next loop beginning For *n* = 1 To 5. However, such a loop would unnecessarily search the entire list when the sought-after item is found early. The wasted time could be significant for a large array.

In some applications, arrays are needed only temporarily to help a procedure complete a task. Visual Basic also allows us to create array variables that are local to a specific procedure and that exist temporarily while the procedure is executing. If the statement

```
Dim arrayName(1 To n) As varType
```

is placed inside an event procedure or general procedure, then space for *n* subscripted variables is set aside in memory each time the procedure is invoked and released when the procedure is exited.

In Example 1, values were assigned to the elements of the array with assignment statements. However, data for large arrays are more often stored in a data file and read with Input # statements. Example 3 uses this technique. Also, because the task of the program is likely to be performed only once during a run of the program, a local array is used.

EXAMPLE 3

Table 6.1 gives names and test scores from a mathematics contest given in 1953. Write a program to display the names of the students scoring above the average for these eight students.

TABLE 6.1
The Top Scores on the Fourth Annual Mathematics Contest Sponsored by the Metropolitan NY Section of the MAA

Richard Dolen	135	Paul H. Monsky	150
Geraldine Ferraro	114	Max A. Plager	114
James B. Fraser	92	Robert A. Schade	91
John H. Maltby	91	Barbara M. White	124

Source: The Mathematics Teacher, February 1953.

SOLUTION:

The following program creates a string array to hold the names of the contestants and a numeric array to hold the scores. The first element of each array holds data for the first contestant, the second element of each array holds data for the second contestant, and so on. See Figure 6-3. Note that the two arrays can be dimensioned in a single Dim statement by placing a comma between the array declarations.

```
Private Sub cmdShow_Click()
  Dim total As Integer, student As Integer, average As Single
  'Create arrays for names and scores
  Dim nom(1 To 8) As String, score(1 To 8) As Integer
  'Assume the data has been placed in the file "SCORES.TXT"
  '(The first line of the file is "Richard Dolen", 135)
  Open "SCORES.TXT" For Input As #1
  For student = 1 To 8
    Input #1, nom(student), score(student)
  Next student
  Close #1
```

```
'Analyze exam scores
total = 0
For student = 1 To 8
  total = total + score(student)
Next student
average = total / 8
'Display all names with above-average grades
picTopStudents.Cls
For student = 1 To 8
  If score(student) > average Then
    picTopStudents.Print nom(student)
  End If
Next student
End Sub
```

[Run, and click the command button.]

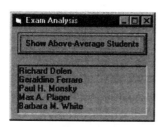

---

	nom(1)	nom(2)	. . .	nom(8)
nom( )	Richard Dolen	Geraldine Ferraro	. . .	Barbara M. White

	score(1)	score(2)	. . .	score(8)
score( )	135	114	. . .	124

FIGURE 6-3   *Arrays Created by Example 3*

In Example 3, the number of students to be processed had to be known at the time the program was written. In actual practice, the amount of data that a program will be processing is not known in advance. Programs should be flexible and incorporate a method for handling varying amounts of data. Visual Basic makes this possible with the statement

```
ReDim arrayName (1 to n) As varType
```

which can use variables or expressions when indicating the subscript range. However, ReDim statements can only be used inside procedures.

EXAMPLE 4

The following program reworks Example 3 for the case when the amount of data is not known in advance.

```
Private Sub cmdShow_Click()
  Dim numStudents As Integer, nTemp As String, sTemp As Integer
  Dim student As Integer, total As Integer, average As Single
```

```
'Determine amount of data to be processed
numStudents = 0
Open "SCORES.TXT" For Input As #1
Do While Not EOF(1)
   Input #1, nTemp, sTemp
   numStudents = numStudents + 1
Loop
Close #1
'Create arrays for names and scores
ReDim nom(1 To numStudents) As String, score(1 To numStudents) As Integer
Open "SCORES.TXT" For Input As #1
For student = 1 To numStudents
   Input #1, nom(student), score(student)
Next student Close #1
'Analyze exam scores
total = 0
For student = 1 To numStudents
   total = total + score(student)
Next student
average = total / numStudents
'Display all names with above-average grades
picTopStudents.Cls
For student = 1 To numStudents
   If score(student) > average Then
      picTopStudents.Print nom(student)
   End If
Next student
End Sub
```

An alternative approach to program flexibility that does not require reading the data file twice is to require that the data file begin with a line that holds the number of records to be processed. If SCORES.TXT is modified by adding a new first line that gives the number of students, then the fourth through eighteenth lines of Example 4 can be replaced with

```
'Create arrays for names and scores
  Open "SCORES.TXT" For
  Input As #1
  Input #1, numStudents
  ReDim nom(1 To numStudents) As String, score(1 To numStudents) As Integer
  For student = 1 To numStudents
    Input #1, nom(student), score(student)
  Next student
Close #1
```

In Example 4, the ReDim statement allowed us to create arrays whose size was not known before the program was run. On the other hand, the arrays that were created were local to the event procedure cmdShow_Click. Many applications require form-level arrays whose size is not known in advance. Unfortunately, Dim statements cannot use variables or expressions to specify the subscript range. The solution offered by Visual Basic is to allow the (Declarations) section of (General) to contain Dim statements of the form

```
Dim arrayName() As varType
```

where no range for the subscripts of the array is specified. An array created in this manner will be form-level but cannot be used until a ReDim statement is executed in a procedure to establish the range of subscripts. The "As *varType*" clause can be omitted from the ReDim statement.

EXAMPLE 5

Suppose the data file WINNERS.TXT contains the names of the teams who have won each of the World Series, with the first line of the file giving the number of World Series that have been played. Write a program that displays the numbers, if any, of the World Series that were won by a team specified by the user.

```
'Create form-level array
   Dim teamName() As String
Dim seriesCount As Integer

Private Sub cmdDidTheyWin_Click()
   Dim teamToFind As String, numWon As Integer, series As Integer
   'Search for World Series won by user's team
   teamToFind = UCase(txtName.Text)
   numWon = 0
   picSeriesWon.Cls
   For series = 1 To seriesCount
      If UCase(teamName(series)) = teamToFind Then
         numWon = numWon + 1
         If numWon = 1 Then
            picSeriesWon.Print "The "; teamName(series);
            picSeriesWon.Print " won the following World Series: ";
         Else
            'Separate from previous
            picSeriesWon.Print ",";
            If (numWon = 5) Or (numWon = 16) Then
               'Start a new line at 5th and 16th win
               picSeriesWon.Print
            End If
         End If
         'First world series played in 1903
         picSeriesWon.Print Str(series + 1902);
      End If
   Next series
   If numWon = 0 Then
      picSeriesWon.Print "The "; teamToFind; " did not win any World Series."
   End If
End Sub

Private Sub Form_Load()
   Dim series As Integer
   'Fill array with World Series winners
   Open "WINNERS.TXT" For Input As #1
   Input #1, seriesCount
   ReDim teamName(1 To seriesCount) As String
   For series = 1 To seriesCount
      Input #1, teamName(series)
   Next series
   Close #1
End Sub
```

[Run, type Yankees into the text box, and click the command button.]

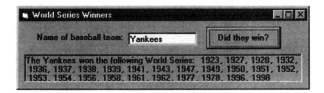

The range of an array need not just begin with 1. A statement of the form

```
Dim arrayName(m To n) As varType
```

where *m* is less than or equal to *n*, creates an array with elements *arrayName(m)*, *arrayName(m* + 1), *arrayName(m* + 2), . . . , *arrayName(n)*. The same holds for ReDim.

EXAMPLE 6

The following program segment stores the names of the 13th, 14th, and 15th Chief Justices of the U.S. Supreme Court in the array pictured in Figure 6-4.

```
'Place names of last three Chief Justices in an array
Dim chiefJustice(13 To 15) As String

    Private Sub Form_Load()
  chiefJustice(13) = "Earl Warren"
  chiefJustice(14) = "Warren Burger"
  chiefJustice(15) = "William Rehnquist"
End Sub
```

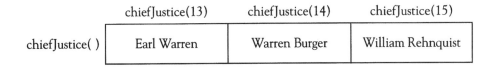

	chiefJustice(13)	chiefJustice(14)	chiefJustice(15)
chiefJustice( )	Earl Warren	Warren Burger	William Rehnquist

FIGURE 6-4   *The Array Created by Example 6*

An array can be used as either a checklist or frequency table, as in the next example. The function Asc associates each character with its position in the ANSI table.

EXAMPLE 7

The following program requests a sentence as input and records the number of occurrences of each letter of the alphabet. The array *charCount( )* has range Asc("A") To Asc("Z"), that is, 65 To 90. The number of occurrences of each letter is stored in the element whose subscript is the ANSI value of the uppercase letter.

```
Private Sub cmdAnalyze_Click()
  Dim index As Integer, letterNum As Integer, sentence As String
  Dim letter As String, column As Integer
  'Count occurrences of different letters in a sentence
  ReDim charCount(Asc("A") To Asc("Z")) As Integer
  For index = Asc("A") To Asc("Z")
    charCount(index) = 0
  Next index
  'Consider and tally each letter of sentence
  sentence = UCase(txtSentence.Text)
  For letterNum = 1 To Len(sentence)
    letter = Mid(sentence, letterNum, 1)
    If (letter >= "A") And (letter <= "Z") Then
```

```
            index = Asc(letter)
            charCount(index) = charCount(index) + 1
      End If
   Next letterNum
   'List the tally for each letter of alphabet
   picLetterCount.Font = "Courier"
   picLetterCount.Cls
   column = 1 'Next column at which to display letter & count
      For letterNum = Asc("A") To Asc("Z")
      letter = Chr(letterNum)
      picLetterCount.Print Tab(column); letter;
      picLetterCount.Print Tab(column + 1); charCount(letterNum);
      column = column + 6
      If column > 42 Then 'only room for 7 sets of data in a line
         picLetterCount.Print
         column = 1
      End If
   Next letterNum
End Sub
```

[Run, type in the given sentence, and click the command button.]

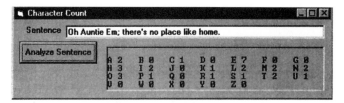

COMMENTS

1. Arrays must be dimensioned in a Dim or ReDim statement before they are used. If a statement such as $a(6) = 3$ appears without a previous Dim or ReDim of the array $a(\ )$, then the error message "Sub or Function not defined" will be displayed when an attempt is made to run the program.

2. Subscripts in ReDim statements can be numeric expressions. Subscripts whose values are not whole numbers are rounded to the nearest whole number. Subscripts outside the range of the array produce an error message as shown below when the last line of the event procedure is reached.

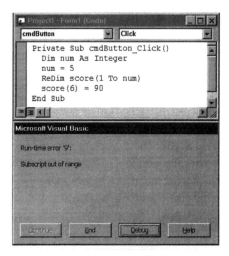

3. The two arrays in Example 3 are referred to as **parallel arrays** because subscripted variables having the same subscript are related.

4. The integers *m* and *n* in the statement Dim *arrayName*(*m* To *n*) As *varType* can be positive, negative, or zero. The only restriction is that *m* cannot be greater than *n*. The same holds true for ReDim statements.

5. Until a value is assigned to an element of an array, the element has its default value. Numeric variables have a default value of 0, and string variables have the default value "", the empty string.

6. The statement Dim *arrayName*(0 To *n*) As *varType* can be replaced by the statement Dim *arrayName*(*n*) As *varType*. The same holds for the ReDim statement.

7. An array whose range has been specified by a ReDim statement is said to be **dynamic**. If *array1*() is a dynamic array, and *array2*() is another array of the same data type (such as String), then the line

```
array1 = array2
```

makes *array1*() an exact duplicate of *array2*(). It will have the same size and contain the same information. This feature was added in Visual Basic 6.0.

8. A dynamic array can be resized with another ReDim statement. However, the resized array loses all its information. If it is resized with the words **ReDim Preserve**, as much information as possible will be retained.

6.2 USING ARRAYS

This section considers three aspects of the use of arrays: processing ordered arrays, reading part of an array, and passing arrays to procedures.

■ ORDERED ARRAYS

An array is said to be **ordered** if its values are in either ascending or descending order. The following arrays illustrate the different types of ordered and unordered arrays. In an ascending ordered array, the value of each element is less than or equal to the value of the next element. That is,

[each element] ≤ [next element].

For string arrays, the ANSI table is used to evaluate the "less than or equal to" condition.

Ordered Ascending Numeric Array

dates( )	1492	1776	1812	1929	1969

Ordered Descending Numeric Array

discov( )	1610	1541	1513	1513	1492

Ordered Ascending String Array

king( )	Edward	Henry	James	John	Kong

Ordered Descending String Array

lake( )	Superior	Ontario	Michigan	Huron	Erie

Unordered Numeric Array

rates( )	8.25	5.00	7.85	8.00	6.50

Unordered String Array

char( )	G	R	E	A	T

Ordered arrays can be searched more efficiently than unordered arrays. In this section we use their order to shorten the search. The technique used here is applied to searching sequential files in Section 7.

EXAMPLE 1

The following program places an ordered list of names into an array, requests a name as input, and informs the user if the name is in the list. Because the list is ordered, the search of the array ends when an element is reached whose value is greater than or equal to the input name. On average, only half the ordered array will be searched. Figure 6-5 shows the flowchart for this search.

```
'Create array to hold 10 strings
Dim nom(1 To 10) As String

Private Sub cmdSearch_Click()
   Dim n As Integer, name2Find As String
   'Search for a name in an ordered list
   name2Find = UCase(Trim(txtName.Text))
   n = 0 'n is the subscript of the array
   Do
     n = n + 1
   Loop Until (nom(n) >= name2Find) Or (n = 10)
   'Interpret result of search
   picResult.Cls
   If nom(n) = name2Find Then
        picResult.Print "Found."
     Else
        picResult.Print "Not found."
   End If
End Sub

Private Sub Form_Load()
   'Place the names into the array
   'All names must be in uppercase
   nom(1) = "AL"
   nom(2) = "BOB"
   nom(3) = "CARL"
   nom(4) = "DON"
   nom(5) = "ERIC"
   nom(6) = "FRED"
   nom(7) = "GREG"
   nom(8) = "HERB"
   nom(9) = "IRA"
   nom(10) = "JUDY"
End Sub
```

[Run, type Don into the text box, and click the command button.]

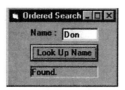

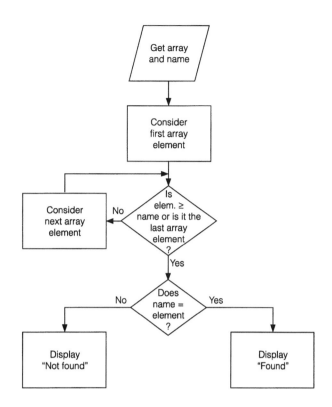

FIGURE 6-5   *Flowchart for a Search of an Ordered Array*

■ USING PART OF AN ARRAY

In some programs, we must dimension an array before knowing how many pieces of data are to be placed into it. In these cases, we dimension the array large enough to handle all reasonable contingencies. For instance, if the array is to hold exam grades, and classes sizes vary from 5 to 100 students, we use a statement such as Dim grades(1 To 100) As Integer. In such situations we must employ a **counter variable** to keep track of the number of values actually stored in the array. We create this counter variable using a Dim statement in the (Declarations) section of (General) so that all procedures will have access to it.

EXAMPLE 2

The following program requests a list of companies and then displays them along with a count.

```
'Demonstrate using only part of an array
  Dim stock(1 To 100) As String
  Dim counter As Integer

Private Sub cmdResult_Click()
  If (counter < 100) Then
    counter = counter + 1
    stock(counter) = txtCompany.Text
    txtCompany.Text = ""
    txtCompany.SetFocus
    Else
      MsgBox "No space to record additional companies.", , ""
      txtCompany.Text = ""
      cmdSummarize.SetFocus
  End If
End Sub
```

```
Private Sub cmdSummarize_Click()
  Dim i As Integer
  'List stock companies that have been recorded
  picStocks.Cls
  picStocks.Print "You own the following"; counter; "stocks."
  For i = 1 To counter
    picStocks.Print stock(i) & " ";
    'Move to new line after every 5 stocks
    If Int(i / 5) = i / 5 Then
      picStocks.Print
    End If
  Next i
End Sub

Private Sub Form_Load()
  'Initialize count of companies
  counter = 0
End Sub
```

[Run, type in eleven companies (press Record Name after each company) and press Summarize.]

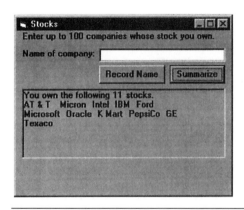

Suppose you have two ordered lists of customers (possibly with some customers on both lists) and you want to consolidate them into a single ordered list. The technique for creating the third list, called the **merge algorithm**, is as follows.

1. Compare the two names at the top of the first and second lists.

    (a) If one name alphabetically precedes the other, copy it onto the third list and cross it off its original list.

    (b) If the names are the same, copy the name onto the third list and cross out the name from the first and second lists.

2. Repeat Step 1 with the current top names until you reach the end of either list.

3. Copy the names from the remaining list onto the third list.

EXAMPLE 3

The following program stores two lists of names in arrays and merges them into a third list. Although at most 10 names will be placed into the third array, duplications will reduce this number. Because the variable r identifies the next position to insert a name in the third array, $r - 1$ is the number of names in the array.

```
'Create arrays to hold list of names
  Dim list1(1 To 5) As String, list2(1 To 5) As String
Dim newList(1 To 10) As String
```

```
Private Sub cmdMerge_Click()
   Dim m As Integer, n As Integer, r As Integer
   Dim numNames As Integer, i As Integer
   'Merge two lists of names
   m = 1 'Subscript for first array
   n = 1 'Subscript for second array
   r = 1 'Subscript and counter for third array
   Do While (m <= 5) And (n <= 5)
      Select Case list1(m)
         Case Is < list2(n)
            newList(r) = list1(m)
            m = m + 1
         Case Is < list2(n)
            newList(r) = list2(n)
            n = n + 1
         Case list2(n)
            newList(r) = list1(m)
            m = m + 1
            n = n + 1
      End Select
      r = r + 1
   Loop
   'If one of the lists has items left over, copy them into the third list
   'At most one of the following two loops will be executed
   Do While m <= 5 'Copy rest of first array into third
      newList(r) = list1(m)
      r = r + 1
      m = m + 1
   Loop
   Do While n <= 5 'Copy rest of second array into third
      newList(r) = list2(n)
      r = r + 1
      n = n + 1
   Loop
   numNames = r - 1
   'Show result of merging lists
   picMergedList.Cls
   For i = 1 To numNames
      picMergedList.Print newList(i) & " ";
   Next i
End Sub

Private Sub Form_Load()
   'Fill list1 with names
   list1(1) = "Al"
   list1(2) = "Carl"
   list1(3) = "Don"
   list1(4) = "Greg"
   list1(5) = "Judy"
   'Fill list2 with names
   list2(1) = "Bob"
   list2(2) = "Carl"
   list2(3) = "Eric"
   list2(4) = "Greg"
   list2(5) = "Herb"
End Sub
```

[Run and click the command button.]

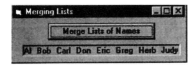

■ PASSING ARRAYS BETWEEN PROCEDURES

An array that is not dimensioned in the (Declarations) section of (General) but rather is declared in a procedure is local to that procedure and unknown in all other procedures. However, an entire local array can be passed to another procedure. The name of the array, followed by an empty set of parentheses, must appear as an argument in the calling statement, and an array variable name of the same type must appear as a corresponding parameter in the procedure definition of the procedure that is to receive the array.

EXAMPLE 4

The following program illustrates passing an array to both a Sub procedure and a Function procedure.

```
Private Sub cmdDisplayAverage_Click()
   'Pass array to Sub procedure and Function procedure
   Dim score(1 To 10) As Integer
   Call FillArray(score())
   picAverage.Cls
   picAverage.Print "The average score is"; Sum(score()) / 10
End Sub

Private Sub FillArray(s() As Integer)
   'Fill array with scores
   s(1) = 85
   s(2) = 92
   s(3) = 75
   s(4) = 68
   s(5) = 84
   s(6) = 86
   s(7) = 94
   s(8) = 74
   s(9) = 79
   s(10) = 88
End Sub]

Private Function Sum(s() As Integer) As Integer
   Dim total As Integer, index As Integer
   'Add up scores
   total = 0
   For index = 1 To 10
     total = total + s(index)
   Next index
   Sum = total
End Function
```

[Run and click the command button.]

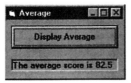

Sometimes it is also necessary to pass a form-level array from one procedure to another. For example, you might have a sorting procedure (discussed in Section 6.3) and three form-level arrays to be sorted. The sorting procedure would be called three times, each time passing a different form-level array. The method for passing a form-level array to another procedure is the same as the method for passing a local array.

EXAMPLE 5

The following program incorporates all three topics discussed in this section. It reads ordered lists of computer languages and spoken languages into form-level arrays, requests a new language as input, and inserts the language into its proper array position (avoiding duplication). The language arrays are dimensioned to hold up to 20 names; the variables *numCompLangs* and *numSpokLangs* record the actual number of languages in each of the ordered arrays. The original contents of the data files are

COMPLANG.TXT:ADA, C, Cobol, Fortran, Pascal, Visual Basic
SPOKLANG.TXT:Cantonese, English, French, Mandarin, Russian, Spanish

Object	Property	Setting
frmAdding	Caption	Adding to an Ordered Array
lblNew	Caption	New language:
txtLang	Text	(blank)
cmdAddComp	Caption	Add to Computer List
cmdAddSpok	Caption	Add to Spoken List
picAllLang		

```
Dim compLang(1 To 20) As String
   Dim spokLang(1 To 20) As String
Dim numCompLangs As IntegerDim numSpokLangs As Integer

Private Sub AddALang(lang() As String, langCount As Integer)
   Dim language As String, n As Integer, i As Integer
   'Insert a language into an ordered array of languages
   language = Trim(txtLang.Text)
   n = 0
   Do
     n = n + 1
   Loop Until (UCase(lang(n))>= UCase(language)) Or (n = langCount)
   If UCase(lang(n)) < UCase(language) Then 'Insert new language at end
       lang(langCount + 1) = language
       langCount = langCount + 1
     ElseIf UCase(lang(n)) > UCase(language) Then 'Insert before item n
       For i = langCount To n Step -1
          lang(i + 1) = lang(i)
       Next i
       lang(n) = language
       langCount = langCount + 1
   End If
End Sub

Private Sub cmdAddComp_Click()
   'Insert language into ordered array of computer languages
   Call AddALang(compLang(), numCompLangs)
   Call DisplayArray(compLang(), numCompLangs)
End Sub

Private Sub cmdAddSpok_Click()
   'Insert language into ordered array of spoken languages
   Call AddALang(spokLang(), numSpokLangs)
```

```
      Call DisplayArray(spokLang(), numSpokLangs)
End Sub

Private Sub DisplayArray(lang() As String, howMany As Integer)
   Dim i As Integer
   'Display the languages in the array
   picAllLang.Cls
   For i = 1 To howMany
      picAllLang.Print lang(i) & " ";
   Next i
End Sub

Private Sub Form_Load()
   'Fill computer language array from COMPLANG.TXT
   numCompLangs = 0 Open "COMPLANG.TXT" For Input As #1
   Do While (Not EOF(1)) And (numCompLangs < 20)
      numCompLangs = numCompLangs + 1
      Input #1, compLang(numCompLangs)
   Loop
   Close #1
   'Fill spoken language array from SPOKLANG.TXT
   numSpokLangs = 0
   Open "SPOKLANG.TXT" For Input As #1
   Do While (Not EOF(1)) And (numSpokLangs < 20)
      numSpokLangs = numSpokLangs + 1
      Input #1, spokLang(numSpokLangs)
   Loop
   Close #1
End Sub
```

[Run, type in German, and click Add to Spoken List.]

[Type in FORTRAN and click Add to Computer List.]

COMMENTS

1. In Examples 1 and 5 we searched successive elements of an ordered list beginning with the first element. This is called a **sequential search**. An efficient alternative to the sequential search is the **binary search**, which is considered in the next section.

2. A single element of an array can be passed to a procedure just like any ordinary numeric or string variable.

```
Private Sub cmdButton_Click()
   Dim num(1 To 20) As Integer
```

```
    num(5) = 10
    picOutput.Print Triple(num(5))
End Sub

Private Function Triple(x As Integer) As Integer
    Triple = 3 * x
End Function
```

> When the program is run and the command button clicked, 30 will be displayed.

3. Visual Basic provides two functions that simplify working with arrays that have been passed to a procedure. If an array has been dimensioned with the range *m* To *n*, then the values of the functions LBound(*arrayName*) and UBound(*array-Name*) are *m* and *n*, respectively.

```
Private Sub cmdButton_Click()
    Dim chiefJustice(13 To 15) As String
    chiefJustice(13) = "Warren"
    chiefJustice(14) = "Burger"
    chiefJustice(15) = "Rehnquist"
    Call Display(pres())
End Sub

Private Sub Display(a() As String)
    Dim i As Integer
    For i = LBound(a) To UBound(a)
        picOutput.Print a(i) & " ";
    Next i
End Sub
```

> When the program is run and the command button clicked, "Warren Burger Rehnquist" will be displayed.

6.3 CONTROL ARRAYS

We have seen many examples of the usefulness of subscripted variables. They are essential for writing concise solutions to many programming problems. Because of the great utility that subscripts provide, Visual Basic also provides a means of constructing arrays of text boxes, labels, command buttons, and so on. Because text boxes, labels, and command buttons are referred to generically in Visual Basic as controls, arrays of these objects are called **control arrays**.

Unlike variable arrays, which can only be created by Dim and ReDim statements once a program is running, at least one element of a control array must be created when the form is designed. The remaining elements can be created either during form design, or, perhaps more typically, with the Load statement when the program is run.

To create the first element of an array of text boxes, create an ordinary text box, then access the Properties window, and select the property called Index. By default this property is blank. Change the Index property to 0 (zero). Your text box is now the first element in a subscripted control array. If the name of a text box is *txtBox* and its Index property is 0, then assigning a value to the text box during run time requires a statement of the form

```
    txtBox(0).Text = value
```

Arrays are not of much use if they contain only a single element. To create additional elements of the *txtBox*( ) control array during form design, make sure that the element you just created is active by clicking on it. Next, press Ctrl+C (or open the Edit menu and select Copy). Visual Basic has now recorded all the properties associated with *txtBox*(0) and is ready to reproduce as many copies as you desire. To create a copy, press Ctrl+V (or open the Edit menu and select Paste). The copy of *txtBox*(0) appears in the upper-left corner of the form. The value of the Index property for this new text box is 1; thus the text box is referred to as *txtBox*(1). Move this text box to the desired position. Press Ctrl+V again and another copy of *txtBox*(0) appears in the upper left corner of the form. Its Index property is 2. Move *txtBox*(2) to an appropriate position. Continue copying *txtBox*(0) in this manner until all desired controls have been created.

It is important to note that all property settings of *txtBox*(0) are being passed (as default settings) to the other elements of the *txtBox*( ) control array, with the exception of the Index, Top, and Left settings. Thus, as a matter of efficiency, before you begin copying *txtBox*(0), set all properties that you want carried over to all elements of *txtBox*( ). For example, if you desire to have the Text property blank for all *txtBox*( ) elements, set the Text property of *txtBox*(0) to (blank) before starting the copying process.

The preceding discussion gave a process for creating an array of text boxes. This same process applies to creating arrays of labels or any other control. In summary, the following steps create an array of controls while designing a form:

1. Add one instance of the desired control to the form.

2. Set the Index property of this control to 0.

3. Set any other properties of the control that will be common to all elements of the array.

4. Click on the control and then press Ctrl+C to prepare to make a copy of the control.

5. Press Ctrl+V to create a copy of the control. Position this control as desired.

6. Repeat Step 5 until all desired elements of the control array have been created.

EXAMPLE 1

A department store has five departments. The following program requests the amount of sales for each department and displays the total sales. We use a control array of five labels and a control array of five text boxes to handle the input. For the label captions we use "Department 1", "Department 2", and so on. Because these labels are the same except for the number, we wait until run time and use a For...Next loop inside the Form_Load ( ) event procedure to assign the captions to each element of the *lblDepart*( ) control array. At design time, before making copies of *lblDepart*(0), we set the Alignment property to "1 – Right Justify" so that all elements of the array inherit this property. Similarly, the Text property of *txtSales*(0) is set to (blank) before copying.

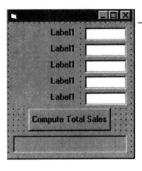

Object	Property	Setting
frm7_3_1	Caption	(blank)
lblDepart()	Index	0 to 4
	Alignment	1 – Right Justify
txtSales( )	Index	0 to 4
	Text	(blank)
cmdCompute	Caption	Compute Total Sales
picTotal		

```
Private Sub Form_Load()
   Dim depNum As Integer
   For depNum = 0 To 4
      lblDepart(depNum).Caption = "Department" & Str(depNum + 1)
   Next depNum
End Sub

Private Sub cmdCompute_Click()
   Dim depNum As Integer, sales As Single
```

```
   sales = 0
   For depNum = 0 To 4
      sales = sales + Val(txtSales(depNum).Text)
   Next depNum
   picTotal.Cls
   picTotal.Print "Total sales were "; FormatCurrency(sales)
End Sub
```

[Run, type the following data into the text boxes, and click the command button.]

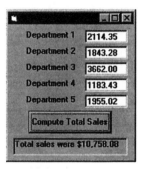

■ CONTROL ARRAY EVENT PROCEDURES

In Section 3 we discussed several events related to text boxes. One example was the GotFocus event procedure. If *txtBox* is an ordinary text box, then the GotFocus event procedure begins with the statement

```
   Private Sub txtBox_GotFocus()
```

If, on the other hand, we make *txtBox* a control array, the GotFocus event procedure begins with the statement

```
   Private Sub txtBox_GotFocus(Index As Integer)
```

Two points should be noted. First, even though we may have a dozen or more elements in the *txtBox*( ) control array, we will have just one txtBox_GotFocus event procedure to deal with. Second, Visual Basic passes to this one event procedure the value of the Index property for the element of the control array that has just received the focus. We may wish to respond in the same manner whenever any element of *txtBox*( ) has the focus, in which case we simply ignore the value of *Index*. If, on the other hand, we wish to respond in different ways, depending on which element has the focus, then we write the GotFocus event procedure in the form

```
Private Sub txtBox_GotFocus(Index As Integer)
   Select Case Index
      Case 0
         action when txtBox( ) gets the focus
      Case 1
         action when txtBox(1) gets the focus . .
   End Select
End Sub
```

In general, all event procedures for a control array have the additional parameter Index As Integer. This additional parameter can be used, if desired, to base the action taken by the event procedure on which element of the control array underwent the event.

EXAMPLE 2

The following program creates an electronic dialing pad. The form contains a control array of 10 command buttons. Each time a command button is clicked, the Index parameter conveys the digit to be added onto the phone number. This program illustrates using the Index parameter without employing a Select Case statement.

Object	Property	Setting
frm7_3_2	Caption	(blank)
cmdDigit( )	Index	0 to 9
Caption	(same as Index)	
lblPhoneNum	BorderStyle	1 - Fixed Single
Caption	(blank)	

```
Private Sub cmdDigit_Click(Index As Integer)
   lblPhoneNum.Caption = lblPhoneNum.Caption & Right(str(index), 1)
   If Len(lblPhoneNum.Caption) = 3 Then
      lblPhoneNum.Caption = lblPhoneNum.Caption & "-"
   ElseIf Len(lblPhoneNum.Caption) = 8 Then
      MsgBox "Dialing ...", , ""
      lblPhoneNum.Caption = ""
   End If
End Sub
```

■ CREATING CONTROL ARRAYS AT RUN TIME

We have discussed the process for creating an entire control array while designing a form, that is, at design time. However, copying and positioning control array elements can become tedious if the number of elements is large. Also, the actual number of elements needed in a control array may not be known until a response from the user is processed at run time. In light of these concerns, Visual Basic provides a solution via the Load statement that only requires us to create the first element of a control array during design time. The remaining elements are then created as needed at run time. Before we discuss creating arrays at run time, we must consider a preliminary topic—the Left, Top, Width, and Height properties of controls. These properties specify the location and size of controls.

The standard unit of measurement in Visual Basic is called a **twip**. There are about 1440 twips to the inch. At design time, when a control is active the two panels on the right side of the toolbar give the location and size of the control, respectively. Figure 6-6(a) shows an active text box, named Text1. The first panel says that the left side of the text box is 960 twips from the left side of the form, and the top of the text box is 720 twips down from the title bar of the form. In terms of properties, Text1.Left is 960, and Text1.Top is 720. Similarly, the numbers 1935 and 975 in the second panel give the width and height of the text box in twips. In terms of properties, Text1.Width is 1935 and Text1.Height is 975. Figure 6-6(b) shows the meanings of these four properties.

The location and size properties of a control can be altered at run time with statements such as

```
Text1.Left = 480
```

which moves the text box to the left or

```
Text2.Top = Text1.Top + 1.5 * Text1.Height
```

which places Text2 a comfortable distance below Text1. As a result of the second statement, the distance between the two text boxes will be half the height of Text1.

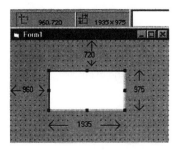
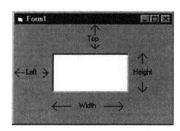

FIGURE 6-6   *The Location and Size of a Control*

If *controlName* is the name of a control whose Index property was assigned a value during form design (thus creating the beginnings of a control array) and *num* is a whole number that has not yet been used as an index for the *controlName*( ) array, then the statement

```
Load controlName(num)
```

copies all the properties of *controlName*(0), including the Top and Left properties, and creates the element *controlName*(*num*) of the *controlName*( ) array. The only property of *controlName(num)* that may differ from that of *controlName*(0) is the Visible property. The Load statement always sets the Visible property of the created element to False. After creating a new element of a control array, you will want to adjust the Top and Left properties so that the new element has its own unique location on the form, and then set the Visible property of the new element to True.

EXAMPLE 3

Write a program to create a control array of 12 labels and a control array of 12 text boxes. Position the labels and text boxes so that they form two columns, with the labels to the left of the text boxes and the text boxes one immediately below the other. Use text boxes whose height is as small as possible. Use labels whose height is just large enough to display a single line. Assign the captions Jan, Feb, and so on, to the labels.

SOLUTION:

When designing the form, we place the first label to the left of the first text box and set the Index property of both controls to 0. The height of the shortest text box is 288 units and the height of a label just tall enough for a single line is 252 units. We use the text box's Height property as the unit of vertical spacing for both the new text box elements and the new label elements. The following is the form at design time and at run time.

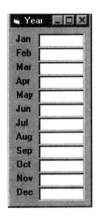

Object	Property	Setting
frm 7_3_3	Caption	Year
lblMonth()	Index	0
Caption	Jan	
Height	252	
txtInfo()	Index	0
Text	(blank)	
Height	288	

```
Private Sub Form_Load()
   Dim i As Integer, monthNames As String
   monthNames = "FebMarAprMayJunJulAugSepOctNovDec"
   For i = 1 To 11
      Load lblMonth(i)
      Load txtInfo(i)
      lblMonth(i).Top = lblMonth(i - 1).Top +
      txtInfo(0).Height txtInfo(i).Top = txtInfo(i - 1).Top + txtinfo(0).Height
      lblMonth(i).Caption = Mid(monthNames, 3 * i - 2, 3)
      lblMonth(i).Visible = True
      txtInfo(i).Visible = True
   Next i
End Sub
```

COMMENTS

1. In the discussion and examples of control arrays, the initial index was always 0. For a particular application it may be more natural to have the lowest index of a control array be 1 or even 1995. To achieve this when creating just the first element at design time and the remaining controls at run time, set the Index property of the first element to the desired lowest index value at design time, then Load the other elements using the desired indexes at run time. (The Load statement copies the properties of the element with the lowest index, whatever that lowest index may be.) For example, at design time you might create *txtSales*(1995) and then at run time execute the statements

```
For yearNum = 1996 to 2005
  Load txtSales(yearNum)
Next yearNum
```

To create an entire control array at design time with indexes starting at a value other than 0, first create the control array using an initial index of 0. Once all elements have been created, use the Properties window to adjust the index of each element of the control array, starting with the element having the highest index.

6.4 SORTING AND SEARCHING

A **sort** is an algorithm for ordering an array. Of the many different techniques for sorting an array we discuss two, the **bubble sort** and the **Shell sort**. Both require the interchange of values stored in a pair of variables. If *var1, var2,* and *temp* are all variables of the same data type (such as all String), then the statements

```
temp = var1
    var1 = var2
var2 = temp
```

assign *var1*'s value to *var2*, and *var2*'s value to *var1*.

EXAMPLE 1

Write a program to alphabetize two words supplied in text boxes.

SOLUTION:

```
Private Sub cmdAlphabetize_Click()
  Dim firstWord As String, secondWord As String, temp As String
  'Alphabetize two words
  firstWord = txtFirstWord.Text
  secondWord = txtSecondWord.Text
  If firstWord > secondWord Then
    temp = firstWord
    firstWord = secondWord
    secondWord = temp
  End If
  picResult.Cls
  picResult.Print firstWord; " before "; secondWord
End Sub
```

[Run, type the following text shown into the text boxes, and click the command button.]

■ BUBBLE SORT

The bubble sort is an algorithm that compares adjacent items and swaps those that are out of order. If this process is repeated enough times, the list will be ordered. Let's carry out this process on the list Pebbles, Barney, Wilma, Fred, Dino. The steps for each pass through the list are as follows:

1. Compare the first and second items. If they are out of order, swap them.

2. Compare the second and third items. If they are out of order, swap them.

3. Repeat this pattern for all remaining pairs. The final comparison and possible swap are between the second-to-last and last elements.

The first time through the list, this process is repeated to the end of the list. This is called the first pass. After the first pass, the last item (Wilma) will be in its proper position. Therefore, the second pass does not have to consider it and so requires one less comparison. At the end of the second pass, the last two items will be in their proper position. (The items that must have reached their proper position have been underlined.) Each successive pass requires one less comparison. After four passes, the last four items will be in their proper positions, and hence, the first will be also.

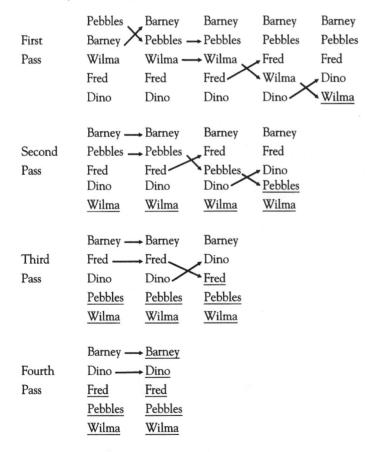

EXAMPLE 2

Write a program to alphabetize the names Pebbles, Barney, Wilma, Fred, Dino.

SOLUTION:

Sorting the list requires a pair of nested loops. The inner loop performs a single pass, and the outer loop controls the number of passes.

```
Dim nom(1 To 5) As String

Private Sub cmdSort_Click()
  Dim passNum As Integer, i As Integer, temp As String
  'Bubble sort names
  For passNum = 1 To 4 'Number of passes is 1 less than number of items
    For i = 1 To 5 - passNum 'Each pass needs 1 less comparison
      If nom(i) > nom(i + 1) Then
        temp = nom(i)
        nom(i) = nom(i + 1)
        nom(i + 1) = temp
      End If
    Next i
  Next passNum
  'Display alphabetized list
    picNames.Cls
  For i = 1 To 5
  picNames.Print nom(i),
  Next i
End Sub


Private Sub Form_Load()
  'Fill array with names
  nom(1) = "Pebbles"
  nom(2) = "Barney"
  nom(3) = "Wilma"
  nom(4) = "Fred"
  nom(5) = "Dino"
End Sub
```

[Run, and click the command button.]

EXAMPLE 3

Table 6.2 contains facts about the 10 most populous metropolitan areas with listings in ascending order by city name. Sort the table in descending order by population.

TABLE 6.2
The 10 Most Populous Metropolitan Areas

Metro Area	Population in Millions	Median Income per Household	% Native to State	% Advanced Degree
Boston	4.2	$40,666	73	12
Chicago	8.1	$35,918	73	8
Dallas	3.9	$32,825	64	8
Detroit	4.7	$34,729	76	7

Houston	3.7	$31,488	67	8
Los Angeles	14.5	$36,711	59	8
New York	18.1	$38,445	73	11
Philadelphia	5.9	$35,797	70	8
San Francisco	6.3	$41,459	60	11
Washington	3.9	$47,254	32	17

Note: Column 4 gives the percentage of residents who were born in their current state of residence. Column 5 gives the percentage of residents age 25 or older with a graduate or professional degree.

Source: The 1990 Census

SOLUTION:

Data are read from a file into parallel arrays by the Form_Load event procedure. When cmdDisplayStats is clicked, the collection of parallel arrays is sorted based on the array *pop*( ). Each time two items are interchanged in the array *pop*( ), the corresponding items are interchanged in each of the other arrays. This way, for each city, the items of information remain linked by a common subscript.

```
Dim city(1 To 10) As String, pop(1 To 10) As Single, income(1 To 10) As Single
Dim natives(1 To 10) As Single, advDeg(1 To 10) As Single

Private Sub cmdDisplayStats_Click()
  Call SortData
  Call ShowData
  End Sub
  Private Sub Form_Load()
  Dim i As Integer
  'Assume the data for city name, population, medium income, % native,
  'and % advanced degree have been placed in the file "CITYSTAT.TXT"
  '(First line of file is "Boston", 4.2, 40666, 73, 12)
  Open "CITYSTAT.TXT" For Input As #1
  For i = 1 To 10
    Input #1, city(i), pop(i), income(i), natives(i), advDeg(i)
  Next i
  Close #1
End Sub

Private Sub ShowData()
  Dim i As Integer
  'Display ordered table
  picTable.Cls
  picTable.Print , "Pop. in", "Med. income", "% Native", "% Advanced"
  picTable.Print "Metro Area", "millions", "per hsd", "to State", "Degree"
  picTable.Print For i = 1 To 10
    picTable.Print city(i); Tab(16); pop(i), income(i), natives(i), advDeg(i)
  Next i
End Sub

Private Sub SortData()
  Dim passNum As Integer, index As Integer
  'Bubble sort table in descending order by population
  For passNum = 1 To 9
    For index = 1 To 10 - passNum
      If pop(index) < pop(index + 1) Then Call
        SwapData(index)
      End If
    Next index
  Next passNum
End Sub
```

```
Private Sub SwapData(index As Integer)
  'Swap entries
  Call SwapStr(city(index), city(index + 1))
  Call SwapNum(pop(index), pop(index + 1))
  Call SwapNum(income(index), income(index + 1))
  Call SwapNum(natives(index), natives(index + 1))
  Call SwapNum(advDeg(index), advDeg(index + 1))
End Sub

Private Sub SwapNum(a As Single, b As Single)
  Dim temp As Single
  'Interchange values of a and b
  temp = a
  a = b
  b = temp
End Sub

Private Sub SwapStr(a As String, b As String)
  Dim temp As String
  'Interchange values of a and b
  temp = a
  a = b
  b = temp
End Sub
```

[Run, and click the command button.]

■ SHELL SORT

The bubble sort is easy to understand and program. However, it is too slow for really long lists. The Shell sort, named for its inventor, Donald L. Shell, is much more efficient in such cases. It compares distant items first and works its way down to nearby items. The interval separating the compared items is called the **gap**. The gap begins at one-half the length of the list and is successively halved until eventually each item is compared with its neighbor as in the bubble sort. The algorithm for a list of n items is as follows:

1. Begin with a gap of $g = \text{Int}(n / 2)$.
2. Compare items 1 and $1 + g$, 2 and $2 + g$, . . . , $n - g$ and n. Swap any pairs that are out of order.
3. Repeat Step 2 until no swaps are made for gap g.
4. Halve the value of g.
5. Repeat Steps 2, 3, and 4 until the value of g is 0.

The Shell sort is illustrated in what follows. Crossing arrows indicate that a swap occurred.
Initial Gap = Int([Number of Items] / 2) = Int(5 / 2) = 2

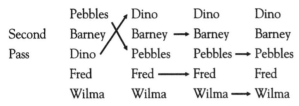

First
Pass

Because there was a swap, use the same gap for the second pass.

Second
Pass

Again, there was a swap, so keep the current gap.

Third
Pass

There were no swaps for the current gap of 2, so

Next Gap = Int([Previous Gap] / 2) = Int(2 / 2) = 1

Fourth
Pass

Because there was a swap (actually two swaps), keep the same gap.

Fifth
Pass

Because there were no swaps for the current gap, then

Next Gap = Int([Previous Gap] / 2) = Int(1 / 2) = 0

and the Shell sort is complete.

Notice that the Shell sort required 14 comparisons to sort the list whereas the bubble sort required only 10 comparisons for the same list. This illustrates the fact that for very short lists, the bubble sort is preferable; however, for lists of 30 items or more, the Shell sort will consistently outperform the bubble sort. Table 6.3 shows the average number of comparisons required to sort arrays of varying sizes.

TABLE 6.3
Efficiency of Bubble and Shell Sorts

Array Elements	Bubble Sort Comparisons	Shell Sort Comparisons
5	10	15
10	45	57
15	105	115
20	190	192
25	300	302
30	435	364
50	1225	926
100	4950	2638
500	124,750	22,517
1000	499,500	58,460

EXAMPLE 4

Use the Shell sort to alphabetize the parts of a running shoe (see Figure 6-7).

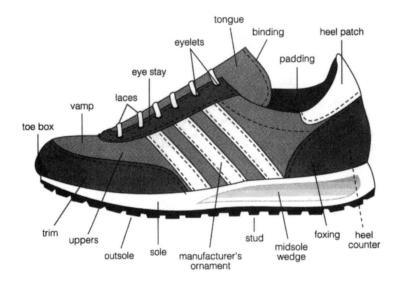

FIGURE 6-7   *Running Shoe*

SOLUTION:
In the following program, the data are read into an array that has been dimensioned so as to guarantee more than enough space. In the event procedure Form_Load, the variable *numParts* provides the subscripts for the array and serves as a counter. The final value of *numParts* is available to all procedures because the variable was created in the (Declarations) section of (General). The Sub procedure SortData uses a flag to indicate if a swap has been made during a pass.

```
Dim part(1 To 50) As String
Dim numParts As Integer

Private Sub cmdDisplayParts_Click()
   'Sort and display parts of running shoe
   Call SortData
   Call ShowData
End Sub

Private Sub Form_Load()
   'Read part names numParts = 0 'Number of parts
```

```
    Open "SHOEPART.TXT"
    For Input As #1
    Do While (Not EOF(1)) And (numParts < UBound(part))
       numParts = numParts + 1
       Input #1, part(numParts)
    Loop
    Close #1
End Sub

Private Sub ShowData()
    Dim i As Integer 'Display sorted list of parts
    picParts.Cls
    For i = 1 To numParts
       picParts.Print part(i),
       If i Mod 5 = 0 Then 'only put 5 items per line
          picParts.Print
       End If
    Next i
End Sub

Private Sub SortData()
    Dim gap As Integer, doneFlag As Boolean
    Dim index As Integer, temp As String
    'Shell sort shoe parts
    gap = Int(numParts / 2)
    Do While gap >= 1
       Do
          doneFlag = True
          For index = 1 To numParts - gap
             If part(index) > part(index + gap)
                Then temp = part(index)
                part(index) = part(index + gap)
                part(index + gap) = temp
                doneFlag = False
             End If
          Next index
       Loop Until doneFlag = True 'Can also be written Loop Until doneFlag
       gap = Int(gap / 2) 'Halve the length of the gap
    Loop
End Sub
```

[Run and click the command button.]

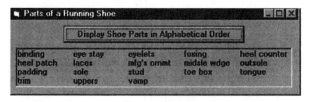

■ SEARCHING

Suppose we had an array of 1000 names in alphabetical order and wanted to locate a specific person in the list. One approach would be to start with the first name and consider each name until a match was found. This process is called a **sequential search**. We would find a person whose name begins with "A" rather quickly, but 1000 comparisons might be necessary to find a person whose name begins with "Z." For much longer lists, searching could be a time-consuming matter. However, when the list has already been sorted into either ascending or descending order, there is a method, called a **binary search**, that shortens the task considerably.

Let us refer to the sought item as *quarry*. The binary search looks for *quarry* by determining in which half of the list it lies. The other half is then discarded, and the retained half is temporarily regarded as the entire list. The process is repeated until the item is found. A flag can indicate if *quarry* has been found.

The algorithm for a binary search of an ascending list is as follows (Figure 6-8 shows the flowchart for a binary search):

1. At each stage, denote the subscript of the first item in the retained list by *first* and the subscript of the last item by *last*. Initially, the value of *first* is 1, the value of *last* is the number of items in the list, and the value of *flag* is False.

2. Look at the middle item of the current list, the item having the subscript *middle* = Int((*first* + *last*) / 2).

3. If the middle item is *quarry*, then *flag* is set to True and the search is over.

4. If the middle item is greater than *quarry*, then *quarry* should be in the first half of the list. So the subscript of *quarry* must lie between *first* and *middle* [minus] 1. That is, the new value of *last* is *middle* – 1.

5. If the middle item is less than *quarry*, then *quarry* should be in the second half of the list of possible items. So the subscript of *quarry* must lie between *middle* + 1 and *last*. That is, the new value of *first* is *middle* + 1.

6. Repeat Steps 2 through 5 until *quarry* is found or until the halving process uses up the entire list. (When the entire list has been used up, *first* > *last*.) In the second case, *quarry* was not in the original list.

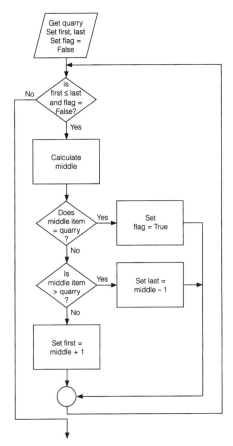

FIGURE 6-8 *Flowchart for a Binary Search*

EXAMPLE 5

In the following program the array *firm*( ) contains the alphabetized names of up to 100 corporations. The program requests the name of a corporation as input and uses a binary search to determine whether or not the corporation is in the array.

```
Dim firm(1 TO 100) As String
Dim numFirms As Integer

Private Sub BinarySearch(corp As String, result As String)
   Dim foundFlag As Boolean
   Dim first As Integer, middle As Integer, last As Integer
   'Array firm() assumed already ordered alphabetically
   'Binary search of firm() for corp
   foundFlag = False
   first = 1
   last = numFirms
   Do While (first <= last) And (Not foundFlag)
      middle = Int((first + last) / 2)
      Select Case UCase(firm(middle))
         Case corp
            foundFlag = True
         Case Is > corp
            last = middle - 1
         Case Is <
            corp first = middle + 1
      End Select
   Loop
   If foundFlag Then
         result = "found"
      Else
         result = "not found"
      End If
End Sub

Private Sub cmdSearch_Click()
   Dim corp As String, result As String
   corp = UCase(Trim(txtCorporation.Text))
   Call BinarySearch(corp, result)
   'Display results of search
   picResult.Cls
   picResult.Print corp; " "; result
End Sub

Private Sub Form_Load()
   'Fill array with data from FIRMS.TXT
   Open "FIRMS.TXT" For Input As #1 'Contains up to 100 companies
   numFirms = 0
   Do While (Not EOF(1)) And (numFirms < UBound(firm))
       numFirms = numFirms + 1
       Input #1, firm(numFirms)
   Loop Close #1
End Sub
```

Run, type IBM into the text box, and click the command button.]

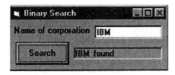

Suppose the array contains 100 corporations and the corporation input in Example 5 is in the second half of the array. On the first pass, *middle* would be assigned Int((1 + 100)/2) = Int(50.5) = 50 and then *first* would be altered to 50 + 1 = 51. On the second pass, *middle* would be assigned Int((51 + 100)/2) = Int(75.5) = 75. If the corporation is not the array element with subscript 75, then either *last* would be assigned 74 or *first* would be assigned 76, depending on whether the corporation appears before or after the 75th element. Each pass through the loop halves the range of subscripts containing the corporation until the corporation is located.

In Example 5, the binary search merely reported whether or not an array contained a certain item. After finding the item, its array subscript was not needed. However, if related data are stored in parallel arrays (as in Table 6.2), the subscript of the found item can be used to retrieve the related information in the other arrays. This process, called a **table lookup**, is used in the following example.

EXAMPLE 6

Use a binary search procedure to locate the data for a city from Example 3 requested by the user.

SOLUTION:
The following program does not include a sort of the data file CITYSTAT.TXT because the file is already ordered alphabetically.

```
Dim city(1 To 10) As String, pop(1 To 10) As Single, income(1 To 10) As Single
Dim natives(1 To 10) As Single, advDeg(1 To 10) As Single

Private Sub cmdDisplayStats_Click()
   Dim searchCity As String, result As Integer
   'Search for city in the metropolitan areas table
   Call GetCityName(searchCity)
   Call FindCity(searchCity, result)
   picResult.Cls
   If result > 0 Then
      Call ShowData(result)
   Else
      picResult.Print searchCity & " not in file"
   End If
End Sub

Private Sub FindCity(searchCity As String, result As Integer)
   Dim first As Integer, middle As Integer, last As Integer
   Dim foundFlag As Boolean
   'Binary search table for city name
   first = 1
   last = 10
   foundFlag = False
   Do While (first <= last) And (Not foundFlag)
      middle = Int((first + last) / 2)
      Select Case UCase(city(middle))
         Case searchCity
            foundFlag = True
         Case Is > searchCity
```

```
            last = middle - 1
         Case Is < searchCity
            first = middle + 1
      End Select
   Loop
      If foundFlag Then
         result = middle
      Else
         result = 0
      End If
End Sub

Private Sub Form_Load()
   Dim i As Integer
   'Assume that the data for city name, population, medium income, % native,
   'and % advanced degree have been placed in the file "CITYSTAT.TXT"
   '(First line of file is "Boston", 4.2, 4066, 73, 12)
   Open "CITYSTAT.TXT" For Input As #1
   For i = 1 To 10
      Input #1, city(i), pop(i), income(i), natives(i), advDeg(i)
   Next i
   Close #1
End Sub

Private Sub GetCityName(searchCity As String)
   'Request name of city as input
   searchCity = UCase(Trim(txtCity.Text))
End Sub

Private Sub ShowData(index As Integer)
   'Display city and associated information
   picResult.Print , "Pop. in", "Med. income", "% Native", "% Advanced"
   picResult.Print "Metro Area", "millions", "per hsd", "to State", "Degree"
   picResult.Print picResult.Print city(index), pop(index), income(index),
   picResult.Print natives(index), advDeg(index)
End Sub
```

[Run, type San Francisco into the text box, and click the command button.]

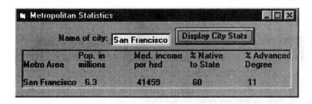

COMMENTS

1. Suppose our bubble sort algorithm is applied to an ordered list. The algorithm will still make $n - 1$ passes through the list. The process could be shortened for some lists by flagging the presence of out-of-order items as in the Shell sort. It may be preferable not to use a flag, because for greatly disordered lists the flag would slow down an already sluggish algorithm.

2. In Example 3, parallel arrays already ordered by one field were sorted by another field. Usually, parallel arrays are sorted by the field to be searched when accessing the file. This field is called the **key field**.

3. Suppose an array of 2000 items is searched sequentially—that is, one item after another—in order to locate a specific item. The number of comparisons would vary from 1 to 2000, with an average of 1000. With a binary search, the number of comparisons would be at most 11 because $2^{11} > 2000$.

4. The built-in function UCase converts all the characters in a string to uppercase. UCase is useful in sorting and searching arrays of strings when the alphabetic case (upper or lower) is unimportant. For instance, Example 5 includes UCase in the Select Case comparisons, and so the binary search will locate "Mobil" in the array even if the user entered "MOBIL".

5. The Visual Basic function Timer can be used to determine the speed of a sort. Precede the sort with the statement t = Timer. After the sort has executed, the statement picOutput.Print Timer – t will display the duration of the sort in seconds.

6.5 TWO-DIMENSIONAL ARRAYS

Each array discussed so far held a single list of items. Such array variables are called **single-subscripted variables**. An array can also hold the contents of a table with several rows and columns. Such arrays are called **two-dimensional arrays** or **double-subscripted variables**. Two tables follow. Table 6.4 gives the road mileage between certain cities. It has four rows and four columns. Table 6.5 shows the leading universities in three disciplines. It has three rows and five columns.

TABLE 6.4
Road Mileage Between Selected U.S. Cities

	Chicago	Los Angeles	New York	Philadelphia
Chicago	0	2054	802	738
Los Angeles	2054	0	2786	2706
New York	802	2786	0	100
Philadelphia	738	2706	100	0

TABLE 6.5
University Rankings

	1	2	3	4	5
Business	U of PA	U of IN	U of MI	UC Berk	U of VA
Comp Sci.	MIT	Cng-Mellon	UC Berk	Cornell	U of IL
Engr/Gen.	U of IL	U of OK	U of MD	Cng-Mellon	CO Sch. of Mines

Source: A Rating of Undergraduate Programs in American and International Universities, Dr. Jack Gourman, 1998

Two-dimensional array variables store the contents of tables. They have the same types of names as other array variables. The only difference is that they have two subscripts, each with its own range. The range of the first subscript is determined by the number of rows in the table, and the range of the second subscript is determined by the number of columns. The statement

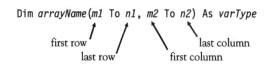

```
Dim arrayName(m1 To n1, m2 To n2) As varType
```
first row   last row   first column   last column

dimensions an array of type *varType* corresponding to a table with rows labeled from $m1$ To $n1$ and columns labeled from $m2$ To $n2$. The entry in the jth row, kth column is *arrayName* (j,k). For instance, the data in Table 6.4 can be stored in an array named rm( ). The statement

```
Dim rm(1 To 4, 1 To 4) As Single
```

will dimension the array. Each element of the array has the form *rm(row, column)*. The entries of the array are

rm(1,1)=0	rm(1,2)=2054	rm(1,3)=802	rm(1,4)=738
rm(2,1)=2054	rm(2,2)=0	rm(2,3)=2786	rm(2,4)=2706
rm(3,1)=802	rm(3,2)=2786	rm(3,3)=0	rm(3,4)=100
rm(4,1)=738	rm(4,2)=2706	rm(4,3)=100	rm(4,4)=0

As with one-dimensional arrays, when a two-dimensional array is created using Dim in the (Declarations) section of (General), the array becomes a form-level subscripted variable, and is therefore accessible in all event procedures and general procedures and retains whatever values are assigned until the program is terminated. Two-dimensional arrays also can be created with Dim that are local to a procedure and cease to exist once the procedure is exited. When the range of the subscripts is given by one or more variables, the proper statement to use is

```
ReDim arrayName(m1 To n1, m2 To n2) As varType
```

The data in Table 7.10 can be stored in a two-dimensional string array named *univ*( ). The statement

```
Dim univ(1 To 3, 1 To 5) As String
```

will dimension the array as form-level. Some of the entries of the array are

univ(1,1) = "U of PA"
univ(2,3) = "UC Berk"
univ(3,5) = "CO Sch. of Mines"

EXAMPLE 1

Write a program to store and access the data from Table 6.4.

SOLUTION:

Data are read from the data file DISTANCE.TXT into a two-dimensional form-level array using a pair of nested loops. The outer loop controls the rows and the inner loop controls the columns.

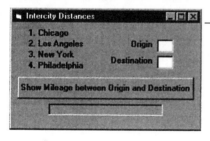

Object	Property	Setting
frmDist	Caption	Intercity Distances
lblCh	Caption	1. Chicago
lblLA	Caption	2. Los Angeles
lblNY	Caption	3. New York
lblPh	Caption	4. Philadelphia
lblOrig	Caption	Origin
txtOrig	Text	(blank)
lblDest	Caption	Destination
txtDest	Text	(blank)
cmdShow	Caption	Show Mileage between Origin and Destination
picMiles		

```
Dim rm(1 To 4, 1 To 4) As Single 'In (Declarations) section of (General)
    Private Sub cmdShow_Click()
    Dim row As Integer, col As Integer
    'Determine road mileage between cities
    row = Val(txtOrig.Text)
    col = Val(txtDest.Text)
```

```
  If (row>= 1 And row <= 4) And (col >= 1 And col <= 4)
    Then
      Call ShowMileage(rm(), row, col)
    Else
      MsgBox "Origin and Destination must be numbers from 1 to 4", , "Error"
  End If
  txtOrig.SetFocus
End Sub

Private Sub Form_Load()
  Dim row As Integer, col As Integer
  'Fill two-dimensional array with intercity mileages
  'Assume the data have been placed in the file "DISTANCE.TXT"
  '(First line of the file is 0, 54, 802, 738)
  Open "DISTANCE.TXT" For Input As #1
  For row = 1 To 4
    For col = 1 To 4
      Input #1, rm(row, col)
    Next col
  Next row
  Close #1
End Sub

Private Sub ShowMileage(rm() As Single, row As Integer, col As Integer)
  'Display mileage between cities
  picMiles.Cls
  picMiles.Print "The road mileage is"; rm(row, col)
End Sub
```

[Run, type 3 into the Origin box, type 1 into the Destination box, and click the command button.]

So far, two-dimensional arrays have been used only to store data for convenient lookup. In the next example, an array is used to make a valuable computation.

EXAMPLE 2

The Center for Science in the Public Interest publishes *The Nutrition Scorebook*, a highly respected rating of foods. The top two foods in each of five categories are shown in Table 6.6 along with some information on their composition. Write a program to compute the nutritional content of a meal. The table should be read into an array and then the program should request the quantities of each food item that is part of the meal. The program should then compute the amounts of each nutritional component consumed by summing each column with each entry weighted by the quantity of the food item.

TABLE 6.6
Composition of 10 Top-Rated Foods

	Calories	Protein (grams)	Fat (grams)	Vit A(IU)	Calcium (mg)
spinach (1 cup)	23	3	0.3	8100	93
sweet potato (1 med.)	160	2	1	9230	46
yogurt (8 oz.)	230	10	3	120	343
skim milk (1 cup)	85	8	0	500	302
whole wheat bread (1 slice)	65	3	1	0	24
brown rice (1 cup)	178	3.8	0.9	0	18
watermelon (1 wedge)	110	2	1	2510	30
papaya (1 lg.)	156	2.4	0.4	7000	80
tuna in water (1 lb)	575	126.8	3.6	0	73
lobster (1 med.)	405	28.8	26.6	984	190

SOLUTION:

Coding is simplified by using a control array of labels to hold the food names and a control array of text boxes to hold the amount input by the user. In the following template, the label captions have been assigned an initial value "(food name)" so that the labels can be seen. The five nutrients of interest and the actual names and nutrient values of the foods to be used in building a meal are read from the data file NUTTABLE.TXT.

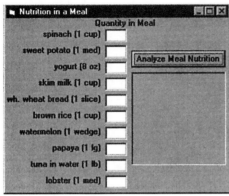

Object	Property	Setting
frmMeal	Caption	Nutrition in a Meal
lblFood()	Caption	(food name)
	Index	0 – 9
lblQnty	Caption	Quantity in Meal
txtQnty()	Text	(blank)
	Index	0 – 9
cmdAnalyze	Caption	Analyze Meal Nutrition
picAnalysis		

```
Dim nutName(1 To 5) As String 'nutrient names
Dim nutTable(1 To 10, 1 To 5) As Single 'nutrient values for each food

Private Sub cmdAnalyze_Click()
   'Determine the nutritional content of a meal
   Dim quantity(1 To 10) As Single 'amount of food in meal
   Call GetAmounts(quantity())
   Call ShowData(quantity())
End Sub

Private Sub Form_Load()
   Dim i As Integer, j As Integer, foodName As String
   'Fill arrays; assign label captions
   Open "NUTTABLE.TXT" For Input As #1
   For i = 1 To 5
     Input #1, nutName(i)
   Next i
   For i = 1 To 10
     Input #1, foodName
     lblFood(i - 1).Caption = foodName
     For j = 1 To 5
       Input #1, nutTable(i, j)
     Next j
   Next i
   Close #1
End Sub

Private Sub GetAmounts(quantity() As Single)
   Dim i As Integer
   'Obtain quantities of foods consumed
     For i = 1 To 10 quantity(i) = Val(txtQnty(i - 1).Text)
   Next i
End Sub

Private Sub ShowData(quantity() As Single)
   Dim col As Integer, row As Integer
```

```
Dim amount As Single, nutWid As Single
'Display amount of each component
picAnalysis.Cls
picAnalysis.Print "This meal contains the"
picAnalysis.Print "following quantities"
picAnalysis.Print "of these nutritional"
picAnalysis.Print "components:"
picAnalysis.Print For col = 1 To 5
  amount = 0
    For row = 1 To 10
      amount = amount + quantity(row) * nutTable(row, col)
    Next row
  picAnalysis.Print nutName(col) & ":"; Tab(16); amount
Next col
End Sub
```

[Run, type the following quantities into each text box, and click the command button.]

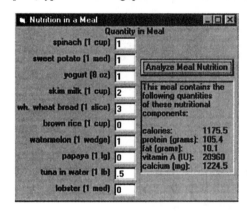

COMMENT

1. We can define three- (or higher-) dimensional arrays much as we do two-dimensional arrays. A three-dimensional array uses three subscripts, and the assignment of values requires a triple-nested loop. As an example, a meteorologist might use a three-dimensional array to record temperatures for various dates, times, and elevations. The array might be created by the statement

```
Dim temps(1 To 31, 1 To 24, 0 To 14) As Single
```

6.6 A CASE STUDY: CALCULATING WITH A SPREADSHEET

Spreadsheets are one of the most popular types of software used on personal computers. A spreadsheet is a financial planning tool in which data are analyzed in a table of rows and columns. Some of the items are entered by the user. Other items, often totals and balances, are calculated using the entered data. The outstanding feature of electronic spreadsheets is their ability to recalculate an entire table after changes are made in some of the entered data, thereby allowing the user to determine the financial implications of various alternatives. This is called "What if?" analysis.

■ THE DESIGN OF THE PROGRAM

Figure 6-9 contains an example of a spreadsheet used to analyze a student's financial projections for the four quarters of a year. Column F holds the sum of the entries in columns B through E, rows 6 and 14 hold sums of the entries in rows 3 through 5 and 9 through 13, respectively, and row 16 holds the differences of the entries in rows 6 and 14. Because the total balance is negative, some of the amounts in the spreadsheet must be changed and the totals and balances recalculated.

	A	B	C	D	E	F
1		**Fall**	**Winter**	**Spring**	**Summer**	**Total**
2	**Income**					
3	Job	1000	1300	1000	2000	5300
4	Parents	200	200	200	0	600
5	Scholarship	150	150	150	0	450
6	**Total**	1350	1650	1350	2000	6350
7						
8	**Expenses**					
9	**Tuition**	400	0	400	0	800
10	**Food**	650	650	650	650	2600
11	**Rent**	600	600	600	400	2200
12	**Books**	110	0	120	0	230
13	**Misc**	230	210	300	120	860
14	Total	1990	1460	2070	1170	6690
15						
16	**Balance**	−640	190	−720	830	−340

FIGURE 6-9   *Spreadsheet for Student's Financial Projections*

The 96 locations in the spreadsheet that hold information are called **cells**. Each cell is identified by its row number and column letter. For instance, cell 14, C contains the amount 1460. For programming purposes, each column is identified by a number, starting with 1 for the leftmost column. Thus cell 14, C will be cell 14, 3 in our program.

This case study develops a program to produce a spreadsheet with the five columns of numbers shown in Figure 6-11, three user-specified categories of income, and five user-specified categories of expenses. The following tasks are to be selected by command buttons:

1. Start a new spreadsheet. All current category names and values are erased and the cursor is placed in the text box of the first income category.
2. Quit.

Three additional tasks need to be performed as the result of other events:

1. Create the spreadsheet when the form is loaded.
2. Limit the user to editing category names and quarterly values.
3. Display totals after a change is made in the spreadsheet.

■ THE USER INTERFACE

Each cell in the spreadsheet will be an element of a text box control array. A control array of labels is needed for the numeric labels to the left of each row and another control array of labels for the alphabetic labels at the top of each column. Finally, two command buttons are required. The task of controlling which cells the user can edit will be handled by a GotFocus event. The task of updating the totals will be handled by a LostFocus event. Figure 6-10 shows one possible form design with all control elements loaded. For this application of a spreadsheet, the headings that have been assigned to cells in rows 1, 2, 6, 8, 14, and 16 are fixed; the user will not be allowed to edit them. The other entries in column A, the category names, may be edited by the user, but we have provided the set from Figure 6-9 as the default.

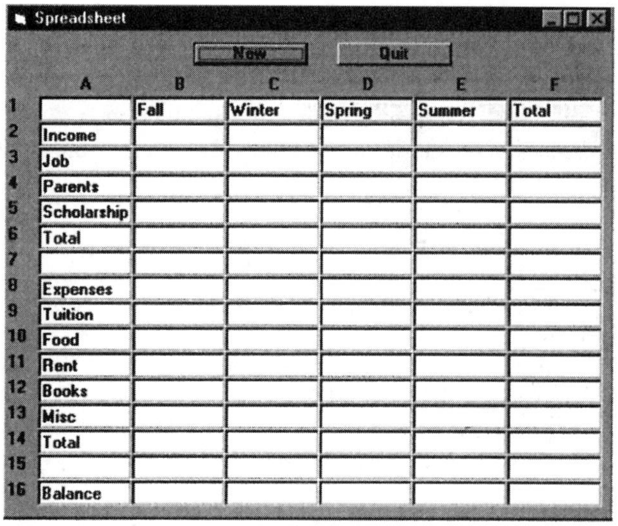

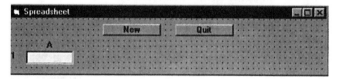

FIGURE 6-10   *Template for Spreadsheet*

Because processing the totals for the spreadsheet involves adding columns and rows of cells, coding is simplified by using a control array of text boxes so that an index in a For...Next loop can step through a set of cells. A two-dimensional array of text boxes seems natural for the spreadsheet. Unfortunately, only a single index is available for control arrays in Visual Basic. However, a single dimensional array of text boxes can be used without much difficulty if we define a function Indx that connects a pair of row (1 to 16) and column (1 to 6) values to a unique index (1 to 96) value. An example of such a rule would be Indx(row,column)=(row–1)*6+column. Successive values of this function are generated by going from left to right across row 1, then left to right across row 2, and so on.

A solution to the spreadsheet problem that uses one control array of text boxes and two control arrays of labels follows. The text box control array *txtCell*( ) provides the 96 text boxes needed for the spreadsheet cells. Because the proposed Indx function advances by one as we move from left to right across a row of cells, the cells must be positioned in this order as they are loaded. The label control array *lblRowLab*( ) provides a label for each of the rows of cells, while label control array *lblColLab*( ) provides a label for each column of cells. Figure 6-11 shows the layout of the form at design time. The properties for the controls are given in Table 6.7. The Height and Width properties given for the text box will assure enough room on the screen for all 96 cells. These dimensions can be obtained by creating a normal size text box, then reducing its width by one set of grid marks and its height by two sets of grid marks.

FIGURE 6-11   *Controls at Design Time*

TABLE 6.7
Objects and Their Properties

Object	Property	Setting
frmSpreadsheet	Caption	Spreadsheet
cmdNew	Caption	New
cmdQuit	Caption	Quit
lblRowLab()	Caption	1

Index	1		
lblColLab()	Caption		A
Index	1		
txtCell()	Text		(blank)
Index	1		
Height	1095		
Width	285		

■ CODING THE PROGRAM

The top row of Figure 6-12 shows the different events to which the program must respond. Table 6.8 identifies the corresponding event procedures and the general procedures they call. Let's examine each event procedure.

1. **Form_Load** assigns the number of rows (16) and columns (6) in our spreadsheet to the form-level variables *maxRow* and *maxCol*. Form_Load then calls three general procedures to create and initialize the spreadsheet.

    The procedure CreateSpreadsheet loads each element of the *txtCell( )* control array in order from left to right, top to bottom. Cell 1, which is to be the first cell in the first row, is not loaded because it was created at design time. The Top property of a new cell is set so that the top edge of the new cell overlaps the bottom edge of the previous cell in the column. The Top property of the first cell in a column is not modified, and so the value of the Top property is the same as cell 1. Similarly, the Left property of a new cell is set so that the left edge of the new cell overlaps the right edge of the previous cell in the row. The Left property of the first cell in a row is not modified, and so the value of the Left property is the same as cell 1. CreateSpreadsheet also loads the additional row and column label elements and assigns an appropriate caption. Create-Spreadsheet's final task is to set the Height and Width properties of frm-SpreadSheet to accommodate all the objects that have been loaded. The numbers 500 and 200, which appear in these statements, were obtained by trial and error and are necessary to account for the space used by the form caption and borders.

    The procedure SetStructure assigns heading values to various cells of the spreadsheet in accordance with the specific application we were asked to program. The user will not be able to alter the value in these cells, because the rules for which cells are to be totaled, and where these totals are to be placed are "hard wired" into the program and cannot be changed by the user. SetStructure also assigns values to a set of form-level variables so that other procedures in the program can be coded using meaningful names rather than possibly obscure numbers. Besides Form_Load, SetStructure is also called by the cmdNew_Click event procedure.

    The procedure SetDefaults assigns the income and expense category headings shown in Figure 6-9 to the appropriate cells. The user may change these headings at any time, and must supply them if the "New" command is issued.

2. **txtCell_GotFocus** checks to see if the cell that has received the focus may, according to the rules of this application, be edited by the user. The row and column numbers for the cell are computed from the cell's index. If the cell that has received the focus is in a column after *stopCol*, the last editable column, then the column to be edited is changed to *startCol*, the first editable column, and the row to be edited is advanced by one. If the row to be edited does not contain any editable cells, then the row to be edited is advanced to the next row containing editable cells. (When the focus goes past the last row of editable cells, the next editable row is the first editable row, that is, *incStartRow*.) Finally, focus is set to the adjusted row and column, but only if an adjustment has been made. If the test Indx(row,col)<>Index were not made and focus were reset to a cell that already

had the focus, then the GotFocus event procedure would be invoked again as a result of the SetFocus, and then again as a result of the SetFocus performed by this invocation of GotFocus, and so on, resulting in an infinite loop.

3. **txtCell_LostFocus** invokes the general procedure DisplayTotals when the cursor leaves one of the spreadsheet cells. DisplayTotals in turn invokes five general procedures that each compute one set of needed totals and display the results by assigning values to appropriate text boxes. TotalIncome adds up the income for each quarter and saves the results in the array *iTot*( ). Similarly, TotalExpenses adds up the expenses for each quarter and saves the results in the array *eTot*( ). ComputeBalances takes the results stored in *iTot*( ) and *eTot*( ) and subtracts them to determine the balance for each quarter. TotalRows adds the four quarters for each category and assigns the results to the text boxes at the right end of each row. Finally, DetermineGrandTotals adds the values in *iTot*( ) and *eTot*( ) to determine the values for the right end of the "balance" row and each "total" row.

4. **cmdNew_Click** prepares for the entry of a new spreadsheet by setting the Text property of each element of the control array *txtCell*( ) to the null string and then setting focus to the first cell in the spreadsheet.

5. **cmdQuit_Click** ends the program.

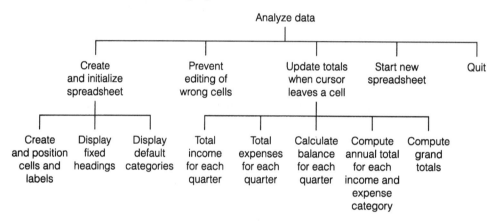

FIGURE 6.12　*Hierarchy Chart for Spreadsheet Program*

TABLE 6.8
Tasks and Their Procedures

1. Create & Initialize spreadsheet Form_Load
   1.1 Create & position cells & labels CreateSpreadsheet
   1.2 Display fixed headings SetStructure
   1.3 Display default categories SetDefaults
2. Prevent editing of wrong cells txtCell_GotFocus
3. Update totals when cursor leaves a cell txtCell_LostFocus (Display Totals)
   3.1 Total income each quarter TotalIncome
   3.2 Total expenses each quarter TotalExpenses
   3.3 Compute balances each quarter ShowBalances
   3.4 Total each income & expense category TotalRows
   3.5 Determine grand totals ShowGrandTotals
4. Start a new spreadsheet cmdNew_Click
5. End program cmdQuit_Click

```
Dim maxCol As Integer                'Number of columns in spreadsheet
    Dim maxRow As Integer            'Number of rows in spreadsheet
    Dim incStartRow As Integer       'Row where income categories begin
    Dim incStopRow As Integer        'Row where income categories end
    Dim incTotRow As Integer         'Row where income total is displayed
    Dim expStartRow As Integer       'Row where expense categories begin
    Dim expStopRow As Integer        'Row where expense categories end
    Dim expTotRow As Integer         'Row where expense total is displayed
    Dim balRow As Integer            'Row where balance is displayed
    Dim startCol As Integer          'Column where numeric data begins
    Dim stopCol As Integer           'Column where numeric data ends
    Dim totCol As Integer            'Column where total for each row is dis-
    played
    'Control Arrays'txtCell()    Control array for data cells
    'lblRowLab() Control array   for numeric row labels
'lblColLab() Control array       for alphabetic column labels

Private Sub cmdNew_Click()
  Dim row As Integer, col As Integer
  'Clear all data and total text boxes
  For col = 1 To maxCol
    For row = 1 To maxRow
      txtCell(Indx(row, col)).Text = ""
    Next row
  Next col
  Call SetStructure
  'Place cursor in first data txtCell
  txtCell(Indx(1, 1)).SetFocus
End Sub


Private Sub cmdQuit_Click()
  End
End Sub


Private Sub CreateSpreadsheet()
  Dim row As Integer, col As Integer, i As Integer
  Dim cellHeight As Single, cellWidth As Single
  Dim cellTop As Single, cellLeft As Single
  cellHeight = txtCell(1).Height
  cellWidth = txtCell(1).Width
  'Create cells For row = 1 To maxRow
    For col = 1 To maxCol
      i = Indx(row, col)
      If Not (col = 1 And row = 1) Then
        Load txtCell(i)
      End If
      If row > 1 Then
        cellTop = txtCell(Indx(row - 1, col)).Top
        txtCell(i).Top = cellTop + cellHeight
      End If
      If col > 1 Then
        cellLeft = txtCell(Indx(row, col - 1)).Left
        txtCell(i).Left = cellLeft + cellWidth
      End If
      txtCell(i).Visible = True
    Next col
```

```
         Next row
         'Create Row Labels
         For row = 2 To maxRow
            Load lblRowLab(row)
            lblRowLab(row).Top = lblRowLab(row - 1).Top + cellHeight
            lblRowLab(row).Caption = LTrim(Str(row))
            lblRowLab(row).Visible = True
         Next row
         'Create Column Labels
         For col = 2 To maxCol
            Load lblColLab(col)
            lblColLab(col).Left = lblColLab(col - 1).Left + cellWidth
            lblColLab(col).Caption = Chr(col + 64)
            lblColLab(col).Visible = True
         Next col 'Set form height and width to accommodate all objects
         i = Indx(maxRow, maxCol)
         frmSpreadsheet.Height = txtCell(i).Top + cellHeight + 500
         frmSpreadsheet.Width = txtCell(i).Left + cellWidth + 200
      End Sub


      Private Sub DisplayTotals()
         ReDim itot(startCol To stopCal) As Single
         ReDim etot(startCol To stopCal) As Single
         'Calculate and show totals for Income each quarter
         Call TotalIncome(itot())
         'Calculate and show totals for Expenses each quarter
         Call TotalExpenses(etot())
         'Calculate and show Balances for each quarter
         Call ShowBalances(itot(), etot())
         'Calculate and show the Total of each Income & Expense category
         Call TotalRows
         'Calculate and show grand totals of quarter totals and balances
         Call ShowGrandTotals(itot(), etot())
      End Sub

         Private Sub Form_Load()
         'Establish number of rows and columns. Trial and error show
         'that a maximum of 20 rows and 8 columns will fit the screen.
         'For this particular application, 16 rows and 6 columns are adequate.
         maxRow = 16
         maxCol = 6
         Call CreateSpreadsheet
         Call SetStructure
         Call SetDefaults
      End Sub

      Private Function Indx(row As Integer, col As Integer) As Integer
         Indx = (row - 1) * maxCol + col
      End Function

      Private Sub SetDefaults()
         'Set default values specific to this application
         txtCell(Indx(3, 1)).Text = "Job"
         txtCell(Indx(4, 1)).Text = "Parents"
         txtCell(Indx(5, 1)).Text = "Scholarship"
         txtCell(Indx(9, 1)).Text = "Tuition"
```

```
    txtCell(Indx(10, 1)).Text = "Food"
    txtCell(Indx(11, 1)).Text = "Rent"
    txtCell(Indx(12, 1)).Text = "Books"
    txtCell(Indx(13, 1)).Text = "Misc"
End Sub

Private Sub SetStructure()
    txtCell(Indx(1, 2)).Text = "Fall"
    txtCell(Indx(1, 3)).Text = "Winter"
    txtCell(Indx(1, 4)).Text = "Spring"
    txtCell(Indx(1, 5)).Text = "Summer"
    txtCell(Indx(1, 6)).Text = "Total"
    txtCell(Indx(1, 6)).ForeColor = vbGreen
    txtCell(Indx(2, 1)).Text = "Income"
    txtCell(Indx(2, 1)).ForeColor = vbMagenta
    txtCell(Indx(6, 1)).Text = "Total"
    txtCell(Indx(6, 1)).ForeColor = vbGreen
    txtCell(Indx(8, 1)).Text = "Expenses"
    txtCell(Indx(8, 1)).ForeColor = vbMagenta
    txtCell(Indx(14, 1)).Text = "Total"
    txtCell(Indx(14, 1)).ForeColor = vbGreen
    txtCell(Indx(16, 1)).Text = "Balance"
    txtCell(Indx(16, 1)).ForeColor = vbGreen
    incStartRow = 3
    incStopRow = 5
    incTotRow = 6
    expStartRow = 9
    expStopRow = 13
    expTotRow = 14
    balRow = 16
    startCol = 2
    stopCol = 5
    totCol = 6
End Sub

Private Sub ShowBalances(itot() As Single, etot() As Single)
    Dim col As Integer
    For col = startCol To stopCol
        txtCell(Indx(balRow, col)).Text = FormatNumber(itot(col) - etot(col), 0)
    Next col
End Sub

Private Sub ShowGrandTotals(itot() As Single, etot() As Single)
    Dim col As Integer, iTotal As Single, eTotal As Single
    'Compute and display grand totals for income, expenses, and balance
    iTotal = 0
    eTotal = 0
    For col = startCol
    To stopCol
        iTotal = iTotal + itot(col)
        eTotal = eTotal + etot(col)
    Next col
    txtCell(Indx(incTotRow, totCol)) = FormatNumber(iTotal, 0)
    txtCell(Indx(expTotRow, totCol)) = FormatNumber(eTotal, 0)
    txtCell(Indx(balRow, totCol)) = FormatNumber(iTotal - eTotal, 0)
End Sub
```

```
Private Sub TotalExpenses(etot() As Single)
   Dim row As Integer, col As Integer
   'Total expenses for each of four quarters
   For col = startCol To stopCol
   etot(col) = 0
   For row = expStartRow To expStopRow
      etot(col) = etot(col) + Val(txtCell(Indx(row, col)).Text)
   Next row
   txtCell(Indx(expTotRow, col)).Text = FormatNumber(etot(col), 0)
   Next col
End Sub

Private Sub TotalIncome(itot() As Single)
   Dim row As Integer, col As Integer
   'Total income for each of four quarters
   For col = startCol To stopCol
   itot(col) = 0
   For row = incStartRow To incStopRow
      itot(col) = itot(col) + Val(txtCell(Indx(row, col)).Text)
   Next row
   txtCell(Indx(incTotRow, col)).Text = FormatNumber(itot(col), 0)
   Next col
End Sub

Private Sub TotalRows()
   Dim row As Integer, col As Integer, rowTot As Single
   'Total each income category
   For row = incStartRow To incStopRow
      rowTot = 0
      For col = startCol To stopCol
         rowTot = rowTot + Val(txtCell(Indx(row, col)).Text)
      Next col
      txtCell(Indx(row, totCol)).Text = FormatNumber(rowTot, 0)
   Next row
   'Total each expense category
   For row = expStartRow To expStopRow
      rowTot = 0
      For col = startCol To stopCal
         rowTot = rowTot + Val(txtCell(Indx(row, col)).Text)
      Next col
         txtCell(Indx(row, totCol)).Text = FormatNumber(rowTot, 0)
   Next row
End Sub

Private Sub txtCell_GotFocus(Index As Integer)
   Dim row As Integer, col As Integer
   'Force focus into a data txtCell for this application
   row = Int((Index - 1) / maxCol) + 1
   col = ((Index - 1) Mod maxCol) + 1
   If col > stopCol Then
         row = row + 1
         col = startCol
   End If
   If row < incStartRow Then
```

```
          row = incStartRow
      ElseIf (row > incStopRow) And (row < expStartRow) Then
          row = expStartRow
      ElseIf row > expStopRow Then
          row = incStartRow
    End If
    If Indx(row, col) ]<> Index Then
          txtCell(Indx(row, col)).SetFocus
    End If
End Sub

Private Sub txtCell_LostFocus(Indx As Integer)
    Call DisplayTotals
End Sub
```

SUMMARY

1. For programming purposes, tabular data are most efficiently processed if stored in an *array*. The *ranges* of variable arrays are specified by Dim or ReDim statements.

2. An array of labels, text boxes, or command buttons, referred to in general as a *control array*, can be created by assigning a value (usually zero) to the *Index* property of the control at design time. Additional elements of the control array are created either at design time by using Ctrl+C and Ctrl+V to copy the first element in the array or at run time by using the Load statement. New elements created in either way inherit all the properties of the first element except the Index, Visible (if created with Load), Top (when copied at design time), and Left (when copied at design time) properties.

3. Two of the best-known methods for ordering (or *sorting*) arrays are the *bubble sort* and the *Shell sort*.

4. Any array can be searched *sequentially* to find the subscript associated with a sought-after value. Ordered arrays can be searched most efficiently by a *binary search*.

5. A table can be effectively stored in a *two-dimensional array*.

PROGRAMMING PROJECTS

1. Table 6.9 contains some lengths in terms of feet. Write a program that displays the nine different units of measure, requests the unit to convert from, the unit to convert to, and the quantity to be converted, and then displays the converted quantity. A typical outcome is shown in Figure 6-13.

TABLE 6.9
Equivalent Lengths

1 inch = .0833 foot	1 rod = 16.5 feet
1 yard = 3 feet	1 furlong = 660 feet
1 meter = 3.2815 feet	1 kilometer = 3281.5 feet
1 fathom = 6 feet	1 mile = 5280 feet

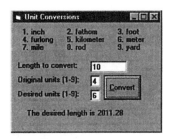

FIGURE 6-13   *Possible Outcome of Project 1*

2. Statisticians use the concepts of **mean** and **standard deviation** to describe a collection of data. The mean is the average value of the items, and the standard deviation measures the spread or dispersal of the numbers about the mean. Formally, if $x_1, x_2, x_3, \ldots, x_n$ is a collection of data, then

$$\text{mean} = m = \frac{x_1 + x_2 + x_3 + \ldots + x_n}{n}$$

$$\text{standard deviation} = s = \sqrt{\frac{(x_1 - m)^2 + (x_2 - m)^2 + (x_3 - m)^2 + \ldots + (x_n - m)^2}{n - 1}}$$

Write a computer program to

(a) Place the exam scores 59, 60, 65, 75, 56, 90, 66, 62, 98, 72, 95, 71, 63, 77, 65, 77, 65, 50, 85, and 62 into an array.

(b) Calculate the mean and standard deviation of the exam scores.

(c) Assign letter grades to each exam score, ES, as follows:

$\text{ES} \geq m + 1.5s$	A
$m + .5s \leq \text{ES} < m + 1.5s$	B
$m - .5s \leq \text{ES} < m + .5s$	C
$m - 1.5s \leq \text{ES} < m - .5s$	D
$\text{ES} < m - 1.5s$	F

For instance, if m were 70 and s were 12, then grades of 88 or above would receive A's, grades between 76 and 87 would receive B's, and so on. A process of this type is referred to as *curving grades*.

(d) Display a list of the exam scores along with their corresponding grades as shown in Figure 6-14.

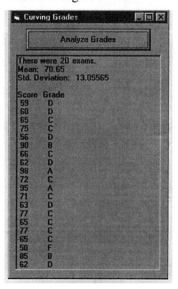

FIGURE 6-14   *Output of Project 2*

3. *Rudimentary Translator.* Table 6.10 gives English words and their French and German equivalents. Store these words in a data file and read them into three parallel arrays, one for each language. Write a program that sorts all three arrays according to the array of English words. The program should then request an English sentence as input from the keyboard and translate it into French and German. For example, if the English sentence given is MY PENCIL IS ON THE TABLE, then the French translation will be MON CRAYON EST SUR LA TABLE, and the German translation will be MEIN BLEISTIFT IST AUF DEM TISCH.

TABLE 6.10
English Words and Their French and German Equivalents

YES	OUI	JA	LARGE	GROS	GROSS
TABLE	TABLE	TISCH	NO	NON	NEIN
THE	LA	DEM	HAT	CHAPEAU	HUT
IS	EST	IST	PENCIL	CRAYON	BLEISTIFT
YELLOW	JAUNE	GELB	RED	ROUGE	ROT
FRIEND	AMI	FREUND	ON	SUR	AUF
SICK	MALADE	KRANK	AUTO	AUTO	AUTO
MY	MON	MEIN	OFTEN	SOUVENT, OFT	

4. Write a program that allows a list of no more than 50 soft drinks and their percent changes in market share for a particular year to be input and displays the information in two lists titled *gainers* and *losers*. Each list should be sorted by the *amount* of the percent change. Try your program on the data for the 8 soft drinks in Table 6.11. *Note:* You will need to store the data initially in an array to determine the number of gainers and losers.

TABLE 6.11
Changes in Market Share from 1996 to 1997 of Leading Soft-Drink Brands

Brand	% Change in Market Share	Brand	% Change in Market Share
Coke Classic	−.2	Sprite	.4
Pepsi-Cola	−.4	Dr. Pepper	.1
Diet Coke	−.2	Diet Pepsi	−.2
Mt. Dew	.5	7-Up	0

Source: Beverage Digest, 1998

5. Each team in a six-team soccer league played each other team once. Table 6.12 shows the winners. Write a program to

   (a) Place the team names in a one-dimensional array.

   (b) Place the data from Table 6.12 in a two-dimensional array.

   (c) Place the number of games won by each team in a one-dimensional array.

   (d) Display a listing of the teams giving each team's name and number of games won. The list should be in decreasing order by the number of wins.

TABLE 6.12
Soccer League Winners

	Jazz	Jets	Owls	Rams	Cubs	Zips
Jazz	—	Jazz	Jazz	Rams	Cubs	Jazz
Jets	Jazz	—	Jets	Jets	Cubs	Zips
Owls	Jazz	Jets	—	Rams	Owls	Owls
Rams	Rams	Jets	Rams	—	Rams	Rams
Cubs	Cubs	Cubs	Owls	Rams	—	Cubs
Zips	Jazz	Zips	Owls	Rams	Cubs	—

6. A poker hand can be stored in a two-dimensional array. The statement

```
Dim hand(1 TO 4, 1 TO 13) As Integer
```

declares a 52-element array, where the first dimension ranges over the four suits and the second dimension ranges over the thirteen denominations. A poker hand is specified by placing ones in the elements corresponding to the cards in the hand. See Figure 6-15.

Write a program that requests the five cards as input from the user, creates the related array, and passes the array to procedures to determine the type of the hand: flush (all cards have the same suit), straight (cards have consecutive denominations—ace can come either before 2 or after King), straight flush, four-of-a-kind, full house (3 cards of one denomination, 2 cards of another denomination), three-of-a-kind, two pairs, one pair, or none of the above.

	A	2	3	4	5	6	7	8	9	10	J	Q	K
Club	0	0	0	0	0	0	0	0	1	0	0	0	0
Diamond	1	0	0	0	0	0	0	0	0	0	0	0	0
Heart	1	0	0	0	0	0	0	0	0	0	0	1	0
Spade	0	0	0	0	1	0	0	0	0	0	0	0	0

FIGURE 6-15   *Array for the Poker Hand A ♥ A ♦ 5 ♠ 9 ♣ Q ♥*

7. *Airline Reservations.* Write a reservation system for an airline flight. Assume the airplane has 10 rows with 4 seats in each row. Use a two-dimensional array of strings to maintain a seating chart. In addition, create an array to be used as a waiting list in case the plane is full. The waiting list should be "first come, first served," that is, people who are added early to the list get priority over those added later. Allow the user the following three options:

(1) Add a passenger to the flight or waiting list.

   (a) Request the passenger's name.

   (b) Display a chart of the seats in the airplane in tabular form.

   (c) If seats are available, let the passenger choose a seat. Add the passenger to the seating chart.

   (d) If no seats are available, place the passenger on the waiting list.

(2) Remove a passenger from the flight.

   (a) Request the passenger's name.

   (b) Search the seating chart for the passenger's name and delete it.

   (c) If the waiting list is empty, update the array so the seat is available.

   (d) If the waiting list is not empty, remove the first person from the list, and give him or her the newly vacated seat.

(3) Quit.

8. The Game of Life was invented by John H. Conway to model some genetic laws for birth, death, and survival. Consider a checkerboard consisting of an *n*-by-*n* array of squares. Each square can contain one individual (denoted by 1) or be empty (denoted by –). Figure 6-16(a) shows a 6-by-6 board with four of the squares occupied. The future of each individual depends on the number of his neighbors. After each period of time, called a *generation*, certain individuals will survive, others will die due to either loneliness or overcrowding, and new individuals will be born. Each nonborder square has eight neighboring squares. After each generation, the status of the squares change as follows:

(a) An individual *survives* if there are two or three individuals in neighboring squares.

(b) An individual *dies* if he has more than three individuals or less than two in neighboring squares.

(c) A new individual is *born* into each empty square with exactly three individuals as neighbors.

Figure 6-16(b) shows the status after one generation. Write a program to do the following:

(a) Dimension an *n*-by-*n* array, where *n* is input by the user, to hold the status of each square in the current generation. To specify the initial configuration, have the user input each row as a string of length *n*, and break the row into 1's or dashes with Mid.

(b) Dimension an *n*-by-*n* array to hold the status of each square in the next generation. Compute the status for each square and produce the display in Figure 6-16(b). *Note:* The generation changes all at once. Only current cells are used to determine which cells will contain individuals in the next generation.

(c) Assign the next-generation values to the current generation and repeat as often as desired.

(d) Display the number of individuals in each generation.

Hint: The hardest part of the program is determining the number of neighbors a cell has. In general, you must check a 3-by-3 square around the cell in question. Exceptions must be made when the cell is on the edge of the array. Don't forget that a cell is not a neighbor of itself.

(Test the program with the initial configuration shown in Figure 6-17. It is known as the figure-eight configuration and repeats after eight generations.)

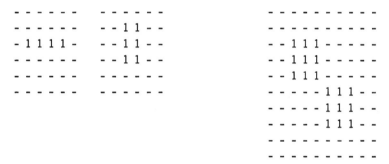

FIGURE 6-16   *Two Generations*   **FIGURE 6-17**   *The Figure Eight*

9. Simulate the game Concentration. The Form_Load routine should create an array of 20 command buttons placed vertically on a form. A list of 10 words should be randomly assigned as potential captions for the buttons, with each word assigned to two command buttons. Initially, none of the buttons should show their words. However, when a button is clicked on, its word is revealed as its caption. After two words have been revealed, either both of the command buttons should become invisible (if their words match) or their captions should again become blank (if the two words do not match). When all matches have been found, a message box should display the number of tries (pairs of words exposed) and an appropriate remark about the user's concentration ability. Possible remarks might be, "You must have ESP" (less than 14 tries), "Amazing concentration" (14 to 20 tries), "Can't hide anything from you" (21 to 28 tries), "Perhaps a nap would recharge your concentration" (29 to 37 tries), and "Better find a designated driver" (more than 37 tries).

SEQUENTIAL FILES

7.1 SEQUENTIAL FILES

Throughout this text we have processed data from files created with Windows' Notepad and saved on a disk. Such files are stored on disk as a sequence of characters. (Two special characters, called the "carriage return" and "line feed" characters, are inserted at the end of each line to indicate where new lines should be started.) Such files are called **sequential files** or **text files**. In this section, we create sequential files from Visual Basic programs and develop techniques for using sequential files.

■ CREATING A SEQUENTIAL FILE

There are many ways to organize data in a sequential file. The technique presented here is easy to implement. The following steps create a new sequential file and write data to it.

1. Choose a file name. A file name can contain up to 255 characters consisting of letters, digits, and a few other assorted characters (including spaces and periods). In this book we use 8.3 format names; that is, each name has a base name of at most 8 characters, and optionally a period followed by a three-letter extension. (Such names are recognized by all utility programs.)

2. Choose a number from 1 through 511 to be the **reference number** of the file. While the file is in use, it will be identified by this number.

3. Execute the statement

   ```
   Open "filespec" For Output As #n
   ```

   where n is the reference number. This process is referred to as **opening a file for output**. It establishes a communications link between the computer and the disk drive for storing data *onto* the disk. It allows data to be output from the computer and recorded in the specified file.

4. Place data into the file with the Write # statement. If a is a string, then the statement

   ```
   Write #n, a
   ```

   writes the string a surrounded by quotation marks into the file. If c is a number, then the statement

   ```
   Write #n, c
   ```

217

writes the number *c*, without any leading or trailing spaces, into file number *n*. The statement

```
Write #n, a, c
```

writes *a* and *c* as before, but with a comma separating them. Similarly, if the statement Write #*n* is followed by a list of several strings and/or numbers separated by commas, then all the strings and numbers appear as before, separated by commas. After each Write # statement is executed, the "carriage return" and "line feed" characters are placed into the file.

5. After all the data have been recorded in the file, execute

```
Close #n
```

where *n* is the reference number. This statement breaks the communications link with the file and dissociates the number *n* from the file.

EXAMPLE 1

The following program illustrates the different aspects of the Write # statement. Notice the absence of leading and trailing spaces for numbers and the presence of quotation marks surrounding strings.

```
Private Sub cmdCreateFile_Click()
  Dim name1 As String, name2 As String
  'Demonstrate use of Write # statement
  Open "PIONEER.TXT" For Output As #1
  Write #1, "ENIAC" Write #1, 1946
  Write #1, "ENIAC", 1946 name1 = "Eckert" name2 = "Mauchly"
  Write #1, 14 * 139, "J.P. " & name1, name2, "John"
  Close #1
End Sub
```

[Run, click the command button, and then load the file PIONEER.TXT into Windows' Notepad. The following will appear on the screen.]

"ENIAC"
1946
"ENIAC",1946
1946,"J.P. Eckert","Mauchly","John"

Caution: If an existing sequential file is opened for output, the computer will erase the existing data and create a new empty file.

Write # statements allow us to create files just like the Notepad files that appear throughout this text. We already know how to read such files with Input # statements. The remaining major task is adding data to the end of sequential files.

■ ADDING ITEMS TO A SEQUENTIAL FILE

Data can be added to the end of an existing sequential file with the following steps.

1. Choose a number from 1 through 511 to be the reference number for the file. It need not be the number that was used when the file was created.

2. Execute the statement

```
Open "filespec" For Append As #n
```

where *n* is the reference number. This procedure is called **opening a file for append**. It allows data to be output and recorded at the end of the specified file.

3. Place data into the file with Write # statements.

4. After all the data have been recorded into the file, close the file with the statement Close #*n*.

The Append option for opening a file is intended to add data to an existing file. However, it also can be used to create a new file. If the file does not exist, then the Append option acts just like the Output option and creates the file.

The three options, Output, Input, and Append, are referred to as **modes**. A file should not be open in two modes at the same time. For instance, after a file has been opened for output and data have been written to the file, the file should be closed before being opened for input.

An attempt to open a nonexistent file for input terminates the program with the "File not found" error message. There is a function that tells us whether a certain file has already been created. If the value of

```
Dir("filespec")
```

is the empty string "", then the specified file does not exist. (If the file exists, the value will be the file name.) Therefore, prudence often dictates that files be opened for input with code such as

```
If Dir("filespec") <> "" Then
    Open "filespec" For Input As #1
  Else
    message = "Either no file has yet been created or "
    message = message & "the file is not where expected."
    MsgBox message, , "File Not Found"
End If
```

There is one file-management operation that we have yet to discuss—deleting an item of information from a file. An individual item of a file cannot be changed or deleted directly. A new file must be created by reading each item from the original file and recording it, with the single item changed or deleted, into the new file. The old file is then erased and the new file renamed with the name of the original file. Regarding these last two tasks, the Visual Basic statement

```
Kill "filespec"
```

removes the specified file from the disk and the statement

```
Name "oldfilespec" As "newfilespec"
```

changes the filespec of a file. (*Note:* The Kill and Name statements cannot be used with open files. So doing generates a "File already open" message.)

EXAMPLE 2

The following program creates and manages a file of names and years of birth.

Object	Property	Setting
frm8_1_2	Caption	Access YOB.TXT
lblName	Caption	Name
txtName	Text	(blank)
lblYOB	Caption	Year of Birth
txtYOB	Text	(blank)
cmdAdd	Caption	Add Above Person to File
cmdLookUp	Caption	Look up Year of Birth
cmdDelete	Caption	Delete Above Person from File

```
Private Sub cmdAdd_Click()
  Dim message As String
```

```vb
  'Add a person's name and year of birth to file
  If (txtName.Text <> "") And (txtYOB.Text "") Then
      Open "YOB.TXT" For Append As #1
      Write #1, txtName.Text, Val(txtYOB.Text)
      Close #1
      txtName.Text = ""
      txtYOB.Text = ""
      txtName.SetFocus
    Else
      message = "You must enter a name and year of birth."
      MsgBox message, , "Information Incomplete"
  End If
End Sub


Private Sub cmdLookUp_Click()
  Dim message As String
  'Determine a person's year of birth
  If txtName.Text <> "" Then
    If Dir("YOB.TXT") <> "" Then
      Call DisplayYearOfBirth
        Else
          message = "Either no file has yet been created or "
          message = message & "the file is not where expected."
          MsgBox message, , "File Not Found"
      End If
    Else
      MsgBox "You must enter a name.", , "Information Incomplete"
  End If
  txtName.SetFocus
End Sub

Private Sub cmdDelete_Click()
  Dim message As String
  'Remove a person from the file
  If txtName.Text <> "" Then
    If Dir("YOB.TXT") <> "" Then
      Call DeletePerson
        Else
          message = "Either no file has yet been created or "
          message = message & "the file is not where expected."
          MsgBox message, , "File Not Found."
      End If
    Else
      MsgBox "You must enter a name.", , "Information Incomplete"
  End If
  txtName.SetFocus
End Sub


Private Sub DeletePerson()
  Dim nom As String, yob As Integer, foundFlag As Boolean
  foundFlag = False Open "YOB.TXT" For Input As #1
  Open "TEMP" For Output As #2
  Do While Not EOF(1)
    Input #1, nom, yob
    If nom <> txtName.Text Then
```

```
            Write #2, nom, yob
         Else
            foundFlag = True
      End If
   Loop
   Close #1
   Close #2
   Kill "YOB.TXT"
   Name "TEMP" As "YOB.TXT"
   If Not foundFlag Then
       MsgBox "The name was not found.", , ""
      Else
         txtName.Text = ""
         txtYOB.Text = ""
   End If
End Sub

Private Sub DisplayYearOfBirth()
   Dim nom As String, yob As Integer
   'Find the year of birth for the name in txtName
   txtYOB.Text = ""
   Open "YOB.TXT" For Input As #1
   nom = ""
   Do While (nom <> txtName.Text) And (Not EOF(1))
      Input #1, nom, yob
   Loop
   If nom = txtName.Text Then
       txtYOB.Text = Str(yob)
      Else
         MsgBox "Person is not in file.", , ""
         txtName.Text = ""
   End If
   Close #1
End Sub
```

[Run. After several names have been added, the file might look as shown in Figure 7-1.]

```
"Barbra",1942
"Ringo",1940
"Sylvester",1946
```

FIGURE 7-1   *Sample Contents of YOB.TXT*

■ ERROR TRAPPING

If you try to Open a file on a diskette in drive A and there is no diskette in drive A, the program will crash with the error message "Disk not ready." Visual Basic has a device, called **error-trapping,** for preventing this and many other types of errors. If an error occurs while error-trapping is active, two things happen. An identifying number is assigned to the Number property of an object called Err, and the program jumps to some lines of code called an **error-handling routine,** which takes corrective measures based on the value of Err.Number. Some errors and the values they generate are as follows:

Type of error	Value of Err.Number
Subscript out of range	9
Division by zero	11
File not found	53
File already open	55
File already exists	58
Disk full	61
Disk not ready	71

To set up error-trapping inside a procedure, do the following:

1. Make the first line of the procedure

```
On Error GoTo ErrorHandler
```

2. Type in the lines to carry out the purpose of the procedure.

3. Make the last lines of the procedure

```
Exit SubErrorHandler:error-handling routineResume
```

The statement "On Error GoTo ErrorHandler" activates error-trapping. If an error occurs during the execution of a line of the procedure, the program will jump to the error-handling routine. The statement "Resume" causes the program to jump back to the line causing the error. The statement "Exit Sub", which causes an early exit from the procedure, prevents the error-handling routine from being entered when no error occurs. For instance, the following procedure has an error-handling routine that is called when a file cannot be found.

```
Private Sub OpenFile()
   On Error GoTo ErrorHandler
   Dim fileName As String
      fileName = InputBox("Enter the name of the file to be opened.")
      Open fileName For Input As #1
      Exit Sub
   ErrorHandler:
   Select Case Err.Number
      Case 53
         MsgBox "File not found. Try Again."
         fileName = InputBox("Enter the name of the file to be opened.")
      Case 71
         MsgBox "The drive door might be open - please check."
   End Select
   Resume
End Sub
```

The word "ErrorHandler", which is called a **line label**, can be replaced by any word of at most 40 letters. The line, which is placed just before the error-handling routine, must start at the left margin and must end with a colon. If "Resume" is replaced by "Resume Next", then the program will jump to the line following the line causing the error.

The line label must be in the same procedure as the On Error statement. However, the error-handling routine can call another procedure.

There are two variations of the On Error statement. The statement "On Error GoTo 0" turns off error-trapping. The statement "On Error Resume Next" specifies that when a run-time error occurs, execution continues with the statement following the statement where the error occurred.

COMMENTS

1. Sequential files make efficient use of disk space and are easy to create and use. Their disadvantages are as follows:

(a) Often a large portion of the file must be read in order to find one specific item.

(b) An individual item of the file cannot be changed or deleted easily.

Another type of file, known as a **random-access file**, has neither of the disadvantages of sequential files; however, random-access files typically use more disk space, require greater effort to program, and are not flexible in the variety and format of the stored data. Random-access files are discussed in Section 8.

2. Consider the sequential file shown in Figure 7-1 at the end of Example 2. This file is said to consist of three records of two fields each. A **record** holds all the data about a single individual. Each item of data is called a **field**. The three records are

"Barbra", 1942

"Ringo", 1940

"Sylvester", 1946

and the two fields are

name field, year of birth field

7.2 USING SEQUENTIAL FILES

In addition to being accessed for information, sequential files are regularly updated by modifying certain pieces of data, removing some records, and adding new records. These tasks can be performed most efficiently if the files are first sorted.

■ SORTING SEQUENTIAL FILES

The records of a sequential file can be sorted on any field by first reading the data into parallel arrays and then sorting on a specific array.

EXAMPLE 1

The following program sorts the sequential file YOB.TXT of the previous section by year of birth.

```
Private Sub cmdSort_Click()
  Dim numPeople As Integer
  'Sort data from YOB.TXT file by year of birth
  numPeople = NumberOfRecords("YOB.TXT")
  ReDim nom(1 To numPeople) As String
  ReDim yearBorn(1 To numPeople) As Integer
  Call ReadData(nom(), yearBorn(), numPeople)
  Call SortData(nom(), yearBorn(), numPeople)
  Call ShowData(nom(), yearBorn(), numPeople)
  Call WriteData(nom(), yearBorn(), numPeople)
End Sub

Private Function NumberOfRecords(filespec As String) As Integer
  Dim nom As String, yearBorn As Integer
  Dim n As Integer 'Used to count records
  n = 0
  Open filespec For Input As #1
  Do While Not EOF(1)
    Input #1, nom, yearBorn
    n = n + 1
  Loop
  Close #1
```

```
     NumberOfRecords = n
End Function


Private Sub ReadData(nom() As String, yearBorn() As Integer, numPeople As _
Integer)
   Dim index As Integer
   'Read data from file into arrays
   Open "YOB.TXT" For Input As #1
      For index = 1 To numPeople Input #1, nom(index), yearBorn(index)
   Next index
   Close #1
End Sub


Private Sub ShowData(nom() As String, yearBorn() As Integer, numPeople As _
Integer)
   Dim index As Integer
   'Display the sorted list
   picShowData.Cls
   For index = 1 To numPeople
      picShowData.Print nom(index), yearBorn(index)
   Next index
End Sub


Private Sub SortData(nom() As String, yearBorn() As Integer, numPeople As
Integer)
   Dim passNum As Integer, index As Integer
   'Bubble sort arrays by year of birth
   For passNum = 1 To numPeople - 1
      For index = 1 To numPeople - passNum
         If yearBorn(index) > yearBorn(index + 1) Then
            Call SwapData(nom(), yearBorn(), index)
         End If
      Next index
   Next passNum
End Sub


Private Sub SwapData(nom() As String, yearBorn() As Integer, index As Integer)
   Dim stemp As String, ntemp As Integer
   'Swap names and years
   stemp = nom(index)
   nom(index) = nom(index + 1)
   nom(index + 1) = stemp
   ntemp = yearBorn(index)
   yearBorn(index) = yearBorn(index + 1)
   yearBorn(index + 1) = ntemp
End Sub


Private Sub WriteData(nom() As String, yearBorn() As Integer, numPeople As
Integer)
   Dim index As Integer
   'Write data back into file
   Open "YOB.TXT" For Output As #1
   For index = 1 To numPeople
      Write #1, nom(index), yearBorn(index)
   Next index
```

```
    Close #1
End Sub
```

[Run, and then click on the command button. The following is displayed in the picture box.]

Ringo 1940
Barbra 1942
Sylvester 1946

■ MERGING SEQUENTIAL FILES

In Section 6.2, we considered an algorithm for merging two arrays. This same algorithm can be applied to merging two ordered files.

Suppose you have two ordered files (possibly with certain items appearing in both files), and you want to merge them into a third ordered file (without duplications). The technique for creating the third file is as follows.

1. Open the two ordered files For Input and open a third file For Output.

2. Try to get an item of data from each file.

3. Repeat steps (a) and (b) below until an item of data is not available in one of the files.

   (a) If one item precedes the other, write it into the third file and try to get another item of data from its file.

   (b) If the two items are identical, write one into the third file and try to get another item of data from each of the two ordered files.

4. At this point, an item of data has most likely been retrieved from one of the files and not yet written to the third file. In this case, write that item and all remaining items in that file to the third file.

5. Close the three files.

EXAMPLE 2

The following program merges two ordered files of numbers into a third file.

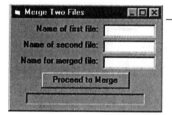

Object	Property	Setting
frmMerge	Caption	Merge Two Files
lblNameFirst	Caption	Name of first file:
txtNameFirst	Text	(blank)
lblNameSecond	Caption	Name of second file:
txtNameSecond	Text	(blank)
lblNameMerged	Caption	Name for merged file:
txtNameMerged	Text	(blank)
cmdProceed	Caption	Proceed to Merge
picProgress		

```
Private Sub cmdProceed_Click()
    Dim file1 As String, file2 As String, file3 As String
    Dim have1data As Boolean, have2data As Boolean
    Dim num1 As Single, num2 As Single
    Dim recCount As Integer 'Number of records in merged file
    'Merge two ordered files
    picProgress.Cls
    file1 = txtNameFirst.Text
    file2 = txtNameSecond.Text
    file3 = txtNameMerged.Text
    Open file1 For Input As #1
```

```
        Open file2 For Input As #2
        Open file3 For Output As #3
        have1data = Get1data(num1)
        have2data = Get2data(num2)
        recCount = 0
        Do While have1data And have2data
          Select Case num1
            Case Is < num2
              Write #3, num1
              have1data = Get1data(num1)
            Case Is > num2
              Write #3, num2
              have2data = Get2data(num2)
            Case num2
              Write #3, num1
              have1data = Get1data(num1)
              have2data = Get2data(num2)
          End Select
          recCount = recCount + 1
        Loop
        Do While have1data
          Write #3, num1
          recCount = recCount + 1
          have1data = Get1data(num1)
        Loop
        Do While have2data
          Write #3, num2
          recCount = recCount + 1
          have2data = Get2data(num2)
        Loop
        Close #1, #2, #3
        picProgress.Print recCount; "records written to "; file3
    End Sub

    Private Function Get1data(num1 As Single) As Boolean
        'If possible, read next value from file 1
        'Return value of True when new data are read; False if data not available
        If Not EOF(1) Then
            Input #1, num1
            Get1data = True
          Else
            Get1data = False
        End If
    End Function

    Private Function Get2data(num2 As Single) As Boolean
        'If possible, read next value from file 2
        'Return value True when new data are read; False if data not available
        If Not EOF(2) Then
            Input #2, num2
            Get2data = True
          Else
            Get2data = False
        End If
    End Function
```

■ CONTROL BREAK PROCESSING

Suppose a small real estate company stores its sales data for a year in a sequential file in which each record contains four fields: month of sale, day of sale (1 through 31), address, and price. Typical data for the sales of the first quarter of a year are shown in Figure 7-2. The records are ordered by date of sale.

Month	Day	Address	Price
January	9	102 Elm Street	$203,000
January	20	1 Main Street	$315,200
January	25	5 Maple Street	$123,450
February	15	1 Center Street	$100,000
February	23	2 Vista Drive	$145,320
March	15	205 Rodeo Circle	$389,100

FIGURE 7-2   *Real Estate Sales for First Quarter of Year*

Figure 7-3 shows the output of a program that displays the total sales for the quarter year, with a subtotal for each month.

```
January   9    102 Elm Street      $203,000.00
January   20   1 Main Street       $315,200.00
January   25   5 Maple Street      $123,450.00

          Subtotal for January:    $641,650.00

February  15   1 Center Street     $100,000.00
February  23   2 Vista Drive       $145,320.00

          Subtotal for February:   $245,320.00

March     15   205 Rodeo Circle    $389,100.00

          Subtotal for March:      $389,100.00

Total for First Quarter: $1,276,070.00
```

FIGURE 7-3   *Output of Example 3*

A program to produce the output of Figure 7-3 must calculate a subtotal at the end of each month. The variable holding the month triggers a subtotal whenever its value changes. Such a variable is called a **control variable** and each change of its value is called a **break**.

EXAMPLE 3

The following program produces the output of Figure 7-2. The data of Figure 7-2 are stored in the sequential file HOMESALE.TXT. The program allows for months with no sales. Because monthly subtotals will be printed, the month-of-sale field is an appropriate control variable.

```
Private Sub cmdCreateReport_Click()
  Dim currentMonth As String, newMonth As String
  Dim dayNum As Integer, address As String
  Dim price As Single, monthTotal As Single
  Dim yearTotal As Single, doneFlag As Boolean
  'Display home sales by month
  picReport.Cls
  Open "HOMESALE.TXT" For Input As #1
  currentMonth = "" 'Name of month being subtotaled
  monthTotal = 0
  yearTotal = 0
  doneFlag = False 'Flag to indicate end of list
  Do While Not doneFlag
```

```
        If Not EOF(1) Then
            Input #1, newMonth, dayNum, address, price
        Else
            doneFlag = True 'End of list
        End If
        If (newMonth <> currentMonth) Or (doneFlag) Then 'Control break processing
            If currentMonth <> "" Then 'Don't print subtotal before 1st month
                picReport.Print
                picReport.Print Tab(15); "Subtotal for "; currentMonth; ":";
                picReport.Print Tab(38); FormatCurrency(monthTotal)
                picReport.Print
            End If
            currentMonth = newMonth
            monthTotal = 0
        End If
        If Not doneFlag Then
            picReport.Print newMonth;
            picReport.Print Tab(11); FormatNumber(dayNum, 0);
            picReport.Print Tab(18); address;
            picReport.Print Tab(38); FormatCurrency(price)
            yearTotal = yearTotal + price
        End If
        monthTotal = monthTotal + price
    Loop
    Close #1
    picReport.Print "Total for First Quarter: "; FormatCurrency(yearTotal)
End Sub
```

COMMENTS

1. In the examples of this and the previous section, the files to be processed have been opened and closed within a single procedure. However, the solution to some programming problems requires that a file be opened just once the instant the program is run and stay open until the program is terminated. This is easily accomplished by placing the Open statement in the Form_Load event procedure and the Close and End statements in the click event procedure for a command button labeled "Quit."

7.3 A CASE STUDY: RECORDING CHECKS AND DEPOSITS

The purpose of this section is to take you through the design and implementation of a quality program for personal checkbook management. Nothing in this chapter shows off the power of Visual Basic better than the program in this section. That a user-friendly checkbook management program can be written in less than five pages of code clearly shows Visual Basic's ability to improve the productivity of programmers. It is easy to imagine an entire finance program, similar to programs that have generated millions of dollars of sales, being written in only a few weeks by using Visual Basic!

■ THE DESIGN OF THE PROGRAM

Though there are many commercial programs available for personal financial management, they include so many bells and whistles that their original purposes—keeping track of transactions and reporting balances—have become obscured. The program in this section was designed specifically as a checkbook program. It keeps track of expenditures and deposits and produces a printed report. Adding a reconciliation feature would be easy enough, although we did not include one.

The program is supposed to be user-friendly. Therefore, it showcases many of the techniques and tools available in Visual Basic.

The general design goals for the program included the abilities to

- Automatically enter the user's name on each check and deposit slip.

- Automatically provide the next consecutive check or deposit slip number. (The user can override this feature if necessary.)

- Automatically provide the date. (Again, this feature can be overridden.)

- For each check, record the payee, the amount, and optionally a memo.

- For each deposit slip, record the source, the amount, and optionally a memo.

- Display the current balance at all times.

- Produce a printout detailing all transactions.

■ THE USER INTERFACE

With Visual Basic we can place a replica of a check or deposit slip on the screen and let the user supply the information as if actually filling out a check or deposit slip. Figure 7-4 shows the form in its check mode. A picture box forms the boundary of the check. Below the picture box are two labels for the current balance and four command buttons.

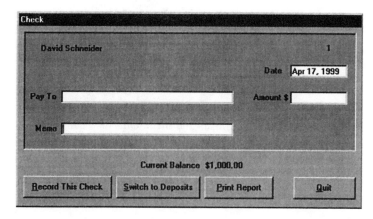

FIGURE 7-4 *Template for Entering a Check*

The first time the program is run, the user is asked for his or her name, the starting balance, and the numbers of the first check and deposit slip. Suppose the user's name is David Schneider, the first check has number 1, the starting balance is $1000, and the first deposit slip is also number 1. Figure 7-4 shows the form after the three pieces of input. The upper part of the form looks like a check. The check has a color of light turquoise blue (or cyan). The Date box is automatically set to today's date, but can be altered by the user. The user fills in the payee, amount, and optionally a memo. When the user pushes the Record This Check button, the information is written to a file, the balance is updated, and check number 2 appears.

To record a deposit, the user pushes the Switch to Deposits button. The form then appears as in Figure 7-5. The form's title bar now reads Deposit Slip, the words Pay To changes to Source, and the color of the slip changes to yellow. Also, in the buttons at the bottom of the form, the words Check and Deposit are interchanged. A deposit is recorded in much the same way as a check. When the Print Report button is pushed, a printout similar to the one in Figure 7-5 is printed on the printer.

Deposit Slip

David Schneider   1

                                                        Date [May 5, 1999]

Source [   ]   Amount $ [   ]

Memo [   ]

Current Balance $1,000.00

[Record This Deposit] [Switch to Checks] [Print Report]   [Quit]

FIGURE 7-5　*Template for Entering a Deposit*

			May 5, 1999
Name: David Schneider	Starting balance: $1,000.00		
Date	Transaction	Amount	Balance
Apr 21, 1999	Check #: 1	$75.95	$924.05
		Paid to: Land's End	
		Memo: shirts	
Apr 29,1999	Check #: 2	$125.00	$799.05
		Paid to: Bethesda Coop	
		Memo: groceries	
May 5,1999	Deposit #: 1	$245.00	$1,044.05
		Source: Prentice Hall	
		Memo: typing expenses	
		Ending Balance: $1,044.05	

FIGURE 7-6　*Sample Printout of Transactions*

The common design for the check and deposit slip allows one set of controls to be used for both items. Figure 7-7 shows the controls and their suggestive names. The caption of the label lblToFrom will change back and forth between Pay To and Source.

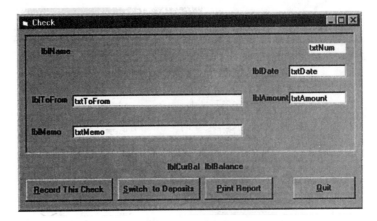

FIGURE 7-7　*Control Names for Checkbook Management Program.*

Table 7.1 lists the objects and their initial properties. Because the program will always begin by displaying the next check, the various captions and the BackColor property of the picture box could have been set at design time. We chose instead to leave these assignments to the SetupCheck Sub procedure, which is normally used to switch from deposit entry to check entry, but also can be called by the Form_Load event procedure to prepare the initial mode (check or deposit) for the form.

TABLE 7.1
Objects and Initial Properties for the Checkbook Management Program

Object	Property	Setting
frmCheckbook		
picBox		
lblName	BackStyle	0 – Transparent
txtNum	BorderStyle	0 – None
lblDate	BackStyle	0 – Transparent
	Caption	Date
txtDate		
lblToFrom	BackStyle	0 – Transparent
txtToFrom		
lblAmount	BackStyle	0 – Transparent
	Caption	Amount $
txtAmount		
lblMemo	BackStyle	0 – Transparent
	Caption	Memo
txtMemo		
lblCurBal	Caption	Current Balance
lblBalance		
cmdRecord		
cmdMode		
cmdPrint	Caption	&Print Report
cmdQuit	Caption	&Quit

The transactions are stored in a data file named CHKBOOK.TXT. The first four entries of the file are the name to appear on the check or deposit slip, the starting balance, the number of the first check, and the number of the first deposit slip. After that, each transaction is recorded as a sequence of eight items—the type of transaction, the contents of txtToFrom, the current balance, the number of the last check, the number of the last deposit slip, the amount of money, the memo, and the date.

■ CODING THE PROGRAM
....

The top row of Figure 7-8 shows the different events to which the program must respond. Table 7.2 identifies the corresponding event procedures and the general procedures they call.

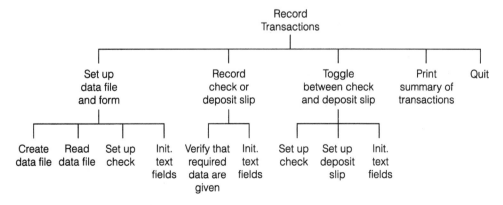

FIGURE 7-8   *Hierarchy Chart for Checkbook Management Program*

TABLE 7.2
Tasks and Their Procedures

Task	Procedure
1. Set up data file and form	Form_Load
1.1 Create data file	CreateDataFile
1.2 Read data file	ReadDataFile
1.3 Set up check	SetupCheck
1.4 Initialize text fields	InitializeFields
2. Record check or deposit slip	cmdRecord_Click
2.1 Verify that required data are given	AllDataGiven
2.2 Initialize text fields	InitializeFields
3. Toggle between check & deposit slip	cmdMode_Click
3.1 Set up check	SetupCheck
3.2 Set up deposit slip	SetupDeposit
3.3 Initialize text fields	InitializeFields
4. Print summary of transaction	cmdPrint_Click
5. Quit	cmdQuit_Click

Let's examine each event procedure.

1. **Form_Load** first looks to see if the file CHKBOOK.TXT has been created. The function Dir returns "CHKBOOK.TXT" if the file exists and otherwise returns the empty string. If CHKBOOK.TXT does not exist, the routine CreateDataFile is called. CreateDataFile prompts the user for the name to appear on the checks and deposit slips, the starting balance, and the numbers of the first check and deposit slip, and then writes these items to the data file. If CHKBOOK.TXT does exist, the routine ReadDataFile is called to read through the entire file to determine all information needed to proceed. The event procedure calls SetupCheck to set the transaction type to Check and set the appropriate captions and background colors for a check. The event procedure then calls InitializeFields, which initializes all the text boxes.

   In the first assignment statement of the procedure, the drive is specified as the A drive. Therefore, the data file will be written to and read from a diskette on the A drive. Feel free to change the letter A to whatever drive you prefer. You may even want to specify an entire path.

2. **cmdRecord_Click** first confirms that the required fields contain entries. This is accomplished by calling the function AllDataGiven. If the value returned is True, then cmdRecord_Click opens the data file for output as Append, sends eight pieces of data to the file, and then closes the file. When AllDataGiven returns False, the function itself pops up a message box to tell the user where information is needed. The user must type in the information and then press the Record button again.

3. **cmdMode_Click** toggles back and forth from a check to a deposit slip. It calls SetupCheck, or its analog SetupDeposit, and then calls InitializeFields.

4. **cmdPrint_Click** prints out a complete history of all transactions, as shown in Figure 7-6.

5. **cmdQuit_Click** ends the program.

```
Dim fileName As String 'Name of data file
Dim nameOnChk As String 'Name to appear on checks
Dim lastCkNum As Integer 'Number of last check written
Dim lastDpNum As Integer 'Number of last deposit slip processed
Dim curBal As Single 'Current balance in account
Dim transType As String 'Type of transaction, check or deposit
```

```
Private Function AllDataGiven() As Boolean
```

```
      Dim message As String
      'If one of the four required pieces of information
      'is missing, assign its name to message
      message = ""
      If txtDate.Text = "" Then
            message = "Date"
            txtDate.SetFocus
        ElseIf txtToFrom.Text = "" Then
        If transType = "Check" Then
            message = "Pay To"
          Else
            message = "Source"
          End If
          txtToFrom.SetFocus
        ElseIf txtAmount.Text = "" Then
          message = "Amount"
          txtAmount.SetFocus
        ElseIf txtNum.Text = "" Then
          If transType = "Check" Then
              message = "Check Number"
            Else
              message = "Deposit Number"
          End If
          txtNum.SetFocus
        End If
      If message = "" Then
            'All required data fields have been filled; recording can proceed
            AllDataGiven = True
        Else
            'Advise user of required data that are missing
            MsgBox "The '" & message & " 'field must be filled", , "Error"
            AllDataGiven = False
      End If
    End If
End Function


Private Sub cmdMode_Click()
    'Toggle from Check to/from Deposit Slip
    If transType = "Check" Then
        Call SetupDeposit
      Else 'transType = "Deposit"
        Call SetupCheck
    End If
    Call InitializeFields
    txtToFrom.SetFocus
End Sub


Private Sub cmdPrint_Click()
    Dim temp As String, lineNo As Integer
    Dim nameOnChk As String, balance As Single, ck As Integer, dp As Integer
    Dim toFrom As String, amount As String, memo As String, theDate As String
    'Print out a detailed list of all transactions.
    temp = frmCheckbook.Caption                 'Save the current form caption
    frmCheckbook.Caption = "Printing..."        'Set form caption to indicate printing
    lineNo = 1                                  'Line number being printed
    Open fileName For Input As #1               'Open the file
    Input #1, nameOnChk, balance, ck, dp        'Read in the file header
```

```vb
'Print the details of the individual transactions.
Do Until EOF(1)
   If lineNo >= 57 Then
'57 or more lines have been printed; start a new page
Printer.NewPage
lineNo = 1
   End If
   If lineNo = 1 Then
      'Print the report header
      Printer.Print
      Printer.Print "Name: "; nameOnChk; Tab(65); FormatDateTime(Now,
      vbLongDate)
      Printer.Print
      Printer.Print , "Starting balance: "; FormatCurrency(balance)
      Printer.Print
      Printer.Print "Date", "Transaction"; Tab(50); "Amount";
      Printer.Print Tab(65); "Balance"
      Printer.Print "____", "_____"; Tab(50); "_____";
      Printer.Print Tab(65); "_____"
      Printer.Print
      Printer.Print
      lineNo = 10
   End If
   Input #1, transType, toFrom, balance, ck, dp, amount, memo, theDate
   If transType = "Check" Then
       Printer.Print theDate, "Check #: "; ck; Tab(50); amount;
       Printer.Print Tab(65); FormatCurrency(balance)
       Printer.Print , "Paid to: "; toFrom
     Else 'Transaction was a deposit
       Printer.Print theDate, "Deposit #: "; dp; Tab(50); amount;
       Printer.Print Tab(65); FormatCurrency(balance)
       Printer.Print , "Source: "; toFrom
   End If
   lineNo = lineNo + 2
   'If there was a memo, then print it.
   If memo <> "" Then
       Printer.Print , "Memo: "; memo
       lineNo = lineNo + 1
   End If
   Printer.Print
   lineNo = lineNo + 1
Loop
Close #1 'Close the file
'Print the ending balance
Printer.Print
Printer.Print , "Ending Balance: "; FormatCurrency(balance)
Printer.EndDoc                          'Send the output to the Printer
frmCheckbook.Caption = temp             'Restore the form caption
txtToFrom.SetFocus                      'Set focus for the next entry
End Sub

Private Sub cmdQuit_Click()
   'Exit the program
   End
End Sub
```

```
Private Sub cmdRecord_Click()
   Dim amt As String, amount As Single, itemNum As Integer
   'Check to ensure all required fields are filled
   If AllDataGiven Then
       amt = txtAmount.Text 'Amount of transaction as string
       amount = Val(amt) 'Amount of transaction as number
       amt = FormatCurrency(amt) itemNum = Val(txtNum.Text)
       If transType = "Check" Then
            curBal = curBal - amount
            lastCkNum = itemNum
         Else 'transType = "Deposit"
            curBal = curBal + amount
            lastDpNum = itemNum
   End If
         lblBalance.Caption = FormatCurrency(curBal)
         Open fileName For Append As #1
         Write #1, transType, txtToFrom.Text, curBal, lastCkNum, lastDpNum, amt, _
            txtMemo.Text, txtDate.Text
         Close #1
         Call InitializeFields
         txtToFrom.SetFocus
   End If
End Sub


Private Sub CreateDataFile()
   Dim startBal As Single, ckNum As integer
   'The first time the program is run, create a data file
   Open fileName For Output As #1
   nameOnChk = InputBox("Name to appear on checks:")
   startBal = Val(InputBox("Starting balance:"))
   ckNum = Val(InputBox("Number of the first check:"))
   lastCkNum = ckNum - 1 'Number of "last" check written
   ckNum = Val(InputBox("Number of the first deposit slip:"))
   lastDpNum = ckNum - 1 'Number of "last" deposit slip processed
   curBal = startBal 'Set current balance
   'First record in data file records name to appear on checks
   'plus initial data for account
   Write #1, nameOnChk, startBal, lastCkNum, lastDpNum
   Close #1
End Sub


Private Sub Form_Load()
   Dim drive As String, today As String
   'If no data file exists, create one. Otherwise, open the
   'data file and get the user's name, last used check and
   'deposit slip numbers, and current balance.
   'In next line adjust drive as necessary drive = "A:"
   'Drive (or path) for data file
   fileName = drive & "CHKBOOK.TXT" 'Program uses one data file
   If Dir(fileName) = "" Then
        'Data file does not exist, so create it and obtain initial data
        Call CreateDataFile
     Else
        Call ReadDataFile
   End If
```

```vb
        'Set name and balance labels
        lblName.Caption = nameOnChk
        lblBalance.Caption = FormatCurrency(curBal)
        'Set the date field to the current date
        today = FormatDateTime(Now, vbLongDate)
        txtDate.Text = Mid(today, 2 + InStr(today, ","))
        Call SetupCheck 'Always start session with checks
        Call InitializeFields
    End Sub


    Private Sub InitializeFields()
        'Initialize all text entry fields except date
        txtToFrom.Text = "" txtAmount.Text = ""
        txtMemo.Text = ""
        If transType = "Check" Then
            'Make  txtNum text box reflect next check number
            txtNum.Text = Str(lastCkNum + 1)
          Else 'transType = "Deposit"
            'Make txtNum text box reflect next deposit slip number
            txtNum.Text = Str(lastDpNum + 1)
        End If
    End Sub


    Private Sub ReadDataFile()
        Dim t As String, s As String, n As String, m As String, d As String
        'Recover name to appear on checks, current balance,
        'number of last check written, and number of last deposit slip processed
        Open fileName For Input As #1
        Input #1, nameOnChk, curBal, lastCkNum, lastDpNum
        Do Until EOF(1)
            'Read to the end of the file to recover the current balance and the
            'last values recorded for ckNum and dpNum.
            't, s, n, m and d are dummy variables and are not used at this point
            Input #1, t, s, curBal, lastCkNum, lastDpNum, n, m, d
        Loop
        Close #1
    End Sub


    Private Sub SetupCheck()
        'Prepare form for the entry of a check
        transType = "Check"
        frmCheckbook.Caption = "Check"
        lblToFrom.Caption = "Pay To"
        cmdRecord.Caption = "&Record This Check"
        cmdMode.Caption = "&Switch to Deposits"
        picBox.BackColor = vbCyan 'color of check is light turquoise blue
        txtNum.BackColor = vbCyan
    End Sub


    Private Sub SetupDeposit()
        'Prepare form for the entry of a deposit
        transType = "Deposit"
        frmCheckbook.Caption = "Deposit Slip"
        lblToFrom.Caption = "Source"
```

```
    cmdRecord.Caption = "&Record This Deposit"
    cmdMode.Caption = "&Switch to Checks"
    picBox.BackColor = vbYellow 'color of deposit slip is yellow
    txtNum.BackColor = vbYellow
End Sub
```

SUMMARY

1. When sequential files are opened, we must specify whether they will be created and written to, added to, or read from by use of the terms Output, Append, or Input. The file must be *closed* before the operation is changed. Data are written to the file with Write # statements and retrieved with Input # statements. The EOF function tells if we have read to the end of the file.

2. A sequential file can be ordered by placing its data in arrays, sorting the arrays, and then writing the ordered data into a file.

PROGRAMMING PROJECTS

1. Table 7.3 gives the leading eight soft drinks in 1997 and their percentage share of the market. Write and execute a program to place these data into a sequential file. Then write a second program to use the file to

   (a) display the eight brands and their gross sales in billions. (The entire soft drink industry grosses about $42 billion.)

   (b) calculate the total percentage market share of the leading eight soft drinks.

TABLE 7.3
Leading Soft Drinks and Percentages of 1997 Market Share

Coke Classic	20.6	Sprite	6.2
Pepsi-Cola	14.5	Dr. Pepper	5.9
Diet Coke	8.5	Diet Pepsi	5.5
Mountain Dew	6.3	7 Up	2.3

Source: Beverage Digest, 2/12/98

2. Suppose the sequential file ALE.TXT contains the information shown in Table 7.4. Write a program to use the file to produce Table 7.5 in which the baseball teams are in descending order by the percentage of games won. *Note:* A batting average can be displayed in standard form with `Format-Number(ave, 3, vbFalse)`.

TABLE 7.4
American League East Games Won and Lost in 1998

Team	Won	Lost
Baltimore	79	83
Boston	92	70
New York	114	48
Tampa Bay	63	99
Toronto	88	74

TABLE 7.5
Final 1998 American League East Standings

| | American League East | | |
	W	L	Pct
New York	114	48	.704
Boston	92	70	.568
Toronto	88	74	.543
Baltimore	79	83	.488
Tampa Bay	63	99	.389

3. Write a rudimentary word processing program. The program should do the following:

(a) Use InputBox to request the name of the sequential file to hold the document being created.

(b) Set the label for a text box to "Enter Line 1" and allow the user to enter the first line of the document into a text box.

(c) When the Enter key is pressed or a "Record Line" command button is clicked, determine if the line is acceptable. Blank lines are acceptable input, but lines exceeding 60 characters in length should not be accepted. Advise the user of the problem with a message box, and then set the focus back to the text box so that the user can edit the line to an acceptable length.

(d) When an acceptable line is entered, write this line to the file and display it in a picture box.

(e) Change the prompt to "Enter Line 2", clear the text box, allow the user to enter the second line of the document into the text box, and carry out (c) for this line using the same picture box. (Determine in advance how many lines the picture box can display and only clear the picture box when the lines already displayed do not leave room for a new line.)

(f) Continue as in (d) with appropriate labels for subsequent lines until the user clicks on a "Finished" command button.

(g) Clear the picture box and display the number of lines written and the name of the data file created.

4. Write a program that counts the number of times a word occurs in the sequential file created in Programming Project 3. The file name and word should be read from text boxes. The search should not be sensitive to the case of the letters. For instance, opening a file that contained the first three sentences of the directions to this problem and searching for "the" would produce the output: "the" occurs six times.

5. *Create and Maintain Telephone Directories.* Write a program to create and maintain telephone directories. Each directory will be a separate sequential file. The following command buttons should be available:

(a) Select a directory to access. A list of directories that have been created should be stored in a separate sequential file. When a request is made to open a directory, the list of available directories should be displayed as part of an InputBox prompt requesting the name of the directory to be accessed. If the user responds with a directory name not listed, the desire to create a new directory should be confirmed, and then the new directory created and added to the list of existing directories.

(b) Add name and phone number (as given in the text boxes) to the end of the current directory.

(c) Delete name (as given in the text box) from the current directory.

(d) Sort the current directory into name order.

(e) Print out the names and phone numbers contained in the current directory.

(f) Terminate the program.

6. Table 7.6 contains the statistics for a stock portfolio. (The current prices are given for October 1, 1998.)

TABLE 7.6
Stock Portfolio

Stock	Number of Shares	Date Purchased	Purchase Price/Share	Current Price/Share
Amgen	200	8/19/97	50.750	75.625
Delta Airlines	100	12/3/97	111.750	97.250
Novell	500	8/27/97	10.375	12.250
PPG	100	12/18/97	56.750	54.500
Timken	300	3/13/98	34.625	15.125

(a) Compose a program to create the sequential file STOCKS.TXT containing the information in Table 7.6.

(b) Compose a program to perform the following tasks. A possible form design is shown in Figure 7-9.

(1) Display the information in the file STOCKS.TXT as in Table 7.6 when the user clicks on a "Display Stocks" command button.

(2) Add an additional stock onto the end of the file STOCKS.TXT when the user clicks on an "Add Stock" command button. The data for the new stock should be read from appropriately labeled text boxes.

(3) Update the Current Price/Share of a stock in the file STOCKS.TXT when the user clicks on an "Update Price" command button. The name of the stock to be updated and the new price should be read from the appropriate text boxes. The file STOCKS.TXT should then be copied to a temp file until the specified stock is found. The update record for this stock should then be written to the temp file, followed by all remaining records in STOCKS.TXT. Finally, the original STOCKS.TXT file should be erased and the temp file renamed to STOCKS.TXT.

(4) Process the data in the file STOCKS.TXT and produce the display shown in Figure 7-10 when a "Show Profit/Loss" command button is clicked.

(5) Quit.

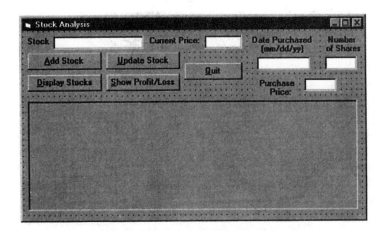

FIGURE 7-9 *Possible Form Design for Programming Project 6*

Stock	Cost	Current Value	Profit (or Loss)
========	===========	===========	===========
Amgen	$10,150.00	$15,125.00	$4,975.00
Delta Airlines	$11,175.00	$9,725.00	($1,450.00)
Novell	$5,187.50	$6,125.00	$937.50
PPG	$5,675.00	$5,450.00	($225.00)
Timken	$10,387.50	$4,537.50	($5,850.00)

FIGURE 7-10   *Output of Project 6*

7. A department store has a file containing all sales transacted for a year. Each record contains a customer's name, zip code, and amount of the sale. The file is ordered first by zip code and then by name. Write a program to display the total sales for each customer, the total sales for each zip code, and the total sales for the store. For instance, if the first six records of the file are

```
"Adams, John", 10023, 34.50
"Adams, John", 10023, 60.00
"Jones, Bob", 10023, 62.45
"Green, Mary", 12345, 54.00
"Howard, Sue", 12345, 79.25
"Smith, George", 20001, 25.10
```

then the output in the picture box will begin as shown in Figure 7-11.

Customer	Total Sales
Adams, John	$94.50
Jones, Bob	$62.45
Total sales of zip code 10023: $156.95	
Green, Mary	$54.00

FIGURE 7-11   *Sample Output for Programming Project 7*

8. *Savings Account.* NAMES.TXT is a sequential file containing the name, account number, and beginning-of-month balance for each depositor. TRANS.TXT is a sequential file containing all the transactions (deposits and withdrawals) for the month. Use TRANS.TXT to upgrade NAMES.TXT. For each customer, print a statement similar to the one received from banks that shows all transactions and the end-of-month balance. Also, record all over-drawn accounts in a file. (As an optional embellishment, deduct a penalty if the balance fell below a certain level any time during the month. The penalty could include a fixed fee of $10 plus a charge of $1 for each check and deposit.) **Hint:** Assume no more than 500 transactions have occurred.

9. A fuel economy study was carried out for five models of cars. Each car was driven for 100 miles of city driving, and then the model of the car and the number of gallons used were placed in the sequential file MILEAGE.TXT with the statement

```
Write #1, modelName, gallons
```

Table 7.7 shows the first entries of the file. Write a program to display the models and their average miles per gallon in decreasing order with respect to mileage. The program should utilize three parallel arrays of range 1 to 5. The first array should record the name of each model of car. This array is initially empty; each car model name is added when first encountered in reading the file. The second array should record the number of test vehicles for each model. The third array should record the total number of gallons used by that model.

Note: The first array must be searched each time a record is read to determine the appropriate index to use with the other two arrays.

TABLE 7.7
Gallons of Gasoline Used in 100 Miles of City Driving

Model	Gal	Model	Gal	Model	Gal
LeBaron	4.9	Cutlass	4.5	Cutlass	4.6
Escort	4.1	Escort	3.8	LeBaron	5.1
Beretta	4.3	Escort	3.9	Escort	3.8
Skylark	4.5	Skylark	4.6	Cutlass	4.4

RANDOM-ACCESS FILES

8.1 USER-DEFINED DATA TYPES

Records provide a convenient way of packaging as a single unit several related variables of different types. Before we can explore this powerful variable type, we must first explore a new category of variable, the fixed-length string.

■ FIXED-LENGTH STRINGS

Fixed-length string variables are named following the same rules as other variable types. They are declared by statements of the form

```
Dim var As String * n
```

where n is a positive integer. After such a declaration, the value of *var* will always be a string of length n. Suppose *info* is an ordinary string and a statement of the form

```
var = info
```

is executed. If *info* has more than n characters, then only the first n characters will be assigned to *var*. If *info* has less than n characters, then spaces will be added to the end of the string to guarantee that *var* has length n.

EXAMPLE 1

The following program uses fixed-length strings. In the output, San Francisco is truncated to a string of length 9 and Detroit is padded on the right with two blank spaces.

```
Private Sub cmdGo_Click()
    Dim city As String * 9
    'Illustrate fixed-length strings
    picOutput.Cls
    picOutput.Print "123456789"
    city = "San Francisco"
    picOutput.Print city
    city = "Detroit"
    picOutput.Print city; "MI"
    picOutput.Print Len(city)
End Sub
```

[Set picOutput's Font property to Courier. Run, and click the command button.]

Care must be taken when comparing an ordinary (variable-length) string with a fixed-length string or comparing two fixed-length strings of different lengths.

EXAMPLE 2

In the following program, the strings assigned to the variables *town*, *city*, and *municipality* have lengths 7, 9, and 12, respectively, and therefore are all different.

```
Private Sub cmdGo_Click()
   Dim town As String * 7
   Dim city As String * 9
   Dim municipality As String * 12
   'Illustrate fixed-length strings
   town = "Chicago"
   city = "Chicago"
   municipality = "Chicago"
   picOutput.Cls
   If (city = town) Or (city = municipality) Then
       picOutput.Print "same"
     Else
       picOutput.Print "different"
   End If
   picOutput.Print "123456789012345"
   picOutput.Print city & "***"
   picOutput.Print town & "***"
   picOutput.Print municipality & "***"
End Sub
```

[Set picOutput's Font property to Courier. Run, and click the command button.]

There are times when we want to consider the values assigned to variables of different types as being the same, such as *city* and *town* in Example 2. In this situation, the function RTrim comes to the rescue. If *info* is an ordinary string or a fixed-length string, then the value of

RTrim(info)

is the (variable-length) string consisting of *info* with all right-hand spaces removed. For instance, the value of RTrim("hello") is the string "hello". In Example 2, if the If block is changed to

```
If (RTrim(city) = town) And (RTrim(city) = RTrim(municipality)) Then
    picOutput.Print "same"
  Else
    picOutput.Print "different"
End If
```

then the first line of the output will be "same".

■ RECORDS

In this text, we have worked with numbers, strings, arrays, and now fixed-length strings. Strings and numbers are built-in data types that can be used without being declared, although we have always elected to declare numeric and string variables using Dim statements. On the other hand, arrays and fixed-length strings are user-defined data types that must be declared with a Dim statement before being used. A record is a user-defined data type that groups related variables of different types.

Figure 8-1 shows an index card that can be used to hold data about colleges. The three pieces of data—name, state, and year founded—are called **fields**. Each field functions like a variable in which information can be stored and retrieved. The **length** of a field is the number of spaces allocated to it. In the case of the index card, we see that there are three fields having lengths 30, 2, and 4, respectively. The layout of the index card can be identified by a name, such as collegeData, called a record type.

Name: State: Year Founded:

Name: _

State: _ _

Year Founded: _ _ _ _

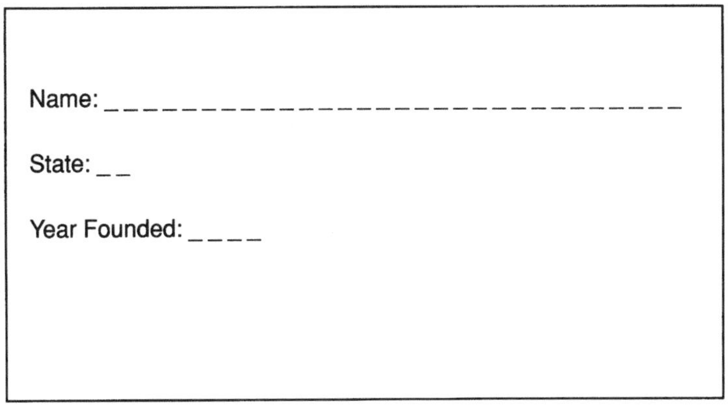

FIGURE 8-1   *An Index Card Having Three Fields*

For programming purposes, the layout of the record is declared by a block of statements similar to

```
Type collegeData
  nom As String * 30
  state As String * 2
  yearFounded As Integer
End Type
```

Each character of a string is stored in a piece of memory known as a byte. Therefore, a field of type String * *n* requires *n* bytes of memory. However, numbers (that is, the integer or single-precision numbers we use in this text) are stored in a different manner than strings. Integer numbers *always* use two bytes of memory, whereas single-precision numbers *always* use four bytes of memory.

Visual Basic requires that Type declarations, such as the preceding record structure *collegeData*, be placed in either (General) or in a special file, referred to as a BAS Module. When placed in the (General) portion of a form, the word "Type" must be preceded by "Private" and the record type is only valid for that form. When placed in a BAS module, the word "Type" may be preceded by either "Private" (valid for the current BAS module) or "Public" (valid throughout the entire program). In this text, we will primarily place our declarations inside BAS Modules and make them Public.

To create a BAS Module for the program currently being designed, press Alt/P/M and double-click on Module. A window like the one in Figure 8-2 will appear. This window is where our Type declarations will be entered. To switch between this BAS Module window and the form(s), press Ctrl+R to activate the Project Explorer and double-click on a form or module. (When the program is saved, the information in the BAS Module will be saved in a separate file with the extension bas.) You can also switch between the BAS Module and form windows by clicking on any portion of the desired window that is sticking out from behind the currently active window.

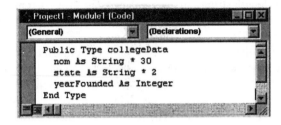

FIGURE 8-2   *BAS Module Window for Type Declarations*

A record variable capable of holding the data for a specific college is declared in the form code by a statement such as

```
Dim college As collegeData
```

Each field is accessed by giving the name of the record variable and the field, separated by a period. For instance, the three fields of the record variable college are accessed as *college.nom*, *college.state*, and *college.yearFounded*. Figure 8-3 shows a representation of the way the record variable is organized.

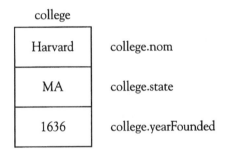

FIGURE 8-3   *Record Variable with Values Assigned to the Fields*

In general, a record type is created in a BAS Module by a Type block of the form

```
Public Type recordType
    fieldName1 As fieldType1
    fieldname2 As fieldType2
    .
    .
    .
End Type
```

where *recordType* is the name of the user-defined data type; *fieldName1, fieldName2,* . . . are the names of the fields of the record variable; and *fieldType1, fieldType2,* . . . are the corresponding field types, either String * *n*, (for some *n*), Integer, Single, or Boolean in this text. In the form code, a record variable *recordVar* is declared to be of the user-defined type by a statement of the form

```
Dim recordVar As recordType
```

EXAMPLE 3

The following program processes records.

```
'In BAS Module
Public Type collegeData
   nom As String * 30
   state As String * 2
   yearFounded As Integer
End Type


'In Form code
Private Sub cmdProcess_Click()
   Dim century As Integer, when As String
   'Demonstrate use of records
   picResult.Cls
   Dim college As collegeData
   college.nom = txtCollege.Text
   college.state = txtState.Text
   college.yearFounded = Val(txtYear.Text)
   century = 1 + Int(college.yearFounded / 100)
   picResult.Print RTrim(college.nom); " was founded in the" & Str(century);
   picResult.Print "th century in "; college.state
   Dim university As collegeData
   university.nom = "M.I.T."
   university.state = "MA"
   university.yearFounded = 1878
   If college.yearFounded < university.yearFounded Then
      when = "before "
    Else
      when = "after "
   End If
   picResult.Print RTrim(college.nom); " was founded ";
   picResult.Print when; RTrim(university.nom)
End Sub
```

[Run, type the following data into text boxes, and press the command button.]

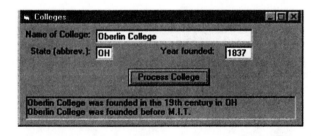

Dim statements can be used in procedures to declare a local record variable. When records are passed to and from procedures, the parameter in the Private Sub or Function statement must have the form

parameter As recordType

EXAMPLE 4

The following program uses Sub procedures to perform the same tasks as the program in Example 3.

```
'In BAS Module
Public Type collegeData
  nom As String * 30
  state As String * 2
  yearFounded As Integer
End Type

'In Form code
Private Sub cmdProcess_Click()
  'Demonstrate use of records
  picBox.Cls
  Dim college As collegeData
  Call GetDat(college)
  Call DisplayStatement(college)
End Sub

Private Sub DisplayStatement(school As collegeData)
  Dim century As Integer, when As String
  century = 1 + Int(school.yearFounded / 100)
  picBox.Print RTrim(school.nom); " was founded in the" & Str(century);
  picBox.Print "th century in "; school.state
  Dim university As collegeData
  university.nom = "M.I.T."
  university.state = "MA"
  university.yearFounded = 1878
  If school.yearFounded < university.yearFounded Then
     when = "before "
   Else
     when = "after "
  End If
  picBox.Print RTrim(school.nom); " was founded ";
  picBox.Print when; RTrim(university.nom)
End Sub

Private Sub GetDat(school As collegeData)
  school.nom = txtCollege.Text
  school.state = txtState.Text
  school.yearFounded = Val(txtYear.Text)
End Sub
```

COMMENTS

1. Record variables are similar to arrays in that they both store and access data items using a common name. However, the elements in an array must be of the same data type, whereas the fields in a record variable can be a mixture of different data types. Also, the different elements of an array are identified by their indices, whereas the fields of a record are identified by a name following a period.

2. If the record variables *recVar1* and *recVar2* have the same type, then all the field values of *recVar2* can be assigned simultaneously to *recVar1* by the statement

   recVar1 = *recVar2*

3. Statements of the form

```
picBox.Print recVar
```

are invalid, where *recVar* is a record variable. Each field of a record must appear separately in a picBox.Print statement. Also, comparisons involving records using the relational operators <, >, =, <>, < =, and > = are valid only with the record fields, and not with the records themselves.

4. In addition to being declared as numeric, Boolean, or fixed-length string data types, the elements of a user-defined variable type can also be declared as other types of records. However, we do not use such structures in this text.

5. An array of fixed-length strings is declared by a statement of the form

```
Dim arrayName (a To b) As String * n
```

6. An array of records would be declared with a statement such as

```
Dim colleges(1 to 8) As collegeData
```

and information would be accessed with statements such as

```
picBox.Print colleges(1).nom
```

7. When fixed-length strings are passed to and from procedures, the corresponding parameter in the Sub or Function statement must be an ordinary (variable-length) string.

8. Most data types can be used as field types appearing in a Type block, including (variable-length) strings. However, the String data type is not allowed in Type blocks that will be used with random-access files.

8.2 RANDOM-ACCESS FILES

A random-access file is like an array of records stored on a disk. The records are numbered 1, 2, 3, and so on, and can be referred to by their numbers. Therefore, a random-access file resembles a box of index cards, each having a numbered tab. Any card can be selected from the box without first reading every index card preceding it; similarly, any record of a random-access file can be read without having to read every record preceding it.

One statement suffices to open a random-access file for all purposes: creating, appending, writing, and reading. Suppose a record type has been defined with a Type block and a record variable, called *recVar*, has been declared with a Dim statement. Then after the statement

```
Open "filespec" For Random As #n Len = Len(recVar)
```

is executed, records may be written, read, added, and changed. The file is referred to by the number *n*. Each record will have as many characters as allotted to each value of *recVar*.

Suppose appropriate Type, Dim, and Open statements have been executed. The two-step procedure for entering a record into the file is as follows.

1. Assign a value to each field of a record variable.

2. Place the data into record *r* of file #*n* with the statement

```
Put #n, r, recVar
```

where *recVar* is the record variable from Step 1.

EXAMPLE 1

The following program creates and writes records to the random-access file COLLEGES.TXT.

```
`In BAS Module
Public Type collegeData
   nom As String * 30 'Name of college
   state As String * 2 'State where college is located
   yrFounded As Integer 'Year college was founded
End Type


'In Form code
Dim recordNum As Integer

Private Sub cmdAddCollege_Click()
   'Write a record into the file COLLEGES.TXT
   Dim college As collegeData
   college.nom = txtCollege.Text
   college.state = txtState.Text
   college.yrFounded = Val(txtYear.Text)
   recordNum = recordNum + 1
   Put #1, recordNum, college
   txtCollege.Text = ""
   txtState.Text = ""
   txtYear.Text = ""
   txtCollege.SetFocus
End Sub


Private Sub cmdDone_Click()
   Close #1
   End
End Sub


Private Sub Form_Load()
    'Create COLLEGES.TXT
   Dim college As collegeData
   Open "COLLEGES.TXT" For Random As #1 Len = Len(college)
   recordNum = 0
End Sub
```

[Run, and type into the text boxes the data shown in the following first window. Click the "Add College to File" command button. Record number 1 is added to COLLEGES.TXT and the text boxes are cleared. Proceed to record the data shown for the other two colleges and then click the "Done" command button.]

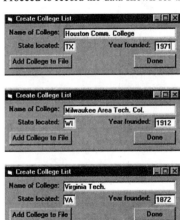

The two-step procedure for reading data from a record is as follows:

1. Execute the statement

```
Get #n, r, recVar
```

to assign record *r* of file *#n* to the record variable *recVar*.

2. Use the field variables of the record variable to either display values with picBox.Print or to transfer values to other variables with assignment statements.

EXAMPLE 2

The following program displays the entire contents of the random-access file COLLEGES.TXT.

```
'In BAS Module
Public Type collegeData
  nom As String * 30 'Name of college
  state As String * 2 'State where college is located
  yrFounded As Integer 'Year college was founded
End Type

'In Form code
Private Sub cmdDisplay_Click()
  Call DisplayFile
End Sub

Private Sub DisplayFile()
  Dim recordNum As Integer
  'Access the random-access file COLLEGES.TXT
  Dim college As collegeData
  Open "COLLEGES.TXT" For Random As #1 Len = Len(college)
  picOutput.Cls
  picOutput.Print "College"; Tab(30); "State", Tab(45); "Year founded"
  For recordNum = 1 To 3
    Get #1, recordNum, college
    picOutput.Print college.nom; Tab(30); college.state; _
                  Tab(45); college.yrFounded
  Next recordNum
  Close #1
End Sub
```

[Run, and click the command button.]

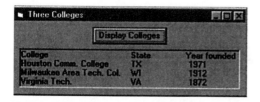

The total number of characters in the file with reference number *n* is given by the value of the function

```
LOF(n)
```

The number of the last record in the file can be calculated by dividing this value by the record length. The LOF function, rather than the EOF function, should be used to determine when the end of the file has been reached. For instance, in Example 2, the For statement in the Sub procedure DisplayFile can be written as

```
For recordNum = 1 To LOF(1) / Len(college)
```

Also, the pair of statements

```
lastRecord = LOF(1) / Len(college)
Put #1, lastRecord + 1, college
```

can be used to add a record to the end of the file.

COMMENTS

1. Random-access files are also known as **direct-access** or **relative** files. Because each record has the same number of characters, the computer can calculate where to find a specified record and, therefore, does not have to search for it sequentially.

2. Unlike sequential files, random-access files needn't be closed between placing information into them and reading from them.

3. Random-access files do not have to be filled in order. For instance, a file can be opened and the first Put statement can be Put #n, 9, recVar. In this case, space is allocated for the preceding eight records.

4. If the record number r is omitted from a Put or Get statement, then the record number used will be the one following the number most recently used in a Put or Get statement. For instance, if the line

```
Put #1, , college
```

   is added to the program in Example 1 after the existing Put statement, then the information on Virginia Tech will occupy records 3 and 4 of the file COL-LEGES.TXT.

5. Users often enter records into a random-access file without keeping track of the record numbers. If file #n is open, then the value of the function

```
Loc(n)
```

   is the number of the record most recently written to or read from file n with a Put or Get statement.

6. Each record in a random-access file has the same length. This length can be any number from 1 to 32767.

7. When the statement Open "COLLEGES.TXT" For Random As #1 Len = Len(college) is typed, the words "For Random" can be omitted. The smart editor will insert them automatically.

8. The decision of whether to store data in a sequential file or in a random-access file depends on how the data are to be processed. If processing requires a pass through all the data in the file, then sequential files are probably desirable. If processing involves seeking out one item of data, however, random-access files are the better choice.

SUMMARY

1. A *fixed-length string* is a variable declared with a statement of the form Dim *var* As String * *n*. The value of *var* is always a string of *n* characters.

2. A *record* is a composite user-defined data type with a fixed number of fields each of which can be of most data types. Type statements [in this text appearing in the (Declarations) section of a BAS Module] define record types and Dim statements are used to declare a variable to be of that type.

3. After a record type has been specified, the associated *random-access file* is an ordered collection of record values numbered 1, 2, 3, and so on. Record values are placed into the file with Put statements and read from the file with Get statements. At any time, the value of LOF(*n*) / Len(*recordVar*) is the number of the highest record value in the file and the value of Loc is the number of the record value most recently accessed by a Put or Get statement.

PROGRAMMING PROJECTS

1. *Balance a Checkbook.* Write an interactive program to request information (payee, check number, amount, and whether or not the check has cleared) for each check written during a month and store this information in a random file. The program should then request the balance at the beginning of the month and display the current balance and the payee and amount for every check still outstanding.

2. A teacher maintains a random-access file containing the following information for each student: name, social security number, grades on each of two hourly exams, and the final exam grade. Assume the random-access file GRADES.TXT has been created with string fields of lengths 25 and 11 and three numeric fields, and all the names and social security numbers have been entered. The numeric fields have been initialized with zeros. Write a program with the five command buttons "Display First Student," "Record Grade(s) & Display Next Student," "Locate Student," "Print Grade List," and "Done" to allow the teacher to do the following.

(a) Enter all the grades for a specific exam.

(b) Locate and display the record for a specific student so that one or more grades may be changed.

(c) Print a list of final grades that can be posted. The list should show the last four digits of the social security number, the grade on the final exam, and the semester average of each student. The semester average is determined by the formula (exam1 + exam2 + 2 * finalExam) / 4.

SECTION

9

THE GRAPHICAL
DISPLAY OF DATA

9.1 INTRODUCTION TO GRAPHICS

Visual Basic has impressive graphics capabilities. Figure 9-1 shows four types of charts that can be displayed in a picture box and printed by the printer.

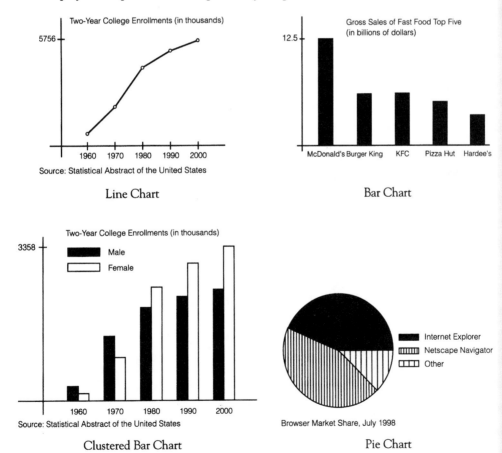

FIGURE 9-1   *Four Types of Charts*

The construction of each of these charts involves three basic steps: (1) define a coordinate system; (2) use graphics methods to draw the appropriate lines, rectangles, and circles;

and (3) place text at appropriate points on the chart. The basic tools for accomplishing each of these steps follow.

■ SPECIFYING A COORDINATE SYSTEM

Suppose we have a piece of paper, a pencil, and a ruler and we want to graph a line extending from (2, 40) to (5, 60). We would most likely use the following three-step procedure:

1. Use the ruler to draw an x axis and a y axis. Focus on the first quadrant because both points are in that quadrant.

2. Select scales for the two axes. For instance, we might decide that the numbers on the x axis range from –1 to 6 and that the numbers on the y axis range from –10 to 80.

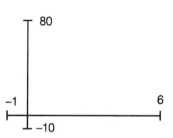

3. Plot the two points and use the ruler to draw the straight-line segment joining them.

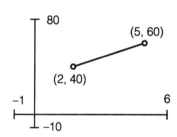

EXAMPLE 1

(a) Draw a coordinate system with the numbers on the x axis ranging from –2 to 10, and the numbers on the y axis ranging from –3 to 18.

(b) Draw the straight line from (1, 15) to (8, 6).

(c) Draw the straight line from (–2, 0) to (10, 0).

SOLUTION:

(a)
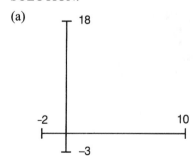

(b)
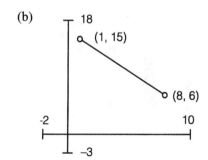

(c) The point (–2, 0) is the left-hand end point of the *x* axis and the point (10, 0) is the right-hand end point; therefore, the line joining them is just the portion of the *x* axis we have already drawn.

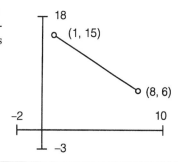

We draw these graphs on the screen with the same three steps we use with paper, pencil, and ruler. The only difference is that we first do Step 2 and then Steps 1 and 3. The Visual Basic method Scale is used to specify the range of values for the axes and the method Line serves as the ruler.

The statement

```
picBox.Scale (a, d)-(b, c)
```

specifies that numbers on the *x* axis range from *a* to *b* and that numbers on the *y* axis range from *c* to *d*. See Figure 9-2. The ordered pair (*a*, *d*) gives the coordinates of the top left corner of the picture box, and the ordered pair (*b*, *c*) gives the coordinates of the bottom right corner of the picture box.

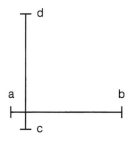   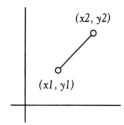

FIGURE 9-2   *Result of Scale Method*   **FIGURE 9-3**   *Result of the Line Method*

■ GRAPHICS METHODS FOR DRAWING LINES, POINTS, AND CIRCLES

After an appropriate coordinate system has been specified by a picBox.Scale statement, graphics can be drawn in the picture box using the Line and Circle methods. The statement

```
picBox.Line (x1, y1)-(x2, y2)
```

draws the line segment from the point with coordinates (*x1*, *y1*) to the point with coordinates (*x2*, *y2*) in the picture box (see Figure 9-3). In particular, the statement picBox.Line (a, 0)–(b, 0) draws the *x* axis and the statement picBox. Line (0, *c*)–(0, *d*) draws the *y* axis.

The following event procedure produces the graph of Example 1, part (b):

```
Private Sub cmdDraw_Click()
   picOutput.Cls picOutput.Scale (-2, 18)-(10, -3) 'Specify coordinate system
   picOutput.Line (-2, 0)-(10, 0) 'Draw x-axis
   picOutput.Line (0, -3)-(0, 18) 'Draw y-axis
   picOutput.Line (1, 15)-(8, 6) 'Draw the straight line
End Sub
```

EXAMPLE 2

Consider Figure 9.4.

(a) Give the statement that specifies the range for the numbers on the axes.

(b) Give the statements that will draw the axes.

(c) Give the statement that will draw the line.

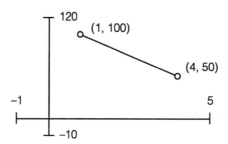

FIGURE 9-4   *Graph for Example 2*

SOLUTION:

(a) picOutput.Scale (-1, 120)-(5, -10)

(b) *x* axis: picOutput.Line (-1, 0)-(5, 0)

    y axis: picOutput.Line (0, -10)-(0, 120)

(c) picOutput.Line (1, 100)-(4, 50)

There are two other graphics methods that are just as useful as the Line method. The statement

```
picOutput.PSet (x, y)
```

plots the point with coordinates (*x*, *y*). The statement

```
picOutput.Circle (x, y), r
```

draws the circle with center (*x*, *y*) and radius *r*.

EXAMPLE 3

Write an event procedure to plot the point (7, 6) in a picture box and draw a circle of radius 3 about the point.

SOLUTION:

The rightmost point to be drawn will have *x* coordinate 10; therefore the numbers on the *x* axis must range beyond 10. In the following event procedure, we allow the numbers to range from –2 to 12. See Figure 9-5.

```
Private Sub cmdDraw_Click()
   'Draw circle with center (7, 6) and radius 3
   picOutput.Cls                          'Clear picture box
```

```
    picOutput.Scale (-2, 12)-(12, -2)        'Specify coordinate system
    picOutput.Line (-2, 0)-(12, 0)           'Draw x-axis
    picOutput.Line (0, -2)-(0, 12)           'Draw y-axis
    picOutput.PSet (7, 6)                    'Draw center of circle
    picOutput.Circle (7, 6), 3               'Draw the circle
End Sub
```

[Run, and then click the command button. The contents of the picture box is shown in Figure 9-5.]

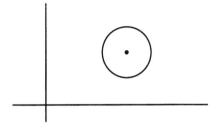

FIGURE 9-5   *Graph for Example 3*

The numbers appearing in the Scale, Line, PSet, and Circle methods can be replaced by variables or expressions. The following example demonstrates this feature.

EXAMPLE 4

Write an event procedure to draw a graph of the square root function.

SOLUTION:
We will graph the function for values of *x* from 0 to 100. See Figure 9.6.

```
Private Sub cmdDraw_Click()
    Dim x As Single
    'Graph the Square Root Function
    picOutput.Cls
    picOutput.Scale (-20, 12)-(120, -2)      'Specify coordinate system
    picOutput.Line (-5, 0)-(100, 0)          'Draw x-axis
    picOutput.Line (0, -1)-(0, 10)           'Draw y-axis
    For x = 0 To 100 Step 0.2                 'Plot about 500 points
        picOutput.PSet (x, Sqr(x))            'Plot point on graph
    Next x
End Sub
```

[Run, and then click the command button. The resulting picture box is shown in Figure 9-6.]

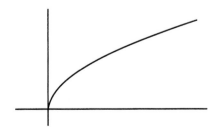

FIGURE 9-6   *Graph of the Square Root Function*

■ POSITIONING TEXT

There are times when text is placed on the screen in conjunction with graphics. This would be the case if a graph were to be titled or a tick mark needed a label. The ability to position such text appropriately in the picture box is essential to good-looking graphs. A picture box has two properties, CurrentX and CurrentY, and two methods, TextHeight and TextWidth, that allow us to precisely position text alongside graphics.

The properties CurrentX and CurrentY record the precise horizontal and vertical location at which the next character of text will be printed. By assigning appropriate values to these properties before executing a Print method, text can be positioned very precisely in the picture box. In the following event procedure, the coordinates of the right end of the tick mark are $(x, y) = (.3, 3)$. As a first attempt at labeling a tick mark on the y axis, the CurrentX and CurrentY properties are set to these coordinates. The results are shown in Figure 9-7(a).

```
Private Sub cmdDraw_Click()
  picOutput.Cls picOutput.Scale (-4, 4)-(4, -4)
  picOutput.Line (-4, 0)-(4, 0)              'Draw x-axis
  picOutput.Line (0, -4)-(0, 4)              'Draw y-axis
  picOutput.Line (-.3, 3)-(.3, 3)            'Draw tick mark
  picOutput.CurrentX = .3                    'Right end of tick mark
  picOutput.CurrentY = 3                     'Same vertical position as tick mark
  picOutput.Print "y=3"                      'Label for tick mark
End Sub
```

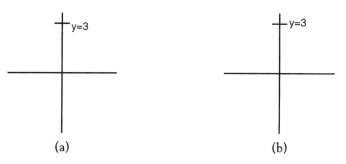

FIGURE 9-7   *Placing Labels: (a) First Attempt and (b) Second Attempt*

Note that the top of the text is even with the tick mark. This reflects the fact that the value of the CurrentY property used by Visual Basic is the location for the **top** of the character cursor. Ideally, the text should be moved up so that the tick mark aligns with the middle of the text. To do this, the value of the CurrentY property needs to be increased by one-half the height of the text. The following statement assigns a corrected value to the CurrentY property by using the TextHeight method to obtain the height of the text being used as the tick mark label. (Since $c < d$ in the scale method, TextHeight returns $(-1) \times$ [height of text].)

```
        picOutput.CurrentY = 3 - picOutput.TextHeight("y=3") / 2
```

The result of using this corrected value for CurrentY is shown in Figure 9-7(b).

When the TextHeight method is used, all characters have the same height. Thus the height of a string can be obtained by asking for the height of any single character. The following procedure uses the TextHeight method with a space character to center the text cursor at the requested graphic point.

```
Private Sub PositionText(x As Single, y As Single)
  'Center text cursor at the point (x, y)
  picOutput.CurrentX = x
  picOutput.CurrentY = y - picOutput.TextHeight(" ") / 2
End Sub
```

Another useful picture box method is TextWidth. Whereas the Len function returns the number of characters in a string, the TextWidth method considers the varying widths of characters and returns the physical width of the entire string in the units of the current scale for the picture box. The TextWidth method is essential when centering text, as illustrated in the following example.

EXAMPLE 5

Write an event procedure to display the phrase "Th-that's all Folks!" centered and double underlined in a picture box with x values ranging from 0 to 6 and y values ranging from 0 to 4.

SOLUTION:

Centering text requires knowing the coordinates of the center of the picture box, which for the given ranges will be the point (3, 2). Next, we need the width and height of the text being centered. These values are available using the TextWidth and TextHeight methods. The text cursor needs to start with a CurrentX that is half the text's width to the left of center and a CurrentY that is half the text's height above center. The first underline can be placed at half the text's height below center. The additional distance down to the second underline should be in proportion to the height of the text. We decided after some experimenting to use a proportion of 1/6th.

```
Private Sub cmdDraw_Click()
    'Center and double underline a phrase
    Dim xCenter As Single, yCenter As Single, phrase as String
    Dim w As Single, h As Single, leftEdge As Single, rightEdge As Single
    Dim ul1Pos As Single, ul2Pos As Single
    picOutput.Scale (0, 4)-(6, 0)
    picOutput.Cls
    xCenter = 3
    yCenter = 2
    phrase = "Th-that's all Folks!"
    w = picOutput.TextWidth(phrase)
    h = picOutput.TextHeight(" ")
    picOutput.CurrentX = xCenter - w / 2
    picOutput.CurrentY = yCenter - h / 2
    picOutput.Print phrase
    leftEdge = xCenter - w / 2
    rightEdge = xCenter + w / 2
    ul1Pos = yCenter + h / 2
    ul2Pos = ul1Pos + h / 6
    picOutput.Line (leftEdge, ul1Pos)-(rightEdge, ul1Pos)
    picOutput.Line (leftEdge, ul2Pos)-(rightEdge, ul2Pos)
End Sub
```

[Run, and then click the command button. The resulting picture box follows.]

COMMENTS

1. In Examples 1 through 4, examples that produce graphs, the range of numbers on the axes extended from a negative number to a positive number. Actually, any value of *a, b, c,* and *d* can be used in a Scale method. In certain cases, however, you will not be able to display one or both of the axes on the screen. (For instance, after picOutput.Scale (1, 10)–(10, −1) has been executed, the *y* axis cannot be displayed.)

2. The following technique can be used to determine a good range of values for a Scale method when graphs with only positive values are to be drawn.

(a) Let r be the x coordinate of the rightmost point that will be drawn by any Line, PSet, or Circle method.

(b) Let h be the y coordinate of the highest point that will be drawn by any Line, PSet, or Circle method.

(c) Let the numbers on the x axis range from about $-[20\%$ of $r]$ to about $r + [20\%$ of $r]$. Let the numbers on the y axis range from about $-[20\%$ of $h]$ to about $h + [20\%$ of $h]$. That is, use

```
picOutput.Scale (-.2 * r, 1.2 * h)-(1.2 * r, -.2 * h)
```

3. Usually one unit on the x axis is a different length than one unit on the y axis. The statement `picBox.Circle (x, y), r` draws a circle whose radius is r x-axis units.

4. If one or both of the points used in the Line method fall outside the picture box, the computer only draws the portion of the line that lies in the picture box. This behavior is referred to as **line clipping** and is used for the Circle method also.

5. A program can execute a picOutput.Scale statement more than once. Executing a new picOutput.Scale statement has no effect on the text and graphics already drawn; however, future graphics statements will use the new coordinate system. This technique can be used to produce the same graphics figure in different sizes and/or locations within the picture box. The output from the following event procedure is shown in Figure 9-8.

```
Private Sub cmdDraw_Click()
   Dim i As Integer
   picOutput.Cls
   For i = 0 To 3
      picOutput.Scale (0, 2 ^ i)-(2 ^ i, 0)
      picOutput.Line (0, 0)-(.5, 1)
      picOutput.Line (.5, 1)-(.8, 0)
      picOutput.Line (.8, 0)-(0, .8)
      picOutput.Line (0, .8)-(1, .5)
      picOutput.Line (1, .5)-(0, 0)
   Next i
End Sub
```

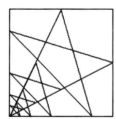

FIGURE 9-8   *Output from Comment 5*

6. The programs in this section can be modified to produce colorful displays.

Lines, points, and circles can be drawn in color through use of the vb*Color* constants. To use color, place ", vb*Color*" at the end of the corresponding graphics statement. For instance, the statement

```
picBox.Line (x1, y1)-(x2, y2), vbRed
```

draws a red line.

9.2 LINE CHARTS

A line chart displays the change in a certain quantity in relation to another quantity (often time). The following steps produce a line chart.

1. Look over the data to be displayed. A typical line chart displays between 3 and 20 items of data corresponding to evenly spaced units of time: years, months, or days. The positions on the x axis will contain labels such as "Jan   Feb   Mar   Apr . . ." or "1996   1997   1998   1999 . . .". These labels can be placed at the locations 1, 2, 3, . . . on the x axis.

2. Choose a coordinate system based on the number of data items and the size of the quantities. A convenient scale for the x axis is from -1 to one more than the number of data items. The scale for the y axis is determined by the largest quantity to be displayed.

3. Draw the line segments. It is a good idea to draw a small circle around the end points of the line segments.

4. Draw and label tick marks on the coordinate axes. The x axis should have a tick mark for each time period. The y axis should have at least one tick mark to indicate the magnitude of the quantities displayed.

5. Title the chart, and give the source of the data.

EXAMPLE 1

Table 9.1 gives enrollment data for 2-year colleges taken from the *Statistical Abstract of the United States* (the data for 2000 is a projection). Write a program to display the total enrollments for the given years in a line chart.

TABLE 9.1
Two-Year College Enrollments (in Thousands)

Year	1960	1970	1980	1990	2000
Male	283	1375	2047	2233	2398
Female	170	945	2479	3007	3358
Total	453	2320	4526	5240	5756

SOLUTION:

Figure 9-9 shows the graph that results from executing the following program. The data in ENROLL.TXT are taken from the first and fourth lines of Table 9.1. For example, the first line in the file is "1960", 453. (Explanatory remarks follow the program.)

```
'In (Declarations) section of (General)
Dim numYears As Integer, maxEnroll As Single

Private Sub cmdDraw_Click()
   'Line Chart of Total Two-Year College Enrollments
   numYears = 5
   ReDim label(1 To numYears) As String
   ReDim total(1 To numYears) As Single
   Call ReadData(label(), total())
   Call DrawAxes
   Call DrawData(total())
   Call ShowTitle
   Call ShowLabels(label())
End Sub

Private Sub DrawAxes()
   'Draw axes
```

```
            picEnroll.Scale (-1, 1.2 * maxEnroll) - (numYears + 1, -.2 * maxEnroll)
            picEnroll.Line (-1, 0)-(numYears + 1, 0)
            picEnroll.Line (0, -.1 * maxEnroll)-(0, 1.1 * maxEnroll)
        End Sub


        Private Sub DrawData(total() As Single)
            i As Integer
            'Draw lines connecting data and circle data points
            For i = 1 To numYears
                If i < numYears Then
                    picEnroll.Line (i, total(i))-(i + 1, total(i + 1))
                End If
                picEnroll.Circle (i, total(i)), .01 * numYears
            Next i
        End Sub

        Private Sub Locate(x As Single, y As Single)
            picEnroll.CurrentX = x
            picEnroll.CurrentY = y
        End Sub

        Private Sub ReadData(label() As String, total() As Single)
            Dim i As Integer
            'Assume the data have been placed in the file "ENROLL.TXT"
            '(First line of the file is "1960",453)
            'Read data into arrays, find highest enrollment
            maxEnroll = 0
            Open "ENROLL.TXT" For Input As #1
            For i = 1 To numYears
                Input #1, label(i), total(i)
                If total(i) > maxEnroll Then
                    maxEnroll = total(i)
                End If
            Next i
            Close #1
        End Sub

        Private Sub ShowLabels(label() As String)
            Dim i As Integer, lbl As String, lblWid As Single
            Dim lblHght As Single, tickFactor As Single
            'Draw tick marks and label them
            For i = 1 To numYears
                lbl = Right(label(i), 2)
                lblWid = picEnroll.TextWidth(lbl)
                tickFactor = .02 * maxEnroll
                picEnroll.Line (i, -tickFactor)-(i, tickFactor)
                Call Locate(i - lblWid / 2, -tickFactor)
                picEnroll.Print lbl
            Next i
            lbl = Str(maxEnroll)
            lblWid = picEnroll.TextWidth(lbl)
            lblHght = picEnroll.TextHeight(lbl)
            tickFactor = .02 * numYears
            picEnroll.Line (-tickFactor, maxEnroll)-(tickFactor, maxEnroll)
            Call Locate(-tickFactor - lblWid, maxEnroll - lblHght / 2)
            picEnroll.Print lbl
        End Sub
```

```
Private Sub ShowTitle()
   'Display source and title
   Call Locate(-.5, -.1 * maxEnroll)
   picEnroll.Print "Source: Statistical Abstract of the United States"
   Call Locate(.5, 1.2 * maxEnroll)
   picEnroll.Print "Two-Year College Enrollments (in thousands)"
End Sub
```

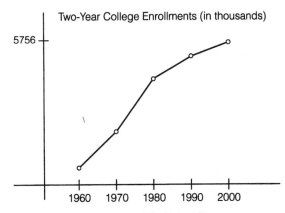

Source: Statistical Abstract of the United States

FIGURE 9-9   *Chart for Example 1*

Remarks on the program in Example 1

1. The value of *tickFactor* in the Sub procedure ShowLabels was set to 2 percent of the scale determiners (*numYears* and *maxEnroll*) for the *x* and *y* axes. This percentage is appropriate for picture boxes that occupy 1/4th to 1/3rd of the screen. Smaller picture boxes might require a factor of 3 percent or 4 percent for good-looking tick marks. Picture boxes that almost fill the screen might have good results with a factor as small as 1 percent.

2. In the Sub procedure ShowLabels, the TextWidth and TextHeight methods were used to obtain the width and height of each label. These values were used together with the coordinates of the appropriate end of the tick mark to assign values to CurrentX and CurrentY for proper placement of the label relative to the graphics.

3. In the event procedure cmdDraw_Click, the number of data points (5) was assigned to the variable *numYears*, and then *numYears* was used as a parameter to all other Sub procedures. This feature makes it easy to add additional data to the line chart. For instance, if we decide to include the data for one additional year, we will only have to change the value of *numYears* and add one more line to the data file.

■ LINE STYLING

Patterned, or "styled," lines can be drawn between two points. Some available line styles are shown in Figure 9-10. Each line has an associated number identifying its style. If *s* is one of the numbers in the figure, then the statements

```
picBox.DrawStyle = s
picBox.Line (a, b)-(c, d)
```

draw the line from (*a, b*) to (*c, d*) in the style corresponding to the number *s*.

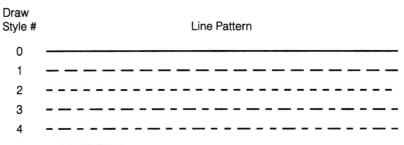

FIGURE 9-10   *Line Patterns*

Styling is useful when displaying several line charts on the same coordinate system.

EXAMPLE 2

Alter the program in Example 1 so that it will draw line charts displaying the male, female, and total enrollments of 2-year colleges.

SOLUTION:

The data file must be changed to contain the enrollment figures for males and females, and arrays must be created to hold this information. The totals can be computed from the other numbers. The styled lines for male and female enrollments must be drawn. Finally, legends must be given to identify the different line charts. Figure 9-11 shows the picture box that results from the modified program.

```
'In (Declarations) section of (General)
Dim numYears As Integer, maxEnroll As Single

Private Sub cmdDraw_Click()
  'Line Charts of Two-Year College Enrollments
  numYears = 5
  ReDim label(1 To numYears) As String
  ReDim male(1 To numYears) As Single
  ReDim female(1 To numYears) As Single
  ReDim total(1 To numYears) As Single
  Call ReadData(label(),male(),female(),total())
  Call DrawAxes
  Call DrawData(male(), female(), total())
  Call ShowTitle
  Call ShowLabels(label())
  Call ShowLegend
End Sub

Private Sub DrawAxes()
  'Draw axes
  picEnroll.Scale (-1, 1.2 * maxEnroll) - (numYears + 1, -.2 * maxEnroll)
  picEnroll.Line (-1, 0)-(numYears + 1, 0)
  picEnroll.Line (0, -.1 * maxEnroll)-(0, 1.1 * maxEnroll)
End Sub

Private Sub DrawData(male() As Single, female() As Single, total() As Single)
  Dim i As Integer
  For i = 1 To numYears
    If i < numYears Then
      'Draw lines connecting data points
      picEnroll.DrawStyle = 2
      picEnroll.Line (i, male(i))-(i + 1, male(i + 1))
      picEnroll.DrawStyle = 1
```

```
         picEnroll.Line (i, female(i))-(i + 1, female(i + 1))
         picEnroll.DrawStyle = 0
         picEnroll.Line (i, total(i))-(i + 1, total(i + 1))
      End If
      'Draw small circles around data points
      picEnroll.Circle (i, male(i)), .01 * numYears
      picEnroll.Circle (i, female(i)), .01 * numYears
      picEnroll.Circle (i, total(i)), .01 * numYears Next i
End Sub

Private Sub Locate(x As Single, y As Single)
   picEnroll.CurrentX = x
   picEnroll.CurrentY = y
End Sub

Private Sub ReadData(label() As String, male() As Single, _ female()
                     As Single, total() As Single)
   'The two lines above should be enter as one line
   Dim i As Integer
   'Assume the data has been placed in the file "ENROLLMF.TXT"
   'as Year, male, female
   '(First line of file is "1960",283,170)
   'Read data into arrays, find highest enrollment Open "ENROLLMF.TXT"
   For Input As #1
   maxEnroll = 0
   For i = 1 To numYears
      Input #1, label(i), male(i), female(i)
      total(i) = male(i) + female(i)
      If maxEnroll < total(i) Then
         maxEnroll = total(i)
      End If
   Next i
   Close #1
End Sub

Private Sub ShowLabels(label() As String)
   Dim i As Integer, lbl As String, lblWid As Single
   Dim lblHght As Single, tickFactor As Single
   'Draw tick marks and label them
   For i = 1 To numYears
      lbl = Right(label(i), 2)
      lblWid = picEnroll.TextWidth(lbl)
      tickFactor = .02 * maxEnroll
      picEnroll.Line (i, -tickFactor)-(i, tickFactor)
      Call Locate(i - lblWid / 2, -tickFactor)
      picEnroll.Print lbl
   Next i
   lbl = Str(maxEnroll)
   lblWid = picEnroll.TextWidth(lbl)
   lblHght = picEnroll.TextHeight(lbl)
   tickFactor = .02 * numYears
   picEnroll.Line (-tickFactor, maxEnroll)-(tickFactor, maxEnroll)
   Call Locate(-tickFactor - lblWid, maxEnroll - lblHght / 2)
   picEnroll.Print lbl
End Sub
```

```
Private Sub ShowLegend()
  'Show legend
  picEnroll.DrawStyle = 2
  picEnroll.Line (.1, 1.05 * maxEnroll)-(.9, 1.05 * maxEnroll)
  Call Locate(1, 1.1 * maxEnroll)
  picEnroll.Print "Male"
  picEnroll.DrawStyle = 1
  picEnroll.Line (.1, .95 * maxEnroll)-(.9, .95 * maxEnroll)
  Call Locate(1, maxEnroll)
  picEnroll.Print "Female"
  picEnroll.DrawStyle = 0
  picEnroll.Line (.1, .85 * maxEnroll)-(.9, .85 * maxEnroll)
  Call Locate(1, .9 * maxEnroll)
  picEnroll.Print "Total"
End Sub

Private Sub ShowTitle()
  'Display source and title
  Call Locate(-.5, -.1 * maxEnroll)
  picEnroll.Print "Source: Statistical Abstract of the United States"
  Call Locate(.5, 1.2 * maxEnroll)
  picEnroll.Print "Two-Year College Enrollments (in thousands)"
End Sub
```

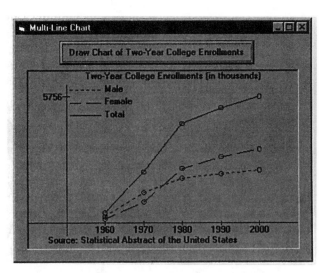

FIGURE 9-11   *Chart for Example 2*

COMMENT

1. The line charts drawn in Examples 1 and 2 can be printed on the printer instead of displayed in a picture box. Just replace each occurrence of `picOutput` with `Printer`, and add

   ```
   Printer.EndDoc
   ```

   as the last statement of the cmdDraw_Click event procedure. Also, the charts will look best in landscape orientation which is invoked with the statement

   ```
   Printer.Orientation = 2
   ```

placed before the Scale method is executed.

9.3 BAR CHARTS

Drawing bar charts requires a variation of the line statement. If $(x1, y1)$ and $(x2, y2)$ are two points on the screen, then the statement

```
picBox.Line (x1, y1) - (x2, y2), , B
```

draws a rectangle with the two points as opposite corners. If B is replaced by BF, a solid rectangle will be drawn (see Figure 9-12).

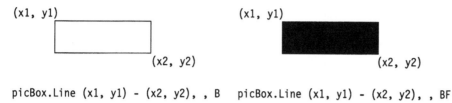

```
picBox.Line (x1, y1) - (x2, y2), , B    picBox.Line (x1, y1) - (x2, y2), , BF
```

FIGURE 9-12   *Line Method with B and BF Options*

EXAMPLE 1

The 1998 populations of California and New York are 32 and 18 million, respectively. Draw a bar chart to compare the populations.

SOLUTION:

The following program produces the chart shown in Figure 9-13. The first five lines are the same as those of a line chart with two pieces of data. The base of the rectangle for California is centered above the point $(1, 0)$ on the x axis and extends .3 unit to the left and right. (The number .3 was chosen arbitrarily; it had to be less than .5 so that the rectangles would not touch.) Therefore, the upper-left corner of the rectangle has coordinates $(.7, 32)$ and the lower-right corner has coordinates $(1.3, 0)$. Figure 9-14 shows the coordinates of the principal points of the rectangles.

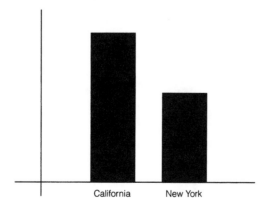

FIGURE 9-13   *Bar Chart for Example 1*

```
Private Sub cmdDisplayPop_Click()
   'Populations of California and New York
   picPop.Scale (-1, 40)-(3, -5)          'Specify coordinates
   picPop.Line (-1, 0)-(3, 0) '           Draw x-axis
   picPop.Line (0, -5)-(0, 40) '          Draw y-axis
   picPop.Line (.7, 32)-(1.3, 0),,BF      'Draw solid rectangle for CA
   picPop.Line (1.7, 18)-(2.3, 0),,BF     'Draw solid rectangle for NY
   picPop.CurrentY = -1                   'Vertical position of labels
```

```
    picPop.CurrentX = .7                    'Beginning horizontal position of
                                            label for CA
    picPop.Print "California";              'Beginning horizontal position of
    label for NY
    picPop.CurrentX = 1.7 picPop.Print "New York";
End Sub
```

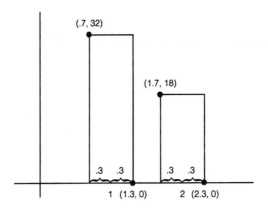

FIGURE 9-14   *Coordinates of Principal Points of Example 1*

Any program that draws a line chart can be easily modified to produce a bar chart. Multiple line charts are converted into so-called **clustered bar charts**.

EXAMPLE 2

Display the 2-year college enrollments for males and females in a clustered bar chart. Use the data in Table 9.2 of Section 9.4.

SOLUTION:

The output of the following program appears in Figure 9-15. This program is very similar to the program that produced Figure 9-11 of Section 9.4.

```
Private Sub cmdDraw_Click()
    Dim numYears As Integer, maxEnroll As Single
    'Bar Chart of Total Two-Year College Enrollments
    numYears = 5
    ReDim label(1 To numYears) As String
    ReDim male(1 To numYears) As Single
    ReDim female(1 To numYears) As Single
    Call ReadData(label(), male(), female(), numYears, maxEnroll)
    Call DrawAxes(numYears, maxEnroll)
    Call DrawData(male(), female(), numYears)
    Call ShowTitle(maxEnroll)
    Call ShowLabels(label(), numYears, maxEnroll)
    Call ShowLegend(maxEnroll)
End Sub

Private Sub
    DrawAxes(numYears As Integer, maxEnroll As Single)
    'Draw axes
    picEnroll.Scale (-1, 1.2 * maxEnroll)-(numYears + 1, -.2 * maxEnroll)
    picEnroll.Line (-1, 0)-(numYears + 1, 0)
    picEnroll.Line (0, -.1 * maxEnroll)-(0, 1.1 * maxEnroll)
End Sub
```

```
Private Sub DrawData(male() As Single, female() As Single, _ numYears As
                     Integer)
   Dim i As Integer
   'Draw rectangles
   For i = 1 To numYears
      picEnroll.Line (i - .3, male(i))-(i, 0), , BF
      picEnroll.Line (i, female(i))-(i + .3, 0), , B
   Next i
End Sub


Private Sub Locate(x As Single, y As Single)
   picEnroll.CurrentX = x
   picEnroll.CurrentY = y
End Sub


Private Sub ReadData(label() As String, male() As Single, _ female() As
Single, numYears As Integer, maxEnroll As Single)
   Dim i As Integer
   'Assume the data have been placed in the file ENROLLMF.TXT
   '(First line is file is "1960",283,170)
   'Read data into arrays, find highest enrollment
   Open "ENROLLMF.TXT" For Input As #1
   maxEnroll = 0
   For i = 1 To numYears
      Input #1, label(i), male(i), female(i)
   If male(i) > maxEnroll Then
         maxEnroll = male(i)
      End If
      If female(i) > maxEnroll Then
         maxEnroll = female(i)
      End If
   Next i
   Close #1
End Sub


Private Sub ShowLabels(|label() As String, numYears As Integer, _ maxEnroll As
                       Single) Dim i As Integer, lbl As String, lblWid As
                       Single
   Dim lblHght As Single, tickFactor As Single
   'Draw tick marks and label them
   For i = 1 To numYears
      lbl = label(i)
      lblWid = picEnroll.TextWidth(lbl)
      tickFactor = .02 * maxEnroll
      picEnroll.Line (i, -tickFactor)-(i, tickFactor)
      Call Locate(i - lblWid / 2, -tickFactor)
      picEnroll.Print lbl
   Next i
   lbl = Str(maxEnroll)
   lblWid = picEnroll.TextWidth(lbl)
   lblHght = picEnroll.TextHeight(lbl)
   tickFactor = .01 * numYears
   picEnroll.Line (-tickFactor, maxEnroll)-(tickFactor, maxEnroll)
   Call Locate(-tickFactor - lblWid, maxEnroll - lblHght / 2)
   picEnroll.Print lbl
End Sub
```

```
Private Sub ShowLegend(maxEnroll As Single) 'Show legend
  picEnroll.Line (.1, 1.05 * maxEnroll)-(.9, .95 * maxEnroll), , BF
  Call Locate(1, 1.05 * maxEnroll)
  picEnroll.Print "Male"
  picEnroll.Line (.1, .9 * maxEnroll)-(.9, .8 * maxEnroll), , B
  Call Locate(1, .9 * maxEnroll)
  picEnroll.Print "Female"
End Sub

Private Sub ShowTitle(maxEnroll As Single)
  'Display source and title Call Locate(-.5, -.1 * maxEnroll)
  picEnroll.Print "Source: Statistical Abstract of the United States"
  Call Locate(.5, 1.2 * maxEnroll)
  picEnroll.Print "Two-Year College Enrollments (in thousands)"
End Sub
```

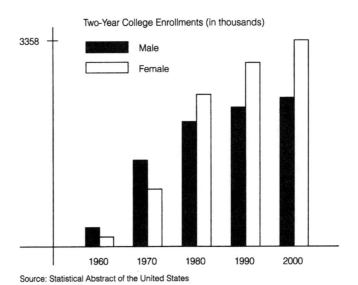

FIGURE 9-15   *Chart for Example 2*

COMMENTS

1. Any line chart can be converted to a bar chart and vice versa. Line charts are best suited for displaying quantities that vary with time. The slopes of the individual line segments clearly portray the rates at which the quantity is changing. Bar charts excel in contrasting the magnitudes of different entities.

2. The Line method can produce colored rectangles. If vb*Color* is one of the 8 color constants, then the statement picBox.Line (*x1, y1*)–(*x2, y2*), vb*Color*, B draws a rectangle in color. A colored solid rectangle will be produced if B is replaced by BF. The use of color permits clustered bar charts with three bars per cluster.

3. In Section 9.4, we discuss a method to fill in rectangles using various patterns, such as horizontal lines and crosshatches. Using this technique, we can create black-and-white clustered bar charts having three or more bars per cluster.

9.4 PIE CHARTS

Drawing pie charts requires the Circle method and the FillStyle property. The Circle method draws not only circles, but also sectors (formed by an arc and two radius lines). The FillStyle property determines what pattern, if any, is used to fill a sector. The FillColor property can be used, if desired, to lend color to the fill patterns.

Figure 9-16 shows a circle with several radius lines drawn. The radius line extending to the right from the center of the circle is called the **horizontal radius line**. Every other radius line is assigned a number between 0 and 1 according to the percentage of the circle that must be swept out in the counterclockwise direction in order to reach that radius line. For instance, beginning at the horizontal radius line and rotating 1/4 of the way around the circle counterclockwise, we reach the radius line labeled .25.

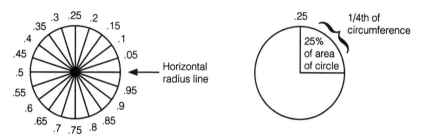

FIGURE 9-16   *Numbers Assigned to Radius Lines*

EXAMPLE 1

In Figure 9-17, what percentage of the area of the circle lies in the shaded sector?

FIGURE 9-17   *Circle for Example 1*

SOLUTION:
The percentage of the circle contained between the radius lines labeled .15 and .35 is 35% − 15%, or 20%.

The statement

```
picBox.Circle (x, y), r
```

draws the circle with center (x, y) and radius r. More precisely, the length of the horizontal radius line will be r units in the scale for the x axis determined by the picBox.Scale statement. If $0 < a < b < 1$ and c is the circumference of the unit circle ($2*\pi$), then the statement

```
picBox.Circle (x, y), r, , a * c, b * c
```

draws an arc from the end of radius line a to the end of radius line b. See Figure 9-18(a). The statement

```
picBox.Circle (x, y), r, , -a * c, -b * c
```

draws the sector corresponding to that arc. See Figure 9-18(b).

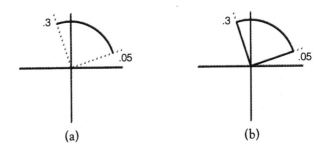

FIGURE 9-18 *(a) Arc of a Circle and (b) Sector of a Circle*

A special case occurs when a is 0. The expression $-a * c$ will be zero rather than a negative number. As a result, Visual Basic does not draw the horizontal radius line associated with $a = 0$. In order to create a sector that has the horizontal radius line as one of its edges, use a small number such as .0000001 for a.

EXAMPLE 2

Write a program to draw a sector whose sides are a horizontal radius line and the radius line that is 40 percent of the way around the circle.

SOLUTION:

The following program draws the sector with its center at the center of the picture box. The radius was arbitrarily chosen to be 2 and the picOutput.Scale statement was chosen so that the circle would be fairly large. The output displayed in the picture box is shown in Figure 9-19.

```
Private Sub cmdDraw_Click()
    Dim c As Single
    picOutput.Cls
    picOutput.Scale (-3, 3)-(3, -3) 'Specify coordinate system
    c = 2 * 3.14159
    a = .0000001
    b = .4
    'Draw sector with radius lines corresponding to 0 and .4
    picOutput.Circle (0, 0), 2, , -a * c, -b * c
End Sub
```

FIGURE 9-19 *Display from Example 2*

A sector can be "painted" using any of the patterns shown in Figure 9-20. Which pattern is used to fill a sector is determined by the value of the FillStyle property. The default value of this property is 1 for transparent. Thus, by default, the interior of a sector is not painted.

Fill Style #	Fill Pattern	Fill Style #	Fill Pattern
0		4	
1		5	
2		6	
3		7	

FIGURE 9-20 *Fill Patterns*

EXAMPLE 3

Write a program to draw the sector consisting of the bottom half of a circle and fill it with vertical lines.

SOLUTION:

Vertical lines correspond to a FillStyle of 3. See Figure 9-21 for the output of the following program.

```
Private Sub cmdDraw_Click()
   Dim c As Single
   'Draw bottom half of circle filled with vertical lines
   c = 2 * 3.14159
   picSector.Cls
   picSector.Scale (-3, 3)-(3, -3)          'Specify coordinate system
   picSector.FillStyle = 3                  'Vertical lines
   picSector.Circle (0, 0), 2, , -.5 * c, -1 * c
End Sub
```

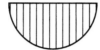

FIGURE 9-21   *Display from Example 3*

The color used to fill the interior of a sector is determined by the value of the FillColor property. If the FillStyle of a picture box is any value except 1, then the statement

```
picBox.FillColor = vbColor
```

where vb*Color* is a color constant, will cause new circles and sectors drawn in the picture box to be filled with a colored pattern.

EXAMPLE 4

Write a program to subdivide a circle into four quadrants and fill in the second quadrant, that is, the quadrant extending from radius line .25 to radius line .5, with magenta crosshatched lines.

SOLUTION:

Crosshatched lines correspond to a FillStyle of 6. See Figure 9-22 for the output of the following program.

```
Private Sub cmdDraw_Click()
   Dim c As Single
   'Draw quarters of circle and paint upper-left quadrant
   c = 2 * 3.14159
   picBox.Cls picBox.Scale (-3, 3)-(3, -3)    'Specify coordinate system
   picBox.Circle (0, 0), 2, , -.0000001 * c, -.25 * c
   picBox.FillStyle = 6                        'Crosshatched
   picBox.FillColor = vbMagenta
   picBox.Circle (0, 0), 2, , -.25 * c, -.5 * c
   picBox.FillStyle = 1                        'Transparent
   picBox.Circle (0, 0), 2, , -.5 * c, -.75 * c
   picBox.Circle (0, 0), 2, , -.75 * c, -1 * c
End Sub
```

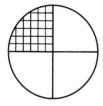

FIGURE 9-22   *Display from Example 4*

The FillStyle and FillColor properties can be used when creating rectangles. The statements

```
picBox.FillStyle = s=
picBox.Fill Color = vbColor
pic Box.Line (x1, y1) - (x2, y2), , 8
```

draw a rectangle filled with the pattern specified by *s* in the color specified by vb*Color*. This capability is often used when creating the legend to accompany a graph.

The procedure for drawing a pie chart is as follows:

1. Read the categories and the quantities into arrays, such as *category*() and *quantity*().

2. Determine the radius lines. The number associated with the *i*th radius line is *cumPercent*(*i*). This number is a total of *quantity*(*i*) and the preceding percentages.

3. Draw and fill each sector with a pattern. The first sector extends from the horizontal radius line to radius line 1, the second sector from radius line 1 to radius line 2, and so on.

4. Draw rectangular legends to associate each sector with its category.

EXAMPLE 5

Table 9.2 gives the market share of Internet browsers for July 1998. Construct a pie chart that displays the market share.

TABLE 9.2
Browser Market Share, July 1998

	Percent of Total Market
Internet Explorer	44
Netscape Navigator	42
Other	14

SOLUTION:
Figure 9-23 shows the output displayed by the following program.

```
Private Sub cmdDraw_Click()
   Dim numItems As Integer, radius As Single
   'Draw pie chart of Browser Market Share
   numItems = 3
   ReDim category(1 To numItems) As String
   ReDim quantity(1 To numItems) As Single
   Call ReadData(category(), quantity(), numItems)
   Call DrawData(quantity(), numItems, radius)
   Call ShowLegend(category(), numItems, radius)
   Call ShowTitle(radius)
End Sub

Private Sub DrawData(quantity() As Single, numItems As Integer, _ radius As
                  Single)
   Dim circumf As Single, leftEdge As Single, rightEdge As Single
   Dim topEdge As Single, bottomEdge As Single, i As Integer
   Dim startAngle As Single, stopAngle As Single
   'Draw and fill each sector of pie chart
   'All scaling and text positioning done as a percentage of radius radius = 1
   'actual value used is not important
   'Make picture 4 radii wide to provide plenty of space for
   'circle and legends. Place origin 1.25 radii from left edge;
```

```
      'space of 1.75 radii will remain on right for legends.
      leftEdge = -1.25 * radius
      rightEdge = 2.75 * radius
      'Force vertical scale to match horizontal scale; 'center origin vertically
      topEdge = 2 * radius * (picShare.Height / picShare.Width)
      bottomEdge = -topEdge
      picShare.Cls
      picShare.Scale (leftEdge, topEdge)-(rightEdge, bottomEdge)
      circumf = 2 * 3.14159
      ReDim cumPercent(0 To numItems) As Single
        cumPercent(0) = .0000001 'a value of "zero" that can be made negative
        For i = 1
        To numItems cumPercent(i) = cumPercent(i - 1) + quantity(i)
        startAngle = cumPercent(i - 1) * circumf
        stopAngle = cumPercent(i) * circumf
        picShare.FillStyle = (8 - i) 'use fill patterns 7, 6, and 5
        picShare.Circle (0, 0), radius, , -startAngle, -stopAngle
      Next i
End Sub


Private Sub Locate (x As Single, y As Single)
    picShare.CurrentX = x
    picShare.CurrentY = y
End Sub


Private Sub ReadData(category() As String, quantity() As Single, _ numItems As
                    Integer)
    Dim i As Integer 'Load categories and percentages of market share
    'Assume the data have been placed in the file BROWSERS.TXT
    '(First line in file is "Internet Explorer", .44)
    Open "BROWSERS.TXT" For Input As #1
    For i = 1 To numItems
      Input #1, category(i), quantity(i)
    Next i
    Close #1
End Sub


Private Sub ShowLegend(category() As String, numItems As Integer, _ radius As
                    Single)
    Dim lblHght As Single, legendSize As Single
    Dim i As Integer, vertPos As Single
    'Place legend centered to right of pie chart
    'Make separation between items equal to one line of text
    '"Text lines" needed for legends is thus (2*numItems-1)
    lblHght = picShare.TextHeight(" ")
    legendSize = lblHght * (2 * numItems - 1)
    For i = 1 To numItems
      picShare.FillStyle = (8 - i)
      vertPos = (legendSize / 2) - (3 - i) * (2 * lblHght)
      picShare.Line (1.1 * radius, vertPos)-(1.4 * radius, _ vertPos +
                    lblHght), ,B
      Call Locate(1.5 * radius, vertPos)
      picShare.Print category(i)
    Next i
End Sub
```

```
Private Sub ShowTitle(radius As Single)
   Dim lbl As String, lblWid As Single
   'Display title right below circle
   lbl = "Browser Market Share, July 1998"
   lblWid = picShare.TextWidth(lbl)
   Call Locate(-lblWid / 2, -(radius + .05))
   picShare.Print lbl
End Sub
```

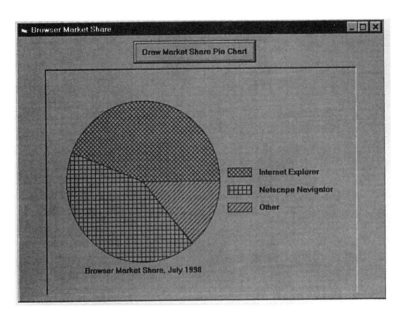

FIGURE 9-23   *Display from Example 5*

SUMMARY

1. Data can be vividly displayed in *line, bar, clustered bar,* and *pie charts*.

2. The programmer can select his or her own coordinate system with the Scale method.

3. The Line method draws lines, rectangles, and solid rectangles. Styled lines can be drawn by assigning appropriate values to the DrawStyle property.

4. The Circle method is used to draw circles, radius lines, and sectors. Each radius line is specified by a number between 0 and 1. The number $2 * \pi$ (or 6.283185) is used by the Circle method when drawing radii and sectors.

5. The PSet method turns on a single point and is useful in graphing functions.

6. The FillStyle property allows circles, sectors, and rectangles to be filled with one of eight patterns, and the FillColor property allows them to appear in assorted colors.

PROGRAMMING PROJECTS

1. Look in magazines and newspapers for four sets of data, one suited to each type of chart discussed in this chapter. Write programs to display the data in chart form.

2. Figure 9-24 is called a *horizontal bar chart*. Write a program to produce this chart.

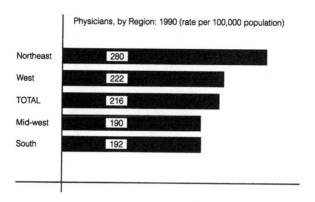

FIGURE 9-24   *Horizontal Bar Chart*

3. Figure 9-25 is called a segmented bar chart. Write a program to construct this chart.

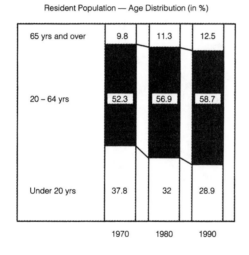

FIGURE 9-25   *Segmented Bar Chart*

4. Figure 9-26 is called a *range chart*. Using the data in Table 9.3, write a program to produce this chart.

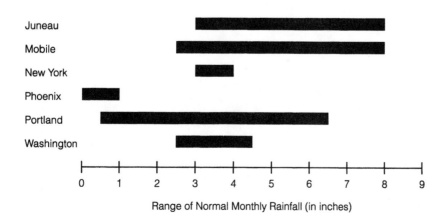

FIGURE 9-26   *Range Chart*

TABLE 9.3
Range of Normal Monthly Rainfall for Selected Cities (in Inches)

	Lowest NMR	Highest NMR
Mobile	2.6	7.7
Portland	.5	6.4
Phoenix	.1	1.0
Washington	2.6	4.4
Juneau	2.9	7.7
New York	3.1	4.2

ADDITIONAL CONTROLS
AND OBJECTS

10.1 LIST BOXES AND COMBO BOXES

The dialog box in Figure 10-1 contains two **list boxes**, one text box, and two **combo boxes**. The Folders list box displays a list of folders (also known as directories). You click on a folder to highlight it and double-click on a folder to open it. A combo box combines the features of a text box and a list box. With the two combo boxes (known as dropdown combo boxes), only the text box part is showing. The associated list drops down when you click on the arrow to the right of the text box part.

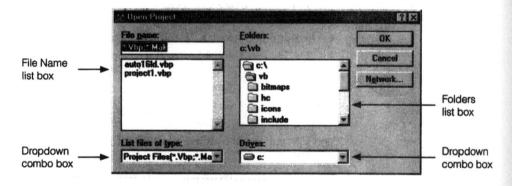

FIGURE 10-1 *Open Project Dialog Box*

 THE LIST BOX CONTROL

The fifth row of the standard toolbox (in most editions of Visual Basic) contains the combo box icon on the left and the list box icon on the right. The list boxes discussed in this text will display a single column of strings, referred to as **items**. The items to appear initially can either be specified at design time with the List property or set with code in a procedure. Then code is used to access, add, or delete items from the list. We will first carry out all tasks with code and then show how the initial items can be specified at design time. The standard prefix for the name of a list box is lst.

The Sorted property is perhaps the most interesting list box property. When it is set to True, the items will automatically be displayed in alphabetical (that is, ANSI) order. The default value of the Sorted property is False.

If *str* is a string, then the statement

```
lstBox.AddItem str
```

adds *str* to the list. The item is added at the proper sorted position if the Sorted property is True, and otherwise is added to the end of the list. At any time, the value of

```
lstBox.ListCount
```

is the number of items in the list box.

Each item in lstBox is identified by an index number ranging from 0 through lstBox.ListCount − 1. The value of

```
lstBox.NewIndex
```

is the index number of the item most recently added to lstBox by the AddItem method. During run time you can highlight an item from a list by clicking on it with the mouse or by moving to it with the up- and down-arrow keys when the list box has the focus. (The second method triggers the Click event each time an arrow key causes the highlight to move.) The value of

```
lstBox.ListIndex
```

is the index number of the item currently highlighted in lstBox. (If no item is highlighted, the value of ListIndex is −1.)

The string array lstBox.List( ) holds the list of items stored in the list box. In particular, the value of

```
lstBox.List(n)
```

is the item of lstBox having index *n*. For instance, the statement picBox.Print lstBox.List(0) displays the first item of the list box lstBox. The value of

```
lstBox.List(lstBox.ListIndex)
```

is the item (string) currently highlighted in lstBox. Alternatively, the value of

```
lstBox.Text
```

is also the currently highlighted item. Unlike the Text property of a text box, you may not assign a value to lstBox.Text.

The statement

```
lstBox.RemoveItem n
```

deletes the item of index *n* from lstBox, the statement

```
lstBox.RemoveItem lstBox.ListIndex
```

deletes the item currently highlighted in lstBox, and the statement

```
lstBox.Clear
```

deletes every item of lstBox.

EXAMPLE 1

An oxymoron is a pairing of contradictory or incongruous words. The following program displays a sorted list of oxymorons. When you click an item (or highlight it with the up- and down-arrow keys), it is displayed in a picture box. A command button allows you to add an additional item with an Input box. You can delete an item by double-clicking on it with the mouse. (*Note:* When you double-click the mouse, two events are processed—the Click event and the DblClick event.) After running the program, click on different items, add an item or two (such as "same difference" or "liquid gas"), and delete an item.

Object	Property	Setting
frmOxyMor	Caption	OXYMORONS
lstOxys	Sorted	True
cmdAdd	Caption	Add an Item
lblDelete	Caption	[To delete an item, double-click on it.]
picSelected		

```
Private Sub cmdAdd_Click()
  Dim item As String
  item = InputBox("Item to Add:")
  lstOxys.AddItem item
End Sub

Private Sub Form_Load()
  lstOxys.AddItem "jumbo shrimp"
  lstOxys.AddItem "definite maybe"
  lstOxys.AddItem "old news"
  lstOxys.AddItem "good grief"
End Sub

Private Sub lstOxys_Click()
  picSelected.Cls
  picSelected.Print "The selected item is"
  picSelected.Print Chr(34) & lstOxys.Text & Chr(34) & "."
End Sub

Private Sub lstOxys_DblClick()
  lstOxys.RemoveItem lstOxys.ListIndex
End Sub
```

[Run, and then click on the second item of the list box.]

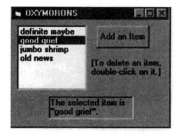

The following steps show how to fill a list box at design time. (This method is used in Example 3.)

1. Select the List property of the list box.
2. Click on the down arrow of the Settings box. (A small box will be displayed.)
3. Type in the first item and press Ctrl+Enter. (The cursor will move to the next line.)
4. Repeat Step 3 for each of the other items.
5. When you are finished entering items, press the Enter key.

When the Sorted property of a list box is True, the index associated with an item will change when a "lesser" item is added to or removed from the list. In many applications it is important to have a fixed number associated with each item in a list box. Visual Basic makes this possible using the ItemData property. The statement

```
lstBox.ItemData(n) = m
```

associates the number m with the item of index n, and the statement

```
lstBox.ItemData(lstBox.NewIndex) = m
```

associates the number m with the item most recently added to the list box. Thus, lstBox can be thought of as consisting of two arrays, lstBox.List( ) and lstBox.ItemData( ). The contents of lstBox.List( ) are displayed in the list box, allowing the user to make a selection while the hidden contents of lstBox.ItemData( ) can be used by the programmer to index records. As illustrated in Example 2, they can also be used to set up parallel arrays that hold other data associated with each item displayed in the list box.

EXAMPLE 2

The following program uses NewIndex and ItemData to provide data about inventions. When an item is highlighted, its ItemData value is used to locate the appropriate entries in the inventor( ) and date( ) arrays. Assume the file INVENTOR.TXT contains the following three lines:

"Ball-point pen", "Lazlo and George Biro", 1938
"Frozen food", "Robert Birdseye", 1929
"Bifocal lenses", "Ben Franklin", 1784

Object	Property	Setting
frmInvent	Caption	Inventions
lstInvents	Sorted	True
lblInventor	Caption	Inventor
lblWho	Caption	(none)
lblYear	Caption	Year
lblWhen	Caption	(none)

```
'In the (Declarations) section of (General)
  Dim inventor(0 To 10) As String
Dim yr(0 To 10) As Integer

Private Sub Form_Load()
  Dim what As String, who As String, when As Integer, index As Integer
  Open "INVENTOR.TXT" For Input As #1
  index = 0
  Do While (index [[ UBound(inventor)) And (Not EOF(1))
    Input #1, what, who, when
    index = index + 1
    lstInvents.AddItem what
    lstInvents.ItemData(lstInvents.NewIndex) = index
    inventor(index) = who
    yr(index) = when
  Loop
  Close #1
End Sub

Private Sub lstInvents_Click()
  lblWho.Caption = inventor(lstInvents.ItemData(lstInvents.ListIndex))
  lblWhen.Caption = Str(yr(lstInvents.ItemData(lstInvents.ListIndex)))
End Sub
```

[Run, and then highlight the second entry in the list.]

THE COMBO BOX CONTROL

A combo box is best thought of as a text box with a help list attached. With an ordinary text box, the user must type information into the box. With a combo box, the user has the option of either typing in information or just selecting the appropriate piece of information from a list. The two most useful types of combo box are denoted as style 0 (Dropdown) and style 1 (Simple) combo boxes. See Figure 10-2. The standard prefix for the name of a combo box is cbo.

Style 0–Dropdown combo box   Style 1–Simple combo box

FIGURE 10-2   *Styles of Combo Boxes*

With a Simple combo box, the list is always visible. With a Dropdown combo box, the list drops down when the user clicks on the arrow, and then disappears after a selection is made. In either case, when an item from the list is highlighted, the item automatically appears in the text box at the top and its value is assigned to the Text property of the combo box.

Combo boxes have essentially the same properties, events, and methods as list boxes. In particular, all the statements discussed before for list boxes also hold for combo boxes. The Style property of a combo box must be specified at design time.

EXAMPLE 3

The following program uses a simple combo box to obtain a person's title for the first line of the address of a letter. (***Note:*** At design time, first set the combo box's Style property to 1, and then lengthen the height of the combo box.)

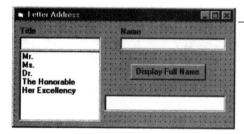

Object	Property	Setting
frmTitle	Caption	Letter Address
lblTitle	Caption	Title
cboTitle	List	Mr.
		Ms.
		Dr.
		The Honorable
		Her Excellency
	Style	1 – Simple Combo
	Text	(blank)
lblName	Caption	Name
txtName	Text	(blank)
cmdDisplay	Caption	Display Full Name
txtDisplay	Text	(blank)

```
Private Sub cmdDisplay_Click()
   txtDisplay.Text = cboTitle.Text & " " & txtName.Text
End Sub
```

[Run, select an item from the combo box, type a name into the Name text box, and click the command button.]

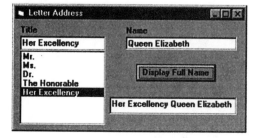

The same program with a style 0 combo box produces the output shown.

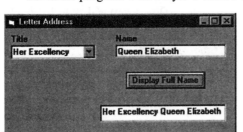

DRIVE, DIRECTORY, AND FILE LIST BOX CONTROLS

Boxes similar to those inside the Open Project dialog box of Figure 10-1 are available to any Visual Basic program via icons from the Toolbox. Visual Basic does much of the work of providing the appropriate lists for the three boxes. Windows determines the contents of the drive box. The programmer determines the contents of directory list boxes and file list boxes with Path properties.

Most of the properties, methods, and events of list boxes are also valid for the three file-related list boxes. For instance, in the file list box File1, File1.ListCount is the number of files and File1.List(n) is the name of the nth file, where counting begins with 0. The selected items for the three controls are identified by the Drive, Path, and FileName properties, respectively. For instance, in the drive list box Drive1, the selected drive is given by the string Drive1.Drive.

Suppose a form contains a drive list box named Drive1, a directory list box named Dir1, and a file list box named File1. (These names are the default names supplied by Visual Basic.) When the user selects a new drive from the Drive1 list box, the directories in Dir1 should reflect this change. The proper event procedure to effect the change is

```
Private Sub Drive1_Change()
    Dir1.Path = Drive1.Drive
End Sub
```

This event is triggered by clicking on the drive name or using the arrow keys to highlight the drive name and then pressing Enter. When the user selects a new directory in Dir1, the files in File1 can be changed with the event procedure

```
Private Sub Dir1_Change()
    File1.Path = Dir1.Path
End Sub
```

This event procedure is triggered by double-clicking on a directory name. If the preceding two event procedures are in place, a change of the drive will trigger a change of the directory, which in turn will trigger a change in the list of files. The standard prefixes for the names of the drive, directory, and file list box controls are drv, dir, and fil, respectively.

EXAMPLE 4

The following program can be used to display the full name of any file on any drive.

Object	Property	Setting
frmFiles	Caption	Select a File
drvList		
dirList		
filList		
cmdDisplay	Caption	Display Complete Name of File
picFileSpec		

```
Private Sub cmdDisplay_Click()
   picFileSpec.Cls
   picFileSpec.Print dirList.Path;
   If Right(dirList.Path, 1) <> "\" Then
      picFileSpec.Print "\";
   End If
   picFileSpec.Print filList.FileName
End Sub

Private Sub dirList_Change()
   filList.Path = dirList.Path
End Sub

Private Sub drvList_Change()
   dirList.Path = drvList.Drive
End Sub
```

[Run, select a drive, double-click on a directory, select a file, and then click the command button.]

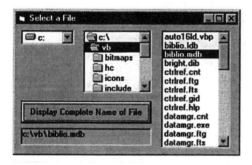

COMMENTS

1. If a list or combo box is too short to display all the items that have been added to it, Visual Basic automatically places a vertical scroll bar on the right side of the list box. The user can then scroll to see the remaining items of the list.

2. When the Style property of a combo box is set to 2, the combo box becomes a dropdown list box. The Drive list box is an example of a dropdown list box.

3. Dropdown combo boxes (Style 0) are used in Windows applications as a text box with a "history list" (list of past entries) from which you can either type a new entry or select an old entry.

4. The standard Windows convention for opening a file is to double-click on a name in a file list box. The program must contain code for a DblClick event procedure to carry out this task.

5. File list boxes can be made to display selective lists based on wildcard characters by setting the Pattern property. For instance, setting File1.Pattern equal to "*.TXT" dictates that only files with the extension TXT will be displayed.

10.2 NINE ELEMENTARY CONTROLS

In this section, we discuss the nine controls indicated on the Toolbox in Figure 10-3.

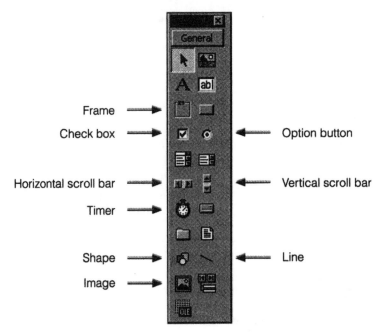

FIGURE 10-3   *Nine Elementary Controls.*

 THE FRAME CONTROL

....

Frames are passive objects used to group related sets of controls for visual effect. You rarely write event procedures for frames. The preceding frame has a group of three text boxes attached to it. When you drag the frame, the attached controls follow as a unit. If you hide the frame, the attached controls will be hidden as well.

A control must be attached to a frame in a special way. You cannot just double-click to create the control and then drag it into a frame. To attach a control to a frame, first create the frame. Next, single-click on the control icon to activate it, then move the mouse pointer inside the frame to the point where you want to place the upper-left corner of the control. Finally, drag the mouse to the right and down, and then release the mouse button when you are satisfied with the size of the control. This is referred to as the **single-click-draw technique**.

A group of controls also can be attached to a picture box. The advantages of using frames are that they have a title sunk into their borders that can be set with the Caption property and that they cannot receive the focus. As shown later in this section, the frame control is particularly important when working with groups of option button controls. The standard prefix for the name of a frame is fra.

 THE CHECK BOX CONTROL

....

A check box, which consists of a small square and a caption, presents the user with a yes/no choice. The form in Example 1 uses four check box controls. The Value property of a check box is 0 when the square is empty and is 1 when the square is checked. At run time, the user clicks on the square to toggle between the unchecked and checked states. So doing also triggers the Click event.

EXAMPLE 1

The following program allows an employee to compute the monthly cost of various benefit packages.

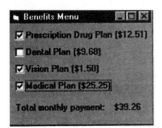

Object	Property	Setting
frmBenefits	Caption	Benefits Menu
chkDrugs	Caption	Prescription Drug Plan
($12.51)		
Value	0 – Unchecked	
chkDental	Caption	Dental Plan ($9.68)
Value	0 – Unchecked	
chkVision	Caption	Vision Plan ($1.50)
Value	0 – Unchecked	
chkMedical	Caption	Medical Plan ($25.25)
Value	0 – Unchecked	
lblTotal	Caption	Total monthly payment:
lblAmount	Caption	$0.00

```
Private Sub chkDrugs_Click()
  Call Tally
End Sub

Private Sub chkDental_Click()
  Call Tally
End Sub

Private Sub chkVision_Click()
  Call Tally
End Sub

Private Sub chkMedical_Click()
  Call Tally
End Sub

Private Sub Tally()
  Dim sum As Single
  If chkDrugs.Value = 1 Then
    sum = sum + 12.51 End If
  If chkDental.Value = 1 Then
    sum = sum + 9.68
  End If
  If chkVision.Value = 1 Then
    sum = sum + 1.5
  End If
  If chkMedical.Value = 1 Then
    sum = sum + 25.25
  End If
  lblAmount.Caption = FormatCurrency(sum)
End Sub
```

[Run and then click on the desired options.]

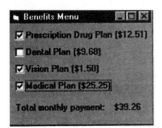

When a check box has the focus, the spacebar can be used to check (or uncheck) the box and invoke the Click event. In addition, the state of a check box can be toggled from the keyboard without first setting the focus to the check box if you create an access key for the check box by including an ampersand in the Caption property. (Access keys appear underlined at run time.) For instance, if the Caption property for the Dental Plan in Example 1 is set as "&Dental Plan", then the user can check (or uncheck) the box by pressing Alt+D.

Notice that the program code for the solution to Example 1 involved four identical click event procedures. This is a good indication that a control array of check boxes will simplify the program, as shown in Example 2.

EXAMPLE 2

The following program reworks Example 1 using a control array of check boxes, with an access key for each check box. The program has been made more general and easy to update by placing the name and cost of each benefit plan in the data file BENEFITS.TXT. Each line of the file consists of the name of the plan followed by the cost of the plan, as illustrated by the first line of the file:

"&Prescription Drug Plan", 12.51

Object	Property	Setting
frmBenefits	Caption	Benefits Menu
chkPlan( )	Index	0 through 3
lblTotal	Caption	Total monthly payment:
lblAmount	Caption	$0.00

```
Dim price(0 To 3) As Single 'In (Declarations) section of (General)
Dim sum As Single

Private Sub Form_Load()
   Dim i As Integer, plan As String, cost As Single
   Open "BENEFITS.TXT" For Input As #1
   For i = 0 To 3
     Input #1, plan, cost
     price(i) = cost
     chkPlan(i).Caption = plan & " (" & FormatCurrency(cost) & ")"
   Next i
   Close 1
   sum = 0
End Sub


Private Sub chkPlan_Click(Index As Integer)
   If chkPlan(Index).Value = 1 Then
     sum = sum + price(Index)
   Else
     sum = sum - price(Index)
   End If
   lblAmount.Caption = FormatCurrency(sum)
End Sub
```

The Value property of a check box also can be set to "2-Grayed". When a grayed square is clicked, it becomes unchecked. When clicked again, it becomes checked.

THE OPTION BUTTON CONTROL

Option buttons are used to give the user a single choice from several options. Normally, a group of several option buttons is attached to a frame or picture box with the single-click-draw technique. Each button consists of a small circle accompanied by text that is set with the Caption property. When a circle or its accompanying text is clicked, a solid dot appears in the circle and the button is said to be "on." At most one option button in a group can be on at the same time. Therefore, if one button is on and another button in the group is clicked, the first button will turn off. By convention, the names of option buttons have the prefix opt.

The Value property of an option button tells if the button is on or off. The property

```
optButton.Value
```

is True when optButton is on and False when optButton is off. The statement

```
optButton.Value = True
```

turns on optButton and turns off all other buttons in its group. The statement

```
optButton.Value = False
```

turns off optButton and has no effect on the other buttons in its group.

The Click event for an option button is triggered only when an off button is turned on. It is not triggered when an on button is clicked.

EXAMPLE 3

The following program tells you if an option button is on.

Object	Property	Setting
frmOptions	Caption	Option Buttons
fraOptions	Caption	Options
optOpt1		
optOpt2		
cmdStatus	Caption	Determine Status
picStatus		

```
Private Sub cmdStatus_Click()
  picStatus.Cls
  If optOpt1.Value Then
    picStatus.Print "Option1 is on."
  ElseIf optOpt2.Value Then
    picStatus.Print "Option2 is on."
  End If
End Sub

Private Sub Form_Load()
  optOpt1.Value = False 'Turn off optOpt1
  optOpt2.Value = False 'Turn off optOpt2
End Sub
```

[Run, click on one of the option buttons, and then click the command button.]

The text alongside an option button is specified with the Caption property. As with a command button and a check box, an ampersand can be used to create an access key for an option button.

EXAMPLE 4

The following program allows the user to select the text size in a text box. The three option buttons have been attached to the frame with the single-click-draw technique.

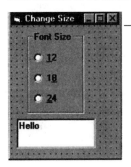

Object	Property	Setting
frmSize	Caption	Change Size
fraFontSize	Caption	Font Size
opt12pt	Caption	&12
opt18pt	Caption	1&8
opt24pt	Caption	&24
txtInfo	Text	Hello

```
Private Sub opt12pt_Click()
   txtInfo.Font.Size = 12
End Sub

Private Sub opt18pt_Click()
   txtInfo.Font.Size = 18
End Sub

Private Sub opt24pt_Click()
   txtInfo.Font.Size = 24
End Sub
```

[Run, and click on the last option button (or press Alt+2).]

A single form can have several groups of option buttons. However, each group must be attached to its own frame or picture box, or to the form itself.

THE ⬚ HORIZONTAL AND ⬚ VERTICAL SCROLL BAR CONTROLS

Figure 10-4 shows the two types of scroll bars. When the user clicks on one of the arrow buttons, the thumb moves a small amount toward that arrow. When the user clicks between the thumb and one of the arrow buttons, the thumb moves a large amount toward that arrow. The user can also move the thumb by dragging it. The main properties of a scroll bar control are Min, Max, Value, SmallChange, and LargeChange, which are set to integers. At any time, hsbBar.Value is a number between hsbBar.Min and hsbBar.Max determined by the position of the thumb. If the thumb is halfway between the two arrows, then hsbBar.Value is a number halfway between hsbBar.Min and hsbBar.Max. If the thumb is near the left arrow button, then hsbBar.Value is an appropriately proportioned value near hsbBar.Min. When an arrow button is clicked, hsbBar.Value changes by hsbBar.SmallChange and the thumb moves accordingly. When the bar between the thumb and one of the arrows is clicked, hsbBar.Value changes by hsbBar.LargeChange and the thumb moves accordingly. When the thumb is dragged, hsbBar.Value changes accordingly. The default values of Min, Max, SmallChange, and LargeChange are 0, 32767, 1, and 1, respectively. However, these values are usually reset at design time. *Note:* The setting for the Min property can be a number greater than the setting for the Max property. The Min property determines the values for the left and top arrows. The Max property determines the values for the right and bottom arrows.

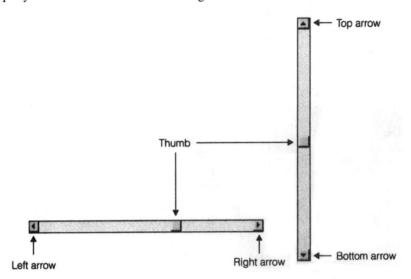

FIGURE 10-4   *Horizontal and Vertical Scroll Bars*

The Change event is triggered whenever an arrow or bar is clicked, or after the thumb has been dragged. The Scroll event is triggered whenever the thumb is being dragged.

EXAMPLE 5

The following program uses scroll bars to move a smiling face around the form. The face is a large Wingdings character J inside a label. The values lblFace.Left and lblFace.Top are the distances in twips of the label from the left side and top of the form. (When printing, 1440 twips equal one inch; on the screen, 1440 twips are more or less an inch.)

Object	Property	Setting
frmFace	Caption	Smiling Face
hsbXPos	Min	0
	Max	3000
	SmallChange	100
	LargeChange	500
	Value	0
vsbYPos	Min	500
	Max	3000
	SmallChange	100
	LargeChange	500
	Value	500
lblFace	Caption	J
	Font	Wingdings
	Font Size	24
	Left	0
	Top	500

```
Private Sub hsbXPos_Change()
  lblFace.Left = hsbXPos.Value
End Sub

Private Sub vsbYPos_Change()
  lblFace.Top = vsbYPos.Value
End Sub
```

[Run and move the thumbs on the scroll bars.]

In Example 5, when you drag the thumb, the face does not move until the dragging is completed. This can be corrected by adding the following two event procedures.
Private Sub hsbXPos_Scroll() lblFace.Left = hsbXPos.ValueEnd SubPrivate Sub vsbYPos_Scroll() lblFace.Top = vsbYPos.ValueEnd Sub

 ## THE TIMER CONTROL

The timer control, which is invisible during run time, triggers an event after a specified amount of time. The length of time, measured in milliseconds, is set with the Interval property to be any number from 0 to 65,535 (about 1 minute and 5 seconds). The event triggered each time Timer1.Interval milliseconds elapses is called Timer1_Timer( ). In order to begin timing, a timer must first be turned on by setting its Enabled property to True. A timer is turned off either by setting its Enabled property to False or by setting its Interval property to 0. The standard prefix for the name of a timer control is tmr.

EXAMPLE 6

The following program creates a stopwatch that updates the time every tenth of a second.

Object	Property	Setting
frmWatch	Caption	Stopwatch
cmdStart	Caption	Start
lblSeconds	Caption	Seconds
lblTime	Caption	(blank)
cmdStop	Caption	Stop
tmrWatch	Interval	100
	Enabled	False

```
Private Sub cmdStart_Click()
   lblTime.Caption = " 0" 'Reset watch
   tmrWatch.Enabled = True
End Sub

Private Sub cmdStop_Click()
   tmrWatch.Enabled = False
End Sub

Private Sub tmrWatch_Timer()
   lblTime.Caption = Str(Val(lblTime.Caption) + .1)
End Sub
```

[Run, click on the Start button, wait 10.8 seconds, and click on the Stop button.]

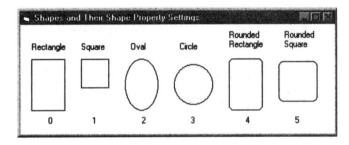

THE SHAPE CONTROL

The shape control assumes one of six possible predefined shapes depending on the value of its Shape property. Figure 10-5 shows the six shapes and the values of their corresponding Shape properties. Shapes are usually placed on a form at design time for decoration or to highlight certain parts of the form. By convention, names of shape controls have the prefix shp.

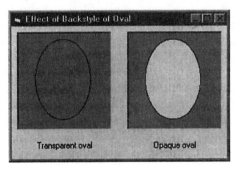

FIGURE 10-5   *The Six Possible Shapes for a Shape Control*

The most useful properties of shapes are BackStyle (transparent vs. opaque; see Figure 10-6), BorderWidth (thickness of border), BorderStyle (solid, dashed, dotted, etc.), BackColor (background color), FillStyle (fill-in pattern: horizontal lines, upward diagonal lines, etc., as in Figure 9.20), FillColor (color used by FillStyle), and Visible.

FIGURE 10-6   *Effect of the Value of the BackStyle Property*

Figure 10-7 shows several effects that can be achieved with shapes. In the first effect, a command button is set off by placing it on top of a rounded rectangle shape whose BackStyle is opaque, BackColor is blue, FillStyle is downward diagonal, and FillColor is yellow. In the second effect, the TRFFC20.ICO icon (displayed in an appropriately sized, borderless picture box) is "framed" by placing it on top of an oval shape whose BackStyle is opaque and BackColor is the same as the background color of the icon. In the last effect, two command buttons are tied together by surrounding them with a circle shape whose FillStyle is transparent, BorderWidth is 8, and BorderColor is green, and by placing behind the command buttons an oval shape whose FillStyle is transparent, BorderWidth is 3, and BorderColor is blue.

FIGURE 10-7   *Several Effects Achieved with Shape Controls*

 ## THE LINE CONTROL

The Line control, which produces lines of various thickness, styles, and colors, is primarily used to enhance the visual appearance of forms. The most useful properties of lines are BorderColor (color of the line), BorderWidth (thickness of the line), BorderStyle (solid, dashed, dotted, etc.), and Visible. Figure 10-8 shows several effects that can be achieved with lines. By convention, names of line controls have the prefix lin.

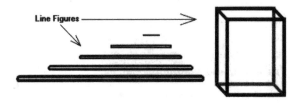

FIGURE 10-8   *Several Effects Achieved with Line Controls*

 ## THE IMAGE CONTROL

The image control is designed to hold pictures stored in graphics files such as .BMP files created with Windows' Paint, .ICO files of icons that come with Visual Basic, or .GIF and JPEG images used on the World Wide Web. Pictures are placed in image controls with the Picture property. If you double-click on the Picture property during design time, a file-selection dialog box appears and assists you in selecting an appropriate file. However, prior to setting the Picture property, you should set the Stretch property. If the Stretch property is set to False (the default value), the image control will be resized to fit the picture. If the Stretch property is set to True, the picture will be resized to fit the image control. Therefore, with Stretch property True, pictures can be reduced (by placing them into a small image control) or enlarged (by placing them into an image control bigger than the picture). Figure 10-9 shows a picture created with Paint and reduced to several different sizes. By convention, names of image controls have the prefix img.

A picture can be assigned to an image control at run time. However, a statement such as

```
imgBox.Picture = "filespec"
```

will not do the job. Instead, we must use the LoadPicture function in a statement such as

```
imgBox.Picture = LoadPicture("filespec")
```

Image controls enhance the visual appeal of programs. Also, because image controls respond to the Click event and can receive the focus, they can serve as pictorial command buttons.

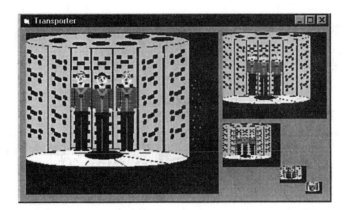

FIGURE 10-9   *A Picture Created with Paint and Reduced Several Times*

COMMENTS

1. When placing Line and Shape controls on a form, greater precision can be achieved by first turning off the "Align Controls to Grid" option in the General tab of the Options submenu of the Tools menu.

2. Although frames cannot receive the focus, they can have an access key that sends the focus to the first control inside the frame that can receive the focus.

3. You can paste a picture into an image control by copying it from your paint program and pressing Crl+V with the image control selected.

10.2 FIVE ADDITIONAL OBJECTS

In this section we discuss three controls and two objects that are not controls. The three controls are the Microsoft FlexGrid control (a custom control), the menu control (not accessed through the toolbox), and the common dialog box control (a custom control). The two objects are the clipboard and the form. The discussion of the form deals with the use of multiple forms.

 ### THE MICROSOFT FLEXGRID CONTROL

The FlexGrid control does not initially appear in your Toolbox. To add the control, click on Components in the Project menu, click the Controls tab, and click on the check box to the left of "Microsoft FlexGrid Control 6.0." Then press the OK button. By convention, names of Microsoft FlexGrids have the prefix *msg*.

A grid is a rectangular array used to display tables or to create spreadsheet-like applications. The grid in Figure 10-10 has 6 rows and 7 columns. The number of rows and columns can be specified at design time with the Rows and Cols properties or at run time with statements such as msgFlex.Rows = 6 and msgFlex.Cols = 7. Rows and columns are numbered beginning with 0. For instance, the rows in Figure 10-10 are numbered (from top to bottom) as 0, 1, 2, 3, 4, and 5.

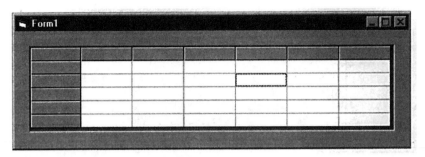

FIGURE 10-10   *A Simple FlexGrid Control*

The width, measured in twips (there are about 1440 twips to an inch), of each column can be specified only at run time with the ColWidth property. A typical statement is msgFlex.ColWidth(3) = 1200, which sets the width of column 3 to 1200 twips. (The default column width is 555 twips.) Similarly, the RowHeight property specifies the height of each row. The width and height of the entire grid can be specified at design time by dragging the mouse or by setting the Width and Height properties.

The grayed row and column in Figure 10-10 are referred to as **fixed**. Fixed rows and columns must be at the top and left sides of the grid. The number of fixed rows and columns is specified by the FixedRows and FixedCols properties. The grid in Figure 10-10 has the default settings FixedRows = 1 and FixedCols = 1.

If the width of the grid is too small to show all the columns, a horizontal scroll bar will automatically appear across the bottom of the grid. Then, during run time, the nonfixed columns can be scrolled to reveal the hidden columns. Similarly, a vertical scroll bar appears when the height of the grid is too small to show all the rows. Scroll bars can be suppressed by setting the ScrollBars property of the grid to 0 – flexScrollBarNone. (The default value of the ScrollBars property is 3 – flexScrollBarBoth.)

The individual small rectangles are called **cells.** Each cell is identified by its row and column numbers. At any time, one cell is singled out as the **current cell.** Initially, the cell in row 1, column 1 is the current cell. The pair of statements msgFlex.Row = m, msgFlex.Col = n set the current cell to the cell in the mth row and nth column. When the user clicks on a nonfixed cell, it becomes the current cell. The cell's border becomes dotted, its row number is assigned to the Row property, and its column number is assigned to the Col property. (In Figure 10-10 the cell in row 2, column 4 is the current cell.) The horizontal and vertical lines forming the cells can be turned off by setting the GridLines property to 0 – flexGridNone.

Unfortunately, you can't just place text into a cell by clicking on the cell and typing, as you would with a text box. The statement msgFlex.Text = *str* places the value of *str* into the current cell and the statement *str* = msgFlex.Text reads the contents of the current cell. The text inside all the nonfixed cells of column n can be displayed left-aligned, right-aligned, or centered with a statement of the form msgFlex.ColAlignment(n) = r, where r is 1 for left-alignment, 7 for right-alignment, and 4 for centered. The fixed cells of column n can be justified with a statement of the form msgFlex.FixedAlignment(n) = r.

EXAMPLE 1

The following program uses a grid to display an improved version of the table of student expenses from Example 5 of Section 2.5. The five expense categories and numeric data for the table are stored in the sequential file STCOSTS.TXT. Each record of the file consists of a string followed by four numbers.

Object	Property	Setting
frmCosts	Caption	Average Expenses of Commuter Students (1995–96)
msgCosts	BorderStyle	0 – flexBorderNone
	Cols	5
	FixedCols	0
	FixedRows	0
	Font	Courier New
	GridLines	0 – flexGridNone

Rows	9
ScrollBars	0 – flexScrollBarNone

```
Private Sub Form_Load()
   Dim rowNum As Integer, colNum As Integer
   Dim strData As String, numData As Single
   'Column headings msgCosts.Row = 0
   msgCosts.Col = 1
   msgCosts.Text = "Pb 2-yr"
   msgCosts.Col = 2
   msgCosts.Text = "Pr 2-yr"
   msgCosts.Col = 3
   msgCosts.Text = "Pb 4-yr"
   msgCosts.Col = 4
   msgCosts.Text = "Pr 4-yr"
   'Read data from data file and obtain column totals
   Dim total(1 To 4) As Single
   Open "STCOSTS.TXT"
   For Input As #1 For rowNum = 2 To 6 'row 0 holds headings, row 1 is blank
      For colNum = 0 To 4
         msgCosts.Row = rowNum
         msgCosts.Col = colNum
         If colNum = 0 Then
             Input #1, strData
             msgCosts.Text = strData
          Else
             Input #1, numData
             msgCosts.Text = FormatCurrency(numData, 0)
             total(colNum) = total(colNum) + numData
         End If
      Next colNum
   Next rowNum
   'Display totals
   msgCosts.Row = 8
   msgCosts.Col = 0
   msgCosts.Text = "Total"
   For colNum = 1 To 4
      msgCosts.Col = colNum
      msgCosts.Row = 7
      msgCosts.Text = "————"
      msgCosts.Row = 8
      msgCosts.Text = FormatCurrency(total(colNum), 0)
   Next colNum
   'Set column widths to accommodate data; right-justify dollar amounts
      msgCosts.ColWidth(0) = 2000              'Space for category names
      msgCosts.ColAlignment(0) = 1             'Left alignment
   For colNum = 1 To 4
   msgCosts.ColWidth(colNum) = 1200            'Space for dollar amounts
   msgCosts.ColAlignment(colNum) = 7.          'Right alignment
   Next colNum
   'Set overall grid size to minimum needed for the data
   msgCosts.Width = 2000 + 4 * 1200
   msgCosts.Height = 9 * msgCosts.RowHeight(0)
End Sub
```

[Run]

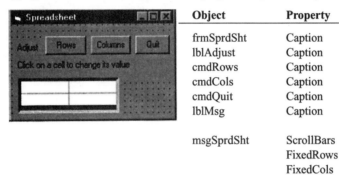

Average Expenses of Commuter Students (1995-96)	Pb 2-yr	Pr 2-yr	Pb 4-yr	Pr 4-yr
Tuition & Fees	$1,387	$6,350	$2,860	$12,432
Books & Supplies	$577	$567	$591	$601
Board	$1,752	$1,796	$1,721	$1,845
Transportation	$894	$902	$929	$863
Other Expenses	$1,142	$1,220	$1,348	$1,169
	-------	-------	-------	-------
Total	$5,752	$10,835	$7,449	$16,910

EXAMPLE 2

The following program creates a simplified spreadsheet. The user places a number into the active cell by typing the number into an input box. The program keeps a running total of the sum of the numbers.

Object	Property	Setting
frmSprdSht	Caption	Spreadsheet
lblAdjust	Caption	Adjust
cmdRows	Caption	Rows
cmdCols	Caption	Columns
cmdQuit	Caption	Quit
lblMsg	Caption	Click on a cell to change its value
msgSprdSht	ScrollBars	0 – flexScrollBarNone
	FixedRows	0
	FixedCols	0
	Font	Courier New

```
'In (Declarations) section of (General)
Dim numRows As Integer 'number of rows
Dim numCols As Integer 'number of columns

Private Sub cmdRows_Click()
  Dim temp As String
  'Adjust the number of rows in the spreadsheet
  temp = InputBox("Enter new number of rows (4-24):")
  If (Val(temp) >= 4) And (Val(temp) < Then
    numRows = Val(temp)
    Call SetUpGrid
    Call ShowValues
    Call ShowTotals
  End If
End Sub

Private Sub cmdCols_Click()
  Dim temp As String
  'Adjust number of columns in the spreadsheet
  temp = InputBox("Enter new number of columns (2-7):")
  If (Val(temp) >= 2) And (Val(temp) <= 7) Then
    numCols = Val(temp)
    Call SetUpGrid
    Call ShowValues
    Call ShowTotals
  End If
End Sub
```

```
Private Sub cmdQuit_Click()
   End
End Sub


Private Sub Form_Load()
   'Set default number of rows and columns
   numRows = 8 'row 0 is for headings, last 2 rows are for totals
   numCols = 2 'column 0 is for category names
   Call SetUpGrid
   Call ShowValues
   Call ShowTotals
End Sub


Private Sub msgSprdSht_Click()
   Dim temp As String, message As String
   'Obtain new value for cell if it is not in the "total" row
   If messageSprdSht.Row < numRows - 2 Then
     message = "Enter new value for the row "
     message = message & Str(msgSprdSht.Row + 1) & " column "
     message = message & Str(msgSprdSht.Col + 1) & " cell:"
     temp = InputBox(message,,msgSprdSht.Text) 'Propose old value as default
     If msgSprdSht.Col = 0 Then
         msgSprdSht.Text = temp
       ElseIf msgSprdsht.Row = 0 Then
   msgSprdSht.Text = temp
       Else
         msgSprdsht.Text = FormatNumber(Val(temp)vbFalse)
         Call ShowTotals
     End If
   End If
End Sub


Private Sub SetUpGrid()
   Dim colNum As Integer
   'Set up grid msgSprdSht.Col = 0
   msgSprdSht.Row = msgSprdSht.Rows - 1
   msgSprdSht.Text = "" 'erase "Total" in case increasing rows
   msgSprdSht.Rows = numRows
   msgSprdSht.Cols = numCols
   'Set column widths; right-justify columns with numeric data
   msgSprdSht.ColWidth(0) = 2000 'space for category names
   msgSprdSht.ColAlignment(0) = 1 'show data left-justified
   For colNum = 1 To numCols - 1
     msgSprdSht.ColWidth(colNum) = 1200 'space for dollar amounts
     msgSprdSht.ColAlignment(colNum) = 7 'show data right-justified
   Next colNum 'Set overall grid size to minimum needed for the data
   msgSprdSht.Width = 2000 + (numCols - 1) * 1200 + 15 * (numCols + 1) + 8
   msgSprdSht.Height = numRows*msgSprdSht.RowHeight(0)+15*(numRows + 1)+8
   'Adjust form to accommodate grid and other controls
   frmSprdSht.Width = msgSprdSht.Left + msgSprdSht.Width + 200
   frmSprdSht.Height = msgSprdSht.Top + msgSprdSht.Height + 500
   frmSprdSht.Top = 0 frmSprdSht.Left = 0
End Sub
```

```
Private Sub ShowTotals()
   Dim colNum As Integer, rowNum As Integer, total As Single
   'Compute and display total of each numeric column
   msgSprdSht.Row = numRows - 1
   msgSprdSht.Col = 0
   msgSprdSht.Text = "Total"
   For colNum = 1 To numCols - 1
     total = 0
     For rowNum = 1 To numRows - 3
       msgSprdSht.Row = rowNum
       msgSprdSht.Col = colNum
       total = total + Val(msgSprdSht.Text)
     Next rowNum
     msgSprdSht.Row = numRows - 2
     msgSprdSht.Text = "————"
     msgSprdSht.Row = numRows - 1
     msgSprdSht.Text = FormatCurrency(total)
   Next colNum
End Sub

Private Sub ShowValues()
   Dim rowNum As Integer, colNum As Integer
   'Refresh values displayed in cells
   For rowNum = 1 To numRows - 1
     For colNum = 1 To numCols - 1
       msgSprdSht.Row = rowNum
       msgSprdSht.Col = colNum
       msgSprdSht.Text = FormatNumber(Val(msgSprdSht.Text)vbFalse)
     Next colNum
   Next rowNum
End Sub
```

[A possible run of the program is shown.]

So far we have used the Text property of grids to place strings into cells. Grids also have a Picture property. A picture (such as a .BMP file created with Paint or an .ICO file from Visual Basic's icon directory) is placed into the current cell with a statement of the form

```
Set msgFlex.CellPicture = LoadPicture("filespec")
```

If both text and a picture are assigned to a cell, then the picture appears in the upper left portion of the cell, and the text appears to the right of the picture.

■ THE MENU CONTROL

Visual Basic forms can have menu bars similar to those in most Windows applications. Figure 10-11 shows a typical menu, with the submenu for the Font menu item dropped down.

Here, the menu bar contains two menu items (Font and Size), referred to as **top-level** menu items. When the Font menu item is clicked, a dropdown list of two second-level menu items (Courier and TimesRm) appears. Although not visible here, the dropdown list under Size contains the two second-level menu items "12" and "24". Each menu item is treated as a distinct control that responds to only one event—the click event. The click event is triggered not only by the click of the mouse button, but also for top-level items by pressing Alt+*accessKey* and for second-level items by just pressing the access key. The click event for the Courier menu item in Figure 10-11 can be activated directly by pressing the shortcut key F1.

FIGURE 10-11 *A Simple Menu*

Menus are created with the Menu Editor window available from the Tools menu on the Visual Basic main menu bar. Figure 10-12 shows the Menu Design window used to create the menu in Figure 10-11. Each menu item has a Caption property (what the user sees) and a Name property (used to refer to the item in the code.) For instance, the last menu item in Figure 10-12 has Caption property "24" and Name property "mnu24". The following steps are used to create the Font-Size menu:

FIGURE 10-12 *The Menu Editor Window Used to Create the Menu in Figure 10-11*

1. Type &Font into the Caption box and type mnuFont into the Name box.
2. Click on the Next button.
3. Click on the Right Arrow button. (This creates the ellipses and indents the next menu item, which will be a second-level item.)
4. Type &Courier into the Caption box and type mnuCourier into the Name box.
5. Click on the arrow to the right of the Shortcut box and select F1 from the dropdown list.
6. Click on the Next button.
7. Type &TimesRm into the Caption box and type mnuTimesRm into the Name box.
8. Click on the Next button:

9. Click on the Left Arrow button. (This causes the next item to appear flush left to indicate that it is a top-level menu item.)

10. Type &Size into the Caption box and type mnuSize into the Name box.

11. Click on the Next button and then click on the Right Arrow button.

12. Type 12 into the Caption box and type mnu12 into the Name box.

13. Click on the Next button.

14. Type 24 into the Caption box and type mnu24 into the Name box. Your Menu Editor window should now appear as in Figure 10-12.

15. Click the OK button to close the Menu Editor window.

Three of the check boxes on the Menu Editor window are especially useful. When the Checked box is checked, a checkmark appears in front of the menu item. This checkmark can be altered in code with statements such as mnuItem.Checked = False and mnuItem.Checked = True. When the Enable box is unchecked, the menu item appears gray and does not respond to the click event. The enabled state can be altered in code with statements such as mnuItem.Enabled = False and mnuItem.Enabled = True. When the Visible property is unchecked, the menu item is invisible.

EXAMPLE 3

The following program creates the application in Figure 10-11, in which the menu is used to alter the appearance of the contents of a text box. The form has caption "Alter Font & Size" and the properties of the menu items are as created before.

```
Private Sub mnu12_Click()
   txtInfo.Font.Size = 12
End Sub

Private Sub mnu24_Click()
   txtInfo.Font.Size = 24
End Sub

Private Sub mnuCourier_Click()
   txtInfo.Font.Name = "Courier"
End Sub

Private Sub mnuTimesRm_Click()
   txtInfo.Font.Name = "Times New Roman"
End Sub
```

■ THE CLIPBOARD OBJECT

The clipboard object is used to copy or move text from one location to another. It is maintained by Windows and therefore even can be used to transfer information from one Windows application to another. It is actually a portion of memory that holds text and has no properties or events.

If *str* is a string, then the statement

```
Clipboard.SetText str
```

replaces any text currently in the clipboard with *str*. The statement

```
str = Clipboard.GetText()
```

assigns the text in the clipboard to the string variable *str*.

The statement

```
Clipboard.Clear
```

deletes the contents of the clipboard.

A portion of the text in a text box or combo box can be **selected** by dragging the mouse across it or by moving the cursor across it while holding down the Shift key. After you select text, you can place it into the clipboard by pressing Ctrl+C. Also, if the cursor is in a text box and you press Ctrl+V, the contents of the clipboard will be inserted at the cursor position. These tasks also can be carried out in code. The SelText property of a text box holds the selected string from the text box and a statement such as

```
Clipboard.SetText txtBox.SelText
```

copies this selected string into the clipboard. The statement

```
txtBox.SelText = Clipboard.GetText()
```

replaces the selected portion of txtBox with the contents of the clipboard. If nothing has been selected, the statement inserts the contents of the clipboard into txtBox at the cursor position. The clipboard can actually hold any type of data, including graphics. Any time you use the Copy menu item, you are putting information into the clipboard. The Paste menu item sends that data to your program.

■ MULTIPLE FORMS

A Visual Basic program can contain more than one form. Additional forms are created from the Project menu with Add Form (Alt/P/F/Enter). The name of each form appears in the Project Explorer window, and any form can be made the active form by double-clicking on its name in the Project Explorer window. (*Hint:* After creating a new form, move it down slightly so that you can see at least the title bars of the other forms. Then you can activate any form by just clicking on its title bar.) The second form has default name Form2, the third form has default name Form3, and so on. Forms are hidden or activated with statements such as

```
Form1.Hide
```

or

```
Form2.Show
```

When a program is run, the first form created is the only one visible. After that, the Hide and Show methods can be used to determine what forms appear.

Often, additional forms, such as message and dialog boxes, are displayed to present a special message or request specific information. When a message or dialog box appears, the user cannot shift the focus to another form without first hiding the message or dialog box by clicking an OK or Cancel command button. If a form is displayed with a statement of the type

```
formName.Show 1    or    formName.Show vbModal
```

then the form will exhibit this same behavior. The user will not be allowed to shift the focus back to the calling form until *formName* is hidden. Such a form is said to be **modal**. It is customary to set the BorderStyle property of modal forms to "3-Fixed Dialog".

Each form has its own controls and code. However, code from one form can refer to a control in another form. If so, the control must be prefixed with the name of the other form, followed by a period. For instance, the statement

```
Form2.txtBox.Text = "Hello"
```

in Form1 causes text to be displayed in a text box on Form2. (*Note:* Two forms can have a text box named txtBox. Code using the name txtBox refers to the text box in its own form unless prefixed with the name of another form.)

EXAMPLE 4

The following program uses a second form as a dialog box to total the different sources of income. Initially, only frmIncome is visible. The user types in his or her name and then either can type in the income or click on the command button for assistance in totaling the different sources of income. Clicking on the command button from frmIncome causes frmSources to appear and be active. The user fills in the three text boxes and then clicks on the command button to have the amounts totaled and displayed in the income text box of the first form.

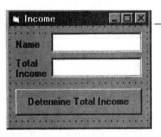

Object	Property	Setting
frmIncome	Caption	Income
lblName	Caption	Name
txtName	Text	(blank)
lblTotal	Caption	Total Income
txtTotal	Text	(blank)
cmdShowTot	Caption	Determine Total Income

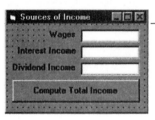

Object	Property	Setting
frmSources	Caption	Sources of Income
	BorderStyle	3 – Fixed Dialog
lblWages	Caption	Wages
txtWages	Text	(blank)
lblInterest	Caption	Interest Income
txtInterest	Text	(blank)
lblDividend	Caption	Dividend Income
txtDividend	Text	(blank)
cmdCompute	Caption	Compute Total Income

```
Private Sub cmdShowTot_Click()
   frmSources.Show vbModal
End Sub

Private Sub cmdCompute_Click()
   Dim sum As Single
   sum = Val(txtWages.Text) + Val(txtInterest.Text) + Val(txtDividend.Text)
   frmIncome.txtTotal.Text = FormatCurrency(Str(sum))
   frmSources.Hide
End Sub
```

[Run, enter name, click the command button, and fill in the sources of income.]

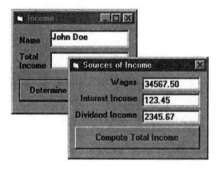

All variables declared and general procedures created in the (General) object of a form are local to that form; that is, they are not available to any other form. Such variables and procedures are said to be of **form level**. However, you can declare global variables and procedures that are available to all forms. To do so, select Add Module from the Project menu and then double-click on the Module icon. A code window will appear with Module1 in the title bar. Procedures created in this window with the Public keyword will be available to all forms. To declare a variable that is available to all forms, declare it in the Module1 window, but use the word Public instead of Dim. For instance, if the statement

```
Public person As String
```

appears in the Module1 code window, the variable *person* can be accessed anywhere in the program.

The contents of this code window are said to form a (Standard) code module. Project Explorer shows the names of all forms and code modules and gives you access to the code from any form or module. When a code module is selected, you can save it by choosing Save Module As from the File menu. You add an existing code module to a program by choosing Add File from the Project menu.

■ THE COMMON DIALOG CONTROL

The common dialog control does not initially appear in your Toolbox. To add the control, select Components from the Project menu, click the Controls tab, and click on the check box to the left of "Microsoft Common Dialog Control 6.0." Then press the OK button. By convention, names of common dialog boxes have the prefix dlg.

The common dialog control can produce each of the useful dialog boxes in Figures 10.13 through 10.17, thereby saving the programmer the trouble of designing custom dialog boxes for these purposes. The common dialog control has no events, only methods and properties. Actually, like the Timer control, the common dialog box control is invisible. However, when you execute a statement of the form

```
CommonDialog1.Show_____
```

where the blank line is filled with Open, Save, Color, Font, or Printer, the specified dialog box is produced. Table 10.1 gives the purposes of the various dialog boxes.

TABLE 10.1
The Different Types of Dialog Boxes

Type of Dialog box	Purpose of Dialog Box
Open	Determine what file to open
Save As	Determine where and with what name to save a file
Color	Select any available color
Font	Select a font for the screen or printer
Print	Help control the printer

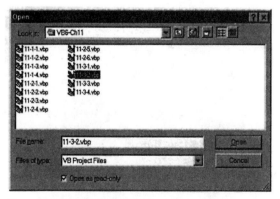

FIGURE 10-13   *An Open Common Dialog Box*

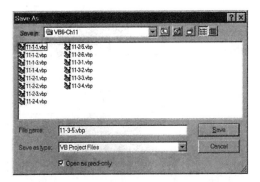

FIGURE 10-14 *A Save As Common Dialog Box*

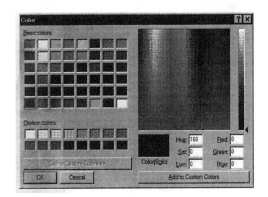

FIGURE 10-15 *A Color Common Dialog Box*

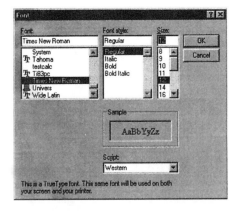

FIGURE 10-16 *A Font Common Dialog Box*

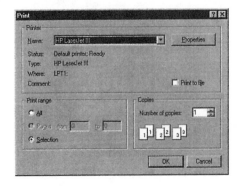

FIGURE 10-17 *A Print Common Dialog Box*

The Flags property influences certain features of the dialog box and should be set prior to setting the Show method. A complete discussion of the Flags property would be too great a digression. For our purposes, we will be well served by always setting the Flags property to 3 with the statement

```
dlgBox.Flags = 3
```

After selections are made from a common dialog box and the OK button is clicked, the values of the selections are stored in properties such as FileName, Color, FontName, FontItalic, FontSize and Copies. For instance, the following event procedure specifies the font for the contents of a text box.

```
Private Sub cmdButton_Click()
  dlgFont.Flags = 3
  dlgFont.ShowFont                    'invoke Font common dialog box
  'Select Font, Font style, and Size and then click on OK
  txtBox.Font.Name = dlgFont.FontName
  txtBox.Font.Bold = dlgFont.FontBold
  txtBox.Font.Italic = dlgFont.FontItalic
  txtBox.Font.Size = dlgFont.FontSize
End Sub
```

Table 10.2 gives the principal properties whose setting are garnered from the common dialog boxes.

TABLE 10.2
Principal Properties of the Common Dialog Boxes

Type of Common Dialog Box	Principal Properties
Open	FileName
Save As	FileName
Color	Color
Font	FontName, FontSize, FontBold, FontItalic
Print	Copies, FromPage, ToPage

With Open and Save As common dialog boxes, a property is needed to specify what types of files should be displayed. A statement of the form

```
dlgFile.Filter = "dscrpt1|filter1|dscrpt2|filter2|dscrpt3|filter3"
```

provides verbal descriptions for the Type box and strings using wildcard characters (filters) to identify the files. A specific statement might be

```
dlgFile.Filter = "Text Files|*.TXT|FRM Files|*.FRM|All Files|*.*"
```

After the filter property is set, the FilterIndex property can be used to set the default filter. For instance, if the preceding statement is followed with

```
dlgFile.FilterIndex = 1
```

the default will be the first pair of filter items. That is, when the dialog box pops up, the Files of type box will display Text Files, and the large box will show only files with the extension TXT.

COMMENT

1. In the Properties window of a FlexGrid control, one setting of the GridLines property is "0 – flexGridNone." In code, this setting can be invoked with either

```
msgFlex.GridLines = 0
```

or

```
msgFlex.GridLines = flexGridNone
```

SUMMARY

1. *List boxes* provide easy access to lists of strings. The lists can be automatically sorted (Sorted property = True), altered (AddItem, RemoveItem, and Clear methods), the currently highlighted item identified (Text property), and the number of items determined (ListCount property). The array List() holds the items stored in the list. Each item is identified by an index number (0, 1, 2, . . .). The most recently inserted item can be determined with the NewIndex property. The ItemData property associates a number with each item of text.

2. *Combo boxes* are enhanced text boxes. They not only allow the user to enter information by typing it into a text box (read with the Text property), but allow the user to select the information from a list of items.

3. *Drive*, *directory*, and *file list boxes* are specialized list boxes managed largely by Windows. The selected items are identified by the Drive, Path, and FileName properties, respectively. A directory list box always displays the subdirectories of the directory identified by its Path property, and a files list box displays the files in the directory identified by its Path property.

4. Selections are made with *check boxes* (allow several) and *option buttons* (allow at most one). The state of the control (*checked* vs. *unchecked* or *on* vs. *off*) is stored in the Value property. Clicking on a check box toggles its state. Clicking on an option button gives it the *on* state and turns *off* the other option buttons in its group.

5. Frames are used to group controls, especially option buttons, as a unit.

6. *Horizontal* and *vertical scroll bars* permit the user to select from among a range of numbers by clicking or dragging with the mouse. The range is specified by the Min and Max properties, and new settings trigger the Click and Change events.

7. The *timer control* triggers an event after a specified amount of time.

8. The *shape* and *line controls* enhance the visual look of a form with rectangles, ovals, circles, and lines of different size, thickness, and color.

9. The *image control*, which displays pictures or icons, can either expand to accommodate the size of the drawing or have the drawing alter its size to fit the image control.

10. A Microsoft FlexGrid control is a rectangular array of cells, each identified by a row and column number. The numbers of rows and columns are specified by the Rows and Cols properties. If the size of the grid is larger than provided by the control, scroll bars can be used to look at different parts of the grid. The FixedRows and FixedCols properties fix a certain number of the top rows and leftmost columns so that they will not scroll. The Row and Col properties are used to designate one cell as *current*. The Text property is used to read or place text into the current cell.

11. *Menus*, similar to the menus of Visual Basic itself, can be created with the Menu Design window.

12. The *clipboard* is filled with the SetText method or by pressing Ctrl+C, and is copied with the GetText function or with Ctrl+V.

13. *Additional forms* serve as new windows or dialog boxes. They are revealed with the Show method and concealed with the Hide method.

14. *Common dialog boxes* provide a standard way of specifying files, colors, and fonts, and of communicating with the printer.

PROGRAMMING PROJECTS

1. *Membership List.* Write a menu-driven program to manage a membership list. (See the following Membership List form.) Assume that the names and phone numbers of all members are stored in the sequential file MEMBERS.TXT. The names should be read into the list box when the form is loaded and the phone numbers should be read into an array. When a name is highlighted, both the name and phone number of the person should appear in the text boxes at the bottom of the screen. To delete a person, highlight his or her name and click on the Delete menu item. To change either the phone number or the spelling of the person's name, make the corrections in the text boxes and click on the menu item Modify. To add a new member, type his or her name and phone number into the text boxes and click on the menu item Add. When Exit is clicked, the new membership list should be written to a file and the program should terminate.

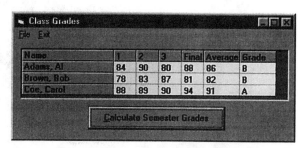

2. *Grade Book.* Write a comprehensive program that a professor could use to record student grades for several classes and save the records in sequential files. (See the preceding Class Grades form.) Each class has three hourly exams and a final exam. The file for a single class should consist of the number of students in the class, call it *n*, and a record of five fields (name, grade1, grade2, grade3, final) for each student, with the records ordered alphabetically by the student's name. (A typical name might appear as "Doe, John".) Initially, the four grade fields should contain zeros. The program should contain a top-level menu item, File, with second-level subitems for Open, Save, Add Student, Remove Student. When a file is opened (via a file list directory or common dialog box), the data for the students should be loaded into a grid of *n* + 1 rows and 7 columns. (The last two columns should remain blank.) The professor should be able to enter (or alter) exam data by clicking on the cell and responding to an input box. When a student is added, the grid should be enlarged by one row and the student inserted in proper alphabetical position. When a student is deleted, the grid should be reduced by one row. When the Calculate Semester Grades button is clicked, the last two columns should be filled in by the program. (Assume that the final exam counts as two hour exams.) If a grade is changed after the last

two columns have been filled in, the corresponding average and grade should be recomputed.

3. *Tic-Tac-Toe.* Write a program that "officiates" a game of tic-tac-toe. That is, the program should allow two players to alternate entering X's and O's into a tic-tac-toe board until either someone wins or a draw is reached. If one of the players wins, the program should announce the winner immediately; in case of a draw, the program should display "Cat's game". The players should enter their plays by clicking on the desired cell in the tic-tac-toe grid, and the program should check that each play is valid. *Optional Enhancement:* Allow the players to enter a number *n*. The program should officiate a best-of-*n* tournament, keeping track of the number of games won by each player until one of them wins more than half of the games. Ignore draws.

4. *Hangman.* Write a program to play Hangman. (See the following Hangman form.) A list of 20 words should be placed in a sequential file and one selected at random with Rnd. The program should do the following:

(a) Draw a gallows on the screen with three line controls.

(b) Create a grid having 1 row and 26 columns, and fill the grid with the 26 letters of the alphabet.

(c) Create a second grid of one row and the number of columns equal to the length of the word selected.

(d) Each time the user clicks on one of the letters of the alphabet, that letter should be removed. If the letter is in the selected word, its location(s) should be revealed in the second grid. If the letter is not in the word, another piece of the man should be drawn with a shape control.

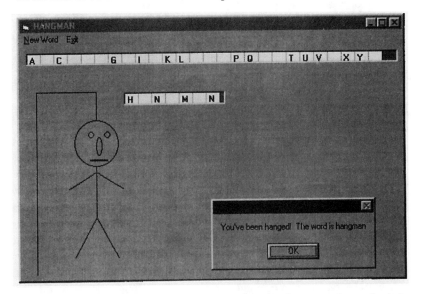

5. *Inventory Control.* Write an inventory program for a book store and save the information in a sequential file. Each record should consist of five fields—title, author, category, wholesale price, and number in stock. (The two categories are fiction and nonfiction.) At any time, the program should display the titles of the books in stock in a list box, for which the user should have the option of displaying either all titles or just those in one of the two categories. When a book is selected from the list, its title, author, category, wholesale price, and number in stock should be displayed in a picture box. The user should be able to add a new book, delete a book, or change the inventory level of a book in stock. At any time, the user should be able to calculate the total value of all books, or the total value of the books in either category.

6. *Voting Machine.* The members of the local Gilligan's Island fan club bring a computer to their annual meeting to use in the election of a new president. Write a program to handle the election. The program should add each candidate to a list box as he or she is nominated. After the nomination process is complete, club members should be able to approach the computer one at a time and double-click on the candidate of their choice. When a "Tally Votes" command button is clicked, a second list box, showing the number of votes received by each candidate, should appear alongside the first list box. Also, the name(s) of the candidate(s) with the highest number of votes should be displayed in a picture box.

7. *Airplane Seating Chart.* An airplane has 30 rows (numbered 1 through 30), with 6 seats (labeled A, B, C, D, E, and F) in each row. Write a program to display a 7-by-31 grid with a cell for each seat. As each passenger selects a seat and a meal (regular, low-calorie, or vegetarian), the ticket agent clicks on the cell corresponding to the seat. A dialog box requests the type of meal and then one of the letters R, L, or V is placed in the cell clicked. At any time, the agent can request the number of seats filled, the number of window seats vacant, and the numbers of each type of meal ordered.

DATABASE MANAGEMENT

11.1 AN INTRODUCTION TO DATABASES

The management of databases is the number one use of computers today. Airlines use databases to handle nearly 1.5 billion passenger reservations per year. The 6500 hospitals in the United States use databases to document the care of over 30 million patients per year. Banks in the United States use databases to monitor the use of 350 million credit cards. Although databases vary considerably in size and complexity, most of them adhere to the fundamental principles of design discussed in this chapter. That is, they are composed of a collection of interrelated tables.

A **table** is a rectangular array of data. Table 11.1 provides information about large cities. Each column of the table, called a **field**, contains the same type of information. (The third column gives the 1995 population in millions and the fourth column gives the projected 2015 population in millions.) The names of the fields are *city*, *country*, *pop1995*, and *pop2015*. Each row, called a **record**, contains the same type of information as every other row. Also, the pieces of information in each row are related; they all apply to a specific city. Table 11.2, Countries, has three fields and nine records.

TABLE 11.1
Cities

city	country	pop1995	pop2015
Beijing	China	12.4	19.4
Bombay	India	15.1	27.4
Calcutta	India	11.7	17.6
Los Angeles	USA	12.4	14.3
Mexico City	Mexico	15.6	18.8
New York	USA	16.3	17.6
Sao Paulo	Brazil	16.4	20.8
Shanghai	China	15.1	23.4
Tianjin	China	10.7	17.0
Tokyo	Japan	26.8	28.7

TABLE 11.2
Countries

Country	pop1995	currency
Brazil	155.8	real
China	1185.2	yuan
India	846.3	rupee
Indonesia	195.3	rupiah
Japan	125.0	yen
Mexico	85.6	peso
Nigeria	95.4	naira
Russia	148.2	ruble
USA	263.4	dollar

Source: An Urbanized World—Global Report on Human Settlements 1996, a report presented at Habitat II, a UN conference on the world's cities held in Istanbul in June 1996.

A **database** (or **relational database)** is a collection of one or more (usually related) tables that has been created with **database management software**. The best known dedicated database management products are Access, Btrieve, dBase, FoxPro, and Paradox. Every version of Visual Basic 6.0 can manage, revise, and analyze a database that has been created with one of these products. Section 11.3 shows how to create a database with Visual Data Manager, a miniversion of Access that is supplied with Visual Basic. Section 11.3 also gives a code template for creating a database programmatically.

The databases used in this chapter can be found in the collection of files accompanying this text. The database files have the extension .MDB. For instance, the file MEGACTY1.MDB is a database file containing the two tables presented on the preceding page. (*Note:* MDB files should be copied from the CD onto a hard drive and accessed from the hard drive.)

 ## The Data Control

Visual Basic communicates with databases through the data control. Data controls can read, modify, delete, and add records to databases. The following walkthrough uses a data control to connect Visual Basic to the database MEGACTY1.MDB.

■ A Data Control Walkthrough

1. Press Alt/File/New Project and double-click on Standard EXE.
2. Double-click on the data control icon. Set its Name property to datCities and its Caption property to Cities.
3. Stretch it horizontally to see the caption Cities.
4. Select the DatabaseName property and set it to the filespec for the file MEGACTY1.MDB.

   An Open File dialog box will help you locate the file.
5. Select the RecordSource property and click on the down-arrow button at the right of the Settings window.

   The names of the two tables in the database, Cities and Countries, are displayed.
6. Select Cities.
7. Place a text box, txtCity, on the form.

   Text boxes are said to be **data-aware** because they can be bound to a data control and access its data.
8. In the Properties window, select the DataSource property of txtCity.

9. Click on the down arrow to the right of the Settings box and select datCities.

10. Select the DataField property and click on the down arrow at the right of the Settings box.

    You will see the names of the different fields in the table.

11. Select the field *city*.

    The text box now is said to be **bound** to the data control. It can now display data from the *city* field of the Cities table.

12. Place another text box, txtPop1995, on the form.

13. Select txtPop1995's DataSource property.

14. Click on the down arrow to the right of the Settings box and select datCities.

15. Select the DataField property, click on the down arrow at the right of the Settings box, and select *pop1995*.

16. Run the program.

    The form will appear as in Figure 11-1. The arrows on the data control, called **navigation arrows**, look and act like VCR buttons. The arrows have been identified by the tasks they perform.

17. Click on the various navigation arrows on the data control to see the different cities and their populations in the Cities table displayed in the text boxes.

18. Change the name of a city or change its population and then move to another record.

    If you look back through the records, you will see that the data have been permanently changed.

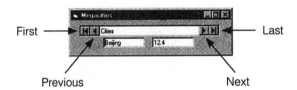

FIGURE 11-1   *A Data Control with Two Text Boxes Bound to It*

■ USING CODE WITH A DATA CONTROL

Only one record can be accessed at a time; this record is called the **current record**. In this walkthrough, the text boxes bound to the data control showed the contents of the *city* and *pop1995* fields of the current record. The user clicked on the navigation arrows of the data control to select a new current record.

Code can be used to designate another record as the current record. The methods MoveNext, MovePrevious, MoveLast, and MoveFirst select a new current record as suggested by their names. For instance, the statement

```
Data1.Recordset.MoveLast
```

specifies the last record of the table to be the current record. (The word Recordset is inserted in most data-control statements that manipulate records for reasons that needn't concern us now.)

The entry of the field *fieldName* of the current record is

```
Data1.Recordset.Fields("fieldName").Value
```

For instance, with the status as in Figure 11-1, the statement

```
strVar = datCities.Recordset.Fields("city").Value
```

assigns "Beijing" to the variable *strVar* and the statements

```
datCities.Recordset.Edit
datCities.Recordset.Fields("city").Value = "Peking"
datCities.Recordset.Update
```

change the *city* field of the current record to "Peking". (The first statement makes a copy of the current record for editing. The second statement alters the copy, and the third statement sends the new copy of the record to the database.)

The number of previously accessed records in the table is given by the RecordCount property. The EOF (End Of File) and BOF (Beginning Of File) run-time properties indicate whether the end or beginning of the file has been reached. For instance, the following two sets of statements each place the cities into a list box.

```
datCities.Recordset.MoveLast 'Needed to set value of RecordCount
   datCities.Recordset.MoveFirst
   For i = 1 to datCities.Recordset.RecordCount
      lstBox.AddItem datCities.Recordset.Fields("city").Value
      datCities.Recordset.MoveNext
Next i
```

```
datCities.Recordset.MoveFirst

   Do
   While Not datCities.Recordset.EOF
      lstBox.AddItem datCities.Recordset.Fields("city").Value
      datCities.Recordset.MoveNext
   Loop
```

The current record can be marked for removal with the statement

```
Data1.Recordset.Delete
```

The record will be removed when a data control navigation arrow is clicked or a Move method is executed. A new record can be added to the end of the table with the statement

```
Data1.Recordset.AddNew
```

followed by

```
Data1.Recordset.Fields("fieldName").Value = entryForField
```

statements for each field and a

```
Data1.Recordset.Update
```

statement. Alternately, the AddNew method can be followed by the user typing the information into text boxes bound to the data control and then moving to another record. (***Note:*** When you add a record and then click on the MovePrevious arrow, you will not see the next-to-last record, but rather will see the record preceding the record that was current when AddNew was executed.)

■ THE VALIDATION EVENT

Visual Basic has a device called **validation** that lets you restrict the values a user can enter into a table. For instance, if the Cities table is only to contain cities with a population of more than 1 million, you can use validation to prevent any record with a number less than 1 in the *pop1995* field from being entered. Validation also allows you to catch (and prevent) errors that might cause a program to crash.

Data controls have an event procedure called Validate that is activated whenever the current record is about to be changed. For instance, it is called when a navigation arrow is clicked or a Move, Update, Delete, or AddNew method is executed. The general form of the Validate event procedure is

```
Private Sub Data1_Validate(Action As Integer, Save As Integer)
    statement(s)
End Sub
```

The value of Action identifies the specific operation that triggered the event and the value of Save specifies whether data bound to the control has changed. You can change the value of the Action argument to perform a different action. Some values of the Action argument are shown in Table 11.3.

TABLE 11.3
Some Values of the Action Argument

Value	Description
1	MoveFirst method
2	MovePrevious method
3	MoveNext method
4	MoveLast method
5	AddNew method
6	Update operation (not UpdateRecord)
7	Delete method
10	Close method

If you assign 0 to the Action argument, the operation will be canceled when the Validate event procedure is exited.

The value of Save is –1 (True) if the data in any control attached to the data control have changed and is 0 (False) otherwise. If you set the value of Save to 0 in the Validate event procedure, any changes will not be saved.

Consider the form created in the walkthrough. Suppose the contents of txtPop1995, the 1995 population text box, is changed to .8 and then a navigator arrow is clicked in an attempt to move to another record. The following code prevents the move.

```
Private Sub datCities_Validate(Action As Integer, Save As Integer)
    Dim strMsg As String
    If val(txtPop1995) < 1 then
        strMsg = "We only allow cities having a population " & _ "at least one
                million."
        MsgBox strMsg"City too small!"
        Action = 0
    End If
End Sub
```

If the statement

```
Action = 0
```

is changed to

```
Save = 0
```

the move will take place, but the previous record will retain its original values. That is, the number .8 will not appear in the table.

EXAMPLE 1

The following program is a general database manager for the Cities table in the MEGACTY1.MDB database. It allows the user to edit the Cities table as needed and to locate information based on the city name. (In the Validate event procedure, the inner If block keeps the message box from appearing when the first or last record is deleted.)

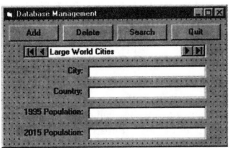

Object	Property	Setting
frmDBMan	Caption	Database Management
cmdAdd	Caption	Add
cmdDelete	Caption	Delete
cmdSearch	Caption	Search
cmdQuit	Caption	Quit
datCities	Caption	Large World Cities
	Database Name	MEGACTY1.MDB
	Record Source	Cities
lblCity	Caption	City:
txtCity	Text	(blank)
	Data Source	datCities
	DataField	City
lblCountry	Caption	Country:
txtCountry	Text	(blank)
	Data Source	datCities
	DataField	Country
lblPop1995	Caption	1995 Population:
txtPop1995	Text	(blank)
	Data Source	datCities
	DataField	pop1995
lblPop2015	Caption	2015 Population:
txtPop2015	Text	(blank)
	Data Source	datCities
	DataField	pop2015

```
Private Sub cmdAdd_Click()
   'Add a new record
   datCities.Recordset.AddNew
   'Data must be entered and a new record moved to
End Sub

Private Sub cmdDelete_Click ()
   'Delete the currently displayed record
   datCities.Recordset.Delete
   'Move so that user sees deleted record disappear
   datCities.Recordset.MoveNext
   If datCities.Recordset.EOF Then
      datCities.Recordset.MovePrevious
   End If
End Sub

Private Sub cmdSearch_Click()
   Dim strSearchFor As String, foundFlag As Boolean
   'Search for the city specified by the user
   strSearchFor = UCase(InputBox("Name of city to find:"))
   If Len(strSearchFor) > 0 Then
      datCities.Recordset.MoveFirst
      foundFlag = False
```

```
       Do While (Not foundFlag) And (Not datCities.Recordset.EOF)
          If UCase(datCities.Recordset.Fields("City").Value) = strSearchFor Then
             foundFlag = True
          Else
             datCities.Recordset.MoveNext
          End If
       Loop
       If Not foundFlag Then
          MsgBox "Unable to locate requested city.""Not Found"
          datCities.Recordset.MoveLast 'move so that EOF is no longer true
       End If
    Else
       MsgBox "Must enter a city.", ,""
    End If
End Sub


Private Sub cmdQuit_Click ()
   End
End Sub


Private Sub datCities_Validate(Action As Integer, Save As Integer)
   'Prevent a user from adding a city of population under 1 million
   Dim strMsg As String
   If Val(txtPop1995) < 1 Then
      If (Not datCities.Recordset.EOF) And (Not datCities.Recordset.BOF) Then
         strMsg = "We only allow cities having a population of " & _
                  "at least one million."
         MsgBox strMsg"City too small!"
         Action = 0
      End If
   End If
End Sub
```

[Run, click the Search button, and enter New York.]

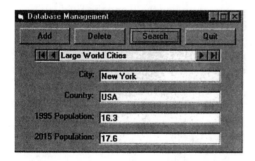

COMMENTS

1. App.Path cannot be used when you set the DatabaseName property of a data control in the Properties window at design time. However, App.Path can be used in the Form_Load event procedure. For instance, if you add the lines

```
Private Sub Form_Load()
   datCities.DatabaseName = App.Path & "\MEGACTY1.MDB"
End Sub
```

to Example 1, the program will find the database when it is located in the same folder as the program. The assignment made in the Form_Load event procedure will override any setting made in the Properties window. (The setting in the Properties window even can be left blank.) The programs for Section 11 on the CD accompanying this textbook contain the above Form_Load event procedure.

2. You will most likely alter the file MEGACTY1.MDB while experimenting with the data control or running the program in Example 1. You can always obtain a fresh copy of MEGACTY1.MDB by recopying it from the CD.

3. You can prevent the user from altering the data in a table by setting the Read-Only property of its data control to True.

4. The following controls can be bound to a data control: text box, check box, image, label, picture box, list box, combo box, data bound list box, data bound combo box, and FlexGrid.

5. A form can contain more than one data control.

6. Some entries in a table can be empty. For instance, in the Cities table, if the 2015 projected value is not known for a particular city, it can be omitted.

7. Do not use a method such as Move, Delete, or AddNew inside the Validate event procedure. Otherwise, an infinite loop will occur.

8. Field names can be up to 64 characters in length and can consist of letters, numbers, and spaces. If spaces are used in a name, then the name must be enclosed in brackets when used in Visual Basic.

9. Both tables in the database MEGACTY1.MDB have fields called *country*. If there is ever any question about which is being referred to, we can distinguish them by using the two (full) names Cities.country and Countries. country.

10. In the MEGACTY1.MDB database, the values in the field *city* are all of data type String and the values in the field *pop1995* are all of data type Single. We say that field *city* has type String (also known as Text) and the field *pop1995* has type Single. Two other common data types are Date/Time and Boolean (also known as Yes/No).

11. When a field is first created, a type must be specified. When that type is String (or Text), a maximum length must also be specified. In the MEGACTY1.MDB database, the fields *city* and *country* have maximum length 20 and the field *currency* has maximum length 10.

12. The database MEGACTY1.MDB was created with Visual Data Manager, which has the same format as Access. When the database to be used has been created with other software, such as FoxPro 3.0 or dBase 5.0, then the walkthrough requires an additional step. Namely, between Steps 3 and 4, the Connect property of the data control has to be set to the name of the software product. (This step was not necessary in our case because Access is the default software.) *Note:* Access database file names end with .MDB, which is an abbreviation for Microsoft Data Base. Btrieve, FoxPro, dBase, and Paradox database file names end with .DAT, .DBF, .DBF, and .DB, respectively.

11.2 RELATIONAL DATABASES AND SQL

■ PRIMARY AND FOREIGN KEYS

A well-designed table should have a field (or set of fields) that can be used to uniquely identify each record. Such a field (or set of fields) is called a **primary key**. For instance, in the Countries table of Section 11.1, the *country* field is a primary key. In the Cities table, because we are only considering very large cities (of over 1 million population), the *city* field is a primary key. Databases of student enrollments in a college usually use a field of social security numbers as the primary key. Names would not be a good choice because there could easily be two students having the same name.

When a database is created, a field can be specified as a primary key. If so, Visual Basic will insist that every record have an entry in the primary key field and that the same entry does not appear in two different records. If the user tries to enter a record with no data in the primary key, the error message "Index or primary key can't contain a null record." will be generated. If the user tries to enter a record with the same primary key data as another record, the error message "Duplicate value in index, primary key, or relationship. Changes were unsuccessful." will be displayed.

When a database contains two or more tables, the tables are usually related. For instance, the two tables Cities and Countries are related by their *country* field. Let's refer to these two fields as Cities.country and Countries.country. Notice that every entry in Cities.country appears uniquely in Countries.country and Countries.country is a primary key. We say that Cities.country is a **foreign key** of Countries.country. Foreign keys can be specified when a table is first created. If so, Visual Basic will insist on the **Rule of Referential Integrity**, namely, that each value in the foreign key must also appear in the primary key of the other table.

The CD accompanying this book contains a database named MEGACTY2.MDB. It has the same information as MEGACTY1.MDB except that Cities.city and Countries.country have been specified as primary keys for their respective tables, and Cities.country has been specified as a foreign key of Countries.country. If the user tries to add a city to the Cities table whose country does not appear in the Countries table, then the error message "Can't add or change record. Referential integrity rules require a related record in table 'Countries'." will be displayed. The message will also be generated if the user tries to delete a country from the Countries.country field that appears in the Cities.country field. Due to the interdependence of the two tables in MEGACTY2.MDB, this database is called a **relational database**.

A foreign key allows Visual Basic to link (or **join**) together two tables from a relational database in a meaningful way. For instance, when the two tables Cities and Countries from MEGACTY2.MDB are joined based on the foreign key Cities.country, the result is Table 11.4. The record for each city is expanded to show its country's population and its currency. This joined table is very handy if, say, we wanted to click on navigation arrows and display a city's name and currency. We only have to create the original two tables; Visual Basic creates the joined table as needed. The request for a joined table is made in a language called SQL.

Table 11.4
A Join of Two Tables

city	Cities. country	Cities. pop1995	Countries. pop2015	Country. country	pop1995	currency
Tokyo	Japan	26.8	28.7	Japan	125.0	yen
Sao Paulo	Brazil	16.4	20.8	Brazil	155.8	real
New York	USA	16.3	17.6	USA	263.4	dollar
Mexico City	Mexico	15.6	18.8	Mexico	85.6	peso
Bombay	India	15.1	27.4	India	846.3	rupee
Shanghai	China	15.1	23.4	China	1185.2	yuan
Los Angeles	USA	12.4	14.3	USA	263.4	dollar
Beijing	China	12.4	19.4	China	1185.2	yuan
Calcutta	India	11.7	17.6	India	846.3	rupee
Tianjin	China	10.7	17.0	China	1185.2	yuan

■ SQL

Structured Query Language (SQL) was developed in the early 1970s at IBM for use with relational databases. The language was standardized in 1986 by ANSI (American National

Standards Institute). Visual Basic uses a version of SQL that is compliant with ANSI-89 SQL. There are some minor variations that are of no concern in this book.

SQL is a very powerful language. One use of SQL is to request specialized information from an existing database and/or to have the information presented in a specified order.

■ FOUR SQL REQUESTS

We will focus on four basic types of requests that can be made with SQL.

Request I: Show the records of a table in a specified order.
  Some examples of orders with MEGACTY2.MDB are

  (a) Alphabetical order based on the name of the city.
  (b) Alphabetical order based on the name of the country, and within each country group, the name of the city.
  (c) In descending order based on the projected 2015 population.

Request II: Show just the records that meet certain criteria.
  Some examples of criteria with MEGACTY2.MDB are

  (a) Cities that are in China.
  (b) Cities whose 2015 population is projected to be at least 20 million.
  (c) Cities whose name begins with the letter S.

Request III: Join the tables together, connected by a foreign key, and present the records as in Requests I and II.
  Some examples with MEGACTY2.MDB are

  (a) Show the cities in descending order of the populations of their countries.
  (b) Show the cities whose currency has "u" as its second letter.

Request IV: Make available just *some* of the fields of either the basic tables or the joined table. (For now, this type of request just conserves space and effort by Visual Basic. However, it will be very useful in Section 11.3 when used with a FlexGrid control.)

Some examples with MEGACTY2.MDB are

  (a) Make available just the city and country fields of the table Cities.
  (b) Make available just the city and currency fields of the joined table.

Normally, we set the RecordSource property of a data control to an entire table. Also, the records of the table are normally presented in the order they are physically stored in the table. We make the requests discussed above by specifying the RecordSource property as one of the following kinds of settings.

Request I: SELECT * FROM *Table1* ORDER BY *field1* ASC
              or SELECT * FROM *Table1* ORDER BY *field1* DESC

Request II: SELECT * FROM *Table1* WHERE *criteria*

Request III: SELECT * FROM *Table1* INNER JOIN *Table2* ON *foreign field* = *primary field* WHERE *criteria*

Request IV: SELECT *field1, field2, . . . fieldN* FROM *Table1* WHERE *criteria*

The words ASC and DESC specify ASCending and DESCending orders, respectively. A *criteria* clause is a string containing a condition of the type used with If blocks. In addition to the standard operators <, >, and =, *criteria* strings frequently contain the operator Like. Essentially, Like uses the wildcard characters ? and * to compare a string to a pattern. A question mark stands for a single character in the same position as the question mark. For instance, the pattern "B?d" is matched by "Bid", "Bud", and "Bad". An asterisk stands for any number of characters in the same position as the asterisk. For instance, the pattern "C*r" is matched by "Computer", "Chair", and "Car". See Comments 3 through 5 for further information about Like.

In the sentence

```
SELECT fields FROM clause
```

fields is either * (to indicate all fields) or a sequence of the fields to be available (separated by commas), and *clause* is either a single table or a join of two tables. A join of two tables is indicated by a *clause* of the form

```
table1 INNER JOIN table2 ON foreign key of table1=primary key of table2
```

Appending

```
WHERE criteria
```

to the end of the sentence restricts the records to those satisfying *criteria*. Appending

```
ORDER BY field(s) ASC (or DESC)
```

presents the records ordered by the specified *field* or *fields*.

In general, the SQL statements we consider will look like

```
SELECT www FROM xxx WHERE yyy ORDER BY zzz
```

where SELECT *www* FROM *xxx* is always present and accompanied by one or both of WHERE *yyy* and ORDER BY *zzz*. In addition, the *xxx* portion might contain an INNER JOIN phrase.

The settings for the examples mentioned earlier are as follows:

I (a) Show the records from Cities in alphabetical order based on the name of the city.

```
SELECT * FROM Cities ORDER BY city ASC
```

I (b) Show the records from Cities in alphabetical order based first on the name of the country and,, within each country group,, the name of the city.

```
SELECT * FROM Cities ORDER BY country,, city ASC
```

I (c) Show the records from Cities in descending order based on the projected 2015 population.

```
SELECT * FROM Cities ORDER BY pop2015 DESC
```

II (a) Show the records for the Cities in China.

```
SELECT * FROM Cities WHERE country = 'China'
```

II (b) Show the records from Cities whose 2015 population is projected to be at least 20 million.

```
SELECT * FROM Cities WHERE pop2015 >= 20
```

II (c) Show the records from Cities whose name begins with the letter S.

```
SELECT * FROM Cities WHERE city Like 'S*'
```

III (a) Show the records from the joined table in descending order of the populations of their countries.

```
SELECT * FROM Cities INNER JOIN Countries ON Cities.country =
Countries.country ORDER BY Countries.pop1995 DESC
```

III (b) Show the records from the joined table whose currency has "u" as its second letter.

```
SELECT * FROM Cities INNER JOIN Countries ON Cities.country =
Countries.country WHERE currency Like '?u*'
```

IV (a) Make available just the city and country fields of the table Cities.

```
SELECT city, country FROM Cities
```

IV (b) Make available just the city and currency fields of the joined table.

```
SELECT city,, currency FROM Cities INNER JOIN Countries ON Cities.coun-
try = Countries.country
```

Note: In several of the statements, the single quote, rather than the normal double quote was used to surround strings. This is standard practice with SQL statements.

We can think of an SQL statement as creating in essence a new "virtual" table from existing tables. For instance, we might regard the statement

```
SELECT city, pop2015 FROM Cities WHERE pop2015 >= 20
```

as creating the "virtual" table

city	pop2015
Tokyo	28.7
Sao Paulo	20.8
Bombay	27.4
Shanghai	23.4

This table is a subtable of the original table Cities, that is, it consists of what is left after certain columns and rows are deleted.

As another example, the statement

```
SELECT Cities.city, Cities.Country, Country.currency FROM Cities INNER JOIN
Countries ON Cities.country = Countries.country WHERE Countries.country>'K'
```

creates in essence the "virtual" table

Cities.city	Cities.country	currency
New York	USA	dollar
Mexico City	Mexico	peso
Los Angeles	USA	dollar

which is a subtable of a join of the two tables Cities and Countries.

These "virtual" tables don't really exist physically. However, for all practical purposes, Visual Basic acts as if they did. In Visual Basic terminology, a "virtual" table is called a **recordset** and SQL statements are said to create a recordset. In standard relational database books, a "virtual" table is called a **view**.

SQL also can be used in code with a statement of the form

```
Data1.RecordSource = " SELECT ... FROM ..."
```

to alter the order and kinds of records presented from a database. However, such a statement must be followed by the statement

```
Data1.Refresh
```

to reset the information processed by the data control.

EXAMPLE 1

The following program allows the user to alter the order and kinds of information displayed from a database. When the first command button is pressed, the cities are presented in ascending order based on their

1995 populations. When the second command button is pressed, the cities are presented in alphabetical order along with their currencies.

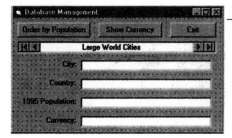

Object	Property	Setting
frmDBMan	Caption	Database Management
cmdOrder ByPop	Caption	Order by Population
cmdShow Currency	Caption	Show Currency
cmdQuit	Caption	Exit
datCities	Caption	Large World Cities
	Database Name	MEGACTY2.MDB
	Record Source	Cities
lblCity	Caption	City:
txtCity	Data Source	datCities
	DataField	city
	Text	(blank)
lblCountry	Caption	Country:
txtCountry	Data Source	datCities
	DataField	country
	Text	(blank)
lblPopulation	Caption	1995 Population:
txtPopulation	Data Source	datCities
	DataField	pop1995
	Text	(blank)
lblCurrency	Caption	Currency:
txtCurrency	Data Source	datCities
	Text	(blank)

```
Private Sub cmdOrderByPop_Click()
  Dim strSQL As String
  txtCurrency.DataField = ""
  txtCurrency.Text = ""
  strSQL = "SELECT * FROM Cities ORDER BY pop1995 ASC"
  datCities.RecordSource = strSQL
  datCities.Refresh
End Sub

Private Sub cmdQuit_Click()
  End
End Sub

Private Sub cmdShowCurrency_Click()

  Dim strSQL As String
  strSQL = "SELECT city, Cities.country, Cities.pop1995, currency " & _ "FROM
          Cities INNER JOIN Countries " & _ "ON
          Cities.country=Countries.country " & "ORDER BY city ASC"
  datCities.RecordSource = strSQL
  datCities.Refresh txtCurrency.DataField = "currency"
End Sub
```

[Run, and click on Order by Population.]

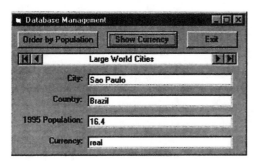

[Click on Show Currency, and then click on the Next navigator arrow six times.]

The program in Example 1 of Section 11.1 searched a table for a specific record by looping through all the records. Whereas this technique is fine for small tables, it is not efficient for searches of large tables. Visual Basic provides a better way with Find methods.

■ FIND METHODS

Suppose a table has been attached to the data control Data1, and an SQL statement has been used to create and order a recordset. Then a statement of the form

Data1.RecordSet.FindFirst *criteria*

starts at the beginning of the recordset, searches for the first record in the recordset that satisfies the criteria, and makes that record the current record. (Here, *criteria* is a string just like a *criteria* phrase that follows WHERE in an SQL statement.) The related methods FindLast, FindNext, and FindPrevious function as their names suggest. (FindLast starts at the end of the recordset. FindNext and FindPrevious start at the current record.) For instance, suppose an SQL statement ordered the cities alphabetically by name. The following statements and their outcomes show the effects of the various Find methods. (In each case, assume that the current record is Mexico City.)

Statement	New Current Record
datCities.Recordset.FindFirst "pop2015 < 20"	Beijing
datCities.Recordset.FindLast "pop2015 < 20"	Tianjin
datCities.Recordset.FindNext "pop2015 < 20"	New York
datCities.Recordset.FindPrevious "pop2015 < 20"	Los Angeles

Visual Basic has two properties, NoMatch and Bookmark, that help when a Find method fails to locate a suitable record.

If BkMk is a string variable, a statement of the form

```
BkMk = Data1.Recordset.Bookmark
```

assigns the location of the current record to the variable BkMk. When desired, the statement

```
Data1.Recordset.Bookmark = BkMk
```

will return to the original location in the table.

If a Find method does not locate a record matching the criteria, the first or last record (depending on where the search is heading) in the recordset becomes the current record and the NoMatch property is set to True. Therefore, the following lines of code can be used to keep the current record current whenever the Find method is unsuccessful.

```
BkMk = Data1.Recordset.Bookmark
   Data1.Recordset.FindNext criteria
   If Data1.Recordset.NoMatch = True Then
   Data1.Recordset.Bookmark = BkMk
End If
```

EXAMPLE 2

The following program displays the large cities in a country specified by the user. Due to the SQL statement in the setting for datCities.RecordSource, the cities will be presented alphabetically. Notice the handling of the string variable *criteria*. Had the Find statement been

```
datCities.Recordset.FindFirst "country = nom"
```

the error message "Can't find name 'nom'." would have been generated.

Object	Property	Setting
frmDBMan	Caption	EXAMPLE 12-2-2
lstCities		
cmdFind	Caption	Find Cities
lblCountry	Caption	Country
txtCountry	Caption	(blank)
datCities	Caption	Large World Cities
	Database Name	MEGACTY2.MDB
	Record Source	SELECT * FROM Cities ORDER BY city ASC

```
Private Sub cmdFind_Click()
   Dim nom As String, criteria As String
   lstCities.Clear
   If txtCountry.Text<> "" Then
       nom = txtCountry.Text
       criteria = "country = " & "'" & nom & "'"
       datCities.Recordset.FindFirst criteria
       Do While datCities.Recordset.NoMatch = False
          lstCities.AddItem datCities.Recordset.Fields("city").Value
          datCities.Recordset.FindNext criteria
       Loop
   If lstCities.ListCount = 0 Then lstCities.AddItem "None"
     Else
       MsgBox "You must enter a country.", , ""
       txtCountry.SetFocus
   End If
End Sub
```

[Run, type China into the text box, and press the command button.]

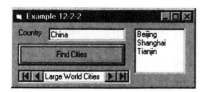

COMMENTS

1. Each record of the Countries table is related to one or more records of the Cities table, but each record of the Cities table is related to only one record of the Countries table. Therefore, we say that there is a **one-to-many relationship** from the Countries table to the Cities table.

2. SQL statements are insensitive to case. For instance, the following choices for *criteria* have the same effect: City='China', city='china', CITY='china', CiTy='CHINA'.

3. When the Like operator is used, the "pattern" must appear on the right of the operator. For instance, the SQL statement

```
SELECT * FROM Cities WHERE city Like 'S*'
```

cannot be replaced by

```
SELECT * FROM Cities WHERE 'S*' Like city
```

4. The operator Like permits a refinement of the wildcard character "?". Whereas "?" is a placeholder for any letter, an expression such as "[*letter1-letter2*]" is a placeholder for any letter from *letter1* to *letter2*. For instance, the pattern "[A-F]ad" is matched by Bad and Dad, but not Sad.

5. The Like operator can be used in If blocks in much the same way as the operators >, =, and <. In this situation, the operator is case-sensitive. For instance, the condition ("bad" Like "[A-F]ad") is False. However, when Like is used in SQL statements, it is case-insensitive. That is, ("bad" Like "[A-F]ad") is True.

6. Sometimes a pair of fields is specified as a primary key. For instance, in a table of college courses, a single course might have several sections—a course might be identified as CMSC 102, Section 3. In this case, the pair of fields *course, section* would serve as a primary key for the table.

7. The requirement that no record may have a null primary key is called the **Rule of Entity Integrity**.

8. If there is no field with unique entries, database designers usually add a "counter field" containing the numbers 1, 2, 3, and so on. This field then can serve as a primary key.

11.3 THREE ADDITIONAL DATA-BOUND CONTROLS; CREATING AND DESIGNING DATABASES

So far, we have used text boxes to display the contents of a single field in a single row. The FlexGrid control can display an entire table (or recordset). Data-bound list boxes and data-bound combo boxes can display the contents of a single field for an entire table or recordset.

There are three ways you can create a database:

1. Use Visual Data Manager, a program supplied with all editions of Visual Basic.

2. Use code.

3. Use database management software, such as Access, Btrieve, FoxPro, or Paradox.

In this section we give a detailed explanation of how to use Visual Data Manager and include a code template that you can modify to create a database programmatically.

Before you can use the three additional data-bound controls, you must add them to the toolbar using the Components dialog box that is invoked from the Project menu. (Place an x in the check box next to "Microsoft FlexGrid Control 6.0" for the FlexGrid control, and place an x in the check box next to "Microsoft Data Bound List Controls 6.0" for the other two controls.)

■ USING THE FLEXGRID CONTROL

When you attach the FlexGrid control to a table via a data control, the FlexGrid control will display the entire contents of the table, including the field names. If the table is too large to be displayed in entirety, scroll bars will automatically appear to allow you to scroll to other parts of the table. The FlexGrid control is discussed in Section 10.3. The gray fixed row at the top will show the field names. You should set the FixedCols property to 0 to avoid having a blank fixed column at the left. If some of the fields have long entries, you should widen the corresponding columns with the ColWidth method in Form_Load. Although you can use code to alter the contents of the cells in a FlexGrid (as shown in Section 10.3), changes in the cells of the FlexGrid will not alter the contents of the database.

You can use an SQL statement to specify the fields displayed in a FlexGrid control. For instance, if the control has datCities as its DataSource and the DatabaseName setting for datCities is MEGACTY2.MDB, then the statement

```
datCities.RecordSource = "SELECT city, country FROM Cities"
```

causes the FlexGrid to display only the first two columns of the Cities table. The same effect can be achieved at design time by setting the RecordSource property of datCities to

```
SELECT city, country FROM Cities
```

EXAMPLE 1

The following program displays the contents of the Cities table of the MEGACTY2.MDB database. When you click on the command button, the FlexGrid displays the cities, their countries, and currency. Also, the caption of the command button changes to "Show City, Country, Populations". The next time you click the command button, the contents of the FlexGrid returns to its original state.

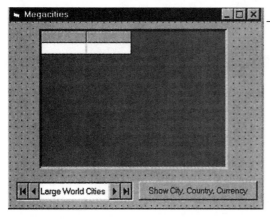

Object	Property	Setting
frm12_3_1	Caption	Megacities
datCities	Caption	Large World Cities
	Database Name	MEGACTY2.MDB
	Record Source	Cities
msgCities	Data Source	datCities
	FixedCols	0
cmdShow	Caption	Show City, Country, Currency

```
Private Sub cmdShow_Click()
If cmdShow.Caption = "Show City, Country, Currency" Then '
    Join the two tables and display cities, countries, and currency
    datCities.RecordSource = "SELECT city, Cities.country, currency FROM " & _
        "Cities INNER JOIN Countries ON Countries.country = Cities.country " & _
        "ORDER BY city"
    datCities.Refresh
    cmdShow.Caption = "Show City, Country, Populations"
Else
    datCities.RecordSource = "Cities"
    datCities.Refresh
    cmdShow.Caption = "Show City, Country, Currency"
```

```
    End If
End Sub

Private Sub Form_Load( )
   msgCities.ColWidth(0) = 1000 'Widen the first column slightly
End Sub
```

[Run]

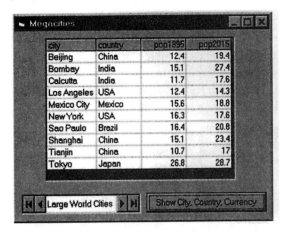

[Click on the command button.]

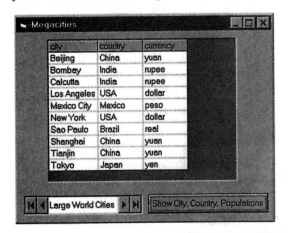

USING THE DATA-BOUND LIST BOX AND COMBO BOX CONTROLS

The data-bound list box and data-bound combo box controls look like the standard list box and combo box controls. They are often used with data-entry forms to speed data entry and ensure that valid data is entered. These controls automatically fill with a column from a table or recordset after you set a few properties. Note that the data-bound controls display data from a table or a recordset. Therefore, three methods (AddItem, Clear, and RemoveItem) and two properties (ListCount and Sorted) used with the regular list box and combo box are not available with the data-bound controls. The count of items displayed in a data-bound control is determined by the RecordCount property of the recordset.

Two key properties determine the entries of a data-bound list or combo box—**Row-Source** and **ListField**. RowSource specifies a data control, and ListField specifies a field from the data control's table or recordset. That field will be used to fill the list.

EXAMPLE 2

The data-bound list box in the following example displays the countries in the Countries table of MEGACTY2.MDB. When the command button is clicked, SQL is used to sort the countries by their 1995 population (in descending order). When an item in the list box is double-clicked, the list box's Text property is used to display the name of the country's unit of currency in a label. (Recall that the value of the Text property is the currently highlighted item.) The data control is made invisible since it is not needed by the user.

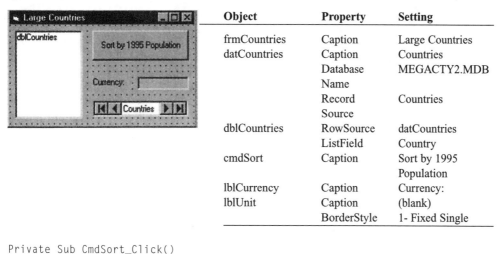

Object	Property	Setting
frmCountries	Caption	Large Countries
datCountries	Caption	Countries
	Database Name	MEGACTY2.MDB
	Record Source	Countries
dblCountries	RowSource	datCountries
	ListField	Country
cmdSort	Caption	Sort by 1995 Population
lblCurrency	Caption	Currency:
lblUnit	Caption	(blank)
	BorderStyle	1- Fixed Single

```
Private Sub CmdSort_Click()
   datCountries.RecordSource = "SELECT * FROM Countries " & _ "ORDER by pop1995
                                 DESC"
   datCountries.Refresh
End Sub

Private Sub dblCountries_dblClick()
   datCountries.Recordset.FindFirst _
                      "Country =" & "'" & dblCountries.Text & "'"
   lblUnit.Caption = datCountries.Recordset.Fields("currency").Value
End Sub
```

[Run, click on the command button, and then double-click on Japan.]

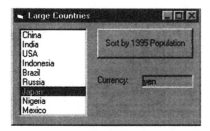

When used to enhance data entry, a data-bound list or combo control is usually linked to two data controls. The first data control is used to fill the list and the second to update a field in a table. As demonstrated in Example 2, the first data control fills the list as designated by the data-bound control's ListField and RowSource properties. The second control updates a field in a table specified by the data-bound control's DataSource and DataField properties. Another property of the data-bound control, the **BoundColumn** property, specifies the name of a field in the first data control's recordset. Once the user chooses one of the items in the list (and thereby one of the rows), the value in the row's specified field is passed to the field to be updated. Usually, the BoundColumn property has the same setting as the DataField property.

EXAMPLE 3

The following program adds cities to the Cities table of MEGACTY2.MDB. Of course, only cities in a country found in the Countries table are acceptable. A data-bound combo box is employed to show the user a list of the acceptable countries. (The experienced data-entry person can just type a name directly into the text box portion of the combo box, whereas the novice must refer to the list.) When the program is first run, the user should press the command button to clear the text boxes. After that, for each new city to be entered into the database, the user should fill the text boxes and then press the command button.

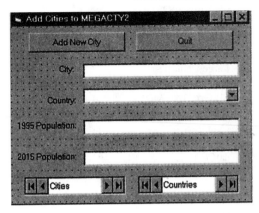

Object	Property	Setting
frm12_3_3	Caption	Add Cities to MEGACTY2
datCountries	Caption	Countries
	DatabaseName	MEGACTY2.MDB
	RecordSource	Countries
Visible	0 – False	
datCities	Caption	Cities
	DatabaseName	MEGACTY2.MDB
	RecordSource	Cities
	Visible	0 – False
cmdAddNew	Caption	Add New City
cmdQuit	Caption	Quit
lblCity	Caption	City:
txtCity	DataSource	datCities
	DataField	city
lblCountry	Caption	Country:
dbcCountry	DataSource	datCities
	DataField	country
	BoundColumn	country
	RowSource	datCountries
	ListField	country
lblPop1995	Caption	1995 Population:
txtPop1995	DataSource	datCities
	DataField	pop1995
lblPop2015	Caption	2015 Population:
txtPop2015	DataSource	datCities
	DataField	pop2015

```
Private Sub cmdAddNew_Click()
   datCities.Recordset.AddNew
End Sub

Private Sub cmdQuit_Click()
   End
End Sub
```

[Run, click on the Add New City command button, add the data for a couple of cities, and click on Quit. Then place the cities table of MEGACTY2.MDB in a FlexGrid to confirm that the cities have indeed been added.]

Some possible cities to add are:

City	country	pop1995	pop2015
Jakarta	Indonesia	11.5	21.2
Osaka	Japan	10.6	10.6
Lagos	Nigeria	10.3	24.4

■ CREATING A DATABASE WITH VISUAL DATA MANAGER

You invoke Visual Data Manager (VisData) from Visual Basic by pressing Alt/Add-Ins/Visual Data Manager. The first two entries of the File menu of VisData are Open Database, used to view and alter an existing database, and New, used to create a new database. See Figure 11-3.

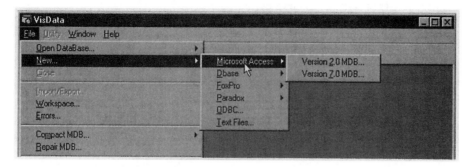

FIGURE 11-2   *Visual Data Manager's File Menu*

Let's focus on creating a new database. After you select New, you are presented with a drop-down menu used to choose the type of database as shown in Figure 11-2. Choose Microsoft Access and then specify a version. (Version 7.0 is the latest version of Access, the one that comes with the Professional Edition of Office 97.) Then a standard file-naming dialog box titled "Select Microsoft Access Database to Create" appears. See Figure 11-3.

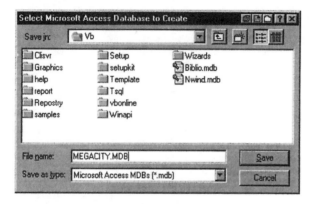

FIGURE 11-3   *Dialog Box Used to Name the Database*

After you name the database, say as MEGACITY.MDB, and click Save, the Database window and SQL Statement box appear. We will work solely with the Database window.

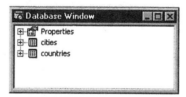

FIGURE 11-4   *Database Window. (Appears After the Database is Named. Initially the Window Will Contain Only the Properties Line. Additional Lines Will Appear as Tables are Created.)*

Suppose you want to create a database with two tables. Starting from the Database window, the basic steps are as follows:

1. Create the database and the two tables.

   (a) Click on the right mouse button within the Database window. Click on New Table and use the Table Structure window (Figure 11-5) to name the first table and to specify the fields and their data types. The steps listed after Figure 11-5 show how to carry out these tasks.

   (b) Repeat Step 1 for the second table.

2. (Optional) Specify a primary key for a table.

(a) Highlight the table name in the Database window.

(b) Press the right mouse button and choose Design to invoke the Table Structure window (Figure 11-5).

(c) Press the Add Index button to invoke the Add Index window (Figure 11-6) and follow the steps listed after the figure.

3. Place records into a table.

(*Note:* The VisData toolbar contains three sets of icons. This discussion assumes that the left icon of each of the first two sets has been selected. These are the "Table type Recordset" and "Use Data Control on New Form" icons.)

(a) Double-click on the table in the Database window to invoke the Table window (Figure 11-7).

(b) Follow the directions listed after Figure 11-7.

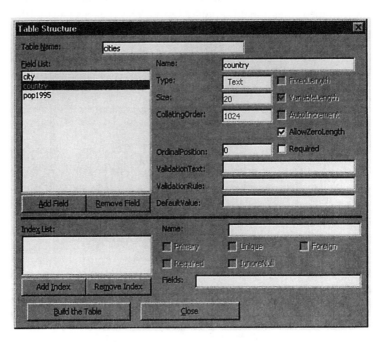

FIGURE 11-5   *Table Structure Window. (Invoked from the Database Window with the Right Mouse Button by Choosing New or Design.)*

How to use the Table Structure window

1. Type the name of the table in the Table Name text box.

2. Click on the Add Field button. (An Add Field window will be displayed.)

3. Type the name of a field in the Name text box.

4. Click on the down arrow of the Type combo box and select a type from the dropdown list. (We use primarily the type "Text" for strings, and "Single" or "Integer" for numbers.)

5. If the data type is "Text," type the length of the largest possible string needed in the Size box. (For instance, length 20 should suffice for names of cities. The length must be no longer than 255 characters.)

6. Press OK to add the field to the table.

7. Repeat Steps 3 through 6 until you have added all the fields to the table. When you are through, click on the Close button to return to the Database window.

8. To delete a field, highlight the field by clicking on it in the list box and then press the Remove Field button.

9. When all fields have been specified, press the "Build the Table" button to save the table and return to the Database window. (If we later decide to add a new field or delete an existing field, we can return to the Table Structure window by highlighting the table in the Database window, clicking the right mouse button, and choosing Design.)

(*Note:* The "Build the Table" button appears only for new tables, otherwise, use the Close button return to the Database window.)

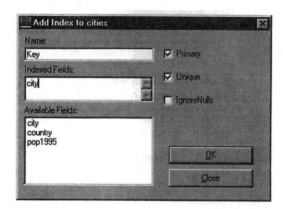

FIGURE 11-6   *Add Index Window (Invoked from the Table Structure Window by Pressing Add Index.)*

How to use the Add Index window to specify a primary key

1. Type in a name for an index, such as Principal, click on the field which is to be the primary field, and place check marks in the Primary and Unique check boxes.

2. Click OK and then click Close.

    Note: To specify an ordinary index, follow all steps except turning on the Primary check box.

3. Press "Build the Table" or Close to return to the Database window.

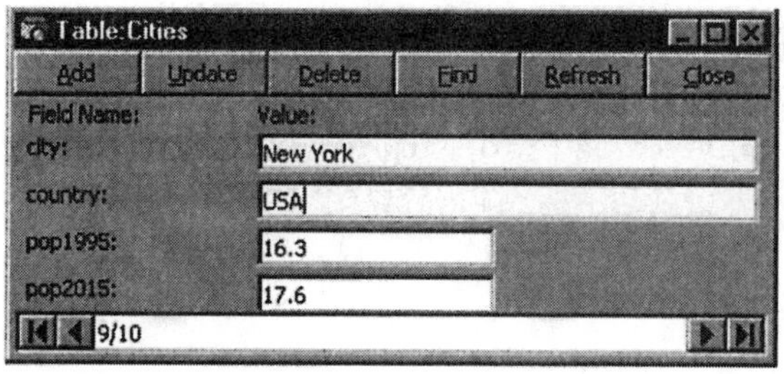

FIGURE 11-7   *Table window (Invoked from the Database Window by Double-Clicking on the Table name. Or, Choose the Table, Click on the Right Mouse Button, and Click on Open.)*

How to use the Table window

1. If the table has no records, the Value text boxes will be blank. To add a record, type data into the fields and press the Update button.

2. To add a new record to the end of a table that already contains records, click the Add button, type data into the fields, and press the Update button. If you make a mistake entering the data, click on the Cancel button.

3. To view an existing record, use the navigator buttons (identical to those of the data control) or the <u>F</u>ind button to move to a record of a specified value.

4. To remove the current record from the table, click the <u>D</u>elete button. The record is immediately deleted and cannot be recovered.

5. To edit an existing record, make changes in the data and click on the <u>U</u>pdate button.

6. Press the <u>C</u>lose button to return to the Database window.

At any time, the main section of the Database window contains a list of the tables you have specified. Initially the main section is blank except for Properties. (This is a list of properties pertaining to the database.) If you click the right mouse button while highlighting a table, a menu will appear with the following options:

Menu Item	Use
Open	Open the table to allow records to be added.
Design	Specify the design (number and types of fields).
Rename	Rename the given table.
Delete	Remove the given table from the database.
Copy Structure	Copies the structure of the given database with or without the data currently contained in the database.
Refresh List	Redisplay the list in the Database window.
New Table	Open the Table Structure window.
New Query	Open the Query Builder window.

■ CREATING A DATABASE IN CODE

The following lines of code create a database named "DBNAME.MDB" with two tables, TABLE1 and TABLE2. TABLE1 has the fields FIELD1A (type Text with maximum length 50) and FIELD1B (numeric of type Single). TABLE2 has analogous fields called FIELD2A and FIELD2B, and also FIELD2C of type Integer. FIELD1A is a primary key of TABLE1 and FIELD2A is a foreign key in TABLE2 referring to FIELD1A of TABLE1. FIELD2C is a primary key of TABLE2. The record ("alpha", 1997) is placed in TABLE1 and the record ("alpha", 2000, 1) is placed in TABLE2. This code, which is contained in the file CREATEDB.TXT accompanying this textbook, is intended as a template that you can modify to create a database programmatically. (*Note:* The code can be placed into an event procedure. Before you run the program, click on References in the Project menu and make sure that "DAO 3.51 Object Library" is selected.)

```
Dim MyDB As Database, MyWs As Workspace
Dim T1, T2 As TableDef
Dim T1Flds(1 To 2), T2Flds(1 To 3) As Field
Dim TempFld As Field
Dim T1Idx, T2Idx As Index
Dim Rel As Relation
Dim MyRec As Recordset
'Create Database
Set MyWs = DBEngine.Workspaces(0)
Set MyDB = MyWs.
CreateDatabase("C:\DBNAME.MDB", dbLangGeneral)'Create first Table, TABLE1
Set T1 = MyDB.CreateTableDef("TABLE1")
'Specify fields for TABLE1
'Note the use of the optional parameter 50 for field size
'If 50 is omitted, the size will default to 20
Set T1Flds(1) = T1.CreateField("FIELD1A", dbText, 50)
Set T1Flds(2) = T1.CreateField("FIELD1B", dbSingle)
'Add the New fields to the field list in the Table
```

```
T1.Fields.Append T1Flds(1)
T1.Fields.Append T1Flds(2)
'Specify a primary field for TABLE1
Set T1Idx = T1.CreateIndex("FIELD1A")
T1Idx.Primary = True
T1Idx.Unique = True
T1Idx.Required = True
Set T1Flds(1) = T1Idx.CreateField("FIELD1A")
'Add this field to the field list of the Index
T1Idx.Fields.Append T1Flds(1)
'Add this Index to the index list of the Table
T1.Indexes.Append T1Idx
'Add the Table to the Database
MyDB.TableDefs.Append T1
'Create TABLE2
Set T2 = MyDB.CreateTableDef("TABLE2")
'Specify fields for TABLE2
Set T2Flds(1) = T2.CreateField("FIELD2A", dbText, 50)
Set T2Flds(2) = T2.CreateField("FIELD2B", dbSingle)
Set T2Flds(3) = T2.CreateField("FIELD2C", dbInteger)
'Add the new fields to the field list of the Table
T2.Fields.Append T2Flds(1)
T2.Fields.Append T2Flds(2)
T2.Fields.Append T2Flds(3)
'Set the primary field for TABLE2Set T2Idx = T2.CreateIndex("FIELD2C")
T2Idx.Primary = True
T2Idx.Unique = True
T2Idx.Required = True
Set T2Flds(3) = T2Idx.CreateField("FIELD2C")
'Add this field to the field list of the Index
T2Idx.Fields.Append T2Flds(3)
'Add this index to the index list of TABLE2
T2.Indexes.Append T2Idx
'Add TABLE2 to the Database
MyDB.TableDefs.Append T2
'Set up the relation between the tables
Set Rel = MyDB.CreateRelation("foreign", "TABLE1", "TABLE2")
Rel.Attributes = 0
'Mark the primary field in TABLE1
Set T2Flds(1) = Rel.CreateField("FIELD1A")
'Mark the foreign key field in TABLE2
T2Flds(1).ForeignName = "FIELD2A"
'Add the field to the field list of the relation
Rel.Fields.Append T2Flds(1)
'Add the relation to the database
MyDB.Relations.Append Rel
'Add a record to each table
'Open a recordset referring to TABLE1
Set MyRec = T1.OpenRecordset
'Create a record
MyRec.AddNew
MyRec("FIELD1A") = "alpha"
MyRec("FIELD1B") = 1997
'Update the recordset
MyRec.Update
```

```
'Close the recordset referring to TABLE1
MyRec.Close
'Open a recordset referring to TABLE2
Set MyRec = T2.OpenRecordset
'Create a record
MyRec.AddNewMyRec("FIELD2A") = "alpha"
MyRec("FIELD2B") = 2000
MyRec("FIELD2C") = 1
'Update the recordset
MyRec.Update
'Close the recordset
MyRec.Close
'Close the database
MyDB.Close
```

■ PRINCIPLES OF DATABASE DESIGN

In order to design a database, you must decide how many tables to use, what fields to include in each table, what fields to make primary or foreign keys, and what validation criteria to specify. The programming paradigm "Plan first, code later" also applies to databases. Before you design a database, you first must understand how the database will be used. For instance, you must know in what way and how often the user will update the data, and what types of reports the user will want to be generated from the database. Failure to plan ahead can be very costly.

You have no doubt read about the "year 2000 crisis." Databases designed in the 1960s and 1970s saved space by using just two digits to refer to each year. As a result, they cannot distinguish between the year 2000 and the year 1900. Correcting this oversight is predicted to cost government and industry billions of dollars.

Good relational database design is more an art than a science. However, there are certain fundamental guidelines that the designer should keep in mind.

Include the necessary data.

After you have a clear picture of the types of reports the user must generate, you will know what fields and relationships to include. On the other hand, some data that seem relevant do not have to be kept.

Be aware that data should often be stored in their smallest parts.

For instance, city, state, and zip code are usually best stored in three fields. So doing will allow you to sort a mailing by zip code or target a mailing to the residents of a specific city.

Avoid redundancy.

The process of avoiding redundancy by splitting a table into two or more related tables is called **data normalization**. For instance, the excessive duplication in Table 11.5(a) can be avoided by replacing the table with the two related tables, Tables 11.5(b) and 11.5(c).

TABLE 11.5(A)
A Table with Redundant Data

course	section	name	time	credits	prerequisite
CS102	1001	Intro to Databases	MWF 8–9	3	CS101
CS102	1002	Intro to Databases	MWF 1–2	3	CS101
CS102	1003	Intro to Databases	MWF 2–3	3	CS101
CS102	1004	Intro to Databases	MWF 3–4	3	CS101
CS105	1001	Visual Basic	MWF 1–2	4	CS200

TABLE 11.5(B)

course	section	time
CS102	1001	MWF 8–9
CS102	1002	MWF 1–2
CS102	1003	MWF 2–3
CS102	1004	MWF 3–4
CS105	1001	MWF 1–2

TABLE 11.5(C)

course	name	credits	prerequisite
CS102	Intro to Databases	3	CS101
CS105	Visual Basic	4	CS200

Avoid tables with intentionally blank entries.

Tables with entries that are intentionally left blank waste space and are inefficient to use. Table 11.6, which serves as a directory of faculty and students, has an excessive number of blank entries. The table should be split into two tables, each dealing with just one of the groups.

TABLE 11.6
A Table with an Excessive Number of Blank Entries

name	ssn	classifi-cation	date hired	dept	office number	gpa	credits earned
Sarah Brown	816-34-9012	student				3.7	78
Pat Riley	409-22-1234	faculty	9/1/90	biology	Y-3014		
Joe Russo	690-32-1108	faculty	9/1/88	math	T-2008		
Juan Lopez	509-43-4110	student				3.2	42

Strive for table clarity.

Each table should have a basic topic and all the data in the table should be connected to that topic.

Don't let a table get unnecessarily large.

A bookstore might keep a permanent record of each purchase for the purpose of targeting mailings. A better solution is to add a couple of extra fields to the customer table that identify the types of books of interest to the customer.

Avoid fields whose values can be calculated from existing fields.

A calculated field is one whose value can be determined from other fields. For instance, if a table has fields for both the population and area of a state, then there is no need to include a field for the population density.

COMMENTS

1. Visual Data Manager can not create foreign keys.
2. You can add additional fields to a database table, but you cannot rename, modify, or delete fields without deleting the entire table and rebuilding each field. For this reason, design your tables carefully.
3. The total length of a record in a table is limited to 2000 bytes.
4. Be careful if you create a database with empty tables. If you pull it into a program and try to move through it with the navigator arrows, an error will be generated. You must add at least one record before starting to navigate.

SUMMARY

1. A *table* is a group of data items arranged in a rectangular array, each containing the same categories of information. Each data item (row) is called a *record*. Each category (column) is called a *field*. Two tables with a common field are said to be *related*. A *database* is a collection of one or more, usually related, tables.

2. The *data control* is used to access a database. When a text box is bound to a data control through its DataSource and DataField properties, the user can read and edit a field of the database. At any time, one record is specified as the *current record*. The user can change the current record with the data control's *navigator arrows* or with *Move* statements. The property *RecordCount* count records, the property *BOF* indicates whether the beginning of the recordset has been reached, and the property *EOF* indicates whether the end of the recordset has been reached. The *Value* property of Fields ("*fieldName*") reads the contents of a field of the current record. The *Validate event*, which can be used to control edits, is triggered whenever the current record is about to be changed.

3. A *primary key* is a field or set of fields that uniquely identifies each row of a table. The *rule of entity integrity* states that no record can have a null entry in a primary key. A *foreign key* is a field or set of fields in one table that refers to a primary key in another table. The *rule of referential integrity* states that each value in the foreign key must also appear in the primary key.

4. Structured Query Language (SQL) is used to create a "virtual" table consisting of a subtable of a table or of a join of two tables and imposes an order on the records. The subtable is specified with the reserved words SELECT, FROM, WHERE, ORDER BY, and INNER JOIN . . . ON. The WHERE clause of an SQL statement commonly uses the Like operator in addition to the standard operators. SQL statements are either employed at design time or run time as the setting of the RecordSource property. During run time, the Refresh method for the data control should be executed after the RecordSource property is set.

5. The *MS FlexGrid grid control* can show an entire "virtual" table in a spreadsheet-like display. *Data-bound list box* and *data-bound combo box* controls can display the contents of a single field for an entire table or recordset.

6. *Visual Data Manager*, a database management program supplied with most versions of Visual Basic, can be used to create a database and specify primary keys and validation criteria. A database can be created by code with the Professional or Enterprise editions of Visual Basic.

7. Although good database design is an art, there are several fundamental principles that usually should be followed.

PROGRAMMING PROJECTS

1. The database MICROLND.MDB (on the accompanying CD) is maintained by the Microland Computer Warehouse, a mail order computer supply company. Tables 11.7 through 11.9 show parts of three tables in the database. The table Customers identifies each customer by an ID number and gives, in addition to the name and address, the total amount of purchases during the current year. The table Inventory identifies each product in stock by an ID number and gives, in addition to its description and price (per unit), the quantity currently in stock. The table Orders gives the orders received today. Suppose it is now the end of the day. Write a program that uses the three tables to do the following:

(a) Update the *quantity* field of the Inventory table.

(b) Display in a list box the items that are out of stock and therefore must be reordered.

(c) Update the *amtOfSales* field of the Customers table.

(d) Print bills to all customers who ordered during the day. (You can assume that each customer only calls once during a particular day and therefore that all items ordered by a single customer are grouped together. The bill should indicate if an item is currently out of stock. You can just display the bills one at a time in a picture window instead of actually printing them.)

TABLE 11.7
First Three Records of the Customers Table

custID	name	street	city	amtPurchases
1	Michael Smith	2 Park St.	Dallas, TX 75201	234.50
2	Brittany Jones	5 Second Ave	Tampa, FL 33602	121.90
3	Warren Pease	7 Maple St	Boston, MA 02101	387.20

TABLE 11.8
First Three Records of the Inventory Table

itemID	description	price	quantity
PL208	Visual Basic – Standard	89.50	12
SW109	MS Office Upgrade	195.95	2
HW913	PaperPort ix	300.25	8

TABLE 11.9
First Four Records of the Orders Table

custID	itemID	quantity
3	SW109	1
1	PL208	3
1	HW913	2
2	PL208	1

2. Most college libraries have a computerized online catalog that allows you to look up books by author or title. Use the database BIBLIO.MDB to design such a catalog. You should create a new database with the necessary tables and fields and copy all needed information from BIBLIO.MDB into the new database. (One field should hold the number of copies that the library owns and another field should hold the number of copies currently on the shelf. Use the Rnd function to fill the first field with numbers from 1 to 3.) The user should be able to do the following.

(a) View the books by author in either alphabetical or chronological order and then obtain relevant information (publisher, ISBN, copyright year, number of copies available and owned) on a specific book.

(b) Determine if a book with a specified title is owned by the library.

(c) Search for all books containing a certain word in its title.

(d) Check out a book that is on the shelf.

(e) Reserve a book that is currently not on the shelf. (A number can be assigned to each reservation to determine priority.)

The librarian should be able to generate a listing of all books for which there is a waiting list.

12

OBJECT-ORIENTED PROGRAMMING

12.1 CLASSES AND OBJECTS

noun   A word used to denote or name a person, place, thing, quality, or act.
verb   That part of speech that expresses existence, action, or occurrence.
adjective   Any of a class of words used to modify a noun or other substantive by limit-
             ing, qualifying, or specifying.

The American Heritage Dictionary of the English Language

"A good rule of thumb for object-oriented programming is that classes are the nouns in your analysis of the problem. The methods in your object correspond to verbs that the noun does. The properties are the adjectives that describe the noun."

Gary Cornell & David Jezak[1]

Practical experience in the financial, scientific, engineering, and software design industries has revealed some difficulties with traditional program design methodologies. As programs grow in size and become more complex, and as the number of programmers working on the same project increases, the number of dependencies and interrelationships throughout the code increases exponentially. A small change made by one programmer in one place may have many effects, both intended and unintended, in many other places. The effects of this change may ripple throughout the entire program, requiring the rewriting of a great deal of code along the way.

A partial solution to this problem is "data hiding" where, within a unit, as much implementation detail as possible is hidden. Data hiding is an important principle underlying object-oriented programming. An object is an encapsulation of data and procedures that act on the data. The only thing of concern to a programmer using an object is the tasks that the object can perform and the parameters used by these tasks. The details of the data structures and procedures are hidden within the object.

Two types of objects will be of concern to us, **control objects** and **code objects**. Examples of control objects are text boxes, picture boxes, command buttons and all the other controls that can be created from the Visual Basic toolbox. Code objects are specific instances of user-defined types that are defined similarly to record types in a separate module. Both types of objects have properties and respond to methods. The main differences are that control objects are predefined and have physical manifestations, whereas code objects must be created by the programmer and exist solely in a portion of memory. In this section, when we use the word "object" without a qualifier, we mean "code object."

---

[1]FActiveX Visual Basic 5 Control Creation Edition, Prentice-Hall, 1997.

Whenever you double-click on the TextBox icon in the toolbar, a new text box is created. Although each text box is a separate entity, they all have the same properties and methods. Each text box is said to be an instance of the class TextBox. In some sense, the TextBox icon in the toolbox is a template for creating text boxes. (When you look at the properties window for a text box, the dropdown list box at the top of the window says something like "Text1 TextBox". "Text1" is the name of the control object and "TextBox" is the name of its class.) You can't set properties or invoke methods of the TextBox icon, only of the specific text boxes that it creates. The analogy is often made between the TextBox icon and a cookie cutter. The cookie cutter is used to create cookies that you can eat, but you can't eat the cookie cutter.

Object-oriented programs are populated with objects that hold data, have properties, respond to methods, and raise events. (The generation of events will be discussed in the next section.) Six examples are as follows:

1. In a professor's program to assign and display semester grades, a student object might hold a single student's name, social security number, midterm grade, and final exam grade. A SemGrade method might calculate the student's semester grade. Events might be raised when improper data is passed to the object.

2. In a payroll program, an employee object might hold an employee's name, hourly wage, and hours worked. A CalculatePay method would tell the object to calculate the wages for the current pay period.

3. In a checking account program, a check register object might record and total the checks written during a certain month, a deposit slip object might record and total the deposits made during a certain month, and an account object might keep a running total of the balance in the account. The account object would raise an event to alert the bank when the balance gets too low.

4. In a bookstore inventory program, a textbook object might hold the name, author, quantity in stock, and wholesale price of an individual textbook. A RetailPrice method might instruct the book object to calculate the selling price of the textbook. An event could be triggered when the book goes out of stock.

5. In a game program, an airplane object might hold the location of an airplane. At any time, the program could tell the object to display the airplane at its current location or to drop a bomb. An event can be triggered each time a bomb moves so that the program can determine if anything was hit.

6. In a card game, a card object might hold the denomination and suit of a specific card. An IdentifyCard method might return a string such as "Ace of Spades." A deck of cards object might consist of an array of card objects. A ShuffleDeck method might thoroughly shuffle the deck and a Shuffling event might indicate the progress of the shuffle.

The most important object-oriented term is **class**. A class is a template from which objects are created. The class specifies the properties and methods that will be common to all objects that are instances of that class. Classes are formulated in class modules. An object, which is an instance of a class, can be created in a program with a pair of statements of the form

```
Private objectName As className 'In General Declarations section
Set objectName = New className  'In procedure
```

In the program, properties of the object is accessed with statements of the form shown in the following table.

Task	Statement
Assign a value to a property	objectName.propertyName = value
Display the value of a property	picBox.Print objectName.propertyName
Carry out a method	objectName.methodName(arg1, ...)
Raise an event	RaiseEvent eventName

The following walkthrough creates a student class and a program that uses that class. The data stored by an object of this class are name, social security number, and grades on two exams (midterm and final).

1. Start a new program.

2. From the Project menu on the toolbar, click on Add Class Module.

3. Double-click on Class Module in the Add Class Module dialog box. (The window that appears looks like an ordinary code window.)

4. If the Properties window is not visible, press F4 to display it. (Notice that the class has the default name Class1.)

5. Change the setting of the Name property to CStudent. (We will follow the common convention of beginning each class name with the uppercase letter C.)

6. Type the following lines into the code module.

```
Private m_name As String
Private m_ssn As String
Private m_midterm As Single
Private m_final As Single
```

(These lines of code declare four variables that will be used to hold data. The word Private guarantees that the variables cannot be accessed directly from outside the object. In object-oriented programming terminology, these variables are called **member variables** (or **instance variables**). We will follow the common convention of beginning the name of each member variable with the prefix "m_".)

7. From the Tools menu on the toolbar, click on Add Procedure. (As before, an Add Procedure dialog box will appear.)

8. Type "Name" into the Name text box, click on Property in the Type frame, and click on OK. The following lines will appear in the class module window.

```
Public Property Get Name() As Variant

End Property

Public Property Let Name(ByVal vNewValue As Variant)

End Property
```

9. Change the words Variant to String, the word vNewValue to vName, and type code into the two property procedures as shown below.

```
Public Property Get Name() As String
  Name = m_name
End Property
Public Property Let Name(ByVal vName As String)
  m_name = vName
End Property
```

The first procedure will be called by our program to retrieve the value of the variable *m_name* and the second procedure will be called to assign a value to the variable *m_name*.

10. In the same manner as in Steps 7–9, create the following pair of property procedures that will be used to retrieve and assign values to the variable *m_ssn*.

```
Public Property Get SocSecNum() As String
  SocSecNum = m_ssn
End Property

Public Property Let SocSecNum(ByVal vNum As String)
  m_ssn = vNum
End Property
```

11. Property procedures can be typed directly into the class module without the use of Add Procedure. Also, property procedures needn't come in pairs. For instance, if we wanted the value of a member variable to be "write only," we would use a Property Let procedure and have no Property Get procedure. Type the following two property procedures into the class module. The inclusion of the word Public is optional.

```
Property Let midGrade(ByVal vGrade As Single)
  m_midterm = vGrade
End Property

Property Let finGrade(ByVal vGrade As Single)
  m_final = vGrade
End Property
```

12. Create the following ordinary Public function with the name SemGrade.

```
Public Function SemGrade() As String
  Dim grade As Single
  grade = (m_midterm + m_final) / 2
  grade = Round(grade) 'Round the grade
  Select Case grade
    Case Is = 90
      SemGrade = "A"
    Case Is = 80
      SemGrade = "B"
    Case Is = 70
      SemGrade = "C"
    Case Is = 60
      SemGrade = "D"
    Case Else
      SemGrade = "F"
  End Select
End Function
```

(This function will be used by our program to invoke a method requesting an object to calculate a student's semester grade.)

13. From the File menu, click on Save CStudent As and save the class module with the name 13-1-1S.cls. (We chose this name since the class will be used in Example 1. Another good choice of name would have been Student.cls. The extension cls is normally given to files holding class modules.)

14. Click on the form window to activate it. We can now write a program that creates an object, call it *pupil*, that is an instance of the class and uses the object to calculate a student's semester grade. The object variable is declared (in the general declarations section of the code module) with the statement

```
Private pupil As CStudent
```

and then an instance of the class is created inside a procedure with the statement

```
Set pupil = New CStudent
```

The object *pupil* will be local to the procedure. That is, it will cease to exist after the procedure has ended. The Property Let procedures are used to assign values to the member variables, and the Property Get procedures are used to retrieve values. The function SemGrade becomes a method for obtaining the student's grade.

Some examples are

```
pupil.Name = "Adams, Al"      'Assign a value to m_name
picBox.Print pupil.Name       'Display the student's name
picBox.Print pupil.SemGrade   'Display the student's semester grade
```

The first statement calls the Property Let Name procedure, the second statement calls the Property Get Name procedure, and the third statement calls the method procedure SemGrade.

EXAMPLE 1

The following program uses the class CStudent to calculate and display a student's semester grade.

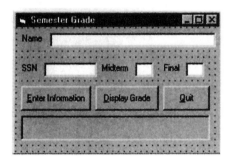

Object	Property	Setting
frm13_1_1	Caption	Semester Grade
lblName	Caption	Name
txtName	Text	(blank)
lblSSN	Caption	SSN
txtSSN	Text	(blank)
lblMidterm	Caption	Midterm
txtMidterm	Text	(blank)
lblFinal	Caption	Final
txtFinal	Text	(blank)
cmdEnter	Caption	&Enter Information
cmdDisplay	Caption	&Display Grade
cmdQuit	Caption	&Quit
picGrade		

```
'Student Class (CStudent)
    Private m_name As String
    Private m_ssn As String
    Private m_midterm As Single
    Private m_final As Single
    Property Get Name() As String
  Name = m_name
End Property

Property Let Name(ByVal vName As String)
  m_name = vName
End Property

Property Get SocSecNum() As String
   SocSecNum = m_ssn
End Property

  Property Let SocSecNum(ByVal vNum As String)
  m_ssn = vNum
End Property
```

```
Property Let midGrade(ByVal vGrade As Single)
   m_midterm = vGrade
End Property

Property Let finGrade(ByVal vGrade As Single)
   m_final = vGrade
End Property

Public Function SemGrade() As String
   Dim grade As Single
   grade = (m_midterm + m_final) / 2
   grade = Round(grade) 'Round the grade
   Select Case grade
       Case Is = 90
         SemGrade = "A"
       Case Is = 80
         SemGrade = "B"
       Case Is = 70
         SemGrade = "C"
       Case Is = 60
         SemGrade = "D"
       Case Else SemGrade = "F"
   End Select
End Function

'Form Code
Private pupil As CStudent 'pupil is an object of class CStudent

Private Sub Form_Load()
   Set pupil = New CStudent
End Sub

Private Sub cmdEnter_Click()
   'Read the values stored in the text boxes
   pupil.Name = txtName
   pupil.SocSecNum = txtSSN
   pupil.midGrade = Val(txtMidterm)
   pupil.finGrade = Val(txtFinal)
   'Clear Text Boxes
   txtName.Text = ""
   txtSSN.Text = ""
   txtMidterm.Text = ""
   txtFinal.Text = ""
   picGrade.Cls
   picGrade.Print "Student recorded."
End Sub

Private Sub cmdDisplay_Click()
   picGrade.Cls
   picGrade.Print pupil.Name; Tab(28); pupil.SocSecNum(); _
                     Tab(48); pupil.SemGrade
End Sub

Private Sub cmdQuit_Click()
   End
End Sub
```

[Run, enter the data for a student (such as "Adams, Al", "123-45-6789", "82", "87"), press the Enter Information button to send the data to the object, and press the Display Grade button to display the student's name, social security number, and semester grade.]

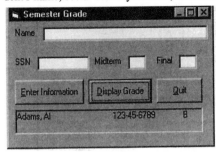

In summary, the following seven steps are used to create a class.

1. Identify a *thing* in your program that is to become an object.
2. Determine the properties and methods you would like the object to have.
3. A class will serve as a template for the object. Add a class module from the Project menu.
4. Set the name property of the class. (A common convention is to begin the name with the letter C.)
5. For each of the properties in Step 2, declare a private member variable with a statement of the form

```
Private m_variableName As dataType
```

6. For each of the member variables in Step 5, create one or two public property procedures to retrieve and assign values of the variable. The general forms of the procedures are

```
Public Property Get ProcedureName() As DataType
  ProcedureName = m_variableName
  (Possibly additional code.)
End Property

Public Property Let Procedurename(ByVal vNewValue As DataType)
  m_variableName = vNewValue
  (Possibly additional code.)
End Property
```

Note: Since the member variables were declared as Private, they cannot be accessed directly from outside an object. They can only be accessed through Property procedures which allow values to be checked and perhaps modified. Also, a Property procedure is able to take other steps necessitated by a change in a member variable.

7. For each method in Step 2, create a Sub procedure or Function procedure to carry out the task.

EXAMPLE 2

Modify the program in Example 1 to calculate semester grades for students who have registered on a "Pass/Fail" basis. Use a class module to calculate the semester grade.

SOLUTION:

We will create a new class, named CPFStudent, with the same member variables and property procedures as the class CStudent. The only change needed in the class module occurs in the SemGrade method. The new code for this method is

```
Public Function SemGrade() As String
   Dim grade As Single
   grade = (m_midterm + m_final) / 2
   grade = Round(grade) 'Round the grade
   If grade = 60 Then
      SemGrade = "Pass"
   Else
      SemGrade = "Fail"
   End If
End Function
```

The only change needed in the Form code is to replace the two occurrences of CStudent with CPFStudent. When the program is run with the same input as in Example 1, the output will be

```
Adams, Al 123-45-6789 Pass
```

■ THE INITIALIZE EVENT PROCEDURE

The Object drop-down combo box in a class module window displays two items General and Class. When you click on Class, the following template appears:

```
Private Sub Class_Initialize()

End Sub
```

This event procedure is automatically invoked when an object is created from the class. Any code you type into the procedure is then executed. This procedure is used to set default values for member variables and to create other objects associated with this object.

Since methods are created with ordinary Function or Sub procedures, arguments can be passed to them when they are called. The graphical program in Example 3 makes use of arguments. The program involves "twips," which are a unit of screen measurement. (One inch is about 1440 twips.) The settings for the Top, Left, Height, and Width properties of a control are given in twips. For instance, the statements

```
Image1.Width = 1440    '1 inch
Image1.Height = 2160   '1.5 inch
Image1.Top = 2880      '2 inches
Image1.Left = 7200     '5 inches
```

set the size of the image control as 1" by 1.5", and place the control 2 inches from the top of the form and 5 inches from the left side of the form. (See Figure 6-6 in Section 6.3.) Programs using the Height property of the form should have the BorderStyle property of the form set to "0-None" since otherwise the height of the border is included in the height of the form.

EXAMPLE 3

Write a program containing a Circle object. The object should keep track of the center and radius of the circle. (The center is specified by two numbers, called the coordinates, giving the distance from the left side and top of the form. Distances and the radius should be measured in twips.) A Show method should display the circle on the form and a Move method should add 500 twips to each coordinate of the center of the circle. Initially, the circle should have its center at (500, 500) and radius 500. The form should have a command button captioned "Move and Show Circle" that invokes both methods.

SOLUTION:

Object	Property	Setting
frmCircles	BorderStyle	0-None
cmdMove	Caption	Move and Show Circle
cmdQuit	Caption	Quit

```
'Class module for CCircle
    Private m_x As Integer  'Dist from center of circle to left side of form
    Private m_y As Integer  'Distance from center of circle to top of form
    Private m_r As Single   'Radius of circle


Private Sub Class_Initialize()
   'Set the initial center of the circle to the upper
   'left corner of the form and set its radius to 500.
   m_x = 0
   m_y = 0
   m_r = 500
End Sub

Public Property Get Xcoord()
   As Integer Xcoord = m_x
End Property

Public Property Let Xcoord(ByVal vNewValue As Integer)
   m_x = vNewValue
End Property

Public Property Get Ycoord() As Integer
   Ycoord = m_y
End Property

Public Property Let Ycoord(ByVal vNewValue As Integer)
   m_y = vNewValue
End Property

   Public Sub Show()
   'Display the circle.
   'See discussion of Circle method in Section 10.4.
   frmCircles.Circle (m_x, m_y), m_r
End Sub

Public Sub Move(Dist)
   'Move the center of the circle Dist twips to the right
   'and Dist twips down.
   m_x = m_x + Dist
   m_y = m_y + Dist
   Call Show
```

```
End Sub

'Form code
Private round As CCircle

Private Sub Form_Load()
   Set round = New CCircle
End Sub

Private Sub cmdMove_Click()
   round.Move (500)
End Sub

Private Sub cmdQuit_Click()
   End
End Sub
```

[Run, and press the command button five times.]

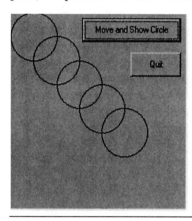

COMMENTS

1. The statement

   ```
   Set objectVar = Nothing
   ```

   dissociates the object variable from the actual object and frees up the memory used by the variable.

2. An object variable declared inside a procedure ceases to exist when the procedure is exited. (We say that the object falls out of scope.) The effect is the same as when the variable is set to Nothing.

3. The counterpart to the Initialize event is the Terminate event procedure which has the template

   ```
   Private Sub Class_Terminate()

   End Sub
   ```

   and is automatically invoked when all references to the object are Set to Nothing or when the object falls out of scope. This procedure is often used to set any objects you may have created inside the class module to Nothing.

4. Methods can be either Function or Sub procedures. A method that returns a value must be a Function procedure; otherwise it can be a Sub procedure.

5. A program with a class module has at least three components: a form, form code, and class module code. Although the View menu gives you access to the form (Alt/V/B) and the form code (Alt/V/C), only the Project Explorer gives access to all three. To view the code for a class module, double-click on the name of the class in the Project Explorer.

6. A class module is saved in a file whose file name has the extension .cls. Therefore, classes have both a name (C*something*) and a file name (*something*.cls).

7. To insert an existing (saved) class module into a program, click on Add Class Module in the Project menu, click on the Existing tab, and enter the filespec for the class module.

8. To delete a class from a program, right click on the class name in the Project Explorer and click on Remove *className*.

9. An object also can be declared with a statement of the form

```
Private pupil As Object
```

However, objects so declared require more time and effort for Visual Basic to access.

10. The set of properties, methods, and events for a class is called the class **interface**. The classes CStudent and CPFStudent have the same interface, even though they carry out the task of computing a grade differently. The programmer need only be aware of the SemGrade method and needn't be concerned about its implementation. The feature that two classes can have behaviors that are named the same and have essentially the same purpose but different implementations is called **polymorphism**.

11. Sometimes you will have difficulty deciding whether an interface item should be a property or a method. As a rule of thumb, properties should access data and methods should perform operations.

12. The ByVal (which stands for "by value") keyword is automatically inserted before parameters in Property Let statements invoked from the Tools menu. However, this keyword is optional. The default way of passing an argument to a parameter is ByRef (which stands for "by reference"). Usually, passing by value is more efficient than passing by reference.

13. The default parameter name in a Property Let procedure is vNewValue. Although we usually substitute a meaningful name, we retain the convention of beginning the name with the prefix v.

14. We could have preceded our member variables with the keyword Public and allowed direct access to the variables. However, this is considered poor programming practice. By using Property Let procedures to update the data, we can enforce constraints and carry out validation.

15. In a class module, a property is implemented by two procedures, one to set and the other to retrieve the property value. These procedures that access properties are sometimes referred to as **accessor** methods.

12.2 COLLECTIONS AND EVENTS

> "An object without an event is like a telephone without a ringer."
>
> *Anonymous*

A collection is an entity, similar to an array, that is especially well-suited to working with sets of objects. This section discusses collections of objects and user-defined events for classes.

■ COLLECTIONS

A collection of objects is an ordered set of objects where the objects are identified by the numbers 1, 2, 3, . . . A collection is declared with a statement of the form

```
Dim collectionName As New Collection
```

and initially contains no objects. (We say that the variable *collectionName* has type Collection.) The statement

```
collectionName.Add objectName
```

adds the named object to the collection and automatically assigns it the next available number. The numbers for the different objects will reflect the order they were added to the collection. The statement

```
collectionName.Remove n
```

deletes the *n*th object from the collection and automatically reduces the object numbers from *n* +1 on by 1 so that there will be no gap in the numbers. At any time, the value of

```
collectionName.Count
```

is the number of objects in the collection. The value of

```
collectionName.Item(n).propertyName
```

is the value of the named property in the *n*th object of the collection. The statement

```
collectionName.Item(n).methodName
```

runs the named method of the *n*th object of the collection.

EXAMPLE 1

In the following program, the user enters four pieces of data about a student into text boxes and selects a type of registration. When the AddStudent button is pressed, the data is used to create and initialize an appropriate object (either from class CStudent or class CPFStudent) and the object is added to a collection. When the Calculate Grades button is pressed, the name, social security number, and semester grade for each student in the collection is displayed in the picture box.

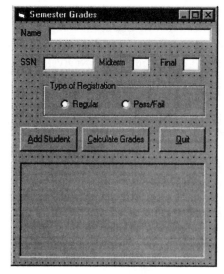

Object	Property	Setting
frm13_2_1	Caption	Semester Grades
lblName	Caption	Name
txtName	Text	(blank)
lblSSN	Caption	SSN
txtSSN	Text	(blank)
lblMidterm	Caption	Midterm
txtMidterm	Text	(blank)
lblFinal	Caption	Final
txtFinal	Text	(blank)
fraType	Caption	Type of Registration
optReg	Caption	Regular
optP	Caption	Pass/Fail
cmdAdd	Caption	&Add Student
cmdSemGrade	Caption	&Calculate Grades
cmdQuit	Caption	&Quit
picGrades		

```
'Student Class (CStudent)
Private m_name As String
Private m_ssn As String
Private m_midterm As Single
Private m_final As Single

Property Get Name() As String
   Name = m_name
End Property

Property Let Name(ByVal vName As String)
   m_name = vName
End Property

Property Get SocSecNum() As String
   SocSecNum = m_ssn
End Property

Property Let SocSecNum(ByVal vNum As String)
   m_ssn = vNum
End Property

Property Let midGrade(ByVal vGrade As Single)
   m_midterm = vGrade
End Property

Property Let finGrade(ByVal vGrade As Single)
   m_final = vGrade
End Property

Public Function SemGrade() As String
   Dim grade As Single
   grade = (m_midterm + m_final) / 2
   grade = Round(grade) 'Round the grade
   Select Case grade
        Case Is = 90
          SemGrade = "A"
        Case Is = 80
           SemGrade = "B"
        Case Is = 70
          SemGrade = "C"
        Case Is = 60
           SemGrade = "D"
        Case Else SemGrade = "F"
   End Select
End Function

'Pass/Fail Student Class (CPFStudent)
Private m_name As String
Private m_ssn As String
Private m_midterm As Single
Private m_final As Single
```

```
Property Get Name() As String
  Name = m_name
End Property

Property Let Name(ByVal vName As String)

  m_name = vName
End Property

Property Get SocSecNum() As String
  SocSecNum = m_ssn
End Property

Property Let SocSecNum(ByVal vNum As String)
  m_ssn = vNum
End Property

Property Let midGrade(ByVal vGrade As Single)
  m_midterm = vGrade
End Property

Property Let finGrade(ByVal vGrade As Single)
  m_final = vGrade
End Property

Public Function SemGrade() As String
  Dim grade As Single
  grade = (m_midterm + m_final) / 2
  grade = Round(grade) 'Round the grade
  If grade = 60 Then
     SemGrade = "Pass"
   Else
     SemGrade = "Fail"
   End If
End Function

'Form code
Dim section As New Collection

Private Sub cmdAdd_Click()
  Dim pupil As Object
  If optReg.Value Then
     Set pupil = New CSTudent
    Else
     Set pupil = New CPFStudent
  End If
  'Read the Values stored in the Text boxes
  pupil.Name = txtName
  pupil.SocSecNum = txtSSN
  pupil.midGrade = Val(txtMidterm)
  pupil.finGrade = Val(txtFinal)
  section.Add pupil
  'Clear Text Boxes
  txtName.Text = ""
  txtSSN.Text = ""
  txtMidterm.Text = ""
```

```
   txtFinal.Text = ""
   picGrades.Print "Student added."
End Sub

Private Sub cmdSemGrade_Click()
   Dim i As Integer, grade As String
   picGrades.Cls
   For i = 1 To section.Count
     picGrades.Print section.Item(i).Name; _
               Tab(28); section.Item(i).SocSecNum(); _
               Tab(48); section.Item(i).SemGrade
   Next i
End Sub

Private Sub cmdQuit_Click()
   End
End Sub

Private Sub Form_Load()
   'Initially, regular student should be selected
   optReg = True
End Sub
```

[Run, type in data for Al Adams, press the Add Student button, repeat the process for Brittany Brown and Carol Cole, press the Calculate Grades button, and then enter data for Daniel Doyle.]

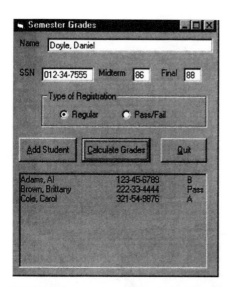

■ KEYS

The items in a collection are automatically paired with the numbers from 1 on. Visual Basic provides an alternative device for accessing a specific item. At the time an item is added to a collection, we can associate a key for the item via a statement of the form

collectionName.Add *objectName, keyString*

After that, the object can be referred to as *collectionName.Item(keyString)*.
   A property of the object can be accessed with

collectionName.Item(*keyString*).*property*

For instance, consider the situation of Example 1. If we are using social security number as a key, and the object *pupil* contains the data for Brittany Brown, then the statement

```
section.Add pupil, "222-33-4444"
```

would assign the string "222-33-4444" as a key for her data. Then her name property can be accessed with

```
section.Item("222-33-4444").Name
```

EXAMPLE 2

Extend the program of Example 1 so that the grade for an individual student can be displayed by giving a social security number.

SOLUTION:
There are no changes in the two classes. In the Sub cmdAdd_Click procedure of the form code, change the line

```
section.Add pupil
```

to

```
section.Add pupil, txtSSN.Text
```

Place an additional command button (cmdDisplay) with the caption "Display Single Grade" on the form and add the following event procedure for this button:

```
Private Sub cmdDisplay_Click()
    Dim ssn As String
    ssn = InputBox("Enter the student's social security number.")
    picGrades.Cls
    picGrades.Print section.Item(ssn).Name; _
            Tab(28); section.Item(ssn).SocSecNum(); _
            Tab(48); section.Item(ssn).SemGrade
End Sub
```

When this command button is pressed, the input box in Figure 12-1 appears. To obtain the output in Figure 12-2, run the program, enter the same data as in the execution of Example 1, press the "Display Single Grade" button, type 222-33-4444 into the input box, and press Enter.

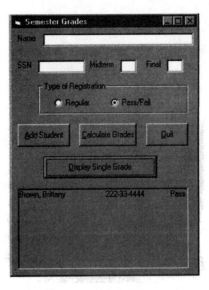

FIGURE 12-1   *Input Box*   **FIGURE 12-2**   *Output of Program*

■ **EVENTS**

In the previous section we drew a parallel between objects and controls and showed how to define properties and methods for classes. In addition to the two predefined events for classes, Initialize and Terminate, other events can be defined by the programmer to communicate changes of properties, errors, and the progress of lengthy operations. Such events are called **user-defined events**. The statement for triggering an event is located in the class module and the event is dealt with in the form code. Suppose the event is named UserDefinedEvent and has the arguments *arg1*, *arg2*, and so on. In the class module, the statement

```
Public Event UserDefinedEvent(arg1, arg2, ...)
```

should be placed in the (Declarations) section of (General), and the statement

```
RaiseEvent UserDefinedEvent(arg1, arg2, ...)
```

should be placed at the locations in the class module code at which the event should be triggered. In the form code, an instance of the class, call it object1, must be declared with a statement of the type

```
Private WithEvents object1 As CClassName
```

in order to be able to respond to the event. That is, the keyword WithEvents must be inserted into the standard declaration statement. The header of an event procedure for *object1* will be

```
Private Sub object1_UserDefinedEvent(par1, par2, ...)
```

EXAMPLE 3

Consider the circle class defined in Example 3 of Section 12.1. Add a user-defined event that is triggered whenever the center of a circle changes. The event should have parameters to pass the center and radius of the circle. The form code should use the event to determine if part (or all) of the drawn circle will fall outside the form. If so, the event procedure should display the message "Circle Off Screen" in a label and cause all future circles to be drawn in red.

SOLUTION:
Let's call the event PositionChanged.

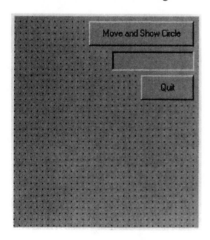

Object	Property	Setting
frmCircles	BorderStyle	0-None
cmdMove	Caption	Move and Show Circle
lblCaution	BorderStyle Caption,	1-Fixed Single (blank)
cmdQuit	Caption,	Quit

```
'Class module for CCircle
Private m_x As Integer 'Dist from center of circle to left side of form
Private m_y As Integer 'Distance from center of circle to top of form
Private m_r As Single 'Radius of circle
Public Event PositionChanged(x As Integer, y as Integer, r As Single)
'Event is triggered by a change in the center of the circle

Private Sub Class_Initialize()
```

```
              'Set the initial center of the circle to the upper
              'left corner of the form and set its radius to 500.
              m_x = 0
              m_y = 0
              m_r = 500
          End Sub

          Public Property Get Xcoord() As Integer
              Xcoord = m_x
          End Property

          Public Property Let Xcoord(ByVal vNewValue As Integer)
              m_x = vNewValue
          End Property

          Public Property Get Ycoord() As Integer
              Ycoord = m_y
          End Property

          Public Property Let Ycoord(ByVal vNewValue As Integer)
              m_y = vNewValue
          End Property

          Public Sub Show()
              'Display the circle.
              'See discussion of Circle method in Section 10.4.
              frmCircles.Circle (m_x, m_y), m_r
          End Sub

          Public Sub Move(Dist)
              'Move the center of the circle Dist twips to the right
              'and Dist twips down.
              m_x = m_x + Dist
              m_y = m_y + Dist
              RaiseEvent PositionChanged(m_x, m_y, m_r)
              Call Show
          End Sub

          'Form code
          Private WithEvents round As CCircle

          Private Sub Form_Load()
              Set round = New CCircle
          End Sub

          Private Sub cmdMove_Click()
              round.Move (500)
          End Sub

          Private Sub round_PositionChanged(x As Integer, y As Integer, _
                                  r As Integer)
              'This event is triggered when the center of the circle changes.
              'The code determines if part of the circle is off the screen.
              If (x + r > frmCircles.Width) Or (y + r ]] frmCircles.Height) Then
                  lblCaution.Caption = "Circle Off Screen"
```

```
          frmCircles.ForeColor = vbRed 'Make future circles red
   End If
End Sub


Private Sub cmdQuit_Click()
   End
End Sub
```

[Run and press the "Move and Show Circle" button seven times. *Note:* The last circle will be colored red.]

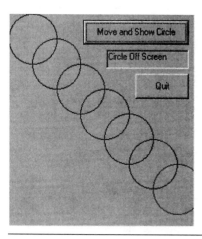

COMMENTS

1. Perhaps a better name for "user-defined events." would be "programmer-defined events."

2. A statement of the form

   ```
   collectionName.Add objectName, keyString
   ```

   can also be written as

   ```
   collectionName.Add Item:=objectName, Key:=keyString
   ```

3. The WithEvents keyword cannot be inserted into a declaration statement of the form

   ```
   Private objectName As Object
   ```

   It can only be used when a specific class follows the word "As."

4. Collections require more memory than arrays and slow down execution time. If either a collection or an array would suffice, choose an array. This will often be the case when the number of items is fixed. For instance, a deck of cards should be represented as an array of card objects rather than a collection of card objects.

12.3 CLASS RELATIONSHIPS

The three relationships between classes are "use," "containment," and "inheritance." One class **uses** another class if it manipulates objects of that class. We say that class A **contains** class B when a member variable of class A has class B as its type. **Inheritance** is a process by which one class (the child class), inherits the properties, methods, and events of another class (the parent class). Visual Basic does not support the strict academic definition of inheritance. In this section, we present programs that illustrate "use" (Example 1) and "containment" (Example 2).

In this section we will be setting variables to existing objects. In that case, the proper statement is

```
Set objVar = existingObject
```

EXAMPLE 1

Write a program to create and control two airplane objects (referred to as a *bomber* and a *plane*) and a bomb object. The airplane object should keep track of its location (that is, the number of twips from the left side and the top side of the form), be capable of moving in a direction (Right, Up, or Down) specified by the user from a combo box, and should be able to drop a bomb when so commanded. The last task will be carried out by the bomb object. In the event that a bomb dropped from the bomber hits the plane, the plane should disappear. The airplanes and the bomb will have physical representations as pictures inside image controls. By their locations we mean the upperleft corners of their respective image controls. The picture files AIRPLANE.BMP and BOMB.BMP can be found in the Pictures directory of the CD accompanying this textbook.

SOLUTION:

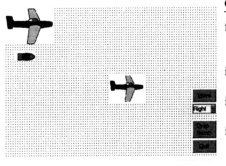

Object	Property	Setting
frmPlanes	BackColor	(white)
	BorderStyle	0-None
	WindowState	2-Maximized
imgBomberPic	Picture	AIRPLANE.BMP
	Stretch	True
imgPlanePic	Picture	AIRPLANE.BMP
	Stretch	True
imgBombPic	Picture	BOMB.BMP
	Stretch	True
	Visible	False
cboDirection	List	Right
		Up
		Down
cmdMove	Caption	Move Bomber
cmdDropBomb	Caption	Drop Bomb
cmdQuit	Caption	Quit

```
'Class module for CPlane
    Private m_imgPlane As Image 'image control associated with plane

Property Let imagePlane(newPlane As Image)
    Set m_imgPlane = newPlane
End Property

    Public Function Present() As Boolean
    'Determine if the plane is visible
    'Will be needed by the bomb object.
    If m_imgPlane.Visible Then
        Present = True
    Else
        Present = False
    End If
End Function
```

```
Public Function X() As Integer
   X = m_imgPlane.Left
End Function

Public Function Y() As Integer
   Y = m_imgPlane.Top
End Function

Public Function W() As Integer
   W = m_imgPlane.Width
End Function

Public Function H() As Integer
   H = m_imgPlane.Height
End Function

Public Sub Fly(ByVal dir As String, ByVal Height As Integer, ByVal Width As
Integer)
   m_imgPlane.Visible = True
   'Meanings of variables
   'dir Direction of airplane (Right, Up, or Down)
   'Height Height of form
   'Width Width of form
   If dir = "Up" Then
      'Prevent airplane from rising off the screen.
      If (m_imgPlane.Top - 500)>= 0 Then
         m_imgPlane.Top = m_imgPlane.Top - 500
      End If
    ElseIf dir = "Down" Then
      'Prevent airplane from falling off the screen.
      If (m_imgPlane.Top + m_imgPlane.Height + 500) <= Height Then
         m_imgPlane.Top = m_imgPlane.Top + 500
      End If
    ElseIf dir = "Right" Then
      'Prevent airplane from moving off the screen.
      If (m_imgPlane.Left + m_imgPlane.Width + 500) <= Width Then
         m_imgPlane.Left = m_imgPlane.Left + 500
      End If
   End If
End Sub

Public Sub Destroy()
   m_imgPlane.Visible = False
End Sub

Private Sub Class_Terminate()
   Set m_imgPlane = Nothing
End Sub

'Class module for CBomb
Private imgBomb As Image
Public Event BombPositionChanged(X As Integer, Y As Integer, _
                        W As Integer, H As Integer)
Property Let imageBomb(bomb As Image)
   Set imgBomb = bomb
End Property
```

```
Public Sub GoDown(plane As CPlane, ByVal FormHeight As Integer)
   Dim j As Integer
   imgBomb.Left = plane.X + 0.5 * plane.W
   imgBomb.Top = plane.Y + plane.H
   imgBomb.Visible = True
   Do While imgBomb.Top < FormHeight
     imgBomb.Top = imgBomb.Top + 5
     RaiseEvent BombPositionChanged(imgBomb.Left, imgBomb.Top, _
                          imgBomb.Width, imgBomb.Height)

     'Pause
     For j = 1 To 2000
     Next j
   Loop
   imgBomb.Visible = False
End Sub


Public Sub Destroy()
   imgBomb.Visible = False
End Sub


Private Sub Class_Terminate()
   Set imgBomb = Nothing
End Sub


'Form code
Private bomber As CPlane
Private plane As CPlane
Private WithEvents bomb As CBomb

Private Sub Form_Load()
   Set bomber = New CPlane
   Set plane = New CPlane
   Set bomb = New CBomb
   bomber.imagePlane = imgBomberPic
   plane.imagePlane = imgPlanePic
   bomb.imageBomb = imgBombPic
End Sub

Private Sub bomb_BombPositionChanged(X As Integer, Y As Integer, H As Inte-
ger, W As Integer)
   'Check to see if Plane is hit, i.e. the bomb is inside plane or vice
   versa.
   If plane.Present() Then
     If (plane.X <= X) And (plane.X + plane.W >= X) And _
        (plane.Y <= Y) And (plane.Y + plane.H >= Y) Or _
        (X <= plane.X) And (X + W >= plane.X) And _
        (Y <= plane.Y) And (Y + H >= plane.Y) Then
        plane.Destroy
        bomb.Destroy
     End If
   End If
End Sub


Private Sub cmdMove_Click()
   bomber.Fly cboDirection.Text, frmPlanes.Height, frmPlanes.Width
```

```
End Sub

Private Sub cmdDropBomb_Click()
   bomb.GoDown bomber, frmPlanes.Height
End Sub

Private Sub cmdQuit_Click()
   End
End Sub
```

[Run, press the Move button twice, and then press the Drop Bomb button.]

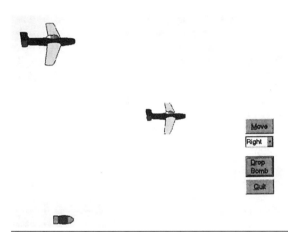

EXAMPLE 2

Write a program to deal a five-card poker hand. The program should have a deck-of-cards object containing an array of 52 card objects.

SOLUTION:

Our card object will have two properties, Denomination and Suit, and one method, IdentifyCard. The IdentifyCard method returns a string such as "Ace of Spades." In the DeckOfCards object, the Initialize event procedure assigns denominations and suits to the 52 cards. The method ReadCard(*n*) returns the string identifying the *n*th card of the deck. The method ShuffleDeck uses Rnd to mix-up the cards while making 200 passes through the deck. The event Shuffling(n As Integer, nMax As Integer) is triggered during each shuffling pass through the deck and its parameters communicate the number of the pass and the total number of passes, so that the program that uses it can keep track of the progress.

Object	Property	Setting
frmPokerHand	Caption	Poker Hand
picHand		
cmdShuffle	Caption	&Shuffle
cmdDeal	Caption	&Deal
cmdQuit	Caption	&Quit

```
'Class module for CCard
Private m_Denomination As String
Private m_Suit As String

Public Property Let Denomination(ByVal vDenom As String)
   m_Denomination = vDenom
End Property
```

```vb
Public Property Let Suit(ByVal vSuit As String)
  m_Suit = vSuit
End Property

Public Property Get Denomination() As String
  Denomination = m_Denomination
End Property

Public Property Get Suit() As String
  Suit = m_Suit
End Property

Public Function IdentifyCard() As String
  Dim Denom As String
  Select Case Val(m_Denomination)
      Case 1
        Denom = "Ace"
      Case Is <= 10
        Denom = m_Denomination
      Case 11
        Denom = "Jack"
      Case 12
        Denom = "Queen"
      Case 13
        Denom = "King"
  End Select
  IdentifyCard = Denom & " of " & m_Suit
End Function

'Class module for CDeckOfCards
Private m_deck(1 To 52) As CCard
Public Event Shuffling(n As Integer, nMax As Integer)

Private Sub Class_Initialize()
  Dim i As Integer
  For i = 1 To 52
      Set m_deck(i) = New CCard
      'Make the first thirteen cards hearts, the
      'next thirteen cards diamonds, and so on.
      Select Case i
        Case Is <= 13
          m_deck(i).Suit = "Hearts"
        Case Is <= 26
          m_deck(i).Suit = "Diamonds"
        Case Is <= 39
          m_deck(i).Suit = "Clubs"
        Case Else
          m_deck(i).Suit = "Spades"
      End Select
      'Assign numbers from 1 through 13 to the
      'cards of each suit.
      If (i Mod 13 = 0) Then
          m_deck(i).Denomination = Str(13)
        Else m_deck(i).Denomination = Str(i Mod 13)
      End If
```

```vb
      Next i
End Sub

Public Function ReadCard(cardNum As Integer) As String
   ReadCard = m_deck(cardNum).IdentifyCard
End Function

Private Sub Swap(ByVal i As Integer, ByVal j As Integer)
   'Swap the ith and jth card in the deck
   Dim TempCard As New CCard
   TempCard.Denomination = m_deck(i).Denomination
   TempCard.Suit = m_deck(i).Suit
   m_deck(i).Denomination =
   m_deck(j).Denomination
   m_deck(i).Suit = m_deck(j).Suit
   m_deck(j).Denomination = TempCard.Denomination
   m_deck(j).Suit = TempCard.Suit
End Sub

Public Sub ShuffleDeck()
   'Do 200 passes through the deck. On each pass
   'swap each card with a randomly selected card.
   Dim index As Integer, i As Integer, k As Integer
   Randomize 'Initialize random number generator
   For i = 1 To 200
     For k = 1 To 52
       index = Int((52 * Rnd) + 1)
       Call Swap(k, index)
     Next k
     RaiseEvent Shuffling(i, 200)
   Next i
End Sub

'Form Code
Public WithEvents cards As CDeckOfCards

Private Sub Form_Load()
   Set cards = New CDeckOfCards
End Sub

Private Sub cmdShuffle_Click()
   Call cards.ShuffleDeck
End Sub

Private Sub cmdDeal_Click()
Dim str As String
Dim i As Integer
   picHand.Cls
   For i = 1 To 5
     str = cards.ReadCard(i)
     picHand.Print str
   Next i
End Sub
```

```
Private Sub cards_shuffling(n As Integer, nMax As Integer)
   'n is the number of the specific pass through the deck (1, 2, 3..)
   'nMax is the total number of passes when the deck is shuffled
   picHand.Cls
   picHand.Print "Shuffling Pass:"; n; "out of"; nMax
End Sub

Private Sub cmdQuit_Click()
   End
End Sub
```

[Run, click on the Shuffle button, and click on the Deal button after the shuffling is complete.]

COMMENT

1. Example 1 illustrates "use" since the GoDown object of the bomb object receives a plane object. In general, class A uses Class B if an object of class B is sent a message by a property or method of class A, or a method or property of class A returns, receives, or creates objects of class B.

SUMMARY

1. An *object* is an entity that stores data, has methods that manipulate the data, and can trigger events. A *class* describes a group of similar objects. A m*ethod* specifies the way in which an object's data are manipulated. An *event* is a change in the state of an object.

2. Classes are defined in a separate module called a *class module*. Data is stored in member variables and accessed by procedures called methods.

3. Property Let and Property Get procedures are used to set and retrieve values of member variables. These procedures can also be used enforce constraints and carry out validation.

4. The Initialize and Terminate event procedures are automatically invoked when an object is created and falls out of scope, respectively.

5. An object variable is declared in the declarations section of a program with a statement of the form `Private objectName As className` and created with a statement of the form `Set objectName = New className`.

6. A *collection* is a convenient devise for grouping together diverse objects. Objects are added to collections with the Add method and removed with the

Remove method. The number of objects in a collection is determined with the Count property and object is returned by the Item method using either a number or a key.

7. Events are declared in the general declarations section of class module with a statement of the form `Public Event UserDefinedEvent (arg1, arg2, ...)` and triggered with a RaiseEvent statement. In the form code, the declaration statement for an object, must include the keyword WithEvents in order for the events coming from the object to be processed.

8. Objects interact through *use* and *containment*.

PROGRAMMING PROJECTS

1. *Son of Deep Blue.* Write a program that plays a game of tic-tac-toe in which a person competes with the computer. The game should be played in a control array of nine labels. See Figure 12-3. After the user moves by placing an X in a label, the program should determine the location for the O. The program should use a tic-tac-toe object that raises events when a player moves and when the game is over. The outcome of the game should be announced in a message box.

FIGURE 12-3   *Tic-Tac-Toe*

2. *Bank Account.* Write a program to maintain a person's Savings and Checking accounts. The program should keep track of and display the balances in both accounts, and maintain a list of transactions (deposits, withdrawals, fund transfers, and check clearings) separately for each account. The two lists of transactions should be stored in sequential files so that they will persist between program sessions.

Consider the form in Figure 12-4. The two drop-down combo boxes should each contain the items Checking and Savings. Each of the four frames corresponds to a type of transaction. (When Savings is selected in the Account combo box, the Check frame should disappear.) The user makes a transaction by typing data into the text boxes of a frame and pressing the command button. The items appearing in the transactions list box should correspond to the type of account that has been selected. The caption of the second label in the Transfer frame should toggle between "to Checking" and "to Savings" depending on the item selected in the "Transfer from" combo box. If a transaction cannot be carried out, a message (such as "Insufficient funds") should be displayed.

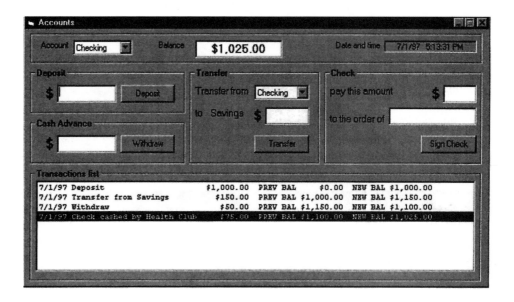

FIGURE 12-4   *Bank Accounts*

The program should use two classes, CTransaction and CAccount. The class CTransaction should have properties for transaction type, amount, paid to, previous balance, new balance, and transaction date. It should have a method that puts the data into a string that can be added to the Transaction list box, and methods that place data into and retrieve data from a sequential file.

The class CAccount, which will have both a checking account and a savings account as instances, should contain a collection of CTransaction objects. In addition, it should have properties for name (Checking or Savings) and balance. It should have methods to carry out a transaction (if possible), display the list of transactions, and to load and retrieve the set of transactions into or from a sequential file. The events InsufficientFunds and TransactionCommitted should be triggered at appropriate times. [**Hint:** In order to make CAccount object to display a list of transactions, a list box should be passed to a method as an argument. The method might begin with `Public Sub EnumerateTransactions(LB As ListBox).]`

13

COMMUNICATING WITH OTHER APPLICATIONS

13.1 OLE

OLE, which stands for Object Linking and Embedding, is the evolving technology that allows programmers to use Visual Basic to glue together applications like spreadsheets and word processors. The three types of OLE are known as automation, linking, and embedding. With automation, you control an application from outside. With linking and embedding, you bring an application into your program. In this section, OLE is illustrated with Microsoft Excel and Word. However, the programs and walkthroughs can be modified for other spreadsheet and word processing software packages.

■ OLE AUTOMATION

The objects in the Visual Basic toolbox have both properties and methods, and Visual Basic controls them by manipulating their properties and methods. In general, anything that can be controlled by manipulating its properties and methods is called an **object**. In particular, an Excel spreadsheet or a Word document can be specified as an **OLE Automation object**.

We have worked extensively with the data types String, Integer, and Single. There are eight other data types, including one called **Object**. A variable that has been declared as an Object variable can be assigned to refer to an OLE Automation object. The CreateObject function is used to create an OLE Automation object and the Set statement is used to assign the object to an object variable. For instance, the pair of statements

```
Dim objExcel As Object
Set objExcel = CreateObject("Excel.sheet")
```

creates an Excel spreadsheet object and assigns it to the Object variable objExcel. The pair of statements

```
Dim objWord As Object
Set objWord = CreateObject("Word.Basic")
```

creates a Word document object and assigns it to the Object variable objWord. After the object is no longer needed, a statement of the form

```
Set objVar = Nothing
```

should be executed to discontinue association of objVar with the specific object and release all the resources associated with the previously referenced object.

An object is controlled by manipulating its properties and methods. For instance, the statement

```
objExcel.Application.Cells(4, 3).Value = "49"
```

places the number 49 into the cell in the fourth row and third column (that is, C4) of the spreadsheet. Some other Excel statements are

```
objExcel.Application.Visible = True          'Display spreadsheet
objExcel.Application.Cells(4, 3).Font.Bold = True 'Make cell bold
objExcel.Application.Cells(7, 3).Formula = "=SUM(C1:C5)" 'Specify that
           'cell C7 hold the sum of the numbers in cells C1 through C5
objExcel.Application.Quit                     'Exit Excel
```

With the Word object, the statement

```
objWord.Insert = "We'll always have Paris."
```

inserts the sentence into the document at the current insertion point. Some other Word statements are

```
objWord.FileNewDefault      'Create a new document based on
                            'the Normal template
objWord.WordLeft            'Move the insertion point left one word
                            '(Counts period as a word.)
objWord.Bold                'Change font to bold
objWord.FileSaveAs filespec 'Save document with specified name
objWord.FilePrint           'Print the current document
objWord.FileClose           'Close the current document
```

OLE Automation involves the following four steps:

1. Declare an Object variable with a Dim statement.
2. Create an OLE Automation object with a CreateObject function and assign it to the variable with a Set statement.
3. Transfer commands and/or data to the OLE Automation object to carry out the desired task.
4. Close the object and assign the value Nothing to the Object variable.

EXAMPLE 1

The following program, which requires that Microsoft Excel be present in your computer, creates a spreadsheet for college expenses and uses the spreadsheet to add up the values for the different categories. The user should place numbers into the text boxes and then press the first command button to tabulate total college expenses. This process can be repeated as many times as desired.

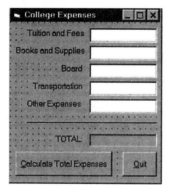

Object	Property	Setting
frm14_1_1	Caption	College Expenses
lblTuitNFees	Caption	Tuition and Fees
txtTuitNFees	Text	blank)
lblBooksNSuppl	Caption	Books and Supplies
txtBooksNSuppl	Text	(blank)
lblBoard	Caption	Board
txtBoard	Text	(blank)
lblTransportation	Caption	Transportation
txtTransportation	Text	(blank)
lblOther	Caption	Other Expenses
txtOther	Text	(blank)
Line1		
LblTotal	Caption	TOTAL:
LblHoldTotal	Caption	(blank)
CmdCalculate	Caption	&Calculate Total Expenses
CmdQuit	Caption	&Quit

```
    Dim objExcel As Object 'In (Declarations) section of (General)

Private Sub cmdCalculate_Click()
    Set objExcel = CreateObject("Excel.Sheet")
    'Make Excel visible objExcel.Application.Visible = True
    'Fill in Rows Values
    objExcel.Application.Cells(1, 3).Value = txtTuitNFees.Text
    objExcel.Application.Cells(2, 3).Value = txtBooksNSuppl.Text
    objExcel.Application.Cells(3, 3).Value = txtBoard.Text
    objExcel.Application.Cells(4, 3).Value = txtTransportation.Text
    objExcel.Application.Cells(5, 3).Value = txtOther.Text
    'Set up a cell to total the expenses
    objExcel.Application.Cells(6, 3).Formula = "=SUM(C1:C5)"
    objExcel.Application.Cells(6, 3).Font.Bold = True
    'Set total as the contents of this cell
    lblHoldTotal = objExcel.Application.Cells(6, 3).Value
    'Make Excel invisible
    objExcel.Application.Visible = False
End Sub

Private Sub cmdQuit_Click()
    'Close Excel
    objExcel.Application.Quit
    'Release the object variable
    Set objExcel = Nothing
    End
End Sub
```

[Run, place numbers into the text boxes, and click on the Calculate Total Expenses button. *Note:* If the form is not visible, click on the College icon in the Window's task bar at the bottom of the screen.]

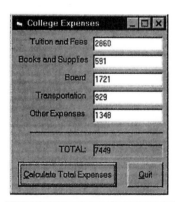

EXAMPLE 2

The following program creates a Word document, prints the contents of the document, and saves the document to a file.

Object	Property	Setting
frm14_1_2	Caption	EXAMPLE 2
cmdCreate	Caption	&Create Word Document

```
Private Sub cmdCreate_Click()
  Dim objWord As Object
  Set objWord = CreateObject("Word.Basic")
  objWord.FileNewDefault
  objWord.Insert "I can resist everything."
  objWord.Wordleft
  objWord.Bold
  objWord.Insert " except temptation"
  objWord.FilePrint 'Make sure your printer is on
  objWord.FileSaveAs "QUOTE.DOC"
  objWord.FileClose Set
  objWord = Nothing
End Sub
```

[Run and click the command button. The printer will produce the following output.]

```
I can resist everything except temptation.
```

THE OLE CONTAINER CONTROL

An OLE Container control provides a bridge to Windows applications, such as spreadsheets and word processors. For instance, it can hold an Excel spreadsheet or a Word document. The application can be either linked or embedded through the OLE Container control. With **linking**, a link is established to the data associated with the application and only a snapshot of the data is displayed. Other applications can access the object's data and modify them. For example, if you link a text file to a Visual Basic application, the text file can be modified by any application linked to it. The modified version appears in all documents linked to this text. With **embedding**, all the application's data are actually contained in the OLE Container control and no other application has access to the data.

When you place an OLE Container control on a form, the dialog box in Figure 13-1 appears. You can select an application from the list and then press the OK button (or double-click on the application) to insert it into the control. Alternately, you can click on the "Create from File" option button to produce the dialog box in Figure 13-2. From this second dialog box, you specify a file (such as a Word .DOC file or an Excel .XLS file) by typing it into the text box or clicking the Browse command button and selecting it from a standard file selection dialog box. After the file has been selected, you have the option of checking the Link check box before clicking on the OK button to insert the contents of the file into the OLE Container control.

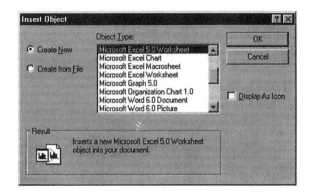

FIGURE 13-1   *An Insert Object Dialog Box*

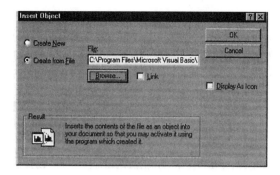

FIGURE 13-2   *Dialog Box for Inserting Contents of a File into an OLE Container Control.*

■ AN EMBEDDING WALKTHROUGH USING EXCEL

1. Press Alt/File/New Project and click on OK.

2. Click the OLE icon in the Toolbox and use the single-click-draw technique to create a very large rectangle on the form.

3. The Insert Object dialog box appears. Double-click on "Microsoft Excel Worksheet" in the Object Type list.

   Excel will be invoked and you will be able to create a spreadsheet. (Most likely, the Excel menu bar will replace the Visual Basic menu bar. In some cases, the Excel menu bar will appear on the form just below the title bar.)

4. Enter data into cells as shown in the first three rows of the spreadsheet in Figure 13-3

5. Drag to select cells A1 through F3.

6. If you are using Excel 97, click Insert, click Chart, and then proceed to Step 8. If you are using Excel 95, click Insert, then Chart, and then On This Sheet.

7. (A new mouse pointer consisting of a thin plus sign and a small bar chart appears.) Move the mouse pointer to cell A5, drag to the bottom-right corner of the OLE Container control, and then release the left mouse button.

   A Chart Wizard dialog box appears.

8. Click on the Finish button.

   Your spreadsheet should be similar to the one in Figure 13-3.

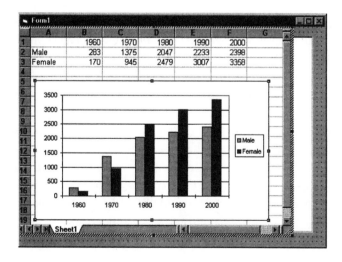

FIGURE 13-3   *An Excel Spreadsheet*

9. Click on the form to exit Excel.

The values you created in Excel are now displayed in the OLE rectangle without any Excel embellishments. If needed, you can resize the OLE rectangle to show any hidden material.

10. Run the program.

11. Double-click on the OLE rectangle to reinvoke Excel.

12. Change the value in one of the cells and then click on any other cell.

Notice that the change is reflected in the bar chart.

13. Click the End icon to end the program.

Notice that the changes to the data and graph have been lost. They are permanently gone.

14. Add a command button to the form and caption it Save Sheet.

15. Double-click on the command button to open the Command1_Click event procedure code window.

16. With Excel 97, enter the following program lines into this code window. (With Excel 95, delete "worksheet("sheet1")".)

```
Dim objExcel As Object
Set objExcel = OLE1.Object
objExcel.worksheet("sheet1").SaveAs "MySheet.xls"
Set objExcel = Nothing
```

The first two lines of this code make the contents of OLE1 into an OLE Automation object.

17. Run the program, double-click on the OLE rectangle to invoke Excel, change the contents of one of the cells, and click on another cell.

18. Click on the Save Sheet command button.

19. Click the End icon to end the program.

Again the changes to the data and graph have been lost. However, the saved file now can be used to recover the changes if you so desire. To do so, go to the SourceDoc property of OLE1, click on the ellipsis, type MYSHEET.XLS into the text box, click on the OK button, and click on Yes in the "Delete Current Embedded Object?" message box.

■ A LINKING WALKTHROUGH USING WORD

1. Before starting Visual Basic, invoke Word, type in a few sentences, and save the document. In this walkthrough we assume that the document you have created now resides on drive A and is named MYWORK.DOC.

2. Invoke Visual Basic.

3. Click the OLE icon in the Toolbox and use the single-click-draw technique to create a large rectangle on the form.

4. Click on the "Create from File" option button, type A:\MYWORK.DOC into the text box, click the Link check box, and click on the OK button.

The document saved in MYWORK. DOC is displayed in the OLE rectangle.

5. Run the program and double-click the OLE rectangle. The complete Word program is invoked and the document in MYWORK.DOC is displayed.

6. Make some changes to the document, and then press Alt/File/Save and Alt/File/Exit to save your changes and exit Word. The modified document is displayed in the OLE rectangle on the Visual Basic form.

7. End the program and display the form if it is hidden.

Notice that the document in the OLE rectangle is the original document, not the modified version. Visual Basic maintains an image of this original document in the program to display at run time if it is unable to display the latest version of the data (document).

8. Run the program.

   The document is still the original version.

9. Double-click on the OLE rectangle to invoke Word.

   Notice that the document displayed is the modified version.

10. Exit back to Visual Basic and then end the Visual Basic program.

11. Double-click on the form and add the code

```
Ole1.Action = 6 'Update OLE image
to the Form_Load event procedure.
```

12. Run the program.

   Notice that Visual Basic has updated the document to the last version saved while in Word even though you have not yet accessed Word by double-clicking.

COMMENTS

1. OLE requires a powerful computer to operate at a reasonable speed.

2. An embedded application in the container OLE1 can be made into an OLE Automation object by a pair of statements of the form

```
Dim objVar As Object
Set objVar = OLE1.Object
```

3. After an Excel spreadsheet has been opened as an object, data can be assigned to and read from a single cell with statements such as

```
objExcel.Application.Cells(4, 2).Value = "49"
num = objExcel.Application.Cells(1, 3).Value
```

   These statements can be replaced by the following statements that use the standard spreadsheet notation for cells.

```
objExcel.Application.Range("B4").Value = "49"
num = objExcel.Application.Range("C1").Value
```

4. A linked or embedded application can be activated by double-clicking on the OLE container. They can also be activated with the code

```
OLE1.Action = 7
```

   and deactivated with the code

```
OLE1.Action = 9
```

5. The OLE Automation function GetObject, which is similar to CreateObject, can be used to access existing Excel spreadsheets. For instance, if a worksheet resides in the root directory on a diskette in drive A and has the name EXPENSES.XLS, then the spreadsheet can be accessed with the pair of statements

```
Dim objExcel As Object
Set objExcel = GetObject("A:\EXPENSES.XLS")
```

6. Some other Word statements for use in OLE Automation are

```
objWord.FileOpen filespec        'Open the specified document
objWord.FontSize n               'Assign the value n to the font size
objWord.StartOfLine              'Move the insertion point to the 'begin-
                                  ning of the current line
objWord.EndOfLine                'Move the insertion point to the 'end of
                                  the current line
objWord.StartOfDocument          'Move the insertion point to the 'begin-
                                  ning of the document
objWord.EndOfDocument            'Move the insertion point to the 'end of
                                  the document
objWord.FileSave                 'Save the current document
```

7. The following key combinations can be used to carry out tasks with an embedded Excel application:

Ctrl+;	Insert the date in the current cell
Alt+=	Sum continuous column of numbers containing the current cell
Ctrl+Z	Undo the last operation
Shift+F3	Invoke the Function Wizard
F7	Check spelling

8. The standard prefix for the name of an OLE container control is ole.

9. OLE replaces an earlier technology known as Dynamic Data Exchange (DDE) that was used to integrate applications into Visual Basic programs. DDE is slower and more difficult to use than OLE.

13.2 ACCESSING THE INTERNET WITH VISUAL BASIC

■ WHAT IS THE INTERNET?

The Internet began in the late 1960s as a plan to link computers at scientific laboratories across the country so that researchers could share computer resources. This plan was funded by the Defense Department's Advanced Research Projects Agency (ARPA) and initially was known as ARPANET. Over time, many research institutions and universities connected to this network. Eventually, the National Science Foundation took over ARPANET and ultimately it became what we now know as the Internet. The past few years has seen an amazing amount of growth in this global network. It more than doubles in size every 6 months.

The Internet often is confused with one of its most popular components, the **World Wide Web** (WWW) or "the Web." The Internet is much more than the Web. It also consists of electronic mail (e-mail), file transfer (FTP), news groups, and remote login capabilities. E-mail allows people to send messages to one another over the Internet. FTP allows people to transfer files from one machine to another. This is often the preferred method of retrieving shareware or freeware programs over the Internet. Usenet is a large collection of electronic discussion groups called newsgroups. There are newsgroups dedicated to every topic imaginable. People can post messages that all members of the group can read and answer.

The World Wide Web is made up of documents called pages, which contain pictures and text. The pages are accessed through programs called **browsers**. The best known Web browsers are Netscape, Mosaic, Lynx, and Internet Explorer. Web pages usually include links to other pages. These links are often set apart from the regular text by using boldface, underlining, or color. When you click on a link, you call up the page referred to by that link. This technology for connecting documents is called **hypertext**.

To access an initial Web page, you must specify an address called a Uniform Resource Locator (**URL**). You can do this by typing in a URL (or Locator) text box found toward the top of your browser or by typing in the dialog box that appears when selecting the Open command from the File menu or clicking the Open button in the toolbar.

■ A WEB BROWSER WALKTHROUGH

1. Connect to the Internet either through your commercial service provider or by using your school's network computers.
2. Start up a Web browser such as Netscape, Mosaic, Lynx, or Internet Explorer.
3. In the Location or URL text box toward the top of the browser, type in http://www.whitehouse.gov
4. Press Enter.
5. Click on one of the highlighted or underlined phrases (links) in the document.

   The page associated with this link will load. For instance if you click on "The President & Vice President:" you will see pictures of them and their wives along with information on how to send e-mail to them.
6. Click on some other links to see what pages are brought up.
7. When you are through exploring the White House page, try other URL addresses such as:

Microsoft's Visual Basic Page	http://www.microsoft.com/vbasic
Carl and Gary's Visual Basic Page	http://www.apexsc.com/vb
Prentice-Hall's Home Page	http://www.prenhall.com

The remainder of this section is devoted to using Visual Basic to create our own Web browser. The requirements for this task are as follows:

1. A modem, or a direct internet connection.
2. A Windows TCP/IP stack, usually referred to as a Winsock. (If you are using an Internet connection through your school, it almost certainly meets this requirement. If you are using a dialup connection from home, the Microsoft hookup to the network that comes with Windows will work.)
3. Microsoft Internet Explorer 4.0 (or higher) must be installed.

To Add the Web Browrser Control to Your Visual Basic Toolbox

1. Invoke Visual Basic.
2. Press Ctrl+T to invoke the Components dialog box.
3. Click the check box next to Microsoft Internet Controls.
4. Click the OK button.

   The Web Browser icon should now appear in your toolbox.

EXAMPLE 1

The following program creates a simplified Web browser. (Before running the program, be sure you are connected to the Internet as discussed above.) The primary task of the program, accessing the Web, is accomplished with the single statement

```
WebBrowser1.Navigate(txtURL.Text)
```

The On Error Resume Next statement specifies that when a run-time error occurs, control goes to the statement immediately following the statement where the error occurred where execution continues. This statement is needed because the LocationURL of the Web Browser control can easily return an error and crash the program. (For instance, this would happen if the intended web site was down.)

After you run the program as specified in what follows, click on one of the links. *Note:* The home page of Internet Explorer will also be the home page of the Web Browser control.

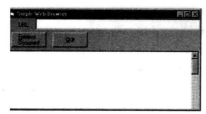

Object	Property	Setting
frm14_2_1	Caption	Simple Web Browser
txtURL	Text	(blank)
mdRetrieve	Caption	&Retrieve Document
Default	True	
CmdQuit	Caption	&Quit
LblURL	Caption	URL:
WebBrowser1		

```
Private Sub Form_Load()
    WebBrowser1.GoHome            'Calls up Internet Explorer's home page
End Sub

Private Sub cmdRetrieve_Click()
    'Calls up the URL typed in the text box
    WebBrowser1.Navigate(txtURL.Text)
End Sub

Private Sub Form_Resize()
    'Resizes the WebBrowser control with the Form,
    'as long as the form is not minimized.
    'occurs when the Form is first displayed
    If frm14_2_1.WindowState > 1 Then
        WebBrowser1.Width = frm14_2_1.ScaleWidth
        WebBrowser1.Height = frm14_2_1.ScaleHeight - 740 'Subtract toolbar
        height
    End If
End Sub

Private Sub WebBrowser1_NavigateComplete (ByVal URL As String)
    'Is activated when the HTML control finishes retrieving the
    'requested Web page.
    'Updates the text box to display the URL of the current page.
    On Error Resume Next 'Eliminates error messages
    txtURL.Text = WebBrowser1.LocationURL
End Sub

Private Sub cmdQuit_Click()
    End
End Sub
```

[Run. The Internet Explorer's home page will be displayed. Type http://www.whitehouse.gov/ into the text box, and click on the "Retrieve Document" command button.]

EXAMPLE 2

The following enhancement of Example 1 adds a label that shows the status of the Web Browser control, a command button that returns you back to the most recently accessed page, and a command button that displays the Prentice-Hall web site. (The picture of the Prentice-Hall trademark is contained in the Pictures directory of the accompanying CD.)

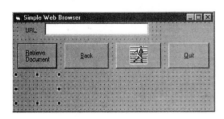

Object	Property	Setting
frm14_2_2	Caption	Simple Web Browser
lblURL	Caption	URL:
txtURL	Text	(blank)
lblStatus	Caption	(blank)
cmdRetrieve	Caption	&Retrieve Document
	Default	
cmdBack	Caption	&Back
cmdPH	Caption	(none)
	Style	Graphical
	Picture	PHICON.BMP
CmdQuit	Caption	&Quit
WebBrowser1		

Add the following code to the program in Example 1.

```
Private Sub WebBrowser1_StatusTextChange(ByVal Text As String)
   'Event is called whenever the address of the page being
   'displayed changes. The address is assigned to the string Text.
   lblStatus.Caption = Text
End Sub
```

```
Private Sub cmdBack_Click()
  WebBrowser1.GoBack 'Return to the previous web site or page
End Sub

Private Sub cmdPH_Click()
  WebBrowser1.Navigate ("http://www.prenhall.com")
End Sub
```

[Run. After the Internet Explore home page appears, click on the command button with the picture of the Prentice-Hall trademark.]

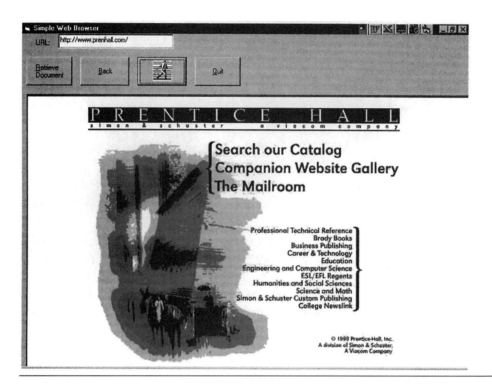

COMMENTS

1. The abbreviation HTTP stands for HyperText Transfer Protocol.
2. Some additional properties of the Web Browser control are

LocationURL	Gives the URL of the current page.
LocationName	Gives the title of the current page.
Busy	Has the value True if the control is downloading a file or navigating to a new location.

3. Some additional methods of the Web Browser control are

GoForward	Undoes the most recent GoBack method.
GoSearch	Goes to the user's web searching page.
Stop	Cancels the current operation of the control.

4. Some additional events of the Web Browser control are

BeforeNavigate	Triggered right before the control moves to a new location.
ProgressChange	Triggered periodically as the downloading continues.

DownloadComplete   Triggered when the download is complete, halter, or failed.

5. If a file on your disk is an HTML document, you can view it as a web page with the statement WebBrowser1.Navigate "filespec".

6. Three good books about the Internet are

C.L. Clark, *A Student's Guide to the Internet*, Prentice Hall, Inc. 1996.

B. P. Kehoe, *Zen and the Art of the Internet*, Prentice Hall, Inc. 1996.

K. Hafner and M. Lyon, *Where Wizards Stay Up Late: The Origins of the Internet*, Simon & Schuster, 1996.

13.3 WEB PAGE PROGRAMMING WITH VBSCRIPT

Note: This section requires that the Internet Explorer Web browser be installed on your computer.

Web browsers display Web pages created as text files, called HTML[1] [stands for Hyper-Text Markup Language] documents. The text files can be written with Notepad or any other word processor. VBScript is a subset of the Visual Basic programming language that is used to make Web pages interactive. (You can use any VBScript code in VB itself.) In this section, we learn how to create Web pages with HTML, add controls to Web pages, and write VBScript code that manipulates the controls.

■ HTML

Here is a typical line in an HTML document.

<B>This sentence will be printed in bold.</B>

The items <B> and </B> are called **tags**. Here the letter B stands for Bold and the pair of tags tells the browser to display everything between the two tags in boldface. The first tag is called the **begin tag** and the second tag is called the **end tag**. Most tags come in pairs in which the second tag differs from the first only in the addition of a slash (/). The combination of pair of tags and the data characters enclosed by them is called an **element**. In general, a tag defines a format to apply or an action to take. A pair of tags tells the browser what to do with the text between the tags. Some pairs of tags and their effect on the text between them are as follows.

<I>, </I>	Display the text in italics
<U>, </U>	Display the text underlined.
<H*n*>, </H*n*>	Display the text in a size *n* header $(1 \leq n \leq 6)$
<BIG>, </BIG>	Display the text one font size larger.
<SMALL>, </SMALL>	Display the text one font size smaller.
<DIV ALIGN=CENTER>, </DIV>	Center the text.
<TITLE>, </TITLE>	Place the text in the Web page title bar.

An example of a tag that does not come in pairs is <P>, which tells the browser to start a new paragraph and insert a blank line. A similar tag is <BR> which inserts a carriage return and a line feed to start a new line. The lines

```
Line One
Line Two
```

in an HTML document will be displayed as

```
Line One Line Two
```

in the Web page, since browsers combine all the white space (including spaces, tabs, and line breaks) into a single space. On the other hand,

```
Line One <BR> Line Two
```

will be displayed as

```
Line One
Line Two
```

and

```
Line One <P> Line Two
```

will be displayed as

```
Line One

Line Two
```

Sometimes the begin tag of a pair of tags contains additional information needed to carry out the task. The pair of tags <A HREF=*address*> and </A> create a hyperlink to the Web page with the specified address and the text between the tags underlined. For instance, the element

<A HREF="http://www.prenhall.com/"> This is a link to Prentice-Hall.</A>

in an HTML document will be displayed by the browser as

<u>This is a link to Prentice-Hall.</u>

When you click anywhere on this line, the browser will move to the Prentice-Hall Web site.

HTML documents consist of two parts, called the head and the body, that are delineated by the pairs of tags <HEAD>, </HEAD> and <BODY>, </BODY>. In addition, the entire HTML document is usually enclosed in the pair of tags <HTML>, </HTML>. The HTML document in Figure 13-4 produces the Web page shown in Figure 13-5.

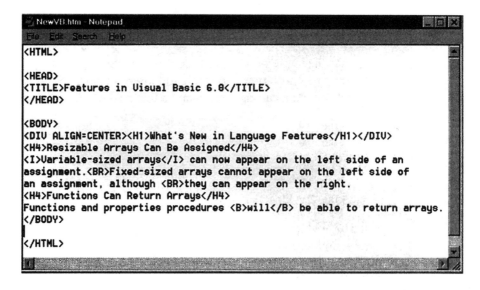

FIGURE 13-4   *HTML Document*

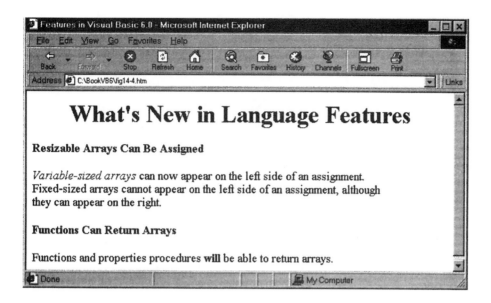

FIGURE 13-5 *Web Page*

■ PLACING ACTIVEX CONTROLS IN HTML DOCUMENTS

With Internet Explorer, ActiveX controls, such as text boxes, command buttons, and user-built controls, can be placed on Web pages. For instance, the element

```
<OBJECT ID="cmdPush" WIDTH=115 HEIGHT=49
 CLASSID="CLSID:D7053240-CE69-11CD-A777-00DD01143C57">
 <PARAM NAME="Caption" VALUE="Push Me">
 <PARAM NAME="Size" VALUE="3037;1291">
 <PARAM NAME="FontCharSet" VALUE="0">
 <PARAM NAME="FontPitchAndFamily" VALUE="2">
 <PARAM NAME="ParagraphAlign" VALUE="3">
 <PARAM NAME="FontWeight" VALUE="0">
</OBJECT>
```

tells Internet Explorer to place a command button (named cmdPush) on the Web page. The string beginning with CLSID is the control's identification number in the Windows registry. The PARAM tags set properties of the control. For instance, the first PARAM tag sets the caption of the command button to "Push Me."

Creating the OBJECT element is so cumbersome that Microsoft has developed a tool, called the ActiveX Control Pad, that makes placing a control on a Web page nearly as easy as placing a control on a Visual Basic form. The ActiveX Control Pad is sometimes included with Internet Explorer. Also, the ActiveX Control Pad can be downloaded separately from the Microsoft Web site. (See Comment 7.)

The ActiveX Control Pad is actually a word processor that looks and acts much like Notepad. The following walkthrough uses the ActiveX Control Pad to create a Web page containing a text box and a command button.

1. Click the Start button on the Windows taskbar, point to Programs, point to Microsoft ActiveX Control Pad, and then click on Microsoft ActiveX Control Pad in the final pop-up list. The window that appears (see Figure 13-6) contains a template for an HTML document.

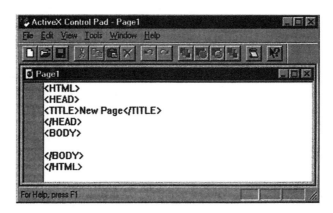

FIGURE 13-6 *ActiveX Control Pad*

2. In the Title element, replace "New Page" with "My First Web Page".

3. Just below the begin Body tag, type the following lines.

```
<BIG>Hello</BIG>
<P>Type your first name into the box.<P>
```

4. Press Alt/Edit/Insert ActiveX Control. (An Insert ActiveX dialog box appears containing a list of all available controls.)

5. Scroll down the list and double-click on Microsoft Forms 2.0 TextBox. (Two windows appear. One window, titled Edit ActiveX Control, contains a text box and is similar to a Visual Basic form. The other window is an abbreviated text box Properties window.)

6. Scroll down the Properties window and click on ID. (The default setting TextBox1 appears next to ID and in the settings text box at the top of the Properties window. The ID property is the same as Visual Basic's Name property.)

7. Replace the words in the settings text box with txtFirstName and click on the Apply button.

8. Go to the Edit ActiveX Control window and make the text box a little larger.

9. Close the windows by clicking on their X buttons. (An OBJECT element for the text box has been added to the ActiveX Control Pad.)

10. Type <P>.

11. Repeat Steps 4 through 9 to add a command button OBJECT element. (Select Microsoft Forms 2.0 Command button, give it the ID cmdShow, and the caption "Show Greeting.")

12. Press Alt/File/Save As, select a location and name (with extension htm) for the file, and click on the Save button.

13. Invoke Internet Explorer. (There is no need to actually connect to the internet via a phone line.)

14. Type the filespec for your saved HTML page into the address box and press Enter. (The window in Figure 13-7 will appear.)

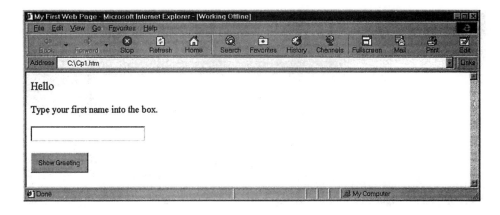

FIGURE 13-7

14. Feel free to type into the text box and click on the command button. Nothing will happen since no code has yet been written for them.

■ ACTIVATING A WEB PAGE WITH VBSCRIPT

The VBScript programming language is an offshoot of Visual Basic. It has most of the familiar features, such as If blocks, Do loops, Select Case blocks, procedures, and arrays. However, VBScript has some differences from Visual Basic. For instance, all variables are of type Variant and are declared with a statement of the form Dim *variableName*. VBScript supports the functions FormatNumber, FormatCurrency, FormatPercent, and FormatDateTime, but not the plain Format function. Some additional differences between Visual Basic and VBScript are listed in Comments 5 and 6.

Code is written into a SCRIPT element with begin tag

```
<SCRIPT LANGUAGE="VBSCRIPT">
```

and end tag </SCRIPT>. Let's continue the walkthrough above by adding some code to the HTML document created in the walkthrough. (If you have already closed the HTML document, you can bring it back into the ActiveX Control Pad with Alt/File/Open.)

15. Type the following code into the body element of the document, just below the OBJECT elements, and then Save the document.

```
<SCRIPT LANGUAGE="VBSCRIPT">
Sub cmdShow_Click()
   Dim nom
   nom = txtFirstName.text
   MsgBox "Greetings " & nom
End Sub
</SCRIPT>
```

16. Return to Internet Explorer and look at the revised Web page. (If you have not changed the Address since the walkthrough, just click on the Refresh icon to load the revised HTML page. Otherwise type in its filespec and press the Enter key.)

17. Type your name, say David, into the text box and click on the command button. A message box will pop up with the message "Greetings David".

COMMENTS

1. You can obtain extensive information about HTML and VBScript from the Help menu in the ActiveX Control Pad. (If the documentation for VBScript is not present on your computer, you can either download the documentation or read it online at http://microsoft.com/scripting.)

2. HTML tags are not case sensitive. For instance, <b> has the same effect as <B>.

3. A TITLE element must placed inside the HEAD portion of an HTML document.

4. VBScript programs can contain code that is not in any procedure. If so, this code is executed by Internet Explorer as soon as the Web page is displayed. It is analogous to Visual Basic code found in the Form_Load event procedure.

5. Some features of Visual Basic that are not available in VBScript are ranges of values and the Is keyword in Case clauses, Str and Val functions, the Open statement, On Error GoTo statement, arrays declared with lower bound $\neq 0$, line labels, collections, and picture box controls.

6. If i is the index of a For...Next loop, in Visual Basic the final statement should be Next i. In VBScript, the i must be dropped from the final statement.

7. To download the ActiveX Control Pad, enter the address http://www.microsoft.com/gallery/tools/contents.htm into your browser and follow the directions.

8. You can place your own custom-built ActiveX controls into an HTML document provided the control has been compiled into an ocx file. However, in order to use these controls you will have to ease Internet Explorer's safety level. To invoke the lowest level of security, select Internet Options from Internet Explorer's View menu, click on the Security tab, and select Low. *Note:* Before you actually connect to the internet, reset the safety level to High.

9. Visual Basic allows you to place controls exactly where you want on a form. The ActiveX Control Pad has a device, called an HTML Layout, that lets you achieve the same result. An HTML Layout is actually an ActiveX control that acts as a container for other controls. It has a grid like a form that allow for precision alignment. The steps for creating an HTML Layout are as follows.

   (a) From the ActiveX Control Pad, click on New HTML Layout in the File menu. (A form-like window and a square toolbar containing about a dozen icons will appear.)

   (b) Place a control on the Layout with the click and drag method. To set the properties of a control in the Layout, double-click on the control to produce a Properties window.

   (c) After all the controls have been drawn and their properties set, save the Layout (in an ALX file).

   (d) To insert the Layout into an HTML document, position the cursor at the insertion point, and click on Insert HTML Layout in the Edit menu to open a file-selection dialog box. Select the location and name of the file, and then press the Open button. (An OBJECT element will be created for the Layout.)

   (e) Whenever you want to alter the Layout, place the cursor anywhere inside the OBJECT element and select Edit HTML Layout from the Edit menu.

SUMMARY

1. OLE, a technology developed by Microsoft, gives Visual Basic access to other applications.

2. OLE Automation allows you to control other applications with Visual Basic code. The other application is declared as an object with the Set statement and CreateObject function.

3. Other applications can be embedded in or linked to a form with the OLE Container control.

4. The WebBrowser control can be used to create a browser for the World Wide Web.

5. The document-formatting language used by Web browsers is called *HTML*. *Tags* are used to mark up text with display instructions. The combination of a pair of tags and the text enclosed is called an *element*.

6. The ActiveX Control Pad is used to place text, controls, and programs into HTML documents.

7. *VBScript* is a subset of Visual Basic that is used to make Web pages interactive.

APPENDIX A

ANSI VALUES

ANSIValue	Character	ANSIValue	Character	ANSIValue	Character
000	(null)	040	(	080	P
001	☐	041	)	081	Q
002	☐	042	*	082	R
003	☐	043	+	083	S
004	☐	044	,	084	T
005	☐	045	−	085	U
006	☐	046	.	086	V
007	☐	047	/	087	W
008	☐	048	0	088	X
009	(tab)	049	1	089	Y
010	(line feed)	050	2	090	Z
011	☐	051	3	091	[
012	☐	052	4	092	\
013	(carriage return)	053	5	093	]
014	☐	054	6	094	^
015	☐	055	7	095	_
016	☐	056	8	096	`
017	☐	057	9	097	a
018	☐	058	:	098	b
019	☐	059	;	099	c
020	☐	060	<	100	d
021	☐	061	=	101	e
022	☐	062	>	102	f
023	☐	063	?	103	g
024	☐	064	@	104	h
025	☐	065	A	105	i
026	☐	066	B	106	j
027	☐	067	C	107	k
028	☐	068	D	108	l
029	☐	069	E	109	m
030	☐	070	F	110	n
031	☐	071	G	111	o
032		072	H	112	p
033	!	073	I	113	q
034	"	074	J	114	r
035	#	075	K	115	s
036	$	076	L	116	t
037	%	077	M	117	u
038	&	078	N	118	v
039	'	079	O	119	w

ANSIValue	Character	ANSIValue	Character	ANSIValue	Character
120	x	166	¦	212	Ô
121	y	167	§	213	Õ
122	z	168	¨	214	Ö
123	{	169	©	215	×
124	|	170	¶	216	Ø
125	}	171	«	217	Ù
126	~	172	¬	218	Ú
127	□	173	-	219	Û
128	□	174	®	220	Ü
129	□	175	¯	221	Ý
130	,	176	°	222	þ
131	ƒ	177	±	223	ß
132	„	178	^{2}	224	à
133	…	179	^{3}	225	á
134	†	180	Ç	226	â
135	‡	181	µ	227	ã
136	^	182	¶	228	ä
137	‰	183	·	229	å
138	Š	184	¸	230	æ
139	‹	185	^{1}	231	ç
140	Œ	186	º	232	è
141	□	187	»	233	é
142	□	188	¼	234	ê
143	□	189	½	235	ë
144	□	190	¾	236	ì
145	'	191	¿	237	í
146	'	192	À	238	î
147	"	193	Á	239	ï
148	"	194	Â	240	õ
149	•	195	Ã	241	ñ
150	–	196	Ä	242	ò
151	—	197	Å	243	ó
152	~	198	Æ	244	ô
153	™	199	Ç	245	õ
154	š	200	È	246	ö
155	›	201	É	247	÷
156	œ	202	Ê	248	ø
157	□	203	Ë	249	ù
158	□	204	Ì	250	ú
159	Ÿ	205	Í	251	û
160		206	Î	252	ü
161	¡	207	Ï	253	ý
162	¢	208	Ð	254	þ
163	£	209	Ñ	255	ÿ
164	¤	210	Ò		
165	¥	211	Ó		

APPENDIX B

HOW TO

HOW TO: INSTALL, INVOKE, AND EXIT VISUAL BASIC

A. Install the Working Model Edition of Visual Basic

   1. Place the CD accompanying this book into your CD drive.

   2. Wait about five seconds. You will most likely hear a whirring sound from the CD drive and then a large window with the words "Visual Basic 6.0 Working Model" will appear. If so, go to Step 5.

   3. If nothing happens automatically after Step 1, double-click on My Computer in the Windows Desktop.

   4. A window showing the different disk drives will appear. Double-click on the icon containing a picture of a CD (along with a drive) and having the drive letter below the label. A large window with the words "Visual Basic 6.0 Working Model" will appear.

   5. The title bar of the large window says "Installation Wizard for Visual Basic 6.0 Working Model." The installation wizard will guide you through the installation process. Click on Next to continue.

   6. An End User License Agreement will appear. After reading the agreement, click on the the circle to the left of the sentence "I accept the agreement." and then click on Next.

   7. The next window to appear has spaces for an ID number, your name, and your company's name. Ignore the ID number. Just type in your name and, optionally, a company name, and then click Next.

   8. Visual Basic 6.0 requires that you have Internet Explorer 4.0 or later version on your computer. If a recent version is not present, the Installation Wizard will install it for you. If so, successive windows will guide you through the installation. At some point you will be required to restart your computer. We recommend doing the standard installation and using the recommended destination folder.

   9. You will next be guided through the installation of DCOM98, which is also needed to Visual Basic 6.0. After installing DCOM98, the installation wizard will automatically restart your computer and then continue with the installation of VB6.0. *Note:* If another widow is covering the Installation Wizard window, then click on the Installation Wizard window. If you can't find the Installation Wizard window, repeat Steps 1–5.

You will now be guided through the installation of the Working Model Edition VB6.0. At the end of the installation, Visual Basic will be invoked.

   10. The next window requests the name of the Common Install Folder. We recommend that you simply click on Next, which will accept the default folder and copy some files into it.

   11. The next window to appear is the Visual Basic 6.0 Working Model Setup. Click on Continue.

   12. The next screen shows your Product ID number. Enter your name and then click on OK.

13. The next window asks you to choose between Typical and Custom installations. We recommend that you click on the Typical icon.

14. About one minute is required for the VB6.0 Working Model to be installed. On the next screen to appear, click on Restart Windows.

15. The next window to appear gives you the opportunity to register your copy of VB6.0 over the web. Uncheck the Register Now box and click on Finish.

B.   Invoke Visual Basic after installation.

1. Click the Start button.

2. Point to Programs.

3. Point to Microsoft Visual Basic 6.0. (A new panel will open on the right.)

4. In the new panel, click on Microsoft Visual Basic 6.0.

C.   Exit Visual Basic.

1. Press the Esc key.

2. Press Alt/F/X.

3. If an unsaved program is present, Visual Basic will prompt you about saving it.

Note: In many situations, Step 1 is not needed.

HOW TO: MANAGE PROGRAMS

A.   Run a program from Visual Basic.

1. Click on the Start icon (right arrowhead) in the Toolbar.

   or

1. Press F5.

   or

1. Press Alt/R and make a selection from the Run menu.

B.   Save the current program on a disk.

1. Press Alt/F/V [or click the Save Project icon (shows a diskette) on the Toolbar].

2. Fill in the requested information. Do not give an extension as part of the project name or the file name. Two files will be created [\m]one with extension .VBP and the other with extension .FRM. The .VBP file holds a list of files related to the project. The .FRM file actually holds the program.

Note: After a program has been saved once, updated versions can be saved with the same filenames by pressing Alt/F/V. Alt/F/E and Alt/F/A are used to save the program with new file names.

C.   Begin a new program.

1. Press Alt/F/N.

2. If an unsaved program is present, Visual Basic will prompt you about saving it.

D.   Open a program stored on a disk.

1. Press Alt/F/O [or click the Open Project icon (shows an open folder) on the Toolbar].

2. Click on one of the two tabs, Existing or Recent.

3. If you selected Existing, choose a folder for the "Look in:" box, type a filename into the "File name:"box, and press the Enter key. Alternatively, double-click on one of the filenames displayed in the large box in the middle of the dialog box.

4. If you selected Recent, double-click on one of the files in the list.

Note 1: (In Steps 3 and 4, if an unsaved program is present, Visual Basic will prompt you about saving it.)

Note 2: The form or code for the program may not appear, but can be accessed through the Project Explorer window. Another way to obtain the Code and Form windows is to run and then terminate the program.

E. Use the Project Explorer.

Note: Just below the Project Explorer title bar are three icons (View Code, View Object, and Toggle Folders), and below them is the List window. At any time, one item in the List window is selected.

1. Click on View Code to see the code associated with the selected item.

2. Click on View Object to see the Object (usually the form) associated with the selected item.

F. Display the form associated with a program.

1. Press Alt/V/B. (If the selection Object is grayed, first run and then terminate the program.)

or

1. Press Shift+F7.

or

1. Press Alt/V/P to activate the Project Explorer window.

2. Select the name of the form.

3. Click on the View Object button.

HOW TO: USE THE EDITOR

A. Mark a section of text as a block.

1. Move the cursor to the beginning or end of the block.

2. Hold down a Shift key and use the direction keys to highlight a block of text.

3. Release the Shift key.

or

1. Move the mouse to the beginning or end of the block.

2. Hold down the left mouse button and move the mouse to the other end of the block.

3. Release the left mouse button.

Note 1: To unblock text, press a direction key or click outside the block.

Note 2: To select a word, double-click on it. To select a line, move the mouse pointer just far enough into the left margin so that the pointer changes to an arrow, and then single-click there.

B. Delete a line of a program.

1. Move the cursor to the line.

2. Press Ctrl+Y.

or

1. Mark the line as a block. (See item A of this section.)

2. Press Alt/E/T or press Ctrl+X.

Note: In the preceding maneuvers, the line is placed in the clipboard and can be retrieved by pressing Ctrl+V. To delete the line without placing it in the clipboard, mark it as a block and press Del.

C. Move a line within the Code window.

    1. Move the cursor to the line and press Ctrl+Y.

    2. Move the cursor to the target location.

    3. Press Ctrl+V.

D. Use the clipboard to move or duplicate statements.

    1. Mark the statements as a block.

    2. Press Ctrl+X to delete the block and place it into the clipboard. Or press Ctrl+C to place a copy of the block into the clipboard.

    3. Move the cursor to the location where you desire to place the block.

    4. Press Ctrl+V to place a copy of the text from the clipboard at the cursor.

E. Search for specific text in the program.

    1. Press Alt/E/F or Ctrl+F.

    2. Type sought-after text into the rectangle.

    3. Select desired options if different from the defaults.

    4. Press the Enter key.

    5. To repeat the search, press Find Next or press Cancel and then F3.

F. Find and Replace.

    1. Press Alt/E/E or Ctrl+H.

    2. Type sought-after text into first rectangle.

    3. Press Tab.

    4. Type replacement text into second rectangle.

    5. Select desired options if different from the defaults.

    6. Press the Enter key.

    7. Press Replace to make the change or press Replace All to make all such changes.

G. Cancel a change.

    1. Press Alt/E/U or Ctrl+Z to undo the last change made to a line.

HOW TO: Get Help

(Available only with Learning, Professional, and Enterprise Editions.)

A. Obtain information about a Visual Basic topic.

    1. Press Alt/H/M.

    2. Click on the Index tab and follow the instructions.

    3. To display a topic, double-click on it.

    4. If a second list pops up, double-click on an item from it.

B. View the syntax and purpose of a Visual Basic keyword.

    1. Type the word into a Code window.

    2. Place the cursor on, or just following, the keyword.

3. Press F1.

C. Display an ANSI table.

1. Press Alt/H/M and click on the Index tab.

2. Type ANSI and press the Enter key.

3. To move between the displays for ANSI characters 0-127 and 128-255, click on "See Also," and then click on the Display button.

D. Obtain a list of Visual Basic's reserved words.

1. Press Alt/H/M.

2. Type "keywords", press the down-arrow key, and double-click on a category of keywords from the list below the blue bar.

E. Obtain a list of shortcut keys.

1. Press Alt/H/M and click on the Contents tab.

2. Double-click on the Additional Information book.

3. Double-click on the Keyboard Guide book.

4. Double-click on one of the collections of shortcut keys.

F. Obtain information about a control.

1. Click on the control at design time.

2. Press F1.

G. Exit Help.

1. Press Esc.

HOW TO: MANIPULATE A DIALOG BOX

A. Use a dialog box.

A dialog box contains three types of items: rectangles (text or list boxes), option lists, and command buttons. An option list is a sequence of option buttons or check boxes of the form ◯ *option* or ☐ *option*.

1. Move from item to item with the Tab key. (The movement is from left to right and top to bottom. Use Shift+Tab to reverse the direction.)

2. Inside a rectangle, either type in the requested information or use the direction keys to make a selection.

3. In an option list, an option button of the form ◯ *option* can be selected with the direction keys. A dot inside the circle indicates that the option has been selected.

4. In an option list, a check box of the form ☐ *option* can be checked or unchecked by pressing the space bar. An X or ✓ inside the square indicates that the option has been checked.

5. A highlighted command button is invoked by pressing the Enter key.

B. Cancel a dialog box

1. Press the Esc key.

or

1. Press the Tab key until the command button captioned "Cancel" is highlighted and then press the Enter key.

HOW TO: MANAGE MENUS

A. Open a drop-down menu.
   1. Click on the menu name.

   or

   1. Press Alt.
   2. Press the underlined letter in the name of the menu. Alternatively, use the Right Arrow key to move the highlighted cursor bar to the menu name, and then press the Down Arrow key.

B. Make a selection from a drop-down menu.
   1. Open the drop-down menu.
   2. Click on the desired item.

   or

   1. Open the drop-down menu. One letter in each item that is eligible to be used will be underlined.
   2. Press the underlined letter. Alternatively, use the Down Arrow key to move the cursor bar to the desired item and then press the Enter key.

C. Obtain information about the selections in a drop-down menu.
   1. Press Alt/H/M and click on the Contents tab.
   2. Double-click on the Interface Reference book.
   3. Double-click on the Menu book.
   4. Double-click on the name of the menu of interest.
   5. Double-click on the selection of interest.

D. Look at all the menus in the menu bar.
   1. Press Alt/F.
   2. Press the Right Arrow key each time you want to see a new menu.

E. Close a drop-down menu.
   1. Press the Esc key or click anywhere outside the menu.

HOW TO: UTILIZE THE WINDOWS ENVIRONMENT

A. Place a section of code in the Windows clipboard.
   1. Mark the section of code as a block as described in the How to Use the Editor section.
   2. Press Ctrl+C.

B. Access Windows' Notepad.
   1. Click the Start button.
   2. Point to Programs.
   3. Point to Accessories.
   4. Click Notepad.

C. Display all characters in a font.
   1. Click the Start button.

2. Point to Programs.

3. Point to Accessories.

4. Click Character Map.

5. Click on the underlined down arrow at the right end of the Font box.

6. Highlight the desired font and press the Enter key or click on the desired font.

D. Display an ANSI or ASCII code for a character with a code above 128.

1. Proceed as described in item C above to display the font containing the character of interest.

2. Click on the character of interest. Displayed at the right end of the bottom line of the font table is Alt+0xxx, where xxx is the code for the character.

HOW TO: DESIGN A FORM

A. Display the ToolBox.

1. Press Alt/V/X.

B. Place a new control on the form.

Option I: (new control with default size and position)

1. Double-click on the control's icon in the ToolBox. The new control appears at the center of the form.

2. Size and position the control as described in items G and H, which follow.

Option II: (a single new control sized and positioned as it is created)

1. Click on the control's icon in the ToolBox.

2. Move the mouse to the approximate position on the form desired for the upper-left corner of the control.

3. Press and hold the left mouse button.

4. Move the mouse to the position on the form desired for the lower-right corner of the control. A dashed box will indicate the overall shape of the new control.

5. Release the left mouse button.

6. The control can be resized and repositioned as described in items G and H.

Option III: (create multiple instances of the same control)

1. Click on the control's icon in the ToolBox while holding down the Ctrl key.

2. Repeatedly use Steps 2 to 5 of Option II to create instances of the control.

3. When finished creating instances of this control, click on the arrow icon in the ToolBox.

C. Create a related group of controls.

1. To hold the related group of controls, place a picture box or frame control on the form.

2. Use Option II or III in item B of this section to place controls in the picture box or frame.

D. Select a particular control.

1. Click on the control.

   or

1. Press the Tab key until the control is selected.

E. Delete a control.
  1. Select the control to be deleted.
  2. Press the Del key.

F. Delete a related group of controls.
  1. Select the picture box or frame holding the related group of controls.
  2. Press the Del key.

G. Move a control, related group of controls, or form to a new location.
  1. Move the mouse onto the control, the picture box or frame containing the related group of controls, or the title bar of the form.
  2. Drag the object to the new location.

H. Change the size of a control.
  1. Select the desired control.
  2. Move the mouse to one of the eight sizing handles located around the edge of the control. The mouse pointer will change to a double-arrow which points in the direction that resizing can occur.
  3. Drag to the desired size.

I. Change the size of a Project Container window.
  1. Move the mouse to the edge or corner of the window that is to be stretched or shrunk. The mouse pointer will change to a double-arrow which points in the direction that resizing can occur.
  2. Drag to the desired size.

J. Use the Color palette to set foreground and background colors.
  1. Select the desired control or the form.
  2. Press Alt/V/L to activate the Color palette.
  3. If the Color palette obscures the object you are working with, you may wish to use the mouse to grab the Color palette by its title bar and move it so that at least some of the object shows.
  4. To set the foreground color, click on the square within a square at the far left in the Color palette and click on the desired color from the palette.
  5. To set the background color, click on the region within the outer square but outside the inner square and click on the desired color from the palette.
      or
  1. Select the desired control or the form.
  2. Press Alt/V/W or F4 to activate the Properties window.
  3. To set the foreground color, click on the down-arrow to the right of the Fore-Color settings box, click on the Palette tab, and click on the desired color.
  4. To set the background color, click on the down-arrow to the right of the Back-Color settings box, click on the Palette tab, and click on the desired color.

HOW TO: WORK WITH THE PROPERTIES OF AN OBJECT

A. Activate the Properties window.
  1. Press Alt/V/W.
      or

    1. Press F4.

        or

    1. Click on an object on the form with the right mouse button.

    2. In the shortcut menu, click on Properties.

B. Highlight a property in the Properties window.

    1. Activate the Properties window and press the Enter key.

    2. Use the Up or Down Arrow keys to move the highlight bar to the desired property.

        or

    1. Activate the Properties window.

    2. Click on the up or down arrow located at the ends of the vertical scroll bar at the right side of the Properties window until the desired property is visible.

    3. Click on the desired property.

C. Select or specify a setting for a property.

    1. Highlight the property whose setting is to be changed.

    2. Click on the settings box or press Tab to place the cursor in the settings box.

        a. If a black down-arrow appears at the right end of the settings box, click on the down-arrow to display a list of all allowed settings, and then click on the desired setting.

        b. If an ellipsis (three periods: . . .) appears at the right end of the settings box, press F4 or click on the ellipsis to display a dialog box. Answer the questions in the dialog box and click on OK or Open, as appropriate.

        c. If the cursor moves to the settings box, type in the new setting for the property.

D. Change a property setting of an object.

    1. Select the desired object.

    2. Activate the Properties window.

    3. Highlight the property whose setting is to be changed.

    4. Select or specify the new setting for the property.

E. Let a label change size to accommodate its caption.

    1. Set the label's AutoSize property to True. (The label will shrink to the smallest size needed to hold the current caption. If the caption is changed, the label will automatically grow or shrink horizontally to accommodate the new caption. If the WordWrap property is set to True as well, the label will grow and shrink vertically, keeping the same width.)

F. Let a label caption use more than one line.

    1. Set the label's WordWrap property to True. [If the label is not wide enough to accommodate the entire caption on one line, part of the caption will wrap to additional lines. If the label height is too small, then part or all of these wrapped lines will not be visible (unless the AutoSize property is set to True).]

G. Let a text box display more than one line.

    1. Set the text box's MultiLine property to True. (If the text box is not wide enough to accommodate the text entered by the user, the text will scroll down to new

lines. If the text box is not tall enough, lines will scroll up out of view, but can be redisplayed by moving the cursor up.)

H. Assign an access key to a label or command button.

   1. When assigning a value to the Caption property, precede the desired access key character with an ampersand (&).

I. Allow a particular command button to be activated by a press of the Enter key.

   1. Set the command button's Default property to True.

Note: Setting the Default property True for one command button automatically sets the property to False for all the other command buttons on the form.

J. Adjust the order in which the Tab key moves the focus.

   1. Select the first control in the tabbing sequence.

   2. Change the setting of the TabIndex property for this control to 0.

   3. Select the next control in the tabbing sequence.

   4. Change the setting of the TabIndex property for this control to 1.

   5. Repeat Steps 3 and 4 (adding 1 to the Tab Index property) until all controls on the form have been assigned a new TabIndex setting.

Note: In Steps 2 and 4, if an object is moved to another position in the sequence, then the TabIndex property for the other objects will be renumbered accordingly.

K. Allow the pressing of Esc to activate a particular command button.

   1. Set the command button's Cancel property to True. (Setting the Cancel property to True for one command button automatically sets it to False for all other command buttons.)

L. Keep the contents of a picture box from being erased accidentally.

   1. Set the picture box's AutoRedraw property to True. (The default is False. Unless the property is set to True, the contents will be erased when the picture box is obscured by another window.)

HOW TO: MANAGE PROCEDURES

A. Access the Code window.

   1. Press Alt/V/C or F7. (If the Code window does not appear, run and then terminate the program.)

   or

   1. Press Alt/V/P to activate the Project Explorer window.

   2. Select the name of the form.

   3. Click on the "View Code"button.

B. Look at an existing procedure.

   1. Access the Code window.

   2. Press Ctrl+Down Arrow or Ctrl+Up Arrow to see all the procedures.

   or

   1. Access the Code window.

   2. Click on the down arrow at the right of the Object box and then select an object. [For general procedures select (General) as the Object.]

3. Click on the down arrow at the right of the Procedure box and then select a procedure.

C. Create a general procedure.

   1. Access the Code window.

   2. Move to a blank line that is not inside a procedure.

   3. Type Private Sub (for a Sub procedure) or Private Function (for a Function procedure) followed by the name of the procedure and any parameters.

   4. Press the Enter key. (The Code window will now display the new procedure heading and an End Sub or End Function statement.)

   5. Type the procedure into the Code Window.

      or

   1. Access the Code window.

   2. Press Alt/T/P. (A dialog box will appear.)

   3. Type the name of the procedure into the Name rectangle.

   4. Select the type of procedure.

   5. Select the Scope by clicking on Public or Private. (In this book, we always use Private.)

   6. Press the Enter key. (The Code window will now display the new procedure heading and an End Sub or End Function statement.)

   7. Type the procedure into the Code Window.

D. Alter a procedure.

   1. View the procedure in the Code Window as described in item B of this section.

   2. Make changes as needed.

E. Remove a procedure.

   1. Bring the procedure into the Code Window as described in item B of this section.

   2. Mark the entire procedure as a block. That is,

      a. Press Ctrl+PgUp to move the cursor to the beginning of the procedure.

      b. Hold down the Shift key and press Ctrl+PgDn to move the cursor to the start of the next procedure.

      c. Press the Up Arrow key until just after the end of the procedure to be deleted.

   3. Press the Del key.

F. Insert an existing procedure into a program.

   1. Open the program containing the procedure.

   2. View the procedure in the Code Window as described in item B of this section.

   3. Mark the entire procedure as a block, as described in step 2 of item E of this section.

   4. Press Ctrl+C to place the procedure into the clipboard.

   5. Open the program in which the procedure is to be inserted and access the Code Window.

   6. Move the cursor to a blank line.

   7. Press Ctrl+V to place the contents of the clipboard into the program.

HOW TO: MANAGE WINDOWS

A. Enlarge the active window to fill the entire screen.

1. Click on the Maximize button (page icon; second icon from the right) on the Title bar of the window.

2. To return the window to its original size, click on the Restore (double-page) button that has replaced the Maximize button.

B. Move a window.

1. Move the mouse to the title bar of the window.

2. Drag the window to the desired location.

C. Change the size of a window.

1. Move the mouse to the edge of the window which is to be adjusted or to the corner joining the two edges to be adjusted.

2. When the mouse becomes a double arrow, drag the edge or corner until the window has the desired size.

D. Close a window.

1. Click on the X button on the far right corner of the title bar.

HOW TO: USE THE PRINTER

A. Obtain a printout of a program.

1. Press Alt/F/P.

2. Press the Enter key.

Note: To print just the text selected as a block or the active (current) window, use the direction keys to select the desired option.

B. Obtain a printout of the form during run time.

1. Place the statement PrintForm in the Form_Click( ) or other appropriate procedure of the program which will be executed at the point when the desired output will be on the form.

HOW TO: USE THE DEBUGGER

A. Stop a program at a specified line.

1. Place the cursor on the desired line.

2. Press F9 or Alt/D/T to highlight the line in red. (This highlighted line is called a *breakpoint*. When the program is run it will stop at the breakpoint before executing the statement.)

Note: To remove this breakpoint, repeat Steps 1 and 2.

B. Remove all breakpoints.

    1. Press Alt/D/C or Ctrl+Shift+F9.

C. Run a program one statement at a time.

    1. Press F8. The first executable statement will be highlighted. (An event must first occur for which an event procedure has been written.)

    2. Press F8 each time you want to execute the currently highlighted statement.

Note: You will probably need to press Alt+Tab to switch back and forth between the form and the VB environment. Also, to guarantee that output is retained while stepping through the program, the AutoRedraw property of the form and any picture boxes may need to be set to True.

D. Run the program one statement at a time, but execute each general procedure call without stepping through the statements in the procedure one at a time.

    1. Press Shift+F8. The first executable statement will be highlighted.

    2. Press Shift+F8 each time you want to execute the currently highlighted statement.

E. Continue execution of a program that has been suspended.

    1. Press F5.

Note: Each time an attempt is made to change a suspended program in a way that would prevent the program from continuing, Visual Basic displays a dialog box warning that the program will have to be restarted from the beginning and gives the option to cancel the attempted change.

F. Have further stepping begin at the line containing the cursor (no variables are cleared).

    1. Press Alt/D/R or Ctrl+F8.

G. Set the next statement to be run in the current procedure.

    1. Place the cursor anywhere in the desired statement.

    2. Press Alt/D/N or Ctrl+F9.

H. Determine the value of an expression during run time.

    1. Press Alt/D/A (Add Watch)

    2. Type the expression into the Expression text box, adjust other entries in dialog box (if necessary), and click on OK.

Note: The value of the expression will appear in the Watches window during break mode.

    or

    1. In Break mode, hover the cursor over the variable to have its value displayed.

APPENDIX C

VISUAL BASIC STATEMENTS, FUNCTIONS, METHODS, PROPERTIES, EVENTS, DATA TYPES, AND OPERATORS

This appendix applies to the following objects: form, printer, text box, command button, label, and picture box. The last four are also called *controls*. Terms in brackets follow some of the discussions. These terms refer to supporting topics presented at the end of this appendix.

ABS The function Abs strips the minus signs from negative numbers while leaving other numbers unchanged. If x is any number, then the value of Abs(x) is the absolute value of x.

ACTION The type of a common dialog box can be determined by the setting of the Action property (1-Open, 2-Save As, 3-Color, 4-Font, 5-Print). This use is obsolete. Instead, use the methods ShowOpen, ShowSave, ShowColor, ShowFont, and ShowPrinter. For an OLE control, the setting of the Action property during run time determines the action to take.

ADD A statement of the form *collectionName*.Add *objectName* adds the named object to a collection. A statement of the form *collectionName*.Add *objectName keyString* adds the named object to a collection with the key keyString.

ADDITEM The AddItem method adds an additional item to a list box or combo box and adds an additional row to a grid. A statement of the form List1.AddItem *str* inserts the string either at the end of the list (if Sorted = False) or in its proper alphabetical position (if Sorted = True). The statement List1.AddItem *str*, *n* inserts the item at the position with index *n*. The use of an index is not recommended when Sorted = True. The statement MSFlexGrid1.AddItem "", *n* inserts a new row into the grid at position *n*.

ADDNEW The AddNew method is used with a data control to set the stage for the addition of a new record to the end of a file. It clears any controls bound to the data control. The actual addition takes place after Value and Update statements are executed.

ALIGNMENT The Alignment property of a text box or label affects how the text assigned to the Text property is displayed. If the Alignment property is set to 0 (the default), text is displayed left-justified; if set to 1, text is right-justified; and if set to 2, text is centered.

AND (Logical Operator) The logical expression *condition1* And *condition2* is true only if both *condition1* and *condition2* are true. For example, (3<7) And ("abc">"a") is true because 3<7 is true as is "abc">"a". Also, ("apple">"ape") And ("earth">"moon") is false because "earth">"moon"is false.

AND (Bitwise Operator) The expression *byte1* And *byte2* is evaluated by expressing each byte as an 8-tuple binary number and then Anding together corresponding digits, where 1 And 1 equals 1, 1 And 0, 0 And 1, and 0 And 0 all equal 0. For example, the expression 37 And 157 translated to binary 8-tuples becomes 00100101 And 10011101. Anding together corresponding digits gives the binary 8-tuple 00000101 or decimal 5. Thus, 37 And 157 is 5.

ARRAY If *arglist* is a comma-delimited list of values, then the value of the function Array(*arglist*) is a variant containing an array of these values. See Dim for discussion of arrays.

ASC Characters are stored as numbers from 0 to 255. If *str* is a string of characters, then Asc(*str*) is the number corresponding to the first character of *str*. For any *n* from 0 to 255, Asc(Chr(*n*)) is *n*.

ATN The trigonometric function Atn, or *arctangent*, is the inverse of the tangent function. For any number x, Atn(x) is an angle in radians between $-\pi/2$ and $\pi/2$ whose tangent is x. [radians]

AUTOREDRAW The AutoRedraw property determines what happens to graphics and Printed material on a form or picture box after another object (for example, another picture box) or program temporarily obscures part of the form or picture box. If AutoRedraw is True, then Visual Basic will restore the graphics and Printed material from a copy that it has saved in memory. If AutoRedraw is False, then Visual Basic does not keep track of graphics and Printed material that have been obscured, but it does invoke the Paint event of the form or picture box when the obstruction is removed. Thus, only graphics and Printed material generated by the Paint event will be restored when AutoRedraw is False.

AUTOSIZE If the AutoSize property of a label or picture box is True, Visual Basic automatically sets the width and height of the label so that the entire caption can be accommodated. If the AutoSize property is False, the size of the label is not adjusted by Visual Basic, and captions are clipped if they do not fit.

BACKCOLOR The BackColor property determines the background color of an object. For a command button, the background color is only valid when the style property is set to "1-Graphical." (Such a command button can display a picture.) If the BackColor of a form or picture box is changed while a program is running, all graphics and Printed text directly on the form or picture box are erased. [color]

BACKSTYLE The BackStyle property of a label or shape is opaque (1) by default. The rectangular, square, circular, or oval region associated with the control is filled with the control's background color and possibly caption. If the BackStyle is set to transparent (0), whatever is behind the control remains visible; the background color of the control essentially becomes "see through."

BEEP The statement Beep produces a sound of frequency 800 Hz that lasts a fraction of a second.

BOF When the BOF property of a data control is True, the current record position in the file is before the first record.

BOOLEAN A variable of type Boolean requires 2 bytes of memory and holds either the value True or False. If boolVar is a Boolean variable, then the statement Print boolVar displays True when the value is True and displays False when the value is False.

BORDERCOLOR The BorderColor property determines the color of a line or shape control. [color]

BORDERSTYLE The BorderStyle property determines the border style for a form [0-none, 1-fixed single, 2-sizeable (default), 3-fixed double, 4-Fixed ToolWindow, 5-Sizable Tool-Window], line or shape [0-transparent, 1-solid, 2-dash, 3-dot, 4-dash-dot, 5-dash-dot-dot, 6-inside solid], grid image, label, picture box, and text box [0-none, 1-fixed single (default)]. You cannot change the borders of forms and text boxes during run time.

BORDERWIDTH The BorderWidth property (with settings from 1 through 8192) determines the thickness of a line or shape control.

BYTE A variable of type Byte uses a single byte of memory and holds a value from 0 to 255.

CALL A statement of the form Call *ProcedureName(argList)* is used to execute the named Sub procedure, passing to it the variables and values in the list of arguments. Arrays appearing in the list of arguments should be specified by the array name followed by empty parentheses. The value of a variable argument may be altered by the Sub procedure unless the variable is surrounded by parentheses. After the statements in the Sub procedure have been executed, program execution continues with the statement following Call. *Note:* The keyword Call may be omitted. In this case, the parentheses are omitted and the statement is written *ProcedureName argList*.

CANCEL The Cancel property provides a means of responding when the user presses the Esc key. At most one command button on a form may have its Cancel property set to True. If the Esc key is pressed while the program is running, Visual Basic will execute the click event procedure of the command button whose Cancel property is True.

CAPTION The Caption property holds the text that is to appear as the caption for a form, command button, data control, or label. If an ampersand (&) is placed in the caption of a command button or label, the ampersand will not be displayed, but the character following the ampersand will become an underlined access key. Access keys provide a quick way to access a command button or the control (usually a text box) following (in tab index order) a label. Access keys are activated by holding down the Alt key and pressing the access key character.

CBOOL The function CBool converts byte, currency, double-integer, integer, long integer, and single-precision numbers to the Boolean values True or False. Nonzero values are converted to True and zero is converted to False. If x is any number, then the value of CBool(x) is the Boolean value determined by x.

CBYTE The function CByte converts integer, long integer, single-precision, double-precision, and currency numbers to byte numbers. If x is any number, then the value of CByte(x) is the byte number determined by x.

CCUR The function CCur converts byte integer, long integer, single-precision, and double-precision numbers to currency numbers. If x is any number, then the value of CCur(x) is the currency number determined by x.

CDATE The function CDate converts byte, currency, double-integer, integer, long integer, and single-precision numbers to dates. If x is any number, then the value of CDate(x) is the date determined by x.

CDBL The function CDbl converts byte, integer, long integer, single-precision, and currency numbers to double-precision numbers. If x is any number, then the value of CDbl(x) is the double-precision number determined by x.

CHANGE The Change event occurs when the contents of a combo box, directory list box, drive list box, label, picture box, scroll bar, or text box are altered in a specific way. The alterations are: (a) change of text (combo box or text box), (b) user selects a new directory or drive (directory and drive list boxes), (c) thumb moves (scroll bar), (d) change of Caption property (label), and (e) change of Picture property (picture box).

CHDIR The statement ChDir *path* changes the current directory on the specified disk drive to the subdirectory specified by *path*. For example, ChDir "C:\"specifies the root directory of the C drive as the current directory. Omitting a drive letter in *path* causes the default drive to be used. [directories]

CHDRIVE The statement ChDrive *drive* changes the default drive to the drive specified by *drive*. For example, ChDrive "A"specifies the A drive as the new default drive.

CHR If n is a number from 0 to 255, then a statement of the form *objectName*.Print Chr(n) displays the nth character of the current font.

CINT The function CInt converts byte, long integer, single-precision, double-precision, and currency numbers to integer numbers. If x is any number from –32768 to 32767, the value of CInt(x) is the (possibly rounded) integer constant that x determines.

CIRCLE The graphics method *objectName*.Circle (x, y), r, c, $r1$, $r2$, a draws on *objectName* a portion, or all, of an ellipse. The center of the ellipse is the point (x, y) and the longer radius is r. The color of the ellipse is determined by c. If $r1$ and $r2$ are present, then the computer draws only the portion of the ellipse that extends from the radius line at an angle of Abs($r1$) radians with the horizontal radius line to the radius line at an angle of Abs($r2$) radians with the horizontal radius line in a counterclockwise direction. If either $r1$ or $r2$ is negative, the computer also draws its radius line. The ratio of the length of the vertical diameter to the length of the horizontal diameter will be *a*. After the Circle method is executed, the value of *objectName*.CurrentX becomes *x* and the value of *objectName*.CurrentY becomes *y*. [color] [coordinate systems] [radians]

CLEAR   The method ClipBoard.Clear clears the clipboard, setting its contents to the null string. The statements List1.Clear and Combo1.Clear remove all items from the control's list.

CLICK   The Click event applies to check boxes, combo boxes, command buttons, directory list boxes, file list boxes, forms, frames, grids, images, labels, list boxes, menu items, OLE controls, option buttons, picture boxes, and text boxes. A Click event occurs whenever the left mouse button is pressed and released while the mouse cursor is over the control or over a blank area on the form. In the case of a command button, the Click event is also called if the spacebar or Enter key is pressed while the command button has the focus, or if the button's access key is used.

CLNG   The function CLng converts byte, integer, single-precision, double-precision, and currency numbers to long integer numbers. If x is any number from $-2,147,483,648$ to $2,147,483,647$, the value of CLng(x) is the (possibly rounded) long integer constant that x determines.

CLOSE   The statement Close #*n* closes the file that has been opened with reference number *n*. By itself, Close closes all open files. The Close method for a data control closes the database.

CLS   The method *formName*.Cls clears the form *formName* of all text and graphics that have been placed directly on the form with methods like *formName*.Print, formName.Circle, and so on. The method *pictureBox*.Cls clears the named picture box. The Cls method resets the CurrentX and CurrentY properties of the cleared object to the coordinates of the upper-left corner [usually (0, 0)].

COL and ROW   The Col and Row properties specify the current cell of a grid. The statements MSFlexGrid1.Col = *m* and MSFlexGrid1.Row = *n* specify the cell in column *m* and row *n* to be the current cell. The statement MSFlexGrid1.Text = *str* places the string into the current cell. When the user clicks on a nonfixed cell, its column number is assigned to the Col property and its row number is assigned to the Row property.

COLALIGNMENT   The statement MSFlexGrid1.ColAlignment(*m*) = *n*, aligns the text in column *m* both vertically and horizontally according to the following table.

n	Horizontally	Vertically
0	Left	Top
1	Left	Centered
2	Left	Bottom
3	Centered	Top
4	Centered	Centered
5	Centered	Bottom
6	Right	Top
7	Right	Centered
8	Right	Bottom
9	Strings left-justified Numbers right-justified	

COLOR   The value of the Color property of a Color common dialog box identifies the selected color.

COLS and ROWS The Cols and Rows properties of a grid specify the numbers of rows and columns.

COLWIDTH The statement MSFlexGrid1.Colwidth(m) = n specifies that column m of the grid be n twips wide. (There are about 1440 twips in an inch.)

CONST The statement Const *constantName* = *expression* causes Visual Basic to treat every occurrence of *constantName* as the value of the expression. This replacement takes place before any lines of the program are executed. Unlike an assignment statement, Const does not set up a location in the program's memory for a variable. A *constantName* may appear in only one Const statement and may not appear on the left side of an assignment statement. We call *constantName* a "symbolic constant" or "named constant."

CONTROL The Control data type may be used in the parameter lists of Sub and Function definitions to allow the passing of control names to the procedure.

CONTROLBOX The ControlBox property determines whether or not a form has a Control-menu button displayed in the upper left corner. If the ControlBox property is set to True (the default), the Control-menu button is displayed. Among the operations available from the ControlBox menu is the ability to close the form and thereby end the program. If the ControlBox property of a form is set to False, the Control-menu button is not displayed. Because, in this case, the user cannot end the program by using the Control-menu button or by pressing Alt+F4, it is important to provide a command button for this purpose.

CONNECT The Connect property of a data control identifies the format (such as Access, FoxPro, Dbase) of the database determined by the DatabaseName property.

COS The value of the trigonometric function Cos(x) is the cosine of an angle of x radians. [radians]

COUNT The value of *collectionName*.Count is the number of objects in the collection.

CREATEOBJECT If *appName* is the name of an application and *objectType* is the type or class of the object to create, then the value of the function CreateObject(*appName. objectType*) is an OLE Automation object. For instance, CreateObject("Excel.sheet") creates an Excel worksheet and CreateObject("Word. Basic") creates a Word document.

CSNG The function CSng converts byte, integer, long integer, and double-precision~ numbers to single-precision numbers. If x is any number, the value of CSng(x) is the single-precision number that x determines.

CSTR The function CStr converts byte, integer, long integer, single-precision, double-precision, currency, and variant numbers to strings. If x is any number, the value of CStr(x) is the string determined by x Unlike the Str function, CStr does not place a space in front of positive numbers. [variant]

CURDIR The value of the function CurDir(*drive*) is a string specifying the current directory on the drive specified by *drive*. The value of CurDir("") or CurDir is a string specifying the current directory on the default drive. [directories]

CURRENCY The currency data type is extremely useful for calculations involving money. A variable of type Currency requires 8 bytes of memory and can hold any number from −922,337,203,685,477.5808 to 922,337,203,685,477.5807 with at most four decimal places. Currency values and variables may be indicated by the type tag @: 21436587.01@, Balance@.

CURRENTX, CURRENTY The properties CurrentX and CurrentY give the horizontal and vertical coordinates of the point on a form, picture box, or the printer at which the next Print or graphics method will begin. Initially, CurrentX and CurrentY are the coordinates of the upper-left corner of the object. [coordinate systems]

CVAR The function CVar converts strings and byte, integer, long integer, single-precision~, double-precision, and currency numbers to variants. If *x* is any string or number, the value of CVar(*x*) is the variant determined by *x*. [variant]

CVDATE The function CVDate converts a numeric or string expression to an equivalent serial date. If *x* is any expression representing a valid date, the value of CVDate(*x*) is the serial date determined by *x*. Valid numeric values are –657434 (January 1, 100 AD.) to 2958465 (December 31, 9999). Valid string expressions either look like one of these valid numeric values (for example, "19497"corresponding to May 18, 1953) or look like a date (for example, "10 Feb 1955", "August 13, 1958", etc.) [date]

DATABASENAME The value of the DatabaseName property of a data control is the file-spec of the file containing the database.

DATAFIELD After the DataSource property of a data-aware control has been set to bind the control to a data control, the DataField property is set to a field of the table accessed by the data control.

DATASOURCE To bind a data-aware control to a data control at design time, set the value of the DataSource property of the data-aware control to the name of the data control.

DATE The value of the function Date is the current date. If *dateStr* is a string representing a date, the statement Date = *dateStr* changes the date as specified by *dateStr*.

DATE A variable of type Date requires 8 bytes of memory and holds numbers representing dates from January 1, 100 to December 31, 9999. Literal date values can be assigned to date variables with statements such as *dateVar* = #5/12/1999#, *dateVar* = #5 Jan, 1997#, and *dateVar* = #February 10, 2004#. However, values of *dateVar* are displayed in the form month/day/year (for example, 5/12/99).

DATESERIAL The value of the function DateSerial(*year, month, day*) is the serial date corresponding to the given year, month, and day. Values from 0 to 9999 are acceptable for *year*, with 0 to 99 interpreted as 1900 to 1999. Values of 1 to 12 for *month*, and 1 to 31 for *day* are normal, but any integer value is acceptable. Often, numeric expressions are used for *month* or *day* that evaluate to numbers outside these ranges. For example, DateSerial(1993, 2, 10 + 90) is the date 90 days after Feb. 10, 1993. [date]

DATEVALUE The value of the function DateValue(*str*) is the serial date corresponding to the date given in *str*. DateValue recognizes the following date formats: "2-10-1955", "2/10/1955", "February 10, 1955", "Feb 10, 1955", "10-Feb-1955", and "10 February 1955". For the years 1900 through 1999, the initial "19"is optional. [date]

DAY The function Day extracts the day of the month from a serial date. If *d* is any valid serial date, the value of Day(*d*) is an integer from 1 to 31 giving the day of the month recorded as part of the date and time stored in *d*. [date]

DBLCLICK The DblClick event applies to combo boxes, file list boxes, forms, frames, grids, images, labels, list boxes, OLE controls, option buttons, picture boxes, and text boxes. A DblClick event occurs whenever the left mouse button is pressed and released twice, in quick succession, while the mouse cursor is over the control or over a blank area on the form. Double-clicking on an object will first cause that object's Click event to occur, followed by its DblClick event. *Note:* When you double-click on an item in a drive list box, the item is automatically assigned to the Path property. When you double-click on an item in a file list box, the item is automatically assigned to the FileName property.

DEFAULT When the Default property of a command button is set to True and the focus is on an object that is not another command button, pressing the enter key has the same effect as clicking on the button. At most, one command button on a form can have True as the value of its Default property.

DEFINT, DEFLNG, DEFSNG, DEFDBL, DEFSTR, DEFCUR, DEFVAR, DEFBYTE, DEFBOOL, DEFDATE, DEFOBJ A variable can be assigned a type by either a type-declaration tag or an As clause. A statement of the form DefInt *letter* specifies that any "untyped" variable whose name begins with the specified letter will have integer type. A statement of the form DefInt *letter1-letter2* specifies that all "untyped" variables whose names begin with a letter in the range *letter1* through *letter2* will have integer type. The statements DefLng, DefSng, DefDbl, DefStr, DefCur, DefVar, DefByte, DefBool, DefDate, and DefObj specify the corresponding types for long integer, single-precision, double-precision, string, currency, variant, byte, boolean, date, and object variables, respectively. Def*Type* statements are placed in the (Declarations) section of (General). [variant]

DELETE The Delete method for a data control deletes the current record.

DIM The statement Dim *arrayName*(*m* To *n*) As *variableType* declares an array with subscripts ranging from *m* to *n*, inclusive, where *m* and *n* are in the normal integer range of –32768 to 32767. The *variableType* must be Integer, Long, Single, Double, Currency, String, String*n, Variant, Boolean, Byte, Date, or a user-defined type. A statement of the form Dim *arrayName*(*m* To *n*, *p* To *q*) As *variableType* declares a doubly subscripted, or two-dimensional, array. Three- and higher-dimensional arrays are declared similarly. If *m* and *p* are zero, the preceding Dim statements may be changed to Dim *arrayName*(*n*) As *variableType* and Dim *arrayName*(*n*, *q*) As *variableType*. The statement Dim *arrayName*( ) As *variableType* defines an array whose size is initially unknown but must be established by a ReDim statement before the array can be accessed. The statement Dim *variableName* As *variableType* specifies the type of data that will be stored in *variableName*. Variables and arrays Dimmed in the (Declarations) section of (General) are available to all procedures. In procedures, Dim is used to declare variables, but ReDim is often used to dimension arrays. [dynamic vs. static] [variant]

DIR If *fileTemplate* specifies a file (or a collection of files by including ? or *), then the value of the function Dir(*fileTemplate*) is the filename of the first file matching the pattern specified by *fileTemplate*. If this value is not the null string, the value of the function Dir is the name of the next file that matches the previously specified pattern. For example, the value of Dir("*.VBP") will be the name of the first file in the current directory of the default drive whose name has the .VBP extension. [directories] [filespec]

DO/LOOP A statement of the form Do, Do While *cond*, or Do Until *cond* is used to mark the beginning of a block of statements that will be repeated. A statement of the form Loop, Loop While *cond*, or Loop Until *cond* is used to mark the end of the block. Each time a statement containing While or Until followed by a condition is encountered, the truth value of the condition determines whether the block should be repeated or whether the program should jump to the statement immediately following the block. A Do loop may also be exited at any point with an Exit Do statement.

DOEVENTS Executing the statement DoEvents permits Visual Basic to act on any events may have occurred while the current event procedure has been executing.

DOUBLE A variable of type Double requires 8 bytes of memory and can hold 0, the numbers from $4.9406520 \times 2010^{-324}$ to $1.797693134862316 \times 10^{308}$ with at most 17 significant digits and the negatives of these numbers. Double values and variables may be indicated by the type tag #: 2.718281828459045#, Pi#.

DRAWMODE The property DrawMode determines whether graphics are drawn in black, white, foreground color, or some interaction of these colors with the current contents of the form or picture box. The following table lists the allowed values for the DrawMode property and the rules for what RGB color number will be assigned at a given point when the RGB color number for the color currently displayed at that point is *display* and the RGB color number for the draw color is *draw*. [color]

DrawMode	Color Produced	
1	&H00000000& (Black)	
2	Not draw And Not display	(inverse of #15)
3	display And Not draw	(inverse of #14)
4	Not draw	(inverse of #13)
5	draw And Not display	(inverse of #12)
6	Not display	(inverse of #11)
7	draw Xor display	
8	Not draw Or Not display	(inverse of #9)
9	draw And display	
10	Not (draw Xor display)	(inverse of #7)
11	display	(transparent)
12	display Or Not draw	
13	draw (draw color)	
14	draw Or Not display	
15	draw Or display	
16	&H00FFFFFF& (White)	

DRAWSTYLE When DrawWidth is 1 for a form or picture box (the default), the property DrawStyle determines whether graphics are drawn using a solid line or some combinations of dots and dashes. Use a DrawStyle of 0 (the default) for solid lines, 1 for dashed lines, 2 for dotted lines, 3 for dash-dot lines, or 4 for dash-dot-dot lines. A DrawStyle of 5 produces "invisible" graphics.

When thick lines are drawn as a result of setting DrawWidth to values greater than 1, graphics are always drawn using solid lines. In this case, DrawStyle can be used either to center the thick line over where a line with a DrawWidth of 1 would be drawn or, when drawing closed figures like ellipses and rectangles, to place the thick line just inside where the line with a DrawWidth of 1 would be drawn. To draw thick graphics inside the normal closed figure, use a DrawStyle of 6. DrawStyles 1 through 4 will center thick graphics over the normal location.

DRAWWIDTH The property DrawWidth determines the width in pixels of the lines that are drawn by graphics methods. The default is 1 pixel. Values from 1 to 32,767 are permitted.

DRIVE The Drive property of a drive list box gives the contents of the currently selected item.

ENABLED The property Enabled determines whether or not a form or control responds to events. If the Enabled property of a form or control is set to True (the default), and if an event occurs for which an event procedure has been written, the event procedure will be executed. When the Enabled property of a form or control is set to False, all events relating to that control are ignored; no event procedures are executed.

END The statement End terminates the execution of the program and closes all files. Also, the statements End Def, End Function, End If, End Select, End Sub, and End Type are used to denote the conclusion of multiline function definitions, function blocks, If blocks, Select Case blocks, Sub procedures, and user-defined, record-type declarations.

ENDDOC The method Printer.EndDoc is used to indicate that the document currently being printed is complete and should be released to the printer.

ENVIRON Visual Basic has an environment table consisting of equations of the form "*name=value*"that is inherited from DOS when Windows is invoked. If *name* is the left side of an equation in Visual Basic's environment table, then the value of the function Environ("*name*") will be the string consisting of the right side of the equation. The value of Environ(*n*) is the *n*th equation in Visual Basic's environment table.

EOF Suppose a file has been opened for sequential input with reference number *n*. The value of the function EOF(*n*) will be True (–1) if the end of the file has been reached and False (0) otherwise. [*Note:* The logical condition Not EOF(*n*) is true until the end of the file is reached.] When used with a communications file, EOF(*n*) will be true if the communications buffer is empty and false if the buffer contains data.

ERR After an error occurs during the execution of a program, the value of Err.Number will be a number identifying the type of error. Err.Number is used in conjunction with the On Error statement. If *n* is a whole number from 0 to 32,767, then the statement Err.Raise *n* generates the run-time error associated with the number *n*.

EQV The logical expression *condition1* Eqv *condition2* is true if *condition1* and *condition2* are both true or both false. For example, (1>2) Eqv ("xyz"<"a") is true because both 1>2 and "xyz"<"a" are false, whereas ("apple">"ape") Eqv ("earth">"moon") is false because "apple">"ape" is true but "earth">"moon" is false.

ERASE For static arrays, the statement Erase *arrayName* resets each array element to its default value. For dynamic arrays, the statement Erase *arrayName* deletes the array from memory. *Note:* After a dynamic array has been Erased, it may be ReDimensioned. However, the number of dimensions must be the same as before. [dynamic vs. static]

ERROR The statement Error *n* simulates the occurrence of the run-time error identified by the number *n*, where *n* may range from 1 to 32,767. It is a useful debugging tool.

ERROR The value of the function Error is the error message corresponding to the run-time error that has most recently occurred. The value of the function Error(*errNum*) is the error message corresponding to the run-time error designated by *errNum*.

EVENT A statement of the form Public Event *UserDefinedEvent*(arg1, arg2, . . .), appearing in the general declarations section of a code module, declares a user-defined event and passes the arguments to the event procedure. After this declaration is made, the RaiseEvent statement can be used to fire the event.

EXIT The Exit statement may be used in any of five forms: Exit For, Exit Sub, Exit Function, Exit Property, Exit Def, and Exit Do. The Exit statement causes program execution to jump out of the specified structure prematurely: Exit For jumps out of a For/Next loop to the statement following Next, Exit Sub jumps out of a Sub procedure to the statement following the Call statement, and so on.

EXP The value of the function Exp(*x*) is e^x, where *e* (about 2.71828) is the base of the natural logarithm function.

FALSE A keyword of Boolean type. False is used when setting the value of properties that are either True or False. For example, Picture1.Font.Italic = False.

FIELDS The Fields property of a recordset is used to read or set the Value property of the Recordset. For instance, a statement of the form Print Data1.RecordSet.Fields(*field-Name*).Value displays the value in the specified field of the current record of the database table associated with the data control. The preceding Print statement can be abbreviated to Print Data1.RecordSet(*fieldName*).

FILEATTR After a file has been opened with reference number *n*, the value of the function FileAttr (*n*, 1) is 1, 2, 4, 8, or 32 depending on whether the file was opened for Input, Output, Append, Random, or Binary, respectively. The value of the function FileAttr (*n*, 2) is the file's DOS file handle, a number that uniquely identifies the file and is used in assembly language programming.

FILECOPY The statement FileCopy *source, destination* creates the file specified by *destination* by making a copy of the file specified by *source*. Both *source* and *destination* may specify drive and path information. If the file specified by *destination* already exists, it will be overwritten without a warning being issued.

FILEDATETIME The value of the function FileDateTime(*filename*) is a string giving the date and time that the file specified by the *filename* was created or last modified.

FILELEN The value of the function FileLen(*filename*) is the length in characters (bytes) of the file specified by *filename*.

FILENAME The FileName property of a file list box is the contents of the currently selected item.

FILLCOLOR When the FillStyle property of a form or picture box is set to a value other than the default of 1, the property FillColor determines what color is used to paint the interior of ellipses and rectangles drawn with the Circle and Line graphics methods. The Fill-Color property may be assigned any valid RGB color number. The default value for FillColor is black (0). [color]

FILLSTYLE The property FillStyle determines what pattern is used to paint the interior of ellipses and rectangles drawn on forms or picture boxes with the Circle and Line methods. The default value for FillStyle is transparent (1), which means that interiors are not painted. Other values available for FillStyle are solid (0), horizontal lines (2), vertical lines (3), diagonals running upward to the right (4), diagonals running downward to the right (5), vertical and horizontal lines [crosshatched] (6), and diagonal crosshatched (7). *Note:* Using BF in a Line method has the same effect as setting the FillStyle to 0 and the FillColor to the color of the bordering line.

FINDFIRST, FINDLAST, FINDNEXT, FINDPREVIOUS A statement of the form Data1.RecordSet.Find*What criteria* selects a new current record in the table of the database associated with the data control in the expected way, based on the specifications of the string *criteria*.

FIX The value of the function Fix(*x*) is the whole number obtained by discarding the decimal part of the number *x*.

FIXEDALIGNMENT The statement MSFlexGrid1.FixedAlignment(*m*) = *n,* where *n* = 0 (left-align (default)), 1 (right-align), or 2 (centered), aligns the text in the fixed cells of the *m*th column of the grid.

FIXEDCOLS and   The FixedCols and FixedRows properties of a grid specify the number of fixed rows and fixed columns of a grid. Fixed rows and columns are used for headings and never disappear due to scrolling.

FLAGS The Flags property of a common dialog box sets a variety of options.

FONT.BOLD or **FONTBOLD** These properties determine whether the characters Printed on a form, picture box, or printer, or assigned to a text box, command button, or label appear in bold or normal type. If the property is set to True (the default), then for a form, picture box, or printer, subsequent Printed characters appear bold. For a text box, command button, or label, the text or caption is immediately changed to bold. If the property is set to False, subsequent characters are Printed in normal type and characters assigned to the text or caption property change immediately to normal type.

FONTCOUNT The value of the property Screen.FontCount is the number of fonts available for use on the screen. Similarly, the value of the property Printer. FontCount is the number of fonts available on the printer. The FontCount property is set according to your Windows environment and is generally used to determine the limit on the index for the Fonts property.

FONT.ITALIC or FONTITALIC These properties determine whether or not the characters Printed on a form, picture box, or printer, or assigned to a text box, command button, or label appear in italic or upright type. If the property is set to True, then for a form, picture box, or printer, subsequent characters appear in italic. For a text box, command button, or label, the text or caption is immediately changed to italic. If the property is set to False (the default), subsequent characters are Printed in upright type and characters assigned to the text or caption property change immediately to upright type.

FONT.NAME or FONTNAME These properties determine what type face is used when characters are Printed on a form, picture box, or printer, or assigned to a text box, command button, or label. If the property of a form, picture box, or printer is set to a font obtained from the Fonts property, all subsequently Printed characters will appear in the new type face. When the property of a text box, command button, or label is set to a new font, characters assigned to the text or caption property change immediately to the new type face.

FONTS The value of the property Screen.Fonts(*fontNum*) is the name of a screen font available in the current Windows environment. The index *fontNum* can range from 0 to Screen.FontCount–1. Similarly, the value of the property Printer.Fonts(*fontNum*) is the name of an available printer font. The values in the Fonts property are set by your Windows environment and are generally used to determine which fonts are available for setting the FontName property.

FONT.SIZE or FONTSIZE These properties determine the size, in points, of characters Printed on forms, picture boxes, and the printer or displayed in text boxes and on command buttons and labels. Available font sizes depend on your Windows environment, but will always be between 1 and 2048. Default font sizes are usually between 8 and 12 point. ***Note:*** One point equals 1/72nd of an inch.

FONT.STRIKETHROUGH or FONTSTRIKETHRU These properties determine whether or not the characters Printed on a form, picture box, or printer, or assigned to a text box, command button, or label appear in a strikethru or standard font. If the property is set to True, then for a form, picture box, or printer, subsequent Printed characters appear with a horizontal line through the middle of each character. For a text box, command button, or label, the text or caption is immediately changed so that a horizontal line goes through the middle of each character. If the property is set to False (the default), subsequent characters are Printed in standard type and characters assigned to text or caption property change immediately to standard type.

FONTTRANSPARENT The property FontTransparent determines the degree to which characters Printed to forms and picture boxes obscure existing text and graphics. If the FontTransparent property is set to True (the default), the existing text and graphics are obscured only by the dots (pixels) needed to actually form the new character. If the FontTransparent property is set to False, then all text and graphics are obscured within the character box (small rectangle surrounding a character) associated with the new character. Those dots (pixels) not needed to form the character are changed to the background color.

FONT.UNDERLINE or FONTUNDERLINE These properties determine whether or not the characters printed on a form, picture box, or printer, or assigned to a text box, command button, or label appear with an underline. If the property is set to True, then for a form, picture box, or label, subsequent characters Printed appear underlined. For a text box, command button, or label, the text or caption is immediately changed to underlined. If the property is set to False (the default), subsequent characters are Printed without underlines characters assigned to the text or caption property change immediately to nonunderlined.

FOR EACH/NEXT A multistatement block beginning with For Each *var* In *arrayName* and ending with Next *var*, where *arrayName* is an array of type variant and *var* is a variant variable, executes the statements inside the block for each element of the array.

FOR/NEXT The statement For *index* = *a* To *b* Step *s* sets the value of the variable *index* to *a* and repeatedly executes the statements between itself and the statement Next *index*. Each time the Next statement is reached, *s* is added to the value of *index*. This process continues until the value of *index* passes *b*. Although the numbers *a*, *b*, and *s* may have any numeric type, the lower the precision of the type, the faster the loop executes. The statement For *index* = *a* To *b* is equivalent to the statement For *index* = *a* To *b* Step 1. The index following the word Next is optional.

FORECOLOR The property ForeColor determines the color used to display text, captions, graphics, and Printed characters. If the ForeColor property of a form or picture box is changed, subsequent characters will appear in the new color. For a text box, command button, or label, text or caption is immediately changed to the new color. [color]

FORMAT The value of the function Format(*expression*, *str*) is a string representing *expression* (a number, date, time, or string) formatted according to the rules given by *str*. Format is useful when assigning values to the Text property and when Printing to a form, picture box, or the printer.

Numeric output can be formatted with commas, leading and trailing zeros, preceding or trailing signs (+ or –), and exponential notation. This is accomplished either by using for *str* the name of one of several predefined numeric formats or by combining in *str* one or more of the following special numeric formatting characters: #, 0, decimal point (period), comma, %, E–, and E+. The expression to be formatted can evaluate to one of the numeric types or a string representing a number.

Predefined numeric formats include "General Number," which displays a number as is; "Currency," which displays a number with a leading dollar sign and with commas every three digits to the left of the decimal, displays two decimal places, and encloses negative numbers in parentheses; "Fixed," which displays two digits to the right and at least one digit to the left of the decimal point; "Standard," which displays a number with commas and two decimal places but does not use parentheses for negative numbers; "Percent," which multiplies the value by 100 and displays a percent sign after two decimal places; and "Scientific," which displays numbers in standard scientific notation. For example, Format(–5432.352, "Currency") gives the string "($5,432.35)".

The symbol # designates a place for a digit. If the number being formatted does not need all the places provided by the #'s given in *str*, the extra #'s are ignored. The symbol 0, like #, designates a place for a digit. However, if the number being formatted does not need all the places provided by the 0's given in *str*, the character 0 is displayed in the extra places. If the number being converted has more whole part digits than there is space reserved by #'s and 0's, additional space is used as if the format string had more #'s at its beginning. For example, Format(56, "####") yields "56", Format(56, "#") yields "56", Format(0, "#") yields "", Format(56, "0000") yields "0056", Format(56, "0") yields "56", and Format(0, "0") yields "0".

The decimal point symbol (.) marks the location of the decimal place. It separates the format rules into two sections, one applying to the whole part of the number and the other to the decimal part. When included in the format string, a decimal point will always appear in the resulting string. For example, Format(56.246, "#.##") yields "56.25", Format(.246, "#.##") yields ".25", Format(.246, "0.##") yields "0.25", and Format(56.2, "0.00") yields "52.20".

The comma symbol (,) placed to the left of the decimal point between #'s and/or 0's causes commas to be displayed to the left of every third digit to the left of the decimal point, as appropriate. If commas are placed to the immediate left of the decimal point (or to the right of all #'s and 0's when the decimal-point symbol is not used), then before the number is formatted, it is divided by 1000 for each comma, but commas will not appear in the result. In order to divide by201000's and display commas in the result, use format strings like "#,#,.00", which displays the number with commas in units of thousands, and "#,#,,.00", which displays the number with commas in units of millions. For example, Format(1234000, "#,#") yields "1,234,000", Format(1234000, "#,") yields "1234", Format(1234000, "#,.")

yields "1234.", Format(1234000, "#,,.0") yields "1.2", and Format(1234000, "#,0,.0") yields "1,234.0".

The percent symbol (%) placed to the right of all #'s, 0's, and any decimal point causes the number to be converted to a percentage (multiplied by 100) before formatting and the symbol % to be displayed. For example, Format(.05624, "#.##%") yields "5.62%", and Format(1.23, "#%") yields "123%".

The symbols E+ and E− placed to the right of all #'s, 0's, and any decimal point cause the number to be displayed in scientific notation. Places for the digits in the exponent must be reserved to the right of E+ or E− with #'s or 0's. When E+ is used and the exponent is positive, a plus sign appears in front of the exponent in the result. When E− is used and the exponent is positive, no sign or space precedes the exponent. When scientific notation is used, each position reserved by #'s to the left of the decimal point is used whenever possible. For example, Format(1234.56, "#.##E+##") yields "1.23E+3", Format(1234.56, "##.##E−##") yields "12.34E2", Format(1234, "###.00E+##") yields "123.40E+1", and Format(123, "###E+00") yields "123E+00".

Date and time output can be formatted using numbers or names for months, putting the day, month, and year in any order desired, using 12-hour or 24-hour notation, and so on. This is accomplished either by letting *str* be the name of one of several predefined date/time formats or by combining in *str* one or more special date/time formatting characters. The expression to be formatted can evaluate to a number that falls within the range of valid serial dates or to a string representing a date/time.

Predefined date/time formats include "General Date," which displays a date in mm/dd/yyyy format and, if appropriate, a time in hh:mm:ss PM format; "Long Date,"which displays the day of week, the full name of month, the day, and a four-digit year; "Medium Date,"which displays the day, abbreviated month name, and two-digit year; "Short Date,"which displays "mm/dd/yy"; "Long Time,"which displays the time in hh:mm:ss PM format; "Medium Time,"which displays time in hh:mm PM format; and "Short Time,"which display time in 24-hour format as hh:mm. For example, let dt = DateSerial(55,2,10) + Time~Serial(21,45,30). Then Format(dt, "General Date") yields "2/10/55 9:45:30 PM", Format(dt, "Medium Date") yields "10-Feb-55", and Format(dt, "Short Time") yields "21:45".

Format symbols for the day, month, and year include d (day as number but no leading zero), dd (day as number with leading zero), ddd (day as three-letter name), dddd (day as full name), m (month as number but no leading zero), mm (month as number with leading zero), mmm (month as three-letter name), mmmm (month as full name), yy (year as two-digit number), and yyyy (year as four-digit number). Separators such as slash, dash, and period may be used as desired to connect day, month, and year symbols into a final format. For example, Format("August 13, 1958", "dddd, d.mmm.yy") yields "Wednesday, 13.Aug.58" and Format("July 4, 1776", "ddd: mmmm dd, yyyy") yields "Thu: July 04, 1776". Additional format symbols for dates include w (day-of-week as number 1–7), ww (week-of-year as number 1–53), q (quarter-of-year as number 1–4), y (day-of-year as number 1–366), ddddd (same as short date), and dddddd (same as long date).

Format symbols for the second, minute, and hour include s (seconds with no leading zero), ss (seconds as two-digit number), n (minutes with no leading zero), nn (minutes as two-digit number), h (hours with no leading zero), hh (hours as two-digit number), AM/PM (use 12-hour clock and uppercase), am/pm (use 12-hour clock and lowercase), A/P (use 12-hour clock and single uppercase letter), a/p (use 12-hour clock and single lowercase letter), and ttttt (same as general date). Separators such as colons and periods may be used as desired to connect hour, minute, and second symbols into a final format. For example, Format("14:04:01", "h:nn AM/PM") yields "2:04 PM", Format("14:04:01", "h.n.s") yields "14.4.1", and Format(0.75, "h:nna/p") yields "6:00p".

String output can be formatted as all uppercase, all lowercase, left-justified or right-justified. Symbols used to format strings are @ (define a field for at least as many characters as there are @ symbols; if less characters than @ symbols, fill remainder of field with spaces; if more characters than @ symbols, display the extra characters—don't clip), & (reserve space for entire output string), < (convert all characters to lowercase before displaying), > (convert all characters to uppercase before displaying), ! (left justify within field defined by @ symbols; default is to right justify). For example, Format("Red", "@") yields "Red", Format("Red", "@@@@@@") yields "Red"(3 leading spaces), Format("Red", "!>@@@@@@") yields "RED"(3 trailing spaces), and Format("Red", "<&") yields "red".

FORMATCURRENCY The value of the function FormatCurrency(*exp*) is the string representation of the expression as dollars and cents. Fractional values are preceded by a leading zero, and negative values are surrounded by parentheses instead of beginning with a minus sign. FormatCurrency(*exp*, *r*) displays a value rounded to *r* decimal places. The function has additional optional parameters. FormatCurrency(*exp*, , vbFalse) suppresses leading zeros for fractional values. FormatCurrency(*exp*, , , vbFalse) uses minus signs for negative numbers.

FORMATNUMBER The value of the function FormatNumber(*exp*, *r*) is the string representation of the expression as a number with *r* decimal places. Fractional values are preceded by a leading zero. FormatNumber(*exp*) displays a value rounded to 2 decimal places. The function has additional optional parameters. FormatNumber(*exp*, , vbFalse) suppresses leading zeros for fractional values. FormatNumber(*exp*, , vbTrue) surrounds a negative value with parentheses instead of a leading minus sign. FormatNumber(exp, , , , vbFalse) suppresses commas.

FORMATPERCENT The value of the function FormatPercent(*exp*, *r*) is the string representation of the expression as a percentage (multiplied by 100) with *r* decimal places. Fractional values are preceded by a leading zero. Format~Percent(*exp*) displays the percentage rounded to 2 decimal places. The function has additional optional parameters. FormatPercent(*exp*, , vbFalse) suppresses leading zeros for fractional values. FormatPercent(*exp*, , , vbTrue) surrounds a negative value with parentheses instead of a leading minus sign.

FREEFILE When files are opened, they are assigned a reference number from 1 to 255. At any time, the value of the function FreeFile is the next available reference number.

FROMPAGE and TOPAGE The FromPage and ToPage properties of a Print common dialog box identify the values selected for the From and To text boxes.

FUNCTION A function is a multistatement block usually beginning with a statement of the form Private Function *FunctionName*(*parList*) As *returnType*, followed on subsequent lines by one or more statements for carrying out the task of the function, and ending with the statement End Function. The parameter list, *parList*, is a list of variables through which values will be passed to the function when the function is called. Parameter types may be numeric, (variable-length) string, variant, object, user-defined record type, or array. The types of the parameters may be specified with type-declaration tags, Def*Type* statements, or As clauses. Array names appearing in the parameter list should be followed by an empty pair of parentheses. Functions are named with the same conventions as variables. The value of a variable argument used in calling a function may be altered by the function unless the variable is surrounded by parentheses. The value returned can be of any type (declared in *returnType*). Variables appearing in a function are local to the function unless they have been declared in the (Declarations) section of (General) and are not redeclared in Dim or Static statements within the function. A statement of the form Function *FunctionName*(*parList*) Static specifies that all variables local to the function be treated as static by default, that is, they are invisible outside of the function but retain their values between function calls. Functions may invoke themselves (called *recursion*) or other procedures. However, no procedure may be defined inside a function.

GET User-defined record types provide an efficient means of working with random-access files. After a user-defined record type is defined and a variable of that type, call it *recVar*, is declared, the file is opened with a length equal to Len (*recVar*). The *r*th record of the random-access file is retrieved and assigned to *recVar* with the statement Get #*n*, *r*, *recVar*.

The Get statement is also used to retrieve data from a binary file and assign it to any type of variable. Suppose *var* is a variable that holds a value consisting of *b* bytes. (For instance, if *var* is an integer variable, then *b* is 2. If *var* is an ordinary string variable, then *b* will equal the length of the string currently assigned to it.) The statement Get #*n*, *p*, *var* assigns to the variable *var*, the *b* consecutive bytes beginning with the byte in position *p* of the binary file having reference number *n*. (***Note:*** The positions are numbered 1, 2, 3, ...) If *p* is omitted, then the current file position is used as the beginning position. [binary file]

GETATTR The value of the function GetAttr(*filename*) is a number indicating the file attributes associated with the file specified by *filename*. Let *attrib* be a variable holding the value returned by GetAttr. Then the file specified by *filename* is a read-only file if *attrib* And 1 = 1, is a hidden file if *attrib* And 2 = 2, is a system file if *attrib* And 4 = 4, is a volume label if *attrib* And 8 = 8, is a directory name if *attrib* And 16 = 16, or has been modified since the last backup if *attrib* And 32 = 32. See SetAttr.

GETOBJECT If *filespec* specifies a file for an application that supports OLE Automation, then the value of the function GetObject(*filespec*) is an OLE Automation object.

GETTEXT The value of the method ClipBoard.GetText is a string containing a copy of the data currently stored in the clipboard.

GLOBAL The Global statement is used to create variables, including arrays, that are available to all procedures in all forms and BAS modules associated with a project. The Global statement must be placed in the (Declarations) section of a BAS module, and has the same structure as a Dim statement. For example, the statement `Global classList (1 to 30) As String, numStudents As Integer` creates an array and a variable for use in all procedures of the project.

GOSUB A statement of the form GoSub *lineLabel* causes a jump to the first statement following the specified line label. When the statement Return is reached, the program jumps back to the statement following the GoSub statement. The GoSub statement and its target must be in the same procedure. [line label] [subroutine]

GOTFOCUS A GotFocus event occurs when an object receives the focus, either through a user action or through code, via the SetFocus method.

GOTO The statement GoTo *lineLabel* causes an unconditional jump to the first statement after the specified line label. The GoTo statement and its target must be in the same procedure. [line label]

GRIDLINES Grid lines are the light gray lines in a grid that separate columns and rows. The GridLines property determines whether the grid lines are visible (GridLines = True) or not (GridLines = False.)

HEIGHT The property Height determines the vertical size of an object. Height is measured in units of twips. For the Printer object, Height may be read (ph = Printer.Height is OK) but not assigned (Printer.Height = 100 causes an error).

HEX If *n* is a whole number from 0 to 2,147,483,647, then the value of the function Hex(*n*) is the string consisting of the hexadecimal representation of *n*.

HIDE The Hide method removes a form from the screen.

HOUR The function Hour extracts the hours from a serial date. If *d* is any valid serial date, then the value of Hour(*d*) is a whole number from 0 to 23 indicating the hours recorded as part of the date and time store in *d*. [date]

IF (block) A block of statements beginning with a statement of the form If *condition* Then and ending with the statement End If indicates that the group of statements between If and End If are to be executed only when *condition* is true. If the group of statements is separated into two parts by an Else statement, then the first part will be executed when *condition* is true and the second part when *condition* is false. Statements of the form ElseIf *condition* may also appear and define groups of statements to be executed when alternate conditions are true.

IF (single line) A statement of the form If *condition* Then *action* causes the program to take the specified action if *condition* is true. Otherwise, execution continues at the next line. A statement of the form If *condition* Then *action1* Else *action2* causes the program to take *action1* if *condition* is true and *action2* if *condition* is false.

IF TYPEOF To test for the type of a control when the control name is passed to a procedure, use If TypeOf *controlName* Is *controlType* Then *action1* Else *action2* in either the single line or block form of the If statement. ElseIf TypeOf is also permitted. For *controlType*, use one of the control names that appear in the Form Design ToolBox (CommandButton, Label, TextBox, etc.)—for example, If TypeOf objectPassed Is Label Then. . . .

IMP The logical expression *condition1* Imp *condition2* is true except when *condition1* is true and *condition2* is false. For example, (3<7) Imp ("abc">"a") is true because both 3<7 and "abc">"a"are true, and ("apple">"ape") Imp ("earth"> "moon") is false because "apple">"ape"is true but "earth">"moon"is false. Imp is an abbreviation for "logically implies."

INDEX When a control is part of a Control array, it is identified by the number specified by its Index property.

INPUT The statement *strVar* = Input(*n*, *m*) assigns the next *n* characters from the file with reference number *m* (opened in Input or Binary mode) to *strVar*.

INPUT # The statement Input #*n*, *var* reads the next item of data from a sequential file that has been opened for Input with reference number *n* and assigns the item to the variable *var*. The statement Input #*n*, *var1*, *var2*, . . . reads a sequence of values and assigns them to the variables.

INPUTBOX The value of the function InputBox(*prompt*) is the string entered by the user in response to the prompt given by *prompt*. The InputBox function automatically displays the prompt, a text box for user input, an OK button, and a Cancel button in a dialog box in the center of the screen. If the user selects Cancel, the value of the function is the null string (""). For greater control, use the function InputBox(*prompt*, *title*, *defaultStr*, *xpos*, *ypos*), which places the caption *title* in the title bar of the dialog box, displays *defaultStr* as the default value in the text box, and positions the upper-left corner of the dialog box at coordinates (*xpos*, *ypos*) on the screen. [coordinate systems]

INSTR The value of the function InStr(*str1*, *str2*) is the position of the string *str2* in the string *str1*. The value of InStr(*n*, *str1*, *str2*) is the first position at or after the *n*th character of *str1* that the string *str2* occurs. If *str2* does not appear as a substring of *str1*, the value is 0.

INT The value of the function Int(*x*) is the greatest whole number that is less than or equal to *x*.

INTEGER A variable of type Integer requires 2 bytes of memory and can hold the whole numbers from –32,768 to 32,767. Integer values and variables may be indicated by the type tag %: 345%, Count%.

INTERVAL The Interval property of a Timer control is set to the number of milliseconds (1 to 65535) required to trigger a Timer event.

ISDATE The value of the function IsDate(*str*) is True if the string *str* represents a date between January 1, 100 and December 31, 9999. Otherwise, the value is False. [date]

ISEMPTY The value of the function IsEmpty(*v*) is True if *v* is a variable of unspecified type (that is, is a variant) that has not yet been assigned a value. In all other cases the value of IsEmpty is False. [variant]

ISNULL The value of the function IsNull(*v*) is True if *v* is a variant variable that has been assigned the special value Null. In all other cases the value of IsNull is False. [variant]

ISNUMERIC The value of the function IsNumeric(v) is True if v is a number, numeric variable, or a variant variable that has been assigned a number or a string that could be obtained by Formatting a number. In all other cases the value of IsNumeric is False. [variant]

ITEM The value of *collectionName*.Item(n) is the nth object in the named collection. The value of *collectionName*.Item(*keyString*) is the nth object in the named collection, where *keyString* is the key given to the object when it was added to the collection. If the value of n or *keyString* doesn't match an existing object of the collection, an error occurs.

ITEMDATA When you create a list or combo box, Visual Basic automatically creates a long integer array referred to as ItemData. The statement List1. ItemData(m) = n assigns the value n to the mth subscripted variable of the array. It is commonly used with the NewIndex property to associate a number with each item in a list, and thereby create a minidatabase. The ItemData property is especially useful for lists in which Sorted = True.

KEYPRESS The KeyPress event applies to command buttons, text boxes, and picture boxes. A KeyPress event occurs whenever the user presses a key while one of the preceding controls has the focus. A code identifying which key was pressed will be passed to the event procedure in the KeyAscii parameter. This information can then be used to determine what action should be taken when a given key is pressed.

KILL The statement Kill *"filespec"* deletes the specified disk file. [filespec]

LARGECHANGE When a scroll bar is clicked between the thumb and one of the arrow buttons, the Value property of the scroll bar changes by the value of the LargeChange property and the thumb moves accordingly.

LBOUND For a one-dimensional array *arrayName*, the value of the function LBound(*arrayName*) is the smallest subscript value that may be used. For any array *arrayName*, the value of the function LBound(*arrayName*, n) is the smallest subscript value that may be used for the nth subscript of the array. For example, after the statement Dim example(1 To 31, 1 To 12, 1990 To 1999) is executed, the value of LBound(example, 3) is the smallest value allowed for the third subscript of example( ), which is 1990.

LCASE The value of the string function LCase(*str*) is a string identical to *str* except that all uppercase letters are changed to lowercase.

LEFT The property Left determines the position of the left edge of a form or control. The units of measure are twips for forms. The units of measure for a control are determined by the ScaleMode property of the container (form, picture box, etc.) upon which the control has been placed, with the position of the control measured from the edge of its container using the coordinate system established by the various Scale. . . properties for the container. By default, the unit of measure for a container is twips, with a value of 0 for the Left property placing the control against the left edge of the container.

LEFT The value of the function Left(*str*, n) is the string consisting of the leftmost n characters of *str*. If n is greater than the number of characters in *str*, the value of the function is *str*.

LEN The value of Len(*str*) is the number of characters in the string *str*. If *var* is not a variable-length string variable, the value of Len(*var*) is the number of bytes needed to hold the value of the variable in memory. That is, Len(*var*) is 1, 2, 2, 4, 4, 8, or 8 for byte, Boolean, integer, long integer, single-precision, double-precision, and currency variables. Len(*var*), when *var* is a variable with a user-defined record type, is the number of bytes of memory needed to store the value of the variable. If *var* is a variant variable, Len(*var*) is the number of bytes needed to store var as a string. [variant]

LET The statement Let *var* = *expr* assigns the value of the expression to the variable. If *var* is a fixed-length string variable with length n and Len(*expr*) is greater than n, then just the first n characters of *expr* are assigned to *var*. If Len(*expr*) < n, then *expr* is padded on the right with spaces and assigned to *var*. If *var* has a user-defined type, then *expr* must be of the same type. The statement *var = expr* is equivalent to Let *var = expr*.

LINE The graphics method *objectName*.Line (*x1, y1*)–(*x2, y2*) draws a line connecting the two points. The graphics method *objectName*.Line –(*x2, y2*) draws a line from the point (*objectName*.CurrentX, *objectName*.CurrentY) to the specified point. The object *objectName* can be a form, picture box, or the Printer. The line is in color *c* if *objectName*.Line (*x1, y1*)–(*x2, y2*), *c* is executed. The statement *objectName*.Line (*x1, y1*)–(*x2, y2*), ,B draws a rectangle with the two points as opposite vertices. (If B is replaced by BF, a solid rectangle is drawn.) After a Line method is executed, the value of *objectName*.CurrentX becomes *x2* and the value of *objectName*.CurrentY becomes *y2*. [color] [coordinate systems]

LINE INPUT # After a file has been opened as a sequential file for Input with reference number *n*, the statement Line Input #*n*, *str* assigns to the string variable *str* the string of characters from the current location in the file up to the next pair of carriage return/line feed characters.

LIST The List property of a combo box, directory list box, drive list box, file list box, or list box is used to access items in the list. When one of these controls is created, Visual Basic automatically creates the string array List to hold the list of items stored in the control. The value of List1.List(*n*) is the item of List1 having index *n*. The value of List1.List (List1.ListIndex) is the item (string) currently highlighted in list box List1.

LISTCOUNT For a list or combo box, the value of List1.ListCount or Combo1.ListCount is the number of items currently in the list. For a directory list box, drive list box, or file list box, the value of *control*.ListCount is the number of subdirectories in the current directory, the number of drives on the computer, or the number of files in the current directory that match the Pattern property, respectively.

LISTINDEX The ListIndex property gives the index of the currently selected item is a combo box, directory list box, drive list box, file list box, or list box.

LOAD The Load event applies only to forms and usually occurs only once, immediately when a program starts. This is the appropriate place to put code that should be executed every time a program is run, regardless of the user's actions.

LOAD If *controlName* is the name of a control in a control array whose Index property was assigned a value during form design and *num* is a whole number that has not yet been used as an index for the *controlName*() array, then the statement Load *controlName*(*num*) copies properties of *controlName*(0) and creates the element *controlName*(*num*) of the *controlName*() array.

LOADPICTURE The statement *objectName*.Picture = LoadPicture(*pictureFile*), where *objectName* is a form or picture box, places the picture defined in the file specified by *pictureFile* on *objectName*.

LOC This function gives the current location in a sequential, random-access, or binary file. For a sequential file with reference number *n*, Loc(*n*) is the number of blocks of 128 characters read from or written to the file since it was opened. For a random-access file, Loc(*n*) is the current record (either the last record read or written, or the record identified in a Seek statement). For a binary file, Loc(*n*) is the number of bytes from the beginning of the file to the last byte read or written. For communications, the value of Loc(*n*) is the number of bytes waiting in the communications buffer with reference number *n*. [binary file]

LOCK The Lock command is intended for use in programs that operate on a network. After a file has been opened with reference number *n*, the statement Lock #*n* denies access to the file by any other process. For a random-access file, the statement Lock #*n*, *r1* To *r2* denies access to records *r1* through *r2* by any other process. For a binary file, this statement denies access to bytes *r1* through *r2*. The statement Lock #*n*, *r1* locks only record (or byte) *r1*. For a sequential file, all forms of the Lock statement have the same effect as Lock #*n*. The

Unlock statement is used to remove locks from files. All locks should be removed before a file is closed or the program is terminated. [binary file]

LOF After a file has been opened with reference number n, the number of characters in the file (that is, the length of the file) is given by LOF(n). For communications, the value of LOF(n) equals the number of bytes waiting in the communications buffer with reference number n.

LOG If x is a positive number, the value of Log(x) is the natural logarithm (base e) of x.

LONG A variable of type Long requires 4 bytes of memory and can hold the whole numbers from –2,147,483,648 to 2,147,483,647. Long values and variables may be indicated by the type tag &: 12345678&, Population&.

LOSTFOCUS A LostFocus event occurs when an object loses the focus, either through a user action or through code, via the SetFocus method.

LSET If *strVar* is a string variable, then the statement LSet *strVar* = *str* replaces the value of *strVar* with a string of the same length consisting of *str* truncated or padded on the right with spaces. LSet also can be used to assign a record of one user-defined type to a record of a different user-defined type.

LTRIM The value of the function LTrim(*str*) is the string obtained by removing all the spaces from the beginning of the string *str*. The string *str* may be either of fixed or variable length.

MAX and MIN The Max and Min properties of scroll bars give the values of horizontal (vertical) scroll bars when the thumb is at the right (bottom) and left (top) arrows, respectively.

MAXBUTTON The MaxButton property determines whether or not a form has a Maximize button in the upper-right corner. If the value of the MaxButton property is set to True (the default), a Maximize button is displayed when the program is run. The user then has the option to click on the Maximize button to cause the form to enlarge and fill the entire screen. If the value of the MaxButton property is set to False, the maximize button is not displayed when the program is run, and the user is thus unable to "maximize" the form.

MAXLENGTH The property MaxLength determines the maximum number of characters that a text box will accept. If the MaxLength property for a text box is set to 0 (the default), an unlimited number of characters may be entered in the text box.

MID The value of the function Mid(*str*, *m*, *n*) is the substring of *str* beginning with the *m*th character of *str* and containing up to *n* characters. If the parameter *n* is omitted, Mid(*str*, *m*) is all the characters of *str* from the *m*th character on. The statement Mid(*str*, *m*, *n*) = *str2* replaces the characters of *str*, beginning with the *m*th character, by the first *n* characters of the string *str2*.

MINBUTTON The MinButton property determines whether or not a form has a Minimize button in the upper-right corner. If the value of the MinButton property is set to True (the default), a Minimize button is displayed when the program is run. The user then has the option to click on the Minimize button to cause the form to be replaced by a small icon in the Taskbar at the bottom of the screen. If the value of the MinButton property is set to False, the Minimize button is not displayed when the program is run, and the user is thus unable to "minimize" the form.

MINUTE The function Minute extracts the minutes from a serial date. If d is any valid serial date, the value of Minute(d) is a whole number from 0 to 59 giving the minutes recorded as part of the date and time stored in d. [date]

MKDIR The statement MkDir *path\dirName* creates a subdirectory named *dirName~* in the directory specified by *path*. [directories]

MOD   The value of the expression *num1* Mod *num2* is the whole number remainder when *num1* is divided by *num2*. If either *num1* or *num2* is not a whole number, it is rounded to a whole number before the Mod operation is performed. If one or both of *num1* and *num2* are negative, the result of the Mod operation will have the same sign as *num1*. For example, 25 Mod 7 is 4, 18.7 Mod 3.2 is 1, –35 Mod –4 is –3, and 27 Mod –6 is 3.

MONTH   The function Month extracts the month from a serial date. If *d* is any valid serial date, the value of Month(*d*) is a whole number from 1 to 12 giving the month recorded as part of the date and time stored in *d*. [date]

MOUSEPOINTER   The property MousePointer determines what shape the mouse pointer takes when the mouse is over a particular form or control. Valid values for the MousePointer property are whole numbers from 0 to 12. A value of 0 (the default) indicates that the mouse pointer should take on the normal shape for the control it is over. (The normal shape over text boxes is an I-beam, and for a form, picture box, label, or command button it is an arrow.) Use a MousePointer value of 1 for an arrow, 2 for crosshairs, 3 for an I-beam, 4 for a small square within a square, 5 for a four-pointed arrow, 6 for a double arrow pointing up to the right and down to the left, 7 for a double arrow pointing up and down, 8 for a double arrow pointing up to the left and down to the right, 9 for a double arrow pointing left and right, 10 for an up arrow, 11 for an hourglass, and 12 for a "do not" symbol (circle with diagonal line).

MOVE   The method *objectName*.Move *xpos*, *ypos* moves the named form or control so that its upper left corner has coordinates (*xpos*, *ypos*). For forms, positioning is relative to the upper left corner of the screen. For controls, positioning is relative to the upper left corner of the form, frame, or picture box to which the control is attached. The method *objectName*.Move *xpos*, *ypos*, *width*, *height* also resizes the named form or control to be *width* units wide and *height* units high. The Move method may be used whether or not a form or control is visible. If you wish to specify just a new width for an object, you CANNOT use *objectName*.Move , , *width*. Instead, use *objectName*.Move *objectName*.Left, *objectName*.Top, *width*. Similar considerations apply for changing just *ypos*, *height*, *width* and *height*, and so on.

MOVEFIRST, MOVELAST, MOVENEXT, MOVEPREVIOUS   The data control methods MoveNext, MovePrevious, MoveLast, and MoveFirst select new current records in the expected way.

MSGBOX (Statement and Function)   The statement MsgBox *prompt* displays *prompt* in a dialog box with an OK button. The more general statement MsgBox *prompt*, *buttons*, *title* displays *prompt* in a dialog box with *title* in the Title bar and containing from one to three buttons as determined by the value of *buttons*. The value of *buttons* also determines which button is the default (has the focus) and which, if any, of four icons is displayed. The value to use for *buttons* can be computed as follows:

$$buttons = \text{set number} + \text{default number} + \text{icon number}$$

where set number, default number, and icon number are determined from the following tables:

Buttons Set	Set Number
OK	0
OK, Cancel	1
Abort, Retry, Ignore	2
Yes, No, Cancel	3
Yes, No	4
Retry, Cancel	5

Focus Default	Default Number
First Button	0
Second Button	256
Third Button	512

Icon	Icon Number
Stop sign	16
Question mark	32
Exclamation mark	48
Information	64

The value of the function MsgBox(*prompt*, *buttons*, *title*) indicates which of the displayed buttons the user pushed; in all other aspects the MsgBox statement and function act in the same manner. The values returned for each of the possible buttons pressed are 1 for OK, 2 for Cancel (or Esc), 3 for Abort, 4 for Retry, 5 for Ignore, 6 for Yes, and 7 for No.

MULTILINE The property MultiLine determines whether or not a text box can accept and display multiple lines. If the MultiLine property of a text box is set to True, then text entered in the text box will wrap to a new line when the right side of the text box is reached. Pressing the Enter key will also start a new line. If the MultiLine property of a text box is set to False (the default), input is restricted to a single line that scrolls if more input is entered than can be displayed within the width of the text box.

NAME (Property) The property Name is used at design time to give a meaningful name to a form or control. This new name will then be used by Visual Basic in naming all event procedures for the form or control.

NAME (Statement) The statement Name *"filespec1"* As *"filespec2"* is used to change the name and/or the directory of *filespec1* to the name and/or directory specified by *filespec2*. The two filespecs must refer to the same drive. [filespec]

NEW The keyword New is used with Set, to create an instance of a class. A typical statement is Set *objectVariable* As New *className*.

NEWINDEX The NewIndex property of a combo box or list box gives the index number of the item most recently added to the list.

NEWPAGE The method Printer.NewPage indicates that the current page of output is complete and should be sent to the printer.

NOT (Bitwise Operator) The expression Not *byte1* is evaluated by expressing the byte as an 8-tuple binary number and then Notting each individual digit, where Not 1 is equal to 0, while Not 0 is equal to 1. For example, the expression Not 37 translated to binary 8-tuples becomes Not 00100101. Notting each digit gives the binary 8-tuple 11011010 or decimal 218; thus Not 37 is 218.

NOT (Logical Operator) The logical expression Not *condition1* is true if *condition1* is false and false if *condition1* is true. For example, Not (3<7) is false because 3<7 is true, and Not ("earth">"moon") is true because "earth">"moon" is false.

NOTHING The keyword Nothing is used with Set to discontinue the association of an object variable with a specific object. A typical statement is Set *objectVariable* = Nothing. Assigning Nothing to an object variable releases all the system and memory resources associated with the previously referenced object when no other variable refers to it.

NOW The value of the function Now( ) is the serial date for the current date and time as recorded on the computer's internal clock. [date]

OCT If *n* is a whole number between 0 and 2,147,483,647, Oct(*n*) is the octal (that is, base 8) representation of *n*.

ON ERROR The statement On Error GoTo *lineLabel* sets up error-trapping. An error then causes a jump to the error-handling routine beginning with the first statement following the specified line label. The On Error statement and its target must be in the same procedure. [line label]

ON . . . GOSUB and ON . . . GOTO The statement On *expression* GoSub *lineLabel1*, *lineLabel2*, . . . causes a GoSub to *lineLabel1*, *lineLabel2*, . . . depending on whether the value of the expression is 1, 2, .20.20.20. Similarly, the GoTo variation causes an unconditional jump to the appropriate line label. The GoSub or GoTo statement and its target must be in the same procedure. [line label]

OPEN The statement Open "*filespec*"For *mode* As #*n* allows access to the file *filespec* in one of the following modes: Input (information can be read sequentially from the file), Output (a new file is created and information can be written sequentially to it), Append (information can be added sequentially to the end of a file), or Binary (information can be read or written in an arbitrary fashion). The statement Open "*filespec*"For Random As #*n* Len = *g* allows random-access to the file *filespec* in which each record has length *g*. Throughout the program, the file is referred to by the reference number *n* (from 1 through 255). Another variation of the Open statement is Open "LPT1"For Output As #*n*, which allows access to the printer as if it were a sequential file.

In a network environment, two enhancements to the Open statement are available. Visual Basic accesses data files in two ways: it reads from them or writes to them. When several processes may utilize a file at the same time, accurate file handling requires that certain types of access be denied to anyone but the person who has opened the file. The statement Open "*filespec*"For *mode* Lock Read As #*n* or Open "*filespec*"For Random Lock Read As #*n* Len = *g* opens the specified file and forbids any other process from reading the file as long as the file is open. Lock Write forbids any other process from writing to the file as long as the file is open. Lock Read Write forbids any other process from reading or writing to the file as long as the file is open. Lock Shared grants full access to any other process, except when a file is currently opened and locked by a process for a certain access mode, then another process attempting to open the file for the same mode will receive the message "Permission denied"and be denied access. [filespec] [binary file]

OPTION BASE After the statement Option Base *m* is executed, where *m* is 0 or 1, a statement of the form Dim *arrayName*(*n*) defines an array with subscripts ranging from *m* to *n*. Visual Basic's extended Dim statement, which permits both lower and upper subscript bounds to be specified for each array, achieves a wider range of results, making its use preferable to Option Base.

OPTION COMPARE The statement Option Compare Text, placed in the (Declarations) section of (General), causes string comparisons to be case-insensitive. Thus, if Option Compare Text is in effect, the comparison "make"= "MaKe"will be true. The statement Option Compare Binary placed in the (Declarations) section produces the default comparison rules, which are case-sensitive and use the character order given in the ANSI/ASCII character tables.

OPTION EXPLICIT If the statement Option Explicit appears in the (Declarations) section of (General), each variable must be declared before it is used. A variable is declared by appearing in a Const, Dim, Global, ReDim, or Static statement, or by appearing as a parameter in a Sub or Function definition.

OR (Bitwise Operator) The expression *byte1* Or *byte2* is evaluated by expressing each byte as an 8-tuple binary number and then Oring together corresponding digits, where 1 Or 1, 1 Or 0, and 0 Or 1 are all equal to 1, while 0 And 0 is equal to 0. For example, the expression 37 Or 157 translated to binary 8-tuples becomes 00100101 Or 10011101. Oring together corresponding digits gives the binary 8-tuple 10111101 or decimal 189. Thus, 37 Or 157 is 189.

OR (*Logical Operator*) The logical expression *condition1* Or *condition2* is true except when both *condition1* and *condition2* are false. For example, ("apple">"ape") Or ("earth">"moon") is true because "apple">"ape"is true, and (1>2) Or ("moon"<"earth") is false because both (1>2) and ("moon"<"earth") are false.

PATH The Path property for a directory list box is the contents of the currently selected item, and for a files list box is the path identifying the directory whose files are displayed.

PATHCHANGE For a files list box, the PathChange event is triggered by a change in the value of the Path property.

PATTERN The Pattern property of a files list box uses wildcard characters to determine which file names are displayed. A typical statement is File1.Pattern = "*.TXT."

PATTERNCHANGE For a files list box, the PatternChange event is triggered by a change in the value of the Pattern property.

PICTURE The property Picture allows a form, command button, option button, check box, or picture box to be assigned a picture or icon for display. If *iconOrPicture* is a file defining an icon or bitmapped picture, then *objectName*.Picture = LoadPicture(*iconOrPicture*) places the icon or picture on the object identified by *objectName*.

POINT The value of the method *objectName*.Point(x, y) is the RGB number of the color of the point with coordinates (x, y) on the form or picture box identified by *objectName*. Thus, if the point with coordinates (x, y) has been painted using color RGB(r, g, b), then the value of Point(x, y) will be $r+256*g+65536*b$. If the coordinates (x, y) identify a point that is not on *objectName*, the value of Point(x, y) will be -1. [color] [coordinate systems]

PRINT The print method is used to display data on the screen or printer. The statement *objectName*.Print *expression* displays the value of the expression at the current position of the cursor in the named object (form, picture box, or Printer) and moves the cursor to the beginning of the next line. (Numbers are displayed with a trailing space and positive numbers with a leading space.) If the statement is followed by a semicolon or comma, the cursor will not move to the next line after the display, but will move to the next position or print zone, respectively. Several expressions may be placed in the same Print method if separated by semicolons (to display them adjacent to one another) or by commas (to display them in successive zones).

PRINT # After a file has been opened as a sequential file for output or append with reference number *n*, the statement Print #*n*, *expression* places the value of the expression into the file in the same way the Print method displays it in a picture box.

PRINTER The Printer object provides access to the printer. Methods available are Print to send text to the printer, NewPage to execute a form feed to begin a new page, EndDoc to complete the printing process, and the graphics methods. Many properties available for forms and picture boxes, such as fonts and scaling, are also available for the printer.

PRINTFORM The method *formName*.PrintForm prints on the printer an image of the named form and all its contents.

PROPERTY GET/END PROPERTYA Property Get procedure is a multistatement block in a class module beginning with a statement of the form Public Property Get *name(parList)*, followed on subsequent lines by one or more statements for carrying out the task of the procedure, and ending with the statement End Property. The parameter list *parList* is a list of variables through which values will be passed to the procedure when the property value of an associated object is retrieved. The name and data type of each parameter in a Property Get procedure must be the same as the corresponding parameter in a Property Let procedure (if one exists).

PROPERTY LET/END PROPERTY A Property Let procedure is a multistatement block in a class module beginning with a statement of the form Public Property Let *name(parList)*, followed on subsequent lines by one or more statements for carrying out the task of the procedure, and ending with the statement End Property. The parameter list *parList* is a list of variables through which values will be passed to the procedure when an assignment is made to the property of an associated object. The name and data type of each parameter in a Property Let procedure must be the same as the corresponding parameter in a Property Get procedure (if one exists).

PSET The graphics method *objectName*.PSet(*x*, *y*) displays the point with coordinates (*x*, *y*) in the foreground color. The method *objectName*.PSet(*x*, *y*), *c* causes the point (*x*, *y*) to be displayed in the RGB color specified by *c*. The size of the point is determined by the value of the DrawWidth property. The actual color(s) displayed depend on the values of the Draw-Mode and DrawStyle properties. After a PSet method is executed, the value of *object-Name*.CurrentX becomes *x* and the value of *objectName*.CurrentY becomes *y*. [color] [coordinate systems]

PUT The Put statement is used to place data into a random-access file. Suppose *recVar* is a variable of a user-defined record type and that a file has been opened with a statement of the form Open *fileName* For Random As #*n* Len = Len(*recVar*). The statement Put #*n*, *r*, *recVar* places the value of *recVar* in the *r*th record of the file.

The Put statement is also used to place data into a file opened as a binary file. Suppose *var* is a variable that holds a value consisting of *b* bytes. (For instance, if *var* is an integer variable, then *b* is 2. If *var* is an ordinary string variable, then *b* will equal the length of the string currently assigned to it.) The statement Put #*n*, *p*, *var* writes the successive bytes of *var* into the *b* consecutive locations beginning with position *p* in the binary file with reference number *n*. (***Note:*** The positions are numbered 1, 2, 3, ...) If *p* is omitted, the current file position is used as the beginning position. [binary file]

QBCOLOR The function QBColor provides easy access to 16 standard colors. If *colorAttrib* is a whole number from 0 to 15, the value of the functions QBColor (*colorAttrib*) is the RGB color number associated with *colorAttrib*. The following table names the colors produced by each of the possible values of *colorAttrib*.

0 Black	4 Red	8 Gray	12 Light Red
1 Blue	5 Magenta	9 Light Blue	13 Light Magenta
2 Green	6 Brown	10 Light Green	14 Yellow
3 Cyan	7 White	11 Light Cyan	15 Intense White

RAISEEVENT After an event has been declared in the general declarations section of a class module, the statement RaiseEvent *EventName(arg1, arg2, . . .)* generates the event.

RANDOMIZE The statement Randomize automatically uses the computer's clock to seed the random-number generator. If a program includes a Randomize statement in the Form_Load event procedure, the list of numbers generated by Rnd will vary each time the program is executed. Randomize *n* seeds the generator with a number determined by *n*. If a program does not seed the random-number generator or seeds it with a set number, the list of numbers generated by Rnd will be the same each time the program is executed.

RECORDCOUNT The value of Data1.Recordset.RecordCount is the number of records in the database table associated with the data control.

RECORDSOURCE The value of the RecordSource property of a data control is the table of the database determined by the DatabaseName property. The value can also be an SQL statement used to specify a virtual table.

REDIM The statement ReDim *arrayName*(...) erases the array from memory and recreates it. The information inside the parentheses has the same form and produces the same results as that in a Dim statement. After the ReDimensioning, all elements have their default values. Although the ranges of the subscripts may be changed, the number of dimensions must be the same as in the original Dimensioning of the array. ReDim may be used only within procedures; it may not be used in the (Declarations) section of (General). To establish an array that is available to all procedures and also can be resized, Dim it with empty parentheses in the (Declarations) section of (General) and then ReDim it as needed within appropriate procedures.

REFRESH The method *objectName*.Refresh causes the named form or control to be refreshed, that is, redrawn reflecting any changes made to its properties. Generally, refreshing occurs automatically, but if not, it may be forced with the Refresh method.

REM The statement Rem allows documentation to be placed in a program. A line of the form Rem *comment* is ignored during execution. The Rem statement may be abbreviated as an apostrophe.

REMOVE A statement of the form *collectionName*.Remove *n* deletes the *n*th object from the collection and automatically reduces the object numbers from *n* on by 1 so that there is no gap in the numbers. A statement of the form *collectionName*.Remove *keyString* deletes the object identified by the key *keyString*. If the value of *n* or *keyString* doesn't match an existing object of the collection, an error occurs.

REMOVEITEM The RemoveItem method deletes items from list and combo boxes and deletes rows from grids. The statement List1.RemoveItem *n* (where *n* is 0, 1, . . .) deletes the item with index *n*. For instance, List1.RemoveItem 0 deletes the top item and List1.RemoveItem ListCount − 1 deletes the bottom item in the list. The statement MSFlexGrid1.RemoveItem *n* deletes row *n* from the grid.

RESET The statement Reset closes all open files. Using Reset is equivalent to using Close with no file reference numbers.

RESUME When the statement Resume is encountered at the end of an error-handling routine, the program branches back to the statement in which the error was encountered. The variations Resume *lineLabel* and Resume Next cause the program to branch to the first statement following the indicated line label or to the statement following the statement in which the error occurred, respectively. (The combination of On Error and Resume Next is similar to the combination GoSub and Return.) [line label]

RETURN When the statement Return is encountered at the end of a subroutine, the program branches back to the statement following the one containing the most recently executed GoSub. The variation Return *lineLabel* causes the program to branch back to the first statement following the indicated line label. [line label] [subroutine]

RGB The value of the function RGB(*red, green, blue*) is the color number corresponding to a mixture of *red* red, *green* green, and *blue* blue. This color number is assigned to color properties or used in graphics methods to produce text or graphics in a particular color. Each of the three color components may have a value from 0 to 255. The color produced using RGB(0, 0, 0) is black, RGB(255, 255, 255) is white, RGB(255, 0, 0) is bright red, RGB(10, 0, 0) is a dark red, and so on. (The value of the function RGB(*r, g, b*) is the long integer *r*+256*g*+65536*b*.) [color]

RIGHT The value of the function Right(*str, n*) is the string consisting of the rightmost *n* characters of *str*. If *n* is greater than the number of characters of *str*, then the value of the function is *str*.

RMDIR If *path* specifies a directory containing no files or subdirectories, then the statement RmDir *path* removes the directory. [directories]

RND The value of the function Rnd is a randomly selected number from 0 to 1, not including 1. The value of Int(*n*Rnd)+1 is a random whole number from 1 to* n.

ROUND The value of the function Round(*n, r*) is the number *n* rounded to *r* decimal places. If *r* is omitted, *n* is rounded to a whole number.

ROWHEIGHT The statement MSFlexGrid1.RowHeight(*m*) = *n* specifies that row *m* of the grid be *n* twips high. (There are about 1440 twips in an inch.)

RSET If *str1* is a string variable, the statement RSet *str1* = *str2* replaces the value of *str1* with a string of the same length consisting of *str2* truncated or padded on the left with spaces.

RTRIM The value of the function RTrim(*str*) is the string obtained by removing all the spaces from the end of the string *str*. The string *str* may be either fixed-length or variable-length.

SCALE The method *objectName*.Scale (*x1, y1*)–(*x2, y2*) defines a coordinate system for the form, picture box, or printer identified by *objectName*. This coordinate system has horizontal values ranging from *x1* at the left edge of *objectName* to *x2* at the right edge and vertical values ranging from *y1* at the top edge of *objectName* to *y2 at the bottom edge. Subsequent graphics methods and control positioning place figures and controls in accordance with this new coordinate system. As a result of using the Scale method, the ScaleMode property of* objectName is set to 0, the ScaleLeft property to *x1*, the ScaleTop property to *y1*, the Scale-Height property to *y2–y1*, and the ScaleWidth property to *x2–x1*. The method *object-Name*.Scale without arguments resets the coordinate system of *objectName* to the default coordinate system where the unit of measure is twips and the upper-left corner of *object-Name* has coordinates (0, 0).

SCALEHEIGHT The property ScaleHeight determines the vertical scale on a form or picture box. After the statement *objectName*.ScaleHeight = *hght* is executed, the vertical coordinates range from *objectName*.ScaleTop at the top edge of *objectName* to *objectName*.ScaleTop + *hght* at the bottom edge. The default value of the ScaleHeight property is the height of *objectName* when measured in the units specified by *objectName's* ScaleMode property.

SCALELEFT The property ScaleLeft determines the horizontal coordinate of the left edge of a form or picture box. After the statement *objectName*.ScaleLeft = *left* is executed, the horizontal coordinates will range from *left* at the left edge of *objectName* to *left + object-Name*.ScaleWidth at the right edge. The default value of the ScaleLeft property is 0.

SCALEMODE The property ScaleMode determines the horizontal and vertical unit of measure for the coordinate system on a form or picture box. If the ScaleMode property of a form or picture box is set to 1 (the default), the unit of measure becomes twips. Other possible values for ScaleMode are 2 for points (72 points = 1 inch), 3 for pixels, 4 for characters (1 horizontal unit = 120 twips; 1 vertical unit = 240 twips), 5 for inches, 6 for millimeters, and 7 for centimeters. A value of 0 for the ScaleMode property indicates that units of measure are to be determined from the current settings of the ScaleHeight and ScaleWidth properties. Visual Basic automatically sets the ScaleMode property of an object to 0 when any of the object's Scale... properties are assigned values.

SCALETOP The property ScaleTop determines the vertical coordinate of the top edge of a form or picture box. After the statement *objectName*.ScaleTop = *top* is executed, the vertical coordinates range from *top* at the top edge of *objectName* to *top + objectName*.ScaleHeight at the bottom edge. The default value for the ScaleTop property is 0.

SCALEWIDTH The property ScaleWidth determines the horizontal scale on a form or picture box. After the statement *objectName*.ScaleWidth = *wdth* is executed, the horizontal coordinates range from *objectName*.ScaleLeft at the left edge of *objectName* to *objectName*.ScaleLeft + *wdth* at the right edge. The default value of the ScaleWidth property is the width of *objectName* when measured in the units specified by *objectName's* Scale-Mode property.

SCROLLBARS The ScrollBars property of a grid or text box specifies whether the control has horizontal (setting = 1), vertical (setting = 2), both (setting = 3), or no (setting = 0) scroll bars. In order for a text box to have scroll bars, the MultiLine property must be set to True.

SECOND The function Second extracts the seconds from a serial date. If *d* is any valid serial date, the value of Second(*d*) is a whole number from 0 to 59 giving the seconds recorded as part of the date and time stored in *d*. [date]

SEEK The statement Seek #*n*, *p* sets the current file position in the binary or random-access file referenced by *n* to the *p*th byte or record of the file, respectively. After the statement is executed, the next Get or Put statement will read or write bytes, respectively, beginning with the *p*th byte or record. The value of the function Seek(*n*) is the current file position either in bytes or by record number. After a Put or Get statement is executed, the value of Seek(*n*) is the number of the next byte or record. [binary file]

SELECT CASE The Select Case statement provides a compact method of selecting for execution one of several blocks of statements based on the value of an expression. The Select Case block begins with a line of the form Select Case *expression* and ends with the statement End Select. In between are clauses of the form Case *valueList* and perhaps the clause Case Else. The items in the *valueList* may be individual values or ranges of values such as "*a* To *b*"or "Is < *a*". Each of these Case statements is followed by a block of zero or more statements. The block of statements following the first Case *valueList* statement for which *valueList* includes the value of *expression* is the only block of statements executed. If none of the value lists includes the value of expression and a Case Else statement is present, then the block of statements following the Case Else statement is executed.

SENDKEYS The statement SendKeys *str* places in the keyboard buffer the characters and keystrokes specified by *str*. The effect is exactly the same as if the user had typed the series of characters/keystrokes at the keyboard. The statement SendKeys *str*, True places keystrokes in the keyboard buffer and waits until these keystrokes are processed (used) before allowing program execution to continue with the next statement in the procedure containing the SendKeys statement. Keystrokes can be specified that do not have a displayable character or that result from using the Shift, Ctrl, or Alt keys.

SET Essentially, Set is "Let for objects." Whereas the Let statement is used to assign ordinary values to variables or properties, the Set statement is used to assign objects to variables or properties.

The statement Set *controlVar* = *objectExpression* associates the name *controlVar* with the object identified by *objectExpression*. For example, if the statements Dim Scenery As PictureBox and Set Scenery = Picture1 are executed, then Scenery becomes another name for Picture1, and references like Scenery.Print *message* are equivalent to Picture1.Print *message*. Also, the Set statement assigns an object to an object variable. When you want to release the memory used for the object, execute Set *objVar* = Nothing.

SETATTR The statement SetAttr *fileName*, *attribute* sets the file attribute of the file specified by *fileName*. A file's attribute can be 0 for "Normal"or a combination of 1, 2, or 4 for "Read-only", "Hidden", and "System." In addition, a file can be marked as "changed since last backup"by adding 32 to its attribute. Thus, for example, if a file's attribute is set to 35 (1 + 2 + 32), the file is classified as a Read-only Hidden file that has been changed since the last backup.

SETFOCUS The method *objectName*.SetFocus moves the focus to the named form or control. Only the object with the focus can receive user input from the keyboard or the mouse. If *objectName* is a form, the form's default control, if any, receives the focus. Disabled and invisible objects cannot receive the focus. If an attempt is made to set focus to a control that cannot receive the focus, the next control in tab order receives the focus.

SETTEXT The method ClipBoard.SetText *info* replaces the contents of the clipboard with the string *info*.

SGN The value of the function Sgn(*x*) is 1, 0, or −1, depending on whether *x* is positive, zero, or negative, respectively.

SHELL If *command* is a DOS command, the function Shell(*command*) causes *command* to be executed. If the DOS command requires user input, execution of the Visual Basic program will be suspended until the user input is supplied. Using the function Shell with no arguments suspends program execution and invokes a copy of DOS. Entering the command Exit resumes execution of the Visual Basic program. The value returned by the Shell function is a number used by Windows to identify the new task being performed.

SHOW The Show method makes an invisible form visible. The statement Form1.Show 1 also makes a form modal. No user input to any other form will be accepted until the modal form is hidden.

SIN For any number *x*, the value of the trigonometric function Sin(*x*) is the sine of the angle of *x* radians. [radians]

SINGLE A variable of type Single requires 4 bytes of memory and can hold 0, the numbers from 1.40129×10^{-45} to 3.40283×10^{38} with at most seven significant digits, and the negatives of these numbers. Single values and variables may be indicated by the type tag !: 32.156!, Meters!.

SMALLCHANGE When a scroll bar arrow button is clicked, the Value property of the scroll bar changes by the value of the SmallChange property and the thumb moves accordingly.

SORTED When the Sorted property of a list or combo box is set to True, the items are automatically presented in alphabetical order.

SPACE If *n* is an integer from 0 to 32767, the value of the function Space(*n*) is the string consisting of *n* spaces.

SPC The function Spc is used in Print and Print# statements to generate spaces. For instance, the statement Print *str1*; Spc(*n*); *str2* skips *n* spaces between the displays of the two strings.

SQR For any nonnegative number *x*, the value of the square root function Sqr(*x*) is the nonnegative number whose square is *x*.

STATIC A statement of the form Static *var1*, *var2*, .20.20. can be used at the beginning of the definition of a procedure to specify that the variables *var1*, *var2*, .20.20. are static local variables in the procedure. Memory for static variables is permanently set aside by Visual Basic, allowing static variables to retain their values between successive calls of the procedure. The type of each variable is either determined by a Def*Type* statement, a type-declaration tag, or an As clause. Static variables have no connection to variables of the same name outside the procedure, and so may be named without regard to "outside" variables. Arrays created in a procedure by Dim or ReDim are lost when the procedure is exited. Arrays that are local to a procedure yet retained from one invocation of the procedure to the next can be created by dimensioning the array in the procedure with a Static statement rather than a Dim or ReDim statement. Dimensions for static arrays must be numeric constants. A local static array whose size is to be determined at run time is declared by listing its name followed by empty parentheses in a Static statement, and then dimensioning the array in a subsequent ReDim statement.

STOP The statement Stop suspends the execution of a program. Execution can be resumed beginning with the first statement after the Stop statement by pressing F5.

STR The Str function converts numbers to strings. The value of the function Str(*n*) is the string consisting of the number *n* in the form normally displayed by a print statement.

STRCOMP The value of the function StrComp(*str1*, *str2*, *compMode*) is −1, 0, 1, or Null, depending on whether *str1* < *str2*, *str1* = *str2*, *str1* > *str2*, or either of *str1* and *str2* is Null. The comparison will be case-sensitive if *compMode* is 0 and case-insensitive if *compMode* is 1.

STRCONV The value of StrConv(*str*, 3) is the value of *str* with the first letter of every word converted to uppercase. The value of StrConv(*str*, 1) is the same as UCase(*str*) and the value of StrConv(*str*, 2) is the same as LCase(*str*).

STRETCH When the Stretch property of an image control is set to False (the default value), the image control will hold the picture at its normal size. If the Stretch property is set to True, the picture will be resized to fit the image control

STRING A variable of type String can hold a string of up to 32,767 characters. String values are enclosed in quotes: "January 1, 2001". String variables can be indicated by the type tag $: FirstName$. A variable of type String*n holds a string of *n* characters, where *n* is a whole number from 1 to 32,767. Variables of this type have no type tag and must be declared in a Dim, Global, or Static statement. Until assigned a value, these variables contain a string of *n* Chr(0)'s.

STRING If *n* is a whole number from 0 to 32767, the value of String(*n*, *str*) is the string consisting of the first character of *str* repeated *n* times. If *m* is a whole number from 0 to 255, the value of the function String(*n*, *m*) is the string consisting of the character with ANSI value *m* repeated *n* times.

STYLE The Style property of a combo box determine whether the list is always visible (Style = 1) or whether the list drops down when the user clicks on the arrow and then disappears after a selection is made (Style = 0).

SUB/END SUB A Sub procedure is a multistatement block beginning with a statement of the form Sub *ProcedureName(parList)*, followed on subsequent lines by one or more statements for carrying out the task of the Sub procedure, and ending with the statement End Sub. The parameter list *parList* is a list of variables through which values will be passed to the Sub procedure whenever the function is called. (See the discussion of Call.) Parameters may be numeric or (variable-length) string variables as well as arrays.

TAB The function Tab(*n*) is used in Print and Print# statements to move the cursor to position *n* and place spaces in all skipped-over positions. If *n* is less than the cursor position, the cursor is moved to the *n*th position of the next line.

TABINDEX The property TabIndex determines the order in which the tab key moves the focus about the objects on a form. Visual Basic automatically assigns successive tab indexes as new controls are created at design time. Visual Basic also automatically prevents two controls on the same form from having the same tab index by renumbering controls with higher tab indexes when the designer or program directly assigns a new tab index to a control.

TAN For any number *x* (except for *x* = p/2, –p/2, 3 * p/2, –3 * p/2, and so on), the value of the trigonometric function Tan(*x*) is the tangent of the angle of *x* radians. [radians]

TEXT For a text box, the Text property holds the information assigned to a text box. A statement of the form *textBoxName*.Text = *str* changes the contents of *textBoxName* to the string specified by *str*. A statement of the form *str* = *textBoxName*.Text assigns the contents of *textBoxName* to *str*. For a list or combo box, *control*.Text is the contents of the currently highlighted item or the item in the text box, respectively. For a grid, MSFlexGrid1.Text is the contents of the active cell.

TEXTHEIGHT This method applies to forms, picture boxes, and printer objects. The value of the method *objectName*.TextHeight(*str*) is the amount of vertical space required to display the contents of *str* using the font currently assigned for *objectName*. These contents may include multiple lines of text resulting from the use of carriage-return/line-feed pairs (Chr(13) + Chr(10)) in *str*. The units of height are those specified by the ScaleMode and ScaleHeight properties of *objectName*. (The default is twips.)

TEXTWIDTH This method applies to forms, picture boxes, and printer objects. The value of the method *objectName*.TextWidth(*strVar*) is the amount of horizontal space required to display the contents of *strVar* using the font currently assigned for *objectName*. When carriage return/line feed pairs (Chr(13) + Chr(10)) create multiple lines in *strVar*, this will be the space required for the longest line.

TIME The value of the function Time is the current time expressed as a string of the form hh:mm:ss. (The hours range from 0 to 23, as in military time.) If *timeStr* is such a string, the statement Time = *timeStr* sets the computer's internal clock to the corresponding time.

TIMER The value of the function Timer is the number of seconds from midnight to the time currently stored in the computer's internal clock.

TIMER The Timer event is triggered by the passage of the amount of time specified by the Interval property of a timer control whose Enabled property is set to True.

TIMESERIAL The value of the function TimeSerial(*hour, minute, second*) is the serial date corresponding to the given hour, minute, and second. Values from 0 (midnight) to 23 (11 p.m.) for *hour*, and 0 to 59 for both *minute* and *second* are normal, but any Integer value may be used. Often, numeric expressions are used for *hour*, *minute*, or *second* that evaluate to numbers outside these ranges. For example, TimeSerial(15–5, 20–30, 0) is the serial time 5 hours and 30 minutes before 3:20 p.m.

TIMEVALUE The value of the function TimeValue(*str*) is the serial date corresponding to the time given in *str*. TimeValue recognizes both the 24-hour and 12-hour time formats: "13:45:24"or "1:45:24PM".

TOP The property Top determines the position of the top edge of a form or control. The units of measure are twips for forms. The units of measure for a control are determined by the ScaleMode property of the container (form, picture box, etc.) on which the control has been placed, with the position of the control measure from the edge of its container using the coordinate system established by the various Scale... properties for the container. By default, the unit of measure for a container is twips, with a value of 0 for the Top property placing the control against the top edge of the container.

TRIM The value of the function Trim(*str*) is the string obtained by removing all the spaces from the beginning and end of the string *str*. The string *str* may be either fixed-length or variable-length.

TRUE A keyword of the Boolean type. True is used when setting the value of properties that are either True or False. For example, Picture1.Font.Italic = True.

TYPE/END TYPE A multistatement block beginning the Type *typeName* and ending with End Type creates a user-defined record type. Each statement inside the block has the form *elt* As *type*, where *elt* is a variable and *type* is either Integer, Boolean, Byte, Date, Long, Single, Double, Currency, Variant, String*n (that is, fixed-length string), or another user-defined record type. After a statement of the form Dim *var* As *typeName* appears, the element corresponding to the statement *elt* As *type* is referred to as *var.elt*. Type declaration blocks must be placed in the (Declarations) section of a BAS module. [variant]

TYPENAME If var is variable, then the value of the function TypeName(var) is a string identifying the type of the variable. The possible values of the function are Byte, Integer, Long, Single, Double, Currency, Date, String, Boolean, Error, Empty (uninitialized), Null (no valid data), Object (an object that supports OLE Automation), Unknown (an OLE Automation object whose type is unknown), and Nothing (an object variable that doesn't refer to an object).

UBOUND For a one-dimensional array *arrayName*, the value of the function UBound(*arrayName*) is the largest subscript value that may be used. For any array *arrayName*, the value of the function UBound(*arrayName, n*) is the largest subscript value that may be used for the *n*th subscript of the array. For example, after the statement Dim example(1 To 31, 1 To 12, 1990 To 1999) is executed, the value of UBound(example, 3) is the largest value allowed for the third subscript of example( ), which is 1999.

UCASE The value of the string function UCase(*str*) is a string identical to *str* except that all lowercase letters are changed to uppercase.

UNLOCK The Unlock command is intended for use in programs that operate on a network. After a Lock statement has been used to deny access to all or part of a file (see the discussion of Lock for details), a corresponding Unlock statement can be used to restore access. Suppose a data file has been opened as reference number n. The locks established by the statements Lock #n; Lock #n, r1; and Lock #n, r1 To r2 are undone by the statements Unlock #n; Unlock #n, r1; and Unlock #n, r1 To r2, respectively. There must be an exact correspondence between the locking and the unlocking statements used in a program, that is, each set of paired statements must refer to the same range of record numbers or bytes.

UPDATE The Update method of a data control is used to save changes made to the database.

VAL The Val function is used to convert strings to numbers. If the leading characters of the string *str* corresponds to a number, then Val(*str*) will be the number represented by these characters. For any number n, Val(Str(n)) is n.

VALIDATE The Validate event procedure is activated whenever the current record of a database table is about to be changed. The heading of the procedure has the form Private Sub Data1_Validate(Action As Integer, Save As Integer), where the value of Action identifies the specific operation that triggered the event and the value of Save specifies whether data bound to the control has changed. You can change the value of the Action argument to convert one operation into another.

VALUE The Value property of a scroll bar is a number between the values of the Min and Max properties of the scroll bar that is related to the position of the thumb. The Value property of an option button is True when the button is on and False when the button is off. The Value property of a check box is 0 (unchecked), 1 (checked), or 2 (grayed). The Value property of Fields("*fieldName*") reads the contents of a field of the current record.

VARIANT A variable of type variant can be assigned numbers, strings, and several other types of data. Variant variables are written without type-declaration tags. [variant]

VARTYPE The value of the function VarType(*var*) is a number indicating the type of value stored in *var*. This function is primarily used to check the type of data stored in a variant variable. Some values returned by VarType are 0 for "Empty," 1 for "Null," 2 for Integer, 3 for Long Integer, 4 for Single Precision, 5 for Double Precision, 6 for Currency, 7 for Date, 8 for String, 9 for OLE Automation object, 10 for Error, 11 for Boolean, 13 for Non-OLE Automation object, and 17 for Byte. For nonvariant arrays, the number assigned is 8192 plus the number assigned to the type of the array. [variant]

VISIBLE The property Visible determines whether or not a form or control is displayed. If the Visible property of an object is True, the object will be displayed (if not covered by other objects) and respond to events if its Enabled property is True. If the Visible property of an object is set to False, the object will not be displayed and cannot respond to events.

WEEKDAY The value of the function WeekDay(*d*) is a number giving the day of the week for the date store in *d*. These values will range from 1 for Sunday to 7 for Saturday.

WHILE/WEND A While ... Wend loop is a sequence of statements beginning with a statement of the form While *condition* and ending with the statement Wend. After the While statement is executed, the computer repeatedly executes the entire sequence of statements inside the loop as long as the condition is true.

WIDTH (Property) The property Width determines the horizontal size of an object. Width is measured in units of twips. For the Printer object, Width may be read (pw = Printer.Width is OK) but not assigned (Printer.Width = 100 causes an error).

WIDTH (Statement) If s is an integer less than 255 and n is the reference number of a file opened in sequential mode, the statement Width #n, s causes Visual Basic to permit at most s characters to be printed on a single line in the file. Visual Basic will send a carriage-return/line-feed pair to the file after s characters have been printed on a line, even if the Print # or Write # statement would not otherwise start a new line at that point. The statement Width

#n, 0 specifies infinite width, that is, a carriage return/line feed pair will be sent to the printer only when requested by Print # or Write #.

WITH/END WITH A multistatement block begun by With *recName* or With *objName* and ended by End With is used to assign values to the fields of the named record variable or to properties of the named object. The statements inside the block have the form *.fieldName = fieldValue* or *.propertyName = propertyValue*. When you use this block, you only have to refer to the record variable or object once instead of referring to it with each assignment.

WITHEVENTS If a class has events attached to it, and form code intends to make use of these events, then the keyword WithEvents should be inserted into the statement declaring an instance of the class. A typical declaration statement is Private WithEvents *objectVariable* As *className*.

WORDWRAP The WordWrap property of a label with AutoSize property set to True determines whether or not long captions will wrap. (When a label's AutoSize property is False, word wrap always occurs, but the additional lines will not be visible if the label is not tall enough.) Assume a label's AutoSize property is True. If its WordWrap property is set to True, long captions will wrap to multiple lines; if its WordWrap property is False (the default), the caption will always occupy a single line. If a label has its WordWrap and AutoSize properties set to True, the label's horizontal length is determined by the length of its longest word, with long captions being accommodated by having the label expand vertically so that word wrap can spread the caption over several lines. If a label's WordWrap property is set to False while its AutoSize property is True, the label will be one line high and will expand or shrink horizontally to exactly accommodate its caption.

WRITE # After a sequential file is opened for output or append with reference number *n*, the statement Write #*n*, *exp1*, *exp2*, . . . records the values of the expressions one after the other into the file. Strings appear surrounded by quotation marks, numbers do not have leading or trailing spaces, all commas in the expressions are recorded, and the characters for carriage return and line feed are placed following the data.

XOR (Logical Operator) The logical expression *condition1* Xor *condition2* is true if *condition1* is true or *condition2* is true, but not if both are true. For example, (3<7) Xor ("abc">"a") is false because both 3<7 and "abc">"a" are true, and ("apple">"ape") Xor ("earth">"moon") is true because "apple">"ape" is true and "earth">"moon" is false.

XOR (Bitwise Operator) The expression *byte1* Xor *byte2* is evaluated by expressing each byte as an 8-tuple binary number and then Xoring together corresponding digits, where 1 Xor 0 and 0 Xor 1 both equal 1, while 1 Xor 1 and 0 Xor 0 both equal 0. For example, the expression 37 Xor 157 translated to binary 8-tuples becomes 00100101 Xor 10011101. Xoring together corresponding digits gives the binary 8-tuple 10111000 or decimal 184. Thus, 37 Xor 157 is 184.

YEAR The function Year extracts the year from a serial date. If *d* is any valid serial date, then the value of Year(*d*) is a whole number from 100 to 9999 giving the year recorded as part of the date and time stored in *d*. [date]

SUPPORTING TOPICS

[BINARY FILE]: A file that has been opened with a statement of the form Open "*filespec*" For Binary As #*n* is regarded simply as a sequence of characters occupying positions 1, 2, 3, ... At any time, a specific location in the file is designated as the "current position." The Seek statement can be used to set the current position. Collections of consecutive characters are written to and read from the file beginning at the current position with Put and Get statements, respectively. After a Put or Get statement is executed, the position following the last position accessed becomes the new current position.

[COLOR]: Numbers written in base 16 are referred to as hexadecimal numbers. They are written with the digits 0, 1, 2, 3, 4, 5, 6, 7, 8, 9, A (=10), B (=11), C (=12), D (=13), E (=14), and F (=15). A hexadecimal number such as *rst* corresponds to the decimal integer $t + 16 * s + 16 * r$. Each color in Visual Basic is identified by a long integer (usually expressed as a hexadecimal number of the form &H...&) and referred to as an RGB color number. This number specifies the amounts of red, green, and blue combined to produce the color. The amount of any color is a relative quantity, with 0 representing none of the color and 255 representing the maximum available. Thus, black corresponds to 0 units each of red, green, and blue, and white corresponds to 255 units each of red, green, and blue. The RGB color number corresponding to *r* units of red, *g* units of green, and *b* units of blue is $r + 256 * g + 65536 * b$, which is the value returned by the function RGB(r, g, b). Hexadecimal notation provides a fairly easy means of specifying RGB color numbers. If the amount of red desired is expressed as a two-digit hexadecimal number, *rr*, the amount of green in hexadecimal as *gg*, and the amount of blue in hexadecimal as *bb*, then the RGB color number for this color is &H00*bbggrr*&. For example, the RGB color number for a bright green would come from 255 (FF in hexadecimal) units of green, so the RGB color number in hexadecimal is &H0000FF00&.

[COORDINATE SYSTEMS]: The default coordinate system for a form, picture box, or the printer defines the upper-left corner as the point (0, 0). In this coordinate system, the point (*x, y*) lies *x* units to the right of and *y* units below the upper-left corner. The unit of measure in the default coordinate system is a twip. A twip is defined as 1/1440 of an inch (though varying screen sizes may result in 1440 twips not appearing as exactly an inch on the screen). Custom coordinate systems can be created using the Scale method and ScaleMode property.

[DATE]: Functions dealing with dates and times use the type 7 variant data type. Dates and times are stored as serial dates, double-precision numbers, with the whole part recording the date and the decimal part recording the time. Valid whole parts range from –657434 to 2958465, which correspond to all days from January 1, 100 to December, 31, 9999. A whole part of 0 corresponds to December 30, 1899. All decimal parts are valid, with .0 corresponding to midnight, .25 corresponding to 6 a.m., .5 corresponding to noon, and so on. In general, the decimal equivalent of *sec*/86400 corresponds to *sec* seconds past midnight. If a given date corresponds to a negative whole part, then times on that day are obtained by adding a negative decimal part to the negative whole part. For example, October, 24, 1898, corresponds to a whole part of –432. A time of 6 p.m. corresponds to .75, so a time of 6 p.m. on 10/24/1898 corresponds to –432 +–.75 = –432.75.

[DIRECTORIES]: Think of a disk as a master folder holding other folders, each of which might hold yet other folders. Each folder, other than the master folder, has a name. Each folder is identified by a *path:* a string beginning with a drive letter, a colon, and a backslash character, ending with the name of the folder to be identified, and listing the names of the intermediate folders (in order) separated by backslashes. For instance the path "C:\DAVID\GAMES" identifies the folder GAMES, which is contained in the folder DAVID, which in turn is contained in the master folder of drive C.

Each folder is called a *directory* and the master folder is called the *root directory*. When a folder is opened, the revealed folders are referred to as its *subdirectories*. Think of a file as a piece of paper inside one of the folders. Thus, each directory contains files and subdirectories.

[DYNAMIC VS. STATIC ARRAYS]: Visual Basic uses two methods of storing arrays: dynamic and static. The memory locations for a static array are set aside the instant the program is executed and this portion of memory may not be freed for any other purpose. The memory locations for a dynamic array are assigned when a particular procedure requests that an array be created (a Dim or ReDim statement is encountered) and *can* be freed for other purposes. Although dynamic arrays are more flexible, static arrays can be accessed faster. Arrays Dimensioned in the (Declarations) section of (General) use static allocation, except for arrays declared using empty parentheses. Arrays created in procedures use dynamic allocation.

[FILESPEC]: The filespec of a file on disk is a string consisting of the letter of the drive, a colon, and the name of the file. If directories are being used, the file name is preceded by the identifying path.

[LINE LABEL]: Program lines that are the destinations of statements such as GoTo and GoSub are identified by placing a line label at the beginning of the program line or alone on the line proceeding the program line. Line labels may be placed only at the beginning of a line, are named using the same rules as variable, and are followed by a colon. Line numbers may be used in place of line labels, but program readability is greatly improved by using descriptive line labels.

[RADIANS]: The radian system of measurement measures angles in terms of a distance around the circumference of the circle of radius 1. If the vertex of an angle between 0 and 360 degrees is placed at the center of the circle, the length of the arc of the circle contained between the two sides of the angle is the radian measure of the angle. An angle of d degrees has a radian measure of (pi/180) * d radians.

[SUBROUTINE]: A subroutine is a sequence of statements beginning with a line label and ending with a Return statement. A subroutine is meant to be branched to by a GoSub statement and is usually placed after an Exit Sub or Exit Function statement at the bottom of a procedure so that it cannot be entered inadvertently.

[VARIANT]: Variant is a generic variable type. Any variable that is used without a type declaration tag ($, %, &, !, #, @) or without being declared as a specific type using an As clause or a Def*Type* statement is treated as a variant variable. A variable of type Variant can hold any type of data. When values are assigned to a variant variable, Visual Basic keeps track of the "type" of data that has been stored. Visual Basic recognizes many types of data: type 0 for "Empty" (nothing yet has been stored in the variable; the default), type 1 for "Null" (the special value Null has been assigned to the variable), type 2 for Integer, type 3 for Long integer, type 4 for Single precision, type 5 for Double precision, type 6 for Currency, type 7 for Date/time, type 8 for String, type 10 for Error, type 11 for Boolean, and type 17 for Byte. A single variant variable may be assigned different data types at different points in a program, although this is usually not a good programming technique. The data assigned to a variant array need not all be of the same type. As a result, a variant array can be used in much the same way as a user-defined type to store related data.

APPENDIX D

VISUAL BASIC DEBUGGING TOOLS

Errors in programs are called *bugs* and the process of finding and correcting them is called *debugging*. Since Visual Basic does not discover errors due to faulty logic, they present the most difficulties in debugging. One method of discovering a logical error is by **desk-checking**, that is, tracing the values of variables on paper by writing down their expected value after "mentally executing" each line in the program. Desk checking is rudimentary and highly impractical except for small programs.

Another method of debugging involves placing Print methods at strategic points in the program and displaying the values of selected variables or expressions until the error is detected. After correcting the error, the Print methods are removed. For many programming environments, desk checking and Print methods are the only debugging methods available to the programmer.

The Visual Basic debugger offers an alternative to desk checking and Print methods. It allows you to pause during the execution of your program in order to view and alter values of variables. These values can be accessed through the Immediate, Watch, and Locals windows, known collectively as the three Debug windows.

THE THREE PROGRAM MODES

At any time, a program is in one of three modes[\m]design mode, run mode, or break mode. The current mode is displayed in the Visual Basic title bar.

Title bar during design time.

Title bar during run time.

Title bar during break mode.

At design time you place controls on a form, set their initial properties, and write code. Run time is initiated by pressing the Start button. Break mode is invoked automatically when a run-time error occurs. While a program is running, you can manually invoke Break mode by pressing Ctrl+Break, clicking on Break in the Run menu, or clicking on the Break icon ▮ (located between the Start and Stop icons). While the program is in break mode, you can use the Immediate window to examine and change values of variables and object settings. When you enter Break mode, the Start button on the Toolbar changes to a Continue button. You can click on it to proceed with the execution of the program.

THE IMMEDIATE WINDOW

You can set the focus to the Immediate window by clicking on it (if visible), by pressing Ctrl+G, or by choosing "Immediate Window" from the View menu. Although the Immediate window can be used during design time, it is primarily used in Break mode. When you type a statement into the Immediate window and press the Enter key, the statement is executed at once. A statement of the form

```
Print expression
```

displays the value of the expression on the next line of the Immediate window. In Figure D.1, three statements have been executed. (When the program was interrupted, the variable *numVar* had the value 10.) In addition to displaying values of expressions, the Immediate window also is commonly used to change the value of a variable with an assignment statement before continuing to run the program. *Note 1:* Any statement in the Immediate window can be executed again by placing the cursor anywhere on the statement and pressing the Enter key. *Note 2:* In earlier versions of Visual Basic the Immediate window was called the Debug window.

```
Immediate
Print 2*3
 6
Print "Good" & "bye"
Goodbye
Print numVar
 10
```

FIGURE D.1　　*Three Print Statements Executed in the Immediate Window*

THE WATCH WINDOW

You can designate an expression as a watch expression or a break expression. Break expressions are of two varieties: those that cause a break when they become true and those that cause a break when they change value. At any time, the Watch window shows the current values of all watch and break expressions. In the Watch window of Figure D.2, the type of each expression is specified by an icon as shown in Table 1.

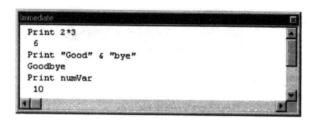

Expression	Value	Type	Context
num1	5	Single	Form1.cmdButton_Click
num2	10	Single	Form1.cmdButton_Click
num2 > 9	True	Boolean	Form1.cmdButton_Click

FIGURE D.2　　*The Watch Window*

TABLE D.1
Watch Type Icons

Icon	Type of expression
👓	Watch expression
👆	Break when expression is true
👆	Break when expression has changed

The easiest way to add an expression to the Watch window is to right-click on a variable in the code window and then click on "Add Watch" to call up an Add Watch dialog box. You can then alter the expression in the Expression text box and select one of the three Watch types. To delete an expression from the Watch window, right-click on the expression and then click on "Delete Watch." To alter an expression in the Watch window, right-click on the expression and click on "Edit Watch."

THE LOCALS WINDOW

The Locals window, invoked by clicking on "Locals Window" in the View menu, is a feature that was new to Visual Basic in version 5.0. This window automatically displays the names, values, and types of all variables in the current procedure. See Figure D.3. You can alter the values of variables at any time. In addition, you can examine and change properties of controls through the Locals window.

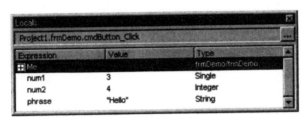

FIGURE D.3   *The Locals Window*

STEPPING THROUGH A PROGRAM

The program can be executed one statement at a time, with each press of an appropriate function key executing a statement. This process is called **stepping** (or **stepping into**). After each step, values of variables, expressions, and conditions can be displayed from the debugging windows, and the values of variables can be changed.

When a procedure is called, the lines of the procedure can be executed one at a time, referred to as "stepping through the procedure," or the entire procedure can be executed at once, referred to as "stepping over a procedure." A step over a procedure is called a **procedure step**. In addition, you can execute the remainder of the current procedure at once, referred to as "stepping out of the procedure."

Stepping begins with the first line of the first event procedure invoked by the user. Program execution normally proceeds in order through the statements in the event procedure. However, at any time the programmer can specify the next statement to be executed.

As another debugging tool, Visual Basic allows the programmer to specify certain lines as **breakpoints**. Then, when the program is run, execution will stop at the first breakpoint reached. The programmer can then either step through the program or continue execution to the next breakpoint.

The tasks discussed previously are summarized below, along with a means to carry out each task. The tasks invoked with function keys can also be produced from the menu bar.

Step Into:	Press F8
Step Over:	Press Shift+F8
Step Out:	Press Ctrl+Shift+F8
Set a breakpoint:	Move cursor to line, press F9
Remove a breakpoint:	Move cursor to line containing breakpoint, press F9
Clear all breakpoints:	Press Ctrl+Shift+F9
Set next statement:	Press Ctrl+F9
Continue execution to next breakpoint or the end of the program:	Press F5
Run to cursor:	Press Ctrl+F8

SIX WALKTHROUGHS

The following walkthroughs use the debugging tools with the programming structures covered in Sections 2, 3, 4, and 5.

STEPPING THROUGH AN ELEMENTARY PROGRAM: SECTION 2
The following walkthrough demonstrates several capabilities of the debugger.

1. Create a form with a command button (cmdButton) and a picture box (picBox). Set the AutoRedraw property of the picture box to True. (During the debugging process, the entire form will be covered. The True setting for AutoRedraw prevents the contents of the picture box from being erased.)

2. Double-click on the command button and enter the following event procedure:

```
Private Sub cmdButton_Click()
    Dim num As Single
    picBox.Cls
    num = Val(InputBox("Enter a number:"))
    num = num + 1
    num = num + 2
    picBox.Print num
End Sub
```

3. Press F8, click the command button, and press F8 again. A yellow arrow points to the picBox.Cls statement and the statement is highlighted in yellow. This indicates that the picBox.Cls statement is the next statement to be executed. (Pressing F8 is referred to as stepping. You can also step to the next statement of a program with the Step Into option from the Debug menu.)

4. Press F8. The picBox.Cls statement is executed and the statement involving InputBox is designated as the next statement to be executed.

5. Press F8 to execute the statement containing InputBox. Respond to the request by typing 5 and clicking the OK button.

6. Press F8 again to execute the statement `num = num + 1`.

7. Let the mouse sit over any occurrence of the word "num" for a second or so. The current value of the variable will be displayed in a small box. See Figure D.4.

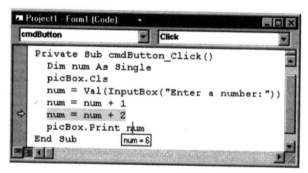

FIGURE D.4   *Obtaining the Value of a Variable*

8. Click on the End icon to end the program.

9. Move the cursor to the line

```
num = num + 2
```

and then press F9. A red dot appears to the left of the line and the line is displayed in white text on a red background. This indicates that the line is a breakpoint. (Pressing F9 is referred to as toggling a breakpoint. You also can toggle a breakpoint with the Toggle Breakpoint option from the Debug menu.)

10. Press F5 and click on the command button. Respond to the request by entering 5. The program executes the first three lines and stops at the breakpoint. The breakpoint line is not executed.

11. Open the Immediate window by pressing Ctrl+G. If necessary, clear the contents of the window. Type the statement

```
Print "num ="; num
```

into the Immediate window and then press Enter to execute the statement. The appearance of "num = 6" on the next line of the Immediate window confirms that the breakpoint line was not executed.

12. Press F7 to return to the Code window.

13. Move the cursor to the line num = num + 1 and then press Ctrl+F9 to specify that line as the next line to be executed. (You can also use the Set Next Statement option from the Debug menu.)

14. Press F8 to execute the selected line.

15. Press Ctrl+G to return to the Immediate window. Move the cursor to the line containing the Print method and press Enter to confirm that the value of *num* is now 7, and then return to the Code window.

16. Move the cursor to the breakpoint line and press F9 to deselect the line as a breakpoint.

17. Press F5 to execute the remaining lines of the program. Observe that the value displayed in the picture box is 9.

General Comment: As you step through a program, the form will become hidden from view. However, the form will be represented by a button on the Windows taskbar at the bottom of the screen. The button will contain the name of the form. You can see the form at any time by clicking on its button.

STEPPING THROUGH A PROGRAM CONTAINING A GENERAL PROCEDURE: SECTION 3

The following walkthrough uses the single-stepping feature of the debugger to trace the flow through a program and a Sub procedure

1. Create a form with a command button (cmdButton) and a picture box (picBox). Set the AutoRedraw property of the picture box to True. Then enter the following two Sub procedures:

```
Private Sub cmdButton_Click()
   Dim p As Single, b As Single
   picBox.Cls p = 1000    'Principal
   Call GetBalance(p, b)
   picBox.Print "The balance is"; b
End Sub

Private Sub GetBalance(prin As Single, bal As Single)
   'Calculate the balance at 5% interest rate
   Dim interest As Single
   interest = .05 * prin
   bal = prin + interest
End Sub
```

2. Press F8, click the command button, and press F8 again. The picBox.Cls statement is highlighted to indicate that it is the next statement to be executed.

3. Press F8 two more times. The Call statement is highlighted.

4. Press F8 once and observe that the heading of the Sub procedure GetBalance is now highlighted in yellow.

5. Press F8 three times to execute the assignment statements and to highlight the End Sub statement. (Notice that the Dim and Rem statements were skipped.)

6. Press F8 and notice that the yellow highlight has moved back to the cmdButton_Click event procedure and is on the statement immediately following the Call statement.

7. Click on the End icon to end the program.

8. Repeat Steps 2 and 3, and then press Shift+F8 to step over the procedure GetBalance. The procedure has been executed in its entirety.

9. Click on the End icon to end the program.

COMMUNICATION BETWEEN ARGUMENTS AND PARAMETERS

The following walkthrough uses the Locals window to monitor the values of arguments and parameters during the execution of a program.

1. If you have not already done so, type the preceding program into the Code window.

2. Press F8 and click on the command button.

3. Select "Locals Window" from the View window. Notice that the variables from the cmdButton_Click event procedure appear in the Locals window.

4. Press F8 three more times to highlight the Call statement. Notice that the value of the variable p has changed.

5. Press F8 to call the Sub procedure. Notice that the variables displayed in the Locals window are now those of the procedure GetBalance.

6. Press F8 three times to execute the procedure.

7. Press F8 to return to cmdButton_Click event procedure. Notice that the value of the variable b has inherited the value of the variable bal.

8. Click on the End icon to end the program.

STEPPING THROUGH PROGRAMS CONTAINING SELECTION STRUCTURES: SECTION 4

If Blocks

The following walkthrough demonstrates how an If statement evaluates a condition to determine whether to take an action.

1. Create a form with a command button (cmdButton) and a picture box (picBox). Set the AutoRedraw property of the picture box to True. Then open the Code window and enter the following procedure:

Private Sub cmdButton_Click()

```
Dim wage As Single
  picBox.Cls
  wage = Val(InputBox("wage:"))
  If wage < 5.15 Then
      picBox.Print "Below minimum wage."
    Else
      picBox.Print "Wage Ok."
  End If
End Sub
```

2. Press F8, click the command button, and press F8 twice. The picBox.Cls statement will be highlighted and executed, and then the statement containing Input-Box will be highlighted.

3. Press F8 once to execute the statement containing InputBox. Type a wage of 3.25 and press the Enter key. The If statement is highlighted, but has not been executed.

4. Press F8 once and notice that the highlight for the current statement has jumped to the statement picBox.Print "Below minimum wage." Because the condition "wage < 5.15" is true, the action associated with Then was selected.

5. Press F8 to execute the picBox.Print statement. Notice that Else is skipped and End If is highlighted.

6. Press F8 again. We are through with the If block and the statement following the If block, End Sub, is highlighted.

7. Click on the End icon to end the program.

8. If desired, try stepping through the program again with 5.75 entered as the wage. Since the condition "wage < 5.15" will be false, the Else action will be executed instead of the Then action.

SELECT CASE BLOCKS

The following walkthrough illustrates how a Select Case block uses the selector to choose from among several actions.

1. Create a form with a command button (cmdButton) and a picture box (picBox). Set the AutoRedraw property of the picture box to True. Then open the Code window and enter the following procedure:

```
Private Sub cmdButton_Click()
    Dim age As Single, price As Single
    picBox.Cls age = Val(InputBox("age:"))
    Select Case age
      Case Is < 12
        price = 0
      Case Is < 18
        price = 3.5
      Case Is >= 65
        price = 4
      Case Else
        price = 5.5
    End Select
    picBox.Print "Your ticket price is ";FormatCurrency(price)
End Sub
```

2. Press F8, click on the command button, and press F8 twice. The picBox.Cls statement will be highlighted and executed, and then the statement containing InputBox will be highlighted.

3. Press F8 once to execute the statement containing InputBox. Type an age of 8 and press the Enter key. The Select Case statement is highlighted, but has not been executed.

4. Press F8 twice and observe that the action associated with Case Is < 12 is highlighted.

5. Press F8 once to execute the assignment statement. Notice that End Select is highlighted. This demonstrates that when more than one Case clause is true, only the first is acted upon.

6. Click on the End icon to end the program.

7. If desired, step through the program again, entering a different age and predicting which Case clause will be acted upon. (Some possible ages to try are 12, 14, 18, 33, and 67.)

STEPPING THROUGH A PROGRAM CONTAINING A DO LOOP: SECTION 5

Do Loops

The following walkthrough demonstrates use of the Immediate window to monitor the value of a condition in a Do loop that searches for a name.

1. Access Windows' Notepad, enter the following line of data, and save the file on the A drive with the name DATA.TXT

```
Bert, Ernie, Grover, Oscar
```

2. Return to Visual Basic. Create a form with a command button (cmdButton) and a picture box (picBox). Set the AutoRedraw property of the picture box to True. Then double-click on the command button and enter the following procedure:

```
Private Sub cmdButton_Click()
  'Look for a specific name
  Dim searchName As String, nom As String
  picBox.Cls
  searchName = InputBox("Name:") 'Name to search for in list
  Open "A:DATA.TXT"For Input As #1
  nom = ""
  Do While (nom [%6][lt>]20searchName) And Not EOF(1)
    Input #1, nom
  Loop
  Close #1
  If nom = searchName Then
      picBox.Print nom
    Else
      picBox.Print "Name not found"
  End If
End Sub
```

3. Press F8 and click on the command button. The heading of the event procedure is highlighted in yellow.

4. Double-click on the variable *searchName*, click the right mouse button, click on "Add Watch," and click on OK. The variable *searchName* has been added to the Watch window.

5. Repeat Step 4 for the variable *nom*.

6. Drag the mouse across the words

```
(nom <> searchName) And Not EOF(1)
```

to highlight them. Then click the right mouse button, click on "Add Watch," and click on OK. Widen the Watch window as much as possible in order to see the entire expression.

7. Press F8 three more times to execute the picBox.Cls statement and the statement containing InputBox. Enter the name "Ernie" at the prompt.

8. Press F8 repeatedly until the entire event procedure has been executed. Pause after each keypress and notice how the values of the expressions in the Watch window change.

9. Click on the End icon to end the program.

A

Access key, 24, 296-297, 303, 309, 418, 425-426
Accumulator, 138, 153
Action argument, 327, 453
Action property, 423
ActiveX Control Pad, 399-403
Add Index window, 344-345
Add method, 380
Algorithm, 4-5, 7, 9, 11-12, 174, 184-185, 188, 192, 195, 225
Align Controls to Grid option, 303
Alignment property, 24, 180, 423
Ampersand, 24, 43, 296-297, 418, 425
ANSI, 6, 45-47, 103-104, 116, 169, 171, 287, 331, 407, 413, 415, 444, 451
ANSI Table, 104, 169, 171, 413
Apostrophe, 56, 447
App.Path, 57, 329
Arc of a circle, 278
Argument, 52, 65, 78, 81-83, 176, 327, 365, 382, 424, 436, 453
Arithmetic operation, 105
Array, 161-165, 167-184, 186-187, 190-191, 193-194, 196-205, 209-213, 223, 240-241, 250-251, 288, 296, 303, 316-317, 323, 350, 356, 365, 373, 377, 381, 423-424, 429, 431, 433, 436-440, 444, 446-447, 450, 452-453, 455-456
ASCII, 45-46, 103, 415, 444
ASCII Table, 103
Assignment statement, 37-38, 40, 43, 107, 232, 427, 458, 463
AutoRedraw property, 87, 418, 421, 424, 460-464
AutoSize property, 417, 424, 454

B

BackColor property, 230, 424
BackStyle property, 26, 301, 424
Bar chart, 273-274, 276, 283, 389-390
BAS module, 247-250, 252-253, 255, 437, 452
Base, 41, 181, 217, 273, 330, 431, 444, 455
Begin tag, 397-398, 401

binary File, 436-437, 440-441, 444, 446, 449, 454
binary search, 178, 192-194, 196, 209
Body, 142, 145-146, 398, 400-401
Boolean data type, 139
BorderColor property, 424
BorderStyle property, 311, 362, 424
BorderWidth property, 424
Branching, 12, 95
Break, 4, 8, 41, 69, 73, 93, 107-108, 120, 134, 213, 227-228, 421, 457-458
Break mode, 41, 421, 457-458
Breakpoint, 420, 459-461
browser, 280, 282, 393-398, 402-403
Bubble sort, 184-190, 195, 209, 224
byte, 247, 423-429, 437, 439-440, 443-444, 449, 452-454, 456

C

Call statement, 74, 76-78, 80-83, 431, 462
Cancel a change, 412
Cancel property, 418, 425
Capitalization, 79
Caption property, 23-24, 26, 29, 294, 296-297, 309, 324, 418, 425, 432-433
Carriage return, 39, 217-218, 397, 407, 440, 451, 454
Case study, 119, 121, 123, 125, 146-147, 149, 151, 200-201, 203, 205, 207, 228-229, 231, 233, 235
Change event, 31, 299, 425
Character Map, 27, 415
check box, 294, 296-297, 303, 313, 316, 330, 338-339, 345, 388, 390, 393, 413, 445, 453
Check box control, 294
Circle method, 266, 277, 282, 363, 372, 426
Circle shape, 301
Class, 3, 11-12, 317, 355-367, 371, 373-382, 427, 443, 445-446, 454
Class module, 357-358, 361-365, 371, 374-375, 377-378, 380-381, 445-446
Click event, 81-82, 164, 203, 228, 272, 288, 295-297, 302, 309-310, 390, 425-426, 428, 462

clipboard, 22, 303, 310-311, 316, 412, 414, 419, 426, 437, 449
Clipboard object, 310
Close method, 327, 426
Clustered Bar chart, 274
Code window, 27, 29, 33, 41, 48, 55, 73, 80, 85, 88, 162, 313, 357, 390, 412, 418-419, 458, 461-463
Coding, 4, 13, 96, 199, 202-203, 231
Col property, 304, 426
Collections, 64, 162, 365-367, 369, 371, 373, 380, 402, 413, 454
ColWidth property, 304
combo box, 287, 290-293, 311, 330, 340-341, 344, 350, 362, 374, 381, 423, 425, 439-440, 443, 450-451
Combo box control, 290, 451
Comment statement, 80
Common dialog box, 303, 313-315, 317, 423, 426, 432, 436
Common dialog box control, 303, 313
Comparison, 6, 156, 185-186, 444, 450
concatenation, 42-43, 46, 48, 67
Condition, 10, 95, 103-108, 110, 112, 126, 131-137, 153, 171, 332, 338, 429, 431, 437-438, 453, 462-464
Confusing If block, 112
Connect property, 330, 427
Containment, 373-374, 381
control array, 179-184, 199, 201-205, 209, 296, 381, 438, 440
Coordinate systems, 426-427, 438, 440, 445-446, 455
Count property, 381
Counter variable, 173
CreateObject function, 385-386, 403
Creating a Database, 324, 342, 346
Creating a Database with Visual Data Manager, 342
Criteria clause, 332
Ctrl+Break, 134, 457
Ctrl+Y, 411-412
Current cell, 304, 308, 316, 392, 426
Current Record, 325-326, 336-337, 346, 350, 424, 429, 431-432, 440, 453
CurrentY property, 264
Curving grades, 210

D

Data control, 324-327, 329-330, 332, 334, 336, 339-341, 344, 346, 350, 423-429, 431-432, 442, 446, 453

Data hiding, 355

Data normalization, 348

database, 321, 324, 326-328, 330-332, 334-335, 337-339, 341-351, 426-428, 431-432, 446, 453

Database management software, 324, 338

DatabaseName property, 324, 329, 427-428, 446

Data-bound combo box, 340-341, 350

Data-bound list box, 340, 350

DataField property, 325, 341, 428

DataSource property, 324-325, 428

DblClick event, 288, 293, 428

Debug window, 458

debugging, 4, 41, 92, 112, 119, 140, 431, 457, 459-460

Decision structures, 9, 112

Declarations, 85-86, 97, 162-165, 167, 173, 176, 190, 197, 247-248, 255, 267, 270, 290, 296, 306, 356, 358, 371, 380-381, 387, 429-431, 436-437, 444, 446-447, 452, 455

Declaring variables, 44, 48

Default property, 418, 428

Default value, 47, 83-84, 163, 171, 278, 287, 302, 304, 431-432, 438, 448, 451

Delete method, 327, 429

Depreciation, 157

Descending order, 171, 186-187, 192, 237, 332-333, 341

Design Time, 34, 180, 182-184, 202-203, 209, 230, 287, 289, 291, 299, 301-304, 329, 339, 350, 413, 428, 443, 451, 457-458

Desk-checking, 457

Dim statement, 44, 48, 85, 97, 162, 165, 173, 247, 251, 386, 437, 444, 446

Directory, 50, 136-137, 238-239, 292-293, 308, 316-317, 349, 374, 391, 395, 425-427, 429, 437, 440-441, 443, 445, 447, 455

Directory list box, 292, 316, 425, 440, 445

Dividend, 60, 312

Division, 35, 40, 60, 65, 147, 222

Divisor, 60

Do loop, 131-133, 135-136, 140-141, 153, 429, 464

documentation, 5, 56-57, 402, 447

DrawStyle property, 282

Drive list box, 292-293, 425, 428, 430, 440

Drive property, 430

Driver, 96, 213

Dynamic array, 171, 431, 455

E

Editor, 30, 33-34, 40, 44, 48, 52, 79, 119, 254, 309-310, 411, 414

Element of an array, 171, 178-179

empty String, 47, 66, 83-84, 171, 219, 232

Enabled property, 300, 430, 452-453

End Function, 87-93, 97, 111, 118, 123-125, 144, 150-151, 176, 179, 206, 224, 226, 233, 358, 360, 362, 367-368, 374-375, 378-379, 419, 430, 436

End icon, 22, 33, 390, 460, 462-464

End Select, 113, 115-118, 125, 175, 181, 193, 195, 222, 226, 358, 360, 367, 378, 430, 449, 463

End Sub, 28-29, 33, 35-39, 42-47, 50-57, 59-63, 65, 73-86, 88-93, 97, 107-111, 113, 115-118, 123-124, 132, 134-136, 138-141, 143-145, 151-153, 161, 163-170, 172-184, 186-188, 190-191, 193-195, 198-200, 205-209, 218, 220-226, 228, 233-237, 245-246, 249-250, 252-253, 261, 263-272, 274-276, 278-282, 289-293, 295-300, 305-308, 310, 312, 315, 327-329, 335, 337, 340-342, 360-364, 369-370, 372-373, 375-377, 379-380, 387-388, 394-396, 401, 419, 430, 451, 460-464

End tag, 397, 401

End Type, 247-250, 252-253, 430, 452

EOF Function, 135-136, 153, 237, 253

error trapping, 221

Esc key, 410, 413-414, 425

Event procedure, 28-33, 37-38, 41, 44, 46-47, 67, 75, 77, 80-87, 97, 121, 164-165, 167, 170, 180-181, 187, 190, 203-204, 228, 231-232, 261-266, 269, 272, 292-293, 315, 326-327, 329-330, 346, 362, 364, 370-371, 377, 390-391, 402, 421, 425, 429-431, 439, 446, 453, 459-460, 462, 464

Events, 27-29, 31, 33, 135, 181, 201, 203, 231, 288, 291-292, 310, 313, 316, 356, 365, 367, 369, 371, 373-374, 380-382, 396, 423, 429-430, 453-454

Excel, 276, 385-392, 427

Exit statement, 431

Exponent, 36, 41, 435

Exponentiation, 35

F

FICA tax, 110, 119-121, 123-125

Field, 62, 155, 196, 223, 227, 233, 236, 247-248, 250-251, 253, 323, 325-326, 330-333, 338-341, 344-347, 349-351, 428, 431, 435-436, 453

Field of a record, 251

Fields property, 431

File list box, 292-293, 428, 432, 440

File name, 22-23, 53, 217, 219, 238, 365, 410, 456

File not found error, 219

FileName property, 428, 432

Filespec, 41, 49, 217-219, 223, 251, 302, 308, 324, 365, 386, 392, 397, 400-401, 428-429, 437, 439, 443-444, 454, 456

FillColor property, 277, 279, 282, 432

FillStyle property, 277-278, 282, 432

Filter property, 315

FilterIndex property, 315

Find methods, 336

FixedCols property, 339

Fixed-length string, 245-246, 251, 255, 439, 452

Flag, 139, 153, 190, 192, 195, 227

Flags property, 315, 432

FlexGrid, 303-304, 315-316, 330, 332, 338-339, 342, 350

FlexGrid control, 303-304, 315-316, 332, 338-339

flowchart, 5-12, 95, 106, 114, 131, 133, 136-137, 142, 172-173, 192

Flowline, 6

Focus, 7, 23, 26, 30, 32-33, 46-47, 67, 74, 80, 86, 96, 181, 203-204, 208, 234, 238, 260, 288, 294, 296, 302-303, 311, 332, 343, 418, 426, 428, 437, 439, 441-443, 449, 451, 458

Font common dialog box, 314-315

Font dialog box, 21

For...Next loop, 141-146, 153, 165, 180, 202, 402, 431

ForeColor property, 21, 434

Foreign key, 331-333, 346-347, 350

Form Layout window, 18

Form_Load event, 87, 97, 164, 180, 187, 228, 231, 329-330, 391, 402, 446

Format Function, 66, 401

Form-level variable, 85, 97

Frame control, 294, 415

Function procedure, 92-93, 98, 127, 176, 361, 365

G

General procedure, 97, 164-165, 204, 419, 421, 461

Get statement, 254-255, 436, 449, 454

GoSub statement, 437, 456

GotFocus event, 31, 181, 201, 204, 437

GoTo, 12, 95, 222, 402, 437, 444, 456

GridLines property, 304, 315, 437

H

Height property, 183, 362

Help, 4, 27, 41, 49, 66, 80, 97, 165, 290, 313, 324, 336, 402, 412-413

Hide method, 317, 437

Hierarchy chart, 8-10, 12-13, 94-95, 121, 148, 204, 231

Horizontal radius line, 277-278, 280, 425

HTML, 394, 397-403

Hypertext, 392, 396-397

I

If block, 106-112, 114, 119, 126, 246, 327, 437, 463
Image control, 302-303, 316, 362, 374, 451
Immediate window, 457-458, 461, 464
Income tax, 99, 119-121, 123-125, 127
Indenting, 111, 118, 135, 146
Index property, 179-181, 183-184, 209, 418, 438, 440
Inequality, 114, 119
infinite Loop, 10, 135, 204, 330
Inheritance, 373-374
initial Value, 142, 144, 153, 199
Initialize event, 362, 364, 377
Input # statement, 49-51, 57-58, 162
Input box, 49, 52-53, 57-58, 288, 306, 317, 370
InputBox function, 132, 438
Insert Object dialog box, 388-389
Integer division, 65
Integer variable, 46, 436, 446
interface, 4, 21, 27-29, 122, 148, 201, 229, 365, 414
internet, 280-281, 392-397, 399-402, 409
Interval property, 300, 438, 452
ItemData property, 289, 316, 439

K

KeyPress event, 46-48, 439
Keyword, 33-34, 40, 56, 153, 313, 365, 371, 373, 381, 402, 412, 424, 431, 443, 452, 454

L

Leading space, 39, 445
Least-squares approximation, 155
Left property, 203, 439
Library, 86, 92, 346, 351
Like Operator, 338, 350
Line chart, 267, 269, 273-274, 276
Line feed, 39, 217-218, 397, 407, 440, 451, 454
Line method, 261-262, 266, 273, 276, 282, 432, 440
List box, 85, 287-290, 292-293, 316-319, 326, 330, 340-341, 344, 350-351, 356, 381-382, 423, 425, 428, 430, 432, 440, 443, 445
List Properties/Methods, 30, 34
List property, 287, 289, 440
Load statement, 179, 182-184, 209
LoadPicture function, 302
Local Array, 165, 176-177
Locals window, 459, 462
Logical error, 41, 457
Logical operator, 104-105, 108, 423, 443, 445, 454
Long division, 60, 65

M

Member Variable, 357-358, 361, 374
Memory, 37-38, 44, 81, 83, 162-163, 165, 247, 310, 355, 364, 373, 424, 427-429, 431, 438-439, 441, 443, 446, 449-450, 455

Menu bar, 18, 309, 389, 414, 459
Menu control, 303, 308
Message box, 33, 55, 93, 213, 232, 238, 327, 381, 390, 401
Modular design, 93, 95-97
Module, 8, 94, 96, 247-250, 252-253, 255, 313, 355, 357-358, 361-365, 371, 374-375, 377-378, 380-381, 431, 437, 445-446, 452
Mouse, 18-21, 27, 29, 31, 33, 48, 288, 294, 304, 309, 311, 316, 343-346, 389, 411, 415-417, 420, 426, 428, 442, 449, 460, 464
MsgBox statement, 67, 442-443
MultiLine property, 22, 417, 443, 448
Multiple forms, 303, 311

N

Name property, 26, 309, 324, 357, 361, 370, 400, 443
Navigation arrows, 325, 331
New program, 23-24, 357, 410
NewIndex property, 316, 439, 443
Notepad, 49-50, 58, 217-218, 397, 399, 414, 464
null String, 47, 204, 426, 429, 438
Number property, 221
Numeric Expression, 38, 55, 62
Numeric function, 87
numeric Variable, 42, 44-45, 47, 50, 53, 57, 64, 104, 115, 138, 141-142, 439

O

Object box, 19, 26, 29, 31, 48, 80, 418
Object-oriented programming, 353, 355, 357
OLE, 385-392, 403, 423, 426-428, 437, 452-453
OLE automation, 385-386, 390-391, 403, 427, 437, 452-453
OLE automation object, 385-386, 390-391, 427, 437, 452-453
OLE container control, 388-389, 392, 403
On Error, 222, 393-394, 402, 431, 444, 447
On Error GoTo statement, 402
Open common dialog box, 313
Open statement, 50, 57, 228, 402, 444
Opening a file for append, 218
Opening a file for input, 49
Opening a file for output, 217
Option button, 294, 296-298, 316, 388, 390, 413, 445, 453
Option button control, 296
Option Explicit, 48, 444
Ordered array, 171-173, 177
Output, 3-7, 9, 11-12, 18, 39, 45, 49-51, 53, 55-58, 65, 68-69, 83, 87, 94, 97-99, 119, 148, 154, 157, 163, 210, 217-220, 224-227, 232, 234-235, 237-238, 240, 245-246, 266, 274, 278-280, 292, 362, 370, 388, 420-421, 431, 434-435, 443-445, 454

P

Parameter, 58, 76-77, 80-81, 83, 92, 97, 176, 181, 249, 251, 269, 346, 365, 427, 436, 439, 441, 444-446, 451
Parenthesis, 52, 80
Pascal, 135, 177
passed by reference, 81, 92
passed by value, 83, 92-93
Passing an array, 176
Passing by reference, 81, 365
Passing by value, 83, 365
Path property, 316, 428, 445
Pattern property, 293, 440, 445
Pie chart, 280-281
Poker, 212, 377
Polymorphism, 365
Positioning text, 263
Primary key, 330-331, 333, 338, 344-346, 350
Print common dialog box, 314, 436
Print method, 38-39, 42-43, 49, 53, 67, 87, 96, 264, 445, 461
Print zone, 53, 58, 445
Printer object, 67, 437, 445, 453
Procedure box, 29-30, 80, 419
Program development cycle, 3-5
Program documentation, 5, 56
Program modes, 41, 457
Programming style, 111, 118, 135, 146
Project Container window, 26-27, 416
Project Explorer window, 18, 311, 411, 418
Properties window, 18-20, 22-27, 179, 184, 315, 324, 329-330, 356-357, 400, 402, 416-417
PSet method, 282, 446
pseudocode, 4-5, 7-10, 12-13, 93, 106, 114, 121, 131, 133, 135-137, 142, 150
Public keyword, 313
Put statement, 254, 446, 449

Q

Quadratic formula, 127
Question mark, 333, 443
Quick Info, 48, 52
Quotient, 5, 60, 65

R

Radian measure, 456
RaiseEvent statement, 381, 431
Random number, 64, 379
Random-access file, 223, 251-255, 436, 440, 446, 449
Range chart, 283
Range of an array, 169
record Variable, 248-251, 253, 454
RecordCount property, 326, 340
RecordSet, 325-326, 328-329, 334, 336-338, 340-342, 344, 346-348, 350, 431-432, 446
RecordSource property, 324, 332, 339, 350, 446
Rectangle shape, 301
ReDim statement, 167, 170-171, 429, 450, 455
Referential integrity, 331, 350
Refresh method, 350, 447

Relational database, 324, 331, 334, 348
Remainder, 35, 60, 65, 393, 435, 442
Remove method, 381
RemoveItem method, 447
Reserved word, 35, 40
Reusable, 96
Right arrow, 309-310, 414
Rnd Function, 64, 351
Row property, 304, 426
RowHeight property, 304
Rule of entity integrity, 338, 350
Rule of referential integrity, 331, 350
Run time, 18, 27, 34, 179-180, 182-184, 209, 288, 294, 296, 300, 302-304, 350, 391, 420-421, 423-424, 450, 457

S

Save As common dialog box, 314
Save File As dialog box, 22
Save Project icon, 22, 410
Scale method, 261, 264-266, 273, 282, 448, 455
scientific Notation, 36, 434-435
scroll bar, 293, 298, 304, 417, 425, 439, 450, 453
Scroll bar controls, 298
Scroll event, 299
ScrollBars property, 304, 448
Sector of a circle, 278
Segmented bar chart, 283
Select Case block, 112-114, 117-119, 126, 449, 463
Select statement, 118
Selected object, 19, 23, 26
Selected text, 19
Selector, 112-119, 126, 463
SelText property, 311
Semicolon, 39, 445
Sequence structure, 8
sequential file, 217-218, 223, 227, 237-240, 254, 304, 317-318, 382, 438, 440, 444-445, 454
sequential Search, 178, 191
Set statement, 385-386, 403, 449
SetFocus method, 437, 441
Settings box, 20-21, 289, 325, 416-417
Shape control, 301, 318, 424
Shell Sort, 184, 188-191, 195, 209
shortcut Key, 309
Shortcut keys, 413
Show method, 315, 317, 362, 450
Simple variable, 161
Sizing handles, 19, 27, 416
SmallChange property, 450
Smart editor, 40, 119, 254

Social Security tax, 124
Sorted property, 287-289, 316, 450
SQL, 330-340, 343, 350, 446
Start button, 17, 27, 58, 300, 400, 410, 414, 457
Start icon, 22, 410
Static Array, 450, 455
Step keyword, 153
step Value, 143-144
Stepwise refinement, 93, 121, 148
Str function, 427, 450
Stretch property, 302, 451
String constant, 42, 47, 76
String expression, 43, 116, 428
String function, 439, 452
String Variable, 42, 45, 50, 52, 77, 104, 115, 117, 178, 310, 336-337, 436, 439-441, 446, 448
strings, 26, 42-48, 55, 57, 60-62, 65, 67-68, 103-104, 163-164, 172, 196, 212, 218, 245-247, 251, 287, 308, 315-316, 332, 334, 344, 426-428, 434-435, 450, 453-454
Structure, 8-10, 28, 47, 96, 112, 162, 247, 343-346, 431, 437
structured programming, 12, 93, 95-97
structured query language, 331, 350
Stub programming, 96
Sub procedure, 73-84, 86, 93, 98, 121, 127, 150, 176, 190, 231, 253, 269, 361, 365, 419, 424, 431, 451, 461-462
Subdirectory, 50, 425, 441
Subroutine, 437, 447, 456
Subscript, 166-167, 169, 171-172, 175, 187, 192, 194, 196, 209, 222, 439, 444, 452
Subscripted variable, 162, 197, 439
substring, 60-61, 65, 438, 441
Subtraction, 35

T

Tab function, 49, 54, 58
Tab key, 26-27, 32-33, 47, 58, 413, 415, 418, 451
Tab order, 449
TabIndex property, 418
Tag, 397-401, 427, 429, 438, 441, 450-451, 456
Terminate event, 364, 380
Terminating value, 142, 144, 153
Testing, 4, 131, 135
Text box control, 201-202
Text property, 20, 29, 180, 204, 288, 291, 308, 316, 341, 423, 434, 451
TextWidth method, 264-265

Thumb, 5, 49, 298-300, 355, 365, 425, 439, 441, 450, 453
Tic-tac-toe, 318, 381
Timer control, 300, 313, 316, 438, 452
Timer event, 438, 452
Toolbar, 18-19, 22, 33-34, 182, 338, 344, 356-357, 393-394, 402, 410, 457
Toolbox, 18-19, 23-25, 287, 292, 294, 303, 313, 355-356, 385, 389-390, 393, 415, 438
Top property, 203, 452
Top-down design, 80, 86, 93-94
Trailing space, 39, 445
Truth value, 112, 127, 131, 133, 429
Twip, 182, 455
Two-dimensional Array, 196-198, 202, 209, 211-212, 429

U

URL, 393-396
User-defined event, 371, 431
User-defined function, 89, 91, 156

V

Validate event procedure, 327, 330, 453
validation event, 326
Value property, 294, 296-297, 316, 350, 431, 439, 450, 453
VBScript, 66, 397, 399, 401-403
View, 18-19, 27, 33, 41, 117, 334, 342, 346, 351, 365, 397, 402, 411-412, 418-419, 457-459, 461-462
Virtual table, 334, 350, 446
Visible property, 26, 183, 310, 453
Visual Basic controls, 17, 385
Visual Basic Notation, 35
Visual Basic objects, 17, 19, 21, 23, 25, 27
Visual Basic statements, 106, 145, 423
Visual Data Manager, 324, 330, 338, 342-343, 349-350

W

Watch type icons, 458
Watch window, 458-459, 464
Web browser control, 393-396
Web page, 393-394, 397-402
Wildcard characters, 293, 315, 332, 445
Windows environment, 414, 432-433
WithEvents keyword, 373
Word Basic, 385, 388, 427
WordWrap property, 417, 454
World Wide Web, 302, 392, 403
Write # statement, 217-218, 453

Accompanying CD for Microsoft Visual Basic 6.0, Working Edition

The CD in this book contains the files needed to install the Working Model Edition of Visual Basic 6.0. To install the software, follow the steps in the first part of Appendix B.

In addition, the CD contains all the programs from the examples and case studies of this textbook, most of the TXT files needed for the exercises, and several BMP (picture) files. The programs (and TXT files) are contained in the folder PROGRAMS, in subfolders called CH3, CH4, CH5, and so on. The picture files are contained in the folder PICTURES. We recommend that you copy the entire contents of the folder PROGRAMS onto your hard drive or a diskette.

Each program has a name of the form chapter-section-number. VBP. For instance, the program in Chapter 3, Section 2, Example 4 has the name 3-2-4.VBP. Many of the programs make use of TXT files that are also in the subfolder. When one of these programs access a text file, the filespec for the text file is preceded with App.Path. This tells Visual Basic to look for the program in the folder from which the program has been opened.

END-USER LICENSE AGREEMENT FOR MICROSOFT SOFTWARE

IMPORTANT—READ CAREFULLY: This Microsoft End-User License Agreement ("EULA") is a legal agreement between you (either an individual or a single entity) and Microsoft Corporation for the Microsoft software product identified above, which includes computer software and may include associated media, printed materials, and "online" or electronic documentation ("SOFTWARE PRODUCT"). The SOFTWARE PRODUCT also includes any updates and supplements to the original SOFTWARE PRODUCT provided to you by Microsoft. Any software provided along with the SOFTWARE PRODUCT that is associated with a separate end-user license agreement is licensed to you under the terms of that license agreement. By installing, copying, downloading, accessing or otherwise using the SOFTWARE PRODUCT, you agree to be bound by the terms of this EULA. If you do not agree to the terms of this EULA, do not install, copy, or otherwise use the SOFTWARE PRODUCT

Software PRODUCT LICENSE

The SOFTWARE PRODUCT is protected by copyright laws and international copyright treaties, as well as other intellectual property laws and treaties. The SOFTWARE PRODUCT is licensed, not sold.

1. GRANT OF LICENSE. This EULA grants you the following rights:

1.1 **License Grant.** You may install and use one copy of the SOFTWARE PRODUCT on a single computer. You may also store or install a copy of the SOFTWARE PRODUCT on a storage device, such as a network server, used only to install or run the SOFTWARE PRODUCT over an internal network; however, you must acquire and dedicate a license for each separate computer on or from which the SOFTWARE PRODUCT is installed, used, accessed, displayed or run.

1.2 **Academic Use.** You must be a "Qualified Educational User" to use the SOFTWARE PRODUCT in the manner described in this section. To determine whether you are a Qualified Educational User, please contact the Microsoft Sales Information Center/One Microsoft Way/Redmond, WA 98052-6399 or the Microsoft subsidiary serving your country. If you are a Qualified Educational User, you may either:

(i) exercise the rights granted in Section 1. 1, OR

(ii) if you intend to use the SOFTWARE PRODUCT solely for instructional purposes in connection with a class or other educational program, this EULA grants you the following alternative license models:

(A) Per Computer Model. For every valid license you have acquired for the SOFTWARE PRODUCT, you may install a single copy of the SOFTWARE PRODUCT on a single computer for access and use by an unlimited number of student end users at your educational institution, provided that all such end users comply with all other terms of this EULA, OR

(B) Per License Model. If you have multiple licenses for the SOFTWARE PRODUCT, then at any time you may have as many copies of the SOFTWARE PRODUCT in use as you have licenses, provided that such use is limited to student or faculty end users at your educational institution and provided that all such end users comply with all other terms of this EULA. For purposes of this subsection, the SOFTWARE PRODUCT is "in use" on a computer when it is loaded into the temporary memory (i.e., RAM) or installed into the permanent memory (e.g., hard disk, CD ROM, or other storage device) of that computer, except that a copy installed on a network server for the sole purpose of distribution to other computers is not "in use". If the anticipated number of users of the SOFTWARE PRODUCT will exceed the number of applicable licenses, then you must have a reasonable mechanism or process in place to ensure that the number of persons using the SOFTWARE PRODUCT concurrently does not exceed the number of licenses.

2. DESCRIPTION OF OTHER RIGHTS AND LIMITATIONS.

- **Limitations on Reverse Engineering, Decompilation, and Disassembly.** You may not reverse engineer, decompile, or disassemble the SOFTWARE PRODUCT, except and only to the extent that such activity is expressly permitted by applicable law notwithstanding this limitation.

- **Separation of Components.** The SOFTWARE PRODUCT is licensed as a single product. Its component parts may not be separated for use on more than one computer.

- **Rental.** You may not rent, lease or lend the SOFTWARE PRODUCT

- **Trademarks.** This EULA does not grant you any rights in connection with any trademarks or service marks of Microsoft

- **Software Transfer.** The initial user of the SOFTWARE PRODUCT may make a one-time permanent transfer of this EULA and SOFTWARE PRODUCT only directly to an end user. This transfer must include all of the SOFTWARE PRODUCT (including all component parts, the media and printed materials, any upgrades, this EULA, and, if applicable, the Certificate of Authenticity). Such transfer may not be by way of consignment or any other indirect transfer. The transferee of such one-time transfer must agree to comply with the terms of this EULA, including the obligation not to further transfer this EULA and SOFTWARE PRODUCT.

- **Termination.** Without prejudice to any other rights, Microsoft may terminate this EULA if you fail to comply with the terms and conditions of this EULA. In such event, you must destroy all copies of the SOFTWARE PRODUCT and all of its component parts.

3. COPYRIGHT. All title and intellectual property rights in and to the SOFTWARE PRODUCT (including but not limited to any images, photographs, animations, video, audio, music, text, and "applets" incorporated into the SOFTWARE PRODUCT), the accompanying printed materials, and any copies of the SOFTWARE PRODUCT are owned by Microsoft or its suppliers. All title and intellectual property rights in and to the content which may be accessed through use of the SOFTWARE PRODUCT is the property of the respective content owner and may be protected by applicable copyright or other intellectual property laws and treaties. This EULA grants you no rights to use such content. All rights not expressly granted are reserved by Microsoft.

4. BACKUP COPY. After installation of one copy of the SOFTWARE PRODUCT pursuant to this EULA, you may keep the original media on which the SOFTWARE PRODUCT was provided by Microsoft solely for backup or archival purposes. If the original media is required to use the SOFTWARE PRODUCT on the COMPUTER, you may make one copy of the SOFTWARE PRODUCT solely for backup or archival purposes. Except as expressly provided in this EULA, you may not otherwise make copies of the SOFTWARE PRODUCT or the printed materials accompanying the SOFTWARE PRODUCT

5. U.S. GOVERNMENT RESTRICTED RIGHTS. The SOFTWARE PRODUCT and documentation are provided with RESTRICTED RIGHTS. Use, duplication, or disclosure by the Government is subject to restrictions as set forth in subparagraph (c)(1)(ii) of the Rights in Technical Data and Computer Software clause at DFARS 252.227-7013 or subparagraphs (c)(1) and (2) of the Commercial Computer Software-Restricted Rights at 48 CFR 52.227-19, as applicable. Manufacturer is Microsoft Corporation/One Microsoft Way/Redmond, WA 98052-6399.

6. EXPORT RESTRICTIONS. You agree that you will not export or re-export the SOFTWARE PRODUCT, any part thereof, or any process or service that is the direct product of the SOFTWARE PRODUCT (the foregoing collectively referred to as the "Restricted Components"), to any country, person, entity or end user subject to U.S. export restrictions. You specifically agree not to export or re-export any of the Restricted Components (i) to any country to which the U.S. has embargoed or restricted the export of goods or services, which currently include, but are not necessarily limited to Cuba, Iran, Iraq, Libya, North Korea, Sudan and Syria, or to any national of any such country, wherever located, who intends to transmit or transport the Restricted Components back to such country; (ii) to any end-user who you know or have reason to know will utilize the Restricted Components in the design, development or production of nuclear, chemical or biological weapons; or (iii) to any end-user who has been prohibited from participating in U.S. export transactions by any federal agency of the U.S. government. You warrant and represent that neither the BXA nor any other U.S. federal agency has suspended, revoked, or denied your export privileges.

7. NOTE ON JAVA SUPPORT. THE SOFTWARE PRODUCT MAY CONTAIN SUPPORT FOR PROGRAMS WRITTEN IN JAVA. JAVA TECHNOLOGY IS NOT FAULT TOLERANT AND IS NOT DESIGNED, MANUFACTURED, OR INTENDED FOR USE OR RESALE AS ONLINE CONTROL EQUIPMENT IN HAZARDOUS ENVIRONMENTS REQUIRING FAIL-SAFE PERFORMANCE, SUCH AS IN THE OPERATION OF NUCLEAR FACILITIES, AIRCRAFT NAVIGATION OR COMMUNICATION SYSTEMS, AIR TRAFFIC CONTROL, DIRECT LIFE SUPPORT MACHINES, OR WEAPONS SYSTEMS, IN WHICH THE FAILURE OF JAVA TECHNOLOGY COULD LEAD DIRECTLY TO DEATH, PERSONAL INJURY, OR SEVERE PHYSICAL OR ENVIRONMENTAL DAMAGE.

MISCELLANEOUS

If you acquired this product in the United States, this EULA is governed by the laws of the State of Washington.

If you acquired this product in Canada, this EULA is governed by the laws of the Province of Ontario, Canada. Each of the parties hereto irrevocably attorns to the jurisdiction of the courts of the Province of Ontario and further agrees to commence any litigation which may arise hereunder in the courts located in the Judicial District of York, Province of Ontario.

If this product was acquired outside the United States, then local law may apply.

Should you have any questions concerning this EULA, or if you desire to contact Microsoft for any reason, please contact Microsoft, or write: Microsoft Sales Information Center/One Microsoft Way/ Redmond, WA 98052-6399.

LIMITED WARRANTY

LIMITED WARRANTY. Microsoft warrants that (a) the SOFTWARE PRODUCT will perform substantially in accordance with the accompanying written materials for a period of ninety (90) days from the date of receipt, and (b) any Support Services provided by Microsoft shall be substantially as described in applicable written materials provided to you by Microsoft, and Microsoft support engineers will make commercially reasonable efforts to solve any problem. To the extent allowed by applicable law, implied warranties on the SOFTWARE PRODUCT, if any, are limited to ninety (90) days. Some states/jurisdictions do not allow limitations on duration of an implied warranty, so the above limitation may not apply to you.

CUSTOMER REMEDIES. Microsoft's and its suppliers' entire liability and your exclusive remedy shall be, at Microsoft's option, either (a) return of the price paid, if any, or (b) repair or replacement of the SOFTWARE PRODUCT that does not meet Microsoft's Limited Warranty and that is returned to Microsoft with a copy of your receipt. This Limited Warranty is void if failure of the SOFTWARE PRODUCT has resulted from accident, abuse, or misapplication.

Any replacement SOFTWARE PRODUCT will be warranted for the remainder of the original warranty period or thirty (30) days, whichever is longer. Outside the United States, neither these remedies nor any product support services offered by Microsoft are available without proof of purchase from an authorized international source.

NO OTHER WARRANTIES. To the maximum extent permitted by applicable law, Microsoft and its suppliers disclaim all other warranties and conditions, either express or implied, including, but not limited to, implied warranties OR CONDITIONS of merchantability, fitness for a particular purpose, title and non-infringement, with regard to the SOFTWARE PRODUCT, and the provision of or failure to provide Support Services. This limited warranty gives you specific legal rights. You may have others, which vary from state/jurisdiction to state/jurisdiction.

LIMITATION OF LIABILITY. TO THE MAXIMUM EXTENT PERMITTED BY APPLICABLE LAW, IN NO EVENT SHALL MICROSOFT OR ITS SUPPLIERS BE LIABLE FOR ANY SPECIAL, INCIDENTAL, INDIRECT, OR CONSEQUENTIAL DAMAGES WHATSOEVER (INCLUDING, WITHOUT LIMITATION, DAMAGES FOR LOSS OF BUSINESS PROFITS, BUSINESS INTERRUPTION, LOSS OF BUSINESS INFORMATION, OR ANY OTHER PECUNIARY LOSS) ARISING OUT OF THE USE OF OR INABILITY TO USE THE SOFTWARE PRODUCT OR THE FAILURE TO PROVIDE SUPPORT SERVICES, EVEN IF MICROSOFT HAS BEEN ADVISED OF THE POSSIBILITY OF SUCH DAMAGES. IN ANY CASE, MICROSOFT'S ENTIRE LIABILITY UNDER ANY PROVISION OF THIS EULA SHALL BE LIMITED TO THE GREATER OF THE AMOUNT ACTUALLY PAID BY YOU FOR THE SOFTWARE PRODUCT OR U.S.$5.00; PROVIDED, HOWEVER, IF YOU HAVE ENTERED INTO A MICROSOFT SUPPORT SERVICES AGREEMENT, MICROSOFT'S ENTIRE LIABILITY REGARDING SUPPORT SERVICES SHALL BE GOVERNED BY THE TERMS OF THAT AGREEMENT. BECAUSE SOME STATES/JURISDICTIONS DO NOT ALLOW THE EXCLUSION OR LIMITATION OF LIABILITY, THE ABOVE LIMITATION MAY NOT APPLY TO YOU.

CD-ROM INSTRUCTIONS

SYSTEM REQUIREMENTS

Windows PC

- — 386, 486, or Pentium processor-based personal computer
- — Microsoft Windows 95, Windows 98, or Windows NT 3.51 or later
- — Minimum RAM: 8 MB for Windows 95 and NT
- — Available space on hard disk: 8 MB for Windows 95 and NT
- — 2X speed CD-ROM drive or faster
- — Browser: Netscape Navigator 3.0 or higher or Internet Explorer 3.0 or higher*
- — Reader: Adobe Acrobat Reader 4.0* (on the enclosed CD-ROM)*

Macintosh

- — Macintosh with a 68020 processor or higher, or Power Macintosh
- — Apple OS version 7.0 or later
- — Minimum RAM: 12 MB for Macintosh
- — Available space on hard disk: 6 MB for Macintosh
- — 2X speed CD-ROM drive or faster
- — Browser: Netscape Navigator 3.0 or higher or Internet Explorer 3.0 or higher*
- — Reader: Adobe Acrobat Reader 4.0*

* You can download any of these products using the URL below:

- — **NetscapeNavigator: http://www.netscape.com/download/index.html**
- — **Internet Explorer: http://www.microsoft.com/ie/download**
- — **Adobe Acrobat Reader: http://www.adobe.com/proindex/acrobat/readstep.html**

GETTING STARTED

Insert the CD-ROM into your drive.

- — Windows PC users should double click on My Computer, then on the CD-ROM drive. Find and double-click on the Index.html file.
- — Macintosh users should double click on the CD-ROM icon on the screen, then find and double-click on the Index.html folder. (Index.html may come up automatically on the Macintosh.)

You will see an opening screen with the Welcome page and other navigation buttons. From this screen, you can click on any button to begin navigating the CD-ROM contents.

MOVING AROUND

If you have installed one of the required browsers, you will see three frames on your screen. The frame on the left-hand side contains a navigational toolbar with buttons. From this toolbar you can click on the buttons to navigate through the CD-ROM, which will then appear in the frame on the right-hand side. Note: At any time, you can use the Back button on your browser to return to the previous screen.